A TREATISE

ON

TRIGONOMETRY,

PLANE AND SPHERICAL,

WITH ITS APPLICATION TO

NAVIGATION AND SURVEYING, NAUTICAL AND PRACTICAL ASTRONOMY AND GEODESY,

WITH

LOGARITHMIC, TRIGONOMETRICAL, AND NAUTICAL

TABLES.

FOR THE USE OF SCHOOLS AND COLLEGES.

A NEW EDITION, WITH EXTENSIVE ADDITIONS AND IMPROVEMENTS.

BY THE

REV. CHARLES W. HACKLEY, S.T.D.,

Prof of Mathematics and Astronomy in Columbia College.

FOURTH EDITION.

NEW YORK:

GEORGE P. PUTNAM & CO., 10 PARK PLACE.

1853.

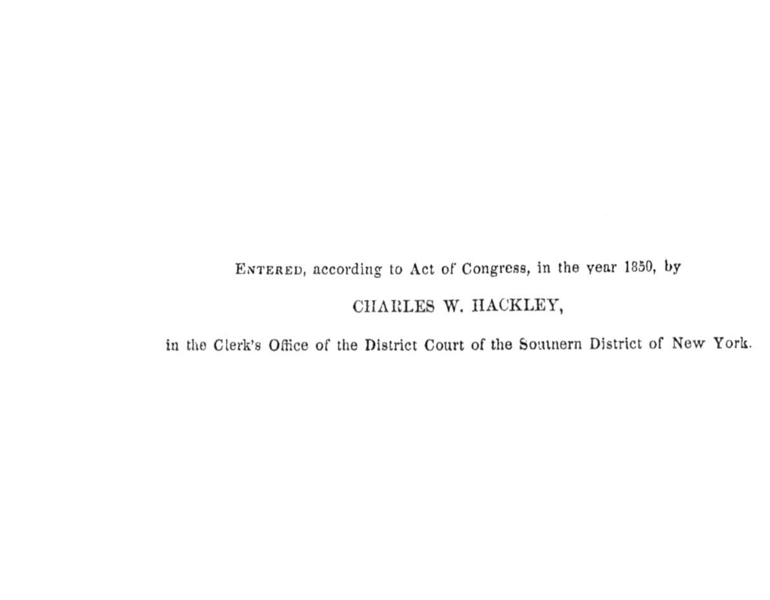

R. CRAIGHEAD, Printer and Stereotyper,
53 Vesey Street.

PART OF

PREFACE TO THE FIRST EDITION.

Analytical Trigonometry has always been to the majority of students a dry and difficult study. A conviction that it might be rendered easy and interesting to all who have a tolerable acquaintance with Algebra and Geometry, has led to the production of the present work. The faults of former treatises on this subject, which have detracted from their usefulness as books of instruction, appear to be these:

1. A too sudden transition from Geometry to Trigonometry, in consequence of which, the first efforts of the learner are in the dark as to the object of his pursuit.

2. A tedious succession of general formulas at the commencement, the use and application of which are so long delayed as to produce weariness and discouragement before there is any apparent fruit to reward labor.

3. Too much abridgment in the demonstration, and particularly in the derivation of the algebraic results.

The author is aware of the importance attached to the exercise of intellect required to discover the connexion between propositions whose mutual dependence is shown by intermediate links which the mind must supply unaided, but it will be admitted on the other hand, that the ordinary term of study is too limited, and the field of knowledge in this department too extensive, to afford the loss of time which such a mode occasions. Besides, there will be abundant scope for this kind of exercise, in a more matured familiarity with mathematical reasoning, for which the shortening of labor here, will leave additional room.

PREFACE TO THE NEW EDITION.

THE old edition has been entirely remodelled, and vast additions of valuable matter which have been some years in collecting, or are the results of recent improvements in science, have been made. The present work begins with some constructions of triangles according to the rules given in geometry, followed by others in which scales of equal parts and protractors are employed, showing at once and distinctly, what is to be understood by the solution of a triangle, and the value of trigonometry in the measurement of inaccessible heights and distances.

The evident inaccuracy in the use of instruments leads the learner to perceive the necessity of a more exact and certain method, and prepares him to enter with satisfaction upon the study of Analytical Trigonometry.

The explanation of the Trigonometrical Lines has been prepared with great care, and it is believed that considerable improvement in the method of exhibiting their changes will be observed. Their application to the solution of triangles is immediately shown in a few cases, with the help of a table of natural sines and cosines at the end.

Then follows a full exposition of the theory and use of logarithms, with every variety of example, including an explanation of the Tables at the end. The use is also taught of the tables of Callet, the tables in highest repute, an American edition of which is known as Hassler's tables.*

Part I. concludes with the application of logarithms and logarithmic sines, tangents, &c., to a number of practical examples in heights and distances, involving every case in the solution of plane triangles.

After this a few pages of miscellaneous exercises occur, which, with those in fine print scattered through the 1st Part, will serve to give greater skill to the better class of students. Appendix I., which follows next in order, contains a vast variety of general formulas, succinct methods of solution, and methods advantageous in particular cases, methods of treating small arcs, resolutions of Algebraic equations by the aid of Trigonometry, various expressions for the area of a triangle in terms of its angles and sides, effects of errors of observation on results; in short, everything necessary for a comprehensive knowledge of Trigonometry.†

* The German tables most in use are those of Vega and those of Köhler.

† Navigation and Surveying, if to be studied, should be taken up immediately after Plane Trigonometry.

Part II. contains Spherical Trigonometry. Particular care has been taken to render the demonstrations here, plain and easy, and to avoid all unnecessary repetition and complication.

It was found that the introduction of a few celestial circles, such for the most part as the study of geography may be supposed to have already rendered familiar, would afford an opportunity for making all the examples of Spherical Trigonometry Astronomical.

The use of the hour angle and of different kinds of time has led also to the introduction of a full description of the transit instrument and its various adjustments, the theory of which depends on Spherical Trigonometry, and is given in all its details.

The practical character of the problems is a peculiar feature in the plan of the present work. The consideration which led to it was that since Trigonometry had grown out of the actual wants of men in these very particulars, if they were sufficiently interesting to stimulate discovery, they would also incite to the study of what is already known. The analytic method, though not always practicable before the mind is somewhat furnished, is doubtless by far the best method of training. Besides this general reason for introducing Astronomical problems here, it was deemed useful thus to prepare the way for the study of Astronomy whilst the formulas and rules of Trigonometry were fresh in the memory, and to prevent that neglect of the Trigonometrical Solutions of Astronomy, which is apt to result from the trouble of recalling what has been long laid aside. It was thought, too, that this foretaste of Astronomy might excite a relish for that study.

The examination questions will be found convenient for students preparing for examination on Trigonometry, or for those studying without the aid of a teacher.

Appendix II., which follows Spherical Trigonometry, is of a character analogous to Appendix I.

Part III. exhibits a pleasing and useful application of Plane Trigonometry to the principles of navigation. This will be found a very complete treatise on the subject in small compass. The appendix to this part, App. III., includes great circle sailing, a method not usually treated in works on navigation, nor much used at present at sea ; but as it serves to shorten voyages, and has no practical inconveniences in the case of steamers, which class of vessels is becoming numerous on the ocean, it cannot longer with propriety be omitted. Sumner's method is also here introduced.

Part IV. is a very complete treatise of surveying, which, by reducing the subject rigorously to its essential elements, is brought within a small space. Besides what is contained in ordinary treatises, including a full description of all the surveying instruments, will be found the methods of surveying railroads and canals, the principles of Topography, and a new method of Hydrographic Surveying.

Part V., which treats of Nautical and Practical Astronomy, contains a complete description of all the Astronomical instruments used at sea and in observatories, a thorough investigation of the theory of their adjustments, and of the corrections to be applied to the observations for errors of adjustment, the use of nearly every part of the nautical almanac and tables of corrections for determining the co-ordinates of the true places of the heavenly bodies, and the solutions in Spherical Trigonometry necessary for converting one set of co-ordinates into another, with all the best methods of determining latitude and longitude, either on land or at sea. App. V. contains the description of the reflecting circle and mural circle, the determination of latitude by circummeridian altitudes, by the method of Littrow, and by an altitude of *the pole star* out of the meridian.

Part VI. contains the necessary instruction for conducting a geodetic survey on a scale of sufficient magnitude to require not merely the spherical figure, but also the spheroidal figure of the earth to be taken into consideration. When the formulas in this part involve the theory of conic sections, they are given and the use taught, but the demonstrations are reserved for the last appendix, in which the calculus is freely introduced when necessary. The subject commences with the modes of measuring bases, with an account of the beautiful improvements in the base apparatus recently made in this country, and the formulas of reduction to the level of the neighboring seas. Then follows a description of the great theodolite, and the methods of conducting the observations of the great or primary triangulation, the modes of verifying and correcting the observed spherical angles, and of computing the elements of the spherical triangles. Then the methods of determining geodetically the differences of latitude, longitude, and azimuth of the stations at the vertices of the triangles, with the construction of maps and the explanation of the necessary tables. Then the best methods of conducting the Astronomical observations for latitude, longitude, and azimuths. The description of the instruments and modes of conducting the magnetic observations, and the use of the formulas for determining the elements of terrestrial magnetism.

App. VI. describes the equatorial, the altitude and azimuth instrument, the prime vertical transit, and gives theorems for determining the size and figure of the earth, &c.

The methods given in this geodetic treatise are those employed upon the coast survey of the United States.*

The tables include a table of logarithms, of numbers, of logarithmic sines, tangents, cosines, cotangents, secants and cosecants ;† a table of natural sines and cosines, a table of difference of latitude and departure for every point and quarter point of the quadrant, a table of Rhumbs, a table of meridional parts, Workman's table for the correction of the middle latitude, a table of refractions, with corrections for the states of the barometer and thermometer, a table for dip or depression of the horizon, a table of the sun's parallax in altitude, of the contraction of the

* These are in some respects superior to the latest and best European methods. The author has to acknowledge the politeness of the accomplished superintendent of the coast survey in furnishing every facility for obtaining information.

† The last two are not usually found in the best tables. The method of taking out the difference for the seconds in these tables is new and expeditious.

sun's or moon's vertical semi-diameter from refraction, ot the augmentation of the moon's semi-diameter with its altitude, a table of proportional logarithms, a table of the reductions of the moon's equatorial parallax for the spheroidal figure of the earth, and finally a table of natural versed sines for reducing observations to the meridian.

Besides these, other small tables and specimens of tables are scattered throughout the w .rk.

Most of the tables are printed from the beautiful and accurate stereotype plates of the tables accompanying Bowditch's Navigator, by permission of the proprietor, Mr. G. W. Blunt.

The author has to acknowledge the kindness of Prof. CHAUVENET, of the U. S. Naval Academy, in permitting the use of his valuable paper on Unlimited Spherical Triangles, first introduced by Gauss. It will be found in Appendix II., as contained in the Astronomical Journal, with some slight modifications and explanatory notes.

N. B. The fine print in the following pages may be omitted without breaking the continuity of the treatise.

CONTENTS.

PART I.

PLANE TRIGONOMETRY.

APPENDIX I.

PART II.

SPHERICAL TRIGONOMETRY AND PRACTICAL ASTRONOMY.

APPENDIX II.

ON UNLIMITED SPHERICAL TRIANGLES AND THEIR SOLUTION.

PART III.

NAVIGATION.

APPENDIX III.

PART IV.

SURVEYING.

PART V.

NAUTICAL ASTRONOMY.

APPENDIX TO PART V.

PART VI.

GEODESY.

APPENDIX TO PART VI.

PART I.

PLANE TRIGONOMETRY.

1. The term Trigonometry is compounded of two Greek words, τριγωνος, a triangle, and μετρον, measure, signifying literally the measurement of triangles. It has for its object to determine the unknown parts of a triangle when a sufficient number of the parts is known.

By parts or elements of a triangle are understood commonly the sides and angles, though trigonometry properly includes the measurement of the surface also.

There will accordingly be six elements of every triangle, namely the three sides and the three angles.

2. It has been proved (Plane Geom., Theorems 1, 2, and 5), that when two triangles have three elements, one of which is a side, in the one, equal respectively to the corresponding elements in the other, the triangles are identical.

One element must be a side, because if the three angles only were equal respectively in the two triangles they would be but similar (Plane Geom., Theorem 63); that is, alike in shape but not necessarily in size.

Since all triangles which have three elements equal, are by consequence equal, it is said that three given elements determine a triangle; that is, with these three given elements, but one triangle can be formed.

There is one exception to this principle, pointed out in Prob. 8, Plane Geom., where two sides and the angle opposite one of them are given, in which case two triangles can be constructed with the given elements.

3. Three elements of a plane triangle being given then (except they be the three angles), it ought to be possible to find the other three, since these are fixed by their dependence upon the three given.

This may be accomplished with sufficient accuracy for many purposes, by means of constructions such as are exhibited at Problems 5 and 8 of Plane Geometry.

We shall repeat one of these constructions, enunciating the problem somewhat differently.

The two sides and included angle of a triangle being given, let it be required to find the remaining side and the other two angles.

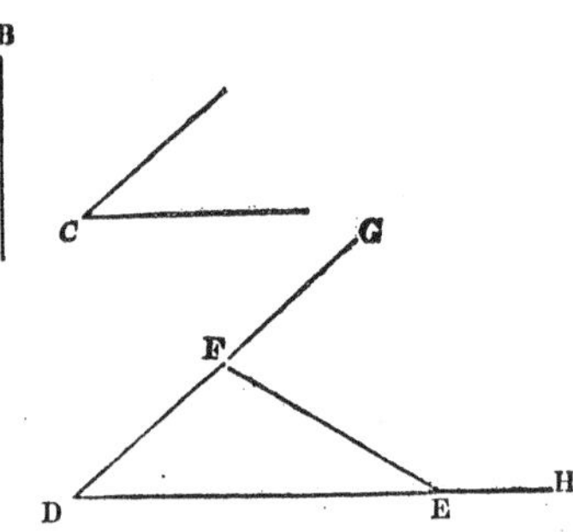

Let A and B be the two given sides, and C the given included angle. Draw two lines DH and DG of indefinite length, making with each other an angle equal to the given angle C. Lay off on the first of these the given line A from D to E, and on the second the given line B from D to F. Join EF. The only possible triangle DEF will thus be formed with the three given elements, in which EF will be the required side, and E and F the required angles.

The finding the unknown elements of a triangle by means of those which are given is called its solution.

4 The method of solution just exhibited is rendered more practically useful by the employment of scales of equal parts and protractors.

The most simple form of the scale of equal parts is shown in the annexed figure.

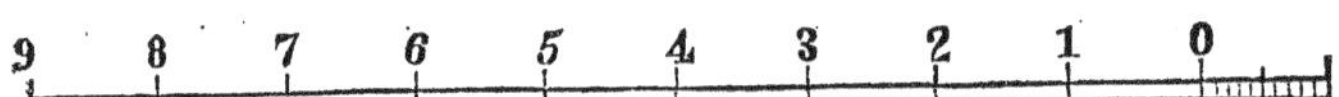

It is a straight rule divided into any number of equal parts; in this example ten, and one of these again into ten, so that the smallest division is one hundredth of the whole length of the rule.

The following is the manner of using it.

Suppose that it is required to draw upon paper a line equal in length to 56.

Place one foot of a pair of dividers at the line of division marked 5, and extend them till the other foot reaches exactly to the sixth smaller division mark on the right of 0; the feet of the dividers will then be at a distance of 56 apart. To draw now the required line upon paper, let A be the point from which it is to be drawn. Placing one foot of the dividers at A, extended the distance 56 obtained from the scale, describe with the other an arc of a circle on the side towards which the line is to be drawn; then from A draw the line in the proper direction, terminating it at the arc before described, and it will be the line required.

Another line of 42 being measured from the scale and laid down upon the paper, the two lines will be in the ratio of 56 to 42. If they are lines upon a map, and the first corresponds to a line of 56 feet upon the ground, the second will correspond to a line of 42 feet. If the first represent 56 yards, or chains, or miles, the second will represent 42 yards, or chains, or miles. And in general lines upon the same drawing which are measured in parts of the same scale must be understood to be expressed in units of the same kind.

The *sectoral* scale of equal parts consists of a ruler of two arms moving on a hinge, each arm being divided into a number (usually 100) of equal parts. To set this scale to any size, say 40 parts to the inch, the arms

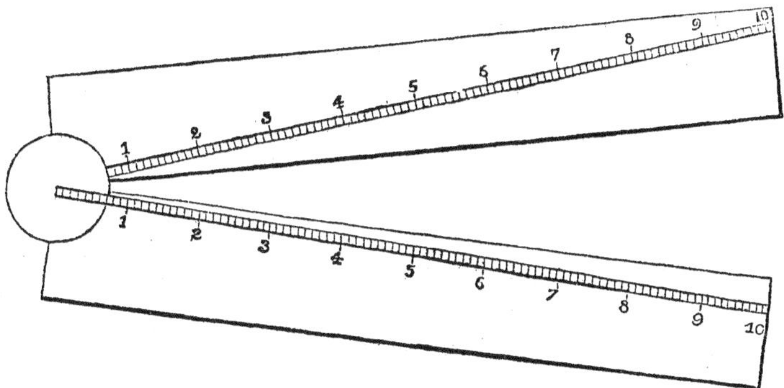

must be separated by turning them round the hinge, till a pair of dividers opened to the distance of an inch will extend exactly from the division marked 40 on one arm, to that marked 40 on the other.

If now any other distance be required upon a scale of 40 parts to the inch, as for instance the distance 65, the dividers must be opened till they will extend from the 65th division on the one arm, to the 65th division on the other.

This kind of scale is constructed on the principle that lines drawn parallel to each other between the sides of an angle are proportional to the parts into which they divide the sides. (See Plane Geom., Theorems 61, 63, 65.)

The diagonal scale of equal parts is constructed as seen in the diagram, by parallel lines drawn along a ruler in sufficient number to embrace 10 spaces between them. Transverse lines are drawn perpendicularly to

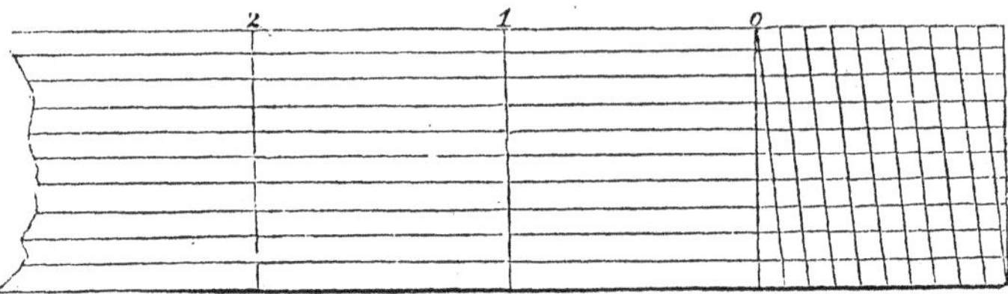

these at intervals usually but not necessarily equal to the whole breadth of the 10 spaces. The last one of these intervals is divided into ten spaces, and the first division at top is joined to the second at bottom, the second at top to the third at bottom, and so on by diagonal lines.

To measure any distance on this scale, as 456, place the dividers on the 6th horizontal line from the top with one foot upon the 4th of the larger divisions, from the 1st on the right, and extend the other foot of the dividers, till it reaches to the 5th smaller division in the right hand square.

5. Before describing the protractor, which is an instrument for laying off angles, it will be necessary to explain the method of estimating the magnitude of angles.

In Geometry, it is shown that angles are proportional to the arcs included between their sides, the arcs being described with equal radii, and it is also there stated that hence such arcs are properly the measures of angles.

So that if an arc included between two sides of one angle be double, or triple, or sextuple, an arc described with the same radius included between the sides of another angle, the first angle is double, triple, or sextuple the second.

The relative magnitudes of angles may therefore be correctly expressed by means of the relative magnitudes of the arcs which measure them.

The relative magnitudes of quantities are commonly given by referring the quantities to be compared to some known standard of measure, which must be always of the same kind with the quantities themselves.

This standard is called a unit. Thus a foot, a yard, &c., are units of length, and the idea of the relative lengths of two lines is obtained by its being said that one is seven feet or yards, and the other nine. Or the just conception of the length of a *single* line is had by being told how many feet, yards, or miles it contains. The mind compares it with one of these well known units, which in imagination it repeats along its length.

Now the unit of measure, which is employed in a similar manner for giving the conception of the magnitude of an arc, is called a degree. A degree is the $\frac{1}{360}$ part of the circumference of a circle. The relation which any given arc bears to the whole circumference may be conveniently expressed by stating the number of degrees which the arc contains. Thus an arc of 90 degrees will be one fourth the whole circumference. An arc of 45 degrees will be one eighth. An arc of 30 degrees will be somewhat less. And it is plain that the length of the arc, as compared with the whole circumference, may be readily conceived, as soon as the number of degrees which it contains is mentioned.

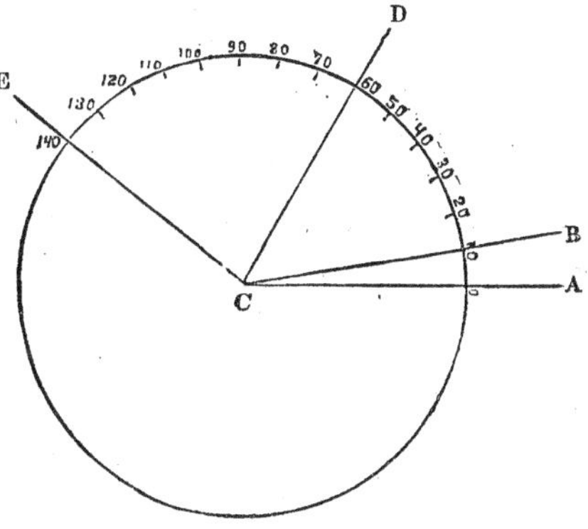

So also the magnitude of the angles subtended by these arcs will, after a little familiarity, be rendered easily sensible to the mind. To speak of an angle of 10 degrees for instance (A C B in the annexed diagram), will suggest the image of a very acute angle, one of 60 degrees (A C D) a much larger acute angle, one of 140 degrees (A C E) an obtuse angle.

A degree being always the $\frac{1}{360}$ part of a circumference, a single degree will be larger in a larger circle than in a smaller, and this, so far from being inconvenient, is particularly advantageous in the measurement of angles; for since arcs described about the vertex of an angle as a centre with different radii, and included between the sides of the angle, bear the same relation to each other as the radii, and since the entire circumferences are also proportional to their radii, it follows that two concentric* arcs included between the sides of the same angle, and having the vertex of that angle for a centre, are the same aliquot parts of their respective circumferences. Consequently, two such arcs will contain the same number of degrees. Hence, to find the number of degrees contained in a given angle, the arc described for the purpose about the vertex, and extending from side to side of the angle, may be with any radius at pleasure.

* Having the same centre.

This may be distinctly seen in the following diagram.

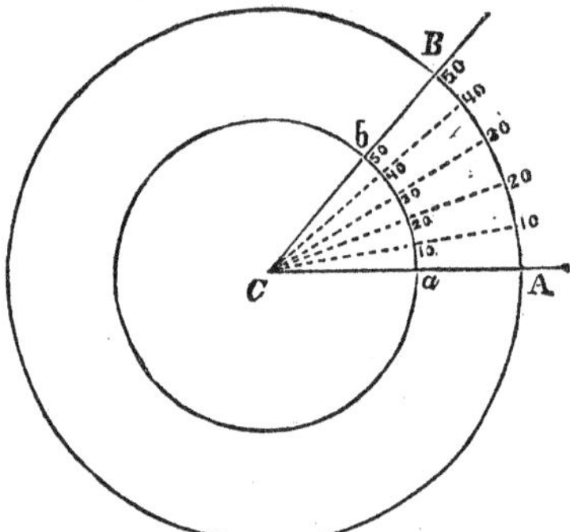

ACB is the angle; the larger arc AB included between its sides contains 50 degrees of the whole circumference; the arc ab with the lesser radius also contains 50 degrees, and so would an arc included between the sides of the given angle described with any other radius whatever.

Where the size of an angle is such that it does not embrace an exact even number of degrees of the circumference, smaller divisions called minutes, 60 of which make a degree, are employed. The angle is then said to contain as many degrees and minutes as there are degrees and parts of a degree, each $\frac{1}{60}$ over, between its sides. If the second side of the angle does not pass exactly through one of these smaller divisions, a still smaller kind termed seconds, 60 of which form a minute, or 360 a degree, must be introduced.

$$90^\circ = 5400' = 324000'', \quad 180^\circ = 10800' = 648000'',$$
$$270^\circ = 16200' = 972000'', \quad 360^\circ = 21600' = 1296000''.$$

When it becomes necessary to use more minute divisions, the same system is continued. The next denomination is thirds, 60 of which make a second; the next fourths, and so on.*

The notation for these denominations is as follows. Degrees are written thus °; minutes thus ′; seconds thus ″; thirds thus ‴, &c.; 30° 20′ 10″ is read thirty degrees, twenty minutes, and ten seconds.

6. It is evident that the numbers used in the system of division, for the circumference of the circle, are entirely arbitrary. Others might be employed with equal propriety, provided the same principles were observed. In fact the attempt has been made, and probably will be successful in France, to subvert the old system of division, and to adopt a decimal system in this as well as in every other sort of measurement. Thus a right angle, which is the unit of angles, is made to contain 100° instead of 90; and the circumference will then contain 400° instead of 360. 100′ instead of 60=1°, 100″=1′. Degrees in the centesimal division of the circumference are called *grades;* and the notation in this division is $^{g}\,{}^{\backprime}\,{}^{\backprime\backprime}$. Grades are converted into degrees by multiplying by $\frac{90}{100}$ or ·9. It will be found more convenient to subtract $\frac{1}{10}$ of the given

* Instead of thirds, fourths, &c., the almost universal practice now is to use decimals of a second, viz. tenths, hundredths, and thousandths.

number of grades from the given number itself. The two methods above described are called the sexagesimal and the centesimal divisions.

EXERCISES.

1. Convert $42^g\ 34^{\backslash}\ 56^{\backslash\backslash}$ or $42^g{\cdot}3456$ into degrees, &c.
   Ans. $38^\circ{\cdot}11104$ or $38^\circ\ 6'\ 39''{\cdot}74$.
2. Convert $24^\circ\ 51'\ 45''$ into grades, &c. *Ans.* $27^g\ 62^{\backslash}\ 50^{\backslash\backslash}$.
3. Prove $45^\circ\ 15'\ 20''=50^g\ 28^{\backslash}\ 39^{\backslash\backslash}{\cdot}50$.
4. Also, $10^\circ\ 15'\ 46''=11^g\ 40^{\backslash}\ 3^{\backslash\backslash}{\cdot}09$. 5. Also, $18^\circ\ 10'\ 48''=20^g\ 20^{\backslash}$.*

The semi-circumference of a circle whose radius is 1 is $3{\cdot}14159265=180^\circ$ $\therefore$ $1^\circ=0{\cdot}017453293$ $\therefore$ $1'=0{\cdot}0002908882$ $\therefore$ $1''=0{\cdot}000004848137$.

Again, $\dfrac{180^\circ}{3{\cdot}14159265}=57^\circ{\cdot}2957795=3437'{\cdot}74677=206264''{\cdot}806$, is the length of the radius of any circle expressed in degrees or minutes or seconds as units of length.

7. Another method of expressing the magnitudes of angles is as follows. A distance at pleasure is laid off from the vertex of the angle upon one of the sides, and a perpendicular there drawn to this side till it meets the other side of the angle. The ratio of this perpendicular to the distance from its foot to the vertex, serves to indicate the size of the angle.

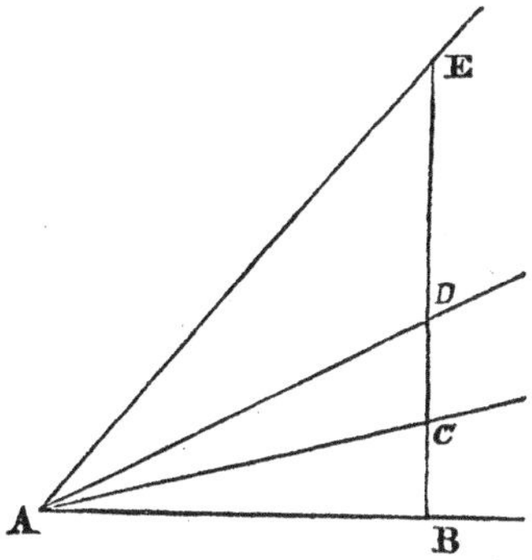

For example, if the line BCDE be perpendicular to the line AB, and BC be one fourth AB, the angle BAC is said to be an angle of $\frac{1}{4}$. If BD be one half AB, the angle BAD is said to be an angle of $\frac{1}{2}$. If BE be equal to AB, BAE is said to be an angle of 1; and so on for other magnitudes. An angle of 1 is plainly half a right angle, or 45°.

This kind of measurement is much used by engineers, to express the degree of slope in excavations and embankments.

8. The protractor which we are now prepared to describe is an instrument for drawing upon paper an angle of any given number of degrees.

This instrument is made in a variety of forms; sometimes with a full circle divided into degrees, sometimes comprising only a semicircle, sometimes upon a rectangular rule having not the circumference but the radii drawn, as they would be through the divisions of the circumference if it were actually described. The first kind is made usually of brass.

* It is quite unnecessary to use the symbols $^{\backslash}$ and $^{\backslash\backslash}$. $148^g{\cdot}5926$ would sometimes be written $1^q{\cdot}485926$, where the symbol ^{q} denotes a quadrant or right angle

It has a metallic radius movable about the centre of the circle, and extending beyond the circumference. This prolonged radius serves to point out the number of degrees, and is armed with a sharp pin under the outer extremity for the purpose of pricking the paper, so that when the instrument is removed a line may be drawn with pencil through this point, and that upon which the centre was placed.

THE SEMI-CIRCULAR PROTRACTOR,

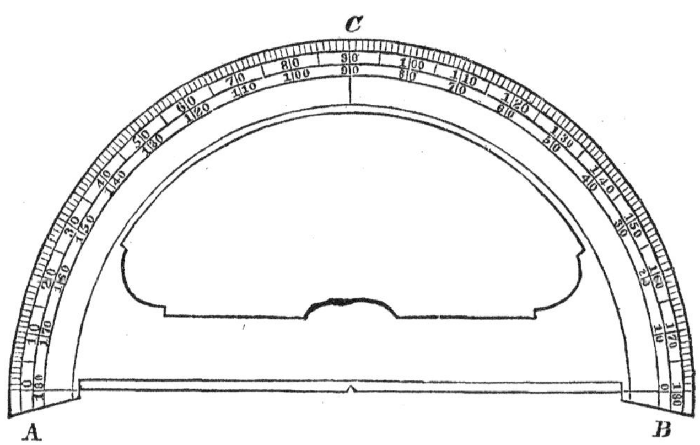

which is the one most commonly seen, is a semicircle of brass (or other metal), having the greater part of the interior cut out to render the instrument less heavy.

The semi-circumference is divided into degrees by marks made in the metal, and these are numbered from 0° to 180 (the number in a semi-circumference) both ways, in order that the counting may commence with convenience at either end.

The degrees are also sometimes divided into half degrees, and lines of different length are employed to mark more distinctly every five and every ten degrees.*

The centre is marked by a notch in the straight side of the instrument, which side is a diameter of the semicircle.†

9. In order to explain the use of the instrument here described, suppose it be required to draw at the point A in the line AB a line making with AB an angle of 22°.

* Such a division of instruments is termed graduation.

† This instrument may be made out of paper, and a large one so made is very accurate.

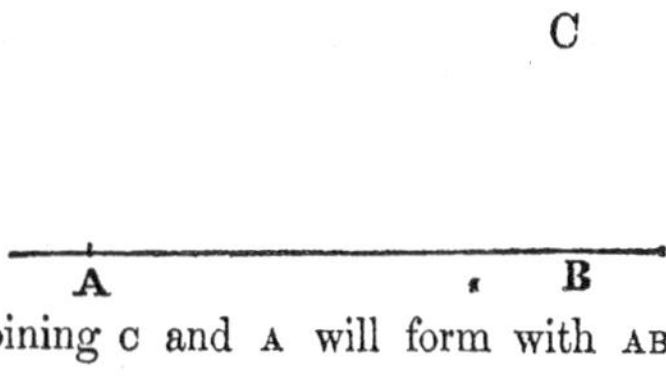

Place the protractor so that its centre shall be upon the point A, and its straight edge or diameter upon the line AB. Then mark the paper at the point C against the 22d division of the protractor, and a line joining C and A will form with AB the angle required.

10. We are now prepared to construct triangles when three of their six elements are given, the angles in degrees and the sides in feet, yards, or other linear units.

In order to show the practical utility of trigonometry at the same time that we explain the solution of a triangle, let us take the following problem in the calculation of distances to inaccessible objects.

Suppose a fort situated upon an island, and a light-house upon the main shore, and let the distance from the light-house to the nearest salient of the fort be required.

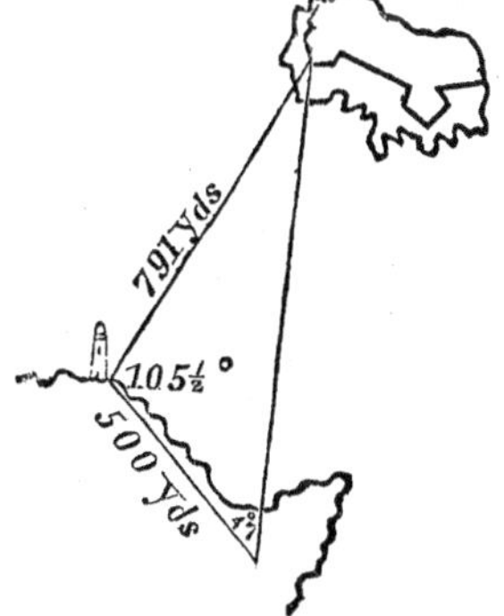

Measure a line along the shore of any length at pleasure, say 500 yards, beginning at the light-house. Then if two lines be imagined to be drawn from the extremities of the line just measured, to the salient of the fort, a large triangle will be formed having its two longest sides resting upon the sea. If now the angles which these two sides form with the first side, which we will call the base, could be determined by observation upon the shore, there would be known in this triangle a side and the two adjacent angles, which would be sufficient data to construct the triangle on a small scale, and to obtain the length of the required side extending from the light-house to the salient of the fort.

A somewhat rude instrument for the purpose of observing such angles as those alluded to above, might easily be made.

Let there be a circle, or flat circular ring of wood, divided into degrees, and having a tin tube movable upon a pivot at the centre of the circle; the tube being closed at one end except a very small orifice, and having two threads crossing at right angles in the centre of the other end, so that in looking through the tube with the eye at the small orifice, the line of sight may coincide with the axis. Let this apparatus be mounted upon a three-legged stand called a tripod, so that the plane of the circle shall be horizontal; then, by placing the instrument thus formed at the light-house, in the example above, and sighting with the tube, first to a staff at the other extremity of the base, and then to the salient of the fort, keeping the circle stationary, the number of degrees passed over

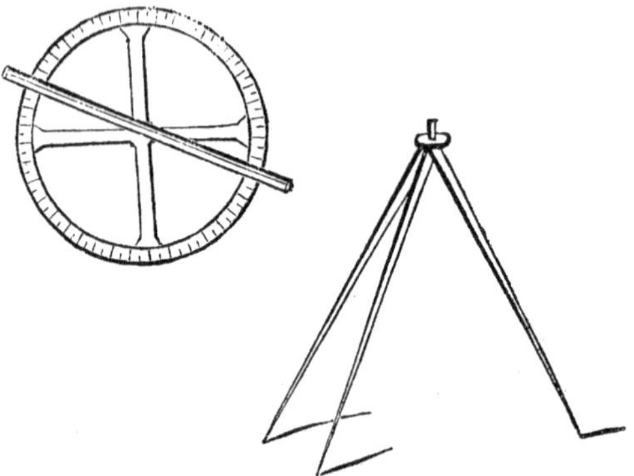

upon its circumference by the tube will indicate the angle of the triangle at the light-house. This angle we shall suppose to be $105\frac{1}{2}°$. The angle at the other extremity of the base might be found in the same manner, and suppose it $47°$.*

To construct the triangle with these data, draw on paper a line AB, and make it equal in length to five hundred divisions of some scale of equal parts.† Then draw an indefinite line AC making with AB an angle of $105\frac{1}{2}°$. Also lay off in a similar manner at the point B an angle of $47°$; the two lines AC and BC will meet at C. Take the line AC in the dividers and apply them to the scale. The number of equal parts upon the scale between the feet of the dividers, will show the number of yards from the light-house to the fort. The number is 791.

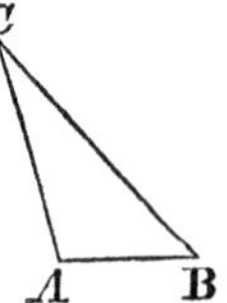

If the angle at C were required, it might be measured by applying to it the protractor; or it is equal to $180°—(A+B) = 27\frac{1}{2}°$.

The side B C, if among the sought parts, might also be measured from the scale.

11. The instrument described above may be rendered suitable for application to the determination of heights. If a round bar be made to project horizontally from the top of the tripod, so that the graduated circular frame can be suspended by the socket at its centre in a vertical position, it will then serve to measure angles in a vertical plane.‡

* The instrument here described is of course very rude. It was deemed advisable to postpone a description of more accurate instruments to a subsequent part of the work.

† This may be done conveniently by taking 50 divisions, and considering each division as equal to ten.

‡ A vertical plane is one perpendicular to the surface of the earth.

To show the use of the instrument thus prepared take the following problem.

Required the height of a tower which stands upon horizontal ground, and the base of which is accessible.

Measure back a distance from the base of the tower, say 200 feet; call this distance the base line; at the extremity of the base line place the instrument arranged for taking vertical angles: suspend a plumb line from the centre of the circle, and the point 90° distant from that in which the plumb line cuts the circumference will be the point through which a horizontal radius would pass. Then sight with the tube to the top of the tower: the number of degrees between the tube and the horizontal radius just mentioned, will be the measure of the angle included between a line drawn to the top of the tower and the base line; let this number be 30°. Constructing a right angled triangle upon paper, having its base 200 and angle at the base 30°, the perpendicular of this triangle, measured by a scale of equal parts, will be the height of the tower. The height of the instrument must be added to the result found.

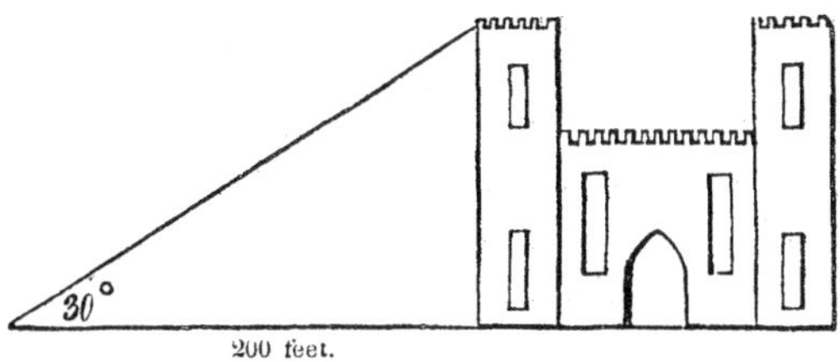

N. B. The sides found will always be expressed in units of the same kind as the base.

12. It is evident that when *any* three parts of a triangle, one of which is a side, are given, the other three may be discovered by a process similar to those just exhibited.

This kind of solution is said to be by construction.

The accuracy of the results must depend upon the niceness of the instruments, and the care with which the construction is made.

A degree of accuracy so uncertain and so variable is quite inadequate for many purposes to which Trigonometry is applied.

A method of *calculating* the required from the given parts of a triangle, which should produce always the same results from the same data, and be either perfectly, or so nearly exact, as to leave an error of no importance, however great the dimensions employed, would be evidently a desideratum. Such a method we have, and it is that which it will be the object of the residue of the present treatise to unfold.

To give the student a general view of what is before him, it will be well to state that a number of equations will be found, each containing four quantities, which quantities will be general expressions for the measures of elements of a triangle. The equation will express the true relation between these elements. By making one of these elements the unknown quantity and resolving the equation with respect to it, its value will be expressed in terms of the other three. If now these three were given, the value of the fourth would be known the moment the values of the three given were substituted for their general representatives.

It is plain that as many such general equations will be required, as there can be formed essentially different combinations of four out of the six elements of a triangle.

Equations like those here alluded to are called formulas, because each is a general form, under which a multitude of particular examples are included.

As these general formulas require of necessity the use of algebraic symbols and processes, and as *algebra*, from its power and application to decompose combinations of quantity so as to extricate their elements, is often called *analysis*, the subject upon which we are now about to enter is called

ANALYTICAL TRIGONOMETRY.

13. The sides and angles of a triangle are not quantities of a similar kind, and therefore do not admit of direct comparison. Since angles are expressed in degrees, and sides in units of length, one of the first principles which governs the formation of equations, namely, that the members and terms should express quantities of the same kind, would be violated by the introduction of angles and sides together, without some modification of one or both.

The expedient which has been invented to accommodate these heterogeneous quantities to each other, is that of employing straight lines, so related to the arcs which measure the angles of a triangle, as to depend upon these arcs for their length, in such a manner that when the arcs are known, these straight lines may be known also; and vice versâ. The chords of arcs are plainly lines of this description, and chords were at one time used for the purpose of which we here speak; but there is a more convenient kind of lines, of which there are three principal sorts, termed sines, tangents, and secants, of an arc or angle, called, when spoken of collectively, ***trigonometrical lines***, the nature and use of which we shall presently explain. These lines being straight and expressed, as they will be found to be, in linear dimensions, like the sides of a triangle, they may be employed with the latter in equations or formulæ; and when, by the resolution of an equation of this description, one of these trigonometrical lines is found in terms of one or more sides of the triangle, the angle to which the trigonometrical line belongs may also be supposed to be known. How the former is known from the latter will be hereafter explained. Let it be taken for granted here that the knowledge of a trigonometrical line is equivalent to the knowledge of its arc or angle, and vice versâ.

The trigonometrical lines are sometimes called trigonometrical functions* of an arc or angle.

Of these trigonometrical lines, we now proceed to explain the nature and properties.

THE SINE.

14. The sine of an arc is a perpendicular let fall from one extremity of the arc upon the diameter drawn through the other extremity.

Thus the line MP is the sine of the arc AM.

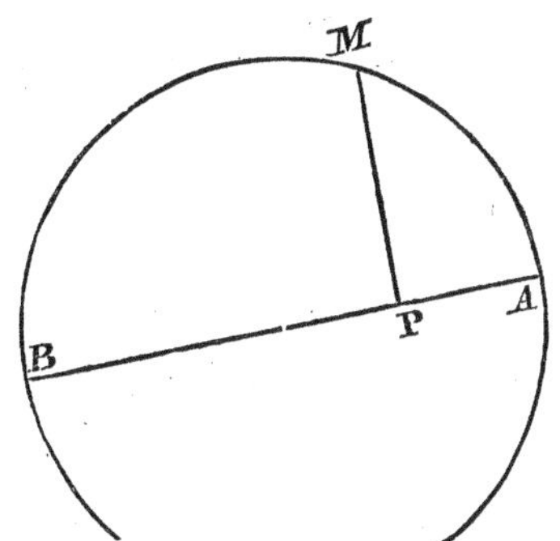

The same line MP is likewise the sine of the arc BM, because it is a perpendicular let fall from one extremity M of the arc upon the diameter drawn through the other extremity B.

15. Two arcs, which together make a semi-circumference, have, it thus appears, the same sine. Two such arcs are called supplements of each other. A semicircle contains 180°. The supplement of an arc is therefore what is left after taking the arc from 180° or 200^g. Thus 80° is the supplement of 100°. 70° is the supplement of 110°. 85^g is the supplement of 115^g; in general 90°—a, or 200^g—a is the supplement of the arc a.

* One quantity is said to be a function of another, when the former depends in any way upon the latter for its value. It is said to be an *increasing* function when it increases as the quantity upon which it depends increases; and a *decreasing* function when it diminishes as the other increases. The latter is called the argument.

EXERCISES.

1. The supplement of $56^\circ\ 20' = 123^\circ\ 40'$.
2. " $186^\circ\ 12' = -(6^\circ\ 12')$.
3. " $37^\circ\ 4'\ 3'' = 142^\circ\ 55'\ 57''$.
4. " $115^\circ\ 13'\ 24''\cdot 66 = 64^\circ\ 46'\ 35''\cdot 34$.
5. " $226^\circ\ 14'\ 17'' = -(46^\circ\ 14'\ 17'')$.
6. " $23^g\ 25^{\backprime} = 176^g\ 75^{\backprime}$.
7. " $110^g\ 40^{\backprime}\ 50^{\backprime\backprime} = 89^g\ 59^{\backprime}\ 50^{\backprime\backprime}$.

Two arcs, then, which are supplements of each other, have the same sine, or, as it is sometimes expressed, the sine of an arc is equal to the sine of its supplement.

If a represent an arc of any number of degrees, the notation employed to express the sine of that arc is sin. a. The proposition* above, stated algebraically, will stand thus, $\sin\ a = \sin\ (180^\circ - a.)$

The sine of an arc is also the sine of the angle measured by that arc.

16. When the arc is very small, it is plain that its sine will be very small also, and that when the arc is 0, the sine will be 0.

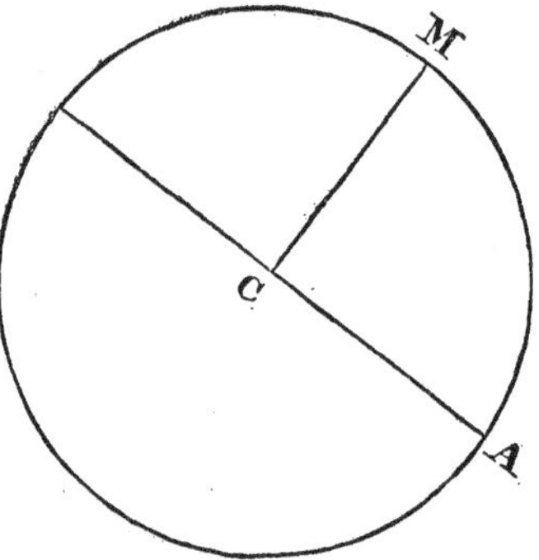

As the arc increases the sine increases till the arc is 90°, which, being a quarter of the circumference, is called a quadrant, the sine of which is R. (R signifying radius; which line this letter, whenever employed hereafter, will be understood to represent.)

As the arc increases beyond 90°, the sine diminishes, i. e. becomes a decreasing function of the arc, till the arc reaches 180°, when the sine is 0 again. Beyond this value of the arc the sine again increases till the arc reaches 270°, or three quadrants, when the sine is again equal in length to R.

From 270° to 360° the sine decreases, till at the latter value it is a third time 0. Beyond 360° we pursue the same round again, and no new variations are developed.

17. The least value of the sine is 0. It has this value at 0°, at 180°, and at 360°.

The greatest value of the sine is R. It has this value at 90° and at 270°. It has all possible values between 0 and R, but it has no different

* The word proposition is here used in the enlarged sense of anything propounded as true.

values, as the arc increases to two, three, and four quadrants, from those which it had in the first. So that when the sine of an arc greater than 90° is required, an arc, having an equal sine, may be found in the first quadrant. To find this arc we have the following rule, the correctness of which the annexed diagram will show. Observe how many degrees distant the termination of the given arc is from 180° or 360°, according to which of these two is nearest, and that number of degrees and fractions of a degree, will be the arc in the first quadrant, having the same sine as the given arc.

For example, let the given arc be 200°. This is nearest 180°, and differs 20°. The sine of 20° is equal in length to the sine of 200°. Or M P, which is the sine of A B M, is also the sine of B M.

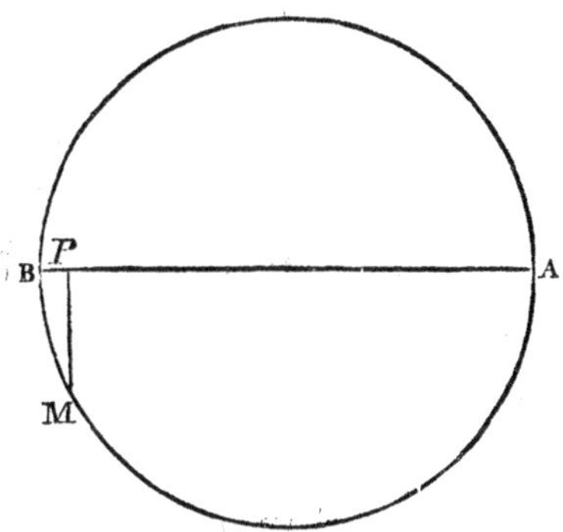

Again, let the given arc be 300°. This is nearest 360°, and differs 60°. The sine of 60° is equal in length to the sine of 300°.

If the given arc exceeds 360°, subtract 360, and then apply the rule just given. If the arc contains a number of circumferences, divide by 360, and apply the rule to the remainder.

18. It is customary, for the purpose of being able to bring the trigonometrical lines as they appear in the figure, the more readily before the mind when the figure is not present, to begin all arcs at the same point; and the point commonly chosen is the extreme right of the circumference, determined by the intersection of the horizontal diameter of the circle with the circumference. This is the point A, in the last figure. An arc of 90° will then reach to the top of the circle, or the upper extremity of a vertical diameter. An arc of 180° will terminate at the left of the circle, or of the horizontal diameter. An arc of 270°, at the lowest point of the circle, or lower extremity of the vertical diameter. An arc of 360°, at the right of the circle, or point of beginning.

One advantage of this plan will readily appear. Since the arc always commences at the same point, namely, the right of the circle, the horizontal diameter will be the diameter which passes through one extremity of the arc, and wherever the arc may terminate, the perpendicular from the other extremity of it, which is the definition of the sine, will be a perpendicular to the horizontal diameter; so that the sines of all arcs, in a diagram so constructed, will be perpendiculars to the horizontal diameter.

The sines of arcs between 0° and 180° will be drawn downwards; and those of arcs between 180° and 360° will be drawn upwards.

According to the general principle of analysis, that quantities estimated in a contrary sense are distinguished by contrary signs, if the sines of arcs between 0° and 180° be considered as positive, those of arcs between 180° and 360° must be regarded as negative.*

THE TANGENT.

19. The tangent of an arc is a perpendicular drawn to the radius at one extremity of the arc, and terminated by the radius produced, which passes through the other extremity.

In the annexed diagram A T is the tangent of the arc A M. It is also the tangent of the angle A C M, measured by the arc.

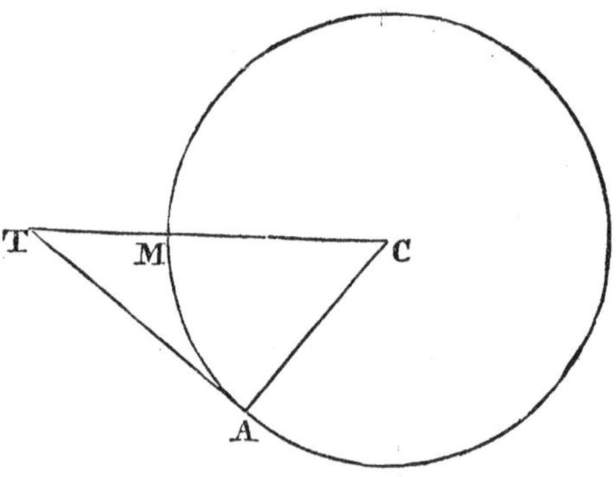

The shorter the arc is, the shorter will be the tangent. When the arc is 0, the tangent will evidently be 0. As the arc increases, the tangent increases, and very rapidly as the arc approaches 90°. In order to trace the tangent through its various changes, we shall suppose the arc to commence at the point on the extreme right of the circle, and the degrees to be counted upwards, towards the left, as in a former case—the tangent of every arc will then be drawn at the extremity of the horizontal radius on the right of the centre, and be terminated by the radius produced, passing through the other extremity of the arc, which extremity will vary its position as the arc varies its magnitude.

* See Algebra, page 182.

When the arc is 90°, the perpendicular to the radius at one extremity is parallel to the radius through the other extremity. These lines will never meet, and the tangent will have no termination. It is in this case said to be infinite. The sign employed to express infinity ∞ is also called the sign of impossibility. The value of the tangent of 90° is expressed algebraically thus, tan. $90 = \infty$.

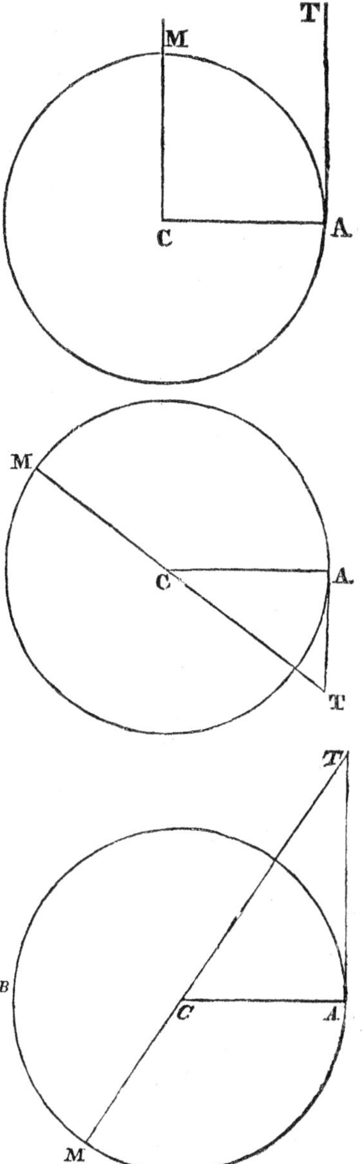

The tangent of an arc, terminating in the second quadrant, will be cut off below the origin* of the arc. Thus A T is the tangent of A M; and according to the principle adopted when treating of the sine, this tangent, being in the opposite direction to that of the tangent of an arc in the first quadrant, is negative.

When the arc is 180°, the negative tangent, which became shorter and shorter as the second extremity of the arc approached this point, again reduces to 0. Beyond 180°, or in the third quadrant, the tangent is cut off above the origin again. Thus A T in the annexed diagram, is the tangent of the arc A B M. The tangent of an arc in the third quadrant is, therefore, positive. When the arc is 270° or 3 quadrants, the tangent becomes parallel to the radius which produced

* A term applied to the point A, where the arc commences.

ought to terminate it, and the tangent is again ∞.*

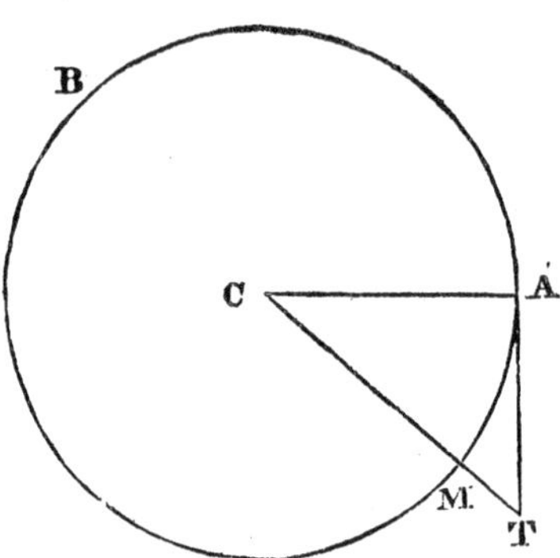

The tangent of an arc in the fourth quadrant is negative, as may be seen from the annexed diagram.

20. The least value of the tangent is 0. The greatest value is ∞. So that the tangent has all possible values. But these it has, if we do not regard the sign, in the first quadrant; and the same rule applies to finding the length of the tangent belonging to any given arc, from that of an arc in the first quadrant, as was given for the sine.

The tangent changes its sign in every quadrant, that is four times in going round the circle. It is positive in the first and third, two diagonal quadrants, and negative in the second and fourth, the other two diagonal quadrants.

The tangent is ∞ at the top and bottom of the circle, and 0 on the right and left.

THE SECANT.

21. The secant of an arc is a line drawn from the centre of the circle to the extremity of the tangent.

In the preceding diagrams, CT is the secant of the arc AM. It is also the secant of the angle measured by the arc.

As the arc with its tangent diminishes, the secant diminishes; and when the arc and tangent are 0, the secant is equal to R. The secant can never be less than radius, because the tangent cannot pass within the circumference, and consequently the line from the centre to the extremity of the tangent, must extend at least to the circumference. When the arc is $90°$ the secant is ∞. When the arc is $180°$ the secant is R. And when the arc is $270°$ or three quadrants, the secant is again ∞. All which will appear from an inspection of the last diagrams.

* The infinity here has the doubtful or double sign $\pm\infty$. Zero may have always the double sign ± 0. Infinity only when it is the transition from a + to a — value or vice versâ. (See Art. 36.)

The tangent and secant have their greatest values, namely ∞, together; that is, at the top and bottom of the circle. They have also their least values, that of the tangent being 0, and that of the secant R, together, to wit, at the right and left points of the circle.

22. In the first quadrant the secant is estimated from the centre towards the second extremity of the arc. In the second and third quadrants it is estimated in the opposite direction. According to the principle which it is necessary to observe, and of which we have before spoken, the secant must in these quadrants be considered as negative. In the fourth quadrant the secant is again estimated towards the second extremity of the arc, and is therefore positive.

The vertical diameter separates the positive from the negative secants, the positive being in the quadrants on the right of this diameter, and the negative being on the left.

23. We have now exhibited three of the trigonometrical lines. There are three others closely connected with these in character, called the cosine, the cotangent, and the cosecant; the reason for which names will presently appear.

The difference between an arc or angle and a right angle or $90^\circ = 100^g$, is called the complement of the arc or angle. Thus 40° is the complement of 50°; 60° is the complement of 30°; 75^g is the complement of 25^g, and in general $90^\circ - a$, or $100^g - a$, is the complement of the arc a.

EXERCISES.

1. The complement of $24^\circ\ 32' = 65^\circ\ 28'$.
2. " $110^\circ\ 15' = -(20^\circ\ 15')$.
3. " $17^\circ\ 36'\ 43'' = 72^\circ\ 23'\ 17''$.
4. " $29^\circ\ 27'\ 6''{\cdot}32 = 60^\circ\ 32'\ 53''{\cdot}68$.
5. " $216^\circ\ 45' = -126^\circ\ 45'$.
6. " $65_g\ 34^{\backprime}\ 27^{\backprime\backprime} = 34^g\ 65^{\backprime}\ 73^{\backprime\backprime}$.
7. " $107^g\ 44^{\backprime}\ 20^{\backprime\backprime} = -7^g\ 44^{\backprime}\ 20^{\backprime\backprime}$.

The cosine, cotangent, and cosecant, are the sine, tangent, and secant of the complement. Thus the cosine of 50° is the sine of 40°; the cotangent of 30° is the tangent of 60°; and in general the cosine, cotangent, or cosecant, of the arc a, is the sine, tangent, or secant of $90^\circ - a$.

THE COSINE.

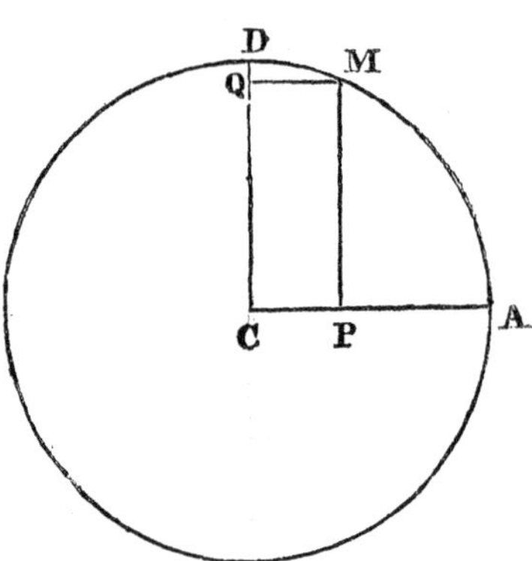

24. In the annexed diagram DM is the complement of the arc AM; and MQ being a perpendicular from one extremity M of the arc DM upon the diameter which passes through the other extremity D, is the sine of the arc DM. Therefore by the definition it is the cosine of the arc AM. But MQ = CP. Hence CP is also the cosine of the arc AM. We have then another definition for the cosine of an arc, viz. *the distance from the foot of the sine of the arc to the centre of the circle.*

25. If the arc terminate on the right of the vertical diameter, i. e. in the first or fourth quadrant, the foot of the sine will fall on the right of the centre; but if the arc terminate on the left of the vertical diameter, i. e. in the 2d or 3d quadrant, the foot of the sine will fall on the left of the centre. The cosine being estimated in opposite directions in these two cases, must have opposite signs. It is therefore positive in the 1st and 4th quadrants, and negative in the 2d and 3d.

It will be recollected that the positive were separated from the negative secants, as the positive are here seen to be from the negative cosines, by the vertical diameter. The secant and cosine have therefore always the same algebraic sign.

It was shown (Art. 15), that sin $(180^\circ - a) = \sin a$; so also cos. $(180^\circ - a)$ is equal in length to cos. a, since they are both the distance from the foot of the same sine (MP in the diagram of Art. 14) to the centre, i. e. if we suppose one of the arcs to originate at A, the other at B, and both to be extended towards M in opposite directions.* But if $a < 90^\circ$, it follows that $180^\circ - a$ terminates in the second quadrant, hence its cosine is negative; if $a > 90^\circ$ then cos. a is negative, and $180^\circ - a$ being in the first quadrant, its cosine is positive; therefore, *the cosine of an arc and the cosine of its supplement are equal with contrary signs.*

* Both arcs a and $180^\circ - a$ are now supposed to originate at the same point A, and to be estimated in the same direction.

26. The cosine of 0° (being equal to the sine of the complement of 0° which is 90°) is R. The cosine of 90° is equal to the sine of 0°, which is 0. The cosine of 180°, being the distance from the foot of the sine to the centre, and being also on the left of the vertical diameter, is — R, as may be seen from the preceding diagram. The cosine of 270°, being the distance from the foot of the sine to the centre, since the sine falls on the centre, is 0.

The least value of the cosine is 0; the greatest value is R. When the sine has its least value, the cosine has its greatest; and vice versâ.

The versed sine of an arc, which is seldom employed in Trigonometry, but often in Mechanics, is the distance from the foot of the sine to the origin of the arc, thus PA in the last diagram is the versed sine of the arc AM.

27. Before noticing the cotangent and cosecant, let us consider the manner of treating negative arcs. Such arcs commencing at the point A in the diagram ought evidently, on the general principle already repeatedly mentioned, to be laid off upon the circumference in the opposite direction from the positive arcs, i. e. downwards.

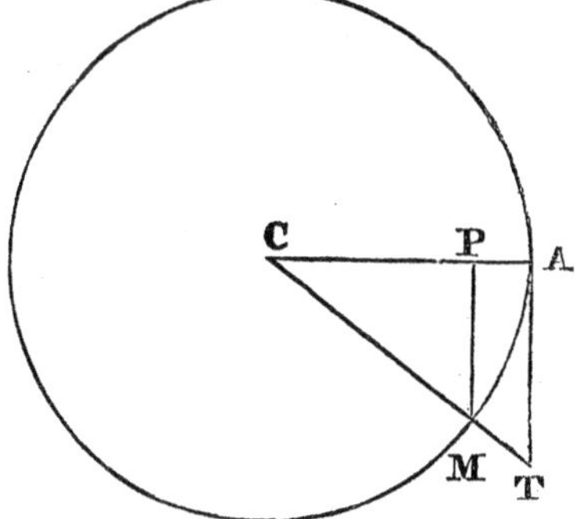

Let us for simplicity suppose the arc in question to be less than a quadrant; being laid off downwards, such an arc will terminate in the fourth quadrant. Hence we see that the trigonometrical lines of a negative arc must be affected with the same signs as those of an arc in the fourth quadrant. Thus *the sine of a negative arc will be* —, *the cosine* +, *the tangent* —, *the secant* +.

Secondly, suppose the given negative arc to be greater than a quadrant; were it positive, some of its trigonometrical lines would be negative. The rule given above, which determines the signs of its trigonometrical lines, by those of an arc in the 4th quadrant, will apply with this modification, that *when the trigonometrical line is* + *in the fourth quadrant, the corresponding trigonometrical line of the negative arc has the same sign as that of a positive arc of the same magnitude, and when the trigonometrical line is* — *in the fourth quadrant, a contrary sign.*

The truth of this assertion may be seen, by trying negative arcs of various magnitudes upon the diagram, laying them off downwards from the right point of the circle, and observing in which quadrant their extremities fall. They will be found in every case to give results agreeable to the rule just stated.

THE COTANGENT AND COSECANT.

28. The cotangent of 0° is equal to the tangent of 90° (Art. 23) and is therefore ∞. The cotangent of 90° is equal to the tangent of 0° and is 0. The cotangent of 180° is equal to the tangent of $90^\circ - 180^\circ =$ the tangent of $-90^\circ = \infty$, since -90° is a negative arc, and terminates at the bottom of the circle, or the 270° point. The cotangent of $270^\circ =$ the tangent of $90^\circ - 270^\circ =$ the tangent of $-180^\circ = 0$.

When the tangent has its least value, which is 0, the cotangent has its greatest which is ∞, and vice versâ.

29. The cosecant of $0^\circ =$ the secant of $90^\circ = \infty$. The cosecant of $90^\circ =$ the secant of $0^\circ = \text{R}$. The cosecant of $180^\circ =$ the secant of $90^\circ - 180^\circ = \infty$. The cosecant of $270^\circ =$ the secant of $-180^\circ = -\text{R}$.

When the secant has its least value, which is R, the cosecant has its greatest, which is ∞, and vice versâ. The cotangent and cosecant have their greatest values together and their least values together, viz. that of the one 0, of the other R, at the top and bottom of the circle, and both ∞ at the right and left points.

30. With regard to the signs of the cotangent and cosecant in the different quadrants, they will be most conveniently discovered from the analytical expressions for these lines which we shall presently have. We add here, however, which so far as the cotangent and cosecant are concerned must be for a moment taken for granted, that the six trigonometrical lines may be arranged in three pairs, each pair having always the same algebraic sign.

We have seen that the secant and cosine go together in this way; so do also the cosecant and sine; and so do the tangent and cotangent. The positive sines and cosecants are separated from the negative by the horizontal diameter; the positive cosines and secants from the negative, by the vertical diameter; and the tangent and cotangent are together $+$ and $-$ alternately in the successive quadrants.

31. The following algebraic notation is employed for the six trigonometrical lines. Let a be the algebraic expression for the number of degrees in any arc, then the trigonometrical lines of the arc a will be expressed thus; sin a, tan a, sec a, cos a, cot a. cosec a.

Cot a tan $a = \text{R}^2$ is read, the cotangent of the arc a multiplied by the tangent of the same arc is equal to the square of the radius of the circle in which these trigonometrical lines are supposed to be drawn. Cot a and tan a are expressions for straight lines, and the equation above expresses that the rectangle formed by the tangent and cotangent of an arc is equivalent to the square formed upon the radius.

The two members of the above equation contain the same number of dimensions, and are therefore homogeneous. This ought to be the case in all trigonometrical equations; because a line cannot be equal to the rectangle of two lines or a surface, nor either of these to a solid.

Sometimes in analytical investigations R is supposed to be equal to 1; R^2 and R^3 would also be equal to 1. Whether this 1 is a unit of length, of surface, or of solidity, must be determined by what is required to preserve the homogeneity of the equation.

32. The tangent, secant, cotangent, and cosecant may be expressed in terms of the sine and cosine.

The values of the four former in terms of the two latter are derived geometrically as follows:

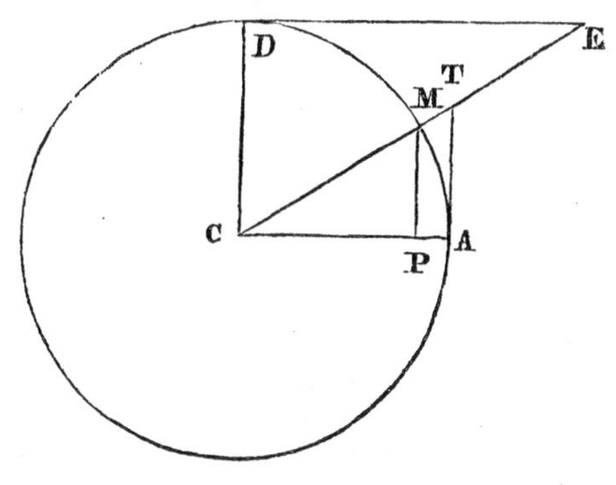

Call the arc AM in the diagram, a; then DM $= 90° - a =$ complement of a, DE $=$ cot a and CE $=$cosec a.

In the similar triangles CPM and CAT, since homologous sides are proportional, we have

$$\text{CP} : \text{PM} :: \text{CA} : \text{AT}$$

or

$$\cos a : \sin a :: \text{R} : \tan a$$

whence multiplying the means and dividing by the first term, we obtain the last

$$\tan a = \frac{\text{R} \times \sin a}{\cos a}$$

that is, *the tangent of any arc is equal to radius multiplied by the sine divided by the cosine of the same arc.* If R be made equal to 1, then

$$\tan = \frac{\sin}{\cos}$$

33. In the same similar triangles we have

$$\text{CP} : \text{CM} :: \text{CA} : \text{CT}$$

or,

$$\cos a : \text{R} :: \text{R} : \sec a$$

hence,

$$\sec a = \frac{\text{R}^2}{\cos a}$$

when $\text{R} = 1$

$$\sec = \frac{1}{\cos}$$

34. In the triangles CMP and CED, which have their sides respectively parallel, and are therefore similar, we have the proportion,*

$$\text{MP} : \text{CD} :: \text{CP} : \text{DE}$$

or,

$$\sin a : \text{R} :: \cos a : \cot a$$

whence,

$$\cot a = \frac{\text{R} \cos a}{\sin a}$$

when $\text{R} = 1$

$$\cot = \frac{\cos}{\sin}$$

35. The same triangles give also the proportion

$$\text{MP} : \text{DC} :: \text{CM} : \text{CE}$$

or,

$$\sin a : \text{R} :: \text{R} : \operatorname{cosec} a$$

whence,

$$\operatorname{cosec} a = \frac{\text{R}^2}{\sin a}$$

R being 1

$$\operatorname{cosec} = \frac{1}{\sin}$$

* The homologous sides are those which are parallel.

36. In the expressions for the tangent and cotangent which we have here derived, it will be observed that we have the quotient of the sine and cosine, and that therefore when the sine and cosine have contrary signs, the tangent and cotangent will be negative. This occurs in the second and fourth quadrants.

It appears hence, that the cotangent changes its sign always with the tangent.

Also that both the tangent and cotangent of an arc are equal to those of its supplement with contrary signs.

From the expressions for the secant and cosecant, it appears that the former must always have the same sign as the cosine, and the latter the same as the sine.

The formulas derived in the last four articles should be committed to memory.

Quantities in changing their signs pass through zero or infinity. (See Alg. Note 3d, p. 176.) Thus the sine changes from $+$ to $-$ or vice versâ, twice in going round the circle; viz. in passing through 0 at 0° and 180°; the cosine twice in passing through 0 at 90° and 270°; the tangent four times, in passing through 0 at 0° and 180°, and ∞ at 90° and 270°; the cotangent four times, in passing through 0 at 90° and 270°, and through infinity at 0° and 180°; the secant twice, in passing through ∞ at 90° and 270°; the cosecant twice, in passing through ∞ at 0° and 180°.

37. Multiplying the expression for the tangent given in Art. 32 by that of the cotangent in Art. 34, we have

$$\tan a \cot a = \text{R}^2$$

whence,

$$\tan = \frac{\text{R}^2}{\cot}$$

and,

$$\cot = \frac{\text{R}^2}{\tan}$$

when $\text{R} = 1$ the above expressions become

$$\tan = \frac{1}{\cot}$$

$$\cot = \frac{1}{\tan}$$

i. e. the tangent and cotangent are reciprocals of each **other.**

EXERCISES.

1. Express each of the six trigonometrical lines in terms of each one of the other five by itself.
2. The sine of an angle being 0·856, find the other trigonometrical functions.
3. The tangent being 2·34, find the others.
4. The cotangent being 1·203.
5. State the equivalents of the following functions of angles greater than 90°, or obtuse angles in equivalent functions of angles less than 90° or acute angles, sin 170°, cos 147°, tan 98° 31′, cot 171° 14′, sec 171°, cosec 155°, sec 215^g, cos 318^g 10`, tan $271_g$ 81`, cot 204^g 18` 94``.
6. Find the versed sine of the angle, the cosine of which is ·93358.
7. Prove the vers. = 1 — cos to be always positive.
8. Prove the greatest value of the versed sine to be 2R.

38. We are now prepared to find formulas for the solution of right angled plane triangles in all cases, and plane triangles in general in a few particular ones. The remaining cases of triangles in general will require further preliminary matter.

DERIVATION OF FORMULAS FOR THE SOLUTION OF RIGHT ANGLED PLANE TRIANGLES.

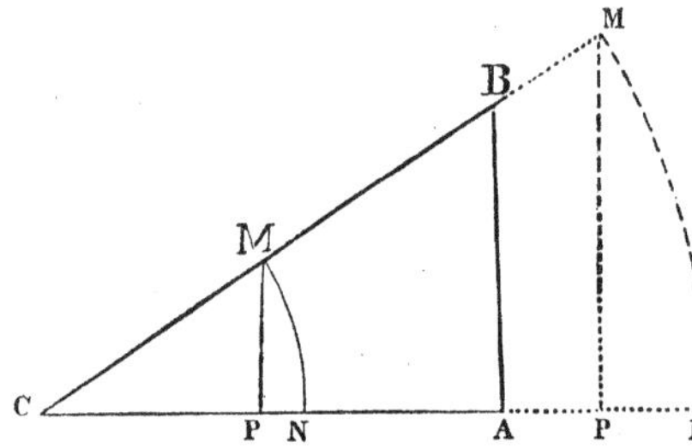

Let ABC be any right angled triangle. With C as a centre describe, with any radius at pleasure, the arc MN terminating at the sides of the angle. This arc will be the measure of the angle C. Draw MP perpendicular to CN. MP will be the sine of the arc MN because it is drawn from one extremity M of the arc perpendicular to the diameter which passes through the other extremity N.

MP is also the sine of the angle C. CM is the radius of the circle to which the arc MN belongs.

The two triangles CMP and CBA are equiangular and similar, and give the proportion

$$\text{CM} : \text{MP} :: \text{CB} : \text{BA} \text{ or } \text{R} : \sin \text{C} :: \text{CB} : \text{BA}.$$

Had an arc been described with B as a centre in a similar manner we should have had R : sin B : : BC : CA, from which it appears that *the radius of any circle whatever* bears the same proportion to the sine in that circle of the arc which measures one of the acute angles of a right angled triangle, that the hypothenuse of the triangle does to the side opposite the acute angle.*

It is customary, for conciseness, to represent the sides opposite the angles of a triangle by small letters of the same name with the large letters which are placed at the angles; which large letters are also employed as the algebraic representatives of the angles. Thus in the triangle above, A being the right angle, the hypothenuse opposite is expressed by a; the side AC opposite B is represented by b, and so the other. The above proportions would, according to this method, be written thus

$$\begin{array}{l} R : \sin B :: a : b \\ R : \sin C :: a : c \end{array} \qquad (1)$$

Both these proportions are expressed in the single rule printed in italics above. When $R = 1$, multiplying the second and third terms, and dividing by the first, in the preceding proportions we have

$$b = a \sin B$$

and

$$c = a \sin C \qquad (2)$$

That is *either perp. side = the hypoth.* $\times$ *the sine of the angle opposite.*

The two acute angles of a right angled triangle are together equal to a right angle or 90° (Plane Geom. Theorem 15, Cor. 5), therefore they are complements of each other; hence $\sin C = \cos B$; and the second of the above proportions (1) may be changed into

$$R : \cos B :: a : c \qquad (3)$$

which may be translated into ordinary language thus; *radius : the cosine of one of the acute angles of a right angled triangle : : the hypothenuse : the side adjacent the acute angle.*

When any three terms of a proportion are given, the remaining term can be found. If the unknown term be one of the extremes, *multiply*

* It is important to observe that the same trigonometrical lines of angles or arcs containing the same number of degrees in two different circles bear the same relation to each other. Thus in the diagram above, CM : MP : CM : MP, or,

(R : sin) of the smaller circ : : (R : sin) of the larger;

also,

CM : CP : : CM : CP or (R : cos) of the one : : (R : cos) of the other.

the two means and divide by the other extreme ; if the required term be a mean, *multiply the two extremes, and divide by the other mean.*

When R = 1 we have from proportion (3) above

$$c = a \cos B \qquad (4)$$

i. e. *either perpendicular side of a right angled triangle, equal to the hypoth.* × *cos of the adjacent angle.*

The above formulas contain each of them two of the sides of a triangle, the sine or cosine of an angle, and radius. If the lengths of the sides be given in numbers, these numbers may be put in place of the small letters which represent the sides in the proportion, and the general form becomes so far adapted to a particular case in the solution of right-angled triangles; but if the angle be given in degrees, how are we to know its sine or cosine, for *that* is the quantity which enters into the formula; and how are we to know the numerical value of R? For the present the student must be satisfied with the reply, that he can find the numerical value of any trigonometrical line corresponding to an angle of any given number of degrees, in a table at the end of the work. This is TABLE XXIV.* of Natural Sines. The degrees for angles or arcs of every magnitude within the quadrant will be found at the top of the columns of the table, and the minutes in the column marked M on the left, if the given angle or arc be less than 45°; but if it be greater than 45°, the degrees will be found at the bottom of the page, and the minutes on the right; the length of the sine or cosine will be found in the column under or over the degrees, as the case may be, and on the same horizontal line with the minutes. The title of the column must be looked for at top if the arc be less than 45°, and at bottom if the arc be greater.† The other trigonometrical lines may be easily calculated from the sines and cosines, as will be seen in the examples.

The trigonometrical lines of this table are computed, by a rule which will be hereafter demonstrated, for a circle whose radius is 1. So far as the *principles* for the solution of triangles are concerned, the length of the radius is entirely immaterial, as it will be recollected that the arc in the last diagram was described with any radius at pleasure.

When, in cases of the solution of right angled triangles, the hypothenuse and one of the acute angles are either given or required by the problem, one of the above formulas is always employed.

* The tables are selected and printed from the stereotype plates of a very large collection.

† A decimal point must be understood at the left of all the numbers in the columns of the table entitled N. sine and N. cos.

39. Let us take an example by which to illustrate their application, and as upon a former occasion, one which shall at the same time exhibit the practical utility of Trigonometry.

A roof is to have a height of 15 feet in the interior at the centre, and an inclination of 35°.

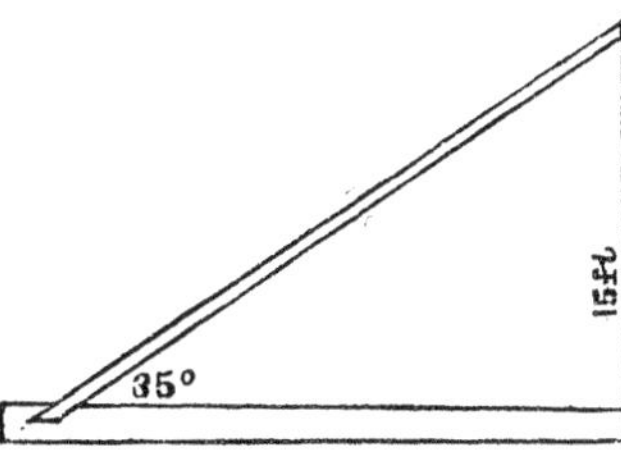

Required the length of the inner line of the rafters.

A right angled triangle will be formed in which the angle at the base will be 35°, and the side opposite 15 feet, and of which the hypothenuse is required. Formula (1) of the last article applied to this case gives*

$$1 : \sin 35° :: a : 15$$

Multiplying the extremes and dividing by the first mean the value of the other mean which is a, the hypothenuse required, will be obtained

$$a = \frac{1 \times 15}{\sin\ 35°}$$

Or formula (2) by a simple transformation gives the same thing.

$$a = \frac{15}{\sin 35°}$$

Looking out the sine of 35° in the tables and performing the operations indicated in the last equation, the value of a will be known, which will be the length of the rafters required. The answer will be in feet.

Sin 35° is found from the tables to be •57358.

thus

$$a = \frac{15}{{\cdot}57358} = 26.1 \text{ feet}$$

If (to vary the problem) half the interior breadth of the roof had been given, say 20 feet, and the angle of inclination, instead of 35° as in the last example, had been 15°, then to find the length of the rafters, it would

* Since in the demonstration of the formulas, the sides and angles of the triangle were supposed to have no particular values, it follows that any numbers, or any other letters compatible with the properties of a triangle, may be put in the place of those employed, and the formulas will still be true. This must be borne in mind throughout the work.

be necessary to find first the angle opposite the given side 20 feet; which is done by subtracting the given angle 15° from 90°, since the two acute angles of a right angled triangle are complements of each other. The remainder is 75°.

Applying the same formula as before, there results the proportion

$$1 : \sin 75° :: a : 20$$

or the equation

$$20 = a \sin 75°$$

whence,

$$a = \frac{20}{\sin 75°} = \frac{20}{\cdot 96600} = 20\cdot 7$$

The same result might be obtained by using the given angle 15°, and employing formula (3) above, which contains the cosine of one of the acute angles. The proportion would stand thus

$$1 : \cos 15° :: a : 20$$

or its equivalent (4)

$$20 = a \cos 15$$

whence,

$$a = \frac{20}{\cos 15°} = 20\cdot 7$$

the same as before. In fact cos 15° = sin 75°. (See Art. 23.)

40. Had the height and half the breadth of the interior of the roof been given, the length of the rafters might have been obtained, by employing the property of the right angled triangle demonstrated at Theorem 26, of Plane Geometry, that the square on the hypothenuse is equivalent to the sum of the squares upon the other two sides. Let the height of the roof be 12 feet, and the semi-breadth 16 feet, then

$$a^2 = 12^2 + 16^2 = 400$$

whence,

$$a = 20$$

If the length of the rafters had been given equal to 20 feet, and the height of the roof equal to 12 feet, then the semi-breadth would have been expressed thus

$$b^2 = 20^2 - 12^2 = (20+12)\,(20-12)^* = 32 \times 8 = 256$$

whence,

$$b = 16$$

* See Algebra, p. 16, ex. 2, and note.

41. Had the semi-breadth or base of the triangle and the inclination of the roof been given, and the height of the roof or perpendicular of the triangle been required, the hypothenuse not entering into the problem, neither of the above formulas, all of which contain the hypothenuse, would serve to find the side required in a direct manner. It might, however, be found indirectly by first finding the hypothenuse, using one of the above proportions, and then by means of the hypothenuse, using the same proportion, the required side might be obtained.

It is, however, objectionable to find one of the required parts in terms of the part which has itself been calculated from the given parts; because in the use of the tables which give the trigonometrical lines of the different angles not with perfect accuracy, but truly for as many decimal places as the table employs, a small error arises from the decimals neglected beyond the last place, and this, though so small as to be unimportant, becomes magnified by repetition, as in the case where one part of a triangle itself not perfectly accurate, is employed to calculate another. It is therefore desirable to find each of the required parts, in terms of the given parts; and this may always be done in right angled triangles. We proceed, therefore, to demonstrate a formula for the direct solution of the last case supposed above.

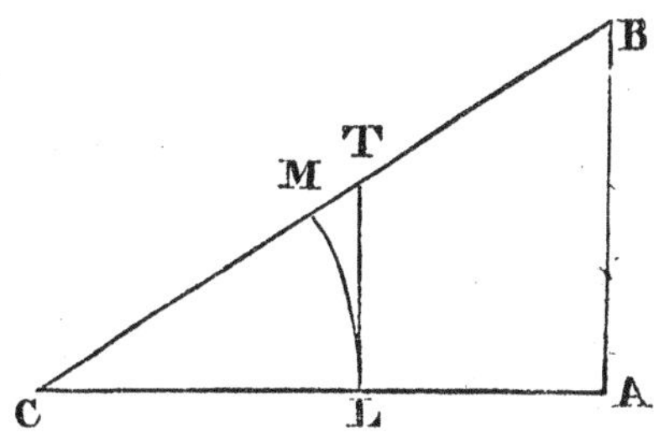

Let ABC be a right angled triangle. With any radius at pleasure describe an arc ML which shall be the measure of the angle C. At the point L draw a perpendicular LT to the line CL, terminating at the line CT. LT is evidently the tangent of the arc ML, since it is a perpendicular to the radius at one extremity of the arc, and is terminated by the radius which passes through the other extremity, according to definition of Art. 19. It is also the tangent of the angle C.

The equiangular and similar triangles CLT and CAB give the proportion

$$\text{CL} : \text{LT} :: \text{CA} : \text{AB}$$

or,

$$\text{R} : \tan \text{C} :: b : c \qquad (1)$$

If $\text{R} = 1$ this proportion gives

$$c = b \tan \text{C} \qquad (2)$$

or,

$$\tan C = \frac{c}{b} \qquad (3)$$

Let the angle of the roof in the above problem be 20° and the semi-breadth 25 feet, then

$$1 : \tan 20^\circ :: 25 : c$$

whence,

$$c = \frac{\tan 20^\circ \times 25}{1}$$

Had the angle B been used instead of C, the resulting proportion would have been

$$R : \tan B :: c : b \qquad (4)$$

Both proportions may be expressed together in common language thus: *Radius : the tangent of one of the acute angles of a right angled triangle :: the side adjacent that angle : the side opposite.*

This last rule applied to the problem at Art. 11, gives

$$1 : \tan 30^\circ :: 200 : c$$

whence,*

$$c = \tan 30^\circ \times 200 = \cdot 57735 \times 200 = 115 \cdot 47000$$

c is the height of the tower.

The same rule will evidently serve to determine either of the acute angles of a triangle when the two perpendicular sides are given.

If the side c were given and the angle B, the side b might be found in the same manner, using the proportion (4) which contains the angle B.

42. We have now exhibited all the cases which can possibly occur in the solution of right angled triangles, with some specimens of their application. The right angle of the triangle is fixed; and any two of the five remaining parts being given, the other three may be found. Let the student select at pleasure any two of the five parts, the two selected to be considered as given, and he will find the case for solution with which he will then be presented, solvable by some one of the formulas above.

The operations in the cases already exhibited, though of the most simple kind, nevertheless involve multiplications and divisions, which, from the number of places of figures, are somewhat tedious. In more complicated cases this evil would be much increased.

* The tangent is found from Table XXIV. by dividing the sine by the cosine. (Art. 32.) Should the cotangent be required, divide the cosine by the sine. (Art. 34.) To find the secant divide 1 by the cosine. (Art. 33.) For the cosecant divide one by the sine. (Art. 35.)

On this account it is customary to employ in trigonometrical calculations, that ingenious invention of Lord Napier's for facilitating numerical calculations, the table of logarithms;* before explaining the use of which we shall give some exposition of the

THEORY OF LOGARITHMS.

43. The logarithm of any given number is the exponent of the power to which it is necessary to raise some particular number in order to produce the given number. Thus, let 10 be the number raised to the power; then 2 is the logarithm of 100, because $10^2 = 100$ and 3 is the logarithm of 1000, because $10^3 = 1000$. Every given number will have a corresponding logarithm or exponent of the power to which it is necessary to raise 10 in order to produce the given number.

The number 10, which is the only number that does not change in the above equalities, is called a constant.

Should the constant number which has been employed be changed for another, the logarithms of numbers would be different from those derived by the use of the first constant. Logarithms derived from different constants are said to belong to different systems of logarithms, and the constant number belonging to each system is called the base of that system. The system most in use has the number 10 for a base, and is called the common system. The relation which this number sustains to the decimal system of notation will readily suggest some reasons for its selection; it will be found, as we proceed, to have many advantages.

44. If b be the base of a system, n a number, and l its logarithm, then by the definition

$$b^l = n$$

If we put b in the place of n, this equation becomes

$$b^l = b$$

Here l is evidently equal to 1. Hence *the logarithm of the base of every system is* 1.

* Table XXVI. at the end. The tables most in repute are the French tables of Callet.

N. B. The tables in this volume having been printed from the accurate stereotype plates of Bowditch's tables, by permission of the proprietor, are numbered as in Bowditch's edition, and as but a part of his tables are necessary to the present work, the Nos. of the table must not be expected to occur in regular order.

If in the equation

$$b^l = n$$

n be made equal to 1, we have

$$b^l = 1$$

Here l is evidently equal to zero. (Algebra, Art. 17.) Hence *in every system, log. of* $1 = 0$.

45. Suppose now the system be the common system; b will be equal to 10. If we substitute for n all possible numbers successively, we shall have a series of equations like the following,

$$10^l = 1$$
$$10^l = 2$$
$$10^l = 3$$
&c.

In the first l is the common logarithm of 1, in the second of 2, in the third of 3, &c. If l be made the unknown quantity, and these equations be successively resolved, we shall have the common logarithms of all numbers.* If now a table be formed having the series of natural numbers, 1, 2, 3, 4, &c., in one column, and their logarithms calculated as above placed in a second column against them, this would be a table of logarithms. The tables in actual use do not differ from such an one in principle, though some arrangements are adopted in them to avoid unnecessary repetitions.†

In the common system the logarithm of 10 is 1, the logarithm of 100 is 2; and the logarithms of all numbers between 10 and 100 are between 1 and 2, that is, they are 1 and a fraction. The logarithm of 1000 is 3, and the logarithms of all numbers between 100 and 1000 are between 2 and 3, that is, they are 2 and a fraction. In the same manner it may be shown that the logarithms of all numbers between 1000 and 10,000 are 3 and a fraction; of all numbers between 10,000 and 100,000, 4 and a fraction, and so on. The logarithms of most numbers, therefore, are mixed numbers. The fractional part is written in the tables; the whole number part, which is called the characteristic, is not written, nor is it necessary that it should be; for numbers between 10 and 100, or those composed of two figures, have 1 for a characteristic, as has just been

* The method of resolving them is given in Art. 325, Alg.

† For a more full exposition of the *theory* of logarithms, see Algebra, Art. 210, page 258, et seq.

seen; numbers between 100 and 1000, or those containing three figures, have 2 for a characteristic; numbers containing four figures have 3 for a characteristic, and so on. Whence it appears that the characteristic is always 1 less than the number of digits in the number to which the logarithm belongs. So that if against any given number, the decimal part of its logarithm be found in the tables, the entire part or characteristic may be supplied by counting the figures in the given number, and making the characteristic, one less.

In proceeding to explain the tables, we will premise that the logarithms of several consecutive numbers, if the numbers be somewhat large, will differ so little as to have several of their first figures the same. Hence, by a proper arrangement of the tables, the first figures of the logarithm may be written but once for several numbers, provided all be designated to which they refer, and thus much repetition be avoided.

The manner in which this is accomplished will be shown in the

EXPLANATION OF THE TABLES.

PROBLEM I.

46. *To find from the tables the logarithm of any given number.*

Case I.—*When the number is between* 100 *and* 10,000, if it be composed of three figures, find it in Table XXVI. at the end of the volume, and in the column at the left entitled No.; in the next column marked 0 at top and on the same horizontal line you will find the decimal part of the logarithm required. This contains five places.* If the given number contain four† figures, find the first three of it in the column No. as before, and the fourth in one of the columns marked 0, 1, 2, 3, &c., at top; under the latter, and on the same horizontal line with the first three, you will find the decimal part‡ of the logarithm sought.

N. B. The characteristic is always one less than the number of figures in the given number.

* In the tables of Callet seven places, the first three of which being the same for several numbers are not repeated, but must be understood before those which follow the number that has them expressed until you come again to seven places.

† In the tables of Callet substitute the word five for four in the above rule, and the word four for three.

‡ In the tables of Callet you find only the last four places, the first three to be prefixed to them must be taken from the numbers projecting to the left in the column marked 0 at top.

EXAMPLES.

1. Required the logarithm of 217.

In the column entitled No. on page 171 of Table XXVI. I find 217; in the next column marked 0 at top, and on the same horizontal line, I find 33646 for the decimal part of the logarithm required. The characteristic is 2, since 217 contains three figures, and the whole logarithm 2·33646.

2. Required the logarithm of 1122

On page 170 and in the column No. I find 112; in the column having the last figure 2 of the given number at top, and on the same horizontal line with the 112 before found, I find 04999 or with the proper characteristic 3·04999.*

3. Required the logarithm of 2188.

Ans. 3·34005.

47. We proceed now to show the use of logarithms in numerical calculations.

MULTIPLICATION.

Let b be the base of the system of logarithms, n any number, and l its logarithm. Then by the definition

$$b^l = n$$

Let n' be another number, and l' its logarithm, we have also

$$b^{l'} = n'$$

Multiplying these two equations, member by member, and observing the rule for exponents in multiplication, which is to add them together, we have

$$b^{l+l'} = nn'$$

From this last expression, it appears that $l+l'$ is the exponent of the power to which it is necessary to raise the base a, in order to produce the number nn'. But nn' is the product of n and n'. Hence the logarithm of the product is equal to the sum of the logarithms of the multiplier and multiplicand.

* At the tops of the pages in the table will be found catch numbers for the eye, in turning over the leaves, to show what numbers and logarithms are contained on the page.

EXAMPLE.

Multiply 2421 by 1613.
The logarithm of 2421 is 3·38399
The logarithm of 1613 is 3·20763

The logarithm of 2421×1613 or 3905073 is* 6·59162, or the sum of the logarithms.

48. If in addition to the numbers n and n' above, we suppose a third number n'' of which the logarithm is l'' we shall have in a similar manner

$$a^{l+l'+l''} = nn'n''$$

and so on.

Or, in general, *the logarithm of a product of several factors is equal to the sum of the logarithms of those factors separately.*

DIVISION.

49. Dividing the equation.

$$b^l = n$$

by the equation

$$b^{l'} = n'$$

we have, observing the rule of division, to subtract the exponent of the divisor from that of the dividend in order to obtain that of the quotient.

$$b^{l-l'} = \frac{n}{n'}$$

Since $l - l'$ is the exponent of the power to which it is necessary to raise b the base, in order to produce $\frac{n}{n'}$, it follows that $l - l'$ is the logarithm of $\frac{n}{n'}$ i. e. *the logarithm of the quotient is equal to the difference between the logarithms of the divisor and dividend.*

EXAMPLE.

Divide 3905073 by 2421
The logarithm of 3905073 is 6·59162
" " " 2421 is 3·38399

The logarithm of $\frac{3905073}{2421} = 1613$ is 3·20763 diff. of logs.

* As the number 3905073 is too large to be found in the tables, the method of finding its logarithm from the tables must be postponed till the explanation of such cases, further in advance.

Before explaining other operations by means of logarithms, we shall exhibit some principles derived from those just demonstrated.

50. The base of the common system being 10, the common logarithm of 10 is 1. (Art. 44.) Hence if any number be multiplied or divided by any number of times 10, the logarithm of the result will be equal to the logarithm of the given number increased or diminished by the same number of times 1. This 1 being an entire number, the decimal part of the logarithm of the given number will not be altered by this addition or diminution, but only the characteristic.

Thus 39794, which is the decimal part of the logarithm of 2500, is also of 25000, and of 250000, or of 250, or of 25.

The characteristics belonging to these different numbers are different. That of the log. of 2500 is 3; that of the log. of 25000 is 4; that of the log of 25 is 1. (See Art. 47.)

Any number is divided by a multiple of 10, by pointing off from the right as many places for decimals, as the divisor is times 10.

Thus 2348 divided by 10, by 10 twice, by 10 three times, becomes successively 234•8, 23•48, 2•348. The decimal part of the logarithms of these last three numbers, will be the same, viz. 37070, the characteristic being one less each time that we divide by 10 or remove the decimal point one place to the left. Because to divide by 10 it is necessary (see the last Art.) to subtract 1, which is the log. of 10, from the log. of the dividend. The characteristic of the first, 234•8, which is between $100 = 10^2$ and $1000 = 10^3$, is 2. The characteristic of the second is 1; and the characteristic of the last is 0, since 2•348 is less than 10, or 10^1.

The decimal part of the logarithm of a number consisting of significant figures, either followed or preceded by ciphers, will be the same as if the ciphers were absent. Thus the decimal part of the logarithm of 482000 or of •00482 is the same as the decimal part of the logarithm of 482.

The following table illustrates the theory of the characteristic.

The characteristic of the log. of 482000 is 5
of 482 is 2
of 4•82 is 0
of •482 is -1
of •0482 is -2
of •00482 is -3

From the above, it appears that the characteristic of the logarithm of a decimal fraction is negative; the decimal part of the same logarithm is, however, positive. The actual value of the whole logarithm will be therefore a negative quantity somewhat less than the characteristic. That the logarithms of proper fractions ought to be negative, appears from the fact, that since a fraction expresses the quotient of the numerator divided by the denominator, applying the rule for division by logarithms, the greater logarithm would have to be subtracted from the lesser, and the remainder would of course be negative.

From the above principles are derived the following rules:

1. To find the logarithm of a number consisting of significant figures with any number of ciphers annexed, *find the logarithm of the significant figures, and make the characteristic one less than the number of figures in the given number including the ciphers.*

2. To find the logarithm of a decimal or mixed number, *consider the number as entire; find the decimal part of its logarithm, and make the characteristic one less than the number of figures in the entire part of the given number.*

3. To find the logarithm of a decimal number having ciphers at the left; *look for the logarithm of the significant figures, and make the characteristic negative* and one more than the number of ciphers at the left of the given decimal.*

EXAMPLES.

The logarithm of	3266000	is 6·51402
of	114·1	is 2·05729
of	·001684	is $\bar{3}$·22634

51. Case II.—We proceed now to the method of determining the logarithm of a number beyond the limits of the table. This method is by a simple calculation from the logarithms of numbers which the table contains, and depends upon the fact that the difference of any two numbers bears the same proportion to the difference of their logarithms, that the difference of two other numbers does to the difference of *their* logarithms, which is nearly true. (See Algebra, p. 284, note.)

Take two numbers in the table differing from each other by 100, as the numbers 843700 and 843800, and a third number 843742 differing from the first of these by 42. The logarithm of the first number 843700, being the same as that of 8437, is given by the tables, and

is 5.92619

The logarithm of the second number 843800 is 5·92624

Their difference is 5

* It is customary to write the negative sign over the characteristic, thus, $\bar{2}$·1756348. It affects the characteristic alone and not the decimal part of the logarithm, which must be considered as +.

which may be found by subtraction, but to save this trouble the subtraction is performed, and the difference is written in the margin (in the tables of Callet in the right hand column marked dif.) Then on the principle that the difference of numbers is proportional to the difference of their logarithms, we have

diff. of numbers.		diff. of logs.		diff. of num.		diff. of logs.
100	:	•00005	: :	42	:	x

hence,

$$x = \frac{\cdot 00005 \times 42}{100} = \cdot 0000210$$

adding this to the logarithm of 843700 which is 5•92619
•0000210

the sum, rejecting the two last places 10 which go beyond the usual number is 5•92621

which is the logarithm of 843742.

Had the first two numbers differed by 1000 instead of 100 the divisor in the value of x would have been 1000, and the quotient would have extended three places beyond the usual. Had they differed by 10, the quotient would have extended one place beyond.

The inaccuracy of this method increases with the number of additional figures beyond four, in the number the logarithm of which is to be found.*

From the above process may be observed the following rule:

To find the logarithm of a number beyond the limits of the table. Enter the table with the first four figures of the given number, and find the corresponding logarithm. From the right hand margin take out the difference between this logarithm and the next in order in the table, and multiply it by the remaining figures of the proposed number, reject from the product as many figures to the right as there are in the multiplier, and add the rest of the product to the logarithm already found.

EXAMPLE.

1. Required the logarithm of 739245.

The decimal part of the log. of 7392 is 86876.

* The same process applies to most other tables as well as tables of logarithms. In all tables the column corresponding to the column of numbers here is called the column of *arguments*. The other columns contain functions depending on these arguments.

The number in the margin is	6
Multiplying this by the remaining figures of the given number	45
Product,	270

From this product reject as many figures to the right as are contained in the multiplier, that is two in this case, and add the rest to the logarithm before found, namely, 86876

The sum is 86879*

which is the decimal part of the log of 739245 required. Prefixing the proper characteristic, we have 5·86879.

EXAMPLE II.

Required the log. of 8193217

log. of 8193	= 91344		217
	1	dif. =	5
log. of 8193217	= 6.91345		1·085

To facilitate the above calculations several smaller tables will be found in the right hand margin of the page, the use of which may be explained from an example. Suppose it be required to find the logarithm of 276738. After cutting off 38 on the right, I find the logarithm of the first four figures, 2767, to be 44201. The difference between this logarithm and the next is 16. In the left hand column of the little table in the margin headed 16, I find the first of the two figures cut off, 3, and against it the number 5, which I place under the logarithm already found, as seen in the scheme below. Again I find in the same way the second of the two figures cut off, 8, and against it 13, which I place as in the scheme below one place to the right. Adding these numbers taken from the little table to the first logarithm found, the sum 44207 is the logarithm sought.

```
44201
    5
    13
44207 or with the characteristic 5·44207
```

The right hand figure 3 of the 13, which would carry the decimal places beyond five, is rejected. If it were any figure greater than 5, we should add 1 to the last figure of the result, 7.

The following example is worked with the tables of Callet in the same manner.

* We add 1 for the $\frac{70}{100}$ rejected which is more than $\frac{1}{2}$.

Find the logarithm of 8193217.

$$
\begin{array}{r}
\text{log. of } 81932 = 9134536 \\
5 \\
37 \\
\hline
6\cdot9134545
\end{array}
$$

The 7 neglected in adding up the above numbers being more than **5**, or $\frac{1}{2}$ of the preceding place, 1 is added to that place.

For the theory of the above see Algebra, at the end of Art. 214.

PROBLEM II.

To find the number corresponding to any given logarithm.

52. By referring to the proportion of Art. 51, and putting the value of x for the fourth term, we have

diff. of num.		diff. of logs.		diff. of num.		diff. of logs.
100	:	00005	: :	42	:	000021

Instead of the 42 being given and the 000021 required as before, the 000021 is now given and the 42 required.

The first term of the proportion is 100 or 1000, &c., and the second term is diff. in the margin, to find the third term multiply the extremes and divide by the second term

$$42 = \frac{000021 \times 100}{00005}$$

Hence the following

RULE.—*To find the number corresponding to any given logarithm.*

Seek for the decimal part of the given logarithm. If we find a logarithm exactly agreeing with that given, then the number, which the table shows us to belong to the logarithm found, will be the required number. If, however, as is most likely, we do not find the proposed logarithm exactly, then we are to take out the number corresponding to the next less logarithm; this number will of course fall short of that required, but the deficiency may be supplied as follows. Subtract the tabular logarithm from the given one, annex ciphers to the remainder at pleasure, and divide it by the diff. number in the margin, and annex the quotient to the number already taken from the table.

N. B. Should there be a quotient figure without annexing a cipher to the dividend, this quotient figure must be added to the last figure of the number taken from the table. Should it be necessary to annex two ciphers before obtaining a quotient figure, a cipher must be placed in the quotient, and annexed with the figures that come after, to the number taken from the table.

The logarithm next greater than that given may be taken from the tables, and the latter subtracted from the former, in which case you would subtract the quotient obtained by dividing the difference as above, instead of adding it.

EXAMPLES.

1. Find the number the log. of which is 5·86879
The decimal part of the next less log. is that of 7392 = ·86876

Their difference is 3

Annex ciphers to this diff. and divide by the diff. number in the margin, which is 6.

$$6\overline{)300}$$
$$50$$

Annex the quotient 50 to the number 7392 before found, and you have the number required corresponding to the given logarithm, namely, 739250. This number contains six figures, one more than the characteristic of the given logarithm. In every case a sufficient number of ciphers must be annexed to obtain quotient figures enough, when appended, to make the whole of the number which thus results contain one more figure at least than is expressed by the characteristic of the given logarithm. If more quotient figures still be obtained, they will occupy the place of decimals.

2. Find the number of which the log. is 2·91345
Next less log. that of 8193 = 91344
Number required is 819·32 5)10
2

53. To find the number corresponding to any given logarithm by the tables of Callet, seek the nearest logarithm in the tables, and subtract it from the given as directed above, then seek the remainder in the right hand column of the little table nearest, and if it be found, or a number not differing more than unity from it, the figure on the left of this number will express the sixth figure of the number required.

EXAMPLE.

2·5386717
The nearest log. is ·5386617 its number is 34567

Subtract and 100 is the remainder.

The nearest number in the right hand column of the little table adjoining is 101, against which on the left is the figure 8, and the number sought is 345·678

If the diff. (100 above) is not found exactly in the little table, take the nearest number to it, and take the difference between these again, and annex to it a cipher, seek this result again in the right hand column of the little table, the figures on the left of the two numbers taken out of the right hand column of the little table will be the sixth and seventh figures of the number required A third remainder might be found in the same manner, and an eighth figure of the required number be found.

EXAMPLE.

	0·4971499	
The nearest log. is	4971371	
Diff.	128	
nearest to which in the little table is	124	number on its left is 9.
diff. with cipher annexed	40	
nearest to this in the little table is	41	number on its left is 3.

The last two figures of the number sought are 93, and the number itself is 3·141593.

The same method is applicable to our tables, though not with the same degree of accuracy.

EXAMPLE.

	4·90835	
Nearest log.	90832	corresponding number 8097
Difference	3	on its left in the marginal table is 5.

The number required is 80975.

EXAMPLE.

	0·06180	
Nearest log.	06145	corresponding No. 1152.
Diff.	35	

The nearest No. to which in the little table is 34 which subtract; on its left is 9.

The rem is.	10	on left of which in the marginal table is 3.

The number required is therefore 1·15293.

EXAMPLES IN MULTIPLICATION AND DIVISION BY LOGARITHMS.

54. 1. Required the product of 26784 and 7·865.

log. of 26784* is	4·42787
log. of 7·865 is	0·89570
Their sum is	5·32357

5·323574 is the log. of 210656, which last number is, therefore, the product required.

* In looking for the log. of this number, look first for that of 2678, multiply the tab. diff. by 4, the last figure of the given number, and cut off one figure from the product.

2. Required the product of 3·586, 2·1046, ·8372, and ·0294.

log. of	3·586	is	0·55461
of	2·1046	is	0·32317
of	·8372	is	$\bar{1}$·92283
of	·0294	is	$\bar{2}$·46835
Product	·18576		$\bar{1}$·26896

Instead of using negative characteristics, a method is sometimes employed of taking the difference between the negative characteristic and 10, which is really adding 10 to the negative characteristic, and writing this difference as a positive characteristic; thus, in the above example,

3·586	log.	0·55461
2·1046	log.	0·32317
·8372	log.	9·92283
·0294	log.	8·46835
·185764	log.	9·26896

twice 10 must be rejected from the sum. That is a 10 for each positive characteristic employed in the place of a negative.

The result thus obtained $\bar{1}$·26896 is written 9·26896, 10 being added again to avoid the negative characteristic.

3. Divide 28·654 by 127·34.

log. of 28·654	is	1·45718
of 127·34	is	2·10496
		difference $\bar{1}$·35222

$\bar{1}$·35222 is, therefore, the log. of the quotient which from the tables, observing the converse rule for pointing off decimals according to the characteristic (3 Art. 50), is ·225020.

Divide ·06314 by ·007241.

log. of ·06314	is	$\bar{2}$·80030
of ·007241	is	$\bar{3}$·85980
Quotient 8·7197		0·94050

55. We shall now demonstrate rules for raising numbers to powers, and for extracting the roots of numbers, by means of logarithms.

Resume the equation,

$$b^l = n$$

raising both members to the mth power, we have, observing the rule of Algebra, which is to multiply the exponent by the degree of the power,

$$b^{lm} = n^m$$

From this last equation, it appears that lm is the power to which it is necessary to raise the base b in order to produce n^m; hence the following

Rule.—To raise a number to any power, by means of logarithms, *multiply the logarithm of the given number by the exponent of the power, and the product will be the logarithm of the power.*

EXAMPLES.

1. Required the 4th power of •09163

log. of •09163 is	$\bar{2}$•96204
Multiply by	4
Product	$\bar{5}$•84816

$\bar{5}$•84816 is the log of •000070494, which last number is the power required.

2. Required the tenth power of •64.

log. of •64	$\bar{1}$•80618
	10
Power •0115293	$\bar{2}$•06180

In multiplying the first decimal place by 10, the product is 80, then 10 times $\bar{1}$ is $\overline{10}$, and 8 to carry is $\bar{2}$.

The same example, with positive characteristics, according to the method pointed out on p. 45 would stand thus

9•80618
10
8•06180

The 10 added to the $\bar{1}$ is repeated 10 times and therefore 100 must be rejected from the product, which leaves $\bar{2}$ for the characteristic to be written 8. The rule for placing the decimal point in the number corresponding to the logarithm will be to place one less cipher after the decimal point than is expressed by the difference between the characteristic and 10.

56. To find a rule for extracting the root of a number by means of logarithms, assume again the equation

$$b^l = n$$

Take the mth root of both members, applying in the first member the rule to divide the exponent by the number expressing the degree of the root, and there results

$$b^{\frac{l}{m}} = \sqrt[m]{n}$$

$\frac{l}{m}$ is here plainly the logarithm of $\sqrt[m]{n}$; hence the following

RULE.—To extract the root of a number by means of logarithms, *divide the logarithm of the given number, by the index of the root, and the quotient will be the logarithm of the root.*

EXAMPLES.

1. Required the 4th root of ·434296.

log. of ·434296	$\bar{1}$·63779

$\frac{1}{4}$ of this logarithm is obtained by observing that the index, which alone is negative, must be divided separately, as we should divide a minus term, followed by a plus term in Algebra; the $\bar{1}$ can be rendered divisible by borrowing $\bar{3}$, and afterwards carrying + 3 before the 6, rendering it 36; that is, the proposed logarithm is viewed under the form $\bar{4} + 3{\cdot}63779$.

The quotient is $\bar{1}$·90945* which is the logarithm of ·8118, the fourth root required.

2. Required the 10th root of 2.

log. of 2	0·30103
Divide this by 10	0·03010 quotient.

which is the log. of 1·07177, the root required.

3. Required the cube root of ·00048.

log. of ·00048	$\bar{4}$·68124
$\frac{1}{3}$ of it	$\bar{2}$·89375 = log. of ·078297, the root.

TABLES OF LOGARITHMIC SINES, TANGENTS, &C.

57. This is Table XXVII. It contains the logarithm of the sine, tangent, cosine and cotangent, secant and cosecant, corresponding to every degree and minute in the quadrant.†

These logarithms are those of the trigonometrical lines in a circle, the radius of which is 10000000000, or the tenth power of 10, the common logarithm of which is 10. As the sine is never greater than radius, its logarithm will always be less than 10, except for the arc 90°, the logarithmic sine of which is equal to 10.

* The last quotient figure is nearer 5 than 4.

† Without this table we should have been obliged to employ the other two tables which have been already described, as follows. First we must have found the natural sine, tangent, &c., of the given arc or angle in Table XXIV. then with this have entered Table XXVI. and found its logarithm. The tables of Callet do not contain the columns of secants and cosecants.

PROBLEM.

58. To find from the table the logarithm of the sine, tangent, or cosine of the number expressing any arc.

CASE I. If the given number be composed of degrees and minutes, seek first for the number of degrees among those which are written at the top or bottom of the pages ; at the top and on the left of the page if it be less than 45° ; at the bottom and on the right of the page if it be greater. Run the eye down the first column which goes on increasing from top to bottom, if the number of degrees is found at the top of the page ; or up the last column, which goes on increasing from the bottom upwards, if the number of degrees is found at the bottom ; run the eye, I say, through one or the other of these columns in the direction in which it increases until you have found the number of minutes given ; upon the same horizontal line with the minutes thus found you will find the logarithm of the sine, cosine, tangent, or cotangent which you seek. In order not to mistake the column, it is necessary to consult the title at the head of the column, if the number of degrees given is at the top of the page, but if it is at the bottom, the inferior title must be consulted.*

EXAMPLES.

1. Required the logarithmic sine, tangent, secant, cosine, cotangent, and cosecant of 19° 55′.

I find 19° at the top of page 204, I descend the first column at the left marked M, which goes on increasing downwards till I find 55′; upon the same horizontal line, and in the column entitled sine at top, I find 9·53231, in the column entitled cosine 9·97322, in the column of tangents 9·55910, and in that of cotangents 10·44090, that of secants 10·02678, that of cosecants 10·46769 ; and these numbers are therefore the numbers required.

2. Required the logarithmic sine and tangent of 70° 10′.

I find 70° at the bottom of p. 204† ; I ascend the last column marked M at bottom which goes on increasing upwards; I find 10′ in that column ; upon the same horizontal line I find in the column marked sine at bottom 9.97344, and in the column marked tangent at bottom 10·44288, which are the logarithms sought.

* The columns marked Hour A. M. and P. M. are connected with Nautical and Practical Astronomy, and will be explained under the proper head.

† For the reason mentioned in note p. 33, the paging of the tables will be found to exhibit gaps.

3. Required the logarithmic sine of 159° 20′.

This will be the same with that of its supplement 20° 40′. For convenience the supplements of arcs in the 1st quadrant are placed on the right of the page in the tables at top, and on the left at bottom. By looking therefore for 159° at top on the right, and immediately under for 20′ in the column M, on the range with this in the column entitled sine at top I find 9·54769, the same that would have been found for 20° 40′.

59. CASE II. If the given number be composed of degrees, minutes, and seconds, find the logarithm of the degrees and minutes as above, and then to know how much this should be increased for the given number of seconds, in case of the sine or tangent, or diminished in case of the cosine or cotangent, observe that the number in the column marked Diff. is the increase of the logarithm for the number of seconds in the column headed M, against which it stands, and will be the quantity to add to the logarithmic sine or tangent before found, or to subtract from the logarithmic cosine or cotangent.

The number in the column Diff. is calculated by subtracting one of two consecutive logarithms in the table, which differ by 1′, from the other,* and dividing the remainder by 60, the number of seconds in a minute; the quotient is the difference of logarithms corresponding to a difference of 1″ in the numbers to which they belong, or is the increase of the logarithm for 1″ increase of arc. This quotient, multiplied by any number of seconds, will give the increase of the logarithm for that number of seconds. This calculation depends upon the principle mentioned at Art. 51, that the differences of logarithms are proportional to the differences of their corresponding numbers. See also Art. 23 App. I.

60. The logarithmic sines and cosecants, cosines and secants, tangents and cotangents, have each pair but one column of differences between them, the reason of which will appear from the following demonstration.

The secant and cosecant may be easily computed from the cosines and sines. Thus (Art. 33):

$$\text{sec.} = \frac{\text{R}^2}{\text{cos}}$$

hence,

$$\text{log. sec} = 20 - \text{log. cos}$$

or log. of the quotient = difference of logs. (Art. 49); and log. of the

* This diff. is given in the first five pages of the table so that the seconds must be calculated as here described when the given arc is 4° or less, and any number of minutes.

square of a number equal to twice the log. of the number (Art. 56), and log of R = 10.

To obtain the log. secant, therefore, we have this

RULE.—*Subtract log. cosine from* 20.

Also (Art. 35),

$$\text{cosec} = \frac{R^2}{\sin}$$

hence,

$$\log.\ \text{cosec} = 20 - \log.\ \text{sine}$$

whence this

RULE.—*To obtain log. cosec, subtract log. sine from* 20.

From the above it appears that as the log. cos decreases with the increase of arc the log. sec increases by the same amount, and as the log. sin increases the log. cosec decreases by the same amount.

Again, by Art. 37, we have

$$\tan \times \cot = R^2$$

applying logarithms to this equation, since the log. of a product = the sum of the logs. of the factors, and the log. of a power = log. of the number raised to the power multiplied by the index of the power, we have

$$\log.\ \tan + \log.\ \cot = 2 \log R = 20$$

log. R being 10. Therefore having two arcs a and b, since log. tan + log. cot in both is 20 we have

$\log.\ \tan a + \log.\ \cot a = \log.\ \tan b + \log.\ \cot b$, or transposing,

$$\log.\ \tan a \sim \log.\ \tan b = \log.\ \cot a \sim \log.\ \cot b,$$

that is, *the difference of the logarithmic tangents of two arcs is equal to the difference of their logarithmic cotangents.*

EXAMPLES.

1. Required the logarithmic sine of 40° 26′ 28″.

I find the log. sine of 40° 26′ to be 9•81195; in the column M, at the left, I find the given number of seconds 28, and on the same horizontal line in the column of diff. I find 7, which added to the log. before found

$$\begin{array}{rr} & 9{\cdot}81195 \\ & 7 \\ \hline \text{gives} & 9{\cdot}81202^{*} \end{array}$$

The logarithmic tangent of any given number of degrees, minutes, and seconds, is found in a similar manner from the column entitled tangent.

* A similar arrangement for finding the difference corresponding to any number of seconds will be found in the table of natural sines and cosines, for the former on the left and for the latter on the right of the page.

2. Required the logarithmic cosine of 8° 40′ 40″.

I find the cosine of 8° 40′ to be 9·99501; the tabular difference in the adjoining column against the seconds 40″ is 1; subtracting* this result from 9·99501, the remainder is 9·99500, the logarithmic cosine sought.

The difference for the seconds may be calculated as follows.

3. Required the log. sine of 32° 10′ 23″.

32° 10′	log. sin	9·72622
32° 11′	" "	9·72643
	Diff.	21
		23
		63
		42
		60)483
	Diff. for 23″	8
32° 10′ log. sin		9·72622
32° 10′ 23″ log. sin		9·72630

61. In the tables of Callet are found the logarithmic sines, tangents, cosines, and cotangents for every 10″ in the quadrant; and the columns of differences contain the differences of the consecutive logarithms, or the increase of the logarithm for 10″ at that part of the quadrant. To take out therefore a logarithmic sine, &c., from these tables, take out for the degrees, minutes, and tens of seconds, and take out also the number from the column of diff.; cut off one figure on the right of the latter, which is equivalent to dividing by 10, and multiply it by the number of seconds by which the given arc differs from an exact number of tens of seconds. The product will be the number by which to increase or diminish the logarithm already taken out, according as the trigonometrical line to which it corresponds is an increasing or decreasing function of the arc.

EXAMPLES OF THE APPLICATION OF THE TABLES OF CALLET.

1. To find the log. tan of 49° 12′ 25″·8

Of 49° 12′ 20″ log. tan is	10·0639854†
Tab. diff. 425×5·8	246·5
	10·0640100 log. required.

* It will be recollected that as the arc increases in the first quadrant the cosine diminishes.

† The characteristic in the column of tangents and cotangents when 10, is printed 0. and when 11, is printed 1., in the tables of Callet.

2. To find the log. cot of 101° 25′ 43″ = log. cot of 78° 34′ 17″

Of 78° 34′ 10″ log. cot is 9•3057605

Diff. for 10″ or 1084×7 758•8

9•3056846 log. required.

In the tables of Callet are to be found the logarithms of trigonometrical lines of arcs given in grades, &c., of the centesimal division of the circle. The following is an example of the use of the table.

To find the log. sine of 92^g 75\` 84\`\`

of 92^g 75\` the log. sin is 9•9971776

tab. diff. 78×84 = 65•52

log. required is 9•9971842

The first 4 figures of the log. 9•997 are taken from the top or bottom of the column, the former when the logarithm is above a black horizontal line drawn across the column, the latter when below.

As the diff. 78 is the diff. of two consecutive logarithms corresponding to 100\`\` two figures must be pointed off to the right after multiplying by the 84.\`\`

PROBLEM.

62. *To find the degrees, minutes, and seconds answering to any given logarithmic sine, cosine, tangent, or cotangent.*

The method is, of course, exactly the reverse of that just given. Look for the given logarithm in the proper column, which you will know from its title, either at the top or bottom, and if you find it exactly, the degrees will be found at the top of the page, and the minutes on the same horizontal line with your logarithm, in the first column at the left, if the title of the column be at top, but the degrees will be found at the bottom of the page, and the minutes in the column at the right, if the title of the column which contains your logarithm be at the bottom.

If the given logarithm cannot be found, take the next less logarithm contained in the tables, subtract it from the given, and seek the remainder in the column marked diff.; the number on the same horizontal line in the column M is seconds, which add to the degrees and minutes belonging to the logarithm found in the tables, if your given logarithm be that of a sine or tangent, but which subtract from the degrees and minutes, if a cosine or cotangent.

Or more accurately, to find the seconds multiply the remainder above mentioned, by 60, and divide the product by the difference between two consecutive logarithms in the table.*

EXAMPLES.

1. Required the number of degrees, minutes, and seconds, of which the logarithmic sine is 9·88005.

I find the next less logarithm in the column marked sine at bottom, to be 9·87996, which subtracted from the given logarithm, leaves 9; this found in the column diff. adjoining, against it in the column M is 50, which is seconds. Taking the degrees from the bottom of the page, and the minutes from the column at the right, and in the same horizontal line with the logarithm 9·87996, I have 49° 20′ 50″ for the number required.

Or more accurately, since the diff. 9 corresponds to any number of seconds from 48″ to 52″ calculate as follows:

Given log.	9·88005		9·87996
Nearest log.	9·87996	consec log.	9·88007
Diff.	9	Diff.	11

```
    9
   60
11)540
   49
```

2. Required the number of degrees, minutes, and seconds, of which the log. cotangent is 10·00869.

I find the next less logarithm in the table to be 10·00859, that of 44° 26′, which subtracted from the given logarithm, leaves 10, corresponding to which in the column M is either 23″ or 24″; more accurately

```
   10
   60
25)600(24″
   50
   100
   100
```

and the required number is 44° 26′—24″ or 44° 25′ 36″.

* This last rule is on the principle that the difference of the logarithmic functions is proportional to the difference of their arguments, the difference of the arguments in this case being 60″.

3. Required the log. sec of 48° 35′ 27″.

BY TABLE XXVII.

48° 35′ log. sec	10•17945
Diff. for 27″	6
48° 35′ 27″ log. sec	10•17951

The tables of Callet not containing the logarithmic secants and cosecants, the calculation of this example from his tables would be as follows, by the rule at Art. 60.

log. cos 48° 35′ 27″ = 9•82049
log. sec 48° 35′ 27″ = (20 — 9•82049) = 10•17951

4. Required log. cosec 35° 27′ 24″. Ans. by Tab. XXVII., 10•23651
or log. sin 35° 27′ 24″ = 9•76349
log. cosec 35° 27′ 24″ = 20–9•76349 = 10•23651

A method of finding with greater accuracy the sine and tangent of a very small arc, or the cosine and cotangent of one near 90°, is pointed out at Art. 8 App. I.

To find the trigonometrical lines of arcs greater than 90°, observe the rule at Art. 17.

SOLUTION OF RIGHT ANGLED TRIANGLES, WITH THE AID OF LOGARITHMS.

EXAMPLE.

63. Referring to the example of Art. 39, where the hypothenuse

$$a = \frac{10^{10} \times 15}{\sin 35^\circ}$$

employing 10^{10} as R, instead of 1, because the tables which we are about to use are constructed with that value of R, we have, by the rules for multiplication and division of logarithms

log. of 10^{10}	=	10•00000
add log. 15	=	1•17609
		11•17609
Subtract log. sin 35°	=	9•75859
Remainder		1•41750 = log. of 26•15 = the hyp.

EXAMPLE II.

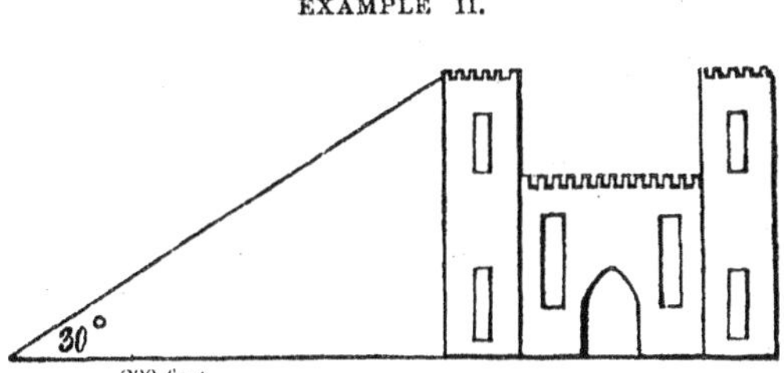

Referring to Art. 41 where the height of the tower c is

$$c = \tan 30° \times 200^{*}$$

which becomes, when the radius 1 in the first term of the proportion is changed into 10^{10}

$$c = \frac{\tan 30° \times 200}{10^{10}}$$

we have, by applying logarithms

$$\begin{array}{rl} \text{log. tan } 30° = & 9{\cdot}76144 \\ \text{add log. } 200 = & 2{\cdot}30103 \\ \hline & 12{\cdot}06247 \\ \text{Subtract log. } 10^{10} = & 10 \\ \hline & 2{\cdot}06247 = \text{log. } 115{\cdot}4 \end{array}$$

64. I. Another definition besides that given at Art. 14 for the sine of an angle, is *the ratio of the hypothenuse to the side opposite the angle* in any right angled triangle of which the angle forms one of the elements.

For from formulas (1) Art. 38 may be obtained.

$$\sin \text{B} = \frac{b}{a} \text{ and } \sin \text{C} = \frac{c}{a} \qquad (1)$$

II. A corresponding definition for the cosine of an angle is *the ratio of the hypothenuse to the side adjacent the angle* in any right angled triangle of which it forms an element. For, form. (3) Art. 38

$$\cos \text{B} = \frac{c}{a} \text{ and } \cos \text{C} = \frac{b}{a}\dagger \qquad (2)$$

* It is evident that radius must be understood in the second member of this expression, because a line c cannot be equal to the rectangle of two lines. (Art. 31.)

† The hypothenuse, which is the greater side, is evidently the denominator of the ratio, as the sine and cosine to radius unity are always fractions.

III. In a similar manner the tangent of an angle is *the ratio of the side adjacent to the side opposite the angle* in any right angled triangle of which the angle forms an element. For Art. 41, (3) and (4)

$$\tan B = \frac{b}{c} \text{ and } \tan C = \frac{c}{b} \qquad (3)$$

From these definitions the following consequences flow.

IV. *The hypothenuse multiplied by the sine of one of the acute angles of a right angled triangle will give the side opposite to the angle.*

For from (1) above clearing of fractions we have

$$a \sin B = b \text{ and } a \sin C = c \qquad (4)$$

V. *The hypothenuse multiplied by the cosine of the angle will give the side adjacent.* For from (2) above

$$a \cos B = c \text{ and } a \cos C = b^* \qquad (5)$$

VI. *The side adjacent multiplied by the tangent* will give the *side opposite.* For from (3) above

$$c \tan B = b \text{ and } b \tan C = c \qquad (6)$$

VII. To *find* the *hypothenuse* when a *side* and *angle* are *given,* we must still use the sine and cosine of the angle, but as a *divisor;* the *sine* when the side opposite is given and serves for a dividend, the *cosine* when the side adjacent. For from formulas (4) and (5) above may be obtained

$$a = \frac{b}{\sin B},\ a = \frac{c}{\sin C},\ a = \frac{c}{\cos B}, \text{ and } a = \frac{b}{\cos C} \qquad (7)$$

VIII. When one of the *perpendicular* sides is given with an angle to find the other, the *tangent* of the angle is the *multiplier* of the side *adjacent* the angle to *find* the side *opposite,* and is the *divisor* of the side *opposite,* to find the side *adjacent.* See (6) above from which also may be obtained

$$c = \frac{b}{\tan B} \text{ and } b = \frac{c}{\tan C} \qquad (8)$$

* When the hypothenuse is given with an acute angle it will be necessary always to multiply the hypothenuse by either the sine or cosine of the acute angle to obtain the other side; by *the sine* when it is the side *opposite* which is required, and by *the cosine* when it is the side *adjacent.* The memory will be aided by observing that for radius unity the sine and cosine are always fractions, and therefore the hypothenuse, which is the larger side, must evidently be *multiplied* by these in order to obtain the other sides.

IX. Radius unity has no effect either as a multiplier or divisor, nevertheless when using the tables in which radius is 10^{10} or 10000000000, it is necessary to know how the radius enters into the products or quotients formed by the above rules. And the following consideration will always show, viz. that two equal quantities must be homogeneous. A line cannot be equal to a surface or the rectangle of two lines. Therefore all the *products* formed by the above rules must be understood to be *divided* by radius. Neither can a line be equal to the ratio or quotient of two lines, for this is an abstract number. Therefore all the *quotients* formed by the above rules must be understood to be *multiplied* by radius.

In the use of logarithms, therefore, for the solution of right angled plane triangles, in every case two logarithms only will have to be employed, and their sum or difference taken according as the rule which applies to the case requires multiplication or division.

When the sum of the two logarithms is taken, 10 must be rejected from the characteristic, which is in effect dividing by radius, and when the difference is taken, 10 must be added to the characteristic of the minuend, which is in effect multiplying by radius. All this will be easily comprehended from the following examples.

EXAMPLE I.

In the right angled triangle ABC right angled at A, given the hypothenuse $a = 493{\cdot}7$, and the angle C $= 65^\circ\ 40'$ to find the side c.

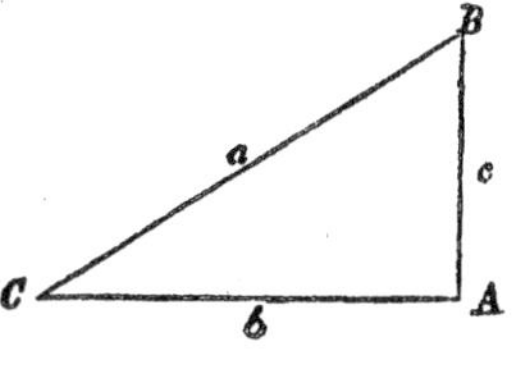

By Rule IV. above, observing that addition of logarithms corresponds to multiplication of the corresponding numbers, and rejecting 10 from the sum, according to IX., the calculation will be as follows :

a	493•7	log.	2•69346
C	65° 40′	log. sin	9•95960
c	449•8	log.	2•65306

The sum of the logarithms 2•69346 and 9•95960 which is 12·65306 after rejecting 10 from index will be the logarithm of 449•8 as may be seen by inspecting the tables, and this number is the value of the required side c.

EXAMPLE II.

The same things being given to find the side *b*. By Rule V. above

a	493·7	log.	2·69346
C	65° 40′	log. cos	9·61494
b	203·4	log.	2·30840

Both the above operations may be conveniently connected together by preparing first a blank form thus:

a	log.	log.
C	log. sin	log. cos
c	log.	
b		log.

in which the *arguments* or elements of the triangle occupy the first column, the trigonometrical functions of these arguments necessary for the calculation of the side *c* the second, and those necessary for the calculation of the side *b* the third. This form is then to be filled up as follows

a 493·7	log.	2·69346	log.	2·69346
C 65° 40′	log. sin	9·95960	log. cos	9·61494
c 449·8	log.	2·65306		
b 203·4			log.	2·30840

The log. of 493 when found in the tables is written in two columns, and the log. sin and log. cos of 65° 40′ can be taken out at one opening of the tables.

EXAMPLE III.

Let *b* = 73·94, C = 57° 20′, to find *a* by VII., subtracting the logarithms for division, adding 10 to the index of the minuend (see IX.) before subtracting, the calculation will be as follows:

b	73·94	log.	1·86888
C	57° 20′	log. cos	9·73219
a	136·9	log.	2·13669

EXAMPLE IV.

Let *c* = 115·3, C = 57° 20′, to find *a*

c	115·3	log.	2·06183
C	57° 20′	log. sin	9·92522
a	136·9	log.	2·13661

EXAMPLE V.

Given $b = 67{\cdot}84$, C = 41° 4′ 36″, to find c and a. By VII. VIII. and IX.

b	67•84	log.	1•8314858*	log.	1•8314858
C	41° 4′ 36″	log. cos	9•8772740	log. tan	9•9403365
a	89•993		1•9542118		
c	59•132				1•7718223

EXAMPLE VI.

Given $a = 84{\cdot}9$, $b = 53{\cdot}4$, to find B, C, and c.
For the rule applicable see I.

a	84•9	log.	1•92891
b	53•4	log.	1•72754
B	38° 58′ 28″	log. sin	9•79863
$a+b$	138•3	log.	2•14082
$a \sim b$	31•5	log.	1•49831
$c^2 = a^2 \sim b^2$†		log.	3•63913 ÷ 2
c	66•0035	log.	1•81957
C = 90°—B = 51° 01′ 32″			

EXERCISES IN THE SOLUTION OF RIGHT ANGLED PLANE TRIANGLES.

1. Given $a = 49{\cdot}63$, $b = 25{\cdot}42$, to find c, B, and C.
   Ans. $c = 42{\cdot}625$, C = 59° 11′ 25″, B = 30° 48′ 35″.
2. " $a = 723{\cdot}1$, $c = 95{\cdot}4$, to find b, C, and B.
   Ans. $b = 716{\cdot}75$, B = 82° 25′ 2″, C = 7° 34′ 58″
3. " $a = 853$, B = 49° 31′ 22″, to find the remaining parts.
   Ans. $b = 648{\cdot}8463$, c 553•725.
4. " $a = 940$, C = 30° 20′ 10″, to find the other elements
   Ans. $c = 474{\cdot}769$, b 811•32.
5. " $b = 25$, $c = 17$, to resolve the triangle.
   Ans. C 34° 12′ 58″ a 30•226, B 55° 47′ 02″.

* The logarithms in this example are taken from the tables of Callet, and extend to seven places of decimals.

† The product of $a + b$ and $a - b$ which is obtained by adding this logarithm, is equal to $a^2 - b^2$. (See Alg. Art. 13.)

6. Given $b = 42173$, $C = 40° 20'$.

Ans. $a = 55324$, c 358·08, B 49° 40'.

7. " $b = 328$, $B = 74° 25' 18''·7$.

Ans. a 340·5025, c 91·436.

8. " $c = 8·76213$, $C = 89°$.

Ans. a 8·7637 b ·15294, B 1°.

9. " $c = 82·94$, $B = 40° 50' 20''·6$.

Ans. a 109·612, b 71·684, C 49° 9' 39''·4.

10. " $b = 81·5$, $c = 92·19$.

Ans. B 41° 28' 42'', C 48° 31' 18'', a 123·33.

65. We shall finish the subject of right angled triangles by presenting a case of their practical application which is likely often to occur.

At the top of a mountain whose height was known by the barometer or otherwise to be 1000 feet above the level of the sea, a ship was observed through the tube of the instrument described at Art. 10, and the number of degrees between the tube and a plumb line from the centre of the circle was found to be 77° 30'; required the distance of the ship.

A right angled triangle is here formed, in which are given the perpendicular and angle at the vertex, and the base is required.

Referring to Rule VI.

$$\tan 77° 30' \times 1000 = \text{dist. required.}$$

1000	log.	3·00000
77° 30'	log. tan	10·65424
		3·65424 = log. of 4510·71 feet.

Therefore the distance of the ship is 4510·71 feet, or a little over $\frac{5}{6}$ of a mile.

EXERCISES.

An upright post being 90 feet high, and its horizontal shadow 117 feet, to find the altitude of the sun. *Ans.* 37° 34' 5''.

The alt. of the sun being 48° 10' and the length of a horizontal shadow = 201, to find the height of the tower which casts it. *Ans.* 224·54.

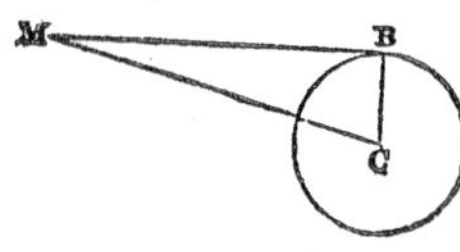

To find the horizontal parallax of the moon (angle M), its distance MC being 240,000 miles, and the rad. of the earth BC 3956.

Ans. 56′ 40″.

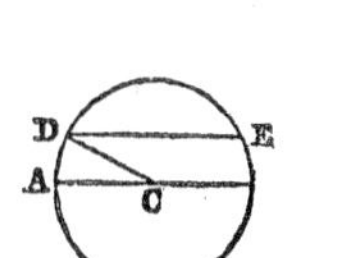

The lat. of a place D being given, DCA $= 38^\circ\ 14'$ and the radius DC of the earth 3956 miles, to find the radius of the parallel DE.

Ans. 3107·43.

To find the side of a regular inscribed figure of 13 sides, when the radius of the circle is 6·7.

Ans. 3·206.

The side of an inscribed regular heptagon being 5·73, find the rad. of the circumscribing circle. *Ans.* 6·6032.

66. It is customary where the subtraction of logarithms, corresponding to the division of numbers, is to be performed, to change this operation into addition by means of what is called the arithmetical complement of each subtractive logarithm. The arithmetical complement of a logarithm is the remainder after taking the logarithm from 10; thus the arithmetical complement of the logarithm 2·32245, is 7·67755.

$$\begin{array}{r} 10\cdot00000 \\ 2\cdot32245 \\ \hline 7\cdot67755 \end{array}$$

It may be formed most conveniently, instead of beginning at the right and subtracting each figure from 10 and carrying one each time throughout, by beginning at the left and subtracting each figure from 9 till you come to the last figure, which subtract from 10.

When we have a logarithm to subtract, we shall obtain the same result by adding its arithmetical complement, and afterwards subtracting 10. Which may be proved as follows:

By the definition arith. comp. log. $b = 10 - \log. b$.

Now add this arith. comp. to some other log. as log. a, the result will be

$$\log. a + 10 - \log. b$$

subtract 10 and there remains

$$\log. a - \log. b$$

The same result as would have been obtained by subtracting log. b from log. a.

Hence to perform operations containing a number of multiplications and divisions, by means of logarithms, we have the following

RULE.—Write the logarithms of all the multipliers, and the arith. complements of those of the divisors in a column. Add up the whole, and reject as many times 10 from the characteristic of the sum as there have been arith. complements employed.

"This use of the arithmetical complement is not expedient in the solution of right angled triangles, but in the solution of oblique angled triangles it always saves one line of numerical work."

SOLUTION OF PLANE TRIANGLES IN GENERAL.

67. Let ABC be any triangle. From the vertex of one of the angles A, let fall upon the side opposite, the perpendicular AD; the given triangle will be divided into two right angled triangles ABD and ACD.

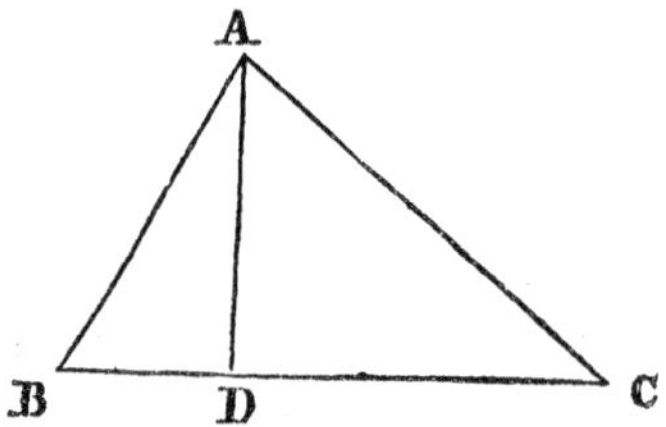

In the first of these (Art. 64, IV.) we have

$$AD = AB \times \sin B$$

Again, in the right angled triangle ACD, we have

$$AD = AC \times \sin C$$

The first members of the two equations above being the same, the second members are equal, hence

$$\sin B \times AB = \sin C \times AC$$

Turning this equation into a proportion, by making the first product the extremes, and the second the means, we have

$$\sin B : \sin C :: AC : AB$$

That is, *the sines of the angles of any plane triangle, bear the same proportion to each other as the opposite sides.**

From the nature of the above demonstration the selection of the vertex from which to let fall the perpendicular being entirely unrestricted, it is plain that this rule applies to all the angles and sides alike.

* The same demonstration will apply when the perpendicular from the vertex of one of the angles falls upon the side opposite produced.

When therefore two of the three given elements of a triangle, are a side and its opposite angle, the element opposite to the third given element may be found by the proportion which has just been established.

We shall according to our custom suppose a practical problem which introduces the case of solution in question.

Let it be required to ascertain accurately the distance from the town in the figure, across an impassable marsh, for the purpose of estimating the expense of a causeway.

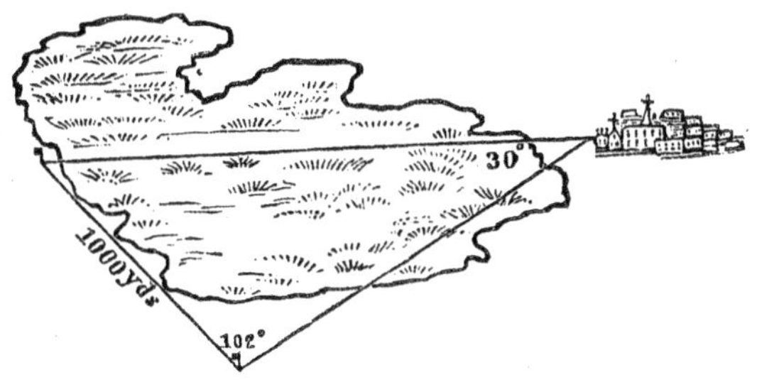

Plant two staves with small flags, the one at the border of the marsh opposite the town where the causeway is to terminate, and the other at some convenient point from which the first and the town may both be seen. Measure the distance between the staves, and let it be 1000 yards; observe also the angle at the second staff by turning the tin tube of the instrument for taking angles first to the staff on the border of the marsh and then to the town; let this angle be 102°; observe also the angle at the town subtended by the line of the two staves, and let this last be 30°. A triangle will be formed in which are known an angle 30°, the side opposite 1000 yards, and another angle 102°, the side opposite to which is required. Then applying the above proportion

sin 30° : sin 102° : : 1000 : length of causeway required.

$$\text{Arith. comp. log. sin. } 30^\circ = 0{\cdot}30103$$
$$\text{(Art. 15) log. sin } 102^\circ = \text{log. sin } 78^\circ = 9{\cdot}99040$$
$$\text{log. } 1000 = 3{\cdot}00000$$
$$3{\cdot}29143 = \text{log. of } 1956$$

The length of the causeway must be 1956 yards.

EXERCISE.

In an oblique angled triangle given

$A = 30^\circ\ 20'\ 10''$, $B = 40^\circ\ 10'\ 30''$, $a = 9754$, to find C, b, and c.

Ans. $C = 109^\circ\ 29'\ 20''$, $b = 12458{\cdot}28$, $c = 18205{\cdot}71$.

67. This proportion is also applicable to the case where two angles and the interjacent side of a triangle are given. Such is the case in the problem at Art. 10.

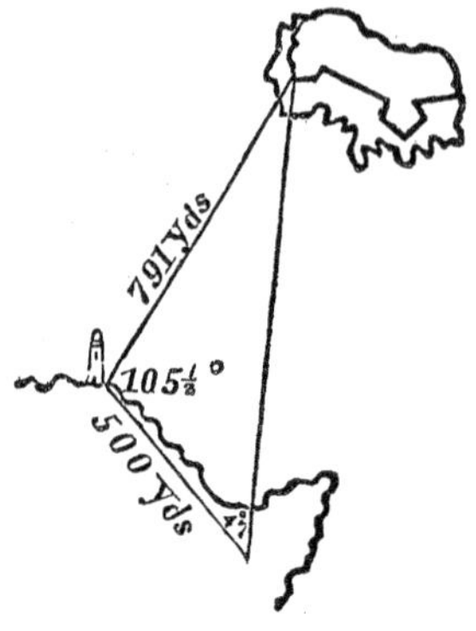

One of the angles of that triangle being given equal to 47°, and the other equal to 105° 30′, it will be easy to find the third angle, by recollecting that the sum of the three angles of a triangle is equal to two right angles (Geom. Theorem 15), or 180°; therefore subtracting the sum of the two given, 47° + 105° 30′ = 152° 30′ from 180°, the remainder 27° 30′ is the third angle of the triangle, and is opposite the given side 500 yards. Thus by the proportion

sin 27° 30′ : sin 47° : : 500 : dist. from lt. house to fort.

arith. comp. log. sin 27° 30′ = 0·33559
log. sin 47° = 9·86413
log. 500 = 2·69897
2·89869 = log. of 791·9

The distance from the light-house to the fort is 791·9 yards.

The importance, where any considerable degree of accuracy is required, of the method of solution by calculation, instead of that by construction, will appear from the fact that with tolerably accurate instruments, and some care in the construction, we made the required side, which we here find to be 791·9 yards, to be 800 yards upon the scale; thus committing an error in the construction of about 8 yards.

EXERCISE.

Given in an oblique angled triangle,
A = 75° 30′ 18″·5, B = 45° 16′, c = 1145·3, to find the other parts of the triangle.

Ans. C = 59° 13′ 41″·5, a = 1290·55, b = 946·949.

We add another practical

EXAMPLE

Involving the same case of solution combined with the solution of a right angled triangle.

An observer upon a plain desires to find the height of a neighboring hill above the level of the plain.

Near the foot of the hill let him take the angle of elevation to the top, and suppose it to be 55° 54′; then let him measure back a distance, say

100 yards, and again take the angle of elevation, which let be 33° 20′. Then in the triangle of which 100 yards is the base, and 33° 20′ is one of the angles at the base, we may have the angle at the vertex, and opposite to the given base, by observing that the exterior angle of a triangle being equal to the two interior and opposite (Geom. Theorem 13), one of the interior is equal to the exterior, minus the other interior, and therefore the angle at the vertex here is equal to 55° 54′—33° 20′ = 22° 34′; then say, as in the last example,

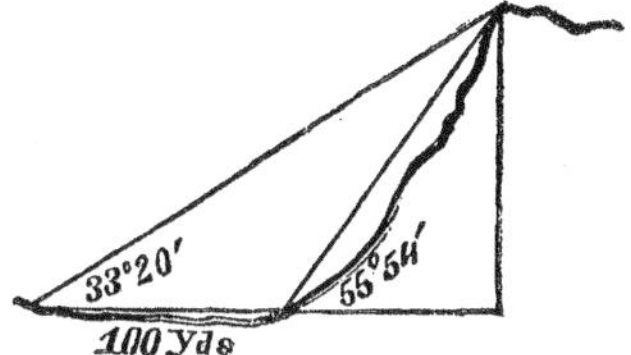

$$\sin 22^\circ\ 34' : \sin 33^\circ\ 20' :: 100 : \text{side opp. to } 33^\circ\ 20';$$

but in the right angled triangle of which 55° 54′ is the angle at the base, and the height of the hill one of the perpendicular sides, we have the proportion

$$10^{10} : \sin 55^\circ\ 54' :: \text{hypoth.} : \text{height required.}$$

from which, multiplying means and dividing by the first term,

$$\text{height req.} = \frac{\sin 55^\circ\ 54' \times \text{hypoth}}{10^{10}}$$

but from the preceding proportion

$$\text{hypoth. or side op. } 33^\circ\ 20' = \frac{\sin 33^\circ\ 20' \times 100}{\sin 22^\circ\ 34'}$$

substituting this value in the last equation, we have

$$\text{height required} = \frac{\sin 55^\circ\ 54' \times \sin 33^\circ\ 20' \times 100}{10^{10} \times \sin 22^\circ\ 34'}$$

arith. comp log. 10^{10} = 0·00000
arith. comp. log. sin 22° 34′ = 0·41594
log. sin 55° 54′ = 9·91806
log. sin 33° 20′ = 9·73997
log. 100 = 2

sum rejecting twice 10 = 2·07397 = log. of 118 6.

118·6 yards, or 355·8 feet is the height of the hill.

* To this result the height of the eye or of the instrument should be added.

EXAMPLE III.

68. Let there be a street in which the front of a triangular block is 216 feet, and another street making an angle of 22° 37′ with the first; under what angle must a third street be laid out from the extremity A of the first, so that the front of a complete row of buildings upon it shall be 117 feet in length?

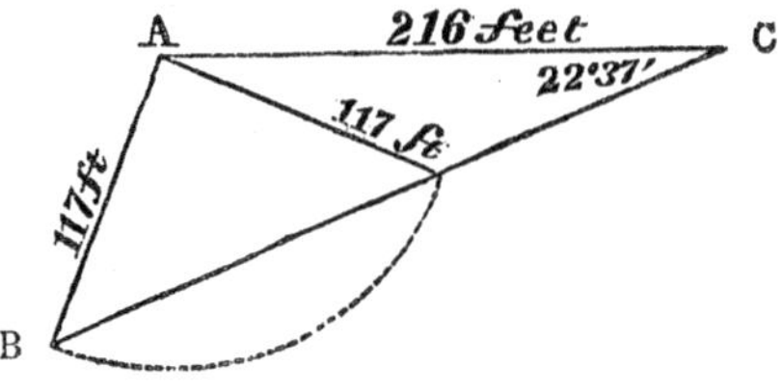

SOLUTION.

117 : sin 22° 37′ : : 216 : sin of the angle B

117 arith comp. of log.	= 7.93181
22° 37′ log. sin	= 9·58497
216 log.	= 2·33445
45° 13′ 55″ log. sin	= 9.85123

B = 45° 13′ 55″ and 180° — B — C = 112° 9′ 5″ = angle A required.

It must be observed that 9·85123 is also the log. sine of the supplement of 45° 13′ 55″, because the sine of an arc is equal to the sine of its supplement. (Art. 15.) Hence 134° 46′ 5″ is also a value of the angle B, and there are two solutions to the problem, which are both exhibited in the diagram. This case corresponds to Problem 8, Geom.

If the given angle were right or obtuse, there could be but one solution, and the required angle must be acute.

The same is the case if the given side opposite the given angle be greater than the other given side, because in every plane triangle the greater angle is opposite the greater side.

69. We shall next derive a formula for the solution of a triangle when the three sides are given, and one or all of the angles required.

Let ABC be any triangle; from the vertex of one of the angles A, let fall a perpendicular A D upon the side opposite. This perpendicular may fall either within or without the triangle. First suppose that it falls within; then (Geom. Th. 29.)

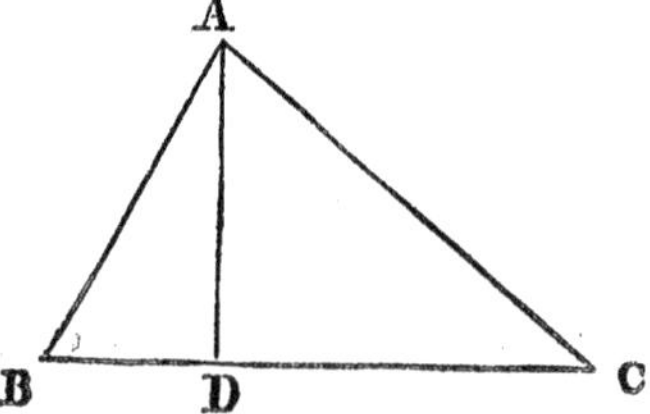

$$AC^2 = AB^2 + BC^2 - 2\,BC \times BD$$

$$\text{whence } BD = \frac{AB^2 + BC^2 - AC^2}{2\,BC}$$

Also in the right angled triangle ABD, we have

$$R : \cos B :: AB : BD \quad \text{(Art. 38)}$$

whence multiplying the extremes and dividing by the third term

$$\cos B = \frac{R \times BD}{AB}$$

substituting in this expression for BD its value obtained above, we have

$$\cos B = R \times \frac{AB^2 + BC^2 - AC^2}{2\,AB \times BC}$$

an expression for the cosine of an angle in terms of the three sides of a triangle.

Suppose now that the perpendicular falls without the triangle.

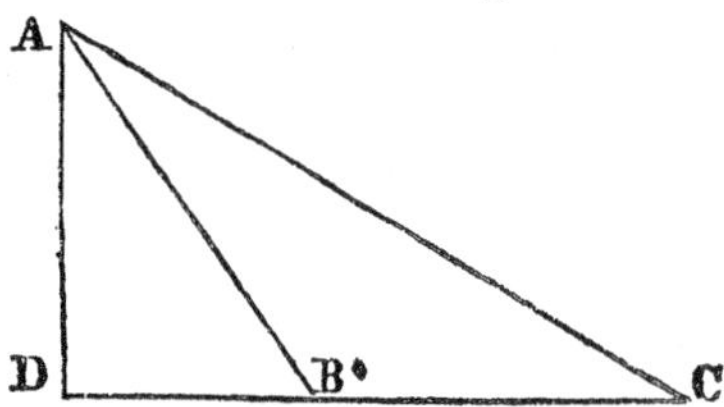

Then (Geom. Theorem 28)

$$AC^2 = AB^2 + BC^2 + 2\,BD \times BC$$

hence

$$-BD = \frac{AB^2 + BC^2 - AC^2}{2\,BC}$$

Again, in the right angled triangle ABD

$$R : \cos ABD :: AB : BD$$

hence,

$$\cos ABD = \frac{R \times BD}{AB}$$

But ABD is the supplement of the angle B of the triangle ABC, hence

$$\cos ABD = -\cos B$$

substituting $-\cos B$ for $\cos ABD$ above, and changing the signs we have

$$\cos B = \frac{-R \times BD}{AB}$$

substituting for $-$ BD in the second member of this equation its value found above, we have as before

$$\cos B = R \times \frac{AB^2 + BC^2 - AC^2}{2 AB \times BC}$$

or employing the small letters to represent the sides opposite the angles which are expressed by the large letters of the same name

$$\cos B = R \frac{a^2 + c^2 - b^2}{2ac}$$

That is to say, *the cosine of either angle of a triangle is equal to the sum of the squares of the two sides which contain it, minus the square of the side opposite, divided by twice the rectangle of the containing sides.*

Let us apply this formula to an

EXAMPLE.

Suppose the three sides of a triangular plat of ground are to be 50, 60, and 70 yards, under what angle must the first two be laid out?

$$\cos \text{required angle} = R \times \frac{2500 + 3600 - 4900}{2 \times 50 \times 60} = \tfrac{1}{5}$$

if we make $R = 1$; hence $\frac{1}{5}$ or ·20000 is the nat. cosine of the angle required. This angle will be found from the table of sines and cosines, to be 78° 27′ 47″.*

This case might also be solved with the table of log. sines, &c., by subtracting the log. of the whole denominator from that of the whole numerator, and adding 10 the log. of R, or adding at once the arith. comp. of the denominator, the logs. of the numerator and R, rejecting 10 from the sum; in either case the result would be log. cosine of the angle required. The solution is left as an exercise for the student.

70. We now proceed to demonstrate some formulas which express relations between the different trigonometrical lines of the same arc, and

* The seconds are found as follows: Take the difference between the two cosines next greater and next less than yours, and also the difference between yours and the next greater, multiply the latter difference by 60 and divide the product by the former fference; the quotient will be the seconds sought. The reason appears from the lowing proportion.

diff. of cosines. in the tab.	:	diff. of numbers. 60″	: :	diff. of cosines. yours and the tab.	:	diff. of numbers. seconds requred.

between the trigonometrical lines of two different arcs. They are introduced here because necessary for the solution of the few cases of plane triangles which remain. We shall first derive formulas by means of which, when the sines and cosines of two arcs are known, the sine and cosine of their sum or difference may be found. Thus if the sine and cosine of 30°, and also those of 20° be given, those of 50° = 30° + 20° or of 10° = 30° — 20° may be found.

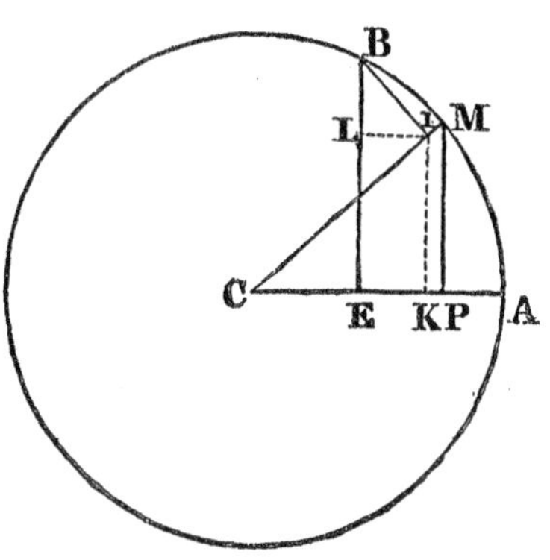

Let A M = a in the diagram be one of the given arcs, and BM = b, be the other. Then M P = sin a, B I = sin b, since it is the perpendicular let fall from one extremity of the arc b, upon the radius which passes through the other extremity. C P = cos a and C I the distance from the foot of the sine to the centre = cos b. A B = A M + M B = $a + b$, B E = sin $(a + b)$ and E C = cos $(a + b)$.

In the triangle C K I we have (Art. 64, IV.)

$$\text{IK} = \sin \text{C} \times \text{CI}$$

or,

$$\text{EL} = \sin a \cos b \qquad (1)$$

and in the triangle B I L (Art. 64, V.)

$$\text{BL} = \text{BI} \cos \text{B}$$

or since B = C their sides being respectively perpendicular

$$\text{BL} = \sin b \cos a \qquad (2)$$

Adding equations (1) and (2) and observing that E L + B L = B E = sin A B we have

$$\sin (a + b) = \sin a \cos b + \sin b \cos a \qquad (3)$$

The second member must be understood to be divided by R = 1, for a line cannot be equal to the sum of two surfaces (See Art. 64, IX.).

Formula (3) is read thus : *the sine of the sum of any two arcs is equal to the sine of the first into the cosine of the second plus the sine of the second into the cosine of the first, divided by radius.*

Again,

$$\text{CK} = \cos \text{C} \times \text{CI} = \cos a \cos b \qquad (4)$$

$$\text{EK} = \text{IL} = \sin \text{B} \times \text{BI} = \sin a \sin b \qquad (5)$$

Subtracting (5) from (4), and observing that $CK - EK = CE = \cos AB$ (Art. 24), we have

$$\cos(a + b) = \cos a \cos b - \sin a \sin b \qquad (6)$$

The second member of (6) must be understood to be divided by R or the first member to be multiplied by R to produce homogeneity.

Formula (6) is read thus: *the cosine of the sum of any two arcs is equal to the rectangle of their cosines minus the rectangle of their sines divided by radius.*

In formula (3) let $a = 60°$ and $b = 20°$ then by the first

$$\sin 80° = \frac{\sin 60° \cos 20° + \sin 20° \cos 60°}{1 \text{ or } 10^{10} \text{ as the case may be}}$$

Performing the operations by the aid of logarithms

	log. sin 60° = 9.93753		
	log. cos 20° = 9.97299		
log. sin 20° = 9.53405	————		
log. cos 60° 9·69897	9·91052*	log. of ·81380	
9·25302		log. of ·17101	
		sin 80° = ·98481	

By formula (6)

$$\cos 80° = \frac{\cos 60° \cos 20° - \sin 60° \sin 20}{1 \text{ or } 10^{10} \text{ or whatever R may be}} \dagger$$

We shall derive expressions for $\sin(a - b)$ and $\cos(a - b)$ or the sine and cosine of the difference of two arcs in terms of the arcs themselves, by making, in the formulas just derived, for $\sin(a + b)$ and $\cos(a + b)$; $b = -b$, observing that $\cos(-b) = \cos b$ and $\sin(-b) = -\sin b$ (Art. 27). By this substitution there results

* From each of the logs. 9·91052 and 9·25302, 10 must be rejected in order to pass from the table of logarithmic sines, &c., in which the radius is 10000000000, the logarithm of which is 10, to the table of natural sines, &c., in which the radius is 1. The characteristics of these logarithms would thus become $\bar{1}$, but they may be read so as they stand according to Art. 54, Ex. 2.

† The student may develope this as an exercise, and compare the result with cos 80° as given by the table of natural sines and cosines.

$$\sin(a - b) = \sin a \cos b - \sin b \cos a \qquad (7)$$

and

$$\cos(a - b) = \cos a \cos b + \sin a \sin b \qquad (8)$$

EXERCISES.

Find the sine of 57° from sin of 15° = ·25882, and cos = ·96593, and sin 42° = ·66913, and cosine = ·74314.

Find the cosine of 9° from sine and cosine of 24° = ·40674 and ·91355 and sine and cosine 15° = ·25882 and ·96593.

These four formulas for the sine and cosine of the sum and difference of two arcs should be committed to memory, as they are constantly recurring in trigonometry, and in the higher analysis. The four may be expressed in two by the use of the double sign, thus

$$\sin(a \pm b) = \sin a \cos b \pm \sin b \cos a$$

$$\cos(a \pm b) = \cos a \cos b \mp \sin a \sin b$$

71. From formula (3) $\sin(a+b) =$ &c., we derive one much used in the higher analysis for expressing twice an arc in terms of the arc itself, by simply making $b = a$ the result is

$$\sin 2a = 2 \sin a \cos a \qquad (1)$$

the two terms of the second member becoming the same.

We also get an analogous expression for the cosine of twice an arc by making $b = a$ in formula (6) of the last article $\cos(a + b) =$ &c. This expression is

$$\cos 2a = \cos^2 a - \sin^2 a \qquad (2)$$

Thus knowing the sine and cosine of 20°, these last two formulas would give us the sine and cosine of 40°.

These two formulas may be modified so as to express the sine and cosine of an arc in terms of half the arc, under which last form they are much used. This is accomplished by making $a = \frac{1}{2} a$, which is legitimate, since a is supposed to have no particular value; then $2a$ becomes a and we have from (1)

$$\sin a = 2 \sin \tfrac{1}{2} a \cos \tfrac{1}{2} a \qquad (3)$$

and from (2)

$$\cos a = \cos^2 \tfrac{1}{2} a - \sin^2 \tfrac{1}{2} a \qquad (4)$$

EXERCISES.

Find the sine of 32° from the sine and cosine of 16°, the former being ·27564 and the latter ·96126. Find also the cosine of 32° from the same data.

NOTE.—This last is best done by observing that the product of the sum and difference is equal to the difference of the squares.

72. By means of this last, and a very simple formula depending upon the well-known property of the right angled triangle, that the square of the hypothenuse is equal to the sum of the squares of the other two sides, a formula expressing the value of the sine of half an arc in terms of the arc itself may be obtained.

The formula depending upon the property of the right angled triangle, will be found by referring to the last diagram, in which the triangle C P M is right angled at P, whence (Geom. Th. 26).

$$\text{C P}^2 + \text{P M}^2 = \text{C M}^2$$

or calling A M $\frac{1}{2}\,a$

$$\cos^2 \tfrac{1}{2}\,a + \sin^2 \tfrac{1}{2}\,a = \text{R}^2 \qquad (5)$$

Introducing R into equation (4) according to the rule for homogeneity at Art. 31, and changing the order of the members it becomes

$$\cos^2 \tfrac{1}{2}\,a - \sin^2 \tfrac{1}{2}\,a = \text{R} \cos a \qquad (6)$$

Subtracting (6) from (5) we have

$$2 \sin^2 \tfrac{1}{2}\,a = \text{R}^2 - \text{R} \cos a$$

Dividing by 2 and taking the square root of both members of this last equation, we have the formula required.

$$\sin \tfrac{1}{2}\,a = \sqrt{\tfrac{1}{2}\,\text{R}^2 - \tfrac{1}{2}\,\text{R} \cos a} \qquad (7)$$

making R = 1

$$\sin \tfrac{1}{2}\,a = \sqrt{\tfrac{1}{2} - \tfrac{1}{2} \cos a} \qquad (8)$$

73. We resume the solution of triangles, having now a formula, by means of which we shall be able to derive an expression for one of the angles of a triangle in terms of the three sides; an expression which will be found much more convenient for the application of logarithms than that contained in Art. 69.

By Art. 69, making R = 1

$$\cos \text{B} = \frac{a^2 + c^2 - b^2}{2\,a\,c} \qquad (1)$$

putting B in the place of a in the formula for sin $\frac{1}{2}$ a (formula (8) of the last article) we have

$$\sin \tfrac{1}{2} \text{B} = \sqrt{\tfrac{1}{2} - \tfrac{1}{2} \cos \text{B}}$$

substituting for cos B in this, its value in (1), we have

$$\sin \tfrac{1}{2} \text{B} = \sqrt{\tfrac{1}{2} - \tfrac{1}{2} \frac{a^2 + c^2 - b^2}{2\, a\, c}}$$

reducing the terms under the radical to a common denominator, there results

$$\sin \tfrac{1}{2} \text{B} = \sqrt{\frac{2\, a\, c - a^2 - c^2 + b^2}{4\, a\, c}}$$

but (Alg. Art. 13, Note 2)

$$2\, a\, c - a^2 - c^2 = -(a - c)^2$$

hence

$$\sin \tfrac{1}{2} \text{B} = \sqrt{\frac{b^2 - (a - c)^2}{4\, a\, c}}$$

but the difference of the squares of two quantities is equal to the product of their sum and difference (Alg. Art. 13, Note 2), hence

$$b^2 - (a - c)^2 = (b + a - c)\ (b - a + c)$$

substituting the second member of this in place of the first in the preceding equation, and separating the 4 of the denominator into two factors 2×2, we have

$$\sin \tfrac{1}{2} \text{B} = \sqrt{\left\{ \frac{\frac{(b + a - c)}{2} \ \frac{(b + c - a)}{2}}{a\, c} \right\}}$$

but

$$\frac{b + a - c}{2} = \frac{b + a + c}{2} - c \text{ and } \frac{b + c - a}{2} = \frac{b + c + a}{2} - a$$

representing $b + a + c$ the sum of the three sides of the triangle by s, the second members of the two last equalities become

$$\tfrac{1}{2}\, s - c \text{ and } \tfrac{1}{2}\, s - a$$

substituting these for their equals in the preceding equation it becomes

$$\sin \tfrac{1}{2} \text{B} = \sqrt{\frac{(\frac{1}{2} s - c)\ (\frac{1}{2} s - a)}{a\ c}} \qquad (2)$$

the formula sought.*

As the angles have each the same relations to the corresponding sides of a triangle, the same formula by a proper modification will furnish the values of the angles A and C.

It may be expressed in ordinary language thus, *the sine of half either angle of a triangle is equal to radius into the square root of half the sum of the three sides minus one of the adjacent sides, into half the sum minus the other adjacent side, divided by the rectangle of the adjacent sides.*

To apply this to an

EXAMPLE.

Let there be three places at distances from each other respectively of 50, 60, and 70 miles. Required the angle under which two roads must depart from that which is 60 and 70 distant from the other two, in the direction of these last. 60 and 70 will be the sides of a triangle adjacent the required angle, and 50 the side opposite; then

$$\sin \tfrac{1}{2} \text{ the angle} = \text{R} \sqrt{\frac{(\frac{1}{2} s - 70)\ (\frac{1}{2} s - 60)}{60 \times 70}}$$

$$\tfrac{1}{2} s = \frac{180}{2} = 90,\ \tfrac{1}{2} s - 70 = 20$$

$$\text{and } \tfrac{1}{2} s - 60 = 30$$

log. of 20 = 1·30103
log. of 30 = 1·47712
ar. comp. of log. of 60 = 8·22185
ar. comp. of log. of 70 = 8·15490

sum rejecting twice 10 = $\bar{1}$·15490

Divide this sum by 2 for √, quot. = — 0·5 + ·07745

Add 10 to multiply by R sum = 9·57745 = log. sin of ½ the required angle.

* Radius must be understood as a factor of the second member for the sake of homogeneity, since the quantity under the radical is the ratio of a surface to a surface, and therefore an abstract number.

From the tables we find ½ the angle to be 22° 12′ 28″.
The whole angle required will be double this or

44° 24′ 56″

The other two angles may be found in a similar manner; the one is 67° 07′ 18″, the other 78° 27′ 40″.

If R in the above formula should be made to pass (by squaring it) under the radical sign, it would be necessary to add twice 10 in order to effect the multiplication by this factor R^2 before taking the square root. But as on the other hand twice 10 must be rejected for the arithmetical complements used, these two operations exactly counterbalance each other, and neither of them need be performed. By adding together the four logarithms, therefore, and dividing by 2, the same result will be obtained. The operation in the above example would be as follows:

log. of 20 = 1·30103
log. of 30 = 1·47712
ar. comp. of log. of 60 = 8·22185
ar. comp. of log. of 70 = 8·15490
2)19·15490
log. sin. of 22° 12′ 28″ = 9·57745

The best mode of proceeding in the solution of a plane triangle when three sides are given, is to prepare a blank form similar to that on p. 58, by ruling four columns, the first for the arguments, and each of the other three for the trigonometrical functions of those arguments necessary to be employed in the calculation of one of the three angles. Thus,
a, *b*, *c*, denoting the given sides, *s* their sum, and A, B, C the required angles,

Column of Arguments.	Column for calculation of A.	Column for calculation of B.	Column for calculation of C.
a		ar. co. log.	ar. co log.
b	ar. co. log.		ar. co. log.
c	ar. co. log.	ar. co. log.	
s			
½ *s*			
½ *s* — *a*		log.	log.
½ *s* — *b*	log.		log.
½ *s* — *c*	log.	log.	
	2)______		
½ A	log. sin	2)______	
½ B		log. sin	2)______
½ C			log. sin

To show how this form is filled up take the following example.

Given $a = 33$, $b = 42\cdot6$, $c = 53\cdot6$, required A, B, C.

Column of Arguments.	Column for calculation of A.	Column for calculation of B.	Column for calculation of C.
a 33		ar. co. log. 8·4814861	ar. co. log. 8·4814861
b 42·6	ar. co. log. 8·3705904		ar. co. log. 8·3705904
c 53·6	ar. co. log. 8·2708352	ar. co. log. 8·2708352	
s 129·2			
$\frac{1}{2} s$ 64·6			
$\frac{1}{2} s - a$ 31·6		log. 1·4996871	log. 1·4996871
$\frac{1}{2} s - b$ 22	log. 1·3424227		log. 1·3424227
$\frac{1}{2} s - c$ 11	log. 1·0413927	log. 1·0413927	
	2)19·0252410		
$\frac{1}{2}$ A 18° 59′ 56″·5	log. sin 9·5126205	2)19·2934011	
$\frac{1}{2}$ B 26° 18′ 53″·3		log. sin. 9·6467005	2)19·6941863
$\frac{1}{2}$ C 44° 41′ 10″			log. sin 9·8470931

A = 37° 59′ 53″, B = 52° 37′ 46″·6, C = 89° 22′ 20″.

There are other forms which have some advantages over the above, and which may be derived in an analogous manner. They are as follows.

$$\sin A = \frac{2R}{bc}\sqrt{\tfrac{1}{2}s\,(\tfrac{1}{2}s-a)\,(\tfrac{1}{2}s-b)\,(\tfrac{1}{2}s-c)} \quad (3)$$

$$\cos \tfrac{1}{2} A = R\sqrt{\frac{\tfrac{1}{2}s\,(\tfrac{1}{2}s-a)}{bc}}\ {}^{*} \quad (4)$$

$$\tan \tfrac{1}{2} A = R\sqrt{\frac{(\tfrac{1}{2}s-b)\,(\tfrac{1}{2}s-c)}{\tfrac{1}{2}s\,(\tfrac{1}{2}s-a)}}\ {}^{\dagger} \quad (5)$$

The student may write the blank forms for these formulas as an exercise.

EXAMPLES.

1. Given in a plane triangle the three sides 120, 112·65, and 112, to find the three angles.

Ans. { 57° 27′
57° 58′ 39″
64° 34′ 21″ }

* Derived from (5) and (6) of Art. 72, and (1) of Art 73. A convenient form.

† By dividing the formula $\sin \frac{1}{2} A = \sqrt{\frac{1}{2} - \frac{1}{2}\cos A}$ by the formula $\cos \frac{1}{2} A = \sqrt{\frac{1}{2} + \frac{1}{2}\cos A}$ is found $\tan \frac{1}{2} A = \frac{\sin A}{1 + \cos A}$ from which (4) above may be derived; or at once dividing (3) by (4). In a similar manner may be found $\cot \frac{1}{2} a = \frac{\sin a}{1 - \cos a}$, $\sec \frac{1}{2} a = \sqrt{\frac{2 \sec a}{\sec a + 1}}$, and $\operatorname{cosec} \frac{1}{2} a = \sqrt{\frac{2 \sec a}{\sec a - 1}}$.

2. Given $a = 6876$, $b = 4231$, $c = 8913{\cdot}24$, to find A, B, and C.

$$Ans. \begin{cases} A = 48° \; 24' \; 36'' \\ B = 27 \; 24 \\ C = 104 \; 11 \; 24 \end{cases}$$

74. Before treating of the only remaining case in the solution of triangles, it will be convenient to demonstrate some additional general formulas which shall present certain important relations of the trigonometrical lines of two different arcs; which formulas are of frequent use in the higher analysis, are employed in the subsequent parts of the work, and will be immediately of service in deriving a formula for the last case of plane trigonometry which we have to consider.

Add together equations (3) and (7) of (Art. 70) which express the values of $\sin(a+b)$ and $\sin(a-b)$ and the resulting equation, cancelling the second terms of the second members which are similar with contrary signs, is

$$\sin(a+b) + \sin(a-b) = 2 \sin a \cos b \qquad (1)$$

make

$$a + b = p \text{ and } a - b = q$$

add these last two equations; there results

$$2a = p + q \text{ whence } a = \tfrac{1}{2}(p+q)$$

subtracting the same equation, the second from the first,

$$2b = p - q \text{ whence } b = \tfrac{1}{2}(p-q)$$

substituting in equation (1) the values of $a+b$, $a-b$, a and b in terms of p and q, that equation becomes

$$\sin p + \sin q = 2 \sin \tfrac{1}{2}(p+q) \cos \tfrac{1}{2}(p-q) \;* \qquad (2)$$

Which may be translated into ordinary language thus: *the sum of the sines of two arcs is equal to twice the sine of half the sum into the cosine of half the difference of those arcs.*

By subtracting the latter of the same equations (3) and (7) of (Art. 69) from the former, and reducing similar terms, there results

$$\sin(a+b) - \sin(a-b) = 2 \sin b \cos a \qquad (3)$$

* R must be understood either as a divisor of the second member or multiplier of the first, because the sum of two lines cannot be equal to a rectangle.

making the same substitutions as above in equation (1) this last equation becomes

$$\sin p - \sin q = 2 \sin \tfrac{1}{2}(p - q) \cos \tfrac{1}{2}(p + q) \qquad (4)$$

or, *the difference of the sines of two arcs is equal to twice the sine of half their difference into the cosine of half their sum.**

Divide equation (2) by equation (4)

$$\frac{\sin p + \sin q}{\sin p - \sin q} = \frac{\sin \frac{1}{2}(p + q) \cos \frac{1}{2}(p - q)}{\cos \frac{1}{2}(p + q) \sin \frac{1}{2}(p - q)} \qquad (5)$$

but

$$\frac{\sin \frac{1}{2}(p + q)}{\cos \frac{1}{2}(p + q)} = \text{tang} \tfrac{1}{2}(p + q) \text{ (Art. 32) and}$$

$$\frac{\sin \frac{1}{2}(p - q)}{\cos \frac{1}{2}(p - q)} = \text{tang} \tfrac{1}{2}(p - q)$$

or inverting this last

$$\frac{\cos \frac{1}{2}(p - q)}{\sin \frac{1}{2}(p - q)} = \frac{1}{\tan \frac{1}{2}(p - q)}$$

substituting in (5) the values of $\frac{\sin \frac{1}{2}(p + q)}{\cos \frac{1}{2}(p + q)}$ and $\frac{\cos \frac{1}{2}(p - q)}{\sin \frac{1}{2}(p - q)}$

the equation becomes

$$\frac{\sin p + \sin q}{\sin p - \sin q} = \frac{\tan \frac{1}{2}(p + q)}{\tan \frac{1}{2}(p - q)} \qquad (6)$$

which may be expressed in a proportion thus: *the sum of the sines of any two arcs is to the difference of their sines as the tangent of half their sum is to the tangent of half their difference.*

75. Let A B C be any triangle; then (Art. 67)

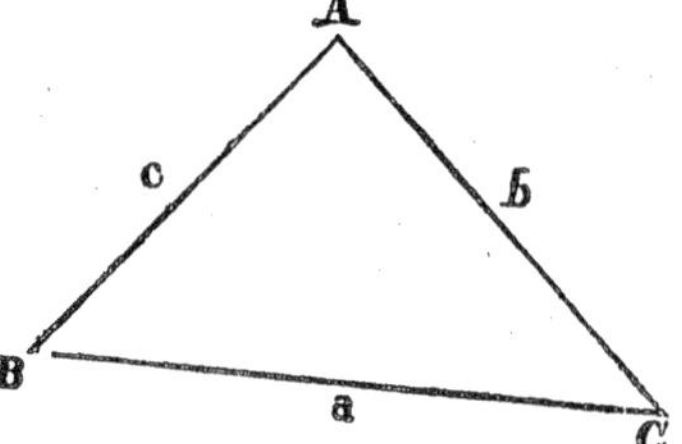

$$a : b :: \sin A : \sin B$$

or by composition, (Alg. Art. 133, IX., Geom. Theorem 47),

$$a + b : a - b :: \sin A + \sin B : \sin A - \sin B$$

* The same remark applies to this form as to (2).

but by equation (6) Art. 74.

$$\sin A + \sin B : \sin A - \sin B :: \tan \tfrac{1}{2}(A + B) : \tan \tfrac{1}{2}(A - B)$$

hence,

$$a + b : a - b :: \tan \tfrac{1}{2}(A + B) : \tan \tfrac{1}{2}(A - B)$$

That is to say, *the sum of two of the sides of a plane triangle is to their difference as the tangent of half the sum of the opposite angles is to the tangent of half their difference.*

76 This proportion is employed when two sides and the included angle of a triangle are given to find the other parts. Since the three angles of every triangle are together equal to two right angles or 180°, subtracting the given included angle from 180°, the remainder is the sum of the two angles opposite the given sides; then substituting for a and b in the above proportion the two given sides, three terms of it are known and the fourth may be found. After which, having half the sum and half the difference of the unknown angles, these angles themselves can be found by adding half the sum to half the difference for the greater, and subtracting half the difference from half the sum from the lesser; when all the parts of the triangle will be known, except one side, which may be found by the proportion *the sines of the angles are as the opposite sides.* (Art. 67.)

EXAMPLE.

An observer wishing to know the length of a small lake, measured two lines from the same point to the two extremities of the lake, which he found to be respectively 153 and 137 yards; he also observed with an instrument for taking angles the angle subtended from this point by the lake to be 40° 33′ 12″.

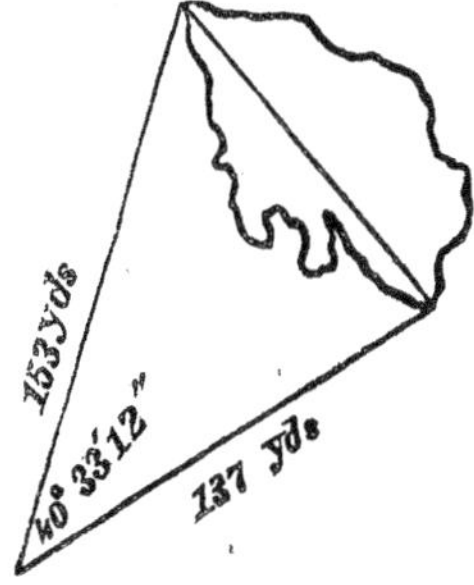

SOLUTION.

I.

To find the two other angles.

As sum of the given sides 290 = arith. comp. of log.–1* 7·53760
: diff. of the sides 16 = log.–1 1·20412
: : tan of $\frac{1}{2}$ sum op. angs. = $\frac{1}{2}$ (180 — 40° 33′ 12″) = 69° 43′ 24″ = log.–1 10·43245

: tan of $\frac{1}{2}$ diff. of op. angs. log. of which is sum rejec. 10 = 9·17417 = log. tan 8° 29′ 37″
Add and subt. with $\frac{1}{2}$ sum of angs. 69° 43′ 24″

sum = greater angle 78° 13′ 1″
diff. = lesser angle 61° 13′ 47″

II.

To find the remaining side.†

As sin 78° 13′ 1″ = arith comp. log.–1 0·00925
: opp. side 153‡ = log.–1 2·18469
: : sin 40° 33′ 12″ = log.–1 9·81302

: side opp. 40° 30′ 12″ =
log.–1 sum rejec. 10 = 2·00696 log of **101·616.**

The length of the lake is 101·616 yards.

The blank form for this case would be as follows:

a		log.
b		
$a + b$	ar. co log.	
$a - b$	log.	
C		log. sin
A ÷ B		
$\frac{1}{2}$ (A + B)	log. tan	
$\frac{1}{2}$ (A — B)	log. tan	
A		ar. co. log. sin
B		
C		log.

* This notation "log.–1" signifies *the number whose log. is.*

† A more direct mode of finding this side when it is the only part required, is given at Art. 77.

‡ 153 is known to be the side opposite 78° 13′ 1″ because the greater angle of a triangle is always opposite the greater side. (Geom. Theorem 9.)

The same form filled up with the given example above is given below.

a 153		log. 2·18469
b 137		
$a+b$ 290	ar. co. log. 7·53760	
$a-b$ 16	log. 1·20412	
C 40° 33′ 12″		log. sin 9·81302
A + B 139° 26′ 48″		
½ (A + B) 69° 43′ 24″	log. tan 10·43245*	
½ (A — B) 8° 29′ 37″	log. tan 9·17417	
A 78° 13′ 1″		ar. co. log. sin 0·00925
B 61° 13′ 47″		
c 101·616		log. 2·00696

77. Given two sides and the included angle of a plane triangle to determine the third side, without finding the remaining angles.

The general expression for the side c, in terms of the two sides a, b, and the included angle C, is (Art. 69) on the supposition of R = 1,

$$\begin{aligned} c^2 &= a^2 + b^2 - 2\,ab\cos C \\ &= (a-b)^2 + 2\,ab\,(1-\cos C) \\ &= (a-b)^2 + 2\,ab\cdot 2\sin^2 \tfrac{1}{2}C \\ &= (a-b)^2 \left\{ 1 + \frac{4\,ab}{(a-b)^2}\sin^2 \tfrac{1}{2}C \right\} \end{aligned} \qquad (1)$$

Assume the second term within the brackets equal to $\tan^2\theta$, then, since $1 + \tan^2\theta = \sec^2\theta = \dfrac{1}{\cos^2\theta}$, we have

$$c = (a-b)\,\frac{\text{rad}}{\cos\theta} \qquad (2)$$

Hence c is determined by these two formulas, viz.,

$$\log.\tan\theta = \log. 2 + \tfrac{1}{2}\log. a + \tfrac{1}{2}\log. b + \log.\sin\tfrac{1}{2}C - \log(a-b)$$
$$\log. c = \log.(a-b) + 10 - \log.\cos\theta.\dagger$$

* Log. cot ½ C might be used instead of log. tan ½ (A + B) since 180° — C = A + B and ∴ 90° — ½ C = ½ (A + B) and tan (90° — ½ C) = cot ½ C. But nothing would be gained, since ½ (A + B) must be employed to add and subtract with ½ (A — B).

† When b is nearly equal to a, the following formulas will give c with greater exactness. For demonstration see App. I. Art. 23.

$$\sin\phi = \frac{2\sqrt{ab}}{a+b}\cos\tfrac{1}{2}C \qquad (3)$$

$$c = (a+b)\cos\phi \qquad (4)$$

EXAMPLE.

Given $a = 562$, $b = 320$, and C $= 128^\circ\ 4'$, to find c.

log. 2	0·30103		
$\frac{1}{2}$ log. 562	1·37487		
$\frac{1}{2}$ log. 320	1·25257		
log. sin 64° 2′	9·95378		
ar. comp. log. 242	7·61618	log. 242 + 10	12·38382
log. tan θ	10·49843	∴ log. cos θ =	9·48072
log. c	800·01		2·90310

EXERCISES.

Given a 5891, b 4562·34, C 30° 20′ 10″·3 to find the other parts of the triangle.

Ans. A 99° 57′ 5″·25, B 49° 42′ 44·45, c 3020·823.

Given A 40° 55′ 31″, b 83·25, c 100, to find a.

Ans. a 65·9574.

This case of the solution of a triangle combined with that exhibited at Art. 67, serves to determine the horizontal distance between two inaccessible objects.

Let the distance between two towns which are in sight be required.

Measure a line upon the ground (which is called the base line) of 2 miles. Take the angles at each extremity formed by this base line and a line to each of the towns. Two triangles will be formed, in each of which a side, viz. the base line, and two adjacent angles will be given. Let the angles in the triangle of which the upper town is the vertex be 159° and 14°; and those in that of which the lower town is the vertex be 25° and 149°. Calculate the distance from one extremity of the base line, say the upper extremity, to each of the towns, as in Art. 67. Then you will know two sides of a triangle the third side of which is the distance between the towns required.

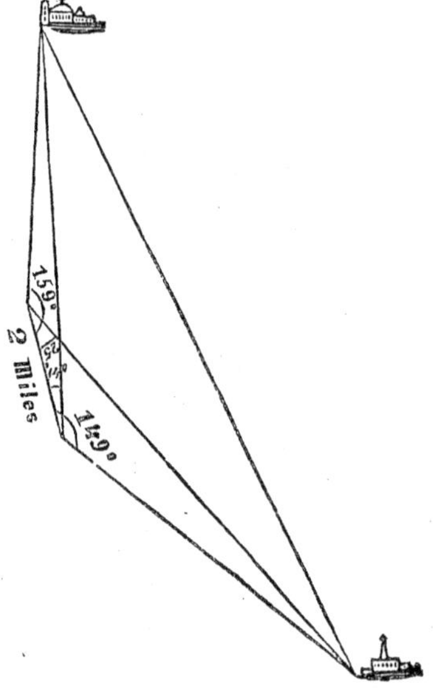

The included angle between these two sides is $159° - 25° = 134°$.

Having then two sides and the included angle, the remainder of the solution is the same as in the last case.

We leave it as an exercise for the learner. *Ans.* 12·932 miles.

MISCELLANEOUS EXAMPLES.

(1.) From the equation $\sin^2 a + 5 \cos^2 a = 3$ to find the value of $\sin a$.

Ans. $\sin a = \frac{1}{\sqrt{2}}$

(2.) If $\sin^2 a = m \cos a - n$ to determine $\cos a$.

Ans. $\cos a = -\frac{1}{2} m \pm \sqrt{\frac{1}{4}m^2 + n + 1}$.

(3.) Given $\sin a = m \sin b$, $\tan a = n \tan b$ to find $\sin a$ and $\cos b$.

Ans. $\sin a = \sqrt{\frac{m^2 - n^2}{1 - n^2}}$ $\cos b = \frac{n}{m}\sqrt{\frac{1 - m^2}{1 - n^2}}$

(4.) Prove $\sin(a + b + c) = \sin a \cos b \cos c + \sin b \cos a \cos c + \sin c \cos a \cos b - \sin a \sin b \sin c$.

(5.) Given $\tan^2 a + 4 \sin^2 a = 6$ to find a.

Ans. $a = 60°$.

(6.) Sin $a = \sin 2a$ to find $\sin a$.

Ans. $\sin a = \sqrt{\frac{3}{4}}$

(7.) Given the base of a triangle 87·75, the vertical angle 73° 20′, and the difference of the angles at the base 13° 4′, to find the other parts.

Ans. $\begin{cases} 46° \ 48', \ 59° \ 52'. \\ 79·2194, \ 66·7721. \end{cases}$

(8.) Given the base 117·3, the vertical angle 19° 18′, and the ratio of the other two sides 8 : 11 to solve the triangle.

Ans. 123° 13′ 23″·7, 37° 28′ 36″·3, 215·94, 296·89.

(9.) Find into what two parts the perpendicular from the vertex of the angle C, divides the side c of a triangle when A = 33°, C = 75°, and $a = 2134$.

Ans. 3125·2 and 659·44.

(10.) The side of a regular polygon of 41 sides is 0·736. What is the ratio of the radii of the inscribed and circumscribed circles?

Ans. ·99708.

(11.) Find the extent of the circle of vision, viz. the arc TO, from the top of a mountain M, whose height is 5460 feet, supposing the radius of the earth to be 3956·1 miles.

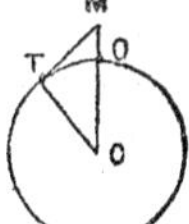

Ans. 91 miles, 1558·88 feet.

(12.) When the sun's altitude is 19° 16′, the peak of a mountain casts its shadow at a certain point, and at another point when the sun's altitude is 20° 42′, distant from the former point 937 ft. Now supposing the sun to be vertical on the top of the mountain at noon, what is its height?

Ans. 4369.1 ft.

(13.) Two forces, one of 410, the other of 320 pounds, act under an angle of 51° 37′, required the direction and intensity of their resultant.*

Ans. { The resultant makes an angle of 29° 13′ 46″·7, with the less force, and 22° 23′ 13″·3 with the greater. Intensity 702·39838 pounds.

(14.) From the edge of a ditch, the width of which was 36 feet, the angle of elevation to the top of an opposite wall was 62° 40′; to find the height of the wall and the length of a ladder which would reach obliquely across the ditch to the top of the wall

Ans. { Height of wall, 69·64.
Ladder, 78·4 feet.

(15.) To find the length of a shoar, which, projecting 11 feet from the perpendicular face of a building, will support a jamb 23 feet 10 inches above the ground?

Ans. 26 feet 3 inches.

(16.) Suppose that a ladder, 40 feet long, will reach a window 33 feet from the ground on one side of a street, and on being turned over, without moving the foot, it will reach a window 21 feet high on the other side; to find the breadth of the street?

Ans. 56·649 feet.

(17.) A liberty-pole whose top was broken off strikes the ground at 15 feet distance from the foot of the pole; to find the height of the whole if the broken piece measures 39 feet in length?

Ans. 75 feet.

(18.) At 170 feet distance from the bottom of a tower, suppose the angle of elevation to be 52° 30′; to find the altitude of the tower?

Ans. 221 feet.

(19.) From the top of a tower by the sea-shore, 143 feet high, the angle of depression of a ship was observed to be 35°; to find the distance of the ship from the bottom of the tower?

Ans. 204·22 feet.

(20.) To find the height of a hill, the angle of elevation at the bottom being 46°, and 200 yards distant from the bottom 31°?

Ans. 286·28 yards.

(21.) To find the height and distance of an inaccessible tower, on a horizontal plane, the angle of elevation being 58°, and at a point 300 feet more distant, the angle being only 32°?

Ans. { Height, 307·53.
Distance, 192·15.

(22.) To find the height of a tower on the top of an inaccessible hill, the angle of elevation to the top of the hill being 40°, the top of the tower 51°, and 200 feet further back the angle to the top of the tower being 33° 45′?

Ans. 93·33148 feet.

(23.) From a window on a level with the bottom of a steeple, the angle of elevation of the top of the steeple being 40°; and from another window, 18 feet directly above the former, the angle was 37° 30′; to find the height and distance of the steeple?

Ans. { Height, 210·44.
Distance, 250·79.

* The resultant of two forces is a single force equivalent to them, and is the diagonal of a parallelogram of which the two forces given are sides.

(24.) A balloon being directly over one of two towns whose distance apart was 8 miles, the angle of depression of the second was observed to be 10°. Required the height of the balloon?

Ans. 1·41 of a mile.

(25.) The horizontal angles were observed from each of two stations, 3000 feet apart, by first sighting to the other station, and then to a balloon, and the angle of elevation at one, as follows:

1st Station.	Hor. angle, 75° 25′	2d.	64° 30′
	Angle of elev. 18°		

Required the height and horizontal distance of the balloon from the first station.

Ans. { Distance, 4205 feet. Height, 1366 feet.

(26.) Two vessels of war anxious to cannonade a fort, are so remote from it that their guns cannot reach it with effect. In order to find the distance they move a quarter of a mile apart, then each vessel observes and measures the angles which the other and the fort subtend; the angles being 83° 45′, and 85° 15′, required the distance between each vessel and the fort?

Ans. { 2292·26, 2298·05 } yards.

(27.) Wishing to know the distance to an object on the other side of a river, I measured a base line of 400 feet in a right line by the side of the river, and found that the two angles, one at each end of this line, subtended by the other end and the object, were 68° 2′ and 73° 15′. Required the distance between each station and the object?

Ans. { 593·08, 612·38 } feet.

(28.) Wanting to know the breadth of a river, I measured a base line of 500 feet in a right line close by its bank; the angles subtended by lines connecting each extremity of this line and an object on the opposite bank, were 53° and 79° 12′. Required the perpendicular breadth of the river?

Ans. 529·48 feet.

(29.) Suppose it be required to find the distance between two headlands, measure from each of them to any point inland, and supposing the distances respectively to be 735 feet and 840 feet, also the horizontal angle subtended between these two lines to be 55° 40′, what was the required distance?

Ans. 741·2 feet.

(30.) Wishing to know the distance between a church and tower, situated at a distance on the other side of a river, I measured a base line along the side where I was, of 600 feet, and at each end of it took the angles subtended by the other end and the church and tower; at one end the angles were 58° 20′ and 95° 20′, and at the other end the angles were 53° 30′, and 98° 45′. Required the distance?

Ans. 959·5866 feet.

(31.) To determine the intensity and direction of a force which, combined with another force expressed by 128, shall produce a resultant of 200, which shall make an angle with the direction of the given force of 18° 24′.

Ans. Intensity, 88·32714. Angle, 27° 13′ 16″·6.

(32.) To determine the force with which a body weighing 516 pounds moves down a plane inclined to the horizon under an angle of 14° 10′.*

Ans. 126·288 lbs.

(33.) The angle of incidence of a ray of light falling upon a surface being 46°, and the angle of refraction being 35° 11′, to find the index of refraction.

NOTE.—The index of refraction is the ratio of the sine of the angle of incidence to the sine of the angle of refraction.

Ans. ·8.

* The force down an inclined plane is to the force of gravity as the height of the plane is to its length.

APPENDIX I.

1. We have postponed to this place the investigation of a few formulas requisite for the study of Analytical Geometry, with other matters of interest.

By resuming the expression for the tangent (Art. 32), and putting $a + b$ for a, we have

$$\tan(a \pm b) = \frac{\sin(a \pm b)}{\cos(a \pm b)}$$

But by Art 70

$$\sin(a \pm b) = \sin a \cos b \pm \cos a \sin b$$

and

$$\cos(a \pm b) = \cos a \cos b \mp \sin a \sin b$$

substituting these values the first equation becomes

$$\tan(a \pm b) = \frac{(\sin a \cos b \pm \sin b \cos a)}{\cos a \cos b \mp \sin a \sin b}$$

dividing both numerator and denominator of the second member of this equation by $\cos a \cos b$ we have

$$\tan(a \pm b) = \frac{\left(\frac{\sin a}{\cos a} \pm \frac{\sin b}{\cos b}\right)}{1 \mp \frac{\sin a \sin b}{\cos a \cos b}}$$

substituting for $\frac{\sin a}{\cos a}$ and $\frac{\sin b}{\cos b}$ their values (Art. 32) $\tan a$ and $\tan b$, the last expression becomes

$$\tan(a \pm b) = \frac{(\tan a \pm \tan b)}{1 \mp \tan a \tan b} \qquad (1)$$

i. e., *the tangent of the sum or difference of two arcs is equal to rad. square into the sum or difference of their tangents divided by rad. square minus or plus the rectangle of their tangents.**

* The mode in which R^2 enters is derived from the principle of homogeneity.

If a represent the tangent of a and a' the tangent of a', then

$$\tan(a - a') = \frac{a - a'}{1 + aa'}$$

Using the upper sines and making $b = a$ in equation (1), we have

$$\tan 2a = \frac{2 \tan a}{1 - \tan^2 a} * \qquad (2)$$

Tan $3a$, tan $4a$, &c., may be found by making b successively equal to $2a$, $3a$, &c.

EXERCISE.

Prove $\tan(a + b + c) = \frac{\tan a + \tan b + \tan c - \tan a \tan b \tan c}{1 - \tan a \tan b - \tan a \tan c - \tan b \tan c}$

2. The sine and cosine of 45° are equal, since the complement of 45° is 45°. These two lines form two sides of a right-angled triangle of which radius is the hypothenuse.

$$\therefore \sin 45^\circ = \cos 45^\circ = \frac{R}{\sqrt{2}} = \tfrac{1}{2} R\sqrt{2}$$

3. *The sine of ½ an arc is equal to ½ the chord of the arc.*

For let MN be the arc ; draw the diameter BA perpendicular to the chord MN of this arc ; this perpendicular bisects the chord, and also the arc subtended by it (Geom. Theorem 34), but MP half the chord is the sine of MA half the arc, since MP is a perpendicular from one extremity M to the diameter which passes through the other extremity A.

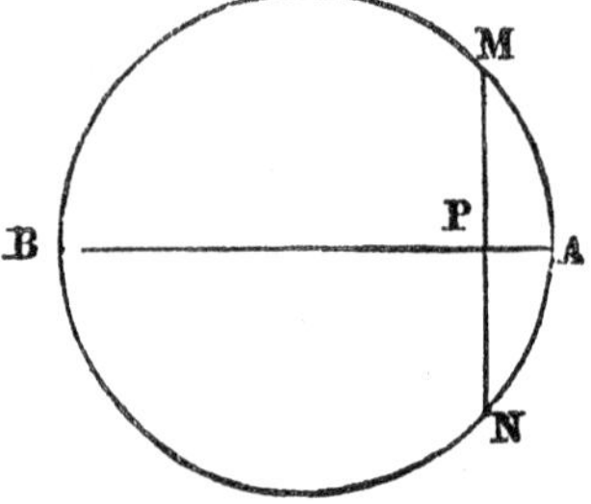

Corollary.—The chord of 60°, or $\frac{1}{6}$ of the circumference, which is the side of the regular hexagon, is equal to R (Geom. Prob. 31), hence the sine of 30° is equal to ½ R.

Again,

$$\cos 30^\circ = \sqrt{1 - \sin^2 30^\circ} = \sqrt{1 - \tfrac{1}{4}} = \frac{\sqrt{3}}{2}$$

Also,

$$\tan 30^\circ = \frac{\sin 30^\circ}{\cos 30^\circ} = \frac{1}{\sqrt{3}}$$

$$\cot 30^\circ = \frac{1}{\tan 30^\circ} = \sqrt{3}$$

* The form employed in Analytical Geometry.

4. Referring to Art. 33, it will be observed that

$$\sec = \frac{R^2}{\cos}$$

but,

$$\cos 60^\circ = \sin 30^\circ = \tfrac{1}{2} R,$$

hence,

$$\sec 60^\circ = \frac{R^2}{\frac{1}{2} R} = 2 R = \textit{the diameter of the circle.}$$

To find the numerical value of the sine, cosine, &c. of 60°.

$$\begin{aligned} \sin 60^\circ &= \cos (90^\circ - 60^\circ) \\ &= \cos 30^\circ \\ &= \frac{\sqrt{3}}{2}, \text{ by last art.} \end{aligned}$$

Again,

$$\begin{aligned} \cos 60^\circ &= \sin (90^\circ - 60^\circ) \\ &= \sin 30^\circ \\ &= \frac{1}{2} \end{aligned}$$

Also,

$$\tan 60^\circ = \sqrt{3}$$

$$\cot 60^\circ = \frac{1}{\sqrt{3}}$$

5. Making $a = 45^\circ$ in equation (1) of Art. 1, App. I., we have

$$\tan (45^\circ \pm b) = \frac{1 \pm \tan b}{1 \mp \tan b}*$$

6. Our demonstration for the sine and cosine of the sum of two arcs at Art. 70, might seem to want generality, since the arcs a and b are there supposed to be less than 90°. That these arcs may extend to the other quadrants, can be shown as follows:

Let $a = 90^\circ + m$, then will the formula

$$\sin (a + b) = \sin a \cos b + \sin b \cos a \qquad (1)$$

still be true, for substituting $90^\circ + m$ for a, we have $\sin (90^\circ + m + b)$ in the place of the first member, which is equal to $\cos (m + b)$†; for the second member by the same substitution we have

$$\sin (90^\circ + m) \cos b + \sin b \cos (90^\circ + m)$$

* Tan 45° = cot 45° = R = 1.

† By referring to either of the diagrams in which a sine is drawn, it will be evident that $\sin (90^\circ + a)$, a being any arc less than a quadrant, is equal in length to $\sin (90^\circ - a) = \cos a$. Also that $\cos (90^\circ + a) = -\cos (90^\circ - a) = -\sin a$.

but $\sin (90^\circ + m) = \cos m$ and $\cos (90^\circ + m) = -\sin m$, hence equation (1) becomes

$$\cos (m + b) = \cos m \cos b - \sin m \sin b$$

which, since m and b are less than 90°, we know to be true, by Art. 70; hence (1), from which it is derived, is true also.

Assuming (1) to be true with $a > 90^\circ$, which we have just proved, make $b = 90^\circ + m$, and in a similar manner the truth of the formula may be established on the supposition of both a and $b > 90^\circ$.

Afterwards make $a = 180^\circ + m$ and observe that $\sin (180^\circ + m + b) = \sin m + b$ and $\cos (180^\circ + m) = -\cos m$, and you will show that the formula extends to the third quadrant, and so on.

7. Not having been sufficiently advanced in the theory of trigonometrical lines to explain the construction of the tables of sines, tangents, &c., at Art. 38, the explanation is here given.

The diameter of a circle being multiplied by $\pi = 3{\cdot}1415926$ the product is the length of its circumference; this divided by 360 gives us the length of one degree, and this by 60 the length of one minute of the circumference. So small an arc as $1'$ may be considered as equal to its sine, without sensible error. Having thus found the sine of $1'$ the sines of other arcs may be found by a formula which will now be deduced.

To determine the sine of $(n + 1)\, a$, in terms of $n\, a$, $(n - 1)\, a$ and a

By formulas (3) and (7) of Art. 70.

$$\sin (b + a) = \sin b \cos a + \sin a \cos b \qquad (a)$$

$$\sin (b - a) = \sin b \cos a - \sin a \cos b \qquad (b)$$

Adding these two equations there results

$$\sin (b + a) + \sin (b - a) = 2 \sin b \cos a \qquad (g)$$

Subtracting $\sin (b - a)$ from each member there remains

$$\sin (b + a) = 2 \sin b \cos a - \sin (b - a)$$

Let $b = n\, a$, then the above becomes

$$\sin (n + 1)\, a = 2 \sin n\, a \cos a - \sin (n - 1)\, a \qquad (l)$$

In the last expression let $n = 1$; then $n + 1 = 2$, $n - 1 = 0$

$$\therefore \sin 2\, a = 2 \sin a \cos a - \sin 0 \qquad (m)$$

$= 2 \sin a \cos a$ the same result as in (g), if $a = b$.

Let $n = 2$; then $n + 1 = 3$, $n - 1 = 1$;

$$\begin{aligned} \text{and } \sin 3\, a &= 2 \sin 2\, a \cos a - \sin a \\ &= 2 \times 2 \sin a \cos a \times \cos a - \sin a \\ &= 4 \sin a \cos^2 a - \sin a \\ &= 4 \sin a\, (1 - \sin^2 a) - \sin a \\ &= 3 \sin a - 4 \sin^3 a \qquad (n) \end{aligned}$$

Let $n = 3$; then $n + 1 = 4$, $n - 1 = 2$;

And by formula (m):

$$\sin 4a = 2 \times \sin 3a \times \cos a - \sin 2a$$
$$= 2(3 \sin a - 4 \sin^3 a) \cos a - 2 \sin a \cos a$$
$$= (8 \cos^3 a - 4 \cos a) \sin a.$$

Continuing the same process, we find successively $\sin 5a$, $\sin 6a$, &c.

To determine the cosine of $(n+1)a$, in terms of na, $(n-1)a$, and a.

By formulas (6) and (8) of Art. 70.

$$\cos(b + a) = \cos b \cos a - \sin b \sin a \qquad (c)$$
$$\cos(b - a) = \cos b \cos a + \sin b \sin a \qquad (d)$$

Adding these two equations, we have

$$\cos(b + a) + \cos(b - a) = 2 \cos b \cos a$$

Subtracting $\cos(b - a)$ from each member there results

$$\cos(b + a) = 2 \cos b \cos a - \cos(b - a)$$

If $b = na$, this becomes

$$\cos(n + 1)a = 2 \cos na \cos a - \cos(n - 1)a \qquad (o)$$

In the formula (o) let $n = 1$; $\therefore n + 1 = 2$, $n - 1 = 0$;

Then, $\cos 2a = 2 \cos a \cos a - \cos 0$

$$= 2 \cos^2 a - 1$$

Let $n = 2$, then $n + 1 = 3$, $n - 1 = 1$;

and $\cos 3a = 2 \cos 2a \cos a - \cos a$

$$= 2(2 \cos^2 a - 1) \cos a - \cos a$$
$$= 4 \cos^3 a - 3 \cos a \qquad (p)$$

Let $n = 3$; then $n + 1 = 4$, $n - 1 = 2$;

and $\cos 4a = 2 \cos 3a \cos a - \cos 2a$

$$= 2(4 \cos^3 a - 3 \cos a) \cos a - (2 \cos^2 a - 1)$$
$$= 8 \cos^4 a - 8 \cos^2 a + 1$$

Continuing the same process, we may find, successively, $\cos 5a$, $\cos 6a$, &c.

Making a equal to $1'$ (m) becomes

$$\sin 2' = 2 \sin 1' \cos 1'$$

observing that $\cos 1' = \sqrt{1 - \sin^2 1'}$ (Art. 72); we have thus the value of the sin $2'$. From (n)

$$\sin 3' = 3 \sin 1' - 4 \sin^3 1'$$

and so on. The cosines are calculated in the same manner from (o) or from the sines by the formula

$$\cos = \sqrt{1 - \sin^2}$$

the tangents by the formula (Art. 32),

$$\tan = \frac{\text{R}\sin}{\cos}$$

the cotangents by (Art. 34),

$$\cot = \frac{\text{R}\cos}{\sin}$$

It is manifest that by continuing the above processes the numerical values of the sines and cosines, &c., of all angles from 1′ up to 90° will be obtained.

The above arithmetical operations are laborious. It is evident that an error in the sine or cosine of the first arcs found will involve errors in the sines, cosines, &c. of all succeeding arcs. Hence the necessity of some check on the computation. For this purpose formulas are employed, called *formulas of verification*.

$\text{Sin}^2 a + \cos^2 a = 1$

And $2 \sin a \cos a = \sin 2a$

Hence,

$$\sin a = \tfrac{1}{2}\sqrt{1 + \sin 2a} \pm \tfrac{1}{2}\sqrt{1 - \sin 2a}$$
$$\cos a = \tfrac{1}{2}\sqrt{1 + \sin 2a} \mp \tfrac{1}{2}\sqrt{1 - \sin 2a}$$

Now if we suppose $a = 12° 30'$

$$\sin 12° 30' = \tfrac{1}{2}\sqrt{1 + \sin 25°} \pm \tfrac{1}{2}\sqrt{1 - \sin 25°}$$
$$\cos 12° 30' = \tfrac{1}{2}\sqrt{1 + \sin 25°} \mp \tfrac{1}{2}\sqrt{1 - \sin 25°}$$

If the values of the sine and cosine of 12° 30′, and of the sine of 25° obtained by the method previously explained, when substituted in these equations, render the two members identical, the results are supposed correct.

The values of the sine and cosine of 30°, 45°, 60°, &c., may be used as formulas of verification.

The following is known as Euler's formula of verification, which we give without demonstration.

$$\sin a + \sin (36° - a) + \sin (72° + a) = \sin (36° + a) + \sin (72° - a)$$

The following is Legendre's formula.

$$\cos a = \sin (54° + a) + \sin (54° - a) - \sin (18° + a) - \sin (18° - a)$$

To exemplify the latter, make $a = 13°$, then

$$\cos 13° = \sin 67° + \sin 41° - \sin 31° - \sin 5°$$

Substituting for these their values from tab. nat. sines

$$97436 = 92050 + 65606 - 51504 - 08716$$

8. **The sines, cosines, &c.,** may be calculated by series.

To develop sin x *and* cos x *in a series containing the ascending powers of* x, *by the method of undetermined co-efficients.*

The series for sin x must vanish when $x = 0$, therefore it can contain no term independent of x, nor can the even powers of x enter into the series; for suppose,

$$\sin x = \mathrm{A}\,x + \mathrm{B}\,x^2 + \mathrm{C}\,x^3 + \mathrm{D}\,x^4 + \mathrm{E}\,x^5 +$$

substitute $(-x)$ for x and the above becomes

$$\sin(-x) = -\mathrm{A}\,x + \mathrm{B}\,x^2 - \mathrm{C}\,x^3 + \mathrm{D}\,x^4 - \mathrm{E}\,x^5 +$$
$$\text{but } \sin(-x) = -\sin x = -\mathrm{A}\,x - \mathrm{B}\,x^2 - \mathrm{C}\,x^3 - \mathrm{D}\,x^4 - \mathrm{E}\,x^5 -$$
$$\therefore \mathrm{B} = -\mathrm{B},\ \mathrm{D} = -\mathrm{D}, \text{ \&c., absurd unless } \mathrm{B} = 0,\ \mathrm{D} = 0, \text{ \&c.}$$
$$\therefore \sin x = \mathrm{A}\,x + \mathrm{C}\,x^3 + \mathrm{E}\,x^5 + \mathrm{G}\,x^7 + \qquad (1)$$

Again, the series for cos x must $= 1$ when $x = 0$, its first term must be 1; and it can contain no uneven powers of x, for suppose

$$\cos x = 1 + \mathrm{A}\,x + \mathrm{B}\,x^2 + \mathrm{C}\,x^3 + \mathrm{D}\,x^4 +$$
$$\text{then } \cos(-x) = 1 - \mathrm{A}\,x + \mathrm{B}\,x^2 - \mathrm{C}\,x^3 + \mathrm{D}\,x^4 -$$
$$\text{but } \cos(-x) = \cos x$$
$$= 1 + \mathrm{A}\,x + \mathrm{B}\,x^2 + \mathrm{C}\,x^3 + \mathrm{D}\,x^4 +$$
$$\because \mathrm{A} = -\mathrm{A},\ \mathrm{C} = -\mathrm{C}, \qquad \therefore \mathrm{A} = 0,\ \mathrm{C} = 0$$
$$\therefore \cos x = 1 + \mathrm{B}\,x^2 + \mathrm{D}\,x^4 + \qquad (2)$$

Adding and subtracting (1) and (2)

$$\cos x + \sin x = 1 + \mathrm{A}\,x + \mathrm{B}\,x^2 + \mathrm{C}\,x^3 + \mathrm{D}\,x^4 + \mathrm{E}\,x^5 + \qquad (3)$$
$$\cos x - \sin x = 1 - \mathrm{A}\,x + \mathrm{B}\,x^2 - \mathrm{C}\,x^3 + \mathrm{D}\,x^4 - \mathrm{E}\,x^5 + \qquad (4)$$

In equation (3) substituting $x + h$ for x, it becomes

$$\cos(x+h) + \sin(x+h) = 1 + \mathrm{A}\,(x+h) + \mathrm{B}\,(x+h)^2 + \mathrm{C}\,(x+h)^3 + \qquad (5)$$

$$\begin{aligned}
\text{but } \cos(x+h) + \sin(x+h) &= \cos x \cos h - \sin x \sin h + \sin x \cos h + \cos x \sin h \\
&= \cos h\,(\cos x + \sin x) + \sin h\,(\cos x - \sin x) \\
&= (1 + \mathrm{B}\,h^2 + \mathrm{D}\,h^4 +)\ (1 + \mathrm{A}\,x + \mathrm{B}\,x^2 + \mathrm{C}\,x^3 +) \\
&+ (\mathrm{A}\,h + \mathrm{C}\,h^3 + \mathrm{E}\,h^5 +)\ (1 - \mathrm{A}\,x + \mathrm{B}\,x^2 - \mathrm{C}\,x^3 +) \\
&= \left.\begin{array}{r} 1 + \mathrm{A}\,x + \mathrm{B}\,x^2 + \mathrm{C}\,x^3 \quad + \\ + \mathrm{A}\,h - \mathrm{A}^2 x h + \mathrm{A}\,\mathrm{B}\,x^2 h + \\ + \mathrm{B}\,h^2 + \mathrm{A}\,\mathrm{B}\,x h^2 + \\ + \mathrm{C}\,h^3 \quad + \\ + \end{array}\right\} \qquad (6)
\end{aligned}$$

Comparing (5) and (6) we have

$$\left.\begin{array}{r} 1 + \mathrm{A}\,x + \mathrm{B}\,x^2 + \mathrm{C}\,x^3 \quad + \\ + \mathrm{A}\,h + 2\mathrm{B}\,xh + 3\mathrm{C}\,x^2h \ + \\ + \mathrm{B}\,h^2 + 3\mathrm{C}\,xh^2 \ + \\ + \mathrm{C}\,h^3 \quad + \end{array}\right\} = \left\{\begin{array}{r} 1 + \mathrm{A}\,x + \mathrm{B}\,x^2 \quad + \mathrm{C}\,x^3 \quad + \\ + \mathrm{A}\,h - \mathrm{A}\,\mathrm{A}\,xh + \mathrm{A}\,\mathrm{B}\,x^2h - \\ + \mathrm{B}\,h^2 \quad + \mathrm{A}\,\mathrm{B}\,xh^2 + \\ + \mathrm{C}\,h^3 \quad - \\ + \end{array}\right.$$

and equating the coefficients of the terms containing the same powers of x h,

$$2\text{B} = -\text{A A}\,;\ \therefore\ \text{B} = -\frac{\text{A A}}{2} = -\frac{\text{A}^2}{1\cdot 2}$$

$$3\text{C} = \quad \text{A P} \qquad \text{C} = \quad \frac{\text{A B}}{3} = -\frac{\text{A}^3}{1\cdot 2\cdot 3}$$

$$4\text{D} = \quad -\text{A C} \qquad \text{D} = -\frac{\text{A C}}{4} = +\frac{\text{A}^4}{1\cdot 2\cdot 3\cdot 4}$$

$$5\text{E} = \quad \text{A D} \qquad \text{E} = \quad \frac{\text{A D}}{5} = +\frac{\text{A}^5}{1\cdot 2\cdot 3\cdot 4\cdot 5}$$

$$\text{hence } \sin x = \text{A}\,x - \frac{\text{A}^3}{1\cdot 2\cdot 3}x^3 + \frac{\text{A}^5}{1\cdot 2\cdot 3\cdot 4\cdot 5}x^5 - \frac{\text{A}^7}{1\cdot 2\cdot 3\cdot 4\cdot 5\cdot 6\cdot 7}x^7 +$$

$$\cos x = 1 - \frac{\text{A}^2}{1\cdot 2}x^2 + \frac{\text{A}^4}{1\cdot 2\cdot 3\cdot 4}x^4 - \frac{\text{A}^6}{1\cdot 2\cdot 3\cdot 4\cdot 5\cdot 6}x^6 +$$

It remains now to determine the value of A. For this purpose we have

$$\sin x = \text{A}\,x - \frac{\text{A}^3}{1\cdot 2\cdot 3}x^3 + \frac{\text{A}^5}{1\cdot 2\cdot 3\cdot 4\cdot 5}x^5 -$$

$$= \text{A}\,x\left(1 - \frac{\text{A}^2}{1\cdot 2\cdot 3}x^2 + \frac{\text{A}^4}{1\cdot 2\cdot 3\cdot 4\cdot 5}x^4 - \right)$$

If x be very small, the first member $\sin x = x$ and the terms in the parenthesis after the first vanish. Hence $x = \text{A}\,x \ \therefore\ \text{A} = 1$, and

$$\sin x = x - \frac{x^3}{1\cdot 2\cdot 3} + \frac{x^5}{1\cdot 2\cdot 3\cdot 4\cdot 5} - \frac{x^7}{1\cdot 2\cdot 3\cdot 4\cdot 5\cdot 6\cdot 7} + \qquad (1)$$

$$\cos x = 1 - \frac{x^2}{1\cdot 2} + \frac{x^4}{1\cdot 2\cdot 3\cdot 4} - \frac{x^6}{1\cdot 2\cdot 3\cdot 4\cdot 5\cdot 6} + \qquad (2)$$

Now, the length of an arc of one degree is so small that if x be equal to this, the third term of the above series will contain no significant figure in the first ten places of decimals.

Retaining therefore only the first two terms of (1) we have, when x is small,

$$\sin x = x - \frac{x^3}{1\cdot 2\cdot 3} = x\left(1 - \frac{x^2}{2\cdot 3}\right) = x\left\{1 - \frac{x^2}{2} + \frac{x^4}{2\cdot 3\cdot 4}\right\}^{\frac{1}{3}} \text{ nearly};$$

that is, the quantity within the brackets being $= \cos x$, by (2)

$$\sin x = x \cos \tfrac{1}{3}\, x\,;$$

therefore introducing radius to render the expression homogeneous, we have

$$\log.\ \sin x = \log.\ x - \tfrac{1}{3}\,(10 - \log.\ \cos x) \qquad (3)$$

Suppose the arc x to contain n seconds, then

$$x = \frac{n\cdot\pi}{180 \times 60 \times 60}$$

* Dividing (1) by (2) we have $\tan x = x + \frac{1}{3}x^3 \ldots$

introducing radius and applying logarithms

$$\log. x = \log. n + \log. 3{\cdot}14159, \&c. + 10 - \log. \overline{180 \times 60^2}$$
$$= \log. n + 4{\cdot}68558\,;$$

substituting this value of $\log. x$ in (3) it becomes

$$\log. \sin x = \log. n + 4{\cdot}68558 - \tfrac{1}{3} \text{ ar. comp. } \log. \cos x. \qquad (4)$$

Hence this rule. To the logarithm of the arc reduced into seconds add the constant 4•68558, and from the sum subtract one-third of the arithmetical complement of the log. cosine; the remainder will be the logarithmic sine of the given arc.

9. *To find the logarithmic tangent of a very small arc.*

By the last article

$$\sin x = x \cos \tfrac{1}{3} x \therefore \frac{\sin x}{\cos x} = \tan x = \frac{x}{\cos \frac{2}{3} x}\ *$$

Introducing the radius and applying logs.

$$\log. \tan x = \log. x + \tfrac{2}{3}\,(10 - \log. \cos x)$$

The second member of this equation may be formed from the second member of (3) in the last article, by adding the arithmetical complement of the log. cos x; therefore from (4)

$$\log. \tan x = \log. n + 4{\cdot}68558 + \tfrac{2}{3} \text{ arith. comp. } \log. \cos x \qquad (5)$$

hence this rule. Add the logarithm of the arc reduced to seconds, the constant 4•68558, and two-thirds of the arithmetical complement of the log. cosine, the sum is the log. tangent required.

10. *To find a small arc from its log. sine.*

From (4) Art. 8, Appendix I.,

$$\log. n = \log. \sin x - 4{\cdot}68558 + \tfrac{1}{3} \text{ arith. comp. } \log. \cos x$$
$$= \log. \sin x + 5{\cdot}31442 + \tfrac{1}{3} \text{ arith comp. } \log. \cos x - 10$$

Hence the rule is this. Add the log. sine of the arc, the constant 5•31442, and $\frac{1}{3}$ of the arithmetical complement of the log. cosine; subtract 10 from the index of the sum, and the remainder will be the logarithm of the number of seconds in the arc.

To find a small arc from its log. tangent.

From (5) last art.

$$\log. n = \log. \tan x - 4{\cdot}68558 - \tfrac{2}{3} \text{ arith. comp. } \log. \cos x$$
$$= \log. \tan x + 5{\cdot}31442 - \tfrac{2}{3} \text{ arith. comp. } \log. \cos x - 10\,;$$

Rule.—Add the log. tangent of the arc, the constant 5•31442, and subtract $\frac{2}{3}$ of the arithmetical complement of the log. cosine, reject 10 from the index, and th result will be the logarithm of the arc in seconds.

* If we substitute for cos x in the last fraction its value $\dfrac{1}{\sqrt{1 + \tan^2 x}}$ we may easily deduce $x = \tan x - \frac{1}{3} \tan^3 x$, &c.

11. The values of a, which satisfy the equation $\sin a = 0$ are $0, \pm \pi$,* $\pm 2\pi, \pm 3\pi$ $\ldots \pm n\pi$

Consequently the series which is the development of $\sin a$ must be divisible by a, $a - \pi, a + \pi, a - 2\pi, a + 2\pi. \ldots$ (Alg. Art. 238, Prop. II.)

If therefore k be a constant whose value is afterwards to be determined, we have

$$\sin a = \pm k\, a\, (\pi - a)\, (\pi + a)\, (2\pi - a)\, (2\pi + a) \ldots$$

$$= \pm k\, a\, \pi \,(1 - \frac{a}{\pi})\, \pi\, (1 + \frac{a}{\pi})\, 2\pi\, (1 - \frac{a}{2\pi})\, 2\pi\, (1 + \frac{a}{2\pi}) \ldots$$

$$= \pm k\, a\, \pi^2 \cdot 2^2\, \pi^2 \cdot 3^2\, \pi^2 \ldots (1 - \frac{a^2}{\pi^2})\;\; (1 - \frac{a^2}{2^2\, \pi^2}) \ldots$$

$$\therefore \frac{\sin a}{a} = \pm k\, \pi^2 \cdot 2^2\, \pi^2 \cdot 3^2\, \pi^2 \ldots (1 - \frac{a^2}{\pi^2})\;\; (1 - \frac{a^2}{2^2\, \pi^2}) \ldots$$

If $a = 0, \dfrac{\sin a}{a} = 1 \;\therefore\; 1 = \pm k\, \pi^2 \cdot 2^2\, \pi^2 \cdot 3^2\, \pi^2 \ldots$

$$\therefore \sin a = a\, (1 - \frac{a^2}{\pi^2})\;\; (1 - \frac{a^2}{2^2\, \pi^2})\;\; (1 - \frac{a^2}{3^2\, \pi^2}) \ldots \qquad (1)$$

In a similar manner may be derived

$$\cos a = (1 - \frac{2^2\, a^2}{\pi^2})\;\; (1 - \frac{2^2\, a^2}{3^2\, \pi^2})\;\; (1 - \frac{2^2\, a^2}{5^2\, \pi^2}) \ldots \qquad (2)$$

If $a = \frac{1}{2}\pi$, (1) becomes

$$1 = \frac{\pi}{2}\, (1 - \frac{1}{2^2})\;\; (1 - \frac{1}{4^2})\;\; (1 - \frac{1}{6^2})\;\; (1 - \frac{1}{8^2}) \ldots$$

$$= \frac{\pi}{2}\; \frac{2^2 - 1}{2^2} \cdot \frac{4^2 - 1}{4^2} \cdot \frac{6^2 - 1}{6^2} \cdot \frac{8^2 - 1}{8^2}$$

$$= \frac{\pi}{2}\; \frac{(2 - 1)\, (2 + 1)}{2^2} \cdot \frac{(4 - 1)\, (4 + 1)}{4^2} \cdot \frac{(6 - 1)\, (6 + 1)}{6^2} \ldots$$

$$\therefore \pi = 2 \cdot \frac{2^2}{1 \cdot 3} \cdot \frac{4^2}{3 \cdot 5} \cdot \frac{6^2}{5 \cdot 7} \cdot \frac{8^2}{7 \cdot 9} \ldots \dagger$$

Applying logarithms to (1) we have, making $a = \dfrac{m}{n}\, \dfrac{\pi}{2}$

$$\log.\, \sin \frac{m}{n}\, \frac{\pi}{2} = \log.\, \left(\frac{m}{n}\, \frac{\pi}{2}\right) + \log.\, \left(1 - \frac{m^2}{2^2\, n^2}\right) + \log.\, \left(1 - \frac{m^2}{4^2\, n^4}\right)$$

$$+ \log.\, \left(1 - \frac{m^2}{6^2\, n^6}\right) + \ldots$$

* π being 180°, or the semi-circumference whose radius is 1.

† This is the theorem of Wallis for determining π. Its successive factors approximate each more and more to 1.

Developing log. $\left(1-\frac{m^2}{4^2\,n^2}\right)$, log. $\left(1-\frac{m^2}{6^2\,n^2}\right)$ &c. Alg. Art. 224.

$$\log.\sin\frac{m}{n}\frac{\pi}{2}=\log.\frac{m}{n}\frac{\pi}{2}+\log.\left(\frac{2^2\,n^2-m^2}{2^2\,n^2}\right)$$

$$-\mathrm{M}\left(\frac{m^2}{4^2\,n^2}+\tfrac{1}{2}\,\frac{m^4}{4^4\,n^4}+\tfrac{1}{3}\,\frac{m^6}{4^6\,n^6}\cdots\right)$$

$$-\mathrm{M}\left(\frac{m^2}{6^2\,n^2}+\tfrac{1}{2}\,\frac{m^4}{6^4\,n^4}+\tfrac{1}{3}\,\frac{m^6}{6^6\,n^6}\cdots\right)$$

$$-\mathrm{M}\left(\frac{m^2}{8^2\,n^2}+\tfrac{1}{2}\,\frac{m^4}{8^4\,n^4}+\tfrac{1}{3}\,\frac{m^6}{8^6\,n^6}\cdots\right)$$

But,

$$\log.\left(\frac{m}{n}\frac{\pi}{2}\right)=\log.m+\log.\pi-\log.n-\log.2$$

And

$$\log.\frac{2^2\,n^2-m^2}{2^2\,n^2}=\log.\left\{(2n+m)\,(2n-m)-\log.2^2\,n^2\right.$$

$$=\log.(2n+m)+\log.(2n-m)-2\,(\log.2+\log.n)$$

$$\therefore\ \log.\sin\frac{m}{n}\frac{\pi}{2}=\log.m+\log.(2n+m)+\log.(2n-m)+\log\pi$$

$$-3\,(\log.n+\log.2.)$$

$$-\mathrm{M}^{*}\left\{\begin{array}{l}\left(\frac{1}{4^2}+\frac{1}{6^2}+\frac{1}{8^2}\cdots\right)\frac{m^2}{n^2}\\ +\tfrac{1}{2}\left(\frac{1}{4^4}+\frac{1}{6^4}+\frac{1}{8^4}\cdots\right)\frac{m^4}{n^4}\\ +\tfrac{1}{3}\left(\frac{1}{4^6}+\frac{1}{6^6}+\frac{1}{8^6}\cdots\right)\frac{m^6}{n^6}\\ +\ \&c.\end{array}\right\}$$

The above form serves to compute a logarithmic sine at once, without first computing the natural sine.†

From (2) in a similar manner may be derived the following formula for calculating logarithmic cosines.

$$\log.\cos\left(\frac{m}{n}\frac{\pi}{2}\right)=\log.(n+m)+\log.(n-m)-2\log.n$$

$$-\mathrm{M}\left\{\begin{array}{l}\left(\frac{1}{3^2}+\frac{1}{5^2}+\frac{1}{7^2}\cdots\right)\frac{m^2}{n^2}\\ +\tfrac{1}{2}\left(\frac{1}{3^4}+\frac{1}{5^4}+\frac{1}{7^4}\cdots\right)\frac{m^4}{n^4}\\ +\tfrac{1}{3}\left(\frac{1}{3^6}+\frac{1}{5^6}+\frac{1}{7^6}\cdots\right)\frac{m^6}{n^6}\\ +\ \&c.\end{array}\right\}$$

* M is the modulus of the system, equal for the common to ·43429448.

† $\frac{m}{n}$ expresses what fraction of a quadrant the arc is.

12. Adding and subtracting (3) and (7) of Art. 70, and adding and subtracting (6) and (8) of the same article, the following formulas are obtained.

$$\left.\begin{aligned}\sin(a+b)+\sin(a-b) &= 2\sin a\cos b\\ \sin(a+b)-\sin(a-b) &= 2\sin b\cos a\\ \cos(a+b)+\cos(a-b) &= 2\cos a\cos b\\ \cos(a+b)-\cos(a-b) &= -2\sin a\sin b\end{aligned}\right\} \qquad (q)$$

The following two are identical equations

$$a=\frac{a+b}{2}+\frac{a-b}{2}$$

$$b=\frac{a+b}{2}-\frac{a-b}{2}$$

$$\therefore \sin a=\sin\left\{\frac{a+b}{2}+\frac{a-b}{2}\right\}$$

$$=\sin\frac{a+b}{2}\cos\frac{a-b}{2}+\sin\frac{a-b}{2}\cos\frac{a+b}{2} \qquad (1)$$

$$\sin b=\sin\left\{\frac{a+b}{2}-\frac{a-b}{2}\right\}$$

$$=\sin\frac{a+b}{2}\cos\frac{a-b}{2}-\sin\frac{a-b}{2}\cos\frac{a+b}{2} \qquad (2)$$

$$\cos a=\cos\left\{\frac{a+b}{2}+\frac{a-b}{2}\right\}$$

$$=\cos\frac{a+b}{2}\cos\frac{a-b}{2}-\sin\frac{a+b}{2}\sin\frac{a-b}{2} \qquad (3)$$

$$\cos b=\cos\left\{\frac{a+b}{2}-\frac{a-b}{2}\right\}$$

$$=\cos\frac{a+b}{2}\cos\frac{a-b}{2}+\sin\frac{a+b}{2}\sin\frac{a-b}{2} \qquad (4)$$

Adding together (1) and (2) there results

$$\sin a+\sin b=2\sin\frac{a+b}{2}\cos\frac{a-b}{2} \qquad (5)$$

Subtracting (2) from (1),

$$\sin a-\sin b=2\sin\frac{a-b}{2}\cos\frac{a+b}{2} \qquad (6)$$

Add together (3) and (4),

$$\cos a+\cos b=2\cos\frac{a+b}{2}\cos\frac{a-b}{2} \qquad (7)$$

Subtract (4) from (3),

$$\cos a - \cos b = -2 \sin \frac{a+b}{2} \sin \frac{a-b}{2} \qquad (8)$$

These formulas might have been immediately deduced from the group (q), by changing $a+b$ into a, $a-b$ into b, a into $\frac{a+b}{2}$ b into $\frac{a-b}{2}$

13. The following are various forms of expressing the principles deduced from Art. 14 to Art. 31 inclusive.

$\sin 0$	$= 0$	$\sin (180^\circ + a)$	$= -\sin a$
$\cos 0$	$= 1$	$\cos (180^\circ + a)$	$= -\cos a$
$\tan 0$	$= 0$	$\tan (180^\circ + a)$	$= \tan a$
$\cot 0$	$= \infty$	$\cot (180^\circ + a)$	$= \cot a$
$\sec 0$	$= 1$	$\sec (180^\circ + a)$	$= -\sec a$
$\text{cosec } 0$	$= \infty$	$\text{cosec } (180^\circ + a)$	$= -\text{cosec } a$
$\sin (90^\circ - a)$	$= \cos a$	$\sin (270^\circ - a)$	$= -\cos a$
$\cos (90^\circ - a)$	$= \sin a$	$\cos (270^\circ - a)$	$= -\sin a$
$\tan (90^\circ - a)$	$= \cot a$	$\tan (270^\circ - a)$	$= \cot a$
$\cot (90^\circ - a)$	$= \tan a$	$\cot (270^\circ - a)$	$= \tan a$
$\sec (90^\circ - a)$	$= \text{cosec } a$	$\sec (270^\circ - a)$	$= -\text{cosec } a$
$\text{cosec } (90^\circ - a)$	$= \sec a$	$\text{cosec } (270^\circ - a)$	$= -\sec a$
$\sin 90^\circ$	$= 1$	$\sin 270^\circ$	$= -1$
$\cos 90^\circ$	$= 0$	$\cos 270^\circ$	$= 0$
$\tan 90^\circ$	$= \infty$	$\tan 270^\circ$	$= -\infty$
$\cot 90^\circ$	$= 0$	$\cot 270^\circ$	$= 0$
$\sec 90^\circ$	$= \infty$	$\sec 270^\circ$	$= -\infty$
$\text{cosec } 90^\circ$	$= 1$	$\text{cosec } 270^\circ$	$= -1$
$\sin (90^\circ + a)$	$= \cos a$	$\sin (270^\circ + a)$	$= -\cos a$
$\cos (90^\circ + a)$	$= -\sin a$	$\cos (270^\circ + a)$	$= \sin a$
$\tan (90^\circ + a)$	$= -\cot a$	$\tan (270^\circ + a)$	$= -\cot a$
$\cot (90^\circ + a)$	$= -\tan a$	$\cot (270^\circ + a)$	$= -\tan a$
$\sec (90^\circ + a)$	$= -\text{cosec } a$	$\sec (270^\circ + a)$	$= \text{cosec } a$
$\text{cosec } (90^\circ + a)$	$= \sec a$	$\text{cosec } (270^\circ + a)$	$= -\sec a$
$\sin (180^\circ - a)$	$= \sin a$	$\sin (360^\circ - a)$	$= -\sin a$
$\cos (180^\circ - a)$	$= -\cos a$	$\cos (360^\circ - a)$	$= \cos a$
$\tan (180^\circ - a)$	$= -\tan a$	$\tan (360^\circ - a)$	$= -\tan a$
$\cot (180^\circ - a)$	$= -\cot a$	$\cot (360^\circ - a)$	$= -\cot a$
$\sec (180^\circ - a)$	$= -\sec a$	$\sec (360^\circ - a)$	$= \sec a$
$\text{cosec } (180^\circ - a)$	$= \text{cosec } a$	$\text{cosec } (360^\circ - a)$	$= -\text{cosec } a$
$\sin 180^\circ$	$= 0$	$\sin 360^\circ$	$= 0$
$\cos 180^\circ$	$= -1$	$\cos 360^\circ$	$= 1$
$\tan 180^\circ$	$= 0$	$\tan 360^\circ$	$= 0$
$\cot 180^\circ$	$= -\infty$	$\cot 360^\circ$	$= \infty$
$\sec 180^\circ$	$= -1$	$\sec 360^\circ$	* $= 1$
$\text{cosec } 180^\circ$	$= 0$	$\text{cosec } 360^\circ$	$= \infty$*

* All the infinities in the above table should perhaps strictly have the doubtful sign, since they are the transition value.

$$\sin a = (\sin n\,360^\circ + a) = \sin(2n\,180^\circ + a)$$
$$\sin a = \sin\left\{(2n+1)\,180^\circ - a\right\}$$
$$\sin a = -\sin\left\{(2n+1)\,180^\circ + a\right\}$$
$$\sin a = -\sin(2n\cdot 180^\circ - a)$$

$$\cos a = \cos(2n\cdot 180^\circ + a) \text{ or } -\cos\left\{(2n+1)\,180^\circ - a\right\}$$
$$\text{or } -\cos\left\{(2n+1)\,180^\circ + a\right\} \text{ or } \cos(2n\cdot 180^\circ - a)$$

$$\tan a = \tan(2n\cdot 180^\circ + a) \text{ or } -\tan\left\{(2n+1)\,180^\circ - a\right\}$$
$$\text{or } \tan\left\{(2n+1)\,180^\circ + a\right\} \text{ or } -\tan(2n\cdot 180^\circ - a)$$

$$\sec a = \sec(2n\cdot 180^\circ + a) \text{ or } -\sec\left\{(2n+1)\,180^\circ - a\right\}$$
$$\text{or } -\sec\left\{(2n+1)\,180^\circ + a\right\} \text{ or } \sec(2n\cdot 180^\circ - a)$$

14. The following are the most useful general relations of arcs or angles deduced in the preceding pages, or deducible from the formulas which they contain.

TABLE II.

(1.) $\sin(a \pm b) = \sin a \cos b \pm \sin b \cos a$

(2.) $\cos(a \pm b) = \cos a \cos b \mp \sin a \sin b$

(3.) $\tan(a \pm b) = \dfrac{\tan a \pm \tan b}{1 \mp \tan a \tan b}$

(4.) $\sin 2a = 2 \sin a \cos a$ also $= \dfrac{2 \tan a}{1 + \tan^2 a} = \dfrac{2\sqrt{\sec^2 a - 1}}{\sec^2 a} = \dfrac{2 \cot a}{1 + \cot^2 a} = \dfrac{2\sqrt{\operatorname{cosec}^2 a - 1}}{\operatorname{cosec}^2 a}$

(5.) $\cos 2a = \cos^2 a - \sin^2 a = 2\cos^2 a - 1 = 1 - 2\sin^2 a = \dfrac{1 - \tan^2 a}{1 + \tan^2 a} = \dfrac{2 - \sec^2 a}{\sec^2 a} = \dfrac{\cot^2 a - 1}{\cot^2 a + 1} = \dfrac{\operatorname{cosec}^2 a - 2}{\operatorname{cosec}^2 a} = 1 - 2\,(2 \operatorname{vers} a - \operatorname{vers}^2 a)$

(6.) $\tan 2a = \dfrac{2 \tan a}{1 - \tan^2 a}$

(7.) $\sin \dfrac{a}{2} = \sqrt{\dfrac{1 - \cos a}{2}}$

(8.) $\cos \dfrac{a}{2} = \sqrt{\dfrac{1 + \cos a}{2}}$

(9.) $\tan \dfrac{a}{2} = \sqrt{\dfrac{1 - \cos a}{1 + \cos a}} = \dfrac{1 - \cos a}{\sin a} = \dfrac{\sin a}{1 + \cos a}$

(10.) $\sin a = 2 \sin \frac{a}{2} \cos \frac{a}{2}$

(11.) $\sin^2 a = -\frac{1}{2} (\cos 2a - 1)$ (See Art. 18, App. I.)

(12.) $\sin^3 a = -\frac{1}{2^2} (\sin 3a - 3 \sin a)$

(13.) $\sin^4 a = -\frac{1}{2^3} (\cos 4a - 4 \cos 2a + \frac{1}{2} \frac{4 \cdot 3}{1 \cdot 2})$

(14.) $\sin^5 a = \frac{1}{2^4} (\sin 5a - 5 \sin 3a + \frac{5 \cdot 4}{1 \cdot 2} \sin a)$

(15.) $\sin^6 a = -\frac{1}{2^5} (\cos 6a - 6 \cos 4a + \frac{6 \cdot 5}{1 \cdot 2} \cos 2a - \frac{1}{2} \frac{6 \cdot 5 \cdot 4}{1 \cdot 2 \cdot 3})$

(16.) $\cos^2 a = \frac{1}{2} (\cos 2a + 1)$

(17.) $\cos^3 a = \frac{1}{2^2} (\cos 3a + 3 \cos a)$

(18.) $\cos^4 a = \frac{1}{2^3} (\cos 4a + 4 \cos 2a + \frac{1}{2} \frac{4 \cdot 3}{1 \cdot 2})$

(19.) $\cos^5 a = \frac{1}{2^4} (\cos 5a + 5 \cos 3a + \frac{5 \cdot 4}{1 \cdot 2} \cos a)$

(20.) $\cos^6 a = \frac{1}{2^5} (\cos 6a + 6 \cos 4a + \frac{6 \cdot 5}{1 \cdot 2} \cos 2a + \frac{1}{2} \frac{6 \cdot 5 \cdot 4}{1 \cdot 2 \cdot 3})$

(21.) $\sin (n + 1) a = 2 \sin na \cos a - \sin (n - 1) a$

(22.) $\cos (n + 1) a = 2 \cos na \cos a - \cos (n - 1) a$

(23.) $\sin a + \sin b = 2 \sin \frac{a + b}{2} \cos \frac{a - b}{2}$

(24.) $\sin a - \sin b = 2 \sin \frac{a - b}{2} \cos \frac{a + b}{2}$

(25.) $\cos a + \cos b = 2 \cos \frac{a + b}{2} \cos \frac{a - b}{2}$

(26.) $\cos a - \cos b = -2 \sin \frac{a + b}{2} \sin \frac{a - b}{2}$

(27.) $\frac{\sin a + \sin b}{\sin a - \sin b} = \frac{\tan \frac{a + b}{2}}{\tan \frac{a - b}{2}}$

(28.) $\frac{\sin a \pm \sin b}{\cos a + \cos b} = \tan \frac{1}{2} (a \pm b)$

(29.) $\frac{\sin a \pm \sin b}{\cos b - \cos a} = \cot \frac{1}{2} (a \mp b)$

(30.) $\sin (a + b) + \sin (a - b) = 2 \sin a \cos b$

(31.) $\sin (a - b) - \sin (a - b) = 2 \sin b \cos a$

(32.) $\cos (a + b) + \cos (a - b) = 2 \cos a \cos b$

(33.) $\cos (a + b) - \cos (a - b) = -2 \sin a \sin b$

(34.) $2 \cos \frac{45^\circ}{2^n} = \sqrt{2 \sqrt{2 \sqrt{2}}}$ &c. to $n + 1$ radicals

(35.) $\cos 36^\circ = \sin 54^\circ = \frac{1}{4}\,(1 + \sqrt{5})$

(36.) $\sin 45^\circ = \cos 45^\circ = \frac{1}{\sqrt{2}}$

(37.) $\tan 45^\circ = \cot 45^\circ = 1$

(38.) $\sin 30^\circ = \cos 60^\circ = \frac{1}{2}$

(39.) $\cos 30^\circ = \sin 60^\circ = \frac{\sqrt{3}}{2}$

(40.) $\tan 30^\circ = \cot 60^\circ = \frac{1}{\sqrt{3}}$

(41.) $\cot 30^\circ = \tan 60^\circ = \sqrt{3}$

The formulas of Trigonometry may be varied to almost any extent, and the same quantity expressed in many different ways.

15. The following, of less frequent occurrence, may be readily deduced from the above.

(42.) $\left\{\begin{array}{l}\sin(45^\circ \pm a) \\ \cos(45^\circ \mp a)\end{array}\right\} = \frac{\cos a \pm \sin a}{\sqrt{2}}$

(43.) $\tan(45^\circ \pm a) = \frac{1 \pm \tan a}{1 \mp \tan a}$

(44.) $\tan^2(45^\circ \pm \frac{a}{2}) = \frac{1 \pm \sin a}{1 \mp \sin a}$

(45.) $\tan(45^\circ \pm \frac{a}{2}) = \frac{1 \pm \sin a}{\cos a} = \frac{\cos a}{1 \mp \sin a}$

(46.) $\frac{\sin(a+b)}{\sin(a-b)} = \frac{\tan a + \tan b}{\tan a - \tan b} = \frac{\cot b + \cot a}{\cot b - \cot a}$

(47.) $\frac{(\cos a + b)}{\cos(a-b)} = \frac{\cot b - \tan a}{\cot b + \tan a} = \frac{1 - \tan a \tan b}{1 + \tan a \tan b}$

(48.) $\sin a = \frac{\varepsilon^{a\sqrt{-1}} - \varepsilon^{-a\sqrt{-1}}}{2\sqrt{-1}}$ *

(49.) $\cos a = \frac{\varepsilon^{a\sqrt{-1}} + \varepsilon^{-a\sqrt{-1}}}{2}$

(50.) $\varepsilon^{a\sqrt{-1}} = \cos a + \sqrt{-1}\sin a$

(51.) $\varepsilon^{-a\sqrt{-1}} = \cos a - \sqrt{-1}\ \text{in}\ a$

(52.) $\frac{\cos a + \cos b}{\cos a - \cos b} = -\cot\frac{a+b}{2}\cot\frac{a-b}{2}$

(53.) $\tan a + \tan b = \frac{\sin(a+b)}{\cos a \cos b}$

(54.) $\cot a + \cot b = \frac{\sin(a+b)}{\sin a \sin b}$

* ε is the base of the Naperian system of logarithms. For the demonstration of the first two of these four formulas see next article.

(55.) $\tan a - \tan b = \dfrac{\sin (a - b)}{\cos a \cos b}$

(56.) $\cot a - \cot b = -\dfrac{\sin (a - b)}{\sin a \sin b}$

(57.) $\cos a + \sin a = \sqrt{1 + \sin 2a}$

(58.) $\cos a - \sin a = \sqrt{1 - \sin 2a}$

If a be less than 45° then

(59.) $\cos a = \frac{1}{2} \left\{ \sqrt{1 + \sin 2a} + \sqrt{1 - \sin 2a} \right\}$

(60.) $\sin a = \frac{1}{2} \cdot \left\{ \sqrt{1 + \sin 2a} - \sqrt{1 - \sin 2a} \right\}$

(61.) $\dfrac{\tan a + \tan b}{\tan a - \tan b} = \dfrac{\sin (a + b)}{\sin (a - b)}$

(62.) $\dfrac{\cos a + \sin a}{\cos a - \sin a} = \sec 2a + \tan 2a$

(63.) $\sin (a + b) \sin (a - b) = \sin^2 a - \sin^2 b = \cos^2 b - \cos^2 a$

(64.) $\cos (a + b) \cos (a - b) = \cos^2 a - \sin^2 b = \cos^2 b - \sin^2 a$

(65.) $\sin 3a = 3 \sin a - 4 \sin^3 a$

(66.) $\cos 3a = 4 \cos^3 a - 3 \cos a$

(67.) $\cos 2a = \dfrac{1}{1 + \tan 2a \tan a}$

(68.) $\tan^2 a - \tan^2 b = \dfrac{\sin (a + b) \sin (a - b)}{\cos^2 a \cos^2 b}$

(69.) $\cot^2 a - \cot^2 b = -\dfrac{\sin (a + b) \sin (a - b)}{\sin^2 a \sin^2 b}$

(70.) $\dfrac{1 - \cos a}{1 + \cos a} = \tan^2 \frac{1}{2} a$

(71.) $\dfrac{\sin a}{1 + \cos a} = \tan \frac{1}{2} a$

(72.) $\dfrac{1 + \cos a}{\sin a} = \cot \frac{1}{2} a$

(73.) $\dfrac{\sin a}{1 - \cos a} = \cot \frac{1}{2} a$

(74.) $\dfrac{1 - \cos a}{\sin a} = \tan \frac{1}{2} a$

(75.) $\sin a = a - \dfrac{a^3}{1 \cdot 2 \cdot 3} + \dfrac{a^5}{1 \cdot 2 \cdot 3 \cdot 4 \cdot 5} - \dfrac{a^7}{1 \cdot 2 \cdot 3 \cdot 4 \cdot 5 \cdot 6 \cdot 7} + \text{\&c.}$

(76.) $\cos a = 1 - \dfrac{a^2}{1 \cdot 2} + \dfrac{a^4}{1 \cdot 2 \cdot 3 \cdot 4} - \dfrac{a^6}{1 \cdot 2 \cdot 3 \cdot 4 \cdot 5 \cdot 6} + \text{\&c.}$

(77.) $\tan a = a + \frac{1}{3} a^3 + \frac{2}{15} a^5 + \frac{17}{315} a^7 + \text{\&c.}$

(78.) $z = \text{arc} (\sin = y) \text{ or } \sin^{-1} y^* = y + \frac{1}{6} y^3 + \frac{3}{40} y^5 + \text{\&c.}$

(79.) $z = \cos^{-1} x = (1 - x) + \frac{1}{6} (1 - x^3) + \frac{3}{40} (1 - x^5) + \text{\&c.}$

(80.) $z = \tan^{-1} t = t - \frac{1}{3} t^3 + \frac{1}{5} t^5 \text{ \&c.}$

15. The following will be found a useful table of reference.

* Arc ($\sin = y$) or $\sin^{-1} y$ are read the arc whose sin is y.

TABLE OF THE MOST USEFUL ANALYTICAL VALUES OF SIN a, COS a, TAN a.

VALUES OF SIN a.	VALUES OF COS a.	VALUES OF TAN a.
1. $\cos a \tan a$	16. $\dfrac{\sin a}{\tan a}$	31. $\dfrac{\sin a}{\cos a}$
2. $\dfrac{\cos a}{\cot a}$	17. $\sin a \cot a$	32. $\dfrac{1}{\cot a}$
3. $\sqrt{1-\cos^2 a}$	18. $\sqrt{1-\sin^2 a}$	33. $\sqrt{\dfrac{1}{\cos^2 a}-1}$
4. $\dfrac{1}{\sqrt{1+\cot^2 a}}$	19. $\dfrac{1}{\sqrt{1+\tan^2 a}}$	34. $\dfrac{\sin a}{\sqrt{1-\sin^2 a}}$
5. $\dfrac{\tan a}{\sqrt{1+\tan^2 a}}$	20. $\dfrac{\cot a}{\sqrt{1+\cot^2 a}}$	35. $\dfrac{\sqrt{1-\cos^2 a}}{\cos a}$
6. $2 \sin\dfrac{a}{2} \cos\dfrac{a}{2}$	21. $\cos^2\dfrac{a}{2}-\sin^2\dfrac{a}{2}$	36. $\dfrac{2\tan\dfrac{a}{2}}{1-\tan^2\dfrac{a}{2}}$
7. $\sqrt{\dfrac{1-\cos 2a}{2}}$	22. $1-2\sin^2\dfrac{a}{2}$	37. $\dfrac{2\cot\dfrac{a}{2}}{\cot^2\dfrac{a}{2}-1}$
8. $\dfrac{2\tan\dfrac{a}{2}}{1+\tan^2\dfrac{a}{2}}$	23. $2\cos^2\dfrac{a}{2}-1$	38. $\dfrac{2}{\cot\dfrac{a}{2}-\tan\dfrac{a}{2}}$
9. $\dfrac{2}{\cot\dfrac{a}{2}+\tan\dfrac{a}{2}}$	24. $\sqrt{\dfrac{1+\cos 2a}{2}}$	39. $\cot a-2\cot 2a$
10. $\dfrac{\sin(30^\circ+a)-\sin(30^\circ-a)}{\sqrt{3}}$	25. $\dfrac{1-\tan^2\dfrac{a}{2}}{1+\tan^2\dfrac{a}{2}}$	40. $\dfrac{1-\cos 2a}{\sin 2a}$
11. $2\sin^2(45^\circ+\dfrac{a}{2})-1$	26. $\dfrac{\cot\dfrac{a}{2}-\tan\dfrac{a}{2}}{\cot\dfrac{a}{2}+\tan\dfrac{a}{2}}$	41. $\dfrac{\sin 2a}{1+\cos 2a}$
12. $1-2\sin^2(45^\circ-\dfrac{a}{2})$	27. $\dfrac{1}{1+\tan a\tan\dfrac{a}{2}}$	42. $\sqrt{\dfrac{1-\cos 2a}{1+\cos 2a}}$
13. $\dfrac{1-\tan^2(45^\circ-\dfrac{a}{2})}{1+\tan^2(45^\circ-\dfrac{a}{2})}$	28. $\dfrac{2}{\tan(45^\circ+\dfrac{a}{2})+\cot(45^\circ+\dfrac{a}{2})}$	43. $\dfrac{\tan(45^\circ+\dfrac{a}{2})-\tan(45^\circ-\dfrac{a}{2})}{2}$
14. $\dfrac{\tan(45^\circ+\dfrac{a}{2})-\tan(45^\circ-\dfrac{a}{2})}{\tan(45^\circ+\dfrac{a}{2})+\tan(45^\circ-\dfrac{a}{2})}$	29. $2\cos(45^\circ+\dfrac{a}{2})\cos(45^\circ-\dfrac{a}{2})$	
15. $\sin(60^\circ+a)-\sin(60^\circ-a)$	30. $\cos(60^\circ+a)+\cos(60^\circ-a)$	

16. *To develop* A^x *in a series of terms arranged according to the ascending powers of* x.

$$a^x = \left\{ 1 + (a-1) \right\}^x = \text{by the binomial theorem}$$

$$1 + x\,(a-1) + x\,\frac{x-1}{2}\,(a-1)^2 + x\,\frac{(x-1)}{2}\;\frac{(x-2)}{3}\;(a-1)^3 + \ldots$$

Representing the coefficient of x, which is $(a-1) - \frac{1}{2}(a-1)^2 + \frac{1}{3}(a-1)^3 \ldots$ by A, those of $x^2, x^3 \ldots$ by B, C, &c. the above becomes

$$a^x = 1 + Ax + Bx^2 + Cx^3 + \ldots \qquad (1)$$

$$\therefore a^z = 1 + Az + Bz^2 + Cz^3 + \ldots$$

$$\therefore a^{x+z} = (1 + Ax + Bx^2 \ldots)\ (1 + Az + Bz^2 \ldots) = \text{by (1) } 1 + A\,(x+z) + B\,(x+z)^2 + \ldots$$

Equating the coefficients of xz, x^2z, x^3z, &c.

$$2B = A\,A \quad \therefore \quad B = \frac{A^2}{2}$$

$$3C = B\,B \quad \therefore \quad C = \frac{A^3}{1\cdot2\cdot3}$$

&c.

But by Alg. Art. 222, $A =$ Nap. logarithm of a. Denoting a Napierian log. by l (1) becomes

$$a^x = 1 + la\;x + \frac{(la)^2}{1\cdot2}\,x^2 + \frac{(la)^3}{1\cdot2.3}\,x^3 + \ldots \qquad (2)$$

Making $a = \varepsilon$ the base of the Napierian system this becomes

$$\varepsilon^x = 1 + x + \frac{x^2}{1\cdot2} + \frac{x^3}{1\cdot2\cdot3} + \ldots \qquad (3)$$

From the above may be deduced remarkable expressions for the sine, cosine, and tangent of an arc.

From (3)

$$\varepsilon^{a\sqrt{-1}} = 1 + a\sqrt{-1} - \frac{a^2}{1\cdot2} - \frac{a^3}{1\cdot2\cdot3}\sqrt{-1} + \frac{a^4}{1\cdot2\cdot3\cdot4}$$

$$\varepsilon^{-a\sqrt{-1}} = 1 - a\sqrt{-1} - \frac{a^2}{1\cdot2} + \frac{a^3}{1\cdot2\cdot3}\sqrt{-1} + \frac{a^4}{1\cdot2\cdot3\cdot4}$$

$$\therefore \varepsilon^{a\sqrt{-1}} + \varepsilon^{-a\sqrt{-1}} = 2\left(1 - \frac{a^2}{1\cdot2} + \frac{a^4}{1\cdot2\cdot3\cdot4} - \ldots\right) = 2\cos a$$

(App. I. Art. 8.)

$$\varepsilon^{a\sqrt{-1}} - \varepsilon^{-a\sqrt{-1}} = 2\sqrt{-1}\left(a - \frac{a^3}{1\cdot2\cdot3} + \ldots\right) = 2\sqrt{-1}\,\sin a$$

$$\therefore \cos a = \tfrac{1}{2}\left(\varepsilon^{a\sqrt{-1}} + \varepsilon^{-a\sqrt{-1}}\right) \qquad (4)$$

$$\sin a = \frac{1}{2\sqrt{-1}}\left(\varepsilon^{a\sqrt{-1}} - \varepsilon^{-a\sqrt{-1}}\right) \qquad (5)$$

Dividing (5) and (4) and multiplying numerator and denominator by $\varepsilon^{a\sqrt{-1}}$ we have

$$\tan a = \frac{1}{\sqrt{-1}} \cdot \frac{\varepsilon^{2a\sqrt{-1}} - 1}{\varepsilon^{2a\sqrt{-1}} + 1}$$

17. Squaring the expression

$$\cos a + \sin a\sqrt{-1} \qquad (1)$$

there results

$$\cos^2 a - \sin^2 a + 2\cos a \sin a\sqrt{-1} = \cos 2a + \sin 2a\sqrt{-1} \quad \{\text{Art. 71, (1) (2)}\}$$

Multiplying by (1) we get, applying the forms for sin and cos of $(a+b)$

$$(\cos a + \sin a\sqrt{-1})^3 = \cos 3a + \sin 3a\sqrt{-1}$$

Finally, proceeding in the same way would be obtained

$$(\cos a + \sin a\sqrt{-1})^n = \cos na + \sin na\sqrt{-1} \qquad (2)$$

Making a negative (2) becomes

$$(\cos a - \sin a\sqrt{-1})^n = \cos na - \sin na\sqrt{-1} \qquad (3)$$

18. *To find the nth power of the sine and cosine.*

Assume

$$\left.\begin{aligned} \cos a + \sin a\sqrt{-1} &= z \\ \cos a - \sin a\sqrt{-1} &= u \end{aligned}\right\} \quad (1)$$

By addition,

$$2\cos a = z + u$$

$$\therefore 2^n \cos^n a = z^n + nz^{n-1}u + \frac{n(n-1)}{1\cdot 2}z^{n-2}u^2 + \frac{n(n-1)(n-2)}{1\cdot 2\cdot 3}z^{n-3}u^3 + \ldots$$

$$= z^n + nz^{n-2}zu + \frac{n(n-1)}{1\cdot 2}z^{n-4}z^2u^2 + \frac{n(n-1)(n-2)}{1\cdot 2\cdot 3}z^{n-6}z^3u^3 + \ldots$$

But $zu = 1 \therefore z^2u^2 = 1$ &c. $\therefore$ these factors will disappear.
Also by the preceding article, form. (2)

$$z^n = \cos na + \sin na\sqrt{-1}$$

$$z^{n-2} = \cos(n-2)a + \sin(n-2)a\sqrt{-1}$$

Making these substitutions

$$2^n \cos^n a = \cos na + n \cos (n-2)\, a + \frac{n(n-1)}{1 \cdot 2} \cos (n-4)\, a + \frac{n(n-1)(n-2)}{1 \cdot 2 \cdot 3}$$

$$\cos (n-6)\, a + \ldots \qquad (2)$$

$$+ \left\{ \sin na + n \sin (n-2)\, a + \frac{n(n-1)}{1 \cdot 2} \sin (n-4)\, a + \frac{n(n-1)(n-2)}{1 \cdot 2 \cdot 3} \right.$$

$$\left. \sin (n-6)\, a + \ldots \right\} \sqrt{-1}$$

When n is a positive whole number, the second part of the series vanishes, and the first part extends only as far as a term containing the factor $(n-n)$. The reason why the second part vanishes will be seen by considering that the arcs in the terms preceding that which with the following terms contains $n-n$ will be negatives of the first, second, &c. terms; their sines will be equal therefore with contrary signs, and the coefficients are also evidently equal at equal distances from the centre, and if n be even, the arc in the middle term, and consequently its sine, will be zero.

Again, take the difference of equations (1) and multiply it by $-\sqrt{-1}$

$$2 \sin a = (z - u)\,(-\sqrt{-1})$$

and the binominal formula proceeding as above gives

$$2^n \sin^n a = \left\{ \begin{array}{l} \cos n\, a - n \cos (n-2)\, a + \frac{n(n-1)}{1 \cdot 2} \cos (n-4)\, a - \ldots \\ + \left\{ \sin n\, a - n \sin (n-2)\, a + \frac{n(n-1)}{1 \cdot 2} \sin (n-4)\, a - \ldots \right\} \sqrt{-1} \end{array} \right\}$$

$$(-\sqrt{-1})^n \qquad (3)$$

If n be even the second part of the series vanishes. If also n be of the form $4m$, $(-\sqrt{-1})^n = 1$. But if $n = 4m + 2$, then $(-\sqrt{-1})^n = -1$, and our formula becomes

$$2^n \sin^n a = \pm \left\{ \cos n\, a - n \cos (n-2)\, a + \frac{n(n-1)}{1 \cdot 2} \cos (n-4)\, a - \ldots \right\}$$

The upper sign applying when $n = 4m$, the lower when $n = 4m + 2$

If n be an odd number, the first part of (3) vanishes, and the formula becomes, $\sqrt{-1}$ outside and inside the parenthesis uniting,

$$2^n \sin^n a = \pm \left\{ \sin n\, a - n \sin (n-2)\, a + \frac{n(n-1)}{1 \cdot 2} \sin (n-4)\, a \ldots \right\}.$$

the upper sign of which is to be used when $n = 4m + 1$ and the lower sign when $n = 4m + 3$.

For examples of the applications of these forms see page 101.

PROBLEM I.

19. To determine the area of a plane triangle when any three parts except the three angles are given.

1. Let two sides, a, c, and the included angle B be given. (See fig. Art. 67.)

The area of the triangle is expressed by $\frac{1}{2}$ BC.AD ; but AD = AB sin B ; hence the expression for the area, in terms of the given quantities, is,

$$\text{area} = \tfrac{1}{2}\, a\, c \sin B \qquad (1)$$

2. Let two angles, B, A, and the interjacent side c, be given
Then, since

$$\sin C : \sin A :: c : a$$

we have

$$a = \frac{\sin A}{\sin C}\, c \therefore ac \sin B = \frac{\sin A \sin B}{\sin C}\, c^2$$

hence the expression for the area is by (1)

$$\text{area} = \tfrac{1}{2}\, \frac{\sin A \sin B}{\sin C}\, c^2$$

3. Let the three sides be given.
By Art. 73, (2)

$$\sin \tfrac{1}{2} B = \sqrt{\frac{(\frac{1}{2} s - a)\,(\frac{1}{2} s - c)}{ac}}$$

Also, by (4) of the same article

$$\cos \tfrac{1}{2} B = \sqrt{\frac{\frac{1}{2} s\,(\frac{1}{2} s - b)}{ac}}$$

$$\therefore 2 \sin \tfrac{1}{2} B \cos \tfrac{1}{2} B, \text{ or (Art. 71) } \sin B = \frac{2}{ac} \sqrt{\tfrac{1}{2} s\,(\tfrac{1}{2} s - b)\,(\tfrac{1}{2} s - a)\,(\tfrac{1}{2} s - c)}$$

Consequently, by substituting this value of sin B in (1) we have

$$\text{area} = \sqrt{\tfrac{1}{2} s\,(\tfrac{1}{2} s - a)\,(\tfrac{1}{2} s - b)\,(\tfrac{1}{2} s - c)}$$

which formula furnishes the well known rule, given in all books on mensuration, for the area of a triangle when the three sides are given.

These expressions for the area of a plane triangle are all adapted to logarithmic computation.

20. In the solution of certain astronomical problems involving the case of solution of triangles at Art. 76, the logarithms of a and b are given, but not the sides themselves ; we can very easily calculate $\frac{A - B}{2}$ without knowing the sides.

$$\tan \frac{A - B}{2} = \frac{a - b}{a + b} \cot \frac{C}{2}$$

$$= \frac{1 - \frac{b}{a}}{1 + \frac{b}{a}} \cot \frac{C}{2}$$

Assume $\frac{b}{a} = \tan \phi$

$$\tan \frac{A - B}{2} = \frac{1 - \tan \phi}{1 + \tan \phi} \cot \frac{C}{2}$$

$$= \tan\ (45^{\circ} - \phi)\ \cot \frac{C}{2}$$

$$\therefore \log.\ \tan \frac{A - B}{2} = \log.\tan(45^{\circ} - \phi) + \log.\cot \frac{C}{2} - \log.\ R.$$

The angle ϕ is known from the equation

$$\tan \phi = \frac{b}{a}$$

Whence $$\log.\ \tan \phi = \log.\ R + \log.\ b - \log.\ a$$

The angle $\frac{A - B}{2}$ thus becomes known from the logs. of a and b, without calculating a and b. In the same way we may have

$$\cot \frac{A - B}{2} = \tan\ (45^{\circ} + \phi)\ \tan \frac{C}{2}$$

And $\therefore \log.\ \cot \frac{A - B}{2} = \log.\ \tan.\ (45^{\circ} + \phi) + \log.\ \tan \frac{C}{2} - \log.\ R.$

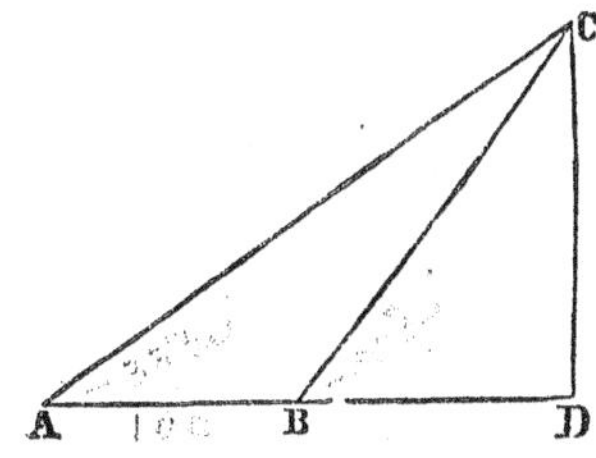

21. A person on one side of a river observes a building CD on the opposite side, and takes the angle of elevation $B = 55^{\circ}\ 54'$, at the place where he stands, then going back the distance $BA = 100$ feet, he again takes the angle of elevation A, and finds it to be $A = 33^{\circ}\ 20'$. The height of the building is required.

The problem may be solved as follows.

Taking CD for radius, DB will be the tangent of the angle DCB, and DA, the tangent of DCA, therefore, AB is the difference of those tangents. By the table of natural sines and cosines,*

$$\begin{aligned} \text{nat. tan } 56^{\circ}\ 40' &= 1{\cdot}520426 \\ \text{nat. tan } 34^{\circ}\ 6' &= {\cdot}677091 \\ \text{difference} &= {\cdot}843335 \end{aligned}$$

$$\therefore {\cdot}843335 : 1 :: 100 : 118{\cdot}57\ \textit{Ans.}$$

PROBLEM II.

From the top of a mountain three miles high, the angle of depression of a line tangent to the earth's surface is taken, and found to be $2^{\circ}\ 13'\ 27''$; it is required thence to determine the diameter of the earth, supposing it to be a perfect sphere.

* A table of natural tangents which some collections of tables contain is often convenient.

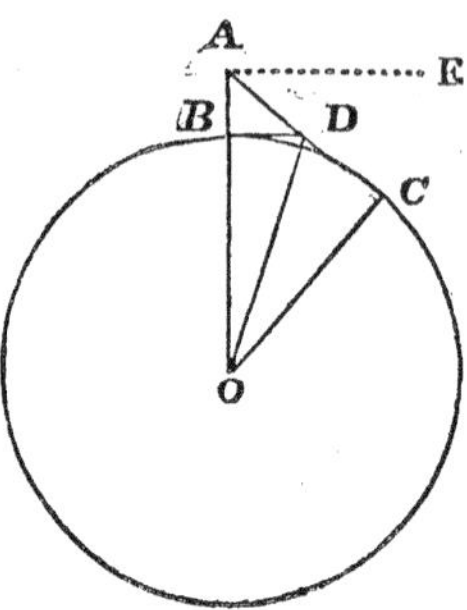

Let O be the centre of the earth, BA the mountain, AC the visual ray or line touching the earth's surface at C. Draw the tangent BD, and join OD, OC; then the angle of depression EAC being given, we have also the angle BAD, the complement of it, equal to 87° 46′ 33″. Also since the tangents BD, CD, are equal (Geom. p. 83), we have the angle BOD = DOC = ½ comp. A = 1° 6′ 43½″, and, therefore, BDO = 88° 53′ 16½″.

Now in the right-angled triangle ABD we have

$$BD = AB \tan A;$$

and in the right-angled triangle OBD,

$$OB = DB \tan BDO;$$

hence, by substitution,

$$OB = AB \tan A \tan BDO;$$

the computation is, therefore, as follows:

A B	3	log.	0·47712
A	87° 46′ 33″	log. tan	11·41074
BDO	88° 53′ 16½″	log. tan	11·71193
OB	3979·15	log.	3·59979

hence the diameter is 7958·3 miles.

PROBLEM III.

Given the distances between three objects, A, B, C, and the angles subtended by these distances at a point D in the same plane with them; to determine the distance of D from each object.

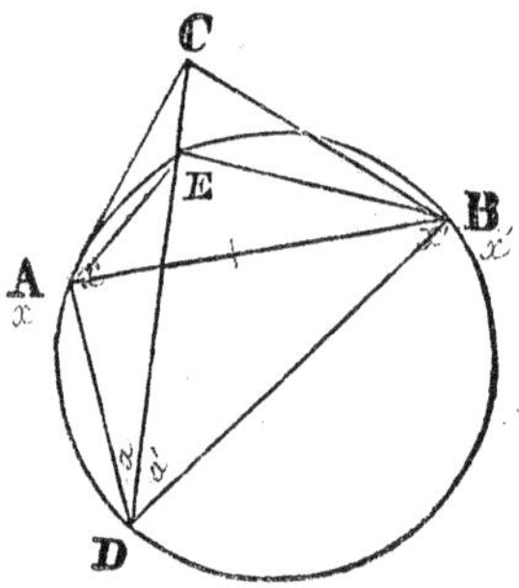

Let a circle be described about the triangle ADB, and join AE, EB, then will the angles ABE, BAE, be respectively equal to the given angles ADE, BDE (Geom. p. 44); thus all the angles of the triangle AEB are known, as also the side AB; we may find, therefore, the remaining sides AE, EB. Again, the sides of the triangle ABC being known, we may find the angle BAC; hence the angle CAE becomes known, so that in the triangle CAE we shall have the two sides AE, AC, and the included angle given, from which we may find the angle AEC in fig. 1, or the angle ACE in fig. 2,

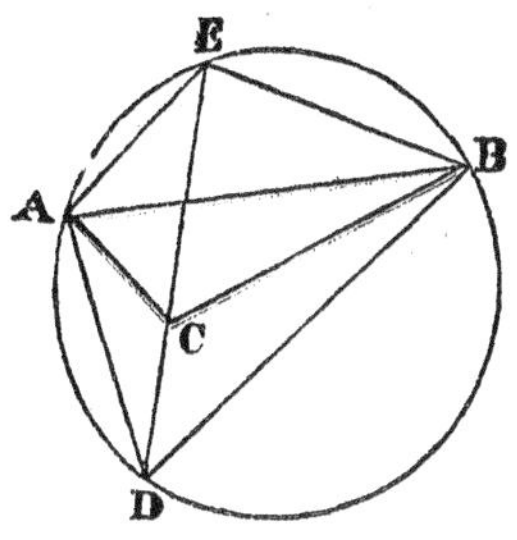

and thence its supplement AED or ACD ; this with the given side AE and angle ADE, in the first figure, or with the given side AC, and angle ADC in the second, will enable us to find AD, one of the required lines, and thence DC and DB the other two.

Or the solution may be conducted more analytically as follows:

Put x for the angle DAC, and x' for the angle DBC ; also call the given angles ADC, BDC α and α' then a, b, c, representing as usual the sides opposite to A, B, C, we have

$$\frac{\sin \alpha}{\sin x} = \frac{b}{\text{DC}} \quad \frac{\sin \alpha'}{\sin x'} = \frac{a}{\text{DC}} \tag{1}$$

$$\therefore \frac{\sin \alpha \sin x'}{\sin \alpha' \sin x} = \frac{b}{a} \therefore a \sin \alpha \sin x' = b \sin \alpha' \sin x \tag{2}$$

This is one equation between the unknown quantities x, x'. Another is easily obtained; for since the four angles of the quadrilateral ABCD make up four right angles or 360°, we have $x + x' + \alpha + \alpha' + \text{ACD} + \text{BCD} = 360°$; the sum of the two latter angles may become known, since in the triangle ABC the angle C is determinable from the three given sides ; therefore all the terms in the first member of this equation are known except x and x'. Call the sum of the known quantities β, and we shall thus have $x' = \beta - x$, and, consequently by substitution, equation (2) becomes

$$a \sin \alpha \sin (\beta - x) = b \sin \alpha' \sin x$$
$$= a \sin \alpha (\sin \beta \cos x - \cos \beta \sin x) ;$$

or dividing by $\sin x$

$$b \sin \alpha' = a \sin \alpha (\sin \beta \cot x - \cos \beta)$$
$$\therefore \cot x = \frac{b \sin \alpha'}{a \sin \alpha \sin \beta} + \frac{\cos \beta}{\sin \beta}$$
$$= \frac{b \sin \alpha'}{a \sin \alpha \sin \beta} + \cot \beta$$

The first term of this second member may be easily calculated by logarithms, and this added to the natural cotangent of β gives the nat. cot. of x, and thence x' is known from the equation $x' = \beta - x$, and CD from either of the equations (1).

This problem has a useful application in the survey of harbors.

Let the angles be taken with a sextant, from a boat, at a point where a sounding is made, to three stations on the shore. After having drawn upon a map the triangle, of which these three stations are the vertices, the following simple and elegant construction will determine the point where the sounding was made.

Upon the line joining two of the stations, on the map, make a segment, capable of containing the angle observed from the place of sounding, and subtended by this line (Plane Geom., Prob. 21) ; upon a line joining one of these two stations and the third, make another segment that will contain the angle observed to be subtended by this last line, and the intersection of the arcs of these two segments will determine the point on the map, corresponding to that at which the sounding was made.

PROBLEM IV.

Given the angles of elevation of an object taken at three places on the same horizontal straight line, together with the distances between the stations; to find the height of the object and its distance from either station.

Let AB be the object, and C, C′, C′′, the three stations, then the triangles BCA, BC′A, BC′′A, will all be right angled at A; and, therefore, to radius BA, AC, AC′, AC′′, will be the tangents of the angles at B, or the cotangents of the angles of elevation; hence, putting a, a', a'', for the angles of elevation, x for the height of the object, and a, b, for the distances CC′, C′C′′, we shall have

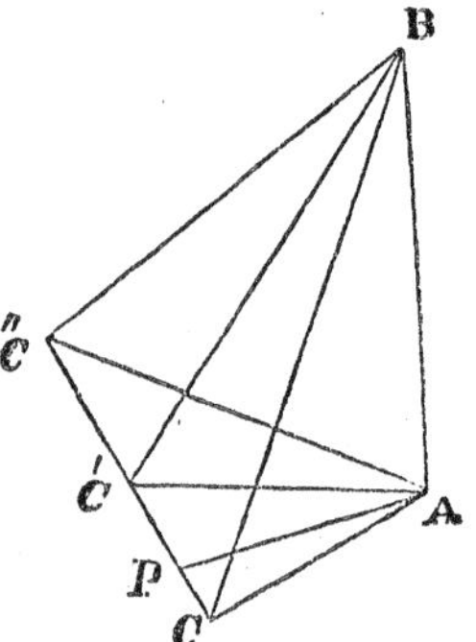

$$AC = x \cot a, \quad AC' = x \cot a', \quad AC'' = x \cot a''$$

Now, if a perpendicular AP be drawn from A to CC′′, we shall have (Geom., p. 34,) from the triangle ACC′

$$AC^2 = AC'^2 + C'C^2 - 2\, C'C \,.\, C'P\,;$$

and from the triangle AC′C′′

$$AC''^2 = AC'^2 + C''C'^2 + 2\, C''C' \,.\, C'P\,;$$

that is, we shall have the two equations

$$x^2 \cot^2 a = x^2 \cot^2 a' + a^2 - 2a \,.\, C'P$$
$$x^2 \cot^2 a'' = x^2 \cot^2 a' + b^2 + 2b \,.\, C'P$$

in order to eliminate C′P, multiply the first by b, the second by a, and add, and we shall have

$$x^2 (b \cot^2 a + a \cot^2 a'') = (a + b)\, x^2 \cot^2 a' + ab\,(a + b)$$

$$\therefore\ x = \sqrt{\frac{ab\,(a+b)}{b \cot^2 a + a \cot^2 a'' - (a+b) \cot^2 a'}}$$

If the three stations are equidistant, then $a = b$, and the expression becomes

$$x = \frac{a}{\sqrt{\frac{1}{2} \cot^2 a + \frac{1}{2} \cot^2 a'' - \cot^2 a'}}$$

The height A B being thus determined, the distances of the stations from the object are found by multiplying this height by the cotangents of the angles of elevation.

EXAMPLE.

22 Given the hypothenuse $a = 6512{\cdot}4$ yards, $b = 6510{\cdot}6$, to find c
By Art. 64

$$\log.\cos c = \log.\text{R} + \log.b - \log.a$$

Now

$$\log.\text{R} = 10$$
$$\log.b = 3{\cdot}8136210$$
$$13{\cdot}8136210$$
$$\log.a = 3{\cdot}8137411$$
$$\log.\cos c = 9.9998799$$
$$c = 1^\circ\,20'\,50''$$

Upon inspecting the tables that are calculated to seven places of decimals only, it will be seen that, when the angles become very small, the cosines differ very little from each other. The same remark applies, of course, to the sines of angles nearly 90°. In cases, therefore, where great accuracy is required, we may commit an important error by calculating a small angle from its cosine, or a large one from its sine. We must consequently endeavor to avoid this, by transforming the expression employed.

In the example before us, c is a small angle which has been calculated from its cosine; we must, therefore, if possible, calculate this angle by means of its sine, or some other trigonometrical function.

Now, by formula (8), Art. 72, we have generally

$$\sin\tfrac{1}{2}c = \sqrt{\frac{1-\cos c}{2}}$$

In the present case, $\cos c = \frac{b}{a}$ substituting this in the above equation,

$$\sin\tfrac{1}{2}c = \sqrt{\frac{b-a}{2a}}$$

$$\therefore \quad \log.\sin\tfrac{1}{2}c = \tfrac{1}{2}\log.(b-a) - \tfrac{1}{2}\log.2a + \log.\text{R}.$$

From which we find

$$\frac{c}{2} = 40'\,24''$$

And $\therefore$ $c = 1^\circ\,20'\,48''$

Instead of $1^\circ\,20'\,50''$, as obtained by the former process.

Or c might first be calculated from a and b, and then c by means of its sine.

No angle which is nearly 90° ought to be calculated from its tangent, for the tangents of large angles increase with so much rapidity, that the results, derived from the column of proportional parts found in the tables, cannot be depended on as accurate.

23. The following is the demonstration of formulas (3) and (4) of Art. 77. By Art. 69

$$c^2 = a^2 + b^2 - 2ab \cos c = a^2 + b^2 - 2ab\,(2 \cos^2 \tfrac{1}{2} c - 1)$$

$$= (a^2 + b^2 + 2ab) - 4ab \cos^2 \tfrac{1}{2} c = (a + b)^2 \left\{ 1 - \left(\frac{2\sqrt{ab}}{a+b} \cos \tfrac{1}{2} c \right)^2 \right\}$$

Making

$$\sin \phi = \frac{2\sqrt{ab}}{a+b} \cos \tfrac{1}{2} c \qquad (1)$$

we have

$$c^2 = (a+b)^2 (1 - \sin^2 \phi) = (a+b)^2 \cos^2 \phi$$

$$\therefore \quad c = (a+b) \cos \phi \qquad (2)$$

These forms (1) and (2) are more suitable than (1) and (2) of Art. 77, if b be nearly equal to a, because then $\tan \phi$, which, in Art. 77, was equal to $\frac{2\sqrt{ab}}{a-b} \sin \frac{1}{2} c$ is very large, or ϕ is near 90°, unless c is very small, and when such is the case the increase of the tangent is not proportioned to the increase of the arc, so that the ordinary mode of calculating logarithms not exactly found in the tables would be inaccurate.

USE OF SUBSIDIARY ANGLES.

24. Formulas not adapted to logarithmic computation may often be rendered so by the use of subsidiary angles. Specimens have been given in the last Art. and Art. 77. The following is another example.

To adapt

$$\sin a = \cos l \cos d \cos a + \sin d \sin l$$

to logarithmic computation.

It may be written

$$\sin a = \sin d \left(\sin l + \cos l \frac{\cos d \cos a}{\sin d}\right)$$

Put the fractional part $\frac{\cos d \cos a}{\sin d} = \tan \phi$ (1)

Our form thus becomes

$$\sin a = \sin d \left(\sin l + \cos l \frac{\sin \phi}{\cos \phi}\right)$$

$$= \frac{\sin d}{\cos \phi} (\sin l \cos \phi + \cos l \sin \phi)$$

$$= \frac{\sin d}{\cos \phi} \sin (l + \phi)$$

From which

$$\sin (l + \phi) = \frac{\sin a \cos \phi}{\sin d} \qquad (2)$$

ϕ may be computed from (1) by logarithms, and then $l+\phi$ from (2), and from ϕ and $l+\phi$, l becomes known.

25. *To resolve a quadratic equation by the aid of Trigonometry.*

The general form of such an equation is

$$x^2 + px = q$$

and the values of x (see Alg. Art. 183) are

$$x = -\frac{p}{2} \pm \sqrt{\frac{p^2}{4} + q} = -\sqrt{q}\left\{\frac{p}{2\sqrt{q}} \mp \sqrt{\frac{p^2}{4q} + 1}\right\}$$

Put $\dfrac{4q}{p^2} = \tan^2\phi$ (1) $\therefore x = -\sqrt{q}\left\{\dfrac{1}{\tan\phi} \mp \dfrac{\sqrt{\tan^2\phi + 1}}{\tan\phi}\right\}$

$$= -\sqrt{q}\,\frac{1 \mp \sec\phi}{\tan\phi} = -\sqrt{q}\,\frac{\cos\phi \mp 1}{\sin\phi}$$

But

$$\frac{\cos\phi + 1}{\sin\phi} = \frac{2\cos^2\frac{1}{2}\phi}{2\sin\frac{1}{2}\phi\cos\frac{1}{2}\phi} = \cot\tfrac{1}{2}\phi$$

and

$$\frac{\cos\phi - 1}{\sin\phi} = \frac{-2\sin^2\frac{1}{2}\phi}{2\sin\frac{1}{2}\phi\cos\frac{1}{2}\phi} = -\tan\tfrac{1}{2}\phi$$

The two values of x therefore will be

$$x_1 = \frac{-\sqrt{q}}{\tan\frac{1}{2}\phi}\ (2),\quad x_2 = \sqrt{q}\tan\tfrac{1}{2}\phi \qquad (3)$$

Logarithms may be applied to the formulas (1), (2), and (3).

If p and q be negative the following forms should be used, which may easily be deduced in a similar manner. Put $\dfrac{4q}{p^2}$ $\sin^2\phi$, then

$$x_1 = \tfrac{1}{2}p\,(1 + \cos\phi) = p\cos^2\tfrac{1}{2}\phi$$

$$x_2 = \tfrac{1}{2}p\,(1 - \cos\phi) = p\sin^2\tfrac{1}{2}\phi^*$$

For the resolution of a cubic equation by the aid of Trigonometry, see Alg. Art. 378.

26. *To find the increment of the sine, tangent, &c. corresponding to a small increment of the angle.*

Let a represent the angle, i its increment, and $\delta \sin a$ the corresponding increment of the sine. Then

* When the coefficients of a quadratic are large, the trigonometric mode of solution is convenient.

$$
\begin{aligned}
\delta \sin a &= \sin (a + i) - \sin a \\
&= \sin a \cos i + \cos a \sin i - \sin a \\
&= \cos a \sin i - \sin a\,(1 - \cos i) \\
&= \cos a \sin i\,(1 - \tan a \frac{2 \sin^2 \frac{1}{2} i}{\sin i}) \quad \text{(Art. 72.)} \\
&= \cos a \sin i\,(1 - \tan a \frac{(2 \sin^2 \frac{1}{2} i)}{2 \sin \frac{1}{2} i \cos \frac{1}{2} i}) \\
&= \cos a \sin i\,(1 - \tan a \tan \tfrac{1}{2} i)
\end{aligned}
$$

The increment i being supposed very small, $\tan \frac{1}{2} i$ will be very small also, and unless $\tan a$ be large, the second term in the parenthesis may be omitted. Then since $\sin i$ is equal to i very nearly, i being very small, it follows that the ratio of $\delta \sin a$ to i is $\cos a$. In other words, the difference of the sines of two angles is proportional to the difference of the angles when the difference is small.

When $\tan a$ is large this principle fails, which is the case with arcs near 90°.

The reasoning for $\delta \cos a$ is very similar.

For the tangent it is as follows:

$$
\begin{aligned}
\delta \tan a = \tan (a + i) - \tan a &= \frac{\sin (a + i)}{\cos (a + i)} - \frac{\sin a}{\cos a} \\
&= \frac{\sin (a + i) \cos a - \cos (a + i) \sin a}{\cos a\,(\cos a \cos i - \sin a \sin i)}
\end{aligned}
$$

The numerator is equal to $\sin \left\{ (a + i) - a \right\} = \sin i$

$$
\therefore\ \delta \tan a = \frac{\sin i}{\cos^2 a \cos i\,(1 - \tan a \tan i)} = \sec^2 a \tan i \frac{1}{1 - \tan a \tan i}.
$$

which if i be very small, and a not near 90°, reduces to $\delta \tan a = \sec^2 a \tan i$.

EXERCISES.

(1). Prove $\text{vers}\,(180° - a) = 2 \text{ vers } \frac{1}{2}\,(180° + a) \text{ vers } \frac{1}{2}\,(180° - a)$.

(2). Find the numerical values of sin 15°, vers 15°, sin 9°, cos 12°.

(3). Prove $\tan 50° + \cot 50° = 2 \sec 10°$.

(4). If $a + b + c = 90°$, prove

$\tan a \tan b + \tan a \tan c + \tan b \tan c = 1$

and $\cot a + \cot b + \cot c = \cot a \cot b \cot c$

and $\tan a + \tan b + \tan c = \tan a \tan b \tan c + \sec a \sec b \sec c$

(5). If $\cos v = \dfrac{\cos u - e}{1 - e \cos u}$ prove $\tan \frac{1}{2} v = \sqrt{\dfrac{1 + e}{1 - e}} \tan \frac{1}{2} u$*

(6). Prove the radii of the inscribed and circumscribed circles of a regular polygon of any given number (n) of sides to be for the former $r = \frac{1}{2} a \cot \dfrac{180°}{n}$, a being the length of one side of the polygon, and for the latter $R = \frac{1}{2} a \operatorname{cosec} \dfrac{180°}{n}$

* This is the formula used in the solution of Kepler's problem in Astronomy.

(7.) Prove the area of a regular circumscribed polygon to be

$$n\, r^2 \tan \frac{180^\circ}{n}$$

That of a regular inscribed polygon to be

$$\frac{n}{2}\, r^2 \sin \frac{360^\circ}{n}$$

(8). Prove the area of a regular polygon of n sides, one of which $= a$ to be

$$\tfrac{1}{4}\, n\, a^2 \cot \frac{180^\circ}{n}$$

(9). Prove the radii of the inscribed and circumscribed circles of a triangle to be

$$r = \sqrt{\frac{(\frac{1}{2}s - a)\,(\frac{1}{2}s - b)\,(\frac{1}{2}s - c)}{\frac{1}{2}s}},\ R = \frac{a\,b\,c}{4\sqrt{\frac{1}{2}s\,(\frac{1}{2}s - a)\,(\frac{1}{2}s - b)\,(\frac{1}{2}s - c)}}$$

PART II.

SPHERICAL TRIGONOMETRY

AND

PRACTICAL ASTRONOMY.

PART II.

SPHERICAL TRIGONOMETRY

AND

PRACTICAL ASTRONOMY.

77. A spherical triangle is formed by three arcs of great circles.

The planes of these arcs produced, form a trihedral angle, the vertex of which is at the centre of the sphere. (Spherical Geom. Prop. 7.)

The angle which two planes make with each other, is called a diedral angle. This angle is equal to the angle formed by two lines, drawn one in each plane and perpendicular to the common intersection of the two planes at the same point. (Geom. of Planes, Def. 6.)

The angles of a spherical triangle are the angles formed by the planes of the arcs. (Spher. Geom., Def. 7.) These are the diedral angles of the trihedral angle mentioned above.

The sides of the spherical triangle are the arcs of the great circles, by which it is bounded. The arcs subtend the plane angles of the trihedral angle, and consequently measure them. The arcs are given in degrees, and since they contain the same number as the plane angles which they subtend, these plane angles may be employed in a demonstration, instead of the arcs, or sides of the spherical triangle; and for a like reason, the diedral angles of the trihedral angle may be employed instead of the angles of the spherical triangle.

If we suppose the trihedral angle, which has its vertex at the centre of a small sphere, to be produced so as to cut out a triangle upon a larger concentric* sphere, the sides of the triangle upon the larger sphere, con-

* Having the same centre.

taining respectively the same number of degrees as the plane angles of the trihedral angle, will contain the same number of degrees respectively as the sides of the spherical triangle cut out by the trihedral angle on the smaller sphere. So that as the number of degrees in the angles and sides which are given or required, and not their absolute length, is taken into consideration in the solution of spherical triangles, the *size* of the sphere need not be regarded.

78. Let ABO be a spherical triangle right angled at A. Let O be the centre of the sphere, and let the planes of the arcs which are the sides of the triangle be produced so as to form the trihedral angle whose vertex is at O.

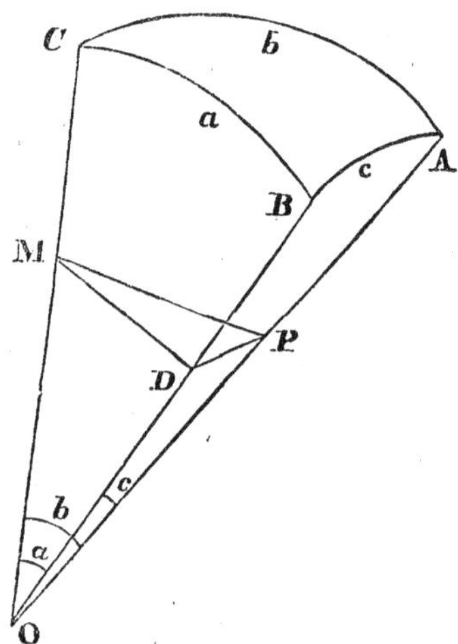

The plane angle COB will contain the same number of degrees as the side a of the spherical triangle; the plane angle COA the same number as the side b; and AOB the same number as c; so that these plane angles may be marked a, b, and c, as in the figure.

It has already been mentioned that the diedral angles of the trihedral angle correspond in the same manner to the angles of the spherical triangle; and that these diedral angles are measured by the angle of two lines, drawn one in each plane, perpendicular to the common intersection of the two planes at the same point. In order to draw these lines so as to be used most conveniently in the following demonstration, take O M = the radius of the tables; draw M P perpendicular to O A, it will be perpendicular to the plane A O B (Geom. of Planes, Prop. 19), since the two planes A O B and A O C are perpendicular to each other, A being by hypothesis a right angle; from P draw P D perpendicular to O B, a line of the plane A O B; join D M; M D will be perpendicular to O B (Geom. of Planes, prop. 8); M D and D P being both perpendicular to O B at the same point D, the angle M D P is the diedral angle of the planes A O B and B O C; or M D P = the angle B of the spherical triangle; O M being equal to radius, M D is the sine of the plane angle a, and M P is the sine of the plane angle b; in the triangle M D P, right angled at P, we have the proportion (Art. 38)

$$R : \sin D :: MD : MP$$

substituting for D its equal B, for M D, its value sin a, and for M P, its value sin b, we have

$$R : \sin B :: \sin a : \sin b$$

That is, *the radius is to the sine of either of the oblique angles of a right angled spherical triangle as the sine of the hypothenuse is to the sine of the side opposite that angle.*

79. The solution of astronomical problems forms one of the most useful and agreeable applications of the theory of spherical trigonometry, which branch of mathematics has grown out of the wants of Astronomy.

To illustrate therefore the above and subsequent formulas of spherical trigonometry we shall introduce a few great circles of the celestial sphere. They are so well known that to define them is perhaps superfluous.

The equator is that great circle the plane of which is perpendicular to the axis of the earth. The *axis* being the line about which the earth performs its diurnal rotation. This produced to the celestial sphere becomes the *axis of the heavens* about which all the stars appear to revolve daily.

The ecliptic is a great circle which makes an angle of about 23° 28′ with the equator. It is the path which the sun appears to describe among the stars once a year.

The points in which the two great circles above defined intersect are called equinoctial points.

The one at which the sun crosses the equator in the spring about the 21st of March, is called the vernal equinox.

The other, which is where the sun crosses in the autumn, viz. about the 23d of September, is called the autumnal equinox.

Declination circles are great circles, the planes of which pass through the axis and the circumferences of which all intersect in the *poles* or points where the axis meets the surface of the celestial sphere. They are also called hour circles. The sun appears to move about the earth once in 24 hours; $\frac{360^\circ}{24} = 15^\circ$ is the number of degrees through which the sun moves in an hour.

That declination circle, the plane of which passes through any place on the surface of the earth and the earth's centre, is called the *meridian* of the place.

The angle contained between the meridian of a place and that declination circle which passes through the sun at any given moment, is called the *hour angle* of the sun, and converted into hours, 15° to the hour, will show the time of day, if we reckon from noon instead of midnight as astronomers do.

This time may be either A. M. or P. M. It is what is called apparent time, which varies a little from mean time, the time given by the clocks, in consequence of the slightly unequal motion of the sun in its annual revolution.

The hour angle of a star is similar to that of the sun.

The horizon of any place is a great circle whose plane touches the surface of the earth at that place, and extends to the celestial sphere. This is called the sensible horizon; the real horizon is a plane parallel to this through the centre of the earth. When any of the fixed stars are in question, the distances of which from the earth are so great that its radius is as nothing comparatively, these two horizons may be regarded as coincident. The *zenith* is the pole of the horizon directly overhead. The *nadir* is the opposite pole.

Great circles passing through the zenith and nadir are called *vertical circles*. They are secondaries to the horizon.

The position of a heavenly body is fixed on the celestial sphere, like that of a place on the globe, by its *latitude* and *longitude*, only it must be observed that on the former these are measured from and upon the *ecliptic* instead of the *equator*.

Similar measurements from and upon the celestial *equator* are called the *declination* and the *right ascension*, the former corresponding to the latitude, and the latter to the longitude.*

Longitude upon the earth is reckoned from some fixed meridian, as that of Greenwich.

Longitude upon the celestial sphere is reckoned from the *vernal equinox* which is called the *first of Aries*; right ascension also from the same point; the former upon the ecliptic, the latter upon the equator.

The *azimuth* of a celestial object is an arc of the horizon, comprehended between the meridian of the observer and the vertical circle which passes through the object.

Or it is the angle which these two vertical circles make with each other having its vertex at the zenith.

80. We are now prepared with materials for a practical application of the formulas of spherical trigonometry, and we commence with that already demonstrated.

* The symbol for right ascension is AR or R. A.; for declination D, or Dec.

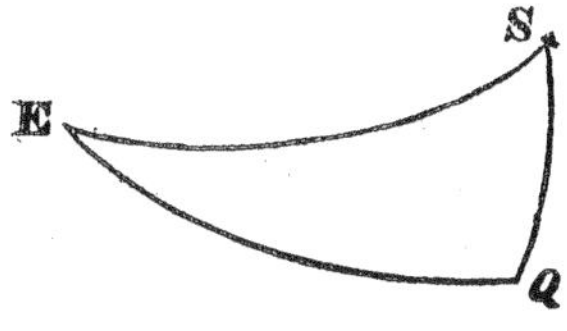

Let E in the annexed diagram be the equinoxial point, EQ a portion of the equator, ES a portion of the ecliptic, S the place of the sun, and SQ a portion of a dec. circle through the sun; then SQ will be the ☉'s declination, which denote by δ, EQ his right ascension, which denote by α, and ES his longitude, which denote by l.

Given the ☉'s declination* equal to 20°, required his longitude.

In the right angled triangle EQS right angled at Q we know E = 23° 28′ the opposite side SQ = 20° required the hypothenuse ES. Hence the proportion

$$R : \sin 23^\circ\ 28' :: \sin l : \sin 20^\circ$$

$$\sin l = \frac{R \times \sin 20^\circ}{\sin 23^\circ\ 28'}$$

δ	20°	log. sin 9·53405
E	23° 28′	log. sin 9·60012
l	59° 11′ 26″	log. sin 9·93393

Hence ES = 59° 11′ 26″ the longitude of the sun required.

* The declination of the sun may be found rudely by taking its meridian altitude with the same instrument and in the same manner as was described at Art. 11. More accurate instruments and methods will be described hereafter. This observation should be made about noon repeatedly, and the greatest observed altitude will be the meridian altitude. A piece of colored glass will be required for the purpose. Let p be a place on the earth; pq its distance from the equator will be the latitude; this contains the same number of degrees as the arc ZQ between the zenith and celestial equator. Let S be the place of the sun, then SQ will be his declination. Let HO be the horizon, then SO is equal ☉'s meridian altitude, SZ = complement of his altitude, and is called the zenith distance, or coaltitude: SQ = ZQ — SZ or declination = latitude — zenith distance.

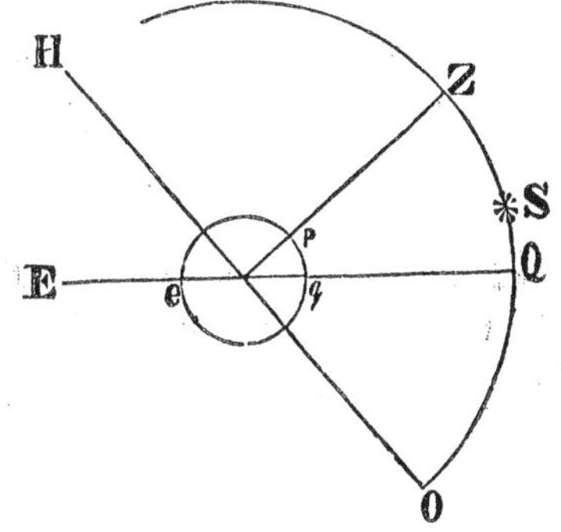

N. B. The altitude of the uppermost point of the circumference of the sun should be first taken, then of the lowermost point, and half their difference added to the latter, or simply half their sum will give the altitude of the ☉'s centre.

Let the student try the following modification of the problem as an exercise.

Given ⊙ = 90° to find his declination.*

81. By means of the proportion for right angled triangles, and of which an application has just been given, one may be derived for triangles in general.

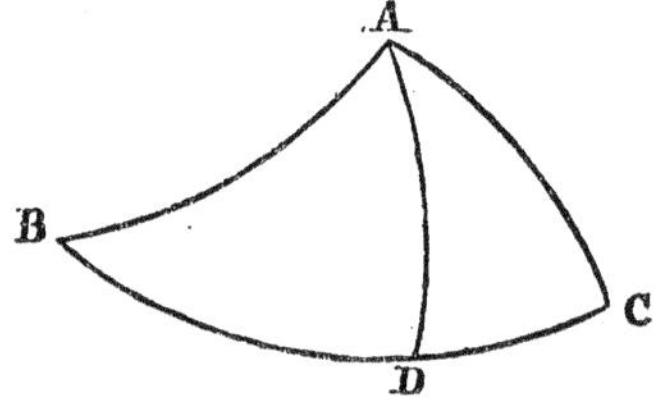

Let ABC be any spherical triangle; let fall from A the arc AD perpendicular to the side BC, the given triangle will be divided into two right angled triangles ABD and ACD. In the right angled triangle ABD we have the proportion (Art. 78)

$$\text{R} : \sin \text{B} :: \sin \text{AB} : \sin \text{AD}$$

and in the right angled triangle ACD, the proportion

$$\text{R} : \sin \text{C} :: \sin \text{AC} : \sin \text{AD}$$

Multiplying the extremes and means of each of these proportions, we have the equations

$$\text{R} \times \sin \text{AD} = \sin \text{B} \times \sin \text{AB}$$

and

$$\text{R} \times \sin \text{AD} = \sin \text{C} \times \sin \text{AC}$$

The first members of these equations being the same the second numbers are equal, hence

$$\sin \text{B} \times \sin \text{A B} = \sin \text{C} \times \sin \text{AC}$$

substituting for the sides AB and AC the small letters of the same name with the angles opposite to them the last equation may be written

$$\sin \text{B} \sin c = \sin \text{C} \sin b$$

or

$$\frac{\sin \text{B}}{\sin b} = \frac{\sin \text{C}}{\sin c}$$

or,

* This symbol ⊙ signifies longitude of the sun.

sin B : sin b : : sin C : sin c*

that is, *the sines of the angles of a spherical triangle are as the sines of the opposite sides.*

EXAMPLE.

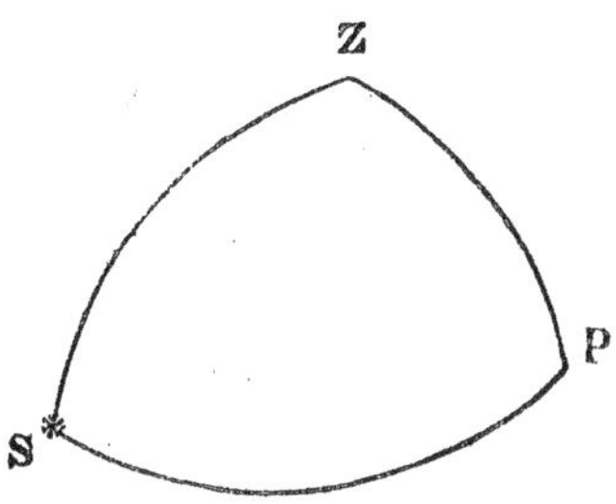

Let Z be the zenith, P the pole of the equator, and S the place of a star; ZS will be the zenith distance of the star, ZPS its hour angle, PS its co-declination or polar distance, and SZP its azimuth. Let the azimuth, zenith distance, and hour angle† be given, to find the polar distance, which is the complement of the declination; Z, ZS and P are given, and PS required.

SOLUTION.

sin P : sin Z : : sin p : sin z

Let P = 32° 26′ 6″, Z = 49° 54′ 38″, and ZS or p = 44° 13′ 45″

P 32° 26′ 6″ ar. comp.	log. sin 0·27056
Z 49° 54′ 38″	log. sin 9·88369
p 44° 13′ 45″	log. sin 9·84357
z 84° 16′	log. sin 9·99782

or declination of the star = 5° 44′

Since the sine of an arc is equal to the sine of its supplement (Art. 15), the required side may be also the supplement of 84° 16′, or 95° 44′ The dec. would then be 5° 44′ south of the equator.

To illustrate this double solution by the diagram, let the student make or conceive to be made the following construction. Draw an arc from S making with PZ an angle equal to Z, meeting PZ in a point which we will call Z′. SZ′ will then be equal to SZ; prolong PZ and PS till they meet in the opposite pole, which we will call P′; a triangle will be formed Z′P′S,

* The student will recollect that a proportion is an equality of ratios, and that ratio, as commonly understood, is the quotient of two quantities. The above is familiarly called the sine proportion.

† The zenith dist. and azimuth may be observed with a theodolite or altitude and azimuth instrument, to be described hereafter; the hour angle by a sidereal clock.

in which the angles z′ and P′, and the side sz′ will be equal to those given in the above example, but in which the side P′s is the supplement of PS.*

The polar distance of the fixed stars will be found to be always the same, hence they describe circles about the poles in their apparent daily motion.

EXERCISE.

Given a 42° 32′ 19″, A 48° 12′, b 55° 7′ 32″ to find B.

Ans. B 64° 46′ 10″.

82. We shall next demonstrate a formula which will express one of the angles of a spherical triangle in terms of the three sides.

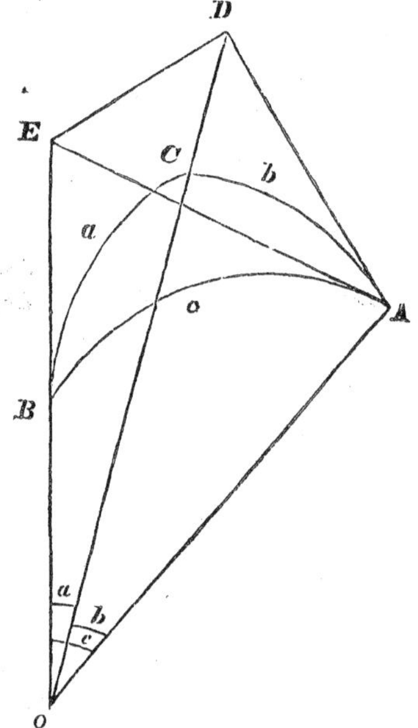

Let ABC be any spherical triangle, O the centre of the sphere; join OA, OB, OC; a trihedral angle is formed having its vertex at O. The plane angles of this trihedral may be called by the same letters as the sides of the spherical triangle for the reason given in Art. 77. By referring to the note of Art. 38, it will be seen that we may choose at pleasure the length of a radius, and the trigonometrical lines will have the same relation as those corresponding to the radius of the tables or any other radius.

Let us take OA as radius, and draw the perpendiculars AD and AE at its extremity and in the planes AOC and AOB; produce these perpendiculars till they meet the lines OC and OB in D and E. AD will be the tangent and OD the secant of the side b of the spherical triangle, and AE the tangent, and OE the secant of the side c.

This being premised, let us take the value of DE, in terms of the other sides and one angle, of each of the two plane triangles DAE and DOE, to both of which it belongs. This may be done by means of the formula

* A rule for determining when there are two solutions, and when but one in such cases, is given at p. 196.

$\cos A = R\,\dfrac{b^2 + c^2 - a^2}{2\,bc}$ (Art. 69), from which, taking the value of the square of the side opposite the angle in the formula, we have

$$a^2 = b^2 + c^2 - \frac{2\,b\,c\cos A}{R}$$

in the triangle EAD this formula becomes

$$ED^2 = AD^2 + AE^2 - \frac{2\,AD \times AE\cos A}{R}$$

and in the triangle EOD

$$ED^2 = DO^2 + EO^2 - \frac{2\,DO \times EO\cos a}{R}$$

subtracting the former from the latter of these two equations and observing that in the right angled triangles OAD and OAE

$$DO^2 - AD^2 = OA^2 \text{ and } EO^2 - AE^2 = OA^2$$

there results

$$0 = 2\,OA^2 - \frac{2\,DO \times EO\cos a}{R} + \frac{2\,AD \times AE\cos A}{R}$$

Finding the value of cos A from this equation, we have

$$\cos A = \frac{DO \times EO\cos a - R \times OA^2}{AD \times AE}$$

substituting for OA its value R for DO its value $\sec b = \dfrac{R^2}{\cos b}$ (Art. 33), for EO, $\sec c = \dfrac{R^2}{\cos c}$ for AD its value $\tan b = \dfrac{R\sin b}{\cos b}$ (Art. 32), and for AE its value $\tan c = \dfrac{R\sin c}{\cos c}$ the above expression becomes

$$\cos A = \frac{\dfrac{R^2}{\cos b} \times \dfrac{R^2}{\cos c}\cos a - R^3}{\dfrac{R\sin b}{\cos b}\;\dfrac{R\sin c}{\cos c}} = \frac{R^4\cos a - R^3\cos b\cos c}{R^2\sin b\sin c}$$

or striking out R^2

$$\cos A = \frac{R^2\cos a - R\cos b\cos c}{\sin b\sin c}$$

or if $R = 1$

$$\cos A = \frac{\cos a - \cos b \cos c}{\sin b \sin c}$$

But the angle A of the plane triangle D A E is the same as the angle A of the spherical triangle (Spher. Geom., Prop. 4) hence, translating the above formula,

The cosine of either angle of a spherical triangle is equal to radius square into the cosine of the side opposite, minus radius into the rectangle of the cosines of the adjacent sides, divided by the rectangle of the sines of the adjacent sides.*

The above formula will serve to calculate one of the angles of a spherical triangle when the three sides are given, if we employ the table of natural sines and cosines; but is unsuitable for the application of logarithms, in consequence of the sign — in the numerator requiring a subtraction to be performed, which operation is impracticable by means of logarithms. We shall therefore derive from this another formula, involving only multiplications, divisions, &c., of the trigonometrical lines contained in it, to which operations logarithms apply.

83. At Art. 74 were derived formulas (2) and (4) for the sum of the sines and difference of the sines of two arcs. In a similar manner two others may be derived for the sum and difference of the cosines. See (7) and (8) of Art. 12, App. I. These four forms would be as follows:

$$\sin m + \sin n = 2 \sin \tfrac{1}{2}(m+n) \cos \tfrac{1}{2}(m-n) \quad (1)$$
$$\sin m - \sin n = 2 \cos \tfrac{1}{2}(m+n) \sin \tfrac{1}{2}(m-n) \quad (2)$$
$$\cos m + \cos n = 2 \cos \tfrac{1}{2}(m+n) \cos \tfrac{1}{2}(m-n) \quad (3)$$
$$\cos n - \cos m = 2 \sin \tfrac{1}{2}(m+n) \sin \tfrac{1}{2}(m-n) \quad (4)$$

The last is read, *the difference of the cosines of any two arcs is equal to twice the sine of half their sum into the sine of half their difference.*

84. A formula for the cosine of half an angle of a spherical triangle, in terms of the three sides, may now be derived. Resume from Art. 82,

$$\cos A = \frac{\cos a - \cos b \cos c}{\sin b \sin c}$$

Add 1 to both members it becomes by (6) of Art. 70,

$$1 + \cos A = \frac{\cos a - \cos (b+c)}{\sin b \sin c}$$

But $\qquad 1 + \cos A = 2 \cos^2 \tfrac{1}{2} A$†

* We say *either* angle, because in the above demonstration no particular angle was selected.

† Deduced similarly to (8) of Art. 72, by adding (5) and (6) of that article.

∴ (4) Art. 83,

$$\cos^2 \tfrac{1}{2} A = \frac{\sin \frac{1}{2}(b+c+a) \sin \frac{1}{2}(b+c-a)}{\sin b \sin c}$$

$$\cos \tfrac{1}{2} A = \sqrt{\frac{\sin \frac{1}{2} s \sin \frac{1}{2}(s-a)}{\sin b \sin c}} \qquad (1)$$

i. e. The cosine of half an angle of a spherical triangle is equal to the square root of the sine of half the sum of the three sides into the sine of half the sum minus the side opposite, divided by the rectangle of the sines of the adjacent sides.

In a similar manner may be derived a formula for the sine of half an angle in terms of the three sides.

$$\sin \tfrac{1}{2} A = \sqrt{\frac{\sin (\frac{1}{2} s - b) \sin (\frac{1}{2} s - c)}{\sin b \sin c}} \qquad (2)$$

Dividing (2) by (1) there results

$$\tan \tfrac{1}{2} A = \sqrt{\frac{\sin (\frac{1}{2} s - b) \sin (\frac{1}{2} s - c)}{\sin \frac{1}{2} s \sin (\frac{1}{2} s - a)}} \qquad (3)$$

Since $\sin A = 2 \sin \frac{1}{2} A \cos \frac{1}{2} A$, by multiplying (1) and (2) a formula for $\sin A$ may be obtained analogous to (2) of Art. 73.

Any of the above forms (1), (2), (3) may be employed for the solution of a spherical triangle when the three sides are given.

(2) is read thus: *the sine of half either angle of a spherical triangle is equal to radius* into the square root of the sine of half the sum of three sides of the triangle minus one of the adjacent sides, into the sine of half the sum minus the other adjacent side, divided by the rectangle of the sines of the adjacent sides.*

* Radius must be introduced as a factor for homogeneity.

The blank form of (2) for examples will be the following.

a		ar. co. log. sin	ar. co. log. sin
b	ar. co. log. sin		ar. co. log. sin
c	ar. co. log. sin	ar. co. log. sin	
s			
$\frac{1}{2}s$			
$\frac{1}{2}s-a$		log. sin	log. sin
$\frac{1}{2}s-b$	log. sin		log. sin
$\frac{1}{2}s-c$	log. sin	log. sin	
	2)	2)	2)
$\frac{1}{2}$ A	log. sin		
$\frac{1}{2}$ B		log. sin	
$\frac{1}{2}$ C			log. sin

Example I.—Given $a=120° \ 17'$, $b=75° \ 3'$, $c=48° \ 56'$.

a	120° 17′			ar. co. log. sine	0·06372	ar. co. log. sine	0·06372
b	75° 3′	ar. co. log. sine	0·01495			ar. co. log. sine	0·01495
c	48° 56′	ar. co. log. sine	0·12266	ar. co. log. sine	0·12266		
s	244° 16′						
$\frac{1}{2}s$	122° 8′						
$\frac{1}{2}s-a$	1° 51′			log. sine	8·50897	log. sine	8·50897
$\frac{1}{2}s-b$	47° 5′	log. sine	9·86472			log. sine	9·86472
$\frac{1}{2}s-c$	73° 12′	log. sine	9·98106	log. sine	9·98106		
			2)19·98339		2)18·67641		2)18·45236
$\frac{1}{2}$ A = 78° 49′ 40″		log. sine	9·99169				
$\frac{1}{2}$ B = 12° 35′ 2″·1				log. sine	9·33820		
$\frac{1}{2}$ C = 9° 41′ 28″·4						log. sine	9·22618

Ans. A = 157° 39′ 20″, B = 25° 10′ 4″·2, C = 19° 22′ 56″·8

The result is not ambiguous in the application of this formula, for half the angle must be less than 90°, since the whole angle cannot exceed 180°. (Spher. Geom., Prop. 8, Note.)

Example II. Given $a=81° \ 17'$, $b=114° \ 3'$, $c=59° \ 12'$.

Ans. A = 62° 39′ 43″·4; B = 124° 50′ 50″; C = 50° 31′ 42″·6

This formula, for the solution of a spherical triangle when the three sides are given, is very convenient for calculation by logarithms. Applied to each of the angles separately, it will serve to determine them all.

An interesting astronomical application of this case of solution is to finding the time of day and error of a watch by an altitude of the sun or other heavenly body. See Nautical Astronomy, p. 287.

85. It is proved (Spher. Geom., Prop. 13), that the three angles of a triangle being given, the triangle is determined. A formula for calculating either of the sides when the three angles are given, may be easily derived from that of the last article, by means of the polar triangles.

It is necessary first to premise that the polar triangles of the whole range of triangles will include all possible triangles: for as each side of a triangle passes through all values from 180° to 0°, the opposite angle of the polar triangle will pass through all values from 0° to 180°. Wherefore whatever can be proved of the polar triangles of all possible triangles may be considered as proved for all triangles.

Resume the equation before (1) of the preceding article.

$$\cos \tfrac{1}{2} A = \sqrt{\frac{\sin \frac{1}{2}(a+b+c) \sin \frac{1}{2}(b+c-a)}{\sin b \sin c}}$$

For the parts of the triangle in this formula, substitute their equivalents in the polar triangle. It will be remembered (Spher. Geom., Prop. 6), that each angle of a spherical triangle is the supplement of the side opposite in the polar triangle, and vice versâ; hence if a', b', and c' represent the sides, and A', B', C', the angles of the polar triangle, we have

$$A = 180^\circ - a' \quad a = 180^\circ - A', \; b = 180^\circ - B' \text{ and } c = 180^\circ - C'$$

putting these values of the letters A, a, b, and c in their places in the formula above, it becomes

$$\cos \tfrac{1}{2}(180^\circ - a')$$

$$= \sqrt{\frac{\sin \frac{1}{2}(540^\circ - (A' + B' + C')) \sin \frac{1}{2}(180^\circ - (B' + C' - A'))}{\sin (180^\circ - B') \sin (180^\circ - C')}}$$

But $\frac{1}{2}(180^\circ - a') = (90^\circ - \frac{1}{2} a')$ and $\cos (90^\circ - \frac{1}{2} a') = \sin \frac{1}{2} a'$ (Art. 23); also $\frac{1}{2}(540^\circ - (A' + B' + C') = 270^\circ - \frac{1}{2}(A' + B' + C')$ and $\sin (270^\circ - \frac{1}{2}(A' + B' + C')) = -\cos \frac{1}{2}(A' + B' + C')$; also $\frac{1}{2}(180^\circ - (B' + C' - A') = 90^\circ - \frac{1}{2}(B' + C' - A')$ and $\sin (90^\circ - \frac{1}{2}(B' + C' - A')) = \cos \frac{1}{2}(B' + C' - A')$; also $\sin (180^\circ - B') = \sin B'$ (Art. 15) and $\sin (180^\circ - C') = \sin C'$.

Making these substitutions, the formula becomes

$$\sin \tfrac{1}{2} a' = \sqrt{\frac{-\cos \frac{1}{2} (A' + B' + C') \cos \frac{1}{2} (B' + C' - A')}{\sin B' \sin C'}} \qquad (1)$$

a formula for the sine of half a side in terms of the three angles of a triangle. We may leave out the accents over the letters, which we have employed only to distinguish the polar from the triangle to which it corresponds, and which are superfluous in a general formula.

This formula will undergo a similar modification to that made in the formula preceding (1) of the last article. Represent $A + B + C$ by S, and the formula becomes

$$\sin \tfrac{1}{2} a = \sqrt{\frac{-\cos \frac{1}{2} S \ \cos (\frac{1}{2} S - A)}{\sin B \sin C}} \qquad (2)$$

or, *the sine of half either side of any spherical triangle is equal to radius* into the square root of minus the cosine of half the sum of the three angles into the cosine of half the sum minus the opposite angle, divided by the rectangle of the sines of the adjacent angles.*

A form for the cosine of half a side may be derived in the same manner from the form from which (2) of Art. 84 is derived.

$$\cos \tfrac{1}{2} a = \sqrt{\frac{\cos \frac{1}{2} (A + B - C) \cos \frac{1}{2} (A + C - B)}{\sin B \sin C}} \qquad (3)$$

from which

$$\cos \tfrac{1}{2} a = \sqrt{\frac{\cos \frac{1}{2} (S - B) \cos \frac{1}{2} (S - C)}{\sin B \sin C}}$$

86. We shall next derive two sets of proportions applicable to the solution of a spherical triangle, the first set when two sides and the included angle are given, and the second when two angles and the included side.

It will be found convenient in the longer analytical processes to represent the angles of a spherical triangle opposite the sides a, b, and c, respectively by α, β, γ. Formula (1) of Art. 84, applied to each of the three angles of a triangle will give

* For homogeneity. In the above form $-\cos \frac{1}{2} S$ is always positive, because S is always more than 180°. (See Spher. Geom., Prop. 14.)

$$\text{A}\left\{\begin{array}{lll}
\cos^2 \frac{1}{2}\alpha = \dfrac{\sin\frac{1}{2}(b+c+a)\sin\frac{1}{2}(b+c-a)}{\sin b \sin c} & & (1) \\[2ex]
\cos^2 \frac{1}{2}\beta = \dfrac{\sin\frac{1}{2}(a+c+b)\sin\frac{1}{2}(a+c-b)}{\sin a \sin c} & & (2) \\[2ex]
\cos^2 \frac{1}{2}\gamma = \dfrac{\sin\frac{1}{2}(a+b+c)\sin\frac{1}{2}(a+b-c)}{\sin a \sin b} & & (3)
\end{array}\right.$$

and the formula from which (2) of the same article is derived.

$$\text{B}\left\{\begin{array}{lll}
\sin^2 \frac{1}{2}\alpha = \dfrac{\sin\frac{1}{2}(a+c-b)\sin\frac{1}{2}(a+b-c)}{\sin b \sin c} & & (4) \\[2ex]
\sin^2 \frac{1}{2}\beta = \dfrac{\sin\frac{1}{2}(b+c-a)\sin\frac{1}{2}(a+b-c)}{\sin a \sin c} & & (5) \\[2ex]
\sin^2 \frac{1}{2}\gamma = \dfrac{\sin\frac{1}{2}(b+c-a)\sin\frac{1}{2}(a+c-b)}{\sin a \sin b} & & (6)
\end{array}\right.$$

By multiplying two of these formulas, and dividing by a third will be obtained

$$\left\{\begin{array}{llll}
\text{from}\ \dfrac{(2)\times(3)}{4} & \text{the formula} & \dfrac{\cos\frac{1}{2}\beta\cos\frac{1}{2}\gamma}{\sin\frac{1}{2}\alpha} = \dfrac{\sin\frac{1}{2}(a+b+c)}{\sin a} & (7) \\[2ex]
\text{"}\ \dfrac{(5)\times(6)}{(4)} & \text{"} & \dfrac{\sin\frac{1}{2}\beta\sin\frac{1}{2}\gamma}{\sin\frac{1}{2}\alpha} = \dfrac{\sin\frac{1}{2}(b+c-a)}{\sin a} & (8)
\end{array}\right.$$

$$\left\{\begin{array}{llll}
\text{"}\ \dfrac{(2)\times(6)}{(1)} & \text{"} & \dfrac{\cos\frac{1}{2}\beta\sin\frac{1}{2}\gamma}{\cos\frac{1}{2}\alpha} = \dfrac{\sin\frac{1}{2}(a+c-b)}{\sin a} & (9) \\[2ex]
\text{"}\ \dfrac{(3)\times(5)}{(1)} & \text{"} & \dfrac{\sin\frac{1}{2}\beta\cos\frac{1}{2}\gamma}{\cos\frac{1}{2}\alpha} = \dfrac{\sin\frac{1}{2}(a+b-c)}{\sin a} & (10)
\end{array}\right.$$

Subtracting and adding (7) and (8), and also (9) and (10), applying to the first members of the results of these operations the formulas deduced in Art. 70, and to the second members formulas (5), (6), (7), (8), of Art. 12, App. I., and afterwards to these same second members formula (3) Art. 71, we obtain the following forms.

$$\text{I.}\quad \frac{\cos\frac{1}{2}(\beta+\gamma)}{\sin\frac{1}{2}\alpha} = \frac{\cos\frac{1}{2}(b+c)}{\cos\frac{1}{2}a}$$

$$\text{II.}\quad \frac{\cos\frac{1}{2}(\beta-\gamma)}{\sin\frac{1}{2}\alpha} = \frac{\sin\frac{1}{2}(b+c)}{\sin\frac{1}{2}a}$$

$$\text{III.}\quad \frac{\sin\frac{1}{2}(\beta+\gamma)}{\cos\frac{1}{2}\alpha} = \frac{\cos\frac{1}{2}(b-c)}{\cos\frac{1}{2}a}$$

$$\text{IV. } \frac{\sin \frac{1}{2}(\beta-\gamma)}{\cos \frac{1}{2}\alpha} = \frac{\sin \frac{1}{2}(b-c)}{\sin \frac{1}{2}a}$$

These four forms (and four others derived similarly from repeating for each side formulas (1) and (3) of Art. 85), are known as the Theorem of Gauss.* By division of III. by I., and IV. by II., in both sets will be obtained four additional forms known as Napier's Analogies;† viz.,

$$\text{V. } \tan \tfrac{1}{2}\alpha \tan \tfrac{1}{2}(\beta+\gamma) = \frac{\cos \frac{1}{2}(b-c)}{\cos \frac{1}{2}(b+c)}$$

$$\text{VI. } \tan \tfrac{1}{2}\alpha \tan \tfrac{1}{2}(\beta-\gamma) = \frac{\sin \frac{1}{2}(b-c)}{\sin \frac{1}{2}(b+c)}$$

$$\text{VII. } \cot \tfrac{1}{2}a \tan \tfrac{1}{2}(b+c) = \frac{\cos \frac{1}{2}(\beta-\gamma)}{\cos \frac{1}{2}(\beta+\gamma)}$$

$$\text{VIII. } \cot \tfrac{1}{2}a \tan \tfrac{1}{2}(b-c) = \frac{\sin \frac{1}{2}(\beta-\gamma)}{\sin \frac{1}{2}(\beta+\gamma)}$$

These each converted into a proportion or equality of ratios by writing $\cot \frac{1}{2}\alpha$ in the denominator for $\tan \frac{1}{2}\alpha$ in V. and VI., and *vice versâ*, in VII. and VIII., will be as follows:

IX. $\cos \frac{1}{2}(b+c) : \cos \frac{1}{2}(b-c) :: \cot \frac{1}{2}\alpha : \tan \frac{1}{2}(\beta+\gamma)$ . . .

X. $\sin \frac{1}{2}(b+c) : \sin \frac{1}{2}(b-c) :: \cot \frac{1}{2}\alpha : \tan \frac{1}{2}(\beta-\gamma)$ . . .

XI. $\cos \frac{1}{2}(\beta+\gamma) : \cos \frac{1}{2}(\beta-\gamma) :: \tan \frac{1}{2}a : \tan \frac{1}{2}(b+c)$ . . .

XII. $\sin \frac{1}{2}(\beta+\gamma) : \sin \frac{1}{2}(\beta-\gamma) :: \tan \frac{1}{2}a : \tan \frac{1}{2}(b-c)$ . . .

That is, *the cosine of half the sum of two sides of a spherical triangle is to the cosine of half their difference, as the cotangent of half the included angle is to the tangent of half the sum of the other two angles.*

The second may be repeated in a similar manner, changing cosine into sine and tangent of the half sum into tangent of the half difference of the other two angles.

The 4th may be translated into ordinary language thus:

The sine of half the sum of two angles of a spherical triangle is to the sine of half their difference as the tangent of half the interjacent side is to the tangent of half the difference of the other two sides.

* Or Gauss equations.

† Analogy is a term synonymous with proportion. The first term bears the same analogy or proportion to the second that the third does to the fourth.

The third may be repeated in a similar manner.

These proportions were first given by Lord Napier, who is celebrated for many useful inventions of a similar character, but chiefly for that of logarithms.

We shall now apply the first set to an

EXAMPLE.

The latitudes and longitudes of two places on the earth's surface being given to find the angles which the arc of a great circle joining them makes with their meridians, and their distance apart, the earth being supposed an exact sphere.

Let P be the pole, S and S′ the places, then PS and PS′ will be their colatitudes, and the angle P will be the difference of their longitudes, since P will be measured by an arc at a quadrant's distance on the equator. (Spher. Geom., Prop. 4.) Let the latitudes of the two places be 51° 30′ and 20°; and let their difference of longitude be 31° 34′ 26″. Their colatitudes will be 38° 30′ and 70°. Then we shall know in the above triangle the two sides opposite S and S′ which we will call s and s', and the included angle P. The greater side $s' = 70°$, $s = 38°$ 30′ and P = 31° 34′ 26″. Applying forms IX. and X. of Napier's analogies with the use of logarithms, the half sum and half difference of the unknown angles will be obtained, by the addition and subtraction of which the angles themselves may be found. The remaining side p of the triangle may be found by the sine proportion, or to avoid ambiguity, by form XI.*

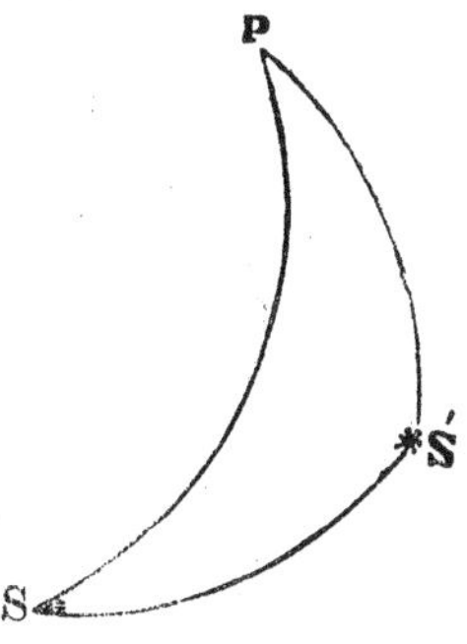

The whole computation is contained in the following table.

* For a highly useful practical application of this problem see Great Circle sailing, App. III.

Arguments.	Logarithms for IX.	Logarithms for X.	Logarithms for XI.
s 38° 30′			
s' 70°			
$\frac{1}{2}(s'+s)$ 54° 15′*	ar. co. log. cos 0·23340	ar. co. log. sin 0·09067	log. tan 10·14273†
$\frac{1}{2}(s'-s)$ 15° 45′	log. cos 9·98338	log. sin 9·43367	
P 31° 34′ 26″			
½ P 15° 47′ 13″	log. cot 10·54863	log. cot 10·54863	
½ (s′ + s) 80° 15′ 40″	log. tan 10·76541		log. cos 9·22828
½ (s′ — s) 49° 47′ 28″		log. tan 10·07297	ar. co. log. cos 0·19005
s′ 130° 3′ 8″			
s 30° 28′ 12″			
½ p 19° 59′ 58″			log. tan 9·56106
p 39° 59′ 56″			

* Had $\frac{1}{2}(s'+s)$ been greater than 90°, its cosine must have been negative, and the first term of the proportion being negative, the fourth must have been negative also, and ½ (s′ + s) would have been the supplement of the angle found in the tables, since the tangent of the supplement is equal to minus the tangent of an arc. (Art. 36.) It is well always to put a small n against those logarithms belonging to trigonometric functions which are negative; then the sign of the result will be indicated by the rule that an even number of negative factors produce a positive result, and an uneven number a negative result.

† This log. need not be found from the tables, but may be obtained by subtracting the ar. comp. of sin $\frac{1}{2}(s'+s)$ above from ar. comp. cos $\frac{1}{2}(s'+s)$ after adding 10 to the latter; for since tan $= \frac{\text{R sin}}{\text{cos}}$, log. tan $= 10 +$ log. sin — log. cos. Calling c the ar. comp. log. cos, and s ar. comp. log. sin, this becomes $10 + (10 - s) - (10 - c) = 10 + c - s$. Q. E. D.

When the first two columns of the above computation are finished, we have the values of ½ (s′ + s) and ½ (s′ — s) the sum of which is equal to s′ and their difference s.

$$\tfrac{1}{2}(s'+s) + \tfrac{1}{2}(s'-s) = 130°\ 3'\ 8'' = s'$$

$$\tfrac{1}{2}(s'+s) - \tfrac{1}{2}(s'-s) = 30°\ 28'\ 12'' = s$$

Since we know now all the parts of the triangle except the side p opposite the angle P, that might be found by the proportion (Art. 81), *the sines of the angles are as the sines of the opposite sides.* But to avoid an ambiguity in the result similar to that of Art. 81, and the trouble of determining which of the two results corresponds to the other parts of the triangle now fixed, it is better to employ XI. of Napier's analogies, inverting it as seen in the last column above. This gives $\frac{1}{2}\ p =$ about 20° and $p =$ about 40° = 2400 geographical miles, the distance required.

EXAMPLE II.

Given the moon's R.A. $11^h\ 38^m\ 27^s{\cdot}15$. Dec. 4° 5′ 40″·4 N.

To find her latitude and longitude, the obliquity of the ecliptic being 23° 27′ 23″·13.

Let P be the pole of the equator, P′ that of the ecliptic, M the place of the moon; then the angle

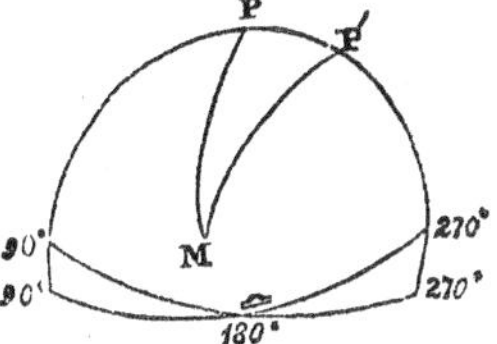

MPP′ = 270° — ☽'s R.A.

the side

PP′ = 23° 27′ 23″·13

the side

PM = 90° — 4° 5′ 40″·4

To find

PP′M = long. of M − 90°

and

P′M = 90° ∓ ☽'s latitude*

Ans. ☽'s lat. = 1° 37′ 3″·3 N.

long. = 173° 25′ 57″·7†

87. When, in the case considered in Art. 86, the only part required happens to be the side opposite the given angle, the finding of the other two angles then becomes merely a subsidiary operation, and the determination of the required side, by Napier's

* The summer solstice is 90° from the vernal equinox, and is N of the equator. The pole of the ecliptic P′ therefore will be south of P and between it and the 270° point. The right ascension of the moon being nearly 12 hours is nearly 180°, which fixes its place in the diagram.

† The determination of the latitude and longitude of a heavenly body from its right ascension and declination as above is one of the most useful problems in Astronomy, the right ascension and declination being observed directly with the astronomical instruments as will be explained in a subsequent part of the work, and the latitude and longitude being required for computing the elements of the orbits of the heavenly bodies.

analogies, seems unnecessarily long. A shorter method of solution is deducible from the fundamental formula, obtained at Art. 82, or

$$\cos c = \cos a \cos b + \sin a \sin b \cos \text{C} \qquad (1)$$

For substituting $\cos a \tan a$ for its equal $\sin a$ it becomes

$$\cos c = \cos a (\cos b + \tan a \sin b \cos \text{C})$$

Assume

$$\tan a \cos \text{C} = \cot \omega = \frac{\cos \omega}{\sin \omega};$$

then

$$\cos c = \cos a \frac{\sin \omega \cos b + \sin b \cos \omega}{\sin \omega}$$

$$= \frac{\cos a \sin (\omega + b)}{\sin \omega}$$

Hence, to find the side c, we must determine a subsidiary angle ω from the equation

$$\cot \omega = \tan a \cos \text{C} \qquad (2)$$

after which c is found by the equation

$$\cos c = \frac{\cos a \sin (\omega + b)}{\sin \omega} \qquad (3)$$

EXAMPLE.

1. In a spherical triangle are given $a = 38° 30'$ $b = 70°$, and $\text{C} = 31° 34' 28''$, to find c.

a	38° 30′ 0″	log. tan	9.90061	log. cos	9·89354
C	31 34 28	log. cos	9·93042		
ω	55 52 30·5	log. cot	9·83103	ar. co. log. sin	0·08207
b	70°				
$\omega + b$	125° 52′ 30″·5			log. sin	9·90864
c	40°			log cos	9·88425

88. If when two angles and the included side are given, the angle opposite to the given side be the only part required, a similar formula should be employed, deduced as follows. From the fundamental formula (1) above, may be obtained by aid of the polar triangles, the formula

$$\cos \text{C} = -\cos \text{A} \cos \text{B} + \sin \text{A} \sin \text{B} \cos c.$$

which becomes when $\cos \text{A} \tan \text{A}$ is substituted for $\sin \text{A}$,

$$\cos \text{C} = \cos \text{A} (\tan \text{A} \sin \text{B} \cos c - \cos \text{B}):$$

or assuming

$$\tan \text{A} \cos c = \cot \omega = \frac{\cos \omega}{\sin \omega}$$

$$\cos \text{C} = \cos \text{A} \frac{\sin \text{B} \cos \omega - \sin \omega \cos \text{B}}{\sin \omega}$$

$$= \frac{\cos A \sin (B - \omega)}{\sin \omega}$$

Hence, having found a subsidiary angle ω, by the equation

$$\cot \omega = \tan A \cos c \qquad (1)$$

the required angle is determined by the equation

$$\cos C = \frac{\cos A \sin (B - \omega)}{\sin \omega} \qquad (2)$$

89. The formulas for the solution of spherical triangles in general, which have now been demonstrated, apply of course to right angled triangles; but if it be recollected that the trigonometrical lines of the right angle or 90° are either R, 0, or ∞, it will be evident that these formulas may, when thus applied, be much simplified.

The student can easily make the substitutions necessary to change the foregoing formulas into such as apply exclusively to right angled triangles, for himself. We shall not occupy space with them here, but be content with observing that after they have been made, all the formulas which result will be found capable of being expressed in two short rules, or these indeed may be united into a single one.*

Amongst all the convenient and useful inventions of mathematicians, none is more ingenious and beautiful than this, the author of which is the celebrated Lord Napier, whose name we already have had occasion repeatedly to mention in connection with the most happy discoveries for facilitating mathematical operations. The rules are known as

NAPIER'S RULES FOR THE CIRCULAR PARTS.

The circular parts of a right angled spherical triangle are
The two sides including the right angle, called

1. The base.
2. The perpendicular.

And

3. The complement of the hypothenuse
4. The complement of the angle at the base.
5. The complement of the angle at the vertex.

The right angle being entirely left out of consideration in the solution of triangles of this kind, the angle at the base is that included between

* The mode of deducing them is given in App. II. p. 194.

the base and the hypothenuse; and the angle at the vertex is that included between the hypothenuse and perpendicular.

The circular parts are then the elements of the triangle itself except the right angle, only that the complements of the hypothenuse and oblique angles are the circular parts, instead of these themselves.

The annexed diagram shows of which elements of the triangle the complements are used.

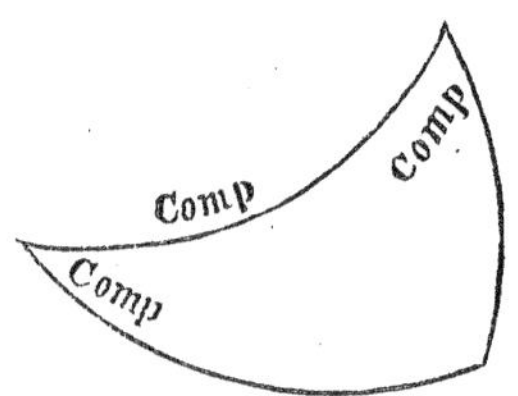

There being five of these circular parts, it is evident that any three of them which you choose to select will either be contiguous or else two will be contiguous, and one will be separated from them by a part on each side.

In the first case, the part intermediate between the other two is called the middle part, and they are called its adjacent parts. In the second case, the part which is separated from the other two is called the middle part, and they its opposite parts. By means of this arrangement, all the relations of a right angled triangle may be expressed in the two following rules of Napier:

1. Radius multiplied by the sine of the middle part is equal to the rectangle of the tangents of the adjacent parts.
2. Radius multiplied by the sine of the middle part is equal to the rectangle of the cosines of the opposite parts.

Or both rules may be given thus: *radius into the sine of the middle part = the rectangle of the tangents of the adjacent parts = the rectangle of the cosines of the opposite parts.**

The memory will be aided by observing that the words *tangents* and *adjacent* in the second clause of the above rule both contain the letter *a*; and that the words *cosines* and *opposite* in the last clause both contain the letter *o*.

As the right angle of a right angled spherical triangle is always known, any other two parts being given, the rest may be found by the above rules.

The method of proceeding is as follows: Take the two given parts and one of the required parts, or if but one of the unknown parts be required, take that, you will thus have under consideration three parts of the triangle. One of these three will be middle, and the other two either adja-

* The rule may be read without radius which must be understood as entering the resulting formulas, in accordance with the principles of homogeneity.

cent or opposite; apply the rule of Napier, and you will have an equation resulting which will contain the two given parts and the required part; make the required part the unknown quantity in the equation, and resolve it, you will thus obtain the value of the required part in terms of the two which were given. By applying logarithms to this value, you will have it in degrees, minutes, and seconds.

EXAMPLE

90. Given the sun's right ascension and declination to find his longitude.

Let the parts of the right angled spherical triangle EQS represent the same circles of the celestial sphere, as at Art. 80; α and δ are given, and l is required.

Of these three parts α, δ and l, α and δ are contiguous, and l is separated from them by a part on each side; therefore l is the middle part and α and δ are opposite parts. Applying Napier's rule, remembering that the complement of the hypothenuse l is to be employed, we have

$$\sin \text{ of comp. } l = \cos \alpha \cos \delta$$

or,

$$\cos l = \cos \alpha \cos \delta$$

91. The same being given, required the obliquity of the ecliptic.

The required part is the angle E in the figure. Of E, α and δ, since the three are contiguous leaving out the right angle, α is the middle part, hence applying the rule of Napier,

$$\sin \alpha = \tan \delta \cot \text{E}$$

We put cot E instead of tan E, because, according to the directions before given, the complements of the oblique angles are to be employed Taking the value of cot E from the above equation, we have

$$\cot \text{E} = \frac{\sin \alpha}{\tan \delta}$$

The sun's R.A on 1st of May 1850 is $2^h\ 33^m\ 10^s{\cdot}42$, and his declination at the same time $15^\circ\ 3'\ 2''{\cdot}4$ required his longitude and the obliquity of the ecliptic.

a 38° 17′ 36″·30	log. cos 9·89479	log. sin 9·79217
δ 15° 3′ 2″·4	log. cos 9·98484	log. tan 9·42959
l 40° 43′ 5″·86	log. cos 9·87963	
E 23° 27′ 25″·46		log. cot 10·36259

In the solution of the above triangle it will be observed that we have found each of the unknown parts in terms of the two given, and have not employed one of those first calculated to obtain another. This is agreeable to the principle laid down at Art. 41, of plane trigonometry, and the reason is the same. Such a method of proceeding is always practicable in the solution of right angled spherical triangles.

In the examples which we have taken above, we have supposed the base and perpendicular of a right angled spherical triangle given. Any other two parts being given, each of the unknown parts may be calculated by the aid of Napier's rules, in a manner entirely similar to what has been just exhibited.

EXERCISES.

1. In the spherical triangle ABC right angled at A, given the hypothenuse a 65° 5′ and the angle C 48° 12′ to find B, b and c

Ans. { B 64° 46′ 14″; b 55 7 32; c 42 32 19

2. Given a 127° 12′, c 141° 11′ to find b, B and C.

Ans. { b 39° 6′ 26″; B 52 22 24; C 128 6 26

3. Given the two oblique angles B 111° 11′, C 91° 11′ to find the three sides.

Ans. { a 89° 32′ 28″; b 111 48 43; c 91 16 8

N. B. If the given quantities in a right angled triangle be a side, and its opposite angle, there will be legitimate ambiguity in the solution.

In all other cases no ambiguity properly exists, but to avoid error it is necessary to observe the two following principles.

1. The greater side is opposite to the greater angle.
2. An angle and the opposite side are of the same affection, *i. e.*, both greater or both less than 90°.

EXAMPLE I.

92. Given the sun's declination to find the time of his rising and setting at any place whose latitude is known.

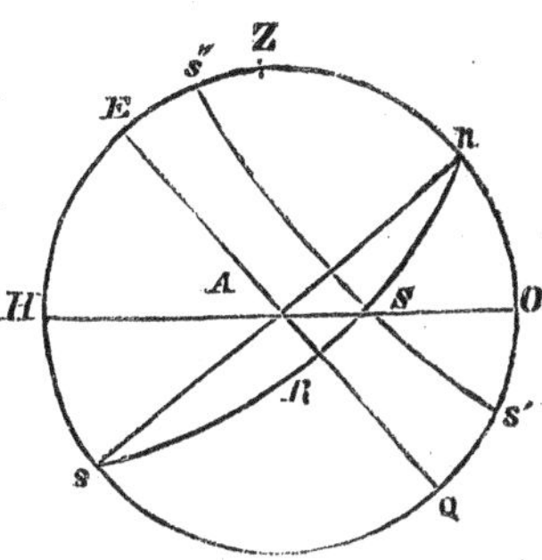

Let n E s Q represent the meridian of the place, Z being the zenith, and HO the horizon, and let s' s'' be the apparent path of the sun on the proposed day, cutting the horizon in S. Then the arc EZ will be the latitude of the place, and consequently EH, or its equal QO, will be the colatitude, and this measures the angle OAQ; also RS will be the sun's declination, and AR, expressed in time, will express the time of sunrise from 6 o'clock, for nAs is the 6 o'clock hour circle.

Hence, in the right angled triangle SAR, we have given RS, and the opposite angle A to find AR, the time from 6 o'clock.

Required the time of sunrise at latitude 40° 43′, when the sun's declination is 23° 27′

By Napier's rule,

Rad. sin AR = cot A tan RS = tan lat. tan dec.

23° 27′	log. tan	9·63726
40° 43′	log. tan	9·93482
21° 55′ 13″	log. sin	9·57208
4*		
60)87° 40 52″		
AR in time 1ʰ 27ᵐ 41ˢ		
6		
4ʰ 32ᵐ 19ˢ	time of sun rising.	

SCHOLIUM.

It should be here remarked that the time thus determined is *apparent time*, which is that which would be shown by a clock so adjusted as to pass over 24 hours during one apparent revolution of the sun, or from its leaving the meridian to its return to it again, the index pointing to 12, when the sun is on the meridian. But it is impossible that any clock can

* Degrees are converted into hours by multiplying by 4 and dividing by 60, which is equivalent to dividing by 15.

be so adjusted, because the interval between the successive returns of the sun to the meridian is continually varying, on account of the unequal motion of the sun in its orbit, and of the obliquity of the ecliptic; each of these varying intervals is called a *true solar day*, and it is the mean of these during the year which is measured by the 24 hours of a well regulated clock, this period of time being a mean solar day; hence, at certain periods of the year, the sun will arrive at the meridian before the clock points to 12, and at other periods the clock will precede the sun; the small interval between the arrival of the index of the clock at 12 and of the sun to the meridian, is called the *equation of time*, and it is given on pages I. and II. of each month of the Nautical Almanac for every day in the month; this correction, therefore, must always be applied to the apparent time determined by trigonometrical calculation to obtain the *mean time* or that shown by a well regulated clock or chronometer, or *vice versâ*, and the Nautical Almanac always indicates whether this correction is additive or subtractive.*

A third kind of time is called siderial time. A siderial day is the period of revolution of the earth upon its axis with reference to the fixed stars, or it is the time which elapses after a fixed star passes the meridian of any place until the same star comes to that meridian again. Owing to the apparent motion of the sun from west to east along the stars about $\frac{360^\circ}{365\frac{1}{4}}$ daily, occasioned by the real motion of the earth in its annular orbit, the solar day is a little longer than the siderial, because when the meridian of a place has revolved with the earth on its axis from west to east to come under a certain star, the sun which the day before may have been on the meridian with the star having moved a little to the east, the meridian has a little farther to revolve towards the east to come under the sun again, and thus complete the solar day. The difference between the siderial and solar day is about $3^m\ 57^s$. The same fixed stars cross the meridian, rise and set about this much earlier† every day. The siderial day is divided into 24 siderial hours, the hour into 60 siderial minutes, and these each into 60 siderial seconds. At pages‡ 584, 585, 586, 587 of the

* To solve the above problem very accurately it would be necessary to compute the sun's declination at the time of sunrise as deduced approximately above, and then to go over the calculation again. The Nautical Almanac gives the declination of the sun at noon for every day in the year, and of the process for determining its declination at any other time of the day we shall have numerous examples in Part V.

† By the common clock. ‡ The Nos. of these pages change a little every year.

Greenwich Nautical Almanac are what are called tables of time equivalents. On pages 584, 585 will be found for any given interval of mean solar hours, or minutes, or seconds, the equivalent interval in siderial time. And similarly on pages 586, 587, for any given siderial interval will be found the equivalent mean solar interval.

EXAMPLE.

Required the equivalent of an interval of $7^h\ 28^m\ 30^s$ of mean solar time in siderial time. From page 584 the equivalent

of	7^h	is found to be	$7^h\ 1^m\ 8^s{\cdot}99$
"	28^m	" "	$28^m\ 4{\cdot}59$
"	30^s	" "	$30{\cdot}08$
Ans.		By addition	$7^h\ 29^m\ 43^s{\cdot}66$

EXAMPLE II.

Required the solar equivalent of $22^{sid.\ h}\ 30^m\ 27^s$ (page 586 N. A.)

$22^h =$	21^h	56^m	$23^s{\cdot}75$
$30^m =$		29	$55{\cdot}08$
$27 =$			$26{\cdot}93$
Ans.	22	26	$45{\cdot}76$

An astronomical clock is one which keeps siderial time. A common clock may be made to do this by shortening a little the pendulum. The weight attached to the pendulum is usually furnished with a screw by which it may be lengthened and shortened at pleasure, and this should be done till the clock goes just 24 hours from the time a star makes its transit over the meridian till the same star makes its meridian transit again.

The exact instant of a star's crossing the meridian is observed with a "Transit Instrument."

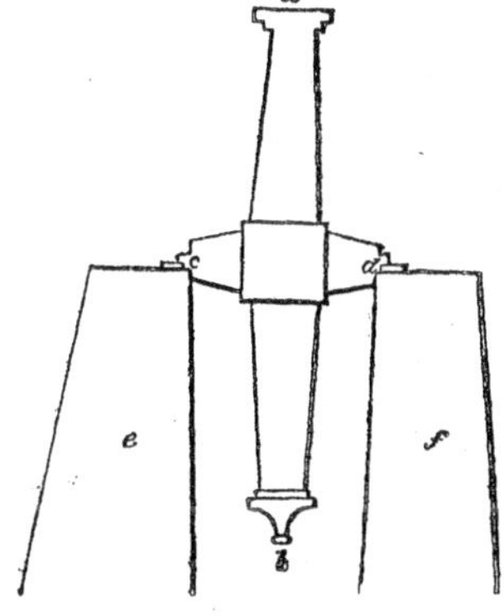

This instrument consists of a telescope *a b* supported by a horizontal axis, each half of which *c* and *d* is a hollow cone of brass, at the outer ends of which are short solid cylindrical pivots which rest upon stone pillars *e* and *f*, called piers, the latter being imbedded in a mass of masonry extending a few feet below the surface of the ground, in order that the vibrations occasioned by passing vehicles or the tread of the observers may not be felt. The pivots of the axis do not rest immediately upon the piers, but upon flat pieces of brass about 4 inches square, and an inch in thickness, which are screwed to the top of the stone. These brass pieces have a notch technically called a Y or V from its shape, in which the pivot of the axis rests. The part of the piece of brass having the notch or V is detached and movable, by means of a screw arranged differently at the opposite ends of the horizontal axis *c d*, so that one end may be moved horizontally, and the other vertically.

The exact line of vision directed to a distant object is marked by two threads of spider's web, technically called wires, crossing each other at right angles, at a point in or near the optical axis of the telescope. They are stretched across a ring or diaphragm to which they are fastened with wax, and this ring, which is smaller in diameter than the tube of the telescope, is held in its place by screws passing through the tube, having their heads outside. By loosening the screw on one side of the tube and tightening the other, the diaphragm, and consequently the point in which the wires cross, receives a lateral motion. The diaphragm is placed at the focus of the object glass near the eye end *b*.†

The whole instrument just described has to be so placed that as it turns on the pivots of the horizontal axis the line of vision along the optical axis of the telescope shall describe the plane of the meridian; narrow trap doors in the roof and sides of the transit room serve to expose the meridian to view. As this plane is vertical, if the line of vision above mentioned be exactly perpendicular to the axis *c d*, whilst at the same time the axis is exactly horizontal, and finally the telescope point due north and south, then will the required position be attained. For this, therefore, three adjustments are requisite. 1. The adjustment of the line of collimation* in a perpendicular to the supporting axis *c d*. 2. The adjustment of the supporting axis to a horizontal position. 3. The adjustment of the line of collimation to the meridian.

The method of making these several adjustments we shall describe in their order.

1. *To collimate the instrument.*—Bring the intersection of the wires upon a well defined point of some distant terrestrial object; take the instrument out of the Y^s and reverse the supporting axis end for end; bring the telescope upon the same distant point, and if the intersection of the wires covers it exactly, the instrument is collimated; if not, move

* *i. e.* the line of vision determined by the intersection of the wires.

† For the illumination of the wires see p. 363.

the diaphragm containing the wires by means of the screws at the side of the tube, till the intersection of the wires is brought half way back to cover the distant* point; bring the cross wire on the same or some other point again, by means of the screw in the Y, which gives a horizontal motion to the whole instrument, and repeat the process already described; after a few trials the point will be found to be exactly covered by the intersection of the wires in both positions of the telescope. This indicates that the line of collimation, or line determined by the intersection of the cross wires, and the distant point, is exactly perpendicular to the axis on which the instrument turns as the object end of the telescope is elevated or depressed.

2. *To render the supporting axis horizontal.*—This is done by means of a spirit level, of which there are two kinds for the purpose, the hanging level, and the riding or striding level.

The former is suspended by hooks from the pivots of the supporting axis, so as to hang parallel to it underneath. The latter is sustained above the supporting axis by two long feet with notches at their bottoms, by means of which it stands upon the pivots of the axis.

First, to adjust the spirit level itself, place it on the pivots, and by means of the screw in the Y at that extremity of the axis which gives it a vertical motion, bring the long air bubble of the level to reach exactly the same distance on either side of the centre marked with a zero on the level scale above the tube; for which purpose the divisions of this scale are numbered in precisely the same manner on the right and left of the zero. Then reverse the level on the pivots, turning it end for end, and if the bubble still reaches the same distance on both sides of the zero, the level requires no adjustment. If not, make half the correction by filing away the notch in one of the feet, or by means of a screw sometimes added for shortening the foot, and the other half by the screw in the Y. Repeat this process till the adjustment is complete. When the level itself is once

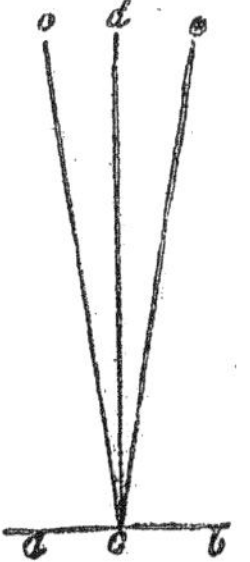

* This may be exhibited with the error of collimation exaggerated in the annexed diagram, in which *a b* represents the supporting axis, *c d* the true line of collimation, *c o* the erroneous position of the line of collimation in the first position of the instrument in the direction *c o* of the object, and *c e* the position of the line of collimation in the reversed position.

adjusted, the supporting axis is made horizontal by placing the level upon it, and turning the screw in the Y till the centre of the air bubble is opposite the zero of the scale.

3. *To adjust the instrument to the meridian.*—Observe the instant that some circumpolar* star (the pole star is the best, from the slowness of its motion) crosses the vertical wire of the transit instrument both at its superior and inferior transit, that is above and below the pole. If the interval of time between the superior and inferior transit be the same with that between the latter and the next superior transit of the same star again, the instrument is in the meridian. If not, it is on that side of the meridian on which the arc described by the star between the two transits is shortest, and must be moved a little by means of the screw in the Y, which gives horizontal motion, and the same observations repeated.† When the instrument is once fixed in the meridian, a meridian mark about half a mile distant may be made upon some object, set up if necessary, upon which the vertical wire is to be brought whenever afterwards an observation is to be made.

Method of observing the meridian transit of a star.—Before describing this we shall observe that for diminishing the error of observation there are inserted on each side of the vertical middle wire, one, two, or three others, making three, five, or seven in all. There is also attached to the supporting axis near one of the pivots a graduated circle, the plane of which is perpendicular to that axis, and consequently vertical. This circle is graduated so that the index points to zero when the telescope points to the zenith, or else when the telescope is horizontal, so that when the telescope is directed to a star, the index will mark the zenith distance of the star in the former case, and its altitude in the latter. The star's declination being known from the Nautical Almanac, or from a catalogue, and the latitude of the place of observation being also known, the instrument may be easily set so that when the star makes its meridian transit it will pass through the middle of the field of view of the telescope. For it is only necessary to bear in mind that the declination is the distance of the star from the equator and the latitude is the distance of the zenith from the equator,‡ so that by simple addition or subtraction of these quanti-

* A circumpolar star is one which never sets, but describes daily a circle round the pole of the heavens, the whole of which is visible above the horizon.

† A method of determining the exact deviation from the meridian, and the consequent error in the time of meridian transit, will be presently given.

‡ These measures are all made on the same great circle of the heavens, viz. the meridian of the place of observation, upon which the star is supposed to be at the instant of transit.

ties the distance of the star from the zenith is obtained. Thus, if the star be south of the zenith and north of the equator its declination must be subtracted from the latitude to obtain the zenith distance. If the star be south of the equator, or its dec. be S., the dec. must be added to the lat. If the star be N. of the zenith, *i. e.* if its N. dec. exceed the N. lat. of the place, then the lat. must be subtracted from the dec. to obtain the zenith distance. The above definitions for dec. and lat. will always be the best guide. If the instrument be graduated for altitudes instead of zenith distances it is only necessary to recollect that the altitude is the complement of the zenith distance. If an inferior transit, or transit *sub polo* of a circumpolar star is to be taken, it may be convenient to remember that the altitude of the pole is equal to the latitude of the place.*

The instrument being set to the proper altitude, so that when the star crosses the meridian it will be sure to be seen in the field of view of the telescope, it remains now only to know when to look for its arrival at the meridian, and its consequent appearance in the field. This is shown by the astronomical clock, which is supported upon a stone pier in the same room with the transit instrument. This clock, when correctly set, should indicate the zero of time, or $0^h\ 0^m\ 0^s$ at the exact instant that the vernal equinox is on the meridian; then at the instant any star is on the meridian, the clock would show the distance of that star in time from the vernal equinox or the right ascension of the star.

A minute or two therefore before the clock shows a time equal to the right ascension of the star, (for whose zenith distance or altitude the instrument is set,) as given by the Nautical Almanac or by catalogue, place the eye at the telescope, and the star will be seen entering the field of view, and moving in a direction contrary to its real motion, *i. e.* from west to east† instead of from east to west, because an astronomical telescope inverts. Bring it near the horizontal wire,‡ by means of a clamp and tangent screw attached to the vertical circle, and before the star reaches the first vertical wire in its motion across the field, look at the clock and take up the count of the seconds, which keep by the ear, applying the eye again to the telescope, and note the instant the star crosses or is bisected by the first vertical wire; record the second in a blank book, then look

* For the zenith being 90° from the horizon, and the pole 90° from the equator, the pole will be just as far from the horizon as the zenith is from the equator.

† Unless it be making its transit *sub polo.*

‡ Or between the two horizontal wires if there are two near together, as is sometimes the case.

at the clock, and record the minute; the hour may be left till the observation is finished. Take up the count of the second again, and apply the eye to the instrument; by this time the star will be seen approaching the second vertical wire. Observe and record the instant of its transit over that wire in the same way, and so on for all the vertical wires. The sum of the minutes and seconds divided by the number of wires will give the minutes and seconds of the time of passing the middle wire, with a probable error of $\frac{1}{5}$ or $\frac{1}{7}$ (according to the number of wires) of the error if the observation had been made upon the middle wire alone.*

* The star will often be seen bisected by a wire between two beats of seconds. The eye then notes how far from the wire the star was at the beat before the bisection and how far at the beat after, and estimates the fraction of a second at which the bisection took place. By the aid of electro-magnetism the exact instant, to a very small fraction of a second, may be not only observed, but recorded without the trouble of keeping count. The arrangement for the purpose is as follows: A wire is made to communicate from one pole of a voltaic battery to the brass work of the clock; the electricity perviates all the brass work, and passes down the pendulum rod; underneath the pendulum a globule of mercury is supported in a little metallic cup from which a wire passes to a magnet, round which it coils, and then passes on to the other pole of the battery. Every time the pendulum vibrates on reaching the lowest point of its arc, it dips into the globule of mercury for an instant, and thus a communication is made between the two poles of the battery, and the magnet acts, drawing back a little hammer which is armed with a sharp point that pricks a narrow strip of paper made to pass along under it, at a uniform rate, by clockwork. The intervals between the points on the paper will correspond to seconds. Two wires communicate also from the opposite poles of a battery (one of them coiling round a magnet close beside the magnet already mentioned) to a wooden block held in the hand of the observer at the instrument, by touching a button in which he connects the wires communicating with it, and the magnet then acts, causing a small hammer to prick with its sharp point the narrow strip of paper a little on one side of the line of points which mark the seconds. The precise position in the interval between two even seconds, of the instant of bisection of the star by the wire, is thus indicated with great precision, and by applying a scale with a vernier, the fraction of a second may be obtained to thousandths, the space on the strip of paper corresponding to a second being usually from half an inch to an inch. The observer at the end of the observation notes on the clock the minute with which the observation closes, and writes it with the hour on the strip of paper in pencil.

The even minutes in the line of dots which marks the seconds on the strip of paper are indicated by the omission of a dot, which is effected as follows. To the axis which carries the second hand of the clock is attached a fork of two prongs, projecting perpendicularly from the axis; when the second hand has made a complete revolution of the clock dial, the two prongs of the fork dip into two globules of mercury communicating by it with the two poles of the battery, one of which wires is the same that communicates the electricity to the brass work of the clock from which

The interval between the wires ought to be exactly the same. As this is scarcely attainable in practice, the mean of the times of transit over all the wires obtained as above will be the time of transit over an imaginary wire situated very near the middle wire. If, by sudden cloudiness or any other accident the transits over some or all the wires but one should be lost, the time of transit over the imaginary middle wire may be obtained as follows:

Having made a complete observation of the times of transit of some star over all the wires, take the difference between the mean of all and the time of transit over each wire. Multiply the intervals thus obtained by the cosine of the star's declination (see Spher. Geom., Prop. 2, Cor. 6, and see Navigation, Art. 99*), and the products will be the equatorial interval between that wire and the imaginary middle wire, or the time that would be occupied by a star situated on the equator in traversing the same interval.† The equatorial intervals being once obtained, to know the time of any star's passing the imaginary middle wire from the time of its passing any other wire, *divide* the equatorial interval between this wire and the middle wire by the cosine of the star's declination.

it goes down the pendulum as before described. When the connexion is made by the fork dipping into the two globules of mercury the electricity goes back to the battery by the shortest path instead of taking the course down the pendulum, and that beat is lost on the magnet.

A number of rapid strokes of the button, which impress a corresponding number of points on the paper, serve to indicate the commencement of the observation.

* The principle alluded to here, which is of frequent use in astronomy, may be stated thus; the arc on a great circle comprehended between two of its secondaries, is to the arc of a small circle parallel to the primary comprehended between the same secondaries, as unity is to the cosine of the distance of the parallel small circle from the primary, this distance being measured on one of the secondaries.

The fourth term of the proportion, instead of the cosine of the distance from the primary, may be the sine of the distance from the pole of the primary or the point in which the two secondaries meet.

† For as the length of arc passed over between two hour circles in the same time on the equator, and on a parallel of declination, is as the cosine of the declination to 1, so the times of passing over the same length of arc (as for instance that included between the wires) on the equator and on a parallel of declination will be in the same ratio.

EXAMPLE.

The transit of the star β Ursæ Minoris, whose declination was 74° 46′ was observed as follows:

Wires.	h.	m.	s.	Intervals.		
I.	14	48	11	I. and III.*	+	131ˢ·18
II.	14	49	16 ·2	II. and III.	+	66ˢ·16
III.	14	50	22 ·5	IV. and III.	—	65ˢ·82
IV.	14	51	28	V. and III.	—	131ˢ·02
V.	14	52	33 ·2			
5)	70^h	250^m	$110^s·9$			
	14^h	50^m	$22^s·18$ Time imag. mid. wire			

I. and III.

	131ˢ·18 log.	2·11787
	74° 46′ log. cos	9·41954
equat intˢ.	34ˢ ·47 log.	1·53741

II. and III.

65ˢ·98 log.	1·81941
	9·41954
17 ·33 log.	1·23895

IV. and III.

	65·82 log.	1·81836
		9·41954
equat intˢ.	17·29	1·23790

V. and III.

131·02 log.	2·11734
	9·41954
34·42 log.	1·53688

March 8th, 1850. The star ϵ, Canis Majoris, was observed on the Vth wire only. Time of transit over that wire 6^h 54^m $3^s·8$

equat. interv.	34ˢ·42	log.	1·53681
star's dec. (N. Alm.)	28° 46′ 16″·89	log. cos	9·94277
int. on par. of dec. 39ˢ·27		log.	1·59404
		Correction	— 39·27
		Transit imaginary middle wire	6^h 53^m 24·53

To compute the effect of error of level upon the time of meridian transit.— It will be first necessary to determine the inclination of the supporting axis to the horizon. For this purpose place the striding level on the pivots, and take the readings at both ends; suppose as in the diagram the

* III. here and below stand for the imaginary middle wire.

west end reads 40 and the east 20. It is evident that each end of the bubble stood at 30 when the level was horizontal, and that each has moved 10 divisions,* which is obtained by taking the difference between the readings of the east and west end, and dividing by 2. So that if i denote the inclination of the supporting axis ab to a horizontal, and i' the inclination of the level to ab, $i + i'$ will denote the inclination of the level to the horizon, and we have (ω denoting the west reading and e the east).

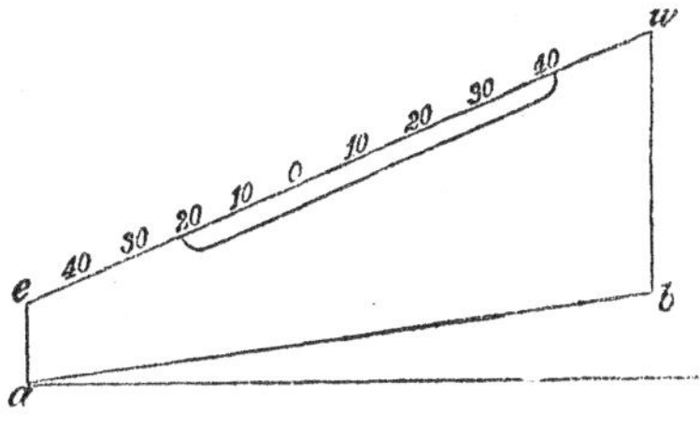

$$\frac{\omega - e}{2} = i + i' \qquad (1)$$

Reversing the level, supposing i' to be greater than i, the east end will now be the highest, but the inclination to the horizon will no longer be the sum, but the difference of the inclinations i and i', hence

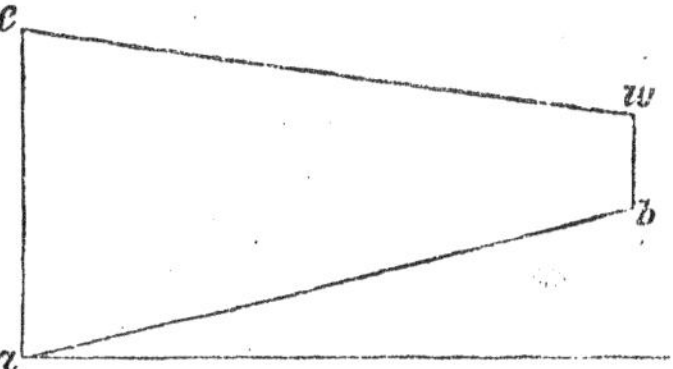

$$\frac{e' - \omega'}{2} = i' - i \qquad (2)$$

subtracting (2) from (1), and dividing by 2 we have

$$\frac{(\omega + \omega') - (e + e')}{4} = i$$

If i be greater than i', after reversing, the west end would still be the highest, and we should have instead of (2)

$$\frac{\omega' - e'}{2} = i - i' \qquad (3)$$

Adding (1) and (3), there results after dividing by 2

* The glass tube is a portion of a circle of large radius, so that the movement of the bubble indicates the angular movement of the level. To find the angular value of a division of the level scale, place the level on the telescope of some instrument to which a large vertical circle is attached. Turn the circle till the bubble passes over a number of divisions of the scale, which will be equal to the degrees, minutes, &c., through which the circle has moved; divide this number of degrees and fractions of a degree by the number of divisions of the level scale passed over, and the quotient will be the value of one division of the scale.

$$\frac{(\omega + \omega') - (e + e')}{4} = i$$

as before.

If the east end of the supporting axis be the highest instead of the west end, as we have supposed above, a similar course of reasoning would produce the formula

$$\frac{(e + e') - (\omega + \omega')}{4} = i$$

which is the same as the above, changing e and e' for ω and ω'. Both formulas may be expressed in one, thus

$$\frac{(e + e') \sim (\omega + \omega')}{4} = i \qquad (4)$$

which is the formula always to be employed for obtaining the inclination of the supporting axis.

N. B. If the sum of the east readings exceed the sum of the west readings the east end of the axis is too high, and *vice versâ.*

EXAMPLE.

First position of the level	e 50	ω 40
Second " " "	e' 24	ω' 66
	$e + e'$ 74	$\omega + \omega'$ 106
		74
	$(e + e') \sim (\omega + \omega')$	32 ÷ 4
	i	8
	value of 1 division of level scale	5″
	i in seconds,	40″

As a verification that the level readings have been correctly noted it may be observed that $e + \omega$ should be the same in both positions of the level, being the length of the bubble which may be supposed not to change from the effects of temperature during an observation. Thus in the above example $50 + 40 = 24 + 66$.

To compute now the effect of the inclination of the axis as determined above, upon the time of transit, let HZO be the vertical circle in which the telescope would play, when the supporting axis was horizontal, HzO the circle in which it plays when the supporting axis is inclined; then ZCz measured by the arc Z z is the inclination of the planes of these two circles, and equal

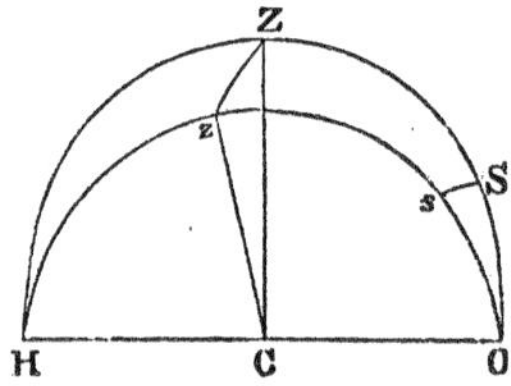

to i the inclination of the supporting axis to the horizon. The length of the arc s_s described by a star at s, in passing from the vertical to the inclined circle in which the telescope plays is expressed by $z_z \sin os$. (See Spher. Geom., Prop. II., Cor. 6), that is

$$s_s = i \sin a$$

a being the altitude of the star. But the length of an arc of the equator similar to s_s is expressed by $s_s \div \cos \delta$, δ being the star's declination. (See note on p. 153, and Spher. Geom., Prop. II. Cor. 6.) This arc of the equator is converted into time by dividing by 15. Hence

$$\frac{i \sin a}{\cos \delta} \div 15 \text{ or } \frac{i \sin a}{15 \cos \delta}$$

is the difference of time between the passage of the star over the middle wire of the telescope when the supporting axis is inclined, and its passage over a vertical circle. N. B. 1. The altitude of the star, designated by a in the above formula, is obtained from its declination given by catalogue, and the latitude of the place as at p. 150. 2. If the east end of the supporting axis is too high, the telescope is thrown to the west of its proper position, and the star, moving as it does from east to west by the diurnal motion, passes the wires too late; the correction therefore found as above is then subtractive. If the west end be too high, the star passes the wires too soon, and the correction is additive.

To compute the azimuth error of the instrument and its effect upon the time of transit.

This error arises from the deviation from the meridian of the vertical circle which the line of collimation describes, or to which the circle that it describes is reduced as above.

The most ready way of determining the amount of deviation and its effect on the time of transit is by "the method of high and low stars," as it is termed, that is by the transit of a star near the zenith, and one remote from it or near the horizon, whose right ascension and consequent time of transit does not differ much from the former.

To understand this let it first be supposed that one star passes the meridian exactly at the zenith, and that the other passes near the horizon, and let it be supposed also that the stars have the same right ascension. If the instrument were exactly adjusted to the meridian so that the optical axis of the telescope moved in the plane of that circle, then the two stars would be on the middle wire at the same instant, if the telescope could be brought down instantaneously from the high to the low star. But if the circle in which the telescope plays make a small angle (called the angle of deviation or azimuth error) with the meridian, then the supporting axis being supposed horizontal, when the telescope is vertical it will point to the zenith, in which all vertical circles as well as the meridian intersect, and the zenith star will be on the middle wire at the same instant as before, but the lower down the other star is, the wider will its time of transit over the middle wire differ from that of its transit over the meridian, because the farther will the vertical circle which the telescope describes be from the meridian, the farther we go from the zenith where they intersect. The greater, therefore, the difference between the time of transit of the zenith star and the low star over the wire of the instrument as compared with the difference of their times of transit over the meridian, which in the case supposed is zero, the greater the deviation of the vertical circle described by the instrument from the meridian. Now it is not necessary that the high star should pass exactly at the zenith, but only near it. If the difference of the observed time of transit of the high and low star be equal to the difference of their right ascensions, that is, of their times of passing the meridian, the optical axis of the telescope moves in the plane of the meridian; if not, this axis describes a vertical circle which deviates from the meridian, and the amount of this deviation and the consequent error in the time of meridian transit, we proceed now to show how to determine.

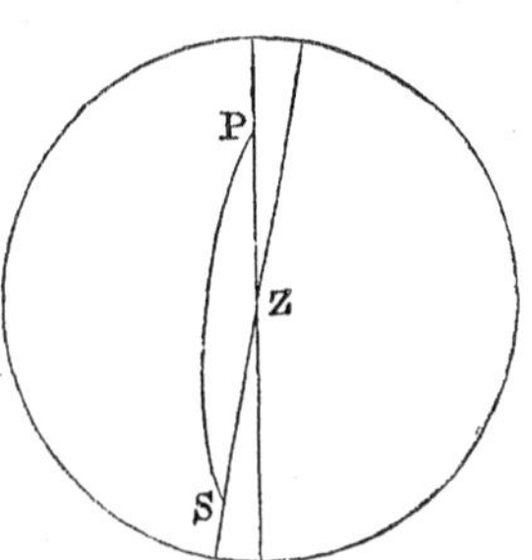

Let the full circle in the diagram represent the horizon, Z the zenith, P the pole, and consequently PZ the meridian. Let ZS represent the vertical circle described by the telescope, S the place of a star where it crosses it, and appears on the middle wire, and PS, the declination circle, passing through the star. In the spherical triangle PZS, in which the hour angle P represents the time that has elapsed since the star S passed the meridian, PZ, before it reached the wire of the telescope in the vertical ZS, we have by the sine proportion

$$\sin P : \sin Z :: \sin ZS : \sin PS$$

From which, taking P in place of sin P, since it is a very small angle, and Z the small angle of deviation of the vertical ZS from the meridian in place of the sine of its supplement PZS, which is also its own sine, and representing ZS by ζ and the complement of PS or the declination of the star by δ, multiplying the means of the proportion and dividing by the last term, we have

$$\text{P} = \text{Z}\,\frac{\sin \zeta}{\cos \delta^*} \qquad (1)$$

ζ may be found as at p. 150, by supposing S to be on the meridian, without sensible error, by means of the latitude of the station and declination of the star.

Represent the fractional part of the above formula by n. It becomes

$$\text{P} = \text{Z}n \qquad (2)$$

Suppose now another star crossing the meridian nearly at the same time. For this we have

$$\text{P}' = \text{Z}n' \qquad (3)$$

Let now t represent the observed time of transit of the later star, α its right ascension, t' and α' the same for the other star, and let e denote the error of the clock which may be supposed unknown. For the former star (since α is the time of its passing the meridian), we shall have for the value of the hour angle when it makes the transit of the middle wire,

$$\text{P} = t + e - \alpha \qquad (4)$$

And for the other star

$$\text{P}' = t' + e - \alpha' \qquad (5)$$

By subtraction of (5) from (4) the error of the clock e is eliminated, and there results

$$\text{P} - \text{P}' = (t - t') - (\alpha - \alpha') \qquad (6)$$

Substituting for P and P′ in (6) their values given by (2) and (3), (6) becomes

$$\text{Z}\,(n' - n) = (t - t') - (\alpha - \alpha')$$

$$\therefore \text{Z} = \frac{(t - t') - (\alpha - \alpha')}{n - n'} \qquad (7)$$

The value of the azimuth error or deviation from the meridian Z is thus found in time. To convert it into space this value must be multi-

* In the later catalogues of stars, their north polar distances (N.P.D.) are given instead of their declinations. In the above formula sin (N.P.D.) would of course be in place of cos δ. When the declination of the star is south, we have still sin PS = cos δ, for sin $(90^\circ + \delta) = \sin (90^\circ - \delta) = \cos \delta$. (See App. Art. 13.)

† N. B. That $t + e$ is the true time of the observed transit.

plied by 15. The instrument may then be adjusted to the meridian by turning the screw of the Y, which admits of horizontal motion, and which has usually upon it a graduated arc, by means of which the movement of the instrument in azimuth is indicated.

To compute the effect of the azimuth error upon the time of transit take the value of Z as given by (7) in time, and substitute it before converting it into space, in either (2) or (3), which will give the value of P or P′ the hour angle in time, n or n' being an abstract number expressing the ratio of two trigonometrical lines.

The value of P is the correction to be applied to the observed time of transit of the later star, to obtain the time of its meridian transit. That of P′ the same for the other star.

If the deviation from the meridian be southwest and northeast, as in the diagram* where we have supposed the zenith to be south of the pole, the correction for a star south of the zenith will be subtractive, for one north additive,† unless the latter make an inferior transit or *sub polo*, in which case the motion being in the opposite direction, the correction is subtractive. This is evident from an inspection of the diagram.

The only remaining correction is for error of collimation. The line of collimation when this error exists describes a cone about the supporting axis as an axis, and the point in which it pierces the surface of the celestial sphere, describes a small circle of that sphere parallel to the meridian, and at a very short distance from it. The distances between these circles measured on parallels of declination may be considered every where the same without sensible error, and the time of traversing this distance by any star will be inversely as the cosine of the star's declination.

The equatorial interval between the circles in question may be found by moving the instrument in azimuth, after reversing, by means of the screw in that Y which gives horizontal motion, till the intersection of the wires is brought back to the terrestrial point on which it was placed before reversing.

The degrees and fractions of a degree passed over on the graduated arc on the Y will indicate double the error of collimation, which, divided

* Which will evidently be indicated by the value of Z being positive. If the deviation be S.E. and N.W. then Z is negative. This may be seen by trying various cases by the diagram, such as one star passing, 1st, N. of the zenith, 2nd, *sub polo*, &c., first writing the numerator in the value of Z in (7) under the form $(t - a) - (t' - a')$.

† The only difference in the above diagram for a star north of the zenith would be that the angle of deviation itself instead of its supplement would be the angle of the triangle, but the proportion would be the same.

by 15, will give the equatorial value of it in time. This divided by the cosine of any star's declination will give the effect of the error of collimation on the time of the star's transit.

The error of collimation is best measured by means of a movable vertical wire, to which motion is given by a micrometer screw, as described in another place.

Should no distant terrestrial object be visible from an observatory, owing to intervening objects near at hand, a small telescope in the building having its object glass turned towards that of the transit instrument may serve as a collimator. The rays of light proceeding from the wires at the focus of the object glass of the small telescope strike this object glass, are refracted by it, and emerge in parallel lines; they then strike the object glass of the transit instrument, and are conveyed to the focus of parallel rays, which is the astronomical focus; so that in looking through the eye end of the transit instrument the wires of the small telescope will be distinctly seen. Care should be taken to throw the light of a window or lamp in at the eye end of the small telescope. A similar contrivance may be employed for a meridian mark.

But the transit instrument may be made its own collimator, by placing a vessel of mercury underneath, and turning the object end of the telescope downwards. If the axis be horizontal, and the instrument truly collimated, the wires being illuminated by an orifice in the side of the eye piece, the rays of light will pass from them to the object glass, emerge in parallel lines, strike the surface of the mercury vertically, be reflected back in the same lines, and converge to the focus of the object glass at the same points which they left, so that the reflected image of the wires will be seen coinciding with the direct image. If not, there is either error of collimation or of level, or both. If the axis had previously been made horizontal by the striding level, it is the latter, and the diaphragm containing the wires must be moved till there is coincidence between their direct and reflected images; or a movable wire may serve to measure the interval between them. This interval is double the collimation error, because the angle of incidence is equal to the angle of reflection, the former being on one side the vertical, the latter on the other. If, therefore, the direct image of the wire be brought to the vertical by the screws of the diaphragm by a movement over half the distance between the direct and reflected image, the reflected image will be brought there too.

The striding level need not be used at all, if the instrument be reversed in the Ys, in using the collimating eye piece with a basin of mercury; for in one position of the instrument the angle obtained by taking half the distance between the direct and reflected image of the wires is the sum, and in the reverse position is the difference of level error and error of collimation. The well-known algebraic formula, "to half the sum add half the difference for the greater of the two quantities, and from half the sum subtract half the difference for the less," will serve to determine those two errors separately. To know which is the greater, the level or collimation error, we have this rule:—If the reflected image in both positions appears on the same side of the direct, then the level error is the greater of the two, but if on different sides, the collimation error is the greater. All this will appear evident if the student make a diagram with a line to represent the supporting axis with level error exaggerated, a line perpendicular to this at the middle, to represent true line of collimation, another line from the same middle point oblique to represent the erroneous line of collimation, a horizontal line below to represent the surface of the mercury, and from the point where the erroneous line of collimation meets it, a vertical and also a line making the same angle with it as does the erroneous line of collimation. In reversing the instrument the only change will be in the erroneous line of collimation, which will now make the same angle on the other side of the true.

The following example will serve to illustrate all the foregoing rules for applying the corrections to an observation with the transit instrument.

STATION AND DATE.	COLLEGE OBSERVATORY.	MARCH 8TH, 1850.
OBSERVER'S NAME.	B.	B.
STAR'S NAME.	δ GEMINORUM.	α CANIS MINORIS.
Wires. I.	$7^h\ 11^m\ 11^s{\cdot}5$	$7^h\ 31^m\ 32^s{\cdot}2$
Wires. II.	7 11 30	7 31 49 •5
Wires. III.	7 11 48 •8	7 32 7
Wires. IV.	7 12 7 •5	7 32 24 •4
Wires. V.	7 12 26	7 32 41 •7
SUM.	5)35 59 03 •8	37 40 34 •8
Mean of Wires.	7 11 48 •76	7 32 06 •96
Corr. for Collim. Error.*	+ •05402	+ •05024
Corr. for Level Error. †	+ •092	+ •07397
Corr. for Azim. Error. ‡	— 2•50	— 1•481
Time of Mer. Transit.	7 11 46 •406	7 32 05 •603
Star's R. Ascen.	7 11 10 •20	7 31 27 •38
Error of Clock.	Secs. 36 •21‖	Secs. 37 •223‖

* Collimation Error (δ Geminorum) thus obtained :

Equatorial Error	0•5	log.	$\bar{2}$•69897
Dec. N. Alm. March 8th, 22° 15′ 4″•9		log. cos	9•96639
Collimation Error	•05402	log.	$\bar{2}$•73258

Collimation Error (α Canis Minoris) :

Equatorial Error	•05	log.	$\bar{2}$•69897
Dec. March 8th, 5° 36′ 6″•5		log. cos	9•99792
	•05024	log.	$\bar{2}$•70105

‖ Mean of the two stars 37^s.

For Notes † and ‡ see next page.

† The level error is computed as follows:

e	96	ω	139
e'	130	ω'	105
$e+e'$	226	$\omega+\omega'$	244

$$\frac{e+e' \sim \omega+\omega'}{4} = 4{\cdot}5$$

Multiplying this result by ·3″ the known value of a division of the level scale, we have 1″·35 as the value of i the inclination of the supporting axis.

δ GEMINORUM.

Dec.	22° 15′ 5″	ar. co. log. cos	0·03360
Lat. of Station,	40 43		
Zenith dist.	18 27 55	log. cos	9·97704
i	1″·35	log.	0·13033
15		ar. co. log.	8·82391
·09223		log.	$\bar{2}$·96488

α CANIS MINORIS.

Dec.	5° 36′ 6″	ar. co. log. cos	0·00208
Lat. of Station,	40 43		
Zenith dist.	35 6 54	log. cos	9·91275
i			0·13033
			8·82391
·07397		log.	$\bar{2}$·86907

‡ Azimuth Error obtained by formulas

$$z = \frac{(t-t')-(a-a')}{n-n'}, P = z\,n, n = \frac{\sin \zeta}{\cos \delta}$$

t	obs'd time transit α Canis Minoris	7ʰ 32ᵐ 6ˢ·96	
t'	" " " δ Geminorum,	7 11 48·76	
$t-t'$	" " "		20ᵐ 18ˢ·20
a	right asc. α Canis Minoris,	7 31 27·38	
a'	" " δ Geminorum,	7 11 10·20	
$a-a'$			20ᵐ 17ˢ·18
$(t-t')-(a-a')$			1ˢ·02

α CANIS MINORIS.

Zenith dist.	35° 6′ 53″·5	log. sin	9·75983
Decli.	5 36 6 ·5	log. cos	9·99792
n	·5779		$\bar{1}$·76191

δ GEMINORUM.

Zenith dist.	18° 27′ 55″·1	log. sin	9·50069
Decli.	22 15 4 ·9	log. cos	9·96639
n'	·3422		$\bar{1}$·53430

The correct siderial time being ascertained by the transit of a star of known right ascension, the correct mean solar time may be found from this, as follows:

The Nautical Almanac gives on p. XXII. of each month the mean time of transit of the first point of Aries, which is the zero of siderial time, and may be called from analogy the siderial noon.* By means of this and the table of time equivalents, explained at p. 147, the mean solar time corresponding to any given siderial time, may be obtained by the following rule.

Mean solar time required = mean time at *preceding* siderial noon + the equivalent to the *given* siderial time.

EXAMPLE.

To convert $7^h\ 11^m\ 10^s{\cdot}20$ siderial time (the true time of meridian transit recorded above) March 8th, 1850, into mean solar time for the meridian of New York.

Mean time at preceding siderial noon, viz. March 8th,					0^h	56^m	$30^s{\cdot}74$
For given siderial time.	7^h	0^m	0^s	Corresponding mean solar intervals by Tab. time equivalents, p. 586, N. A.	6	58	51·19
		11	0			10	58·20
			10				9·97
			0·20				0·20
				Sum mean solar time required	8^h	6^m	$30^s{\cdot}30$
				Correction for longitude of N. Y.†			$48^s{\cdot}68$
					8	5	41·62

$n - n'$	·2357	log.	$\bar{1}{\cdot}37236$
$(t - t') - (a - a')$	1·02	log.	0·00860
z. in time,	$4^s{\cdot}328$	log.	0·63624
	15	log.	1·17609
z. in space,	$6''{\cdot}491$	log.	1·81233

z.	4·328	log.	0·63624			log.	0·63624
n.	·5779	log.	$\bar{1}{\cdot}76191$	n'	·3422	log.	$\bar{1}{\cdot}53430$
P.	$2^s{\cdot}501$	log.	0·39815	P.′	1·481	log.	0·17054

* To obtain the mean time of siderial noon at any place having a different longitude from Greenwich, it is necessary to subtract $9^s{\cdot}8565$ multiplied by the hours and fractions of an hour, by which the place differs in long. from Greenwich if the place be west, and to add this product if the place be east of Greenwich. As the daily gain of siderial time on solar is about $3^m\ 56^s$, this divided by 24 or $9^s{\cdot}8565$ will be the hourly gain or the hourly motion of the sun backward from west to east.

† This is obtained by multiplying $9^s{\cdot}856$ by $4^h{\cdot}94$ the difference of longitude between New York and Greenwich. This correction may be applied here instead

The mean solar time may be obtained by direct observation of a meridian transit of the sun, which is made by taking the transit of each limb of the sun, that is to say observing the times when the sun's disc is tangent to the wires, both upon its western and eastern side, and taking a mean of the times as the time of transit of the sun's centre.* Or more accurately by applying as a correction additively or subtractively to the bserved time of transit of the limb the time occupied by the sun's semidiameter in passing the meridian, which is given for every day in the year in the Nautical Almanac, p. I. of each month.

To convert mean solar time into siderial the rule is as follows.

Siderial time *required* = siderial time at *preceding* mean moon + the equivalents to the *given* mean time.

EXAMPLE.

To convert $8^h\ 5^m\ 41^s{\cdot}62$ mean time at New York, into siderial time.

			h	m	s
Sider. time at preced. mean noon, Gr. viz., March 8th,			23^h	3^m	$19^s{\cdot}98$
		Correction for long. N. Y.		+	48·68
			23	4	8·66
For mean intervals.	$8^h\ 0^m\ 0^s$	The tab. p. 518, N. A. gives the equiv. sid. intervals.	8	1	18·85
	5 0			5	0·82
	41				41·11
	0·62				0·62
		Sum sid. time required	7^h	11^m	$10^s{\cdot}06$†

The reasons for the above rules are sufficiently evident.

PROBLEM.

93. Given the latitude of the place, and the declination of a heavenly body, to determine its altitude and azimuth when on the six o'clock hour circle.

of to the mean time of siderial noon. Strictly the equivalent of $4^s{\cdot}863$ in solar intervals should be applied, or $48^s{\cdot}68$ may be applied to the given siderial time additively before taking out the solar equivalents.

* A colored glass over the eye piece is necessary in observing the sun.

† The sum amounting to more than 24^h, of course 24^h must be rejected from it, as after reaching 24^h the siderial time begins at zero again.

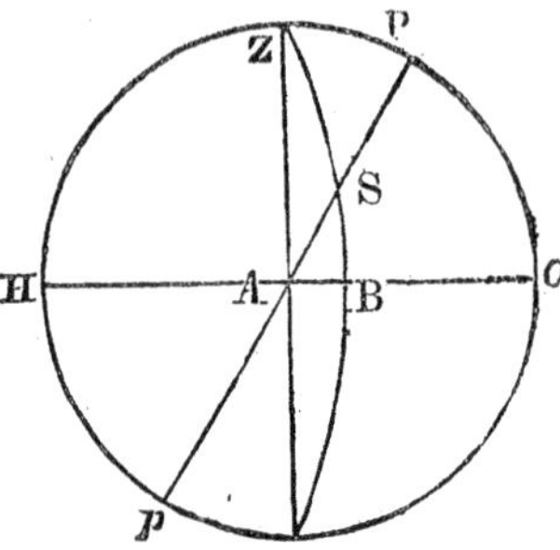

Let HZPO be the meridian of the place, Z the zenith, HO the horizon, S the place of the heavenly body on the six o'clock hour circle PSp, and ZSB the vertical circle passing through it. Then, in the right-angled triangle SBA are known AS,* the declination, and the angle SAB, or arc OP, the latitude of the place, to find the altitude BS, and AB or the complement of the azimuth OB.

EXAMPLE.

1. Required the altitude and azimuth of Arcturus when upon the six o'clock hour circle of New York, lat. 40° 43′ N., on the 1st of Jan. 1850; its declination on that day being 19° 57′·56″ N.

By Napier's rules we have

$$\text{Rad. sin BS} = \text{sin A sin AS}$$

$$\text{Rad. cos A} = \text{tan AB cot AS} \therefore \text{cot BO} = \frac{\text{Rad. cos A}}{\text{cot AS}}$$

	40° 43′		log. sin	9·81446	log. cos	9·87964
	19 57	56	log. sin	9·53334	log. cot	10·43974
alt.	12 52	12	log. sin	9·34780		
az.	74 38	22			log. cot	9·43990

94. There remains one case in the solution of oblique angled spherical triangles, which we have deferred to this place because we wished to employ in it the rules for the solution of right angled triangles.

This is where two sides and the angle opposite† to one of them, or two angles and the side opposite to one of them, are given; or, as it is sometimes expressed, where two of the given parts are a side and its opposite angle. In such a case we may proceed as follows:

By means of the proportion, *the sines of the angles are as the sines of the opposite sides* (Art. 81), the unknown part opposite one of the given parts may be found. Four parts of the triangle will then be known, and two will remain unknown; these two will be a side and its opposite angle, to find which, from the vertex of the unknown angle let fall an arc perpen-

* The horizon and equator intersect at A, 90° from the meridian.

† The term opposite is used in a more exact sense here than in Napier's rules, of which we have just been speaking.

dicular upon the unknown side opposite, and the given triangle will be divided into two partial triangles, which will be right angled, and in each of which two parts will be known. Applying Napier's rules to the solution of these, the partial angles which compose the unknown angle may be found, and their sum will be the value of the unknown angle; then the unknown side opposite may be found by the proportion, the sines of the angles are as the opposite sides; or this last side may be found by calculating the two parts of which it is composed from the right angled triangles, and adding them together, which is the better method, since it avoids ambiguity. If the perpendicular arc drawn from the vertex of the unknown angle to the unknown side falls without the triangle, of course the difference, instead of the sum of the angles and sides found in the right angled triangles, is to be taken.

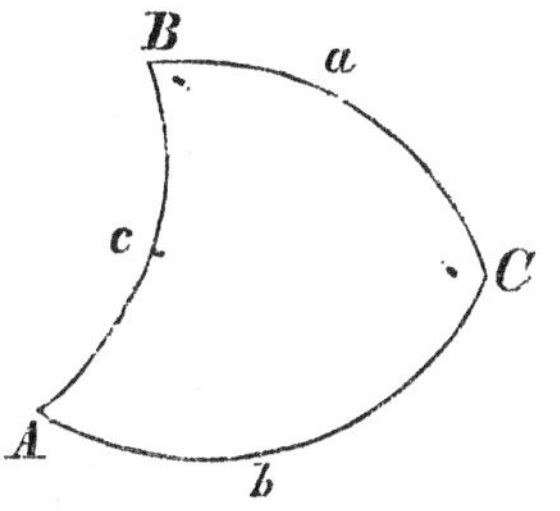

Thus in the annexed diagram triangle let the side and angle opposite given be c and C, and the other given angle B. Then first

$$\sin \text{C} : \sin c :: \sin \text{B} : \sin b$$

by means of which proportion b may be calculated and will be legitimately ambiguous. Then there will be left unknown A and a. From A let fall a perpendicular AD upon a, which we have not drawn, lest it should confuse the diagram, but which the student can imagine; then in the right angled triangle B A D we know two parts B and c, and also in the right angled triangle C A D we know two parts C and b, the latter having been found by the proportion above. To calculate the partial angles at A, calling that in the first right-angled triangle above mentioned ω, and that in the second ω', we have by Napier's rules

$$\text{R} \cos c = \cot \text{B} \cot \omega$$

whence

$$\cot \omega = \frac{\text{R} \cos c}{\cot \text{B}}$$

and in the same manner

$$\cot \omega' = \frac{\text{R} \cos b}{\cos \text{C}}$$

then

$$\omega + \omega' = \text{A}$$

and

$$\sin \text{C} : \sin c :: \sin \text{A} : \sin a$$

whence

$$\sin a = \frac{\sin c \sin \text{A}}{\sin \text{C}}$$

Thus all the parts of the triangle are determined.

For an application of this case of solution take the following

EXAMPLE.

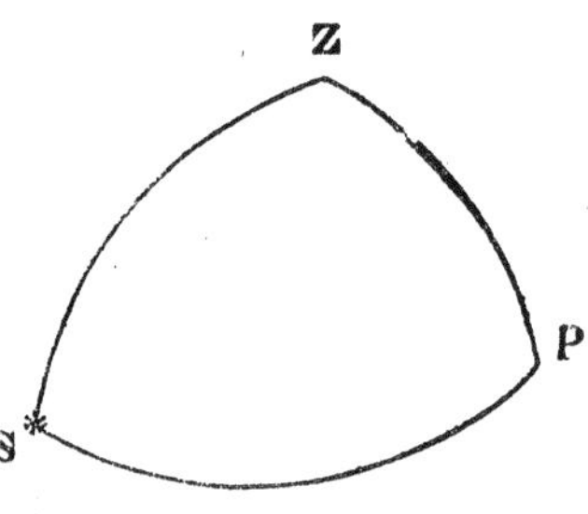

Given the zenith distance, azimuth and polar distance, to find the hour angle and colatitude of the station. Or in the diagram given, ZS, Z, and PS, to find P and PZ.

Supposing the declination of a star, as given by catalogue, to be 16° 11′ N., and its observed altitude and azimuth to be 39° 10′ and 75° 10′ from the south, required the hour angle of the star and latitude of the station.

PS =	90°—16° 11′= 73° 49′	a. c. log. sin 0·01756		log. cot 9·46271
Z =	180°—75° 10′=104° 50′	log. sin 9·98528	log. cos 9·40825	
ZS =	90°—39° 10′= 50° 50′	log. sin 9·88948	log. cot 9·91095	
P =	3^h 25^m 12^s = 51° 18′	log. sin 9·89232		log. cos 9·79605
	17° 26′ 46″		log. tan 9·49730	
	65° 6′ 6″			log. tan 10·33334
PZ =	47 39 20″			
lat. =	42 20 40			

We have now demonstrated formulas for the solution of every possible case of plane and spherical triangles, including the more simple formulas which apply exclusively to the right angled triangles.

The examination questions which follow call attention to the most important results of the investigations in the preceding pages. After these, in Appendix II. will be found many useful matters connected with Spherical Trigonometry, for which it was thought not best to interrupt the general train by which the solutions of triangles are deduced.

Note.—In assuming hypothetical cases, care must be taken not to suppose such as are impossible. The following are the governing principles to be observed.

In plane triangles, 1. One side must be less than the sum of the other two (Geom. Ax. 13 Cor.) 2. The greater side of a triangle is opposite to the greater angle (Geom. Th. 9). 3. The sum of the angles must be exactly two right angles.

In spherical triangles, the first two principles also apply (Spher. Geom., App. III. p. 2, and Prop. 7). 4. The sum of the three angles must not be less than two, nor greater than six right angles (Spher. Geom., Prop. 14). 5. The sum of the three sides must be less than a circumference (Spher. Geom., Prop. 8). 6. Each side must be less than a semicircumference (Spher. Geom., Prop. 8, Note). 7. Ench angle must be less than two right angles (Spher. Geom., Prop. 8, Note).

EXAMINATION QUESTIONS IN TRIGONOMETRY.

What is the object of Trigonometry ?

How many elements are there in a triangle, and what are they ?

How many elements must be given in order to determine the rest ?

In plane triangles what must one element always be ? Why ?

What is the difference between Geometrical and Trigonometrical solutions ?

Which are most accurate ?

Are trigonometrical solutions perfectly accurate ?

Whence arises the very small inaccuracy ? *Ans.* From the decimals neglected in calculating tables of logarithms.

How is the circumference of a circle divided for the purposes of Trigonometry ?

What is the complement of an angle or arc ?

What is the supplement ?

What are complements of each other in a right angled triangle ?

What is the sine of an arc ?

What is the cosine ?

The tangent ? Cotangent ? Secant ? Cosecant ?

What trigonometrical line changes its sign with the sine ? *Ans.* The cosecant.

In which quadrant are they negative ?

What changes with the cosine ? *Ans.* The secant.

Where are they negative ?

What with the tangent ? *Ans.* The cotangent.

Where are they negative ?

In passing through what values do quantities generally change their signs ? *Ans.* Zero and infinity.

What is the least value of the sine ?

Where is it 0 ?

What is the greatest value of the sine ?

Where is it radius ?

How many times does it change its sign in going round the circumference ?

What is the least value of the tangent ?

Where is it 0 ?

What is its greatest value ?

Where is it infinite ?

How many times does it change in going round the circumference ?

N. B. Let these questions be repeated for the secant, cosine, cotangent, and cosecant.

To what is the sine of 45° equal ?
The tangent of 45° ? } Why ?
The sine of 30° ?

To what is the sine of a negative arc equal ?

The cosine of a negative arc ?

The Tangent ? Secant ? Cotangent ? Cosecant ?

To what is the sine of the supplement of an arc equal ?

The cosine of the supplement ?

The Tangent ? Secant ? Cotangent ? Cosecant ?

To what is the sine of 90° plus an arc equal ?

The cosine of 90° plus an arc ?

The Tangent ? Secant ? Cotangent ? Cosecant ?

What formula expresses the relation between the sine and cosine of an arc ? *Ans.* $R^2 = \sin^2 + \cos^2$.

What is the expression for the tangent in terms of the sine and cosine ? *Ans.* $\text{Tan} = \frac{\sin}{\cos}$

The expression for the secant ? *Ans.* $\frac{1}{\cos}$

For the cotangent ? *Ans.* $\frac{\cos}{\sin}$

For the cosecant ? *Ans.* $\frac{1}{\sin}$

How are the tangents of two arcs to each other ?

To what is the tangent equal in terms of the cotangent ? *Ans.* $\frac{1}{\cot}$ or the reciprocal of the cotangent.

What is the formula for the sine of the sum of two arcs ? *Ans.* $\text{Sin}\,(a + b) = \sin a \cos b + \sin b \cos a$ or the sum of the rectangles of the alternate sines and cosines.

The formula for the sine of the difference ? *Ans.* $\text{Sin}\,(a - b) = \sin a \cos b - \sin b \cos a$.

For the cosine of the sum ? *Ans.* $\text{Cos}\,(a + b) = \cos a \cos b - \sin a \sin b$ or the difference of the rectangles of the cosines and sines.

For the cosine of the difference ? *Ans.* $\text{Cos}\,(a - b) = \cos a \cos b + \sin a \sin b$.

For the sine of an arc in terms of half the arc ? *Ans.* $\text{Sin}\,a = 2 \sin \frac{1}{2} a \cos \frac{1}{2} a$, or twice the sine of half the arc into the cosine of half the arc.

From what is this formula deduced ?

The formula for the cosine in terms of half the arc ? *Ans.* $\text{Cos}\,a = \cos^2 \frac{1}{2} a - \sin^2 \frac{1}{2} a$.

Whence derived ?

The formula for the sine of half an arc. *Ans.* $\text{Sin}\,\frac{1}{2} a = \sqrt{\frac{1}{2} - \frac{1}{2} \cos a}$.

For the cosine of half an arc ? *Ans.* $\text{Cos}\,\frac{1}{2} a = \sqrt{\frac{1}{2} + \frac{1}{2} \cos a}$.

For the sum of the sines ? *Ans.* $\text{Sin}\,p + \sin q = 2 \sin \frac{1}{2} (p + q) \cos \frac{1}{2} (p - q)$, or twice the sine of half the sum into the cosine of half the difference.

The difference of the sines? *Ans.* Sin $p - \sin q = 2 \cos \frac{1}{2} (p+q) \sin \frac{1}{2} (p-q)$.

The sum of the cosines? *Ans.* Cos $p + \cos q = 2 \cos \frac{1}{2} (p+q) \cos \frac{1}{2} (p-q)$.

The difference of the cosines? *Ans.* Cos $p - \cos q = 2 \sin \frac{1}{2} (q+p) \sin \frac{1}{2} (q-p)$.

What is the ratio of the sum of the sines to the difference of the sines? *Ans.* $\frac{\tan \frac{1}{2}(p+q)}{\tan \frac{1}{2}(p-q)}$ or tan of half the sum to tan of half the difference.

How derived?

Of the sum of the sines to the sum of the cosines?

Of the difference of the sines to the sum of the cosines?

Of the sine of the sum to the sum of the sines?

Ans. $$\frac{\sin (p+q)}{\sin p + \sin q} = \frac{\frac{2}{R} \sin \frac{1}{2}(p+q) \cos \frac{1}{2}(p+q)}{\frac{2}{R} \sin \frac{1}{2}(p+q) \cos \frac{1}{2}(p-q)} = \frac{\cos \frac{1}{2}(p+q)}{\cos \frac{1}{2}(p-q)}$$

Of the sine of the sum to the difference of the sines? *Ans.* $\frac{\sin \frac{1}{2}(p+q)}{\sin \frac{1}{2}(p-q)}$.

What is the formula for the sine in terms of the tangent? *Ans.* $\sin a = \frac{\tan a}{\sqrt{1+\tan^2 a}}$.

What is the formula for the tangent of the sum of two arcs? *Ans.* $\tan (a+b) = \frac{\tan a + \tan b}{1 - \tan a \tan b}$

For the tangent of the difference? *Ans.* $\tan (a-b) = \frac{\tan a - \tan b}{1 + \tan a \tan b}$

From the tangent of the sum how is the tangent of twice an arc found? Of three times an arc?

RESOLUTION OF RIGHT ANGLED PLANE TRIANGLES.

What are the three formulas for the solution of right angled triangles?

Ans. (1) Radius : the hypothenuse : : sine of one of the acute angles : the side opposite : : cosine : the side adjacent ; or radius being unity, hypothenuse × sine of either acute angle = side opposite and hyp. × cos of either angle = side adjacent.

(2) R : either of the perpendicular sides : : tangent of the angle adjacent or cotangent of the angle opposite : the other side, or R being 1, one perp. side × tan of adjacent angle = side opp.

(3) Square of the hypothenuse = sum of the squares of the other two sides. Square of either perp. side = rectangle of sum and dif. of the other two sides.

In a right angled triangle how many elements must be given? *Ans.* Two.

Why should each required element be found in terms of the two given?

In finding each unknown element how many logarithms will be employed?

When the logarithms are added what must be rejected from their sum?

When one is subtracted from the other what must be added to the latter?

When the hypothenuse is given or required with an angle, which formula is employed?

When the hypothenuse is neither given nor required?

When two sides are given to find the third?

RESOLUTION OF PLANE TRIANGLES IN GENERAL.

Two sides and the included angle of a triangle being given, how are the other elements determined? *Ans.* $a + b : a - b :: \tan \frac{1}{2}(A + B) : \tan \frac{1}{2}(A - B)$

$A + B = 180^\circ - C$

$\frac{1}{2}(A + B) + \frac{1}{2}(A - B) = A$, $\frac{1}{2}(A + B) - \frac{1}{2}(A - B) = B$

$\text{Sin } A : a :: \sin C : c$.

The three sides being given?

Ans. $\text{Sin } \frac{1}{2} A = \sqrt{\frac{(\frac{1}{2}s - b)(\frac{1}{2}s - c)}{bc}}$ or $\cos \frac{1}{2} A = \sqrt{\frac{\frac{1}{2}s(\frac{1}{2}s - a)}{bc}}$.

Two angles and the interjacent side being given? *Ans.* $180^\circ - (A + B) = C$. $\sin C : c :: \sin A : a :: \sin B : b$

Two of the three given parts being a side and its opposite angle? *Ans.* By the sine proportion, or sines of the angles are as the opposite sides.

What is the formula for the cosine of an angle in terms of the three sides of a plane triangle? *Ans.* $\text{Cos } A = \frac{b^2 + c^2 - a^2}{2bc}$ or the sum of the squares of the sides which contain it, minus the square of the opposite side, divided by twice the rectangle of the containing sides.

Which is the fundamental formula in Spherical Trigonometry?

Ans. $\text{Cos } A = \frac{R^2 \cos a - R \cos b \cos c}{\sin b \sin c}$*

SOLUTION OF RIGHT ANGLED SPHERICAL TRIANGLES.

Upon what are Napier's rules founded? *Ans.* Upon the formulas in right angled spherical trigonometry.

How many parts are considered for the application of his rules?

What are they? *Ans.* The base, perpendicular, the complement of the hypothenuse, and the complements of the two oblique angles.

What are the rules? *Ans.* Sin of the middle part = product of the cosines of the opposite parts = product of the tangents of the adjacent parts.

N. B. Radius must be introduced homogeneously.

When two parts are given how are the rules applied?

SOLUTION OF SPHERICAL TRIANGLES IN GENERAL.

Three sides of a spherical triangle being given how are the three angles found?

* All the formulas for the solution of spherical triangles may be derived from this; for applied to the three angles it gives three equations containing the six elements of the triangle from which any two elements being eliminated, an equation results containing the other four elements.

Ans. By the formulas $\sin \frac{1}{2} A = \sqrt{\frac{\sin(\frac{1}{2} s - b) \sin(\frac{1}{2} s - c)}{\sin b \sin c}}$

or $\cos \frac{1}{2} A = \sqrt{\frac{\sin \frac{1}{2} s \sin(\frac{1}{2} s - b)}{\sin b \sin c}}$

Why is not the formula for the cosine of an angle in terms of the three sides suitable for the application of logarithms?

The three angles being given how are the three sides found?

Ans. $\operatorname{Sin} \frac{1}{2} a = R \sqrt{\frac{\cos \frac{1}{2} S \cos(\frac{1}{2} S - A)}{\sin B \sin C}}$

Two sides and the included angle being given how are the other parts found? *Ans.* By Napier's analogies. $\operatorname{Cos} \frac{1}{2} (a + b) : \cos \frac{1}{2} (a - b) : : \cot \frac{1}{2} C : \tan \frac{1}{2} (A + B)$, $\sin \frac{1}{2} (a + b) : \sin \frac{1}{2} (a - b) : : \cot \frac{1}{2} C : \tan \frac{1}{2} (A - B)$. And then $\frac{1}{2} (A + B) + \frac{1}{2} (A - B) = A$ and $\frac{1}{2} (A + B) - \frac{1}{2} (A - B) = B$, and finally the sine proportion $\sin A : \sin B : : \sin C : \sin c$.

Two angles and the interjacent side being given? *Ans.* Napier's Analogies, 2d set.

$\operatorname{Cos} \frac{1}{2} (A + B) : \cos \frac{1}{2} (A - B) : : \tan \frac{1}{2} c : \tan \frac{1}{2} (a + b)$

$\operatorname{Sin} \frac{1}{2} (A + B) : \sin \frac{1}{2} (A - B) : : \tan \frac{1}{2} c : \tan \frac{1}{2} (a - b)$

$\frac{1}{2} (a + b) + \frac{1}{2} (a - b) = a$ and $\frac{1}{2} (a + b) - \frac{1}{2} (a - b) = b$, $\sin a : \sin A : : \sin c : \sin C$.

Two of the three given parts being a side and its opposite angle? *Ans.* From the vertex of that unknown angle which is opposite the unknown side, let fall a perpendicular upon this side and apply Napier's rules to the two right angled triangles thus formed. The parts of the given triangle are by this means found either directly, or by adding the parts of the two right angled triangles together.

QUESTIONS ON LOGARITHMS.

What is a logarithm?

What is the constant number which is raised to a power called?

To what is the logarithm of the base equal?

To what is the logarithm of unity equal?

What is the base of the common system?

In the common system what is the logarithm of 100? Of 1000?

Of all numbers between 100 and 1000?

Of all numbers between 1000 and 10,000?

What is the entire part of a logarithm called?

How does it compare with the number of digits in the number to which the logarithm belongs?

How is the logarithm of a number consisting of three figures found from the tables?

Of one of four?

Of one of more than four?

By the tables of Callet?

How is the number corresponding to any given logarithm found from the tables?

What is the rule for multiplication by logarithms?

For division?

Raising of powers?

Extraction of roots?

How is the logarithmic sine, tangent, &c., of any arc found when consisting of degrees and minutes only?

How the log. sine, tangent, and secant, when of seconds also?

How the cosine, cotangent, and cosecant in the last case?

How are the logarithmic secant and cosecant computed from the logarithmic sine and cosine?

What is the arithmetical complement of a logarithm?

For logarithms entering in what way into formulas are arith. comp[s]. used?

What must be rejected from the logarithmic sum for each ar. comp. used?

QUESTIONS ON THE CIRCLES OF THE CELESTIAL SPHERE.

What is the axis of the earth?

The axis of the heavens?

What is the celestial equator? The ecliptic?

What are the equinoxes?

What are declination circles?

What is the meridian of a place?

What is the hour angle of a heavenly body?

What is the horizon of a place?

What are the poles of the horizon called?

What are vertical circles?

Which is called the prime vertical?

What is the declination of a heavenly body? The right ascension?

What is the celestial latitude? Longitude?

What is the altitude of a heavenly body? The azimuth?

What are the co-ordinates of a heavenly body?

How many sets are there?

Which are obtained from observation?

Which of the observed co-ordinates are preferable, and why? *Ans.* R. A, and D, because they are the same for every place on the earth, whereas altitude and azimuth are different for every place.

QUESTIONS ON THE TRANSIT INSTRUMENT.

What are the different kinds of time?

What is apparent solar time? Mean solar time?

What is siderial time?

How much longer is a mean solar than a siderial day?

How is a mean solar interval of time converted into a siderial interval, and the contrary?

What instrument is employed for observing the time of transit of stars over the meridian?

Of what parts does the transit instrument consist?

How many and what are the adjustments?

How is the instrument collimated?

How is the striding level adjusted ?

How is the instrument adjusted to the meridian ?

When the instrument is completely adjusted, in what plane does the line of collimation move ?

How is an observation made with the transit instrument ?

How is the equatorial interval of the wires determined ?

How the interval between any wire and the middle wire for a particular star ?

What is the use of knowing the intervals of the wires ?

How does the probable error of observation compare with the number of wires observed upon ?

What is the formula for the inclination of the supporting axis ?

What the formula for the correction of the time of meridian transit for level error ?

What the formula for determining error in azimuth or deviation from the meridian ?

What for consequent error in the time of meridian transit ?

How is the equatorial error of collimation found ?

How from this the collimation error for any star ?

What is used with the transit instrument ?

If the clock keep true siderial time, what does the time of meridian transit show ?

If the right ascension of the object observed is known by catalogue, what does the difference between this and the time of meridian transit show ?

How is siderial time converted into solar and the converse ?*

* The above questions will suffice to show the nature of those which should be put upon the subsequent parts of the work with which we shall not take up further space.

APPENDIX II.

ON UNLIMITED SPHERICAL TRIANGLES AND THEIR SOLUTION.*

OF THE VARIOUS TRIANGLES FORMED BY THE SAME THREE POINTS ON THE SPHERE.

1. If any two points, A and B, be taken upon the surface of the sphere, the arc of a great circle joining them may be considered to be either the arc A B ($< 180^\circ$), or $360^\circ -$ A B; or if we do not limit the arcs to values less than a circumference, we may consider it to have an indefinite number of values expressed generally by the formula $2\,n\,\pi \pm a$, a denoting that value which is less than π or a semicircumference, and n any whole number or zero.

2. If two arcs of great circles intersect in a point A, the angle which they form may be considered to be either the angle A ($< 90^\circ$), or $180^\circ -$ A, or $180^\circ +$ A, or $360^\circ -$ A; or, taking the most general view of angular magnitude, the angle will have an indefinite number of values expressed by the formula $m\,\pi \pm A$, A denoting the value which is less than $\frac{1}{2}\pi$, and m any whole number or zero.

3. If, therefore, any three points, A, B, C, be taken on the surface of the sphere, and great circles, made to pass through each pair, we shall have an infinite series of triangles whose sides will be generally expressed by

$$2\,n\,\pi \pm a, \quad 2\,n\,\pi \pm b, \quad 2\,n\,\pi \pm c \tag{1}$$

and whose angles will be generally expressed by

$$m\,\pi \pm A, \quad m\,\pi \pm B, \quad m\,\pi \pm C; \tag{2}$$

$a, b, c,$ denoting the arcs less than π joining the pairs of points B C, A C, A B, respectively; A, B, C, the angles less than $\frac{1}{2}\pi$ formed at those points by the intersection of these arcs; and n and m, any whole numbers, or zero.

4. It is evident, however, that we cannot assume that any three values of the sides from the series (1), combined with any three values of the angles from (2), will form a spherical triangle. Some general relations of the parts composing a triangle must first be established, from which corresponding values of n and m in (1) and (2)

* Introduced by Gauss. Notwithstanding the elegance and generality thus given, to the solutions of many astronomical problems, nothing is to be found on this subject in our trigonometrical works. The present paper is from Prof. Chauvenet of the U. S. Naval Acad. The explanatory notes are the author's.

may be deduced. Although these general relations are well known, it may not be out of place to add here a concise demonstration of them.

Let the point C,* one of the angular points of the spherical triangle A B C, be referred by rectangular co-ordinates to three planes, one of which, the plane of $x\ y$, is the plane of the great circle A B; let the axis of x be the diameter of the sphere passing through B, and let the origin be the centre of the sphere. The formulas of transformation from these co-ordinates to polar co-ordinates, the origin being the same, the polar axis being the axis of x, and the fixed plane the plane of $x\ y$, are

$$\left.\begin{array}{l} x = \mathrm{R} \cos a \\ y = \mathrm{R} \sin a \cos \mathrm{B} \\ z = \mathrm{R} \sin a \sin \mathrm{B} \end{array}\right\} \quad (3)$$

where B denotes the angle which the plane passing through the polar axis and the point C makes with the fixed plane; R, the radius-vector in this plane, or distance of the point C from the origin; and a the angle which this radius-vector makes with the polar axis. B is an angle of the spherical triangle, and a is the side opposite the angle A; and, according to the principles of analytical geometry, B and a may be altogether unlimited, due regard being had to the signs of their trigonometric functions, and to those of x, y, and z.

Let us now transform from these rectangular co-ordinates to others also rectangular, the origin and the plane of $x\ y$ remaining the same, but the axis of x in the new system passing through the point A, and therefore making with the first axis the angle c, c also expressing the side of the triangle opposite the angle C. The known formulas of transformation become

* The rest of Art. 4 implies some knowledge of Analytical Geometry. It may be readily understood, however, by the mere student of trigonometry from the annexed diagram, with the following explanations. R in formulas (3) is equal to O C in the diagram. The projection of R or of O C, on O B which is called the axis of x, that is to say the distance between the foot of a perpendicular from C on O B and the point O is the value of x in the formulas, the projection of O C on a line called the axis of Y, drawn from O in the plane A O B perpendicular to O B, is the value of y in the formulas, and the projection of R or O C on O Z perpendicular to the plane A O B, is the value of Z in the formulas. The first of formulas (3) is now obvious enough; in the second R sin a evidently expresses the value of a perpendicular from C to OB in the plane C O B, and this perpendicular multiplied by the cosine of the angle which it makes with its projection on the plane A O B equal to the angle of the two planes or the angle B, expresses the length of the projection on the plane A O B, which is evidently equal to the projection of R on the axis of Y; or multiplied by the sin B expresses the height of C above the plane A O B, which is equal to the projection of R on O Z the axis of Z.

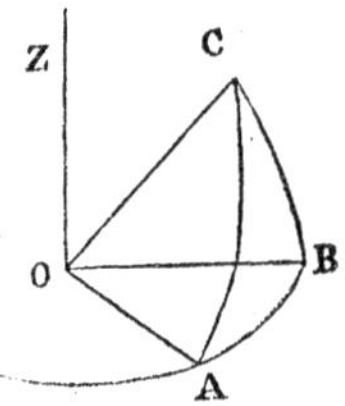

N. B. The axes of x, y, and z are at right angles each to the plane of the other two. So also are those of x', y', and z'.

The student will readily deduce formulas (4) by the rules of Plane Trigonometry.

$$\left.\begin{aligned} x &= x' \cos c - y' \sin c \\ y &= x' \sin c + y' \cos c \\ z &= z' \end{aligned}\right\} \qquad (4)$$

Finally, the formulas of transformation from this last system of rectangular again to polar co-ordinates, the origin being the same, the fixed plane the plane of x' y' and the polar axis the axis of x', are

$$\left.\begin{aligned} x' &= \text{R} \cos b \\ y' &= -\text{R} \sin b \cos \text{A} \\ z' &= \text{R} \sin b \sin \text{A} \end{aligned}\right\} \qquad (5)$$

Now, if the values of x, y, z, x', y', z', given by (3) and (5) be substituted in (4), we have at once the following system of equations:—

$$\left.\begin{aligned} \cos a &= \cos c \cos b + \sin c \sin b \cos \text{A} \\ \sin a \cos \text{B} &= \sin c \cos b - \cos c \sin b \cos \text{A} \\ \sin a \sin \text{B} &= \sin b \sin \text{A} \end{aligned}\right\} \qquad (6)$$

which are the known fundamental formulas of spherical trigonometry, but established without imposing any restrictions upon the values of the parts of the triangle.

From this investigation it appears that these formulas may be regarded as formulas of transformation from one system of polar co-ordinates to another, or rather from one system of spherical co-ordinates to another. For example, the co-ordinates of a star referred to the pole of the equator and the meridian of a place whose colatitude is c, are its polar distance a, and its hour angle B; the co-ordinates of the same star referred to the pole of the horizon and the meridian, are its zenith distance b, and its azimuth A; and the formulas (6) express the relations by means of which we can pass from one of these systems to the other.

(5.) Let us now inquire what are the corresponding values of the sides and angles in the series of triangles expressed by (1) and (2). Let a, b, c, A, B, C, denote the values of the parts of *one* of these triangles, which, if we please, we may suppose to be the triangle whose parts are less than π. Then since

$$\sin (2 n \pi + \phi) = \sin \phi, \cos (2 n \pi + \phi) = \cos \phi,$$

the equations (6) will be satisfied by the substitution of $2 n \pi + a$, $2 n \pi + b$, &c., for a, b, and c; and therefore the triangle (a, b, c, A, B, C) is the first of an infinite series obtained from it by the successive addition of 2π to each or all of its parts, every triangle of the series being such, that the relations of its parts are expressed by (6), when a, b, c, A, B, C, are assumed to represent those parts.

It is evident, also, from the principle of "uniformity of direction" observed in the preceding demonstration in reckoning the sides and angles, that we must be able to satisfy the equations, by making either all the sides, or all the angles, or all the sides and angles, *negative at the same time*,* and, considering each of the triangles

* The student will do well to conceive the position of the angular points of the triangles on the surface of the sphere with these variations.

N. B. That the sides are all negative together, or the angles together, or both together.

The same thing stated in the text may be made evident by referring to equations

thus obtained as the first of a series, as above, we have three more series. We have then the four series following :—

1st Series.	2d Series.
$2n\pi + a,\ 2n\pi + A$	$2n\pi - a,\ 2n\pi + A$
$2n\pi + b,\ 2n\pi + B$	$2n\pi - b,\ 2n\pi + B$
$2n\pi + c,\ 2n\pi + C$	$2n\pi - c,\ 2n\pi + C$

3d Series.	4th Series.
$2n\pi + a,\ 2n\pi - A$	$2n\pi - a,\ 2n\pi - A$
$2n\pi + b,\ 2n\pi - B$	$2n\pi - b,\ 2n\pi - B$
$2n\pi + c,\ 2n\pi - C$	$2n\pi - c,\ 2n\pi - C$

In all the terms of these series, n may have the same or different values; and we thus have all the possible combinations of the values represented by (1) and (2), *so long as* m *in* (2) *is even.* But if we substitute $2n+1$ for m we shall find that the following series will satisfy the equations (6) :—*

5th Series.	6th Series.
$2n\pi + a,\quad 2n\pi + A$	$2n\pi - a,\quad 2n\pi + A$
$2n\pi - b,\ (2n+1)\pi + B$	$2n\pi + b,\ (2n+1)\pi + B$
$2n\pi - c,\ (2n+1)\pi + C$	$2n\pi + c,\ (2n+1)\pi + C$

7th Series.	8th Series.
$2n\pi + a,\quad 2n\pi - A$	$2n\pi - a,\quad 2n\pi - A$
$2n\pi - b,\ (2n+1)\pi - B$	$2n\pi + b,\ (2n+1)\pi - B$
$2n\pi - c,\ (2n+1)\pi - C$	$2n\pi + c,\ (2n+1)\pi - C$

the 6th, 7th, and 8th of which series are derived from the 5th, as the 2d, 3d, and 4th were derived from the 1st, in the preceding paragraph.

By successively exchanging a for b and c, we find eight more series, namely,

9th Series.	10th Series.
$2n\pi - a,\ (2n+1)\pi + A$	$2n\pi + a,\ (2n+1)\pi + A$
$2n\pi + b,\quad 2n\pi + B$	$2n\pi - b,\quad 2n\pi + B$
$2n\pi - c,\ (2n+1)\pi + C$	$2n\pi + c,\ (2n+1)\pi + C$

(6), which involve all the relations of the six elements of a spherical triangle, and which will be satisfied by changing simultaneously a, b, and c into $-a, -b, -c$, or A, B, C, into $-A, -B, -C$ or both; observing the general rule that $\sin(-\phi) = -\sin\phi$ and $\cos(-\phi) = \cos\phi$.

* The student will try these elements given in the 5th series, in eqs. (6), observing that $\cos\{(2n+1)\pi + \phi\} = \cos(180^\circ + \phi) = -\cos\phi$ and $\sin\{(2n+1)\pi + \phi\} = -\sin\phi$.

11th Series.	12th Series.
$2n\pi - a$, $(2n+1)\pi - A$	$2n\pi + a$, $(2n+1)\pi - A$
$2n\pi + b$, $2n\pi - B$	$2n\pi - b$, $2n\pi - B$
$2n\pi - c$, $(2n+1)\pi - C$	$2n\pi + c$, $(2n+1)\pi - C$

13th Series.	14th Series.
$2n\pi - a$, $(2n+1)\pi + A$	$2n\pi + a$, $(2n+1)\pi + A$
$2n\pi - b$, $(2n+1)\pi + B$	$2n\pi + b$, $(2n+1)\pi + B$
$2n\pi + c$, $2n\pi + C$	$2n\pi - c$, $2n\pi + C$

15th Series.	16th Series.
$2n\pi - a$, $(2n+1)\pi - A$	$2n\pi + a$, $(2n+1)\pi - A$
$2n\pi - b$, $(2n+1)\pi - B$	$2n\pi + b$, $(2n+1)\pi - B$
$2n\pi + c$, $2n\pi - C$	$2n\pi - c$, $2n\pi - C$

5. Since three great circles by their mutual intersections (provided they have not a common diameter), divide the surface of the whole sphere into eight primitive triangles (whose parts are all less than π), the three angular points of each of which give sixteen triangles, whose parts are all less than 2π,* therefore, *three great circles of the sphere form in general one hundred and twenty-eight triangles, each of which may be considered as the first term of an infinite series of triangles formed from it by the successive addition of 2π to each or all of its parts.*

AMBIGUITY IN THE SOLUTION OF THE GENERAL SPHERICAL TRIANGLE.

For the sake of brevity, I shall call the spherical triangle, whose parts are only limited by the condition $< 360^\circ$, *the general spherical triangle.* Although any three points of the surface of the sphere may be regarded (in general) as the angular points of sixteen such triangles, yet to the problem " given three parts of the triangle to find the other three," there will in every case be but two solutions, *i. e.* two triangles containing the same data. From the equations (6), and the consequences that flow from them, we can always obtain expressions for both the sine and cosine of each of the required parts, which would fully determine the triangle, were it not that in every case one of these expressions at least involves a radical of the second degree, and has either two different numerical values, or two values numerically equal with opposite signs. To avoid this ambiguity it was thought expedient to limit all the parts of the triangles to values less than 180°, or to consider only the simple geometrical triangle. By this means all the cases in which the required quantities can be found by a cosine or tangent, without involving radicals, become fully determined. But this occurs in but four of the six cases, the other two still having two solutions; so that although six conditions were thus imposed, three limiting the data themselves, and three the quæsita, the object of removing all ambiguity was not reached.

* *i. e.*, making $n = 0$, in each of the 16 series of the last art.

We shall see from the solutions of the general triangle, that *the ambiguity is entirely removed in every case by the imposition of a single condition restricting the sign of either the sine or cosine of but one of the required parts.* The general method here, as in many parts of the mathematics, is therefore the simplest.

FORMULAS REQUIRED FOR THE SOLUTION OF THE GENERAL SPHERICAL TRIANGLE.

1. As the formulas (6) are the same as those deduced in trigonometrical works for limited spherical triangles, we may avail ourselves, for the solution of the general triangle, of all the formulas (found in those works), deduced from them in a general manner. It is not necessary therefore to repeat all those deductions here; but I shall add a demonstration of GAUSS's equations, slightly differing from the common one, in order to establish them in their generality.

2. GAUSS'S THEOREM. If

$$p = \cos \tfrac{1}{2} c \sin \tfrac{1}{2} (A + B), \qquad P = \cos \tfrac{1}{2} C \cos \tfrac{1}{2} (a - b)$$
$$q = \cos \tfrac{1}{2} c \cos \tfrac{1}{2} (A + B), \qquad Q = \sin \tfrac{1}{2} C \cos \tfrac{1}{2} (a + b)$$
$$r = \sin \tfrac{1}{2} c \sin \tfrac{1}{2} (A - B), \qquad R = \cos \tfrac{1}{2} C \sin \tfrac{1}{2} (a - b)$$
$$s = \sin \tfrac{1}{2} c \cos \tfrac{1}{2} (A - B), \qquad S = \cos \tfrac{1}{2} C \sin \tfrac{1}{2} (a + b)$$

then the products p q, p r, p s, q r, q s, r s, *are respectively equal to the products* P Q, P R, P S, Q R, Q S, R S.

To demonstrate this, we have only to form the following equations, which are easily deduced from the fundamental formulas:—

$$\sin c (\sin A \pm \sin B) = \sin C (\sin a \pm \sin b)^*$$
$$\sin c (\cos A \pm \cos B) = (1 \mp \cos C) \sin (a \pm b)^\dagger$$
$$(1 \pm \cos c) \sin (A \pm B) = \sin C (\cos b \pm \cos a)^\ddagger$$

which, transformed by the formulas of the trigonometric analysis,§ give respectively

* By combining $\dfrac{\sin c}{\sin C} = \dfrac{\sin a}{\sin A} = \dfrac{\sin b}{\sin B}$

† By the second of (6) we have

$$\sin c \cos A = \cos a \sin b - \sin a \cos b \cos C$$
$$\sin c \cos B = \cos b \sin a - \sin b \cos a \sin C$$

By addition and subtraction of these we obtain

$$\sin c (\cos A \pm \cos B) = (\sin a \cos b \pm \sin b \cos a) (1 \mp \cos C)$$

whence the formula in the text.

‡ This is obtained from the last by substituting $\pi - C$ &c., for C to produce the supplemental or polar triangle.

§ To wit: formulas which express the factors of the above forms in terms of the sines and cosines of $\tfrac{1}{2}$ C, $\tfrac{1}{2}$ c, $\tfrac{1}{2}$ (A $\pm$ B), $\tfrac{1}{2}$ ($a \pm b$) by means of which we have the following, each of the above forms furnishing two:

$$2 \sin \tfrac{1}{2} c \cos \tfrac{1}{2} c \, 2 \sin \tfrac{1}{2} (A + B) \cos \tfrac{1}{2} (A - B) = 2 \sin \tfrac{1}{2} C \cos \tfrac{1}{2} C \, 2 \sin \tfrac{1}{2} (a + b) \cos \tfrac{1}{2} (a - b)$$
$$2 \sin \tfrac{1}{2} c \cos \tfrac{1}{2} c \, 2 \sin \tfrac{1}{2} (A - B) \cos \tfrac{1}{2} (A + B) = 2 \sin \tfrac{1}{2} C \cos \tfrac{1}{2} C \, 2 \sin \tfrac{1}{2} (a - b) \cos \tfrac{1}{2} (a + b) \text{ \&c., \&c.}$$

$$p\,s = \text{P S}, \qquad q\,r = \text{Q R}$$
$$q\,s = \text{Q S}, \qquad p\,r = \text{P R}$$
$$p\,q = \text{P Q}, \qquad r\,s = \text{R S}$$

3. *The same notation being employed, the quantities* p², q², r², s², *are respectively equal to the quantities* P^2, Q^2, R^2, S^2.

For we have $p\,q \times p\,r = \text{P Q} \times \text{P R}$ and $q\,r = \text{Q R}$, whence by division $p^2 = \text{P}^2$, and in the same way $q^2 = \text{Q}^2$, $r^2 = \text{R}^2$ $s^2 = \text{S}^2$.

4. Gauss's Equations. From the preceding paragraph we deduce

$$p = \pm\,\text{P}$$
$$q = \pm\,\text{Q}$$
$$r = \pm\,\text{R}$$
$$s = \pm\,\text{S}$$

In these equations the positive sign must be taken in all the second members, or the negative sign in all of them.

For if we take $p = +\,\text{P}$, the equations $p\,q = \text{P Q}$, $p\,r = \text{P R}$, $p\,s = \text{P S}$, being divided by this, give $q = +\,\text{Q}$, $r = +\,\text{R}$, $s = +\,\text{S}$. But if we take $p = -\,\text{P}$, the same equations divided by this, give $q = -\,\text{Q}$, $r = -\,\text{R}$, $s = -\,\text{S}$.

Hence the two following groups of equations, the first group comprising those commonly known as Gauss's equations, which are identical with (I.), (II.), (III.) and (IV.) of Art. 86, by clearing the latter of fractions.

$$\left.\begin{aligned}
\cos \tfrac{1}{2} c \sin \tfrac{1}{2} (\text{A}+\text{B}) &= \cos \tfrac{1}{2} \text{C} \cos \tfrac{1}{2} (a-b) \\
\cos \tfrac{1}{2} c \cos \tfrac{1}{2} (\text{A}+\text{B}) &= \sin \tfrac{1}{2} \text{C} \cos \tfrac{1}{2} (a+b) \\
\sin \tfrac{1}{2} c \sin \tfrac{1}{2} (\text{A}-\text{B}) &= \cos \tfrac{1}{2} \text{C} \sin \tfrac{1}{2} (a-b) \\
\sin \tfrac{1}{2} c \cos \tfrac{1}{2} (\text{A}-\text{B}) &= \sin \tfrac{1}{2} \text{C} \cos \tfrac{1}{2} (a-b)
\end{aligned}\right\} \quad (7)$$

$$\left.\begin{aligned}
\cos \tfrac{1}{2} c \sin \tfrac{1}{2} (\text{A}+\text{B}) &= -\cos \tfrac{1}{2} \text{C} \cos \tfrac{1}{2} (a-b) \\
\cos \tfrac{1}{2} c \cos \tfrac{1}{2} (\text{A}+\text{B}) &= -\sin \tfrac{1}{2} \text{C} \cos \tfrac{1}{2} (a+b) \\
\sin \tfrac{1}{2} c \sin \tfrac{1}{2} (\text{A}-\text{B}) &= -\cos \tfrac{1}{2} \text{C} \sin \tfrac{1}{2} (a-b) \\
\sin \tfrac{1}{2} c \cos \tfrac{1}{2} (\text{A}-\text{B}) &= -\sin \tfrac{1}{2} \text{C} \sin \tfrac{1}{2} (a+b)
\end{aligned}\right\} \quad (8)$$

5. Now when the parts of the triangle are limited to values less than 180°, the second of these groups is excluded, since $\cos \frac{1}{2} c$, $\sin \frac{1}{2} (\text{A}+\text{B})$, $\cos \frac{1}{2} \text{C}$, $\cos \frac{1}{2} (a-b)$ are then all positive. But when the triangle is unlimited, both groups must be admitted, and the question arises, when are we to employ the positive, and when the negative sign? Gauss himself has remarked (*Theoria Mot. Corp. Cœl.*, Art. 54), that cases occur in practice in which it is necessary to employ the negative sign, and promises elsewhere a fuller explanation, which, however, I have not been able to find. But the nature of these cases and the answer to the question above propounded will be easily inferred from the following considerations.

We have seen that the formulas (6) apply not only to the triangle whose parts a, b, c, A, B, C, are all less than 360°, or 2π, but also to all the triangles whose parts are $2\,n\,\pi + a$, $2\,n\,\pi + b$, $2\,n\,\pi + c$, $2\,n\,\pi + \text{A}$, $2\,n\,\pi + \text{B}$ $2\,n\,\pi + \text{C}$, n being

---

The first two of the six that would result are all that we have thought necessary to write. They are identical with

$$p\,s = \text{P S} \qquad q\,r = \text{Q R}$$

any whole number or zero, and admitting of different values in each of the parts. Let us, therefore, substitute in (7) the following values of these parts:—

$$2\,n_1\,\pi + a, \qquad 2\,m_1\,\pi + A$$
$$2\,n_2\,\pi + b, \qquad 2\,m_2\,\pi + B$$
$$2\,n_3\,\pi + c, \qquad 2\,m_3\,\pi + C$$

We shall have for the factors of the first members values similar to the following:

$$\cos\,(n_3\,\pi + \tfrac{1}{2}\,c) = (-1)^{n_3} \cos \tfrac{1}{2}\,c^*$$

$$\sin\,(n_3\,\pi + \tfrac{1}{2}\,c) = (-1)^{n_3} \sin \tfrac{1}{2}\,c^*$$

$$\cos\,[(m_1 + m_2)\,\pi + \tfrac{1}{2}\,(A + B)] = (-1)^{m_1 + m_2} \cos \tfrac{1}{2}\,(A + B)$$

$$\sin\,[(m_1 + m_2)\,\pi + \tfrac{1}{2}\,(A + B)] = (-1)^{m_1 + m_2} \sin \tfrac{1}{2}\,(A + B)$$

$$\cos\,[(m_1 - m_2)\,\pi + \tfrac{1}{2}\,(A - B)] = (-1)^{m_1 - m_2} \cos \tfrac{1}{2}\,(A - B)$$

$$\sin\,[(m_1 - m_2)\,\pi + \tfrac{1}{2}\,(A - B)] = (-1)^{m_1 - m_2} \sin \tfrac{1}{2}\,(A - B)$$

Now whatever the values of m_1 and m_2, $m_1 + m_2$ and $m_1 - m_2$ are both even or both odd at the same time, and therefore *the above substitution gives the same sign to all the first members of our equations.* In the same way it is shown that the second members will all have the same sign ; and we may consequently express the result of the substitution thus :—

$$\cos \tfrac{1}{2}\,c \sin \tfrac{1}{2}\,(A + B) = (-1)^n \cos \tfrac{1}{2}\,c \cos \tfrac{1}{2}\,(a - b)$$
$$\cos \tfrac{1}{2}\,c \cos \tfrac{1}{2}\,(A + B) = (-1)^n \sin \tfrac{1}{2}\,c \cos \tfrac{1}{2}\,(a + b)$$
$$\sin \tfrac{1}{2}\,c \sin \tfrac{1}{2}\,(A - B) = (-1)^n \cos \tfrac{1}{2}\,c \sin \tfrac{1}{2}\,(a - b)$$
$$\sin \tfrac{1}{2}\,c \cos \tfrac{1}{2}\,(A - B) = (-1)^n \sin \tfrac{1}{2}\,c \sin \tfrac{1}{2}\,(a + b)$$

which single group involves both (7) and (8). *The group* (7) *will represent one series of triangles, while the group* (8) *will represent another series, the two differing in each of their elements by some multiple of* 2π, *and the primitive triangle may belong to one or the other of these series. We may dispense, therefore, in practice, with group* (8), *by deducting* 360° *or* 2π *from the elements found by group* (7), *till they become less than* 360°, *as required for use.* (*See top of this page.*)

6. When the parts of the triangle are interchanged in GAUSS's equations, it would seem to require proof that the same sign, whether + or —, must continue in these equations; *i. e.* that when the triangle is such as to satisfy the equation,

$$\cos \tfrac{1}{2}\,c \sin \tfrac{1}{2}\,(A + B) = \cos \tfrac{1}{2}\,c \cos \tfrac{1}{2}\,(a - b)$$

* Apply (3) and (6) of Art. 70 to sin and cos of $2\,n_3\,\pi + \tfrac{1}{2}\,c$ to obtain these results. Or observe that $\cos\,(n\pi + \tfrac{1}{2}\,c) = \pm \cos \tfrac{1}{2}\,c$ according as n is even or odd.

it will also satisfy the equations,

$$\left.\begin{array}{l}\cos \tfrac{1}{2} b \sin \tfrac{1}{2} (A + C) = \cos \tfrac{1}{2} B \cos \tfrac{1}{2} (a - c) \\ \cos \tfrac{1}{2} a \sin \tfrac{1}{2} (B + C) = \cos \tfrac{1}{2} A \cos \tfrac{1}{2} (b \quad c)\end{array}\right\} \qquad (e)$$

and that when it is such as to satisfy the equation,

$$\cos \tfrac{1}{2} c \sin \tfrac{1}{2} (A + B) = -\cos \tfrac{1}{2} C \cos \tfrac{1}{2} (a - b)$$

it will also satisfy the equations

$$\left.\begin{array}{l}\cos \tfrac{1}{2} b \sin \tfrac{1}{2} (A + C) = - \cos \tfrac{1}{2} B \cos \tfrac{1}{2} (a - c) \\ \cos \tfrac{1}{2} a \sin \tfrac{1}{2} (B + C) = - \cos \tfrac{1}{2} A \cos \tfrac{1}{2} (b - c)\end{array}\right\} \qquad (f)$$

To demonstrate this, we will show that the groups to which the equations (e) belong may be derived from (7), and those to which (f) belong from (8), by merely linear transformations, and therefore without again introducing the double sign. Let the equations (7) be written thus:—

$$\left.\begin{array}{l}\dfrac{\sin \frac{1}{2} (A + B)}{\cos \frac{1}{2} C} = \dfrac{\cos \frac{1}{2} (a - b)}{\cos \frac{1}{2} c} \\ \dfrac{\cos \frac{1}{2} (A + B)}{\sin \frac{1}{2} C} = \dfrac{\cos \frac{1}{2} (a + b)}{\cos \frac{1}{2} c} \\ \dfrac{\sin \frac{1}{2} (A - B)}{\cos \frac{1}{2} C} = \dfrac{\sin \frac{1}{2} (a - b)}{\sin \frac{1}{2} c} \\ \dfrac{\cos \frac{1}{2} (A - B)}{\sin \frac{1}{2} C} = \dfrac{\sin \frac{1}{2} (a + b)}{\sin \frac{1}{2} c}\end{array}\right\} \qquad (g)$$

The sum and difference of the first two, and the sum and difference of the last two, give*

$$\begin{array}{l}\dfrac{\cos \frac{1}{2} (A + B + C)}{\sin C} = -\dfrac{\sin \frac{1}{2} a \sin \frac{1}{2} b}{\cos \frac{1}{2} c} \\ \dfrac{\cos \frac{1}{2} (A + B - C)}{\sin C} = \dfrac{\cos \frac{1}{2} a \cos \frac{1}{2} b}{\cos \frac{1}{2} c} \\ \dfrac{\cos \frac{1}{2} (A - B + C)}{\sin C} = \dfrac{\cos \frac{1}{2} a \sin \frac{1}{2} b}{\sin \frac{1}{2} c} \\ \dfrac{\cos \frac{1}{2} (-A + B + C)}{\sin C} = \dfrac{\sin \frac{1}{2} a \cos \frac{1}{2} b}{\sin \frac{1}{2} c}\end{array}$$

By differently combining these four equations, two and two, we may either reproduce the group (g) or the two groups represented by (e). Thus the sum and difference of the first and third, and of the second and fourth, give

$$\begin{array}{l}\dfrac{\sin \frac{1}{2} B \sin \frac{1}{2} (A + C)}{\sin C} = \dfrac{\sin \frac{1}{2} b \cos \frac{1}{2} (a - c)}{\sin c} \\ \dfrac{\cos \frac{1}{2} B \cos \frac{1}{2} (A + C)}{\sin C} = \dfrac{\sin \frac{1}{2} b \cos \frac{1}{2} (a + c)}{\sin c} \\ \dfrac{\sin \frac{1}{2} B \sin \frac{1}{2} (A - C)}{\sin C} = \dfrac{\cos \frac{1}{2} b \sin \frac{1}{2} (a - c)}{\sin c} \\ \dfrac{\cos \frac{1}{2} B \cos \frac{1}{2} (A - C)}{\sin C} = \dfrac{\cos \frac{1}{2} b \sin \frac{1}{2} (a + c)}{\sin c}\end{array}$$

* See the mode of deducing (I), (II), &c., of Art. 86.

These multiplied by

$$\frac{\sin C}{\sin B} = \frac{\sin c}{\sin b}$$

give

$$\frac{\sin \frac{1}{2}(A + C)}{\cos \frac{1}{2} B} = \frac{\cos \frac{1}{2}(a - c)}{\cos \frac{1}{2} b}$$
$$\frac{\cos \frac{1}{2}(A + C)}{\sin \frac{1}{2} B} = \frac{\cos \frac{1}{2}(a + c)}{\cos \frac{1}{2} b}$$
$$\frac{\sin \frac{1}{2}(A - C)}{\cos \frac{1}{2} B} = \frac{\sin \frac{1}{2}(a - c)}{\sin \frac{1}{2} b}$$
$$\frac{\cos \frac{1}{2}(A - C)}{\sin \frac{1}{2} B} = \frac{\sin \frac{1}{2}(a + c)}{\sin \frac{1}{2} b}$$

Precisely the same transformations applied to (8) would of course give a similar result with the negative sign. Hence

In the three groups which GAUSS's *equations form by the permutation of the letters, the positive sign must be taken in all the equations, or the negative sign in all of them.*

AUXILIARY ANGLES.

It will be convenient to premise here the following proposition, upon which depends the proper employment of auxiliary angles in preparing our general formulas for logarithmic computation.

In the equations

$$\left.\begin{array}{l} k \sin \phi = m \\ k \cos \phi = n \end{array}\right\} \qquad (9)$$

whatever the values of m *and* n, *we can always determine* k *and* ϕ *so as to satisfy at once these equations, and any one of the following conditions arbitrarily imposed.*

1st k positive, ($\phi < 360°$),
2d k negative, ($\phi < 360°$),
3d $\phi > 0$ and $< 180°$,
4th $\phi > 180°$ and $< 360°$,
5th $\phi < 90°$ and $> -90°$,
6th $\phi > 90°$ and $< 270°$.

The six conditions above stated are obviously equivalent to the following; 1st, $k +$; 2d, $k -$; 3d, $\sin \phi +$; 4th, $\sin \phi -$; 5th, $\cos \phi +$; 6th, $\cos \phi -$. Of these six conditions, however, we commonly employ only the first, third, or fifth.

The quotient of the equations (9), $\tan \phi = \frac{m}{n}$, gives two values of ϕ under 360°.* Hence, also, two values of k, which will be numerically equal with opposite signs,

* Because for any arc less than 360° there is always another arc $< 360°$, having the same tangent. If the former be in the first quadrant, the latter is in the 3d; if the former be in the 2d, the latter is in the 4th quadrant.

since the two values of sin ϕ will be numerically equal with opposite signs, as also the two values of cos ϕ. If we restrict the sign of any one of the three quantities k, sin ϕ, cos ϕ, the signs of the other two will become known, and there will be but one value of k and one of ϕ under that restriction.

SOLUTION OF THE SEVERAL CASES OF THE GENERAL SPHERICAL TRIANGLE.

In the solutions of the various cases of spherical triangles, it is of the first importance to have simple and clear precepts, both for removing the ambiguity that occurs in every case and for determining properly the auxiliary angles. Examples might be pointed out, in recent works on trigonometry, of incorrect numerical solutions resulting from an erroneous application of precepts, in themselves correct, but not sufficiently simple or explicit. I have, therefore, given special attention to this point in arranging the following solutions. These solutions have also been carefully verified by the computation of the two triangles following:—

FIRST TRIANGLE.

$a = 125^\circ\ 0'\ 0''$	$A = 264^\circ\ 51'\ 30''\cdot4$
$b = 140\quad 0\quad 0$	$B = 231\quad 24\quad 6\ \cdot9$
$c = 46\quad 0\quad 0$	$C = 299\quad 0\quad 0\ \cdot6$

SECOND TRIANGLE.

$a = 40^\circ\ 0'\ 0''$	$A = 319^\circ\ 21'\ 21''\cdot4$
$b = 250\quad 0\quad 0$	$B = 107\quad 46\quad 57\ \cdot6$
$c = 230\quad 0\quad 0$	$C = 50\quad 55\quad 9\ \cdot3$

The first of these triangles requires the positive sign in GAUSS's Equations, and the second requires the negative sign.

1. *Given* b, c, *and* A, *to find* a, B, and C. The general relations between the given and required parts are

$$\left.\begin{aligned} \cos a &= \cos c \cos b + \sin c \sin b \cos A \\ \sin a \cos B &= \sin c \cos b - \cos c \sin b \cos A \\ \sin a \sin B &= \sin B \sin A \end{aligned}\right\} \qquad (1)$$

and similar forms to the last two, with C and c interchanged with B and b.

The second members being computed, the numerical value and the sign of cos a will be determined from the first equation. From the second and third sin a and B are determined precisely as k and ϕ in the preceding section and are subject to the same ambiguity.* *The ambiguity will be removed, therefore, when the sign of either sin* a, *sin* B, *or cos* B *is given, and in like manner when the sign of either sin* C *or cos* C *(the other required parts) is given.*

The solution may be adapted for logarithmic computation, and the condition required for removing the ambiguity may be varied.

Let k and ϕ be determined by the conditions (9), taking $m =$ sin b cos A, and $n =$ cos b, and adopting the first arbitrary condition; then these conditions together with equations (1) assume the following form:—

* For the second members of the 2d and 3d of (1) being computed, they will be fixed quantities like m and n in (9), and sin a occupies the place of k, and B that of ϕ in the same equations (9).

$$\left.\begin{array}{rl} k \sin \phi = & \sin b \cos A \\ k \cos \phi = & \cos b \qquad (k \text{ positive}) \\ \cos a = & k \cos (c - \phi) \\ \sin a \cos B = & k \sin (c - \phi) \\ \sin a \sin B = & \sin b \sin A \end{array}\right\} \qquad (2)$$

Or, eliminating k and adopting the third condition imposed on eqs. (9)

$$\left.\begin{array}{rl} \tan \phi = & \tan b \cos A \qquad (\phi < 180^\circ) \\ \cos a = & \dfrac{\cos b}{\cos \phi} \cos (c - \phi) \\ \sin a \cos B = & \dfrac{\cos b}{\cos \phi} \sin (c - \phi)^* \\ \sin a \sin B = & \sin b \sin A \end{array}\right\} \qquad (3)$$

If the quadrant in which a *is to be taken is given,* then

$$\left.\begin{array}{rl} \tan \phi = & \tan b \cos A \qquad (\phi < 180^\circ) \\ \tan a \cos B = & \tan (c - \phi)\dagger \\ \tan a \sin B = & \dfrac{\sin \phi \tan A}{\cos (c - \phi)}\ddagger \end{array}\right\} \qquad (4)$$

In (3) and (4) we may also limit ϕ to values numerically less than 90°, the sign of the tangent being determined according to the fifth arbitrary condition following (9).

If both a *and* b *are less than* 180°, as not unfrequently happens in the applications of this problem, let

$$m = \frac{k}{\sin b} \qquad n = \frac{\sin a}{k}$$

then m and n are both positive (k being positive) and the following form may be employed :—§

$$\left.\begin{array}{rl} m \sin \phi = & \cos A \\ m \cos \phi = & \cot b \\ n \sin B = & \sin \phi \tan A \\ n \cos B = & \sin (c - \phi) \\ \cot a = & \cot (c - \phi) \cos B \| \end{array}\right\} \qquad (5)$$

Check.—For the purpose of verification we may employ with (4) or (5), the formula $\sin a \sin B = \sin b \sin A$; and with any of the preceding solutions the following check :—

$$\frac{\sin (c - \phi)}{\sin \phi} = \frac{\sin a \cos B}{\sin b \cos A} = \frac{\tan A}{\tan B}\P$$

* The value of k which appears in the 2d and 3d of (3) is obtained from the 2d of (2).

† Dividing the 3d by the 2d of (3).

‡ Combining the 1st, 2d, and 4th of (3).

§ Derived from (2).

‖ Dividing the 3d by the 4th of (2).

¶ From 1st, 4th, and 5th of (2).

2. *Given* b, c, *and* A, *to find* B *and* C. We employ GAUSS'S equations as follows :—

$$\left.\begin{aligned}\cos \tfrac{1}{2} a \sin \tfrac{1}{2} (B + C) &= \cos \tfrac{1}{2} A \cos \tfrac{1}{2} (b - c)\\ \cos \tfrac{1}{2} a \cos \tfrac{1}{2} (B + C) &= \sin \tfrac{1}{2} A \cos \tfrac{1}{2} (b + c)\\ \sin \tfrac{1}{2} a \sin \tfrac{1}{2} (B - C) &= \cos \tfrac{1}{2} A \sin \tfrac{1}{2} (b - c)\\ \sin \tfrac{1}{2} a \cos \tfrac{1}{2} (B - C) &= \sin \tfrac{1}{2} A \sin \tfrac{1}{2} (b - c)\end{aligned}\right\} \quad (6)$$

The first two by eliminating $\cos \frac{1}{2} a$ determine $\frac{1}{2}$ (B + C) when the sign of $\cos \frac{1}{2} a$ is known, and the second two determine $\frac{1}{2}$ (B — C) when the sign of $\sin \frac{1}{2} a$ is known. *Hence, these equations present no ambiguity when the sign of sin* a *is given;* for $\sin \frac{1}{2} a$ is always positive, and $\cos \frac{1}{2} a$ has the same sign as $\sin a$ according to the formlua,

$$\sin a = 2 \sin \tfrac{1}{2} a \cos \tfrac{1}{2} a$$

The equations (6) taken with the positive sign only may give values of B and C exceeding 360°, in which case the required solution will be found by diminishing such values by 360°.

3. *Given* B, C, *and* a *to find* A *and* b. The general relations between the given and required parts are

$$\left.\begin{aligned}\cos A &= -\cos C \cos B + \sin C \sin B \cos a\\ \sin A \cos b &= \sin C \cos B + \cos C \sin B \cos a\\ \sin A \sin b &= \sin B \sin a\end{aligned}\right\} \quad (7)^*$$

which determine A and b without ambiguity, *when the sign of either* sin A, sin b, *or* cos b *is given.* In like manner the ambiguity is removed when the sign of either $\sin c$ or $\cos c$ is given.

Adapted for logarithms by the method already used, these equations become†

$$\left.\begin{aligned}k \sin \phi &= \sin B \cos a\\ k \cos \phi &= \cos B \qquad (k \text{ positive})\\ \cos A &= -k \cos (C + \phi)\\ \sin A \cos b &= k \sin (C + \phi)\\ \sin A \sin b &= \sin B \sin a\end{aligned}\right\} \quad (8)$$

Or,

$$\left.\begin{aligned}&\tan \phi = \tan B \cos a \ (\phi < 180^\circ \text{ always}\\ &\text{positive; or } \phi \text{ less than } 90^\circ \text{ with the sign of its tangent,})\\ &\cos A = -\frac{\cos B}{\cot \phi} \cos (C + \phi)\\ &\sin A \cos b = \frac{\cos B}{\cos \phi} \sin (C + \phi)\\ &\sin A \sin b = \sin B \sin a\end{aligned}\right\} \quad (9)‡$$

When the quadrant in which A *is to be taken is known,*

* Derived from equations (6) p. 179 by polar triangles.

† Compare (2). ‡ Compare (3).

$$\left.\begin{aligned} \tan\phi &= \tan B\cos a\ (\phi < 180^\circ) \\ \tan A\cos b &= -\tan(c+\phi) \\ \tan A\sin b &= -\frac{\sin\phi\tan a}{\cos(c+\phi)} \end{aligned}\right\} \quad (10)^*$$

When A *and* B *are both less than* 180° ;

$$\left.\begin{aligned} m\sin\phi &= \cos a \quad (m \text{ positive}) \\ m\cos\phi &= \cot B \\ n\sin b &= \sin\phi\tan a\ (n \text{ positive}) \\ n\cos B &= \sin(c+\phi) \\ \cot A &= -\cot(c+\phi)\cos b \end{aligned}\right\} \quad (11)^\dagger$$

Check.—With (10) or (11) we may employ $\sin a\sin B = \sin b\sin A$, and with any of the solutions (8), (9), (10), (11), the check

$$\frac{\sin(c+\phi)}{\sin\phi} = \frac{\sin A\cos b}{\sin B\cos a} = \frac{\tan a}{\tan b}$$

4. *Given* B, C, *and* a, *to find* b *and* c. We employ GAUSS's equations arranged as follows:

$$\left.\begin{aligned} \sin\tfrac{1}{2}A\sin\tfrac{1}{2}(b+c) &= \sin\tfrac{1}{2}a\cos\tfrac{1}{2}(B-C) \\ \sin\tfrac{1}{2}A\cos\tfrac{1}{2}(b+c) &= \cos\tfrac{1}{2}a\cos\tfrac{1}{2}(B+C) \\ \cos\tfrac{1}{2}A\sin\tfrac{1}{2}(b-c) &= \sin\tfrac{1}{2}a\sin\tfrac{1}{2}(B-C) \\ \cos\tfrac{1}{2}A\cos\tfrac{1}{2}(b-c) &= \cos\tfrac{1}{2}a\sin\tfrac{1}{2}(B+C) \end{aligned}\right\} \quad (12)$$

which present no ambiguity when the sign of $\cos\frac{1}{2}A$ is given ; that is, ***when the sign of*** $\sin A$ ***is given,*** observing that $\sin\frac{1}{2}A$ is always positive, and $\cos\frac{1}{2}A$ has the same sign as $\sin A$.

As before, when these equations lead to values of b or c greater than 360°, the true values are to be found by subtracting 360°.

5. *Given* a, b, *and* A, *to find* B, C, *and* c. The general relations between the given and required parts, are

$$\left.\begin{aligned} \sin a\sin B &= \sin b\sin A \\ -\cos C\cos A + \sin C\sin A\cos b &= \cos B \\ \sin C\cos A + \cos C\sin A\cos b &= \sin B\cos a \\ \cos c\cos b + \sin c\sin b\cos A &= \cos a \\ \sin c\cos b - \cos c\sin b\cos A &= \sin a\cos B \end{aligned}\right\} \quad (13)$$

The first equation determines B ***when the sign of*** $\cos B$ ***is given;*** and B being known, the remaining equations will fully determine C and c. Thus we find first

$$\sin B = \frac{\sin b\sin A}{\sin a} \quad (14)$$

Then from the second and third of (13) if we put

$$\left.\begin{aligned} k\sin\phi &= \cos A \quad (k \text{ positive}) \\ k\cos\phi &= \sin A\cos b \\ k\sin\phi' &= \cos B \\ k\cos\phi' &= \sin B\cos a \quad \text{we obtain} \\ C &= \phi + \phi' \S \end{aligned}\right\} \quad (15)^\ddagger$$

* Compare (4). † Compare (5). ‡ Compare with former check.

§ Because $\sin(C-\phi) = \sin\phi'$ and $\cos(C-\phi) = \cos\phi'$.

From the fourth and fifth, ([1])

$$\left.\begin{aligned} k \sin \theta &= \sin b \cos A \quad (k \text{ positive}) \\ k \cos \theta &= \cos b \\ k \sin \theta' &= \sin a \cos B \\ k \cos \theta' &= \cos a \\ c &= \theta + \theta' \end{aligned}\right\} \quad (16)$$

In these solutions it may happen that $\phi + \phi'$, or $\theta + \theta'$ exceeds 360°, in which case $C = \phi + \phi' - 360°$, or $c = \theta + \theta' - 360°$.

Checks.—One of the following* may be employed when either C or c has alone been computed:—

$$\frac{\sin \phi}{\sin \phi'} = \frac{\cos A}{\cos B} \qquad \frac{\cos \phi}{\cos \phi'} = \frac{\tan a}{\tan b}$$

$$\frac{\sin \theta}{\sin \theta'} = \frac{\tan B}{\tan A} \qquad \frac{\cos \theta}{\cos \theta'} = \frac{\cos b}{\cos a}$$

When both C and c have been computed, the obvious check is

$$\frac{\sin C}{\sin c} = \frac{\sin A}{\sin a}$$

6. *Given* a, b, *and* A, *to find* C *and* c *without finding* B. Observing that k is positive in the preceding article we deduce the following forms and conditions, by eliminating B ;†

$$\left.\begin{aligned} k \sin \phi &= \cos A \qquad (k \text{ positive}) \\ k \cos \phi &= \sin A \cos b \\ \cos \phi' &= \cos \phi \cot a \tan b \ (\phi' \text{ less than } 180°, \text{ with the same sign as } \cos B.)‡ \\ C &= \phi + \phi' \end{aligned}\right\} \quad (17)$$

$$\left.\begin{aligned} k \sin \theta &= \sin b \cos A \qquad (k \text{ positive}) \\ k \cos \theta &= \cos b \\ \cos \theta' &= \frac{\cos \theta \cos a}{\cos b} \ § \qquad (\theta' \text{ less than } 180°, \text{ with the same sign as } \sin a \cos B), \end{aligned}\right\} \quad (18)$$

Check.

$$\frac{\sin C}{\sin c} = \frac{\sin A}{\sin a}$$

([1]) The propriety of employing the same factor k in both (15) and (16) will be seen by comparing the values of k deduced from the two groups. We find in both cases $k^2 = 1 - \sin^2 A \sin^2 b$.

* Deduced from (15) and (16).

† By substituting $\sin A \sin b$ for $\sin B$ in the 4th of (15), and for $\sin A$ its value $\frac{\cos \phi}{\sin a}$ from 2nd of 15.

‡ See 3d of (15.)

§ The value of $\cos \theta'$ is obtained by taking the value of k in the 2d of (16), and substituting it in the 4th.

In these solutions, when $\phi+\phi'$, and $+\theta+\theta'$ exceed 360°, we must take $c=\phi+\phi'-360°$, $c=\theta+\theta'-360°$; and when they are negative we must take $c=\phi+\phi'+360°$, $c=\theta+\theta'+360°$.

7. *Given* A, B, *and* a, *to find* b, c, *and* c. We find b by the formula

$$\sin b = \frac{\sin B \sin a}{\sin A}$$

which determines b *when the sign of* cos b* *is given.* The remainder of the solution is by (15) and (16).

8. *Given* A, B, *and* a, *to find* c *and* c *without finding* b. We may eliminate b from (15) and (16) in their present form, but the conditions for determining the auxiliary angles will not be so simple as in the following method. Let ϕ and ϕ' in (15) be exchanged for $\phi'-90°$, and $\phi+90°$ respectively; then after eliminating b, we find

$$\left.\begin{array}{l} k\sin\phi = -\sin B \cos a \ (k \text{ positive}) \\ k\cos\phi = \cos B \\ \cos\phi' = -\dfrac{\cos\phi\cos A}{\cos B}\dagger\ (\phi' \text{ less than } 180°, \text{ with the sign of } \sin A \cos b.) \\ c=\phi+\phi' \end{array}\right\} \quad (19)$$

In a similar manner from (15) we find

$$\left.\begin{array}{l} k\sin\theta = -\cos a \quad (k \text{ positive}) \\ k\cos\theta = \sin a \cos B \\ \cos\theta' = -\cos\theta \cot A \tan B\ddagger\ (\theta' \text{ less than } 180° \text{ with the sign of } \cos b.) \\ c=\theta+\theta' \end{array}\right\} \quad (20)$$

Check.

$$\frac{\sin C}{\sin c} = \frac{\sin A}{\sin a}$$

In these formulas, as before, when $\phi+\phi'$, and $\theta+\theta'$ exceed 360°, we take $c=\phi+\phi'-360°$, $c=\theta+\theta'-360°$; and when they are negative we take $c=\phi+\phi'+360°$, $c=\theta+\theta'+360°$.

9. *Given* a, b, *and* c, *to find* A, B, *or* C. The formula (see Art. 82)

$$\cos A = \frac{\cos a - \cos b \cos c}{\sin b \sin c} \quad (21)$$

determines A *when the sign of* sin A *is given; or when the sign of either* sin A, sin B, *or* sin C *is given;* when the sign of any one of these functions is known, those of the other two may be discovered by an inspection of the equation

* Which determines the quadrant in which b is, the sign of the sin b only determining whether it is in the first two or last two.

† Compare the 3d of (18).

‡ Compare the 3d of (17).

$$\frac{\sin A}{\sin a} = \frac{\sin B}{\sin b} = \frac{\sin C}{\sin c}$$

The usual formulas for $\sin \frac{1}{2} A$, $\cos \frac{1}{2} A$, $\tan \frac{1}{2} A$ (see Art. 84), derived from (21), may be employed, and the ambiguity removed, by the same conditions.

Check.—Compute two of the functions $\sin \frac{1}{2} A$, $\cos \frac{1}{2} A$, $\tan \frac{1}{2} A$; or one of them in connexion with (21).

10. *Given* A, B, *and* C, *to find* a, b, *or* c. The formula (see Art. 88)

$$\cos a = \frac{\cos A + \cos B \cos C}{\sin B \sin C} \qquad (22)$$

determines *a when the sign of* sin a *is given;* or *when the sign of either* sin a, sin b, *or* sin c *is given,* since when the sign of any one of these functions is known, those of the other two may be discovered by an inspection of the equation

$$\frac{\sin A}{\sin a} = \frac{\sin B}{\sin b} = \frac{\sin C}{\sin c}$$

the usual formulas for $\sin \frac{1}{2} a$, $\cos \frac{1}{2} a$, $\tan \frac{1}{2} a$, may be employed, and the ambiguity removed, by the same conditions.

Check.—Compute two of the functions $\sin \frac{1}{2} a$, $\cos \frac{1}{2} a$, $\tan \frac{1}{2} a$; or one of them in connexion with (22).

10. From the preceding sketch it appears that for the determinate solution of a spherical triangle generally considered, there are required *four* data; namely, the numerical values of three of the six parts composing the triangle, and the algebraic sign of one of the functions of a required part. To recapitulate, the triangle is fully determined by the following data:—

1. b, c, A; and the sign of either $\sin a$, $\sin B$, $\cos B$, $\sin C$, or $\cos C$.
2. B, C, a; and the sign of either $\sin A$, $\sin b$, $\cos b$, $\sin c$, or $\cos c$.
3. a, b, A; and the sign of $\cos B$.
4. A, B a; and the sign of $\cos b$.
5. a, b, c; and the sign of either $\sin A$, $\sin B$, or $\sin C$.
6. A, B, C; and the sign of either $\sin a$, $\sin b$, or $\sin c$.

---

11. Since π is the symbol which represents the circumference of a circle whose diameter is unity, or the semicircumference whose radius is unity, $\frac{1}{2}\pi$ will represent a quadrant of the latter or 90°. We may, therefore, for convenience, represent the supplement of an arc a by $\pi - a$, and its complement by $\frac{1}{2}\pi - a$.

12. A triangle, one side of which is π or 90°, is called a quadrantal triangle; such triangles may be resolved by Napier's rules for the circular parts, if the quadrantal side be neglected, and $\frac{1}{2}\pi - b$, $\frac{1}{2}\pi - c$, B, C, and $A - \frac{1}{2}\pi$ be taken for the circular parts.

For let $A'B'C'$ be the polar triangle. It will be right angled because $A = \pi - a = \frac{1}{2}\pi$. Applying Napier's rule to this triangle we obtain

$$\cos a' = \cos b' \cos c' = \cot B' \cot C' \qquad (1)$$
$$\sin b' = \sin B' \sin a = \cot C' \tan c' \qquad (2)$$
$$\cos B = \cos b \sin C = \cot a' \tan c \qquad (3)$$

These are the expressions for each of the parts of a right angled triangle in terms of two others, because expressions for c' and C' would be exactly like (2) and (3).

Substituting $\pi - A$, $\pi - a$, &c., for A', a', &c. in the above equations, they become

$$-\cos A = \cos B \cos c = \cot b \cot c$$
$$\sin B = \sin b \sin A = \cot c \tan C$$
$$-\cos b = -\cos B \sin c = \cot A \tan c$$

But these last equations are precisely what would be obtained by the application of Napier's rules, using the complements of b and c, and $A - \frac{1}{2}\pi$ as the circular parts.

13. Napier's rules may be deduced as follows :

The following formulas have been derived in the foregoing pages for oblique angled triangles.

Art. 82.

$$\cos a = \cos b \cos c + \sin b \sin c \cos A \quad (1)$$
$$\cos a \sin B \sin C = \cos A + \cos B \cos C \quad (2)*$$
$$\cos c \sin A \sin B = \cos C + \cos A \cos B \quad (3)*$$
$$\sin c \sin A = \sin a \sin C \quad (4)†$$
$$\cot c \sin b = \cos b \cos A + \sin A \cot C \quad (5)‡$$
$$\cot a \sin c = \cos c \cos B + \sin B \cot A \quad (6)‡$$

Making in the above forms $A = 90°$ they become

$$\cos a = \cos b \cos c \quad (1)$$
$$\cos a = \cot B \cot C \quad (2)$$
$$\cos C = \cos c \sin B \quad (3)$$
$$\cos B = \cos b \sin C$$
$$\sin c = \sin a \sin C \quad (4)$$
$$\sin b = \sin a \sin B$$
$$\sin b = \tan c \cot C \quad (5)$$
$$\sin c = \tan b \cot B$$
$$\cos B = \cot a \tan c \quad (6)$$
$$\cos C = \cot a \tan b$$

The above are but expressions of Napier's rules.

14. The case of solution treated at Art. 94, may be solved by Napier's Analogies. Thus if a, b and A be given, B may be calculated by the sin proportion, and C and c by the formulas

$$\sin \tfrac{1}{2}(a - b) : \sin \tfrac{1}{2}(a + b) :: \tan \tfrac{1}{2}(A - B) : \cot \tfrac{1}{2} C$$
$$\sin \tfrac{1}{2}(A - B) : \sin \tfrac{1}{2}(A + B) :: \tan \tfrac{1}{2}(a - b) : \tan \tfrac{1}{2} c$$

15. Napier's rules for the solution of right angled spherical triangles, though applicable to all cases, do not give results of that degree of accuracy which is some-

* (2) and (3) are the same, and are derived from (1) by polar triangles.

† Sine proportion, Art. 81.

‡ Appendix II. See formula at top of p. 200.

times required, when the required part expressed by its sine is very small, or expressed by its cosine is very near 90°. The following formulas may in such cases be used.

I.

By formula (8), Art. 72,

and p. 76, 2d note.

$$\left.\begin{aligned}1-\cos p &= 2\sin^2 \tfrac{1}{2}p \\ 1+\cos p &= 2\cos^2 p\end{aligned}\right\} \quad (m)$$

whence

$$\frac{1-\cos p}{1+\cos p} = \tan^2 \tfrac{1}{2} p$$

But by Napier's rules, R being 1,

$$\cos a = \cot B \cot C$$

changing p into a, and substituting the value of $\cos a$, given by this last, we have

$$\tan^2 \tfrac{1}{2} a = \frac{1-\cot B \cot C}{1+\cot B \cot C} = \frac{\sin B \sin C - \cos B \cos C}{\sin B \sin C + \cos B \cos C}$$

or

$$\tan^2 \tfrac{1}{2} a = -\frac{\cos (B+C)}{\cos (B-C)}$$

which is a formula to be employed, when B and C are given and a required.

II.

With the same data to find b use the formula

$$\tan \tfrac{1}{2} b = \sqrt{\left\{\tan [\tfrac{1}{2}(B-C)+45°] \tan [\tfrac{1}{2}(B+C)-45°]\right\}}$$

derived from Napier's rules, which gives

$\cos b = \dfrac{\cos B}{\sin C}$, from the formulas preceding (1) and (4) of Art. 12, App. I. and from formula (42), Art. 15, App. I.

III.

The hypothenuse a and the side c being given to find the adjacent angle B, use the formula

$$\tan \tfrac{1}{2} B = \sqrt{\frac{\sin (a-c)}{\sin (a+c)}}$$

derived in a manner similar to that in case I.

IV.

Given a and b to find c; by Napier's rules

$$\cos c = \frac{\cos a}{\cos b}$$

add and subtract 1; by App. I., Art. 15, formula (52), and forms. (m) above

$$\tan \tfrac{1}{2} c = \tan \tfrac{1}{2}(a+b) \tan \tfrac{1}{2}(a-b)$$

V.

Finally, to obtain b when the opposite angle B and the hypothenuse a are given, we have, by Napier's rules,

$$\sin b = \sin a \sin B$$

whence, observing that $\frac{1 - \tan x}{1 + \tan x} = \tan (45^\circ - x)$, App. I., Art. 15, form. (43), and making $\tan x = \sin a \sin B$,

$$(\tan 45^\circ - \tfrac{1}{2} b) = \sqrt{\tan (45^\circ - x)}$$

16. The part of a spherical triangle determined by the proportion $\sin a : \sin b :: \sin A : \sin B$ admits of a double value, since two arcs answer to the same sine; it becomes necessary, therefore, for us to inquire under what circumstances both these values are admissible, and how we may know which to choose when but one solution exists.

Referring to the fundamental formula (Art. 82), we have

$$\cos B = \frac{\cos b - \cos a \cos c}{\sin a \sin c}; \qquad (2)$$

in which expression we may remark that if $\cos b$ is numerically greater than either $\cos a$ or $\cos c$, the second member must take the sign of $\cos b$, consequently B and b must be of the same affection if $\sin b < \sin a$, or $\sin b < \sin c$, that is, *an angle must be of the same species as its opposite side, if the sine of this side is less than the sine of either of the other sides.*

But if $\cos b$ is numerically less than $\cos a$, then whether the right hand member be + or — will depend upon the magnitude of $\cos c$, or $\cos c$ will have two values corresponding to $+ \cos B$, and $- \cos B$; hence *an angle has two values, when the sine of its opposite side is greater than the sine of the other given side.*

In the proportion

$$\sin A : \sin B :: \sin a : \sin b$$

a being the required part, the nature of the arc b may be discussed, as in the preceding case.

By means of the polar triangles, we obtain from (2), in the same manner as at Art. 85, the formula

$$\cos b = \frac{\cos B + \cos A \cos C}{\sin A \sin C}$$

from which it follows, as in the foregoing case, that if $\cos B$ is numerically greater than $\cos A$, B and b will be of the same affection. If $\cos B$ is numerically less than $\cos A$, then both the values of b, given by the above proportion, will be admissible, for c may be determined so as to render $\cos b$ positive or negative. Hence *any side will be of the same affection as its opposite angle, if the sine of this angle be less than the sine of either of the other angles; and the affection of the side* b *will be indeterminate if the sine of its opposite angle* B *be greater than the sine of the other given angle* A.

17. In practice, the data for the solution of triangles are obtained by observation and measurement, and are liable to error from obvious and inevitable causes. It is true that from the great excellency of instruments, and the almost inconceivable accuracy of modern observation, these errors are extremely minute, yet in cases where precision is requisite, it becomes necessary to determine the effects which small errors in the data will produce upon the computed quantities, and to select the data and quæsita in such a manner that the given errors in the one shall entail the smallest possible on the other.

The principles of the Differential Calculus present an easy method for the purpose in question, and we shall here indicate the mode of proceeding, for the benefit of the student acquainted with that branch of mathematics.

Let us suppose that of the three data (for there are always three in the solution of a triangle), two have been obtained with sufficient accuracy, but the third x is liable to an error of a given amount, which we shall call h. Let u be the sought quantity. Two of the three data being considered constant, the sought quantity u may be considered as a function of the third x. The quantity x becoming $x + h$, let the quantity u become u', we have by Taylor's theorem,

$$u' - u = \frac{du}{dx} h + \frac{d^2u}{dx^2} h^2 + \frac{d^3u}{dx^3} h^3 + \&c.$$

$u' - u$ is the error sought, and as h is in practice very small, the higher powers of it may be neglected, and we may call

$$u' - u = \frac{du}{dx} h$$

hence the following rule:

Multiply the given error by the differential coefficient of the sought quantity considered as a function of *the given quantity liable to error, and the product will be the error in the sought quantity.*

If two of the data be liable to given errors, the effect upon the sought quantity may be computed on similar principles, by considering the sought quantity as a function of the two data so liable to error, and differentiating it with respect to these two independent variables.

It is evident that the same method extends to the case where all the data are liable to given small errors. In this case the sought quantity is to be regarded as a function of three independent variables, and its differential found as before.

EXAMPLE.

To determine the relation between the minute variations of the perpendicular side of a plane right angled triangle and the opposite angle, the remaining perpendicular side being considered constant.

Let c and c be the side and angle which are subject to variation, and b the constant side. Then (Art. 41),

$$c = b \tan \mathrm{c}$$

and (Dif. Cal.)

$$\frac{dc}{d\mathrm{c}} = b \sec^2 \mathrm{c}$$

which is the multiplier of the given small variation in c to obtain that in c.

The theory of maxima and minima as explained in the Calculus, will here admit of an important and easy application, viz., to find under what circumstances $u' - u$ will be least on the supposition of a given variation h in the variable datum, or in other words, under what circumstances the function $\frac{du}{dx}$ will be a minimum.

17. The effects of small errors may be obtained, but with less brevity and elegance, without the aid of the differential calculus.

The following are specimens of the mode of proceeding.

PROBLEM I.

In a right-angled triangle one of the oblique angles being given, to determine the variation of the opposite side, arising from a small variation in the hypothenuse.

Let C be the angle which does not change, c its opposite side, and a the hypothenuse; then δc denoting the variation of c, and δa of a

$$\sin c = \sin C \sin a$$
$$\sin (c + \delta c) = \sin C \sin (a + \delta a)$$

$\therefore$ by subtraction,

$$\sin (c + \delta c) - \sin c = \sin C \left\{\sin (a + \delta a) - \sin a\right\},$$

that is (Art. 74, formula 4),

$$2 \cos (c + \tfrac{1}{2} \delta c) \sin \tfrac{1}{2} \delta c = 2 \sin C \cos (a + \tfrac{1}{2} \delta a) \sin \tfrac{1}{2} \delta a$$

$$\therefore \sin \tfrac{1}{2} \delta c = \frac{\sin C \cos (a + \frac{1}{2} \delta a) \sin \frac{1}{2} \delta a}{\cos (c + \frac{1}{2} \delta c}$$

and if δa, δc be very small,

$$\delta c = \frac{\sin C \cos a}{\cos c} \delta a;$$

or, substituting for sin C its value from the first equation,

$$\delta c = \frac{\sin c}{\cos c} \cdot \frac{\cos a}{\sin a} \delta a = \tan c \cot a \, \delta a;$$

which variation will be the least possible when cot a is least, or when $a = 90^\circ$. If we restore the $\frac{1}{2} \delta a$ which has been neglected, and write the above result thus:

$$\delta c = \tan c \cot (a + \tfrac{1}{2} \delta a) \delta a;$$

then, in the case of $a = 90^\circ$, the expression becomes

$$\delta c = - \tan c \tan \tfrac{1}{2} \delta a \cdot \delta a;$$

or, considering the very small arc $\frac{1}{2} \delta a$ to be equal to its tangent, we have in the case supposed

$$\delta c = - \tfrac{1}{2} \tan c \, (\delta a)^2.$$

PROBLEM II.

In an oblique-angled spherical triangle given two sides to determine the variation produced in the third side by a small variation of the opposite angle.

Let a, b be the two given sides, C the included angle, and c the opposite side. Then

$$\cos c = \cos a \cos b + \sin a \sin b \cos C$$
$$\cos (c + \delta c) = \cos a \cos b + \sin a \sin b \cos (C + \delta C);$$

∴ by subtraction,

$$\cos (c + \delta c) - \cos c = \sin a \sin b \left\{ \cos (C + \delta C) - \cos C \right\};$$

that is,

$$2 \sin (c + \delta c) \sin \tfrac{1}{2} \delta c = 2 \sin a \sin b \sin (C + \tfrac{1}{2} \delta C) \sin \tfrac{1}{2} \delta C$$

Hence, if δC be very small,

$$\sin c \, \delta c = \sin a \sin b \sin C \, \delta C$$
$$\therefore \delta c = \frac{\sin a \sin b \sin C}{\sin c} \delta C$$
$$= \sin a \sin B \delta C;$$

and δc is therefore the least possible when $\sin C$ is the least possible, that is, when $C = 0$. To find the expression for δc, in this case, restore what has been rejected, and we shall have

$$\delta c = \frac{\sin a \sin b \sin (C + \frac{1}{2} \delta C)}{\sin c} \delta C;$$

which, when $C = 0$, and $\frac{1}{2} \delta C$ very small, becomes

$$\delta c = \frac{\sin a \sin b}{2 \sin c} (\delta C)^2$$

PROBLEM III.

In an oblique angled spherical triangle given two sides and the included angle, to find the variation in one of the opposite angles corresponding to a small variation in the included angle.

Let a, b be the given side, C the included angle, to find what influence a small variation in the value of C will have on A opposite a. Substitute the expression for $\cos c$ above, in the corresponding expression for $\cos a$, and $1 - \sin^2 b$ for $\cos^2 b$, there results

$$\cos A \sin c = \cos a \sin b - \sin a \cos b \cos C;$$

$$\therefore \cos A \frac{\sin c}{\sin a} = \cot a \sin b - \cos b \cos C$$

But

$$\frac{\sin c}{\sin a} = \frac{\sin C}{\sin A}$$

Then, by substitution,

$$\cot A \sin C = \cot a \sin b - \cos b \cos C$$
$$\cot (A + \delta A) \sin (C + \delta C) = \cot a \sin b - \cos b \cos (C + \delta C);$$

and, by subtraction,

$$\cot (A + \delta A) \sin (C + \delta C) - \cot A \sin C = \cos b \{\cos C - \cos (C + \delta C)\} \quad (1)$$

The first member of this equation is equal to

$$\cot (A + \delta A) \{\sin (C + \delta C) - \sin C\} + \sin C \{\cot (C + \delta A) - \cot A\};$$

and the quantities within the brackets are respectively equal to

$$2 \cos (C + \tfrac{1}{2} \delta C) \sin \tfrac{1}{2} \delta C \text{ and } \frac{-\sin \delta A}{\sin A \sin (A + \delta A)}.$$

The second member of (1) is equal to

$$\cos b \cdot 2 \sin (C + \tfrac{1}{2} \delta C) \sin \tfrac{1}{2} \delta C$$

$$\therefore 2 \cot (A + \delta A) \cos (C + \tfrac{1}{2} \delta C) \sin \tfrac{1}{2} \delta C - \frac{\sin C \sin \delta A}{\sin A \sin (A + \delta A)} = 2 \cos b \sin (C + \tfrac{1}{2} \delta C) \sin \tfrac{1}{2} \delta C$$

and consequently when δC and δA are very small,

$$\cot A \cos C \delta C - \frac{\sin C}{\sin^2 A} \delta A = \cos b \sin C \delta C$$

$$\therefore \delta A = \frac{\sin^2 A}{\sin C} (\cot A \cos C - \cos b \sin C) \delta C$$

PART III.

NAVIGATION.

PART III.

When a ship sails from any known place, and a correct account is kept of her various directions, and rates of sailing, her situation at any time may be determined by the rules of Plane Trigonometry. The processes employed for this purpose constitute what is called *Navigation.*

But, owing to the imperfection of the instruments with which a ship's course and the distance sailed are observed, it would be unsafe, after a long passage, to compute the place of the ship from the *dead reckoning*, as the observed direction and distance are called. In such cases recourse must be had to astronomical observations, from which the place of the ship or its *latitude* and longitude are computed by the rules of Spherical Trigonometry. The problem then becomes one of *Nautical Astronomy.* We shall treat successively of each of these important branches.

NAVIGATION.

DEFINITIONS.

96. 1. For the purposes of Navigation the earth may be considered as spherical. It revolves about one of its diameters, called its *axis*, in twenty-four hours. This rotation is from west to east, causing the heavenly bodies to have an apparent motion from east to west.

2. The great circle, whose poles are the extremities of the axis, is called the *equator*. The poles of the equator are called also the *poles* of the earth; the one being the *north pole*, and the other the *south pole.*

3. Great circles passing through the poles are called *meridians.* Through every place on the surface of the earth such a great circle may be drawn, and will be the meridian of the place. The meridian from which the meridians of other places are estimated is called a *first meridian.*

The English have fixed upon the meridian of Greenwich Observatory for the first meridian, which has also been adopted in this country.

4. The *longitude* of any place is the arc of the equator, intercepted between the meridian of that place and the first meridian; the longitude, therefore, is the measure of the angle between the planes of the two meridians. The longitude is east or west, according as the place is situated east or west of the first meridian.

5. The *difference of longitude* between two places is the arc of the equator intercepted between the meridians of those places, or the measure of the angle which their planes include; hence, when the longitudes of the places are of the *same* denomination, that is, either both east or both west, the difference is found by *subtracting* the one from the other; but when they are of *contrary* denominations the difference is found by *adding* the one to the other.

6. The *latitude* of a place is its distance north or south of the equator, measured on the meridian of the place. Latitude cannot exceed 90°.

7. Small circles parallel to the equator, are called *parallels* of latitude. The arc of a meridian, intercepted between two such parallels, drawn through any two places, is the *difference of latitude* of those places; when the latitudes are of the same name, *i. e.*, both N. or both S., the difference of latitude is found by subtraction, but when not, the difference of latitude is found by addition.

8. The *horizon* of any place is an imaginary plane, touching the surface of the earth at that place, and extending to the heavens; such a plane is called the *sensible horizon*, and one parallel to it, but passing through the centre of the earth, the *rational horizon* of the place. The line of intersection of the plane of the horizon, and the plane of the meridian of a place, is called a north and south line; the horizontal line through the same point, and perpendicular to this, is called the east and west line. Besides the North, South, East, and West points, called cardinal points, thus determined on the boundary of the horizon, there are numerous subdivisions corresponding to the divisions in the circle on the next page.

9. The *course* of a ship is the angle which her track makes with the meridians; if this angle continued the same, and the meridians were all parallel, the path of the ship would be a straight line; but as the meridians bend towards the poles, the direction of her path is continually changing, and she moves in a curve, called the *rhumb line* or *loxodromic curve.* The instrument employed on ship-board to show the course of the ship is called the *mariner's compass.*

10. *The Mariner's Compass* consists of a circular card, whose circumference is divided into thirty-two equal parts, called *points*, and each

of these is subdivided into four equal parts, called quarter points; across this card, in the direction of a diameter, and fastened to the card, so that they move together, is fixed a slender bar of magnetized steel, called *the needle;* the extremities of which point to two diametrically opposite divisions of the card. These opposite divisions are marked N. and S., corresponding to the *north* and *south* poles, or ends, of the magnetized bar. The diameter E.W., at right angles to the diameter N.S., points out the east and west points.

One point from the north towards the east, is marked N.E., and called *north by east;* two points, N.N.E., and called *north north-east;* three points, *north-east by north;* and so on. Each quadrant contains eight points, so that a point is $90^{\circ} \div 8 = 11^{\circ}\ 15'$. (See Table of Rhumbs, Table XXVIII., at the end.)

The card thus furnished being now suspended horizontally, so as to move freely, and allow the needle attached to it, to settle itself, will point out the four cardinal points of the horizon, as also the several intermediate points, provided only that it is the property of the magnetic needle to point due north and south. Such, however, is not strictly the case, as is found by comparison with astronomical observations. The card rests at its centre, on a pivot placed in the vertical plane, cutting the ship from stem to stern, and is held stationary in space by the magnetic forces of the earth, whilst the ship turns under it in changing her course, so that that point of the compass which is directed to the ship's head shows the *ship's course*, which must be corrected for the slight variation of the compass from the meridian, a variation which is different in different parts of the earth; the method of determining it will be hereafter given.

11. A ship's *rate* of sailing is determined by means of an instrument called the *log*, and an attached line, called the *log-line*. The log is a piece of wood in the form of the sector of a circle, the rim of which is so loaded with lead, that when *heaved* into the sea it assumes a vertical position, having its centre barely above the water. The log-line is so

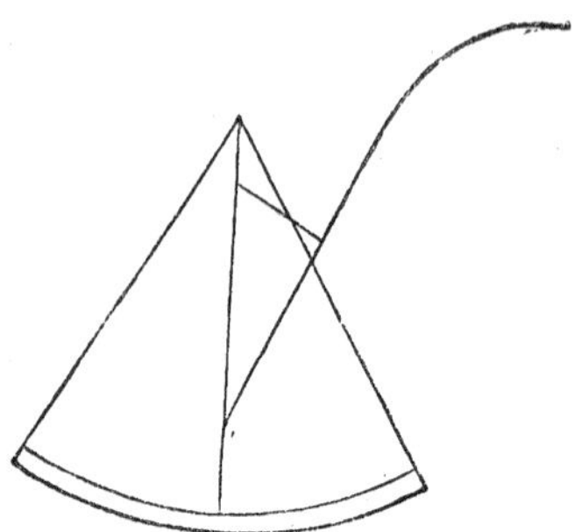

attached as to keep the face of the log towards the ship, that it may offer the greater resistance to being dragged after the ship by the log-line, as it unwinds from a reel on board, by the advancing motion of the ship. The log-line is divided into equal parts, called *knots*, of which each measures the 120th of a nautical or geographical mile.* A half minute sand glass is used in connexion with the log. When the log is heaved, the instant the first knot on the line passes the hand of a sailor, the half minute glass is turned by a word, and the instant the sand is run out, the line is caught by a word; as half a minute is the 120th of an hour, it follows that the number of knots, and parts of a knot, run in half a minute expresses the number of miles, and parts of a mile, run in an hour, at the same rate of sailing.

ON PLANE SAILING.

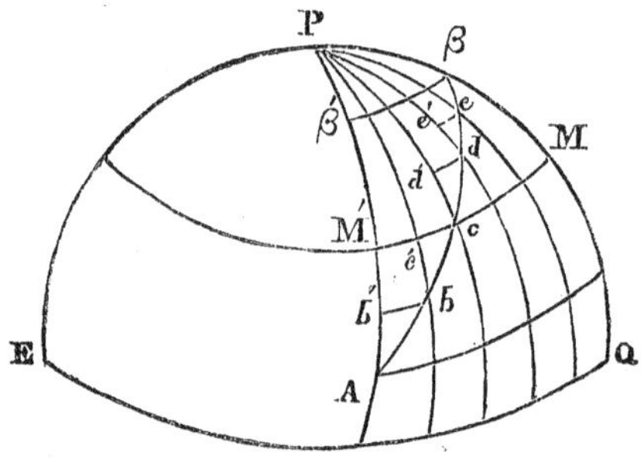

97. Let the annexed diagram represent a portion of the earth's surface, P the pole, and E Q the equator. Let A β be a rhumb line, or path described by a ship in sailing on a single course from A to β Let the rhumb line be divided into portions Ab, bc, cd, &c., so small that each may differ insensibly from a straight line, and draw meridians through these several divisions, as also the parallels of latitude bb', cc', dd', &c.; a series of triangles will thus be described on the surface of the globe, but so small that each may be considered as a plane triangle. These triangles are all similar, for the angles at b', c', d', &c., are right-angles, and the ship's path cuts all the meridians at equal angles; hence (Theorem 63 Geom.),

$$Ab : Ab' :: bc : bc' :: cd : cd', \&c.$$

* The geographical mile is one minute of the earth's circumference. Taking the diameter at 7916 English miles the geographical mile will be about 6079 feet.

therefore, since by the theory of proportion the sum of the antecedents is to the sum of the consequents as any one antecedent is to its consequent,

$$Ab : Ab' :: Ab + bc + cd + \&c., : Ab' + bc' + cd' + \&c.$$

But $Ab + bc + cd + \&c.$, is the whole distance sailed, and $Ab' + bc' + cd' + \&c. = A\beta'$, is the difference of latitude between A and β; consequently, if a right angled triangle ABB', similar to the small triangle Abb' be constructed, that is, one in which the angle A is equal to the course, and the hypothenuse A B is equal to the distance sailed, the side A B' will represent the difference of latitude. Moreover, the other side BB', or that opposite to the course, will represent the sum $b'b + c'c + d'd + \&c.$ of all the minute *departures* which the ship makes from the successive meridians which it crosses; for as the triangle ABB', in this last diagram, is similar to the small triangle Abb', in the former we have

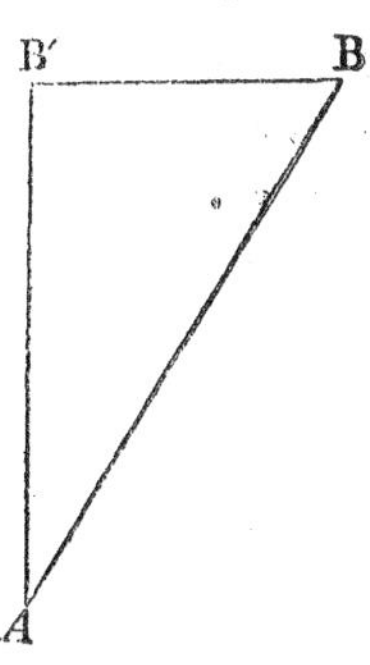

$$Ab : bb' :: AB : BB' \quad (1)$$

but in the first figure we have

$$Ab : bb' :: bc : cc' :: cd : dd', \&c.$$

$$\therefore Ab : bb' :: Ab + bc + cd + \&c. : bb' + cc' + dd' + \&c. \quad (2)$$

consequently, since the three first terms of (1) are respectively equal to those of (2), the fourth term BB', of (1), must be equal to the fourth term, $bb' + cc' + dd +$ of (2), &c. This last quantity is called the *departure* of the ship in sailing from A to β.* It follows, therefore, that the *distance sailed*, the *difference of latitude* made, and the *departure*, are correctly represented by the *hypothenuse* and *sides* of a right angled plane triangle, in which the angle opposite the departure is the *course*, so that when any two of these four things are given, the other two may be found simply by the resolution of a right angled plane triangle; so far, therefore, as these particulars are concerned, the results are the same as if the ship were sailing on a plane surface, the meridians being parallel straight lines, and the parallels of latitude cutting them at right angles; and hence that part of Navigation in which only distance sailed, departure, difference of latitude, and course are considered, is called *Plane Sailing.*

* The departure is not to be confounded with $\beta\beta'$ in the first diagram. It is greater than this, because the small departures bb', cc', &c., whose sum is the whole departure, lap over each other.

The two of the four elements which enter into problems of plane sailing usually given are course and distance, being found from observation.

EXAMPLES.

1. A ship from latitude 47° 30′ N. has sailed S.W. by S. 98 miles. At what latitude has she arrived, and what departure has she made?

Let C be the place sailed from, CB the meridian, the angle C = 3 points = 33° 45′, see Table of Rhumbs, and CA = 98 miles, the distance sailed; then CB will be the difference of latitude, and BA the departure. Then by the formulas for the solution of right angled triangles (forms (4) and (5) Art. 64)

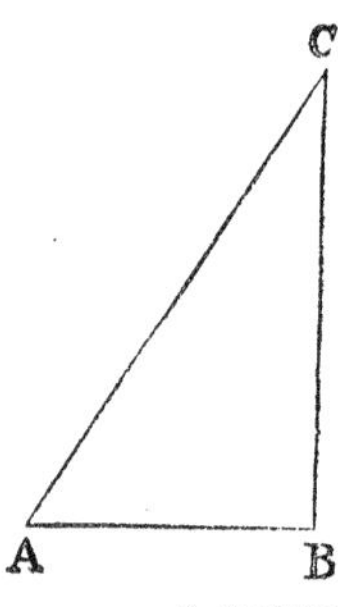

Dist.	98	log.	1·99123	log.	1·99123
Course	33° 45′	log. cos	9·91985	log. sin	9·74474
Diff. of lat.	81·48	log.	1·91108		
Dep.	54·45			log.	1·73597

Latitude left 47° 30′ N.

Diff. of lat. = 81·48* minutes = 1 22 S. Dep. = 52·45 miles W.

Latitude in 46 9 N.

2. A ship sails for 24 hours on a direct course, from lat. 38° 32′ N., till she arrives at lat. 36° 56′ N.; the course is between S. and E., and the rate $5\frac{1}{2}$ miles an hour. Required the course, distance and departure.

Lat. left 38° 32′ N. $24 \times 5\frac{1}{2} = 132$ miles, the distance.

Lat. in 36 56 N.

Diff. 1 36 = 96 miles.

Dist.	132	log.	2·12057	log.	2·12057
Diff. lat.	96	log.	1·98227		
Course	43° 20′	log. cos	9·86170	log. sin	9·83648
Dep.	90·58			log.	1·95705

Hence the course is S. 43° 20′ E., and the departure 90·58 miles E.

3. A ship sails from lat 3° 52′ S. to lat. 4° 30′ N., the course being N.W. by W. $\frac{1}{2}$ W.; required the distance and departure.

Distance, 1065 miles; Departure 939·2 miles W.

* See last note but one. Miles are converted into degrees, &c., by dividing by 60.

4. Two ports lie under the same meridian, one in latitude 52° 30′ N. and the other in latitude 47° 10′ N. A ship from the southernmost sails due east, at the rate of 9 miles an hour, and two days after meets a sloop which had sailed from the northernmost port; required the sloop's direct course and distance run.

Course S. 53° 28′ E., or S.E. ¾ E.; distance run 537·6 miles.

5. If a ship from lat. 48° 27′ S. sail S.W. by W. 7 miles an hour, in what time will she arrive at the parallel of 50° S?

In 23·914 hours.

6. If after a ship has sailed from lat. 40° 21′ N. to lat. 46° 18′ N., she be found 216 miles to the eastward of the port left; required her course and distance sailed. Course N. 31° 11′ E., distance 417·3 miles.

TRAVERSE SAILING

98. Is where a ship, in going from one place to another, sails on different courses; the determination of the single course and distance from the one place to the other is called *working* or *compounding* the traverse. The method of proceeding is to rule seven columns (see next page), the first to contain the courses, the second the number of points and quarter points in these courses which may be found from the table of Rhumbs (Tab, XXVIII.), the third the distances sailed on these courses, the fourth and fifth the differences of latitude in two columns entitled N. and S., in the former of which the dif. of lat. for the N. courses is entered, and in the latter of which the dif. of lat. for the S. courses; the sixth and seventh contain the departures, the former those of the E. courses, the latter those of the W. courses, sometimes called *eastings* and *westings*.

When these several particulars are all inserted, the columns are added up, and the difference of the sums of the N. and S. columns will be the whole difference of the latitude which the ship has made, and the difference of the sums of the E. and W. columns will be her whole departure.

The columns appropriated to the difference of latitude and departures are usually filled up from a table (Table I.), already computed to every quarter point of the compass, and to all distances from one mile up to 300; so that by entering this table with any given course and distance, the proper difference of latitude and departure is found by inspection.

The course is found at the top or bottom of the page, and the distance in the first column, the dif. of lat. in the second column, and the departure in the third, if the course be found at top; but if at the bottom, the lat. and dep. columns are interchanged, as may be seen by the entitling in the bottom of the columns. If the distance sailed be more than 300 miles, it will exceed the limit of the table; but the difference of latitude and departure may still be determined from it by this simple operation: divide the given distance by any number that will give a quotient not exceeding 300; enter the table with this quotient, and multiply the corresponding diff. of lat. and dep. by the assumed divisor, and there will result the diff. of lat. and dep. due to the proposed distance. If there be a remainder add the diff. of lat. and dep. corresponding to this. Or take any two numbers whose sum is equal to the given distance; the sum of their differences of lat. and dep. will be the lat and dep. of the given distance. These rules depend upon the principle that for the same course the differences of latitude and departure are proportional to the distance run, which will be evident if we recollect that dist., diff. of lat. and dep. form a right angled triangle, and that two right angled triangles are similar when an acute angle of one is equal to an acute angle of the other.

EXAMPLE.

1. A ship sails from lat. 24° 32′ N., and runs the following courses and distances, viz.

1st, S.W. by W., distance 45 miles; 2d, E. S. E., distance 50 miles; 3d, S.W., distance 30 miles; 4th, S.E. by E., distance 60 miles; 5th, S.W. by S. ¼ W., distance 63 miles: required her present latitude, with the direct course and distance from the place left, to the place arrived at.

TRAVERSE TABLE.

COURSES.	PTS.	DIST.	DIFFERENCE OF LAT.		DEPARTURE.	
			N.	S.	E.	W.
S. W. by W.	5	45		25·0		37·4
E. S. E.	6	50		19·1	46·2	
S. W.	4	30		21·2		21·2
S. E. by E.	5	60		33·3	49·9	
S. W. by S. ¼ W.	3¼	63		50·6		37·5
				149.2	96·1	96·1

It appears from the results of this table that the difference of latitude made by the ship during the traverse is 149·2 S. =2° 29′ S.

Lat. left	24°	32′	N.
Diff. lat.	2	29	S.
Lat. in	22	3	N.

It appears also that the departures east are equal to the departures west, so that the ship has returned to the meridian she sailed from, consequently the direct course from the place left to that come to is due south, and the distance is equal to the difference of latitude, which is 149·2 miles.

There is another mode of finding the direct course and distance, much practised by seamen, viz., by construction. For this purpose the *mariner's scale* is employed, which is a two foot flat rule exhibiting several scales on each side, by help of which and a pair of compasses the usual problems in sailing may be all solved. One of these scales, which is called a scale of rhumbs, is a scale of chords, to every point and quarter point of the compass; and another is a more enlarged scale of chords to every degree. Both these scales are constructed for a circle with the same common radius, so that the chords on the scale of rhumbs belong to that circle whose radius equals the chord of 60° on the scale of chords; and the method of laying down a traverse from these scales, and a scale of equal parts, and of thence measuring the equivalent single course, and distance made good, will be at once understood from the example.

Construction of the traverse for the last example is as follows:

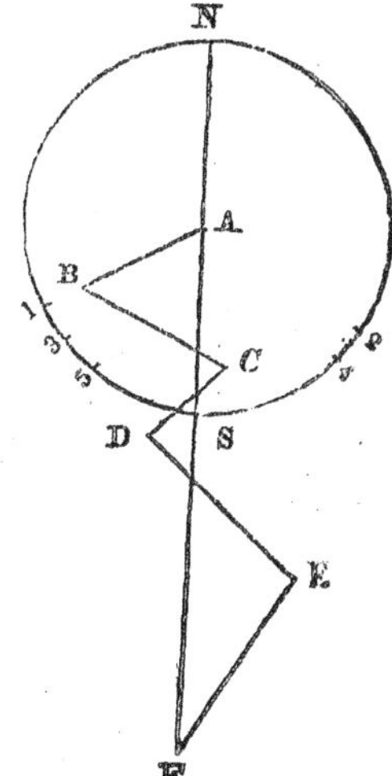

With the chord of 60°, taken from the line of chords on the mariner's scale, describe the horizon circle, and draw the north and south line N. S. From the line of rhumbs take the chords of the several courses, and as these are all southerly they must be laid off from the south point S, those which are westerly to the left, and those which are easterly to the right, their extremities being marked 1, 2, 3, &c., in the order of the courses. This done, lay off from any scale of equal parts, and in the direction of A1, the distance AB sailed on the first course; then in the direction parallel to A2, the distance BC sailed on the second course; in the direction parallel to A3, the distance CD on the third course; in the direction parallel to

A4, the distance DE on the fourth course; and, lastly, in the direction parallel to A5, the distance EF on the fifth course; then F will represent the place of the ship at the end of the traverse; FA, being applied to the scale of equal parts, will show the distance made good, and the chord of the arc included between this distance, and the meridian, being applied to the line of rhumbs, will show the direct course. In the present case the intercepted arc will be 0, showing that F is on the meridian of A.

2. A ship from Cape Clear, in lat 51° 25′ N., sails 1st, S.S.E. ¼ E., 16 miles; 2d, E.S.E., 23 miles; 3d, S.W. by W. ½ W., 36 miles; 4th, W. ¾ N., 12 miles; 5th, S.E. by E. ¼ E., 41 miles: required the distance made good, the direct course, and the latitude reached?

TRAVERSE TABLE.

COURSES.	PTS.	DIST.	DIFFERENCE OF LAT.		DEPARTURE.	
			N.	S.	E.	W.
S.S.E. ¼ E.	2¼	16		14·5	6·8	
E.S.E.	6	23		8·8	21·3	
S.W. by W. ½ W.	5½	36		17·0		31·8
W. ¾ N.	7¼	12	1·8			11·9
S.E. by E. ¼ E.	5¼	41		21·1	35·2	
			1·8	61·4	63·3	43·7
				1·8	43·7	
				59·6	19·6	

Lat. left	51° 25′	N.
Diff. lat 59·6 miles	1 0	S.
Lat. in	50 25	N.

Then by means of the whole dif. of lat. and dep., which are the two perpendicular sides of a right angled triangle, one of the acute angles and hypothenuse, or the direct course and distance, may be computed as follows:

diff. lat. 59·6 log.	1·77525		
departure 19·6 log.	1·29226	log.	1·29226
course 18° 12′ log. tan	9·51701	log. sin	9·49462
			1·79764
distance 62·74			

therefore, as the difference of latitude is south, and the departure east, the direct course is S. 18° 12′ E., and the distance made good 62·74 miles.

To construct this traverse, describe, as before, the horizon circle, with a radius equal to the chord of 60°, and taking from the line of rhumbs the chord of the first course, $2\frac{1}{4}$ points, apply it from S to 1, to the right of S N, as this course is south-easterly; apply, in like manner, the chord of the second course, six points from S to 2, also to the right of the meridian line; apply the chord of the third course, $5\frac{1}{2}$ points from S to 3, to the left of the meridian, the chord of the fourth course, $7\frac{1}{4}$ from N. to 4, to the left of N S, this course being north-westerly, and, lastly, apply the chord of the fifth course, $5\frac{1}{4}$ points, from S to 5, to the right of S N. In the direction A1, lay off the distance AB = 16 miles from a scale of equal parts; in the direction parallel to A2, lay off the distance BC = 23 miles; in the direction parallel to A3, lay off CD = 36; in the direction parallel to A4 lay off DE = 12 miles; and, lastly, in the direction parallel to A5, lay off EF = 41; then F will be the place of the ship at the end of the traverse; consequently, AF will be the distance made good, and the angle FAS the direct course; applying, therefore, the distance AF to the scale of equal parts, we shall find it reach from 0 to $62\frac{3}{4}$; and applying the distance Sa to the line of chords, we shall find it reach from 0 to 18°, or by the scale of rhumbs it will be found to measure one point and a half.

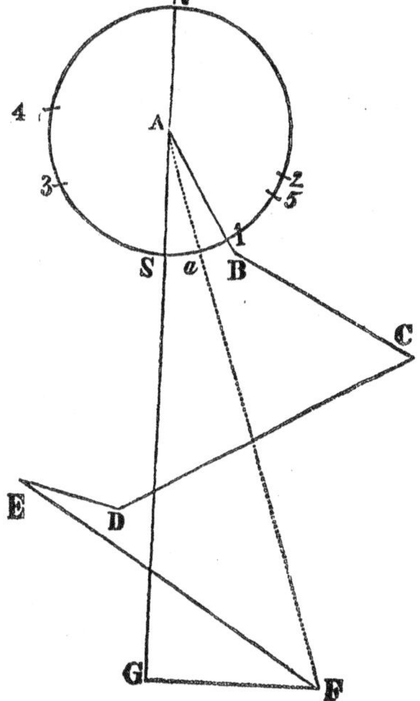

3. A ship from lat. 28° 32′ N., has run the following courses, viz., 1st, N.W. by N., 20 miles; 2d, S.W., 40 miles; 3d, N.E. by E., 60 miles; 4th, S. E. 55 miles; 5th, W. by S., 41 miles; 6th, E. N. E., 66 miles. Required her present latitude, the distance made good, and the direct course from the place left.

The direct course is due east, and distance 70•2 miles, the ship being in the same latitude at the end as at the beginning of the traverse.

4. A ship from lat. 41° 12′ N., sails S.W by W. 21 miles; S.W. ½ S. 31 miles; W. S.W. ½ S., 16 miles; S. ¾ E., 18 miles; S.W. ¼ W., 14 miles; and W. ½ N., 30 miles; required the latitude of the place arrived at, and the direct course and distance.

Lat. 40° 5′ N.; course S. 52° 49′ W.; distance 111•7 miles.

5. A ship runs the following courses, viz.

1st, S. E., 40 miles; 2d, N. E., 28 miles; 3d, S.W. by W., 52 miles; 4th, N.W. by W., 30 miles; 5th, S. S. E., 36 miles; 6th, S. E. by E., 58 miles; required the direct course and distance made good. Direct course S. 25° 42′ E., or S. S. E. ¼ E. nearly; distance 95•69 miles.

These examples will sufficiently illustrate the principles of plane sailing, in which, course, distance, difference of latitude, and departure, are the only quantities which enter into the problem, two of them being always given. The determination of the difference of longitude made on any course, which is the distance between the meridians measured on the equator, cannot be effected by these principles, for this element is not the same as if the meridians were all parallel to each other, as is the case with the other elements. The finding of the difference of longitude is the easiest when the ship sails due east or due west, that is, upon a parallel of latitude; this is called

PARALLEL SAILING.

99. The theory of parallel sailing is comprehended in the following proposition, which admits of a variety of other applications.

The arc of a great circle comprehended between two of its secondaries is to the arc of a parallel small circle, comprehended between the same secondaries, as radius unity is to the cosine of the distance between the great circle and its parallel, measured on one of the secondaries. (See Spherical Geom., Prob. 2, Cor. 6.)

Applied to the case under consideration the above proposition would run as follows, viz:

The cosine of the latitude of the parallel is to the distance run as the radius to the difference of longitude. This may be demonstrated as follows:

Let IQH represent the equator, and BDA any parallel of latitude; CI will be the radius of the equator, and *c*B the radius of the parallel. Let BD be the distance sailed, then the difference of longitude will be measured by the arc IQ of the equator, and since similar arcs are to each as the radii of the circles to which they belong, we have

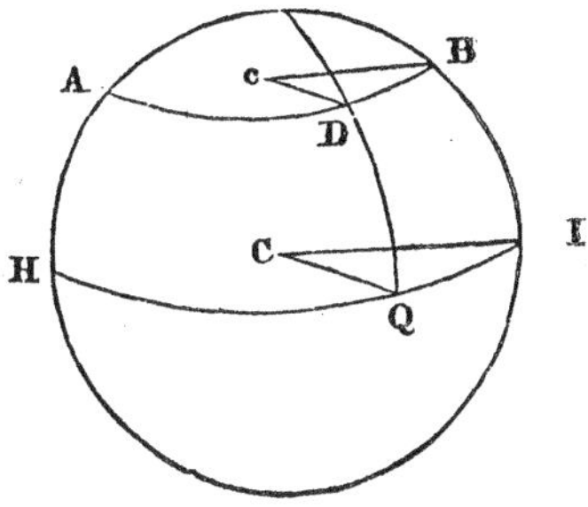

*c*B : CI : : dist. BD : diff. long. IQ

But *c*B is the cosine of the latitude IB to the radius CI, and as cosine and radius are proportional in different circles,

*c*B : CI : : cos lat. : R

The first two terms of these proportions being the same, the last are proportional, and we have

cos lat. : Rad. : : distance : diff. long. (1)

Corollary: hence if the distance between any two meridians, measured on a parallel in latitude L be D, and the distance of the same meridians, measured on a parallel, in latitude L′ be D′, we shall have (Spher. Geom., Prop. II., Cor. 6),

cos L : D : : cos L′ : D′ (2)

for both the ratios of (2) will be equal to R : diff. long.

By referring to proportion (1) it will be seen that if any one of the legs of a right-angled triangle represent the distance run on any parallel, and the adjacent acute angle be equal to the degrees of lat. of that parallel, then the hypothenuse will represent the difference of longitude, since this hypothenuse will be determined by that proportion.

The right angled triangle used in plane sailing may therefore be employed here, changing the names of its elements, viz., *course* into *latitude*, *difference* of *latitude* into *distance*, and *distance* into *difference of longitude.*

And a traverse table computed to degrees and fractions of a degree instead of points and quarter points, may be employed to solve problems in parallel sailing.

Formula (1) above may be expressed by the following rule. *Divide the distance sailed by the cosine of the latitude, and the quotient will be the difference of longitude.*

EXAMPLES.

1. A ship from latitude 53° 56′ N., longitude 10° 18′ E., has sailed due west, 236 miles : required her present longitude.

By the rule

lat.	53° 56	log. cos	9·76991
dist.	236	log.	2·37291
diff. long.	409	log.	2·60300

Long. left	10° 18′ E.
Diff. long. $= \frac{409}{60}$ degrees $=$	6 49 W.
Long. reached	3 29 E.

2. If a ship sail E. 126 miles, from the North Cape, in lat. 71° 10′ N., and then due N., till she reaches lat. 73° 26′ N.; how far must she sail W. to reach the meridian of the North Cape?

Here the ship sails on two parallels of latitude, first on the parallel of 71° 10′, and then on the parallel of 73° 26′, and makes the same difference of longitude on each parallel. Hence by the corollary,

As cos. lat.	71° 10′	arith. comp.	0·49104
: distance	126		2·10037
: : cos lat.	73 26		9·45504
: distance	111·3		2·04645

3. A ship in latitude 32° N. sails due east, till her difference of longitude is 384 miles; required the distance run.

325·6 miles.

4. If two ships in latitude 44° 30′ N., distant from each other 216 miles, should both sail directly south till their distance is 256 miles, what latitude would they arrive at?

32° 17′ N.

5. Two ships in the parallel of 47° 54′ N., have 9° 35′ difference of longitude, and they both sail directly south, a distance of 836 miles

required their distance from each other at the parallel left, and at that reached.

385·5 miles, and 476·9 miles.

MIDDLE LATITUDE SAILING.

100. Having seen how the longitude which a ship makes when sailing on a parallel of latitude may be determined, we come now to examine the more general problem, viz., to find the longitude a ship makes when sailing upon any oblique rhumb.

There are two methods of solving this problem, the one by what is called *middle latitude sailing*, and the other by *Mercator's sailing.* The first of these methods is confined in its application, and is moreover somewhat inaccurate even where applicable; the second is perfectly general, and rigorously true; but still there are cases in which it is advisable to employ the method of middle latitude sailing, in preference to that of Mercator's sailing; it is, therefore, proper that middle latitude sailing should be explained, especially since, by means of a correction to be hereafter noticed, the usual inaccuracy of this method may be rectified.

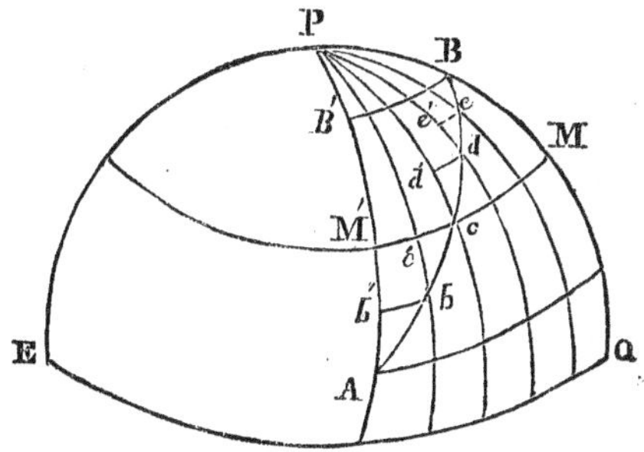

Middle latitude sailing proceeds on the supposition that the departure or sum of all the meridional distances bb', cc', dd', &c. from A to B, is equal to the distance M'M of the meridians of A and B, measured on the middle parallel of latitude between A and B.

This supposition becomes very inaccurate when the course is small, and the distance run great; for it is plain that the middle latitude distance between the extreme meridians will be much greater than the departure, if the track A B cuts the successive meridians at a very small angle.

The principle approaches nearer to accuracy as the angle A of the course increases, because then as but little advance is made in latitude, the several component departures lie more in the immediate vicinity of the middle latitude parallel. But since in very high latitudes, a small advance in latitude makes a considerable difference in meridional distance, this principle is not to be recommended in such latitudes if much accuracy is required.

By means, however, of a small table of corrections, constructed by Mr. WORKMAN, the imperfections of the middle latitude method may be removed, and the result of it rendered in all cases accurate. This table we have given at the end of the present volume.

The rules for middle latitude sailing may be thus deduced.

It has been seen at (Art. 97), that the difference of latitude, departure, and distance sailed on any oblique rhumb, may be all accurately represented by the sides AB′, B′B, AB, of a right angled plane triangle. Now, by the present hypothesis, the departure B′B is equal to the middle latitude distance between the meridians of the places sailed from, and arrived at, so that the difference of longitude of the two places of the ship is the same as if it had sailed the distance B′B on the middle latitude parallel; the determination of this difference of longitude is, therefore, reduced to a case of parallel sailing; and since, as we have seen (p. 215), the formula for parallel sailing is a proportion which expresses the relation between the elements of a right angled plane triangle in which the base is the dist. sailed, the angle at the base the lat., and the hypothenuse the diff. of long., let B′BA′ be this triangle, in which, according to the theory of mid. lat. sailing, the departure B′B takes the place of the dist. sailed. From these triangles, the two partial ones of which are right angled, and the total one not, we have the following theorems, viz., in the triangle A′B′B,

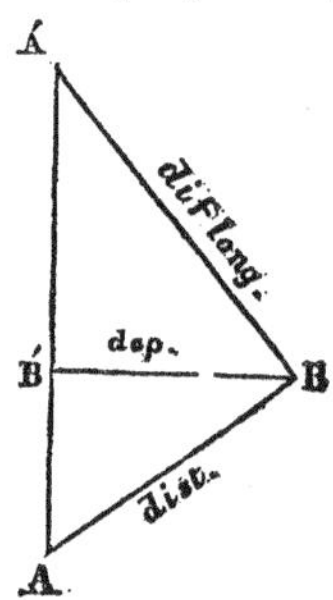

$$\cos A'BB' : BB' :: \text{radius} : BA'$$

that is,

I. Cos. mid. lat. : departure : : radius : diff. of long.

In the triangle A′BA, which is not right angled,

$$\sin A' : AB :: \sin A : A'B ;$$

that is,

II. Cos mid. lat. : distance : sin course : diff. long.

In the triangle ABB′, we have the proportion (Art. 41),

$$R : \tan A :: AB' :: BB'$$

comparing this with the first proportion above, observing that the extremes of this are the means of that, we have

$$AB' : A'B :: \cos A'BB' : \tan A ;$$

that is,

III. Diff. lat. : diff. long. : : cos mid. lat. : tan course.

These three proportions comprise the theory of middle latitude sailing, and when to the middle latitude the proper correction, taken from Mr. Workman's table, is added, these theorems will be rendered strictly accurate.

This is Table XXIX; the middle latitude is to be found in the first column to the left; in a horizontal line with which, and under the given difference of latitude, is inserted the proper correction to be *added* to the middle latitude to obtain the latitude in which the meridian distance is accurately equal to the departure. The formula for constructing this table is obtained as follows:*

Let

$d =$ proper diff. of lat.
$\text{D} =$ meridional diff. of lat.
$m =$ middle latitude.
$\text{M} = m +$ correction.
$\text{L} =$ diff. of longitude.

Then (Art. 100, Form III.),

$$\tan \text{course} = \frac{\cos \text{M} \times \text{L}}{d}$$

But (Art. 101, Rule 1),

$$\tan \text{course} = \frac{\text{rad} \times \text{L}}{\text{D}}$$

$$\therefore \frac{\cos \text{M} \times \text{L}}{d} = \frac{\text{rad} \times \text{L}}{\text{D}} \therefore \cos \text{M} = \frac{\text{rad}\ d}{\text{D}}$$

$$\therefore \text{correction} = \cos^{-1} \frac{\text{rad.}\ d}{\text{D}} - m$$

EXAMPLES.

1. A ship, in latitude 51° 18′ N., longitude 22° 6′ W., has sailed S. 33° 5′ E., required her latitude and longitude.

The required latitude is found by plane sailing, as follows:

Course	33° 5′	log. cos	9·92318
Dist.	1024	log.	3·01030
Diff. Lat.	858		2·93348

* The investigation of this formula should be postponed until after reading the next article, and may be omitted entirely.

Lat. left	51° 18′	N.
Diff. lat.	14 18	
Lat. required	37°	N.

To find the longitude by mid. lat. sailing.

Lat. left	51° 18′
" reached	37°
Sum	88 18
½ Sum	44° 9′ mid. lat.

Then by the proportion III. above,

cos. mid. lat. 44° 9′ ar. comp	log. 0·14418
: tan course 33 5	log. 9·81390
: : diff. lat. 858	log. 2·93349
: diff. long. 779	log. 2·89157

In this operation the middle latitude has not been corrected, so that the difference of longitude here determined is not without error. To find the proper correction, look for the given middle latitude, viz., 44° 9′ in the table of corrections, the nearest to which we find to be 44°; against this and under 14° diff. of lat. we find 27′, also under 15° we find 31′, the difference between the two being 4′; hence corresponding to 14° 18′ the correction will be about 28′. Hence the corrected middle latitude is 44° 37′, therefore,

cos. corrected mid. lat. 44° 37′ ar. comp. log.	0·14763
: tan course 33 5	9·81390
: : diff. lat. 858	2·93349
: diff. long. 785·3	2·89502

therefore, the error in the former result is about 6⅓ miles.

Long. left,	22° 6′ W.
Diff. of long. 785 =	13° 5′
Long. required,	9° 1′ W.

2. A ship sails in the N.W. quarter, 248 miles, till her departure is 135 miles, and her difference of longitude 310 miles; required her course, the latitude left, and the latitude come to.

Course N. 32° 59′ W.; lat. left 62° 27′ N.; lat. in 65° 52′ N.

3. A ship, from latitude 37° N., longitude 9° 2′ W., having sailed between the N. and W., 1027 miles, reckons that she has made 564′ miles of departure; what was her direct course, and the latitude and longitude reached, the middle latitude being uncorrected by Workman's table?

Course N. 33° 19′ W. or N.W. by N. nearly; lat. 51° 18′ N.; long. 22° 8′ W.

4. Required the course and distance from a point in lat. 37° 48′ N., long. 25° 13′ W., to a point in lat. 50° 13′ N., long. 3° 38′ W., the middle latitude being corrected by Workman's Table.

Course N. 51° 11′ E.; distance 1189 miles.

MERCATOR'S SAILING.

This is for the determination of difference of longitude when a ship sails on any oblique rhumb.

101. It has already been seen that when a ship sails on any oblique rhumb, the difference of latitude, the departure, and the distance run, are truly represented by the sides of a right-angled plane triangle. Let AB′B in the annexed diagram be this triangle, A representing the course, AB′ the diff. of lat., and B′B the departure. Let AC′ be a sufficiently greater difference of latitude to make the corresponding departure CC′ equal to the difference of longitude required. This increased difference of latitude AC′ is called the *meridional difference of latitude*, AB′ being called the *proper* difference of latitude, by way of distinction. The solution of the triangle AC′C then will serve to determine the difference of longitude C′C. In this triangle we know the course A, and we shall now show how to construct a table for finding the side AC′, the meridional difference of latitude. The departure B′B represents the sum of all the very small meridian distances, or elementary departures, *b′b*, *c′c*, &c., in the diagram at Art. 100, the difference of latitude AB′ represents the sum of all the corresponding small differences in the figure referred to, and the distance AB the sum of all the corresponding distances A*b*, *bc*, *cd*, &c., and each of these elements is supposed to be taken so exceedingly small as to form on the sphere a series of triangles, differing insensibly from plane triangles.

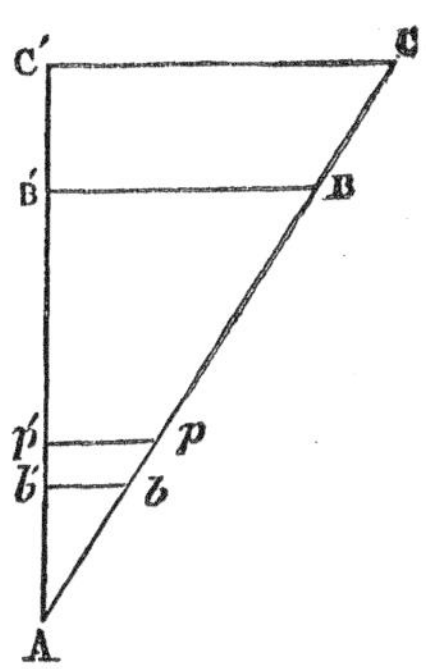

Let A*b′b* in the annexed diagram represent one of these elementary triangles, *b′b* will be one of the elements of the departure, and A*b′*, the corresponding difference of latitude; and as $b'b$ is a small portion of a parallel of latitude, it will be to a similar portion of the equator, or of the meridian, as the cosine of its latitude to radius (Art. 99), this similar portion of the equator, or of the meridian, being the difference of longitude between b' and b. Suppose now the distance Ab prolonged to p, till the departure $p'p$ is equal to the difference of longitude of b', and b, then $b'b$ will be to $p'p$ as the cosine of the latitude of $b\,b$ to the radius; but $b\,b : p'p :: $ Ab' : Ap'; hence the proper difference of Ab' is to the increased difference Ap' as the cosine of the latitude of $b'b$ to the radius. Calling, therefore, the proper difference of latitude d, the increased difference of latitude D, the latitude of $b'b$, l, and the radius 1, which it is in the table of natural sines, this proportion will be in symbols,

$$d : \text{D} :: \cos l : 1$$

$$\therefore \text{D} = \frac{d}{\cos l} = d \sec l \text{ since } \sec = \frac{1}{\cos} \quad \text{(Art. 33.)}$$

The ship, therefore, having made the small departure $b'b$, and the difference of latitude Ab,' must continue her course till the difference of latitude becomes D, in order that her departure may become equal to the difference of longitude corresponding to $b'b$. Conceiving all the elementary distances to be in this manner increased, the sum of all the corresponding increased departures will necessarily be the whole difference of longitude made by the ship during the course. The determination of AC$'$ requires the previous determination of all its elementary parts; if d be taken equal to $1'$, each of these parts will be expressed by D $= 1' \sec l$, or D $= \sec l$, that is, $\sec l$ expresses the meridional difference of latitude corresponding to a proper difference of latitude of $1'$ at the latitude l; giving l successively the values $1'$, $2'$, $3'$, &c., up to 90°, and adding the result of the second substitution to that of the first, and so on, we shall have in succession, the values of the increased latitude corresponding to $1'$, $2'$, $3'$, &c. of proper latitude; these values are called the *meridional parts*, corresponding to the several proper latitudes, and when registered in a table, form a table of meridional parts, given in all books on Navigation.*

The following scheme may serve as a specimen of the manner in which such a table may be constructed, and, indeed, of the manner in which the

* In other words, a table of meridional parts is a table of differences of latitude expressed in geographic miles, each difference of latitude being enough greater than its corresponding proper difference of latitude, to make the departure equal to the difference of longitude. The table gives the meridional difference between the equator and any given latitude.

first table of meridional parts was actually formed by Mr. WRIGHT, the proposer of this ingenious and valuable method.

Mer. parts of 1′= nat. sec 1′.
Mer. parts of 2′= nat. sec 1′+ nat. sec 2′.*
Mer. parts of 3′= nat. sec 1′+ nat. sec 2′+ nat. sec 3′.
Mer. parts of 4′= nat. sec 1′+ nat. sec 2′+ nat. sec 3′+ nat. sec 4′, &c., &c.

Hence, by means of a table of natural secants, we have

			Nat. secs.		Mer. parts.
Mer. parts of 1′=			1·0000000		1·10000000
Mer. parts of 2′=	1·0000000	+	1·0000002	=	2·00000002
Mer. parts of 3′=	2·0000002	+	1·0000004	=	3·00000006
Mer. parts of 4′=	3·0000006	+	1·0000007	=	4·00000013
&c.					&c.

There are other methods of construction, but this is the most simple and obvious. The meridional parts thus determined are all expressed in geographical miles, because in the general expression D = 1′ sec l, 1′ is a geographical mile.

Having thus formed a table of meridional parts (Table III. at the end), if we enter it with the latitudes sailed from, and reached, and take the difference of the corresponding parts in the table, the remainder will be the meridional difference of latitude, or the line AC′ in the preceding diagram.

The angle A is the given course, so that there are known in a right angled triangle AC′C, an angle and the side adjacent, to find the side opposite. The following is the rule.

1. *The tangent of the course × meridional difference of latitude = the difference of longitude;* or if the departure be given instead of the course, then from the similar triangles AB′B, AC′C, the proportion will be

2. *As the proper difference of latitude is to the departure, so is the meridional difference of latitude to the difference of longitude.* Other proportions immediately suggest themselves from the preceding figure.

* Observe that the meridional parts, or meridional diff. of latitude from the equator to 2′ of latitude will be the sum of the meridional parts from the equator to 1′, plus the meridional parts from 1′ to 2′, which latter is nat. sec. 2′. Again, that the meridional parts from the equator to 3′ is the sum of the meridional parts from the equator to 2′, and the meridional parts from 2′ to 3′, which latter is the nat. sec. 3′.

EXAMPLES.

1. A ship from latitude 42° 30′ N., and longitude 58° 51 W., having sailed S.W. by S. 300 miles, required the latitude and longitude at which she has arrived.

To find the diff. of lat. by plane sailing.

Dist.	300	log.	2•47712
Course,	33° 45′	log. cos	9•91985
Proper dif. lat.	249•4	log.	2•39697

To find the diff. of long. by Mercator's sailing.

Lat. left,	42° 30′ N*,	mer. parts 2822
Prop. diff. lat. 249 =	4° 9′	
Lat. reached,	38° 21′*	mer. parts 2495

Long. left,	58° 51′	Mer. diff. lat.	327	log.	2•51455
Diff. long. 219 =	3° 39′	Course,	33° 45′	log. tan	9•82489
Long. reached,	62° 30′	Diff. of long.	218•5	log.	2•33944

2. Required the course and distance from Cape Cod light-house, lat. 42° 3′ N., long 70° 4′ W., to the island of St. Mary's, lat. 36° 59′ N., long. 25° 10′ W.

Cape Cod, lat.	42° 3′ N.	Mer. parts,	2786	Long.	70° 4′ W.
St. Mary's, lat.	36° 59′ N.	Mer. parts,	2391	Long.	25° 10′ W.
	5° 4′	Mer diff. lat.	395		44° 54′
	60				60
Prop. diff. lat.	304			Diff. long.	2694 miles.

To find the Course (by Rule 1.)		To find distance by Plane Sailing.	
Merid. diff. lat. 395 log.	2•59660		
Diff. of long. 2694 log.	3•43040		
Course 81° 40′ log. tan	10•83380	log. cos.	9•16116
Proper diff. lat. 304 miles		log.	2•48287
Distance 2098 miles		log.	3•32171

* Enter tab. of mer. parts with the argument 42° 30′, and take out the mer. parts corresponding, viz., 2822, which is the meridional diff. of lat. from the equator to 42° 30′ N. Again enter the tab. with the argument 38° 21′; the corresponding mer. parts, or mer. diff. of lat., from the equator to lat. 38° 21′ N. will be found to be 2495. Subtract the latter from the former, and the remainder will be the meridional diff. of lat. between 38° 21′ N., and 42° 30′ N.

3. A ship from latitude 37° N., and longitude 32° 16′ W., has sailed in a north-westerly direction 300 miles, till she has reached the latitude of 41° N. Required the precise course on which she has sailed, and the longitude at which she has arrived.

Ans. Course 36° 52′; Long. 36° 8′

APPENDIX III.

GREAT CIRCLE SAILING.

1. The shortest path from one point to another on the surface of a sphere is the arc of a great circle (Geom., App. III., p. 2). A ship, therefore, sailing on the arc of a great circle, joining her point of departure and point of destination on the surface of the earth, will make a shorter voyage than if she sails in the direct course, that is upon the rhumb line joining the same two points.

The practical application of great circle sailing will consist in determining as often as the ship's place is found, that is to say her latitude and longitude, which, under ordinary circumstances, occurs daily, the direction which she ought to take, in order to sail on the great circle from the point where the ship is, to the point of destination. This problem is, in effect, solved in the example on p. 137. In the diagram at that place, S denotes the point where the ship is, S′ the point of destination, and the angle PSS′ the course which the ship ought to steer, in order to sail on the great circle from S to S′. The solution of the problem of Great Circle Sailing, it appears, from the example referred to, requires the application of Napier's Analogies, forms IX. and X. of Art. 86. In a practical treatise on Great Circle Sailing, which appeared in 1846, by S. T. Coit, a table will be found called the "Great Circle Table." It is a table of double entry, in which the logarithm of the ratio of the cosine of the half sum, to the cosine of the half difference, and of the ratio of the sine of the half sum to the sine of the half difference of the colatitudes of S and S′, will be found computed for any two latitudes. You enter this table with the less of the given latitudes at top, and the greater at the side; under the former, and on the range of the latter, in the column entitled sine, is found the logarithm of the ratio of the sine of half the sum to the sine of the half difference, and in the column entitled cosine, the ratio of the cosine of the half sum to the cosine of the half difference; if to each of these be added the log. cotangent of the difference of longitude of the point where the ship is, and the point for which she is destined, the results will be the logarithmic tangent of the half sum and half difference of the angles S and S′, the former of which, viz., S will be the course upon which the ship should be directed.

The example at p. 137 adapted to this place should read as follows:

1. A ship from lat. 20°, long. 41° 34′ 26″, is bound to a point in lat. 51° 30′, long. 10°, upon what course must she sail in order to pursue the shortest path to her destination?

Ans. 30° 28′ 12″.

2. A ship in lat. 40° 30′ N., long. 70° W., is bound for a place in lat. 51° 22′ N., long. 9° 37′ W., required the course for Great Circle Sailing?

Ans. N. 54° 3′ E.

The computation of the third side ss′ in the same triangle gives the distance sailed.

As a steamer in ordinary weather pursues steadily the course of the great circle from port to port, it may be convenient to calculate beforehand the position of the points in which this great circle intersects the meridians for every five degrees of longitude (five degrees being about the daily progress of a first class steamer), and then if the ship lays upon the direct course for these points successively, it will be sufficient, since the rhumb line differs insensibly from the arc of a great circle for so short a distance. The method of determining these is simple. For when the angle s is calculated, it is only necessary to employ the last two forms, XI. and XII. (Art. 86) of Napier's Analogies, which are used for solving a spherical triangle when two angles and the interjacent side are given.

The data will be the colatitude of the point s, the course PSS′ previously calculated, and the angle which the meridian PS makes with the meridian whose point of intersection with the great circle course from s to s′ is to be calculated; in other words, the difference of longitude of these two meridians.

The logarithm of the ratio of the cosines and sines of the half sum and half difference of the given angles may be taken from "The Circle Table," entering it with the complements of these angles; the log. tangent of the given side will be the same in the calculation for each meridian; the solution of the triangle for each meridian giving the colatitude of the point in which the great circle path intersects the meridian, and the course which the ship ought to take in departing from that meridian.

EXAMPLE.

A ship sailing from the port of New York to Havre or Liverpool, by the shortest path, would steer from Sandy Hook, lat. 40° 27′ 30″, long. 74° 00′ 48″ W., E. ½ S.* running on the rhumb line, and thus give the south shoal of Nantucket a berth of about 15 miles; from this she would sail to a point in lat. 41°, long. 68°, on southern part of George's shoal, in 25 fathoms of water. From this point she would commence Great Circle Sailing, nothing being gained in taking the great circle rather than the rhumb line in the previous short distances. As the great circle from this point to that of destination would pass over Newfoundland, it is necessary to divide the voyage between two great circles, the first terminating at Cape Race, and the second terminating at Cape Clear, the south point of Ireland.

Required the course from the south shoal of Nantucket to George's Shoal, and the points at which the great circle from lat. 41° N., long. 68°, W., to Cape Race, in lat. 46°, 39′ 24″, long. 53° 04′ 36″, intersects the meridians of 60° and 55° W.; and the points in which the great circle from Cape Race to Cape Clear, in lat. 51° 22′ N., long. 9° 37′ W., intersects the meridians of 45°, 40°, 35°, 30°, 25°, 20°, and 15° W.

Ans. The course from Nantucket to George's is

* This allows for variation of compass.

The first great circle intersects the meridian of 60° at 44° 24′ 25″, of 55° at 46° 5′ 28″ of N. latitude.

The second great circle intersects the meridian of 45° at 48° 55′ 47·″5, of 40° at 49° 58′ 27″, of 35° at 50° 46′ 6″, of 30° at 51° 19′ 44″, of 25° at 51° 40′ 3″, of 20° at 51° 47′ 28″, and of 15° at 51° 42′ 7″.*

The following, from Mr. Coit's work, to which the student is referred for a variety of useful problems, and interesting information, will furnish a number of exercises.

TRACK OF THE ARC OF A GREAT CIRCLE FROM CHESAPEAKE BAY TO BORDEAUX.

Table showing the longitude of the intersections of the latitudes crossed by the arc of a great circle from Cape Henry's light-house, mouth of Chesapeake Bay, to the Corduan light, near Bordeaux; also showing the courses from the points of intersections of the latitudes crossed, and from intersection to intersection.

	Latitudes crossed.	Long. of the intersec. of the lat. crossed.		Courses towards Corduan from the points of intersection.	Courses towards Cape Henry from the points of intersection.
		From the Meridian of Greenwich.	From the Meridian of Corduan.		
C. Henry.	36°·56′	76°·04′	74°·54′	N. 55°·40′ E.	. . . . . .
	37 ·	75 ·55	74 ·45	– 55 ·46 –	S. 55°·46′ W.
	38 ·	74 ·02	72 ·52	– 56 ·55 –	– 56 ·55 –
	39 ·	72 ·01	70 ·51	– 58 ·10 –	– 58 ·10 –
	40 ·	69 ·52	68 ·42	– 59 ·32 –	– 59 ·32 –
	41 ·	67 ·36	66 ·26	– 61 ·01 –	– 61 ·01 –
	42 ·	64 ·25	63 ·15	– 62 ·41 –	– 62 ·41 –
	43 ·	62 ·22	61 ·12	– 94 ·31 –	– 64 ·61 –
	44 ·	59 ·19	58 ·09	– 66 ·37 –	– 66 ·37 –
	45 ·	56 ·27	55 ·17	– 69 ·03 –	– 69 ·01 –
	46 ·	51 ·52	50 ·42	– 71 ·53 –	– 71 ·53 –
	47 ·	46 ·55	45 ·45	– 75 ·29 –	– 75 ·29 –
	48 ·	39 ·56	38 ·46	– 80 ·38 –	– 80 ·38 –
Max. Lat.	48 ·41	27 ·25	26 ·15	East.	West.
	48 ·	14 ·54	13 ·44	S. 80 ·38 E.	N. 80 ·38 W.
	47 ·	7 ·55	6 ·45	– 75 ·29 –	– 75 ,29 –
	46 ·	2 ·58	1 ·48	– 71 ·53 –	– 71 ·53 –
Corduan.	.45 ·35	1 ·10	0 ·	. . . . . .	– 70 ·36 –

On this track the difference or saving is 110.

* The great circle courses and distances are as follows: From George's Shoal to the meridian of 60°, 57° 14′ and 407 miles. From 60° to 55° N., 62° 40′ E., and 234 miles. From 55° to Cape Race N. 66° 13′ E., and 87 miles. From Cape Race to the meridian of 45°, N. 64° 19′ E., and 353 miles. From 45° to 40°, N. 70° 18′ E., and 205 miles. From 40° to 35°, N. 74° 6′ E., and 197 miles. From 35° to 30°, N. 77° 57′ E., and 191 miles. From 30° to 25°, N. 80° 50′ E., and 188 miles. From 25° to 20°, N. 85° 45′ E., and 186 miles. From 20° to 15° N. 89° 42′ E., and 186 miles. From 15° to Cape Clear S. 86° 23′, and 202 miles.

For further information on Great Circle Sailing, see "The Practice of Navigation and Nautical Astronomy, by Lieut. Raper, of the Royal Navy," Art. 336, in which work will also be found a convenient table (tab. 5) called the Spherical Traverse table, for solving problems in this kind of sailing.

See also a small collection of "Tables to facilitate Great Circle Sailing," by John Thomas Towson, published by order of the Lords Commissioners of the Admiralty.

SUMNER'S METHOD.

This is a method discovered recently by accident, and consists in calculating the ship's longitude by chronometer for two assumed latitudes, the one of which is the next even degree less, the other the next even degree greater (without odd minutes) than the latitude by dead reckoning. The two positions of the ship thus determined from the longitudes found and the assumed latitudes, being projected on a Mercator's chart, the line joining them passes through the true position of the ship, and any land it may happen to pass through in the vicinity, will have the same bearing from the ship that this line makes with the meridian.

The theory is, that this line is a small portion of what the author terms a parallel of equal altitude, that is, a small circle of the terrestrial sphere, the pole of which is the point of the earth's surface, at which the sun is vertical or in the zenith at the instant of observation. To all places situated on this circle the sun will have the same altitude at the instant. Now since in the two computations in the above problem the latitude only is different, the altitude and declination, which are the other data, remaining the same, the altitude of the sun is therefore the same at the two positions determined, and they are in the same parallel of equal altitude, and as the observed altitude of the ship is also the same, the ship, too, is upon the same parallel of equal altitude, a small arc of which may be regarded as a straight line.

A perpendicular to the line determined as above will be in the direction of the sun's bearing, and the angle it makes with the meridian will be the sun's azimuth. For the perpendicular to an arc will pass through the pole of the arc.

If two altitudes of the sun be taken, and two lines projected as above, passing each through the place of the ship, its actual position is determined by their intersection.

For the method of allowing for the change of place of the ship between two observations for altitude, and for a variety of problems based upon the principle above explained, see Sumner's work.

PART IV.

SURVEYING.

PART IV.

SURVEYING

102. HAS for its object to make upon paper an exact delineation called a map, plot, or draft, and sometimes to find the contents of ground.

The most common mode of proceeding is to measure a base line upon the ground, as at Art. 10, and take the angles at each extremity with some instrument suitable for the purpose, thus determining the position of a distinct point. This is transferred to paper, by means of a scale of equal parts, and a semicircular protractor, as described in the same article. As many points upon the ground as may be desirable can thus be transferred to the map. If two points thus determined be the extremities of some straight boundary, as a wall, fence, or side of a building, the boundary itself is drawn by uniting the two points by a straight line. If the boundary be curved or irregular, as the bank of a stream, a coast, the border of a wood, &c., the prominent points should be determined on the map, as above described, and the boundary then traced through them with the hand, by the eye.

The positions of points on a map may also be determined by taking their direction and distance from some point used as a basis or base point for the whole survey. Or, when more convenient, some one of the points determined from the first base point may itself become a base point for the determination of others more in advance. The direction of one point from another is expressed by the angle which the line of direction makes with some known line. A very convenient line for this purpose is a meridian or north and south line, for the direction of this latter may always be known by means of a magnetic needle, and the direction of any line from a north and south line by a compass. Allowance must of course be made for what is called the variation of the needle, which is determined by astronomical observations, in a manner to be hereafter explained. Distances are measured upon the ground with a tape or chain. The measuring tape is covered with wax, to prevent the effects of varying degrees of moisture, in contracting and expanding it. It is divided usually into feet and inches. The chain is of iron wire, each link being the hundredth part of the whole chain, which is 4 rods, or 66 feet, or 792 inches, so that each link is 7·92 inches in length. Every ten links is, for convenience of counting, marked by a piece of brass, with as many tongues as the brass piece is tens of links from the extremity of the chain. A line is measured on the ground, as follows: Two persons take hold, one of each extremity of the chain, and one going in front, towards the point whose distance is to be measured, carries in his hand a staff and ten marking pins, of iron wire, each about two feet in length, sharpened to stick in the ground at the extremity of the chain measured off.

The one behind, by a motion of the hand to the right or left, indicates to the other whether the staff which is held at the end of the stretched chain is on the alignment of the distant point or not. As soon as he discovers it to be so, he makes a motion with his hand downward, and the other places a marking pin. Both then move on, the one behind taking up the marking pins which the other has left in the ground. When all the pins have been passed from one to the other, ten chains have been measured off.

For fixing the position of points of ground upon a map, the best instrument, when the survey is of moderate extent, is one which surveys and plots at the same time, called the

PLANE TABLE.

This consists of a rectangular board, mounted upon a three-legged stand, called a tripod, to which it is attached by a ball and socket movement, that is to say, there is a socket fastened to the tripod and a ball clasped by the socket, which moves in it, the ball being fastened to the underside of the table. This permits the table to be placed exactly horizontal. To ascertain whether it is so or not, a detached spirit level is placed upon the table temporarily, and the table is levelled by means of three screws, which pass through a horizontal circle of wood or brass which projects round the top of the tripod, the screws working against the table underneath. These screws are placed near the outer edge of the circle, and at distances of 120° from each other. If one of them be screwed in one direction, it lifts the table on that side; if in the opposite direction, it lets it down. In order to level the table by means of these screws the spirit level is placed over the line joining two of them, and by moving them the bubble is brought to the centre; this renders one line of the table horizontal. The spirit level is then placed in a direction perpendicular to its former one, and the bubble brought to the centre by turning the third screw, leaving the others untouched; two lines of the table are then horizontal, and consequently the table itself.* The spirit level, which is a tube of glass inclosed in one of brass, and containing spirits of wine, rests on short feet at the ends, one of which is made movable by a screw, and should be adjusted by reversing the level, end for end, on the table, after the bubble is first brought to the centre, when, if it departs from the centre, it must be brought back half by the foot screw of the level itself, and half by the levelling screws of the table. This process is to be repeated till in both positions of the level the bubble remains in the centre. A necessary appendage to the plane table is a brass ruler, with a thin edge, upon which are mounted either plain or telescopic sights, the line of vision being parallel to the edge of the ruler. Plain sights consist of two upright flat pieces of brass, one at each end of the ruler, facing each other with a narrow vertical aperture in each, to look through. Sometimes the aperture is made wider in the one towards the object, and a vertical thread or hair stretched down the middle of it, which serves for a sight. Larger orifices are made at some parts, in which to catch sight of the object, which is then brought down to a fine sight in the narrow part of the aperture.

When the sights are telescopic, the telescope may be mounted like that of a transit instrument (if the ruler is very wide) upon the upright piers of brass, by means of a small horizontal axis. Or upon a narrow ruler the telescope is supported at the top of a single column of brass, by a stout axis projecting from one side. At the focus of the object glass of the telescope two lines of spiders web cross each other exactly in the optical axis of the telescope. When the ruler is placed upon the table, by turning the table round a vertical axis called the axis of the instrument, the line of sights may be turned in any horizontal direction at pleasure. The telescope has a small vertical play also upon the horizontal axis, for the purpose of directing it to objects somewhat elevated or depressed. To use the instrument, place it over one end of the base line on the ground, so that a line to represent the base line drawn upon paper, stretched tightly and immovably upon the table, may be in the same direction. This is done by placing the edge of the ruler upon the line on the paper, and then turning the table upon the vertical axis of the instrument until a staff placed at the other end of the base line is seen upon the line of sights. There is a convenient arrangement for accomplishing this, consisting of what are termed a clamp and tangent screw, or screw of slow

* This operation has generally to be repeated, as the levelling of the second line deranges a little the level of the first.

motion, an arrangement which is applied to almost all instruments. This consists of a screw working near its head, in a collar in which it has no longitudinal motion, the thread of the screw working in a piece of brass which is at pleasure loose from or screwed against the stand below, by a second screw, called the clamp screw, the first being called the tangent screw. When the instrument is "clamped," the tangent screw being turned, pushes the side of the table to which its collar is attached slowly away from the part of the tripod below, thus giving a slight motion to the table on its vertical axis. The line of sights being thus arranged in the direction of the base line on the ground, whilst the edge of the ruler coincides with the base line upon the paper, keeping now the edge of the ruler passing through one extremity of the latter, whilst the table is held immovable by the clamp screw, upon the tripod, turn the line of sights accurately towards one of the points to be plotted, and draw a line along the edge of the ruler upon the paper, marking it 1. Turn the line of sights successively to all the points in view to be plotted, drawing lines on the paper from the extremity of the base line on the paper, in the directions of these points, as before, and numbering them 2, 3, and so on, in order. Let the instrument now be taken up and carried to the other extremity of the base line, levelled, and the edge of the ruler being placed upon the base line on the paper, in a reversed position, bring the line of sights in the direction of the station at the first extremity of the base, by turning the table on its vertical axis, using the clamp and tangent screw, as before. Proceed in the manner just described, to draw lines also from this extremity of the base on paper, in the directions of the same objects, by sighting towards them in the same order, and numbering the lines as before. Where 1 meets 1 will be the position of the first object on the map; where 2 meets 2 the position of the second object, and so on.

The telescope of the plane table has sometimes an arrangement by which distances can be measured without the use of the tape or chain. Two sets of cross wires, as the spider lines are technically called, are placed at the focus of the object glass, the points of intersection of each pair being a small distance apart, the one above the other. If a staff be placed 100 feet from the telescope, and a space of exactly one foot be seen intercepted between the intersection of the wires; if then the staff be removed to a distance of 200 feet, two feet will be seen intercepted on the staff, because, according to an optical law, the size of the image formed at the focus of the object glass is inversely as the distance of the object from the instrument, so that the space between the wires at the focus, where the image is formed, being occupied by 1 foot at the distance of

100 feet, the image of this 1 foot at the distance of 200 feet will occupy only half the space, or it will take an image of two feet to occupy the whole space.

To ascertain the proportions of the instrument by experiment, place a staff at such a distance that 1 foot may be intercepted between the intersections of the wires; measure this distance, and it will be the distance to be multiplied by the number of feet and fractions of a foot seen intercepted when the instrument is used for measuring distances. The staff used should be about two inches broad by one in thickness, and painted white, the divisions and numbers upon it being black or deep red, and made very distinct.

THE SURVEYOR'S COMPASS.

This instrument is a circular box of brass about six inches in diameter, and half an inch deep, mounted upon a tripod with ball and socket motion. The bottom of the box on the interior is silvered, and the circumference of this silvered bottom is graduated. In the centre of the bottom stands up a pivot upon which a long magnetic needle is accurately balanced. The top of the box is of glass, in order that the whole interior may be seen. Upon the box above, in the direction of a diameter, is a line of sights which may be plain or telescopic. The graduation is numbered from each end of the diameter, and runs to 90° each way.*

To survey a polygonal field with this instrument place it at one of the corners of the field, and direct the line of sights to the next corner along one of the straight boundaries of the field, and measure with a chain the length of this boundary line. Enter in a field book, ruled in three columns, in the first column the number of the station beginning with station 1; in the second column the Bearing (which would be, for instance, N. 30° E., if the line of sight were directed to the right of the north end of the needle marked with a cross, and the needle pointed to 30° on the graduated circle;†) and in a third column the distance measured with the tape or chain. Take the instrument now to the corner whose position has just been determined, calling it station number 2, and determine the position of station number 3, a third corner of the field and the bounding line connecting stations 2 and 3 in the same manner, and so proceed quite ound the field. (See p. 233.) To plot this assume the point on the paper at

* Sometimes the graduation is numbered from 0° to 360°, the 0 and 180 diameter being the line of sights.

† If the graduation of the compass box be from 0 to 360, it will only be necessary to record the number to which the north end of the needle points.

which you will have the first corner of the field, draw through it a line to represent a magnetic meridian, or north and south line, and another line making an angle with this, equal to the first bearing, as 30° above, which will be laid off with the semi-circular protractor to the right of the meridian line if the bearing be east, and vice versâ; then from a scale of equal parts lay down the distance taken from the third column of the field book, and this will determine the second station of the map; through this draw a north and south line parallel to the first drawn, and lay off the second boundary by its bearing and distance, in the same manner, and so proceed till the plot is complete. The accuracy of the work will be tested by the last bearing and distance, reaching exactly to the first station from which the work commenced.

The same method may be pursued with the plane table, in an obvious manner. It is only necessary, as the table is moved from corner to corner of the field, to place the line on paper which has just been determined parallel to the corresponding line on the ground, by placing the ruler upon it, and sighting back from the 2d to the 1st station, turning the table on its vertical axis, for the purpose. The line joining the 2d and 3d station may then be drawn by sighting to the 3d station, the edge of the ruler passing through the 2d station in the paper, and by a scale of equal parts the length of this line laid down, and so on.

The compass may be employed to survey an irregular line, as a road, the border of a stream, a wood, a coast, &c., by taking stations sufficiently numerous to include portions nearly straight between them.

Thus:

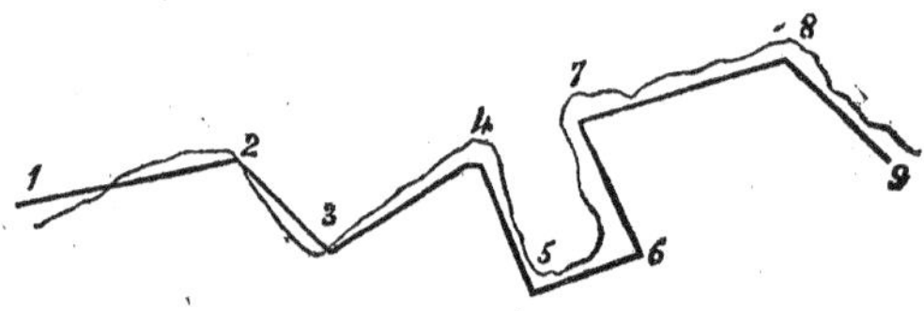

Another mode is to run a straight line along the irregular boundary, and measure *offsets*, that is, perpendiculars to the main line, extending to the boundary at points where there are remarkable changes.

Thus:

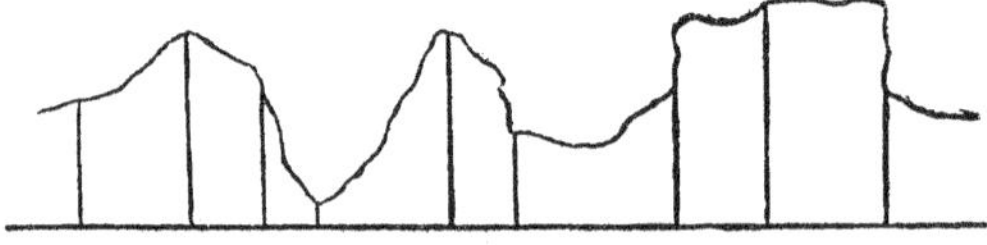

The perpendiculars not only are measured with the chain, but the distances between them. To plot such a piece of surveying, the main line having been laid down on paper by its bearing observed with the compass, the measured distances between the perpendiculars are laid off on this line by a scale of equal parts, the perpendiculars drawn and laid off by the same scale, and the boundary traced by the hand through their extremities. An instrument for taking offsets is the surveyor's cross, consisting of two pairs of plain sights, at right angles to each other. Place the cross on the principal line, sight with one pair to a distant staff upon it, the other pair will be directed in a perpendicular to the principal line. Where a survey is extensive, the relative positions of distant points are fixed with an instrument of greater accuracy for taking angles than any we have yet described, by a process similar to that mentioned at p. 236, called *triangulation*. The instrument used for this purpose, of which that described at Art. 10 is a rude imitation, is called

THE THEODOLITE.

This consists of a horizontal circle of brass resting upon a tripod by three foot-screws or levelling screws. The circumference of the circle is silvered, and divided into degrees and parts of a degree, numbered from 0 to 360. Directly above a diameter of this circle is supported a small telescope, to which is attached a vertical circle, the plane of which is parallel to its optical axis. There are various modes of supporting the telescope. The best is by means of two upright columns of brass, standing upon a horizontal circle concentric with the horizontal limb, and moving upon or within it, round a vertical axis.* Between these columns the telescope is suspended, by means of two projections from the sides of its tubes, resembling the trunnions of a cannon, the ends of which rest in notches in the tops of the upright columns, called Y's. These projections are called the supporting axis, and this passes through the centre of the vertical circle, which is firmly attached to it at one end, and which revolves with this axis. The circumference of the vertical circle is also graduated, and called the vertical limb, the numbers on this limb running from 0 to 90° four times.

The indices which show the number of degrees passed on the horizontal limb in a horizontal direction, or on the vertical limb in a vertical direction, thus indicating the angular motion of the line of vision, or optical axis of the telescope, are of peculiar construction, and called ***verniers***, from the name of their inventor. As they are used upon many instruments, we shall presently describe them in detail.

* This mounting is similar to that of the transit instrument.

There are usually three of these upon the horizontal limb, and two upon the vertical, at distances from each other of 120° in the one, and 180° on the other. The object of having more than one is to correct for wrong centring of the circle, or excentricity. Those which apply to the horizontal limb are attached to the concentric movable circle which supports the telescope, and move with it. A clamp screw serves to fasten this circle to the limb, and a tangent screw to give it a slow motion along the limb. Those which belong to the vertical limb are attached to the supports of the Y^s, immovably except for adjustment, the limb moving past them with the telescope about the supporting axis.

The line of sights is marked by two wires, one vertical, the other horizontal, crossing each other at the focus of the object glass of the telescope.

These wires are fastened across a diaphragm smaller in diameter than the tube of the telescope, and held within it by means of screws passing through from the outside of the tube on the right and left. By tightening the right, and loosening the left, or vice versà, the diaphragm may be moved laterally. The instrument is used for measuring either horizontal or vertical angles. A horizontal angle is one formed by two lines in a horizontal plane; or it is the angle included between two vertical planes which meet. A vertical angle is one formed by two lines in a vertical plane. An angle of elevation is a vertical angle formed by a horizontal line, with an oblique line coming from above to meet it. An angle of depression is a vertical angle formed by a horizontal, with an oblique line meeting it from below. For the measurement of such angles it is evident that the axis about which the verniers of the horizontal limb move, which is called the axis of the instrument, should be truly vertical, that the supporting axis on which the vertical limb turns, should be truly horizontal, and that the line of vision of the telescope should be exactly perpendicular to the latter. The processes of placing them so are called adjustments. The last mentioned, which is the first in order to be made, is called *collimation.* This is accomplished by placing the intersection of the wires upon some distant, well-defined point, then reversing the supporting axis in the Y^s, by turning it end for end. If the intersection of the wires passes through the same object, as the telescope is turned round the supporting axis, the instrument is collimated, and no adjustment is necessary. But if not, the intersection of the wires must be brought half way, by estimation, towards the object by means of the screws of the diaphragm, and the other half by the tangent screw of the horizontal limb. This process must be repeated, owing to the difficulty of estimating just half, till in both positions of the supporting axis the intersection of the wires passes through the same distant point.* The second adjustment in order, consists in rendering the supporting axis horizontal. This is accomplished by means of a spirit level, composed of a glass tube, not quite filled with alcohol, leaving an air bubble at top. This tube is partly encased in a brass one, which rests by its ends upon two feet, notched at the bottom, to stand upon the ends of the supporting axis, so that the tube of the level is above, and parallel to the supporting axis, striding over the telescope, and hence the name of striding level, by which it is known. First, to adjust the axis of the level tube into parallelism with the supporting axis, when the feet of the striding level rest upon its extremities. Bring the bubble to the centre by the levelling screws of the instrument; reverse the level upon the axis, turning it end for end; if the bubble does not continue in the centre, make half the correction by the levelling screws, the other half by filing away the notch in one of the feet, viz., that nearest to the bubble, as being the highest. Sometimes the foot of the striding level is made capable of being lengthened or shortened, by means of a screw, by turning which the adjustment may be made. The parallelism between the axis of the spirit level and the supporting axis being established, whenever the bubble is at the centre, the latter of these axes is horizontal. To make the supporting axis perpendicular to the vertical axis of the instrument, bring the bubble of the level to the centre, by the levelling screws, turn the instrument round the vertical axis 180°; if the bubble now departs from the centre, make half the correction by the levelling screws, the other half by screws which elevate or depress one of the Y^s.

The above are the principal adjustments. To measure an angle, with the instrument thus adjusted, one plane passing through the vertical axis of the instrument, and perpendicular to the supporting axes, is made vertical by bringing the bubble to the centre in one position; then turning the instrument round the vertical axis 90°, bring the bubble again to the centre, and the vertical axis will be truly vertical, because it is perpendicular to two horizontal lines which intersect, viz., the lines determined by the spirit level, and consequently to a horizontal plane. The instrument is now prepared for the measure of either a horizontal or vertical angle, having its vertex at the centre of motion of the instrument. For the former, turn the telescope in the direction of one of the sides of the angle, and take the reading of the degrees from one of the three verniers on the horizontal limb (which are engraved each with one of the letters A, B, C), and of the minutes and seconds from all three. A mean of the minutes and seconds is taken by adding up the three readings for the minutes and

* For the theory of this process see transit instrument, p. 149, note.

seconds, and dividing the sum by three. The telescope is now turned in the direction of the other side of the angle, by sighting to a station at its extremity, and taking the reading from the three verniers as before. The difference between this reading and the former one will give either the angle required in degrees, minutes, and seconds, or else a number which, subtracted from 360°, will give the required angle. As for instance, if the vernier stood first at 350°, moving a short distance past 360° to 10°, the angle passed over would be only 20°, which is obtained by subtracting the difference between 350° and 10°, or 340° from 360°.

In some theodolites the horizontal limb itself as well as the vernier circle, has a motion round the vertical axis of the instrument, and a clamp and tangent screw. This is for the purpose of introducing the repeating process into the measurement of horizontal angles, which is conducted as follows. Sight first to the object in the direction of one of the sides of the angle to be measured, and take the reading; loosen the clamp screw of the vernier circle, and turn this with the telescope round the vertical axis of the instrument to sight to the second object in the direction of the other side of the angle, using the clamp and tangent screw of the vernier circle for making the sight exact. Loosen now the clamp screw of the limb, keeping that of the vernier circle tight, and bring the telescope back to the first object, clamping the limb there, and adjusting the sight by the tangent screw of the limb. Repeat this process several times, ending with a movement of the vernier circle to bring the telescope upon the second object; take now the reading; the difference of the two readings divided by the number of times that the vernier circle has been moved forward, say six times, will be the angle required, with a probable error of observation of $\frac{1}{6}$ what it would have been without the repeating process.

To measure a vertical angle with the theodolite, level the instrument, or make its vertical axis truly vertical as before; elevate or depress the telescope to the object, in the direction of the inclined side of the vertical angle, and take the reading by both verniers of the vertical limb. Turn the instrument on its vertical axis 180°, and bring the telescope to bear upon the same point as before, taking the mean of the two verniers again. Half the sum of the mean of the results of the readings in the two positions of the telescope will be the angle of elevation, or depression, as the case may be corrected for index error.* Half the difference of the same

* Because if the index be a little *behind* the zero on the limb when the telescope is horizontal in the one position, it will be a little *before* the zero in the reverse position, after turning the instrument 180° on its vertical axis.

same results will be the index error which must be applied as a correction if the reading for an observation afterwards is taken only in one position, or with the face of the limb one way, either to the right or left.

It will be proper now to describe the vernier, which serves to read accurately smaller divisions of the limb than could be done with a simple index. The vernier is a short arc of a circle, in which divisions are cut, as in the limb, but smaller; so little smaller however, that the difference between them shall be equal to the smallest denomination which the instrument is intended to read. If the first division of the vernier, marked with a crow-foot, and called the zero of the vernier, be made to coincide with a division of the limb, the last division of the vernier will be observed also to coincide with a division of the limb; and, on counting the divisions, there will be found to be one more on the vernier than upon the same length of the limb. Suppose the smallest division of the limb to be denoted by a, and a division of the vernier by x, and suppose that n' divisions of the vernier are equal to n of the limb, then

$$n'x = na \qquad (1)$$

$$x = \frac{n}{n'}\,a \qquad (2)$$

$$a - x = a\left(1 - \frac{n}{n'}\right) \qquad (3)$$

This last being the difference between a division on the vernier, and a division on the limb, is the expression for the smallest denomination which can be measured with the instrument.

A common division of the limb of the theodolite is into degrees or half degrees, or 30′ spaces; and of the vernier such that 30 of its divisions cover 29 of the limb. The second member of formulas (3) above, by the substitution of these numbers, becomes

$$30'\left(1 - \frac{29}{30}\right) \text{ or } 1'$$

The smallest angular space which the instrument is capable of measuring in this case is one minute of a degree.

The first dividing line or zero of the vernier coinciding with a dividing line of the limb, if the vernier be moved forward, till the second dividing line of the vernier coincides with the next line of the limb, the zero of the vernier will have moved past the dividing line of the limb, at which it stood a distance equal to the difference of a space on the vernier, and a space on the limb, or once the smallest denomination which the instrument measures. If the vernier be moved still farther forward, till its third dividing line, or second from the zero, coincides with the line of the limb, the zero of the vernier will have moved forward again, a distance equal to the difference between a space on the vernier, and a space on the limb, or altogether twice the smallest measure of the instrument. To take a reading, therefore, from a theodolite divided as above mentioned, observe the number of degrees and half degrees pointed out on the limb by the crow-foot or zero of the vernier, and if this line be a little past one of the dividing lines of the limb, count the number of divisions on the vernier from the zero to a dividing line which coincides exactly with one of the limb; this will be the number of single minutes to be added to the degrees and half degrees indicated by the crow foot.

The use of two verniers 180° apart, in correcting for excentricity, may be thus explained. An excentric angle, or one having its vertex not in the centre of a circle, is measured by half the sum of the opposite arcs. The mean of the two opposite verniers, therefore, gives the true angle moved over by the telescope. If the number of verniers be increased beyond two, error of graduation and of figure in the circle are proximately eliminated, as well as error of excentricity, by taking the mean of all the verniers.

TRIANGULATION OF A COUNTRY.

This is a process which consists in measuring a base, and taking the angles at its extremities with the theodolite, for the purpose of determining the positions of points, the sides of the triangles thus determined becoming bases for new triangles.*

SURVEY OF A LARGE ESTATE.

A good instrument for the purpose is a compass with telescopic sights, graduated from 0 to 360°. And a good method of proceeding is to select three stations on elevated ground at remote parts of the estate. Setting out from one of them, go in the direction of one of the others, having previously taken the bearing of the line joining them with the compass. This line may be kept by its bearing in plunging into the low grounds, out of sight of the principal stations. Distances must be measured along the line to points opposite objects on either side of it, which are to be introduced upon the map, and offsets to these objects measured. Oblique instead of perpendicular offsets will sometimes be found more convenient,

* This will be fully treated in our chapter on Geodesy.

in which case their bearing must be observed with the compass as well as their lengths measured. Or if an object be too inaccessible to measure the offset to it, its bearing with the compass may be taken from two points on the principal line, which will serve to fix its position. The method of keeping the field book is exhibited on the next page but one.

The record commences at the bottom of the page, and goes upwards, till one page of the field book is filled, and then commences at the bottom of the next, and so on.* The bearings and distances are entered in the middle column of the page, the offsets on the right and left. Distances are usually measured in chains and links, or decimals of a chain. The objects to which the offsets are measured may have their names written, or still better, may be roughly drawn. The points at which streams, roads, stone walls, hedges, &c. cross the principal line, are indicated in the field book by drawing representations of these in the proper direction on both sides of the central column, and where they cross obliquely, recording their bearings upon them.

On reaching the second station, a line is drawn across the page, and a line is *run* in a similar manner from the second to the third station, and finally from the third to the first.

The sum of all the partial measured distances upon any one of these sides of the great triangle will be the length of that side, and the lengths of the three sides being known, the triangle may be plotted. The offsets will be plotted as described at p. 238, or where they are oblique, in an obvious manner. A turn to the right, on reaching a station, may be marked ┏ at the side of the page, and a turn to the left ┓.

The great triangle with the offsets being completed, other points may be taken within, as the vertices of smaller triangles having the sides of the large triangle for bases, and, if necessary, other points again within these, until all the systems of triangles with the offsets from their sides include every object desirable to be placed upon the map.

On p. 246 is a map of ground with the great triangle and offsets, and on p. 247 is the corresponding field book.

* This is in order that the book and the ground may lie in corresponding positions before the eye of the surveyor.

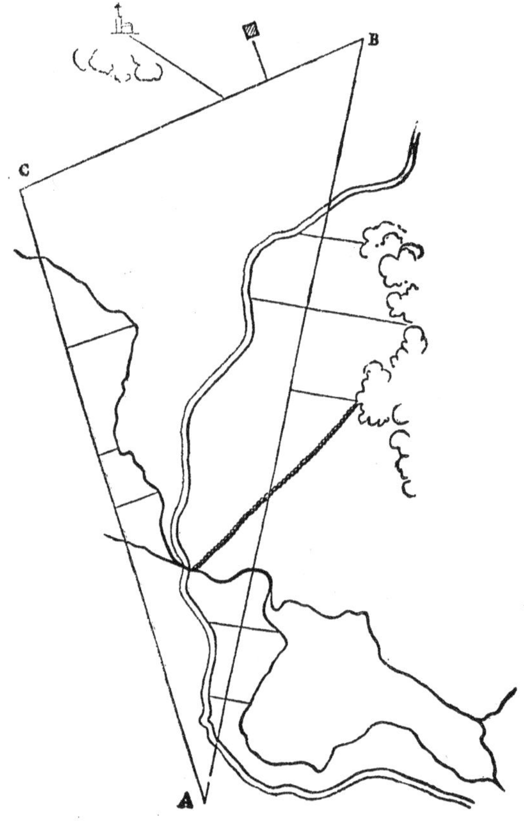
B
C
A

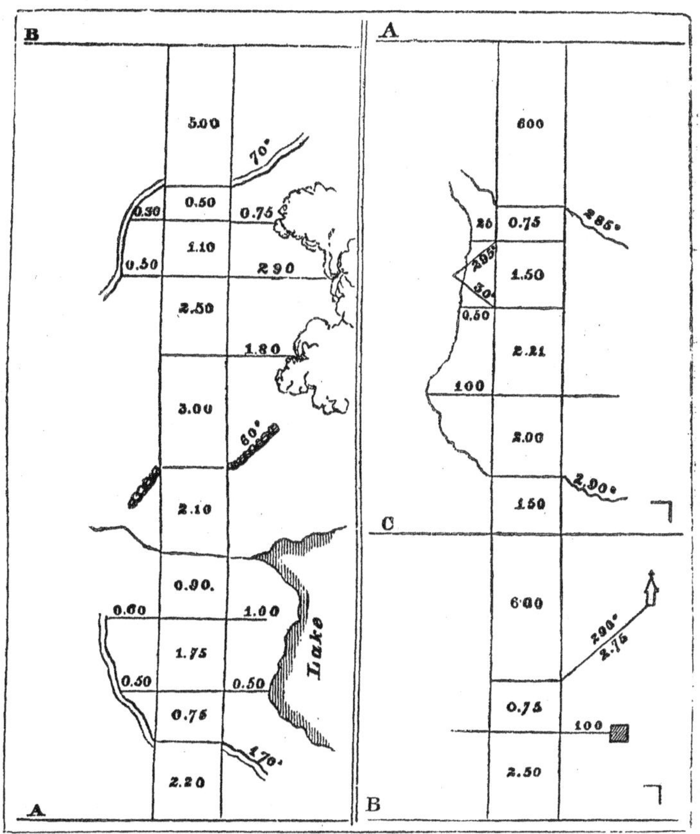

To survey a town or city the same general method would be pursued. The principal lines run with the compass would be the main streets, and the objects on either side would be brought in by either oblique or perpendicular offsets. The points of crossing of the minor streets would be noted, and their bearings taken.

LEVELLING.

The instrument employed for this purpose is called *the level*, and consists of a telescope mounted horizontally upon a tripod. At the top of the tripod, firmly fastened to it, is a small horizontal circular plate of brass, parallel to which, and a few inches above it, is another of the same size, the two being separated by levelling screws, and called levelling plates. From the centre of the upper levelling plate rises vertically a spindle, which fits into a socket in the middle of a horizontal bar, about a foot or more in length. At the extremities of this bar are two stout uprights of two or three inches in length, the tops of which are formed as Y^s, in which the telescope rests, in a position parallel to the horizontal bar. One of these Y^s has a vertical motion by means of a screw underneath it, which passes up through the end of the horizontal bar. A spirit level is suspended below the telescope and parallel to it, having a horizontal movement by means of a screw at one end, and a vertical movement by the same means, at the other.

1. To collimate the instrument, bring the intersection of the wires upon some well-defined distant point, and then turn the telescope on its optical axis in the Y^s, till the spirit level comes at top. If the intersection of the spider lines be not in the axis of motion, it will depart from the object, and will be as much on the opposite side of the axis after this demi-revolution. It must, therefore, be brought back half way to the object, by the screws which move the wires. This experiment must be repeated till the intersection remains on the object, during the revolution of the telescope on its optical axis.

There are three lines of the instrument which ought to be parallel to each other, horizontal, and perpendicular to the vertical axis about which the instrument turns, viz., the line of collimation, the axis of the spirit level, and the horizontal bar.

2. To render the axis of the spirit level parallel to the line of collimation, bring the air bubble to the centre by turning the levelling screws, having previously placed the level in the direction of the line joining two of them; take the telescope out of the Y^s, and reverse it, turning it end for end; if the bubble remains in the centre, both lines, that is to say, the line of collimation and the axis of the level, are horizontal; if not, bring the bubble half way back to the centre, by means of the screws at the end of the spirit level, and the other half by the levelling screws. Repeat this process until, in both positions of the telescope, the bubble remains in the centre. The axis of the spirit level may also be oblique to the line of collimation in a lateral direction. To ascertain whether it is so or not, turn the telescope on its optical axis as it rests in the Y^s, till the spirit level comes out at one side, not so far, however, as to cause the bubble to disappear; the lateral obliquity will then be converted into an obliquity partially vertical, which the departure of the bubble from the centre will render sensible. This obliquity must be corrected by the screws at the other end of the spirit level, which give a lateral motion to its tube.

3. To render the line of collimation and axis of the spirit level now

parallel to each other, both parallel to the horizontal bar, or rather perpendicular to the vertical axis of the instrument, round which the horizontal bar turns, by means of the spindle fitting into the socket at its centre; bring the bubble to the centre, by means of the levelling screws, turn the instrument round the vertical axis 180°,* and if the bubble remains in the centre,† the axis of the spirit level, and consequently its parallel, the axis‡ about which the telescope revolves, are perpendicular to the vertical axis of the instrument, and the latter, though not vertical, is in a vertical plane, perpendicular to the line of collimation. To make it vertical, which must be done every time an observation is made with the instrument, the above adjustments being completed, bring the bubble to the centre by means of the levelling screws, then turn the bar 90° on the vertical axis, and bring the bubble to the centre again; the vertical axis will then be truly vertical.

In connexion with this instrument two rectangular staves, called levelling staves, are used, divided into feet, tenths and hundredths of a foot. The staves are painted white, and the division lines are made very distinct, in black or red, the feet being numbered with distinct numerals; the hundredths are painted, the whole of each division, alternately white, and black or red. Two or three lengths of 6 feet of staff fit together by joints, so as to make a length of 12 or 18 feet. A plumb line suspended at the side of the staff, or in a groove covered, the lead part with glass so as to be visible, serves to place the staff exactly vertical.

In order to find the difference of level between two points of ground or the height of one above the other with these instruments, let an assistant hold one of the levelling staves vertically, standing upon one of the points in question, and another assistant the other staff, at some point in the direction of the second point; the observer turns the telescope, after the vertical axis of the instrument has been made truly vertical, and takes the reading cut by the horizontal wire, first on one of the levelling staffs, and then on the other,§ recording them in separate columns of a field

* If there is a horizontal compass box attached to the instrument this may be done by observing the number of degrees to which the needle points. If not, the instrument must be placed on the line of two staves, and between them, sighting first to one, and then to the other.

† If not, half the correction must be made by the screw under the Y, which affects the relative direction of the horizontal bar to the axis of the telescope, the other half by the levelling screws, and the operation repeated.

‡ This axis, by the first adjustment, is identical with the line of collimation, or line of vision, when the intersection of the wires is brought upon an object. It is not the optical axis of the telescope, though it should be as nearly as possible, but the axis of the cylindrical parts of its tube, which are in contact with the Y's.

§ Not only feet, tenths, and hundredths may be distinctly read, but even thousandths, by estimation.

book, the one in the direction in which he is going, under the title of "forward readings," the other under that of reverse readings.* The staff on the given point of ground is now taken up and carried round the other (which is simply turned about where it stands), to a point still farther in the direction of the second given point; the level is also removed to a point between the levelling staves, and the process just described is repeated, and so on, till the second given point, between which and the first the difference of level is required, is reached, the last levelling staff being placed there. The difference between the sum of the direct readings and the sum of the reverse readings will be the difference of level of the two given points, or height of the one above the other.

To make a section of ground which is the intersection of a vertical plane with the surface of the earth, it is necessary to add three more columns to the field book, a column of differences, a column of heights, and a column of distances. The first contains the difference between each direct and reverse reading ;† the second contains the height of each point upon which the levelling staves are placed above a horizontal plane, assumed at pleasure, usually passing through the first point of the survey. Each number in the column of heights will be computed by adding the number of the column of differences to the preceding number in the column of heights; the first number in the column of heights is the

* The level is always placed nearly half way between the two staffs, to avoid the error which would be occasioned by the difference between true and apparent level, the nature of which may be explained by the annexed diagram. Let the circle in the diagram be a vertical section of the earth through the point A, where the instrument is supposed to stand. The arc AM will be the line of true level, A and M being at equal distances from the centre of the earth C; the line AT tangent at A is the line of apparent level, determined by the optical axis of the instrument. For a point on the opposite side of A, from M, and at the same distance, the difference between apparent and true level will be the same. Hence the advantage of placing the instrument half way between the points whose difference of level is to be observed.

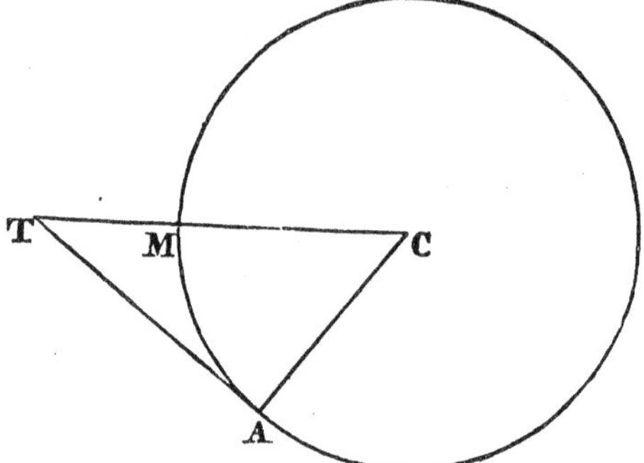

† This should be entered with the negative sign, if the direct exceed the reverse reading.

same as tnat adjoining in the column of differences. The numbers in the column of heights will be negative for points below the plane of reference. The third column contains the horizontal distances between points at which the levelling **staves** were placed, supposed to be measured with a tape or chain. To plot the section or profile of ground from such a field book, a horizontal line must be drawn to represent the section of the profile with the plane of reference; on this the numbers from the column of distances must be laid off from a scale of equal parts, and at the points of division ordinates or perpendiculars must be erected and taken from the scale of equal parts, equal to the numbers in the columns of heights; through the tops of these ordinates the section of ground required can then be traced with the hand. The following example of a field book, and the profile constructed from it, will serve to illustrate this subject.

D R	R R	Dif.	H	Dist.
6•895	2•461	4•434	4•434	1•35
5•321	1•468	3•854	8•287	0•75
8•264	3•812	4•452	12•739	1•00
9•322	2•111	7•211	19•950	1•50
7•444	3•212	4•232	24•280	2•00
4•321	1•211	3•110	27•390	1•25

CONTOUR OF GROUND.

The mode of representing this is by means of horizontal sections formed by planes at regular intervals, one above another, these sections being all projected upon one horizontal plane, viz., that represented by the map.

To survey a hill for the purpose of drawing its horizontal sections upon a map, place an instrument for taking horizontal angles at the top of the hill, and plant stakes along lines diverging from this point down the hill, and take the horizontal angles formed by the vertical planes in which these lines lie; then level along the lines, taking the difference of level and distance at points where the slope changes. In order now from such a survey to plot the horizontal sections of the hill, draw on the map from the point A, corresponding to the one assumed on the top of the hill (supposed to have been previously determined in position on the map by triangulation or otherwise), a system of lines diverging from this point under

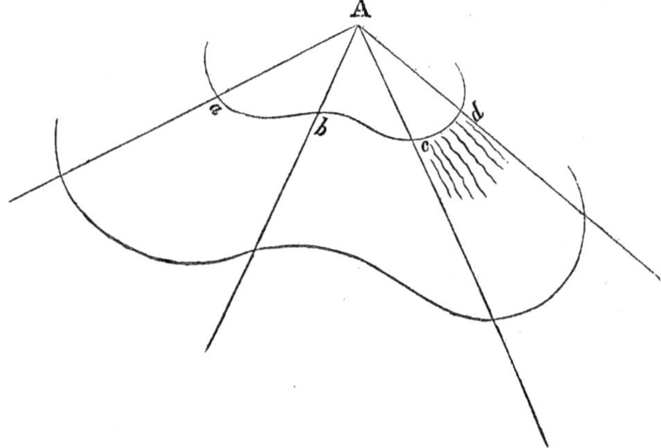

angles equal to the observed angles, and supposing, to render the conception definite, that the planes forming the horizontal sections are taken 10 feet apart, the points in which the projections of the sections cut the diverging line thus drawn, may be ascertained by proportion as follows :— The difference of level between two points on one of these lines is to the horizontal distance between them, as 10 feet is to the horizontal distance from the upper point, at which a plane of section ten feet below this point would cut the diverging line. Commencing with the upper point of all, A, and determining thus the points *a*, *b*, *c*, *d*, at which the projection of the section 10 feet below cuts each of the diverging lines, it may be traced through them by the hand. In a similar manner another section 10 feet lower, and so on to the bottom of the hill. Where the sections are convex, are the ridges, or *back bones* of the hill; where the sections are re-entering are the ravines; and in general, the varying forms of the sections present to a practised eye an exact notion of the general configuration of the hill. In topographical maps these sections are drawn in pencil, and the hill shaded with irregular lines, in India ink, perpendicular to the sections, as seen between *c* and *d*, which is the direction in which water or alluvion would flow down the hill. These shading lines are best drawn with a pen of short coarse nib, and very short portions of a number of them at a time. The light should be supposed to fall obliquely in a certain direction, and the sides of the ravines towards the source of light will be darker than the opposite sides. The tops of the back bones will be quite light. The summits of the hills being usually more nearly perpendicular, will present deeper shades than the bases, which usually slope gently into the level ground.

Water is shaded by making the line of shore quite black, which should be first drawn all round the map, including the islands, then a second and finer line all round, as near the first as possible without touching it, then a third a little more distant, and so on, broader and broader, till the shadings from opposite shores meet midway.*

SURVEY OF ROADS, RAILWAYS, AND CANALS.

The problem ordinarily is to ascertain the shortest and cheapest route from one point to another on the surface of the earth, having no greater and more sudden elevations or depressions than are compatible with the nature of the locomotion to be employed upon it.†

The case frequently presented, not only for the whole route, but in minor instances, along its course, is that of a dividing ridge between two valleys, from one to the other of which it is necessary to pass.

It becomes necessary then to ascertain the lowest point of the dividing ridge. A good indication may be obtained proximately by a simple inspection of the course of the streams upon a map, inasmuch as the direction of their flow must be governed by the topography of the country over which they pass. One or two examples will sufficiently illustrate the principles which are to guide such an inspection.

If two streams run along two valleys, and tributaries proceed from near the same point A of the dividing ridge to empty into them, then the point A is a low point of the dividing ridge. For the waters accumulating for the formation of the sources of the tributaries at the point A must flow from higher ground on both sides of this point.

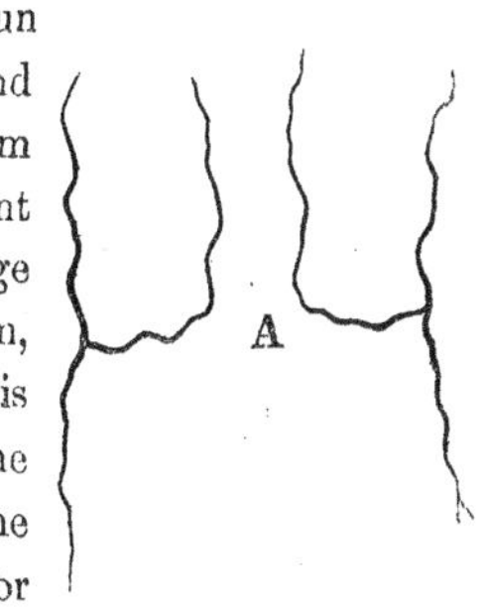

Again, if two tributaries running at first nearly parallel to the principal streams, turn outward at a point A, this is a low point. For the

* For further instruction in topographical drawing see an excellent little work by S. EASTMAN, U.S.A.

† This will of course be modified by various circumstances, such as the greater or less difficulty of working the ground, from the nature of the soil; the vicinity of large towns, to pass through which the construction would turn aside, the existence of mines, or valuable products of any kind, for which it would afford transportation.

tributaries at first descending into a lower country than that at their sources, encounter rising ground, which prevents their progress in that direction, and turns them off towards their principals.

These examples will suffice to point out the nature of the investigation to which an ordinary map should be subjected. A good topographical map, exhibiting contour of ground, would of course be a far better guide. Conflicting points of passage of a ridge may be compared by means of an altitude and azimuth instrument or theodolite; by first levelling the instrument, elevating the telescope till the line of sight passes through one of the points in question, and then turning the instrument in azimuth till the line of sight passes by the other point in question; if it passes above, the latter point is lower than the former, and vice versâ.

Next, a personal reconnoissance of the country should be made, and information sought from the inhabitants as to the nature of the ground, convenience for obtaining constructing materials, the mineral and agricultural wealth of the region, etc., etc. Three or four routes may thus be selected, one or other of which is to be finally decided upon by a rough survey of them all. This survey is conducted with the compass and chain, and level. The former instruments furnish a plot of the route by the method pointed out at p. 238, and the latter, a continuous profile or longitudinal section of the ground along the whole route, as seen at p. 251. A comparison of the compass plots of the different routes will determine which is the shortest, in a horizontal direction, and a comparison of the profiles will show which presents most elevation and depression to be overcome. The route being thus finally selected, it must be surveyed with care, another column being added to the field book, entitled *grade*, the numbers in which express the height of the roadway or bottom of the canal above the plane of reference at the same points of the route, for which the column of heights expresses those of the natural ground. The numbers in the column of grade will depend upon the elevation or depression of the natural ground, and the slope which the construction permits, that of a common road being greater than that of a railroad, and the latter being greater than that of a canal. The determination of these numbers will require an exercise of eye and judgment. A prime object to be had in view is the equalization of excavation and embankment; *i. e.*, the grade should be so adjusted to the natural slope of the ground as to cut off as much earth as would be required to fill the depression adjoining, up to the level of the grade. The survey being finished, a double profile must be made, one of the natural ground in black ink, the other of the grade in red, upon the same base line, and with the same abscissas or horizontal distances between the ordinates or lines of heights. An inspection of this, and a computation, if necessary, of areas between the black and red lines of section, will serve to show how well the excavation and embankment have been equalized, and the result may require a modification of the grade to adapt it better for the purpose in question, to the natural ground; cross-sections of the route must also be surveyed at all points of change in the longitudinal or latitudinal slope, and more frequently, if these occur at long intervals. The amount of excavation and embankment may be then obtained with sufficient accuracy for an estimate of expense, by computing the areas of the cross-sections of the work as it will be when completed, and multiplying half the sum of the areas of two of them by the longitudinal distance between them. The cross-sections, when the work is in embankment, will be of the form exhibited below, and the same turned upside down when the work is in

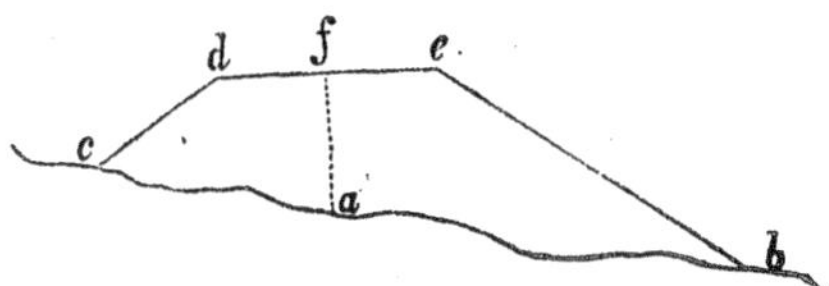

excavation. These are easily drawn from the field book. The cross-section *bac* being plotted, *a* corresponding to the point where it intersects the longitudinal section of ground, *af* will be the difference of the numbers in the columns of height and grade, *df*, *fe*, each equal to half the breadth fixed upon for the top of the road or bottom of the canal, *dc*, *eb* are then drawn at the proper slopes, for common earth $1\frac{1}{2}$ base to 1 in height. These sections may be regarded as quadrilaterals, and each divided into two triangles, for the purpose of obtaining their area.* Where the cross-section of ground is parallel to the top of the road, or bottom of the canal, they are trapezoids, and the area will then be $\frac{1}{2}$ the sum of the

* To compute the area of the cross-section from the numbers in the field book, conceive parallels to be drawn from the points *b* and *c* in the diagram, to *af*, meeting *de*, produced both ways; a trapezoid will be formed, from which, if two right angled triangles be deducted, the area of the sections will be obtained. If *d* denote the difference of level between *b* and *f*, *d* will be one parallel side of the trapezoid, and the altitude of one of the triangles, the base of which if the slope be $1\frac{1}{2}$ will be $\frac{3}{2}d$. And if d' denote the difference of level between *c* and *f*, similar expressions will be had for the other side and altitude; and the expressions for the area of the section will be, *b* being the breadth of the roadway,

$$\tfrac{1}{2}(d+d')\left[b+\tfrac{3}{2}(d+d')\right]-\tfrac{3}{2}d\times\tfrac{1}{2}d-\tfrac{3}{2}d'\times\tfrac{1}{2}d'=\tfrac{1}{2}\left[(d+d')b+3dd'\right]$$

parallel sides *dc*, *cb*, multiplied by the altitude *af*. Notes of the nature of the soil are kept in the field book of the compass, and the amount of digging and wheeling or carting that can be done in a day in different kinds of earth, having been ascertained by experiment, and the price of day labor being known, the data for determining the expense of the work are all known. To the above must be added the accidental expenses of culverts, blasting rocks, construction of tunnels, &c., which are all subjected to the same general rules, and are functions of the price of materials, mechanic labor, and experiments as to relations of time and amount of performance.

TO COMPUTE THE CONTENTS OF FIELDS.

1. Compute the contents of the figures, whether triangles or trapeziums, &c., by the proper rules for the several figures. If the linear measures be in links, the result is acres, after cutting off five figures on the right for decimals. Then bring these decimals to roods and perches, by multiplying first by 4, and then by 40.

2. In small and separate pieces, it is usual to cast up their contents from the measures of the lines taken in surveying them, without making a correct plan of them.

3. In pieces bounded by very crooked and winding hedges, measured by offsets, all the parts between the offsets are most accurately measured separately as small trapezoids.

4. But in larger pieces, and whole estates, consisting of many fields, it is the common practice to make a rough plan of the whole, and from it compute the contents quite independent of the measures of the lines and angles that were taken in surveying. For, then, new lines are drawn in the fields in the plan, so as to divide them into trapeziums and triangles, the bases and perpendiculars of which are measured on the plan by means of the scale from which it was drawn, and so multiplied together for the contents. In this way the work is very expeditiously done, and sufficiently correct; for such dimensions are taken as afford the most easy method of calculation; and, among a number of parts thus taken and applied to a scale, it is likely that some of the parts will be taken a small matter too little, and others too great; so that they will, upon the whole, in all probability, very nearly balance one another. After all the fields and particular parts are thus computed separately, and added all together into one sum, calculate the whole estate independently of the fields, by dividing it into large and arbitrary triangles and trapeziums, and add these also together. Then if this sum be equal to the former, or nearly so, the

work is right; but if the sums have any considerable difference, it is wrong, and they must be examined and recomputed, till they nearly agree.

5. But the chief secret in computing consists in finding the contents of pieces bounded by curved or very irregular lines, or in reducing such crooked sides of fields or boundaries to straight lines, that shall inclose the same or equal area with those crooked sides, and so obtain the area of the curved figure by means of the right-lined one, which will commonly be a trapezium. Now, this reducing the crooked sides to straight ones, is very easily and accurately performed in this manner:—Apply the straight edge of a thin, clear piece of lantern-horn to the crooked line which is to be reduced, in such a manner that the small parts cut off from the crooked figure by it, may be equal to those which are taken in; which equality of the parts included and excluded you will presently be able to judge of very nicely by a little practice; then with a pencil or point of a tracer, draw a line by the straight edge of the horn. Do the same by the other side of the field or figure. So shall you have a straight-sided figure equal to the curved one, the content of which, being computed as before directed, will be the content of the curved figure proposed.

Or, instead of the straight edge of the horn, a horse-hair may be applied across the crooked sides in the same manner; and the easiest way of using the hair is to string a small slender bow with it, either of wire, or cane, or whalebone, or such like slender or elastic matter; for, the bow keeping it always stretched, it can be easily and neatly applied with one hand, while the other is at liberty to make two marks by the side of it, to draw the straight line by.

EXAMPLE.

Let it be required to find the contents of the irregular figure below, to a scale of 4 chains to an inch.

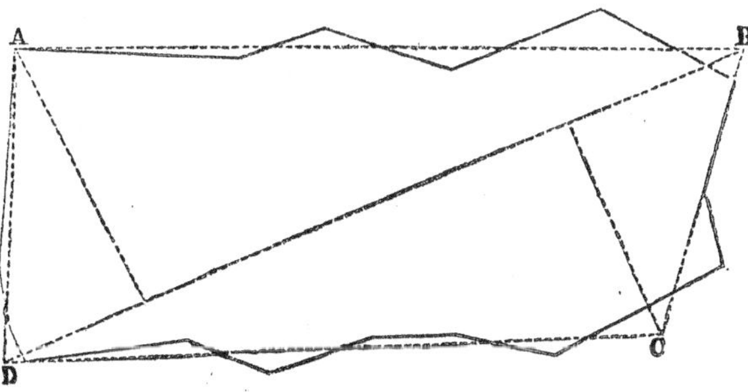

Draw the four dotted straight lines AB, BC, CD, DA, cutting off equal quantities on both sides of them, which they do as near as the eye can judge; so is the crooked figure reduced to an equivalent right-lined one of four sides, ABCD. Then draw the diagonal BD, which, by applying a proper scale to it, measures 1256. Also the perpendicular, or nearest distance, from A to this diagonal measures 456; and the distance of C from it is 428.

Then, half the sum of 456 and 428, multiplied by the diagonal 1256, gives 555,152 square links, or 5 acres, 2 roods, 8 perches, the content of the trapezium, or of the irregular crooked piece.

TO FIND THE CONTENT OF A FIELD WITHOUT PLOTTING.

Take the bearings and lengths of the sides of the field, and enter them in a field book as course and distance, and take out the difference of latitude and departure corresponding to each, and enter them in two double columns, marked N. S. and E. W. as at Art. 98. To obtain these, if the bearings are given in degrees, recourse may be had to a table of difference of latitude and departure for every degree and minute of the quadrant, such as is found in Bowditch's Navigator, or instead of this, the difference of latitude and departure may be calculated for each course and distance.* Another double column must be added, entitled double meridian distances. The meridian distance of any line is the distance of its middle point from an assumed meridian, which should be taken through some corner of the field. The double *meridian distance*, corresponding to *the first course* adjoining the assumed meridian, will be equal to *the departure of that course.* Double the meridian distance of any other course will be equal to the *double meridian distance of the preceding course, plus the departure of the preceding course, plus its own departure.*†

In applying this rule, distances to the right should be considered +, those to the left —. The double meridian distances east of the meridian

* The sum of the numbers in the column marked N. ought to equal that of the numbers in the column marked S. If such be not the case, the difference between the two sums should be half of it subtracted from the numbers in the column having the greater sum, being distributed among them in proportion to their magnitude; the other half should be added in the same way to the numbers in the column producing the less sum. For in going round a field and returning to the same point, the distance gone north must be equal to that gone south. The same remark applies to the columns marked E. and W. New columns will then be derived which may be called corrected diff. of lat. and departure.

† This may be seen by making and inspecting a diagram.

should be entered in a column marked E., and those west in a column marked W., the column of double meridian distances being made double for the purpose. By means of this double column of double meridian distances, and the double column of differences of latitude, the content of the field may be computed by the following rule.

The difference between the northings multiplied by the eastings plus the southings multiplied by the westings, and the northings multiplied by the westings, plus the southings multiplied by the eastings, will be equal to double the area of the land.

The proof of this is left as an exercise for the student.

In the following example the bearings were taken with a compass resembling the mariner's in principle. A metallic graduated circle, one diameter of which, that joining the zero and 180° points, being an attached needle, the graduated circle was held stationary in space by the magnetic force of the earth. The numbering was from zero to 360 in the direction shown in the annexed diagram. The compass sights were plain, and the number on the line of sights towards the extremity next the eye was the one read and recorded in the 1st column p. 261. The equivalents of these readings in bearings of the compass courses or sides of the field from the meridian, are recorded in the 2d column. These are ascertained by considering in what part of the circumference in the diagram above the No. in the 1st column would fall; the course would be in the direction from this point to the centre of the circle.

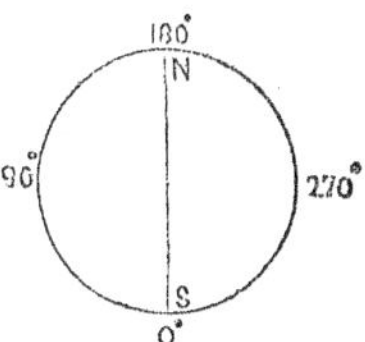

The third column contains the lengths of the courses or sides of the field, measured with a chain. Then follow the columns of difference of latitude and departure,* and the columns of corrected diff. of lat. and departure. The assumed meridian from which to estimate the double meridian distances is taken through the point at which the survey commenced.† The double meridian distance of the first course then, according to the rule, will be equal to its departure 234·1, and is W. because the departure is W. Double the meridian distance of the second course is equal to that of the preceding course 234·1 + the departure of the preceding course 234·1 + its own departure 50·3. (See rule.) All these numbers being W., their sum in the arithmetical sense, 518·5, is taken as the double meridian distance of the 2d course. For the next course the departure 17·6 is E., and on the general analytic principle that quantities estimated in a contrary sense must have contrary signs, this may be

* The sum of the column N. 264·5 exceeds that of the column S. 263·0 by 1·5; half this, or ·8 is subtracted from the numbers of the first column N., ·6 from the 1st No. in the column, and ·1 from each of the other two, to obtain the Nos. in the 2d column N., and ·7, in the same manner, is added by distribution among the five numbers of the 1st column S., to produce those of the 2d column S., &c.

† It would be most simple to assume it through the westernmost point of the land, in the present example at the commencement of the 3d course, where the reading was 163°. Here the courses, which were previously all W., begin to turn E. The advantage of this is that the double meridian distances would be all E.

considered positive, if we regard the previous numbers employed in computing the double meridian distances, which are all W. as negative. To add this 17•6 then, in the algebraic sense, to the sum of 518•5, and 50•3, according to the rule, will be in reality to subtract it, which gives 551•2 for the 3d D. M. D. For a similar reason the sum of 17•6 and 73•2 being both E., must be subtracted from 551•2, which is W., to produce the 4th D. M. D.; and so on till we arrive at the 7th course, marked 80°, in the 1st column. Here the sum of the two departures, 96•7 and 59•2, both E., viz., 155•9 exceeds the last D. M. D., 135•9, which is still W., and as they have contrary signs, their algebraic sum will be their difference with the sign of the greater, which is E., and this difference 20•0 must be entered in the column E. of double meridian distances. The D. M. D. of the last course is obtained by adding 59•2 and 20•0 both E., and subtracting 40•1, which is W., from their sum. The double meridian distances E., which have corresponding difference of latitude, N., are now multiplied by them according to the rule; and the double meridian distances W., which have corresponding differences of latitude S., and the products all entered in a column entitled N. × E. + S. × W., and their sum taken. Of the N. × W. + S. × E., which the remaining part of the rule requires to be formed, there is but one product in this example an N × W. 196•2 by 234•1, or 45930•42, for which an additional column, which would ordinarily be employed, is not worth while. This product is subtracted from the sum of the former, and the remainder, 68103•90, is by the rule equal to double the area of the land in square links, 10,000* of which make a square chain. Half this will be the area, which is converted into square chains by removing the decimal point 4 places to the left; and this again into acres, by removing the decimal point one place further to the left still, since there are 10 sq. chains in an acre. The decimals of an acre are converted into roods and perches by multiplying by 4 and by 40.

The plotting of the above example will be an exercise. A circle should be described on the paper, and points marked on it, according to the compass readings in the first column, the N. and S. line corresponding to the 0° and 180° points, as in the last diagram. Lines drawn from the points thus marked to the centre of the circle will be parallel to the boundary lines of the survey. For further directions see p. 237 at bottom.

* Which is the square of 100, the No. of links in a chain.

EXAMPLE.

Compass Reading.	Bearing from Meridian.	Dist.	Diff. Lat.		Dep.		Cor. Diff. Lat.		Cor. Dep.		D. M. D.		
			N.	S.	E.	W.	N.	S.	E.	W.	E.	W.	N.×E.+S.×W.
310°	N. 50 W.	306	196•8			234•4	196•2			234•1		234•1	
226	S. 46 W.	70		48•6		50•4		48•7		50•3		518•5	25250•95
163	S. 17 E.	60		57•4	17•5			57•5	17•6			551•2	31694•00
133	S. 47 E.	100		68•2	73•1			68•3	73•2			461•4	31513•62
129	S. 51 E.	100		62•9	77•7			63•1	77•8			310•4	19586•24
105	S. 75 E.	100		25•9	96•6			26•1	96•7			135•9	3546•99
80	N. 80 E.	60	10•4		59•1		10•3		59•2		20•0		206•00
325	N. 35 W.	70	57•3			40•2	57•2			40•1	39•1		2236•52
			264•5	263•0	324•0	325•0	263•7	263•7	324•5	324•5			114034•32
													45930•42

2) 68103•90

Area in Square Links, 34051•95
4

Roods, 1•3620780
40

Perches, 14•4831200

The area is therefore 1 rood, 14•48 perches.

HYDROGRAPHIC SURVEYING.

In the survey of harbors, after having surveyed and plotted the outline of the shore, it becomes necessary to set down upon the map the depths of the water in feet or fathoms at a sufficient number of points to serve as a guide to navigators. The depth is ascertained by sounding, and the problem is to fix upon the map the points at which the soundings were made. One method consists in rowing a boat uniformly in a straight line from one point on the shore to another opposite, casting the lead at regular intervals by a watch; this line being drawn on the map and divided into as many equal parts as there were casts, the points of division will be the points required; upon these the numbers obtained by the soundings are to be put down. Another method is to place three signals upon the shore, not in the same straight line, and with a sextant* in the boat to measure the angles subtended by the lines joining these signals; then having these lines plotted upon the map, construct upon each of them a segment capable of containing the observed angle subtended by it (see Plane Geom., Prob. 21), and the intersection of the arcs of these segments will determine the points on the map at which the boat was situated at the time of observation. The sounding of course should be taken at the same point, and recorded at its position (6) thus determined on the map.

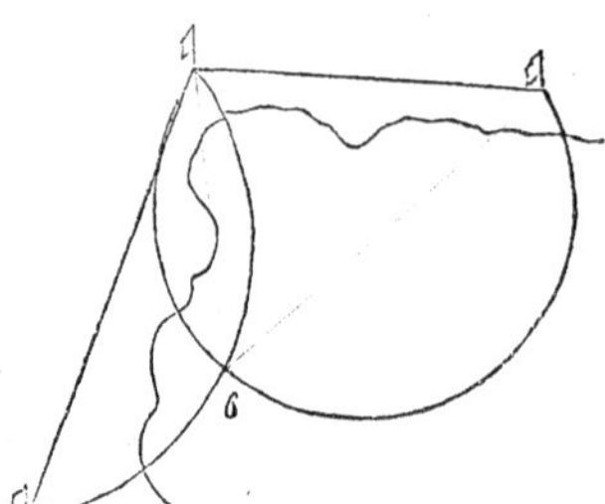

A third method consists in having two theodolites, and taking the angles with them from the extremities of a base line on the shore, by which means the position of the boat is determined. In this method a system of signals is requisite, by which the observers on shore may know the instant at which the sounding is made. A very perfect one was invented by Mr. Thomas H. Norris, of New York, and practised in the survey of the mouths of the Mississippi. This consisted in having at one of the two stations on the shore (which in the low lands of the Mississippi were elevated platforms of wood) a flag which could be run up and a chronometer. The boat also carried a chronometer. The intervals of time at which the soundings should be made having been previously agreed upon, about 10 seconds before one of these intervals expired, the flag was run up, and both theodolites brought to bear upon the boat, or rather upon a staff at its bow, from which the

* See the instrument of this name described at p. 290, note.

sounding was made. The tangent screws served to keep the instruments steadily upon this point, and the instant the 10 seconds were up, the flag was lowered, the lead was cast, and the readings taken from the horizontal limbs of the instruments and recorded. This mode was found to be very rapid and accurate. By way of experiment the boat was frequently made to cross its track, and the agreement was exact. By rowing the boat along at oar's length from the shore, and determining its position at frequent intervals, as above described, the line of shore could be traced upon the map. This was found particularly convenient in the survey of the bayous or inlets of the low muddy banks.

Horizontal sections of the bottom of a harbor may be determined, making the plane of the water a plane of reference, in an obvious manner, and the bottom represented in the same manner as a hill. This, however, is not often practised.

Points at great distances out at sea are obtained by triangulating outward with three vessels successively moored at points more and more remote from the shore.

PART V.

APPLICATION OF SPHERICAL TRIGONOMETRY TO

NAUTICAL ASTRONOMY.

PART V.

APPLICATION OF SPHERICAL TRIGONOMETRY TO

NAUTICAL ASTRONOMY.

103. Navigation, as we have seen, is the determination of the place of a ship at sea, that is to say her latitude and longitude, by the "dead reckoning."

The dead reckoning proceeds upon the hypothesis that the ship's course and the distance she sails are accurately known; and if this were really the case, her true place might be found by the methods given in Part III. But this is impossible. 1. From the difficulty of steering exactly upon the intended course. 2. From the uncertainty of lee-way. 3. From errors of the log, occasioned by the heaving of the sea, unknown currents, and the rudeness of the instrument itself.

The "dead reckoning" is, however, indispensable in determining the ship's place during cloudy weather, and is useful at all times for detecting the existence and velocity of currents.

The main reliance must be upon astronomical observations, and the method of determining a ship's place by means of these constitutes the science of nautical astronomy.

DEFINITIONS.

104. For the purpose of measuring the *angular* distances of the heavenly bodies from each other, and from the horizon, it is convenient to suppose them all situated as they really appear to an observer on the earth, viz., in a spherical concave surrounding the earth, and concentric with it. This imaginary concave, which the student may suppose identical with the blue vault of the sky, is called the celestial sphere.

The position of a point on the celestial sphere, like the position of a point on the terrestrial sphere, is fixed by its latitude and longitude. On the celestial sphere the circle of longitude is the ecliptic; and secondaries passing, therefore, through the poles of the ecliptic, are the circles of celestial latitude; the point from which longitude is measured is the vernal equinoctial point. Commencing at this point, the ecliptic is divided into twelve parts called signs; a sign is, therefore, 30°. The twelve signs are named, and symbolically expressed, as follows:

1. ♈ Aries.	4. ♋ Cancer.	7. ♎ Libra.	10. ♑ Capricornus.
2. ♉ Taurus.	5. ♌ Leo.	8. ♏ Scorpio.	11. ♒ Aquarius.
3. ♊ Gemini.	6. ♍ Virgo.	9. ♐ Sagittarius.	12. ♓ Pisces.

The vernal equinoctial point is called the first point of Aries. The longitude is measured from this point in one direction, viz., in the order of the signs, or from W. to E.

Parallels of latitude on the terrestrial sphere correspond to parallels of declination on the celestial. Of these, the two which touch the ecliptic in the first points of Cancer and Capricorn, are called the *tropics* of Cancer and of Capricorn. These first points of Cancer and Capricorn* are respectively called the summer and winter *solstice;* because for a day or two before and after the sun enters them he appears to be stationary, and the days to be of equal length, so slowly does his declination at those times change, for his motion is obviously very nearly parallel to the equator. The declination circle, through the solstitial points, is called the *solstitial colure,* and that through the equinoctial points the *equinoctial colure.*

Secondaries to the equator, we have said (Art. 79), are called *declination* or *hour circles.*

The declination of a heavenly body is its distance from the equator in degrees, minutes, and seconds, measured on the declination or hour circle which passes through the body.

The right ascension of a heavenly body is the number of degrees and fractions of a degree measured on the equator, between the vernal equinox or first of Aries, and the circle of declination which passes through the body. Another definition of right ascension is the angle at the pole of the equator or of the earth, comprehended between the hour or declination circle through the vernal equinox, and the hour circle through the heavenly body.

Right ascension is now commonly expressed in hours, minutes, and

* At the first of these points the sun, which up to the time of its arrival there had been moving north, begins to move backwards towards the south; at the second from going south he begins to climb upwards towards the north, whence it appears that the points in question are named in allusion to the habits of the animals after which they are called.

seconds of time, allowing 15° to the hour, 15′ to the minute, and 15″ to the second of time.

The right ascension is also the difference in the time of transit of the heavenly body and of the first point of Aries over the meridian of any place.

The difference of right ascension of two stars is the difference in their times of meridian transit at the same place. Or it is the angle comprehended between the two hour circles which pass through the stars.

A *catalogue* of stars is a list of them with the right ascension and the declination of each annexed.*

Having described the principal circle and points of the celestial sphere which are considered as permanent, or which do not alter with the situation of the observer on the earth, we come now to describe those which change with his place. The principal of these is the *horizon*, which has been defined already (Art. 79), and *vertical circles*, which are secondaries to the horizon, and on which the altitudes of celestial objects are measured.

These vertical circles all meet in two points diametrically opposite, viz., the poles of the horizon; one of which is directly over the head of the observer, and called his *zenith*, and the opposite one his *nadir*. The ver-

* The late catalogue of the British Association, the name of which is abbreviated B. A. C., gives the north polar distances (N. P. D.) of the stars instead of their declinations. The north polar distance of a star is its distance from the north pole of the heavens, measured on the circle of declination passing through the star. The right ascension of the star fixes the position of this circle in the heavens, and the north polar distance fixes the place of the star upon the circle, so that its position is completely determined by these two co-ordinates. In the British Catalogue is a column containing the annual variation in R. A., and four columns marked a, b, c, d, at top; also a column containing the annual variation in N. P. D., and four columns marked a', b', c', d'. The numbers whose logarithms are in these columns may be regarded as constant for a period of about ten years. In the Nautical Almanac, on p. XXII. of each month, will be found four columns marked A, B, C, D, at top, containing the logs. of numbers, which vary with the time, or are ephemeral.

To find the R. A. of a star for any given time, take out its R. A. for the epoch of the catalogue, viz., 1850, to which add the product of the annual variation in R. A., by the number of years between the given time and 1850. The result will be the mean R. A. at the beginning of the given year. Take out from the columns a, b, c, d, the logs. opposite the given star, and from the Nautical Almanac, from the columns A, B, C, D, the logs. corresponding to the given date, for which the apparent R. A. is required, and with these logs. compute the following formula:

$$da = \mathrm{A}a + \mathrm{B}b + \mathrm{C}c + \mathrm{D}d$$

da being the correction to be applied to the result before found, to obtain the R. A. required. This will be the time at which a star ought to make its meridian transit by the siderial clock. The formula for the correction in declination is

$$d\delta = \mathrm{A}a' + \mathrm{B}b' + \mathrm{C}c' + \mathrm{D}d'$$

tical circle which passes through the east and west points of the horizon is called the *prime vertical;* it necessarily intersects the meridian of the place (which passes through the north and south points) at right angles.

The *azimuth* of a celestial object has been already defined to be an arc of the horizon, comprised between the meridian of the observer and the vertical circle through the object, and hence vertical circles are sometimes called azimuth circles.

The *amplitude* of a celestial object is the arc of the horizon comprised between the east point and the point where the object rises, or between the west point and that where it sets; the one is called the rising amplitude, the other the setting amplitude.

ON THE CORRECTIONS TO BE APPLIED TO THE OBSERVED ALTITUDES OF CELESTIAL OBJECTS.

105. The *true altitude* of a celestial object is always understood to mean its angular distance from the rational horizon of the observer. This is not obtained directly by observation; but is the result of certain corrections applied to the observed altitude.* These we shall now enumerate and explain.

* The observed altitude is obtained by means of an instrument called a quadrant of reflection, or simply a quadrant. This instrument is a frame of wood in the form of a sector of a circle, the arc of which is graduated to degrees and parts of a degree. This frame is suspended so that the plane of the circle shall be vertical. It has an arm, one extremity of which is attached to the centre of the circle, and which is movable about this point; upon this arm is a small mirror, and opposite to it is a plane glass, half of which is mirror, and half transparent. When a heavenly body, seen by double reflection in these two mirrors, is brought by the movement of the arm, upon which one of the mirrors is placed, to coincide with the line of the horizon at sea as seen through the transparent part of the opposite glass, the outer extremity of the arm points out upon the graduated arc the number of degrees of altitude of the heavenly body above the horizon.

The construction of this instrument depends upon the optical principle that the angle of incidence is equal to the angle of reflection. The angular movement of the image of the heavenly body is double the angular movement of the arm, so that to measure the greatest altitudes, the limit of which is 90°, the graduated arc need be but the eighth of a circumference; the degrees upon it are however numbered as if it were a quadrant, to save the trouble of doubling them. The instrument takes its name from the amount which it measures, instead of from the magnitude of its arc. There are colored glasses attached, which can be interposed so that the rays of light, coming from the heavenly body to the eye, can be made to pass through them when taking the altitude of the sun.

More complete instruments of this nature are the sextant and repeating circle, or circle of reflection, for full descriptions of which see p. 290, and p. 299.

DIP OR DEPRESSION OF THE HORIZON.

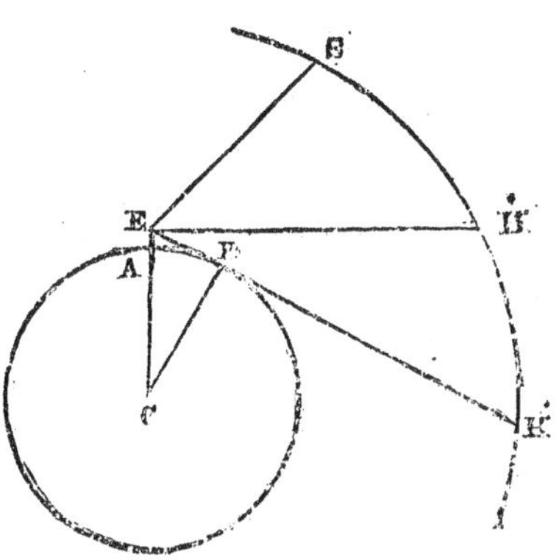

106. Let E represent the place of the observer's eye, elevated to the height EA above the surface of the earth, and S the place of a heavenly body; the first object is to obtain its apparent altitude above the horizontal line EH; that is, the angle SEH. Now, since to the observer, the *visible* horizon is in the direction EBH', the altitude taken with the instrument is the angle SEH'; hence from this observed altitude the angle HEH', called the *Dip or Depression of the Horizon*, must be subtracted to obtain the apparent altitude SEH.

The angle HEH', or its equal C, is calculated for various elevations, AE, of the eye above the surface of the sea, by resolving the right angled triangle EBC, in which are known CB, the radius of the earth, and EC equal to the radius increased by the height of the eye. The results are registered in a table (Table XXXI.), the argument of which is the height of the eye.

The depression thus obtained must be lessened by the amount of terrestrial refraction, which is very uncertain; $\frac{1}{10}$ of the whole quantity has been allowed in computing this table.

SEMIDIAMETER.

107. The foregoing correction for dip having been applied, the result will be the apparent altitude of the object observed, above the sensible horizon. If this be the upper or lower edge of the disc of the sun or moon, called the upper and lower limb, a further correction will be necessary to obtain the apparent altitude of the centre. The angle at the eye of the observer, subtended by the semidiameter or radius of the sun or moon, must be added to the altitude of the lower limb, and subtracted from that of the upper limb. This quantity, which is continually varying both for the sun and moon, in consequence of the variation of their distance from the

earth, is given in the Nautical Almanac for every day in the year.* But in the case of the moon the semidiameter itself requires a small correction depending upon the observed altitude. For the semidiameter, furnished by the Nautical Almanac, is the apparent *horizontal* semidiameter, *i. e.* the apparent semidiameter when the moon is in the horizon, where the distance from the observer is greater than when she is in the zenith by the semidiameter of the earth. Consequently her apparent semidiameter, which is inversely as her distance, will be least in the horizon, and greatest in the zenith; and its value between these limits will vary with the sine of the altitude, as may be easily seen by constructing a diagram.

The distance of the moon being about 60 semidiameters of the earth, the moon's horizontal semidiameter will be increased about $\frac{1}{60}$ part in the zenith. Therefore, if to the logarithm of the sine of $\frac{1}{60}$ of the ☽'s horizontal semidiameter or the log. of the arc itself, which is small, we add

* It is given for noon of each day for the sun, and for noon and midnight for the moon, and is found for any other time of day by the proportion: As 24 or 12 hours : the variation in 24 or 12 hours : : the time after noon or midnight, at Greenwich : the variation in that time, which must be added to the semidiameter given in the Almanac or subtracted, according as the semidiameter is increasing or diminishing from day to day, in order to have the semidiameter at the required time.

Proportions of this kind, in which the terms contain two or three denominations, as hours and minutes, minutes and seconds, or hours, minutes, and seconds, degrees and minutes, &c., may be resolved conveniently by means of the table of proportional logarithms, Table XXII.

The following example will illustrate the mode of proceeding.

$$24^h : 16' \; 19'' : : 8^h \; 2^m$$

Taking the first and third terms one grade lower, we find their proportional logarithms (P. L.) on pp. 134 and 132, writing the arith. comp. of the former, and taking from p. 133 the P. L. of 16′ 19″, the calculation will be as follows:

24^m	ar. comp. P. L.	9·1249
16′ 19″	P. L.	1·0426
$8^m \; 2^s$	P. L.	1·3504
5′ 28″	P. L.	1·5179

In this as in many other problems of Nautical Astronomy, the time at Greenwich at the instant of observation is required, and may be found by adding or subtracting the difference of longitude in time, according as the place is W. or E. of Greenwich. Thus the time at Greenwich, corresponding to any given time at New York, is found by adding $4^h \; 56^m \; 4^s$ (the difference of longitude between the two places) to the latter.

the log. sine of the ☽'s altitude, the result will be the log. of the apparent semidiameter at the given altitude.

In this way is formed the Table at the end, entitled *Augmentation of the Moon's Semidiameter* (Table XXXIII.), which contains the proper correction to be *added* to the given horizontal semidiameter, to obtain the true semidiameter.

On account of the great distance of the sun, no such correction of his semidiameter is necessary.

The corrections for dip and semidiameter being thus applied, the result is called *the apparent altitude of the centre.* In the case of the stars, the only correction for the apparent altitude is the dip.

To obtain the *true* altitude requires two other corrections, viz. for *refraction* and for *parallax.* The former of these has indeed an effect upon the two preceding corrections, dip and semidiameter, which require certain modifications in consequence, which we shall notice after explaining the nature and effect of

REFRACTION.

108. The rays of light coming from a heavenly body, having to pass through the atmosphere, are bent towards the vertical by refraction. As the atmosphere grows more and more dense in approaching the surface of the earth, the light bending continually towards the vertical pursues a curvilinear path in a vertical plane, and enters the eye in the last direction of its motion, which prolonged is a tangent to the curve, and it is in the direction of this tangent that the object emitting the light appears. The curve being convex upward, the tangent lies above it, and the effect of refraction is therefore to elevate the object, or to make the apparent place above the true place. The correction for refraction, therefore, like the correction for dip, is always *subtractive;* it decreases from the horizon, where it is greatest, to the zenith, where it vanishes (as the rays from objects in the zenith enter the atmosphere perpendicularly) in accordance with the optical law that the ratio of the sine of the angle of incidence to the sine of the angle of refraction is constant.

At the end of the volume we have given a table of refractions containing the correction for refraction to be applied to every altitude, from the horizon to the zenith,* and adapted to the mean state of the atmo-

* It will be observed that there is in the table a column of differences for 1′ of altitude. The number in this opposite the degrees in the given altitude must be multiplied by the given minutes and the result subtracted from the correction, or added to the altitude.

sphere (Table XXX.).* When the temperature of the atmosphere is raised, which is indicated by the thermometer, the refraction decreases; and when the density of the atmosphere is increased (indicated by the rising of the mercury in the barometer), its refractive power increases. The change in refraction for a difference of 1° of Fahrenheit, and of 1 inch in the barometer from the mean state, is given in separate columns, and must be multiplied the one by the number of degrees which the thermometer differs from 50°, and the other by the number of inches and fractions of an inch which the barometer differs from 30°, and the result added or subtracted, as the case may require. It should be observed that below 4° the refraction is very variable and uncertain, and such low altitudes should be avoided as much as possible at sea.

It will be unnecessary to use the correction for the state of the barometer and thermometer, when the latitude of the ship is the only object of the observation, as this could seldom make a difference so great as half a mile in the resulting latitude; but, in determining the longitude by the *Lunar Observations*, the neglect of these small corrections would sometimes introduce an error in the resulting longitude of more than thirty miles.

When the foregoing corrections have been applied to the observed altitude, the result will be the true altitude of the centre above the sensible horizon, and it now remains to apply the correction necessary to reduce this to the true altitude of the centre above the rational horizon; that is, to the altitude which the body would have if the observer were situated at the centre of the earth instead of on its surface. This last correction is called

PARALLAX.

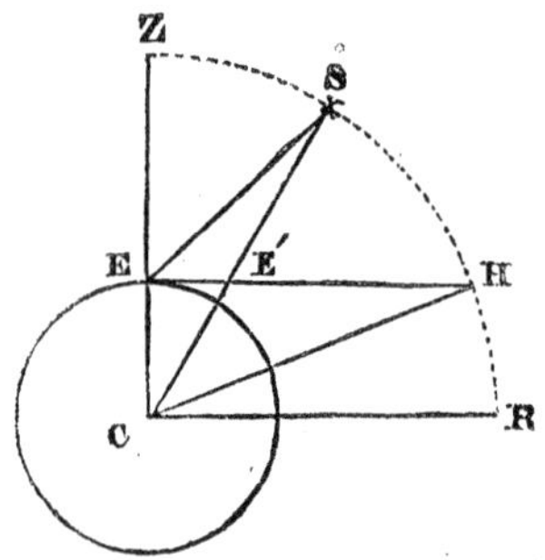

109. In order to explain the nature and effect of parallax, let S represent the place of the object observed from the surface of the earth, at E; then the angle SEH, that is, the observed angle, when corrected for dip, semidiameter, and refraction, will be the true altitude of the object, in reference to the observer's sensible horizon EH; and the angle SCR will be the true altitude

* Such a table might be formed by comparing the observed altitude of a star with its altitude computed from the declination or N.P.D. hour angle and latitude.

in reference to the rational horizon CR; and the difference of these angles is the parallax called *parallax in altitude* when the object is above the horizon as at S, and *horizontal parallax* when it is in the horizon as at H.

Since the angle SE′H is equal to the angle SCR, EH and CR being parallel by definition, we have for the parallax in altitude SE′H — SEH = ESC (Geom. Th. 15), that is, the parallax is the angle which the semidiameter of the earth subtends at the object;* it is obviously greatest in the horizon, and nothing in the zenith, and is the quantity which must be *added* to the true altitude above the sensible horizon to obtain the true altitude above the rational horizon.

The sun's parallax in altitude is given in a Table at the end (Table XXXIV.), his horizontal parallax being nearly constant; and the moon's horizontal parallax is given for the noon and midnight at Greenwich, of every day of the year, in the Nautical Almanac, and from the horizontal parallax thus obtained, parallax in altitude must be calculated. This is easy; for since in the triangle SEC we have the proportion

SC : EC : : sin SEC = sin SEZ = cos SEH : sin ESC;

it follows (since SC, the distance of the heavenly body, as well as EC, the semidiameter of the earth, may be regarded as constant for a single day), that the sine of the parallax in altitude varies as the cosine of the altitude; but when the altitude = 0, as in the case of horizontal parallax, cos. altitude = 1, and the constant ratio SC to EC, the above proportion shows to be equal to the sine of the horizontal parallax. But from the proportion itself we see that it is necessary to multiply this ratio by the cosine of the altitude, to have the sine of the parallax in altitude; but as the parallax is always a very small angle, it is usual to substitute the arc for its sine, or par. in alt. = hor. par. × cos. alt., so that

log. hor. par. in seconds + log. cos. alt. — 10 = log. par. in alt. in seconds.

We must observe here that the horizontal parallax, given in the Nautical Almanac, is calculated to the equatorial radius of the earth;

* This result might be arrived at much more simply by means of our definition of an angle (Geometry, def. 10), viz. "the difference of direction of two lines," and a definition of parallax, viz. the difference of direction in which an object is seen from the centre and surface of the earth, or in a more enlarged sense of the term, from any two points. This in the diagram will be the difference of direction of the two lines CS and ES, *i. e.* the angle CSE, or the angle subtended by the line joining the two points of observation.

and, therefore, except at the equator, a small subtractive correction of the horizontal parallax will be necessary, on account of the spheroidal figure of the earth, in consequence of which the radius of the earth is smaller everywhere else than at the equator, and consequently subtends a smaller parallax. A table of such corrections is given at the end. (See Table XXXV.) It must evidently be a table of double entry, the two arguments being the equatorial horizontal parallax and the latitude, upon which two quantities the correction depends.

110. Such are the corrections necessary to be applied to the observed altitudes of celestial objects, in order to obtain their true altitudes. A few other preliminary, but very simple and obvious operations, must also be performed upon the several quantities taken out of the Nautical Almanac, in order to reduce them to their proper value at the time and place of observation; for the elements furnished by the Nautical Almanac are computed for certain stated epochs, and their values for any intermediate epoch must be found by proportion. But ample directions for these preparatory operations are contained in the "Explanation of the Articles in the Nautical Almanac,"* to be found in the last pages of that work.

* It may be well, however, to give here some general account of the arrangement of the Nautical Almanac. The first twenty-two pages contain the right ascension, declination, semidiameter, and a variety of other elements relating to the sun and moon for every day of the month of January, the right ascension of the sun at mean noon and at apparent noon, that of the moon at the beginning of every hour of mean time throughout the day at Greenwich. The next twenty-two pages contain the same elements for the month of February, and so on, each month occupying twenty-two pages, marked with the Roman numerals, I. II., &c. The year thus being gone through, after a few pages containing the sun's co-ordinates, follows the ephemeris of the planets, beginning with Mercury, the one nearest the sun. This contains the semidiameter and declination, apparent right ascension, as affected by aberration of light, and some other elements of the planet for every day in the year of mean noon at Greenwich, and also at the time of the planet's meridian transit at Greenwich, each month occupying two pages. This Ephemeris extends from p. 275 to p. 455, in the almanac of 1850. The next three pages contain the mean places or right ascension and declination on the 1st of Jan. of 100 principal fixed stars, with their annual variations in right ascension and declination, marked + or — .

The latter multiplied by the fraction of the year which has elapsed, which is given in the last column of p. XXII. of each month, will be the quantity to be added or subtracted, in order to have the mean R. A. and Dec. at the time. To obtain the true places, corrected for nutation, &c., recourse must be had to formulas and tables given in the next three pages of the Almanac, except that of a number of the principal stars, the true R. A. and Dec. are given for every ten days from p. 468 to p. 501, in the edition of 1850. The remaining matters contained in the Nautical Almanac will be noticed as occasion requires.

EXAMPLES OF THE CORRECTIONS.

1. On the 14th of July, 1833, suppose the observed altitude of the sun's lower limb* to be 16° 36′ 4″, the observer's eye to be 18 feet above the level of the sea, the barometer to stand at 29 inches, and the thermometer at 58°; required the true altitude of the sun's centre.

Observed alt. ☉'s L. L.	16°	36′	4″
Depression of the horizon (Tab. XXXI.) . .	—	4	·4
App. alt. of L. L.	16	32	0
Refraction	—	3	14†
Correction for Barometer		+	6·5‡
Correction for Thermometer		+	3·2§
True altitude of L. L. above the visible horizon .	16	28	55·7
Sun's semidiameter (Naut. Alm.)	+	15	45·4
Parallax in altitude		+	8·4‖
True altitude of the sun's centre	16	44	49·5

2. On the 23d of June, 1850, in longitude 4^h 56^m 4^s W., latitude about 40° 43′ N., at 11^h 44^m 55^s mean time, the double altitude of the moon's upper limb was observed by reflection from Mercury to be 58° 14′; the index error of the sextant was 15″ subtractive; the barometer stood at 30·74 in., and the thermometer at 76°, required the true altitude of the moon's centre.

The object in this example being the moon, it is necessary to compute her semidiameter and parallax in altitude at the instant of obser-

* The limb of the sun or moon is the edge or border of the disc.

† Take out the refractions for 16° 30′ of altitude from the table, then the diff. for 1′ of altitude in the column adjoining, multiplying the latter by 2, and subtracting the product from the refraction for 16° 30′; the result will be that for 16° 32′, when the barometer is at 30 in. and the thermometer at 50°. The correction for refraction is always subtractive.

‡ The barometer standing at 29 in. the number taken from the column entitled cor. for + 1 must be subtracted from the refraction or added to the altitude, the atmosphere being less dense than in its medium state.

§ The thermometer standing at 8° above its medium state, the atmosphere is more rare, and the number taken from the column Diff. for 1° Fah., after being multiplied by 8, must be subtracted from the refraction, or added to the altitude.

‖ Table XXXIV., the parallax in alt. for 10° is 9″, and for 20° is 8″. Therefore for 16° by proportion it is 8″·4. This correction for par. in alt. is always additive.

vation since these elements, for the moon changes sensibly in a very short time. The semidiameter of the moon at noon and midnight is given in the Nautical Almanac for every day in the year, at page III. of each month, and the difference between these will be the variation of the semidiameter in 12 hours. Therefore we must say as 12^h : the variation in 12^h : : the interval between the preceding noon or midnight and the instant of observation : the variation of the semidiameter in that interval; the fourth term of this proportion added to or subtracted from the semidiameter at the preceding noon or midnight, according as the semidiameter is observed from the numbers in the almanac to be increasing or decreasing, will give the semidiameter at the instant of observation.

In a similar manner must the moon's horizontal parallax, which is given for every noon and midnight on the same page of the Nautical Almanac, be reduced by proportion to the time of observation.

The computation of these elements is as follows :

Mean time of observation at the station	$11^h\ 44^m\ 55^s$
Add longitude of the place of observation	4 56 4
Corresponding mean time at Greenwich	16 40 59
Time after midnight Gr. June 23d	4 40 59

Semidiameter previous midnight, June 23d (Naut. Alm.).	14′ 50″·3
Semidiam. noon (June 24th),	14 48 ·1
Variat. in 12^h	2 ·2
∴ 12^h : 2″·2 : : $4^h\ 40^m\ 59^s$* :	0 ·8
Semidiam. at midnight (23d),	14 50 ·3
Semidiam. at time of obs.,	14 49 ·5
Augmentation for 29° of alt.†	+ 7 ·8
Apparent semidiam. to obs.,	14 57 ·3
Subtract contraction,‡	— 1 ·1
True semidiam. to observer,	14 56 ·2

Horizontal parallax preceding midnight, June 23d (Naut. Alm.)	54′ 27″·3
Hor. par. noon (24th),	54 19 ·1
Var. in 12^h	8 ·2
∴ 12^h : 8″·2 : : $4^h\ 40^m\ 59^s$:	3 ·1
Hor. par. at midnight,	54 27 ·3
Hor. par. at time of obs.,	54 24 ·2
Ditto in seconds,	3264″·2
Diminut. of par. for lat. 41°§	— 4 ·7
Hor. par. at station,	3259″·5

* This is the interval from midnight at Greenwich to the instant of observation.

† Table XXXIII. This augmentation is in consequence of the moon being nearer to the observer, as it approaches the zenith. See p. 272.

‡ This is occasioned by the effect of refraction, which is to make every vertical arc, such as the vertical semidiameter of the sun or moon, appear shorter in the heavens than it really is. This will obviously be the case, because the lower extremity of the arc is more elevated by refraction than the higher, and consequently the two extremities are brought nearer together, and thus the arc is shortened. The contraction is obtained from Tab. XXXII.

§ Table XXXV., see p. 275, last paragraph of Art. 109.

Observed double altitude ☽'s U. L.	58° 14′ 00
Index error subtractive, ...	15″
Double altitude corrected for index error, . .	58 13 45
Half this is the obs'd altitude of ☽'s U.L. . .	29 6 52•5
Corrected semidiameter, ...	14 56•2
Apparent altitude ☽'s centre, ...	28 51 56•3

FOR THE PARALLAX IN ALTITUDE.*

App. alt. ☽'s centre, ...	28° 51′ 56″•3 cos	9•94238
Horizontal parallax at station, . .	3259″•5 log.	3•51315
Parallax in altitude, ...	2854″•5	3•45553

App. alt. ☽'s centre, ...	28° 51′ 56″•3
Refraction, ...	— 1 44 •9
Barometer, ...	— 2 •7
Thermometer, ...	+ 5 •5
Parallax in altitude, ...	+ 47 34 •5
True alt. of cent. from cent. of the earth, . .	29 37 48 •7

These two examples will serve for specimens of the corrections to be applied to an observed altitude, in order to deduce from it the true altitude of the body's centre. In the case of the moon, the corrections, when the utmost accuracy is sought, are rather numerous, as the last example shows.

But in finding the latitude at sea, it is usual to dispense with some of these, more especially with the corrections for temperature, for the contraction of the moon's semidiameter, and for the spheroidal figure of the earth; because an error of a few seconds in the true altitude will introduce no error worth noticing in the resulting latitude. When, however, the object of the observer is to deduce the longitude of the ship, all the data, furnished by observation, should be as accurate as possible; for the problem is one of such delicacy that by neglecting to allow for the influence of temperature would alone introduce in some cases an error of from 30 to 40 miles in the longitude.

When the object observed is a star, several of the foregoing corrections vanish; the only corrections in this case requisite are those for dip and refraction, modified as usual for the temperature.

111. *To determine the latitude at sea from the meridian altitude of any celestial object whose declination is known.*

The determination of the latitude, by a meridian altitude, is the most

* See p. 275.

easy and safe method of finding that element; the observations and subsequent calculations being few, are readily performed, and with but little liability to error in the result; this method, therefore, is always to be preferred at sea, unless clouds obscure the meridian whilst other portions of the heavens are left visible.

The declination of the object observed is supposed to be given in the Nautical Almanac, when it culminates or makes its meridian transit at Greenwich; its declination when it culminates at the meridian of a ship, may be found by means of the longitude by account,* which will always be sufficiently accurate for this purpose, although it should differ very considerably from the true longitude, because declination changes so slowly that even an error of an hour in the longitude would cause an error in the declination too small to deserve notice.

The declination being the distance of the object from the equator, and the observed altitude, properly corrected, being the distance of the same object from the ship's zenith, the distance of the zenith from the equator, that is, the latitude, immediately becomes known.

Let the full circle in the diagram be the meridian.

1. Let S be the object observed, the zenith Z being to the north of it, and the object itself north of the equator, EQ, then the latitude EZ is equal to the zenith distance, or co-altitude ZS + the declination ES, and it is north.

2. Let S′ be the object, still north of the equator, but so posited that the zenith is south of it, then the latitude EZ is equal to the difference between the zenith distance S′Z, and declination S′E, and is still north.

3. Let now the object be at S″, south of the equator, and the zenith to the north of the object, then the latitude EZ is equal to the difference between the zenith distance S″Z and declination S″E, and it is north.

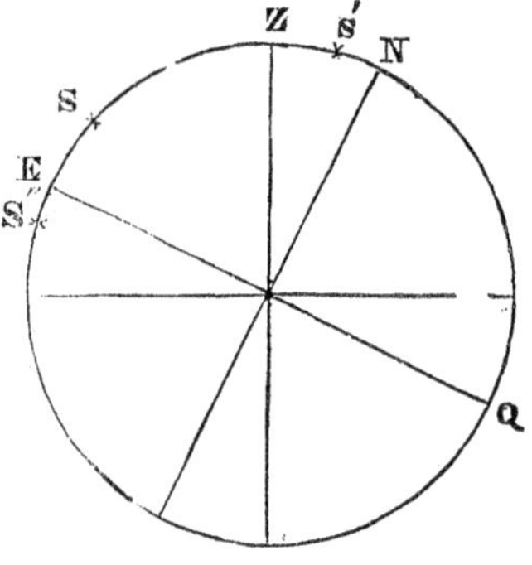

We have here assumed the north to be the elevated pole, but if the south be the elevated pole, then we must write south for north, and north for south. Hence the following rule for all cases.

* For this purpose the variation of the declination in 1 hour, which is given in the Nautical Almanac for the sun, must be multiplied by the longitude in hours and fractions of an hour, and the product added or subtracted will produce the declination at the time of meridian transit at the ship.

Call the zenith distance north or south, according as the zenith is north or south of the object.

If the zenith distance and declination be of the same name, that is, both north or both south, their sum will be the latitude; but if of different names, their difference will be the latitude, of the same name as the greater.

EXAMPLE.

1. Ship Admiral, from New York to Havre, at sea Jan. 4th, 1850. Longitude 25° W.

Observed merid. alt. ☉'s lower limb, ...	18° 54′ 20″
Dip (for height of 17 feet)	— 3 57
App. alt. ☉'s L. L.	18 50 23
Refraction, ...	— 2 49
Parallax in alt.	+ 8
Semidiameter, ...	16 17·3
☉'s true alt.	19 3 59·3
☉'s zenith dist. N.	70 56 00·7
☉'s declination* S.	22 43 37·9
Latitude, N.	48 12 22·8

2. At sea Jan. 11th, 1850. Long. 2° W. ☉'s Dec. 21° 46′ 2″ S.

Observed alt. ☉'s L.L. . . . . . . 18° 4′ 00″
Allowing for semidiameter (Dip 3′ 26″) parallax, &c. + 12 29
Required the latitude.

Ans. 49° 57′ 29″ N.

3. On the 1st of January, 1850, the meridian altitude of Capella was 27° 35′, the zenith being south of the star, and the height of the eye 22 feet; required the latitude.

* This is obtained by taking out from the Nautical Almanac, the declination for apparent noon, p. I., which is 22° 44′ 5″·2. Then computing the change in declination for 1⅔ hours, the time in which the sun is passing from the meridian of Greenwich to that of the ship in long. 25° W., by multiplying the number 16″·38, found in the column in the Almanac entitled Diff. for 1 hour by 1⅔. The product 27″·3, subtracted from 22° 44′ 5″·2, because the declination is decreasing will give the declination at the meridian transit of the sun at the ship.

Observed altitude, ...	27° 35′ 0″
Dip, ...	— 4 30
Apparent altitude, ...	27 30 30
Refraction, ...	— 1 51
True altitude, ...	27 28 39
Zenith distance, ...	62 31 21 S,
Star's dec. (Nautical Almanac), ...	45 50 20 N.
Latitude, ...	16 41 1 S.

4. Suppose that the altitude of the moon, as given in Example 2, p. 277, was observed when the moon was upon the meridian, required the latitude of the place of observation.

The true altitude of the moon's centre being known, after applying the corrections as at p. 278, it remains to find her declination at the instant of observation. The Nautical Almanac gives the moon's declination for every even hour of the day of every day, on pages V. to XII. of each month, and the variation in declination for 10^m of time. The required declination would therefore be computed as follows:

☽'s dec. June 23d, at 16^h (Nautical Almanac),	19° 36′ 48″·8
Diff. dec. for 41^m,*	1 35
Dec. at the inst. of observation, ...	19 38 23 ·8 S.
☽'s zenith dist. = (90° — 29° 37′ 49″·8†) .	60 22 10 ·2 N.
Latitude required, ...	40 43 46 ·4

If the time of observation were not known, it could be computed from the fact that the moon is on the meridian.

The moon passed the Meridian of Greenwich

June 23d (Nautical Almanac, p. IV.), at . .	11^h 33^m 0^s
June 24th, " "	12 21 7
The interval between the two transits is . .	24 48 7

That is in 24^h 48^m 7^s the moon is retarded in coming to the meridian, by her proper motion from W. to E. 48^m 7^s

$$\therefore\ 24^h\ 48^m\ 7^s : 48^m\ 7^s :: 4^h\ 56^m\ 4^s‡ : 9^m\ 39^s$$

* The time of obs. was 40^m 59^s past 6^h or nearly 41^m. The Naut. Alm. gives 23″·17 diff. of dec. for 10^m ∴ 10^m : 23″·17 : : 41^m : 1′ 34″ the change in dec. in 41^m, which as dec. is increasing must be added. Second differences are not used.

† This is the true alt. of the ☽'s centre from the centre of the earth, p. 279.

‡ This is the longitude of the place of observation.

This last number is the retardation of the moon in passing from the meridian of Greenwich to that of the place of observation. The moon having crossed the meridian at Greenwich at $11^h\ 33^m$ on the 23d, will cross that of the station $9^m\ 39^s$ later, so that the time of meridian transit at the station will be $11^h\ 36^m\ 39^s$.*

It saves trouble to note the time of meridian transit by a watch, or still better by a chronometer, keeping Greenwich time.

SCHOLIUM.

These examples will, no doubt, be found sufficient to put the student in possession of the method of applying the various corrections to the observed meridian altitude of a celestial object, in order to deduce from it the latitude of the ship. But it should be remarked, that in most works on Nautical Astronomy, subsidiary tables are inserted for the purpose of abridging some of the foregoing corrective operations; such tables, there fore, offer very acceptable aid to the practical Navigator. Bowditch's Navigator is the most complete work of the kind.

It should also be observed here, that in the preceding examples the celestial object is supposed to be on the meridian *above* the pole; that is, to be higher than the elevated pole. But, if a meridian altitude be taken below the pole, which may be done if the object is *circumpolar*, or so near to the elevated pole as to perform its apparent daily revolution about it without passing below the horizon, then the latitude of the place will be equal to the sum of the true altitude, and the codeclination or polar distance of the object; for this sum will obviously measure the elevation of the pole above the horizon, which is equal to the latitude.†

112. *To determine the latitude at sea, by means of two altitudes of the sun, and the time between the observations.*

In the preceding article we have shown how to determine the latitude of the ship by the meridian altitude of the sun, or of any other heavenly body, whose declination may be found. But, as already remarked, the object we wish to observe may be obscured when it comes to the meridian, and this may happen for many days together, although it may be frequently visible at other times of the day. As therefore the opportunity

* This differs slightly from the time of observation given. The moon changes so rapidly in declination that her greatest altitude is not always the meridian altitude.

† That the elevation of the pole above the horizon is equal to the latitude of the place is evident from the fact that the zenith is 90° from the horizon, and the pole 90° from the equator.

for a meridian observation cannot be depended upon, it becomes an important problem to determine the latitude at sea, by observations made out of the meridian; and considerable attention has accordingly been paid, by scientific persons, to the method of finding the latitude by "double altitudes," and various tables have been computed to facilitate the operation. But the direct method, by spherical trigonometry, though rather long, involving three spherical triangles, will be more readily remembered, and more easily applied by persons familiar with the rules and formulas of trigonometry than any indirect or approximate process; we shall therefore explain the direct method.

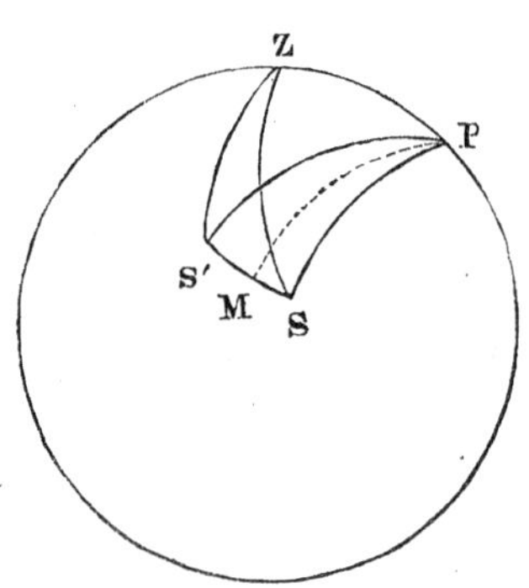

Let P be the elevated pole, Z the zenith of the ship, and S, S′ the two places of the sun, when the altitudes are taken. Then, drawing the great circle arcs as in the figure, we shall have these given quantities, viz., the co-declinations PS, PS′; the coaltitudes ZS, ZS′, and the hour angle SPS′, which measures the interval between the observations; and the quantity sought is the colatitude ZP. Now, in the triangle PSS′, we have given two sides and the included angle to find the third side SS′, and one of the remaining angles, say the angle PSS′. In the triangle ZSS′ we have given the three sides to find the angle S′SZ; having then the angles PSS′, S′SZ, the angle ZSP equal to their difference, becomes known, so that we have, lastly, two sides and the included angle in the triangle ZSP, to find the third side ZP.

Before the application of the trigonometrical process, the observed altitudes must, of course, be reduced to the true altitudes, as in the preceding examples. Moreover, as the ship most probably sails during the interval of the observation, an additional reduction becomes necessary, as follows: Let Z be the zenith of the ship, and S the place of the sun, at the first observation Z′ and S′ the same at the second. Then the angle Z′ZS will represent the bearing of the ship's path from the sun, which may be observed with the compass; considering

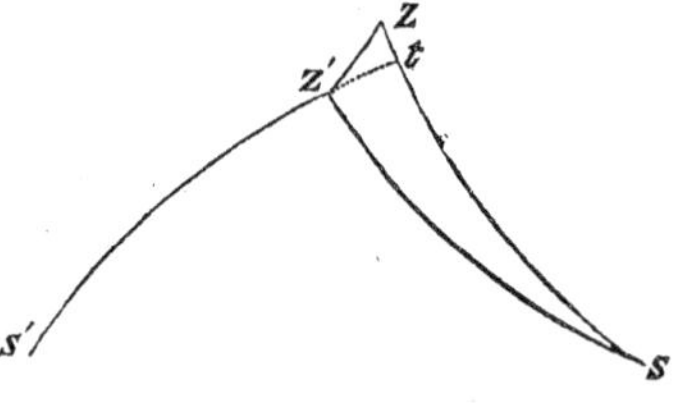

this angle as a course, and the distance sailed, zz′, as the corresponding distance, find by the table (or by the formula zz′ cos z′zt) *zt* which subtracted from zs will give z′s nearly, which, instead of zs, should be used with z′s′ in the solution before given. This must be subtracted from the first zen. dist. if the angle z′zt is less than 90°; but it must be added when the angle exceeds 90°. If the angle is 90°, no correction for the ship's change of place will be necessary.

Where great accuracy is aimed at, account should be taken of the ship's change of longitude during the interval of the observations; when converted into time it must be added to the interval of time between the observations when the ship has sailed eastward, and subtracted when she has sailed westward. *This correction is very easily applied.

Having thus mentioned the necessary preparative corrections, we shall now give an example of the trigonometrical operation.

EXAMPLE.

Let the two zenith distances corrected be (see last figure but one), zs = 73° 54′ 13″, zs′ = 47° 45′ 51″, the corresponding declinations 8° 18′ and 8° 15′ north, and the interval of time three hours; to determine the latitude.

Considering ss′ to be the base of an isosceles spherical triangle, of which one of the equal sides is ½ (PS + PS′)† = 81° 43′ 30″, and the vertical angle equal to 3^h or 45°, let the perpendicular PM be drawn, then we have in the triangle PMS right angled at M, PS = 81° 43′ 30″, and $P = \frac{45°}{2} = 22° 30'$, given, to find SM = ½ ss′ as follows.

1. TO FIND SS′ FROM THE TRIANGLE PMS.

sin PS	81°	43′	30″	9·99545
sin P	22	30	0	9·58284
sin SM	22	15	11·4	9·57829
			2	
ss′ =	44	30	22·8	

* If the student will conceive an addition to the first diagram on the preceding page, to wit, the arc of another great circle, different from PZ, drawn through P, to represent the new meridian of the ship, calling this PZ′, then the hour angle or time of the first observation would be ZPS, as before, but that of the second observation would be Z′PS′, and the difference ZPS — Z′PS′, or the diff. of the times of obs., would evidently be equal to SPS′ + ZPZ′, or SPS′ — ZP′Z, according as PZ′ is in front or behind in the diagram, i. e., east or west of PZ. But ZPZ′ is the difference of longitude of the two meridians.

† Which we may, without sensible error, where the base is so small

II. TO FIND PSS′ FROM THE TRIANGLE PSS′.

sin SS′	44° 30′ 22·8″	arith. comp.	0·15429
sin PS′	81 45 0	. . .	9·99548
sin SPS′	45 0 0	. . .	9·84948
sin PSS′	86 38 53	. . .	9·99925

This angle is acute like its opposite side (see p. 196).

III. TO FIND ZSS′ IN THE TRIANGLE ZSS′.

ZS′	47° 45′ 51″		
sin ZS	73 54 13	arith. comp.	0·01737
sin SS′	44 30 22·8	arith. comp.	0·15429
	2)166 10 26·8		
½ sum =	83 5 13·4		
sin (½ sum — ZS)	9 11 0·4	. . . .	9·20302
sin (½ sum — SS′)	38 34 50·6	. . . .	9·79492
			2)19·16960
sin ½ ZSS′	22 36 26·4	. . . .	9·58480

∴ ZSS′ = 45° 12′ 52·8″
PSS′ = 86 38 53
PSZ = 41 26 0·2

IV. TO FIND THE TWO UNKNOWN ANGLES OF THE TRIANGLE ZSP.

cos ½ (ZS + PS)	77° 48′ 52″	ar. comp.	0·67555	ar. comp. sin	0·00990
* cos ½ (ZS ∼ PS)	7° 49′ 17″	. . .	9·99594	sin	9·13381
cot ½ PSZ	20° 43′ 3″	. . .	10·42228	. . . .	10·42228
tan ½ (ZPS + PZS)	85° 23′ 35″	. .	11·09377	tan ½ (P ∼ Z) 20° 12′ 32″	9·56599
	20° 12′ 32″				
SPZ =	105° 36′ 7″				
ZPS =	65° 11′ 3″				

* This sign ∼ is employed to express the difference between two quantities, whichever may be the greater.

V. TO FIND ZP IN THE TRIANGLE ZSP.

$\cos \frac{1}{2}$ (z — P)	20° 12′ 32′ ar. comp.	0·027593
$\cos \frac{1}{2}$ (z + P)	85° 23′ 31″	8·904822
$\tan \frac{1}{2}$ (zs + PS)	77° 48′ 52″	10·665658
$\tan \frac{1}{2}$ ZP	21° 37′ 14″	9·598073
ZP =	43° 14′ 28″	

Upon the same principles may the latitude be determined from the altitudes of two fixed stars, taken at the same time; in this case S, S′, in the preceding figure, will represent the two stars: PS, PS′, their known polar distances, and the angle SPS′, the difference of their right ascensions; the same quantities are therefore given as in the case of the sun, but, as in the case of two stars, PS, PS′, may differ very considerably, SS′ cannot be considered as the base of an isosceles triangle, but must be computed from the other two sides and their included angle.

For other modes of determining the latitude, see the next Appendix.

ON FINDING THE LONGITUDE.

The determination of the longitude of a place always requires the solution of these two problems, viz.: 1st, to determine the time at the place at any instant; and, 2d, to determine the time at the first meridian, or that from which the longitude is estimated, at the same instant; for the difference of the times converted into degrees, at the rate of 15° to an hour, will obviously give the longitude.

When the latitude of the place is known (and it may be found by the methods already explained), the time may be computed from the altitude of any celestial object whose declination is known; for the coaltitude, codeclination, and colatitude, will be three sides of a spherical triangle given to find the hour angle, comprised between the codeclination and the colatitude.

(See Art. 84.) The following example will illustrate the mode of proceeding.

At Columbia College, January 13th, 1850, the double altitude of the sun's lower limb was observed by reflexion from mercury to be 42° 29′ Thermometer 40°, and Barometer 30 in.

Time by the watch, $10^h\ 6^m\ 10^s$ A.M.

Index error of the sextant, 52″ additive.

Latitude of station 40° 42′ 40″.

Longitude from Greenwich in time, $4^h\ 56^m\ 4^s$.

Required correct time of Observation and error of the watch.

Equation of time at ap. noon, January 13th, 1850, 9^m 00^s •27.
Difference per hour = 0^s •926.*
Sun's declination at ap. noon, January 13th, 1850, 21° 29′ 19″•5 S.
Difference per hour = 26″•1.

Observed double altitude, ...	42°	29′		
Index error of sextant. Additive (see 2d note, p. 290).			52″	
Double altitude corrected for index error, . .	42	29	52	
Altitude, ...	21	14	56	
Refraction (Th. 40), (B. 30), Table XXX., . .		— 2	35	•5
Sun's Parallax in Altitude, Table XXXIV., . .			8	
Semidiameter (Nautical Almanac) . . .		16	16	•8
☉'s true altitude corrected for refraction, parallax, and semidiameter	21	28	45	•3
☉'s zenith distance (90° — Altitude) . . .	68	31	14	•7

Approx. time at station, ...	10^h	6^m	10^s	A.M.
Longitude from Greenwich in time, .	4	56	4	
Time at Greenwich, ...	3	2	14	
Equation of time, subtractive, . .		9	3 •08	
Time after apparent noon at Greenwich,	2	53	10 •92	
☉'s declination at time of observation†,	21	28	4 •18	S.

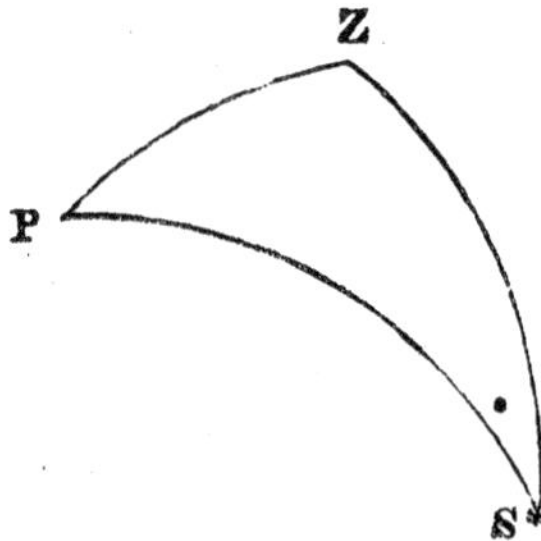

* This must be multiplied by the time after apparent noon at Greenwich, found below, reduced to hours and decimals of an hour, and the product added to the equation of time at noon above, to obtain the equation of time at the instant of observation.

† This is computed from the data in the third and fourth lines from the top of the page, in the same manner as the equation of time.

PS or z = ☉'s N.P.D = $(90^\circ + D)$ =	111°	28′	4″	·18	ar. co. log. sin	0·03122
PZ or s = Colatitude	49	17	20		ar. co. log. sin	0·12033
ZS or p = Zenith distance	68	31	14	·7		
S	229	16	38	·88		
$\frac{1}{2}$ S	114	38	19	·44		
$\frac{1}{2}$ S — z	3	10	15	·26	log. sin	8·74285
$\frac{1}{2}$ S — s	65	20	59	·44	log. sin	9·95850
						2)18·85290
$\frac{1}{2}$ P	15°	29′	1″		log. sin	9·42645

Hour angle = 30° 58″ 2′.

$\frac{P}{15}$ = Hour angle in time, or apparent time before noon,	2^h	3^m	52^s ·1
Subtract hour angle from	12		
Apparent time, A.M. by observation, ...	9	56	7 ·9
Equation of time, additive, ...		9	3 ·08
Mean time by observation, ...	10	5	10 ·98
Mean time by watch, ...	10	6	10
Error of watch (too fast)			59 ·02

2. Ship Admiral at sea, March 5th, 1850, at 10 o'clock, A. M.

Observed altitude sun's lower limb, ...	27° 44
Height of eye above the level sea, 16 feet.	
Time at Greenwich, by mean of three chronometers .	12^h 41^m 12^s
Lat. at time of obs. north, ...	49° 54′ 00″

EXTRACTS FROM NAUTICAL ALMANAC.

At mean noon.

March 6th, ☉'s semidiameter,	16′ 7″·9; eq. of time,	— 11^m 30^s·98*
7th, " "	6 7 ·6 " "	— 11 16 ·56
☉'s dec. at apparent noon Gr. (6th)		5° 40′ 48″·3 S.
Diff. for 1^h, 58″·20†		

Required the time of observation.

Ans. 9^h 19^m 29^s ·4

3. March 12th, at 4 P.M. Astronomical Account.

Alt. of the sun's lower limb, ...	18° 42′ 40″
Time at Greenwich by mean of chronometers, . .	7^h 51^m 30^s
Lat. of ship at time of obs.	41° 41′ 30″

* To be subtracted from mean time.

† The dec. is of course diminishing till the equinox March 21st.

19

At mean noon.

March 12th, eq. of time — 9^m $59^s \cdot 14$ semidiam. $16'$ $6'' \cdot 3$*
" 13th, " " — 9 42 ·71 " 16 6

☉'s dec. at app. noon, March 12th (Gr.) 3° 20 11· 7 S.

Var. of dec. in 1^h is $59'' \cdot 02$.

Required the time. *Ans.* ^{h} ^{m} ^{s}.

To find the time at Greenwich requires the aid of additional data, besides those furnished by observations made at the place. The Greenwich time may, indeed, be obtained at once, independently of any observations at the place, by means of a chronometer, carefully regulated to Greenwich time, provided it be subject to no irregularities after having been once properly adjusted. A ship furnished with such a timepiece always carries the Greenwich time with her, and the longitude then becomes reduced to the problem of finding the time at the place.

EXAMPLE.

Time computed by an altitude of the sun, as at p. 288, was	9^h 45^m 10^s
Chronometer showed Greenwich time at the instant of observation to be	0 50 20
Difference of longitude of the place of observation from Gr. in time, ...	3 5 10
To convert time to space multiply by	15
Longitude of the ship west of Greenwich, ...	46° $17'$ $30''$

The same method applies to examples 2 and 3, p. 289.

Still, however, as the most perfect contrivance of human art is subject to accident, and the more delicate the machine the more liable is it to disarrangement, from causes which we may not be able to control, it becomes highly desirable, in so important a matter as finding the place of a ship at sea, to be possessed of methods altogether beyond the influence of terrestrial vicissitudes, and such methods the celestial motions alone can supply.

The angular motion of the moon in her orbit is more rapid than that of any other celestial body, and sufficiently great to render the portion of her path passed over in so short a time as two or three seconds, a measurable quantity even with a small portable instrument (the sextant).†

* In computing the ☽'s semi-diameter and parallax, second differences need not be used, the consequent error being less than $0'' \cdot 1$.

† THE SEXTANT

is constructed upon the same principles as the quadrant. It consists of a graduated

It is obvious, therefore, that if the distance of the moon's centre from any celestial body, in or near her path, be computed for any Greenwich time, and this distance be found the same as that given by actual observation at any place, then the difference between the time of observing

brazen arc of 60°, numbered double, however, for the same reason as in the quadrant, or to 120°, called the limb, upon which moves a vernier attached to one end of an index, the other end of which is at the centre of the arc. Upon the latter, in a direction parallel with it, and perpendicular to the plane of the limb, is a mirror called the index glass, adjustable by three screws to perpendicularity with the plane of the limb. Opposite the index glass, and parallel with its plane when the index is at zero, is another glass, half mirror and half transparent, called the horizon glass. A small telescope parallel to the plane of the limb is placed before the horizon glass, and directed so as to look through the latter.

There are three adjustments. 1. *To make the index glass perpendicular to the plane of the limb.* This is done by moving forward the index to the middle of the limb, then looking with the naked eye into the index glass; if the part of the limb seen by reflection appear in the same plane with the part seen direct, the index glass is perpendicular to the plane of the limb; if not, it must be adjusted.

2. *To make the horizon glass perpendicular to the plane of the limb.*—The index glass having been adjusted, hold the instrument in a vertical position, and bring the direct and reflected images of the same object to coincide; if this can be done exactly, no adjustment is required, but if one image appear at the right or left of the other, the horizon glass must be adjusted by a screw or screws attached to it for the purpose.

3. *To make the axis of the telescope parallel to the plane of the limb.*—Bring the images of two objects which are more than 90° apart, to coincide upon one of the parallel wires in the telescope, and then by turning the instrument in the hand a little, make the objects appear on the other wire. If the coincidence remains, the position of the telescope is correct; if not, it must be adjusted by the screws of the ring into which the telescope is screwed. N. B. There are usually two telescopes accompanying the sextant, the one an inverting or astronomical telescope, and the other not. There is also a plane tube without glasses, and either of the three may be screwed into the same ring.

There are darkening glasses to be used in observing the sun, four near the index glass, and three before the object glass. They are red and green, of different shades. The latter color is particularly good to take off the glare of the moon. The paler one before the horizon glass may sometimes be used with advantage to take off the glare of the horizon below the sun, occasioned by the reflection of that luminary from the small rippling waves. N. B. The parallelism of the surfaces of the darkening glasses should be tested by inverting them, and observing if the coincidence of objects be preserved.

When the index stands at zero the direct and reflected images of the same object ought to coincide. If not, there is *index error,* the amount of which is determined by observing how far the index stands from zero when the direct and reflected images coincide. The best mode of determining the index error is by measuring the diame-

the phenomenon and the time at Greenwich, when it was predicted to happen, will give the longitude of the place of observation. Now, in the Nautical Almanac the distances of the moon from the sun, and from several of the fixed stars near her path, are given for every three hours of apparent Greenwich time, and for several years to come, and the Greenwich time, corresponding to any intermediate distance, is obtainable by simple proportion; so that by means of the Nautical Almanac we may always determine the time at Greenwich when any distance observed at sea was taken.* (See Nautical Almanac, pp. XIII. to XVIII. inclusive.)

The distances inserted in the Nautical Almanac are the true angular distances between the centres of the bodies, the observer being considered as at the centre of the earth, and to the true distance therefore every observed distance must be reduced; it is this reduction which constitutes the trigonometrical difficulties of this problem. And it consists in *clearing the lunar distance from the effects of parallax and refraction;* how to do this, it is now our business to explain.

ter of the sun by moving the index both forward and backward, the limb being graduated a short distance behind the zero for the purpose. Half this difference of the two measures will be the index error.

To measure an angle with the sextant, bring the two objects, the line joining which subtends the angle, the one as seen direct, and the other by reflection, to coincide, by holding the instrument so that the plane of the limb passes through them, and moving the index forward; the reading shown by the index will be the angle required.

* The proportion would run thus: As the difference between two lunar distances given in the Almanac, the one greater, the other less than that observed with the sextant, is to 3 hours, so is the difference between the distance observed with the sextant corrected for refraction, &c., and one of those in the Alm., to the difference between the time of observation and the time given by the Almanac corresponding to the latter lunar distance. The Nautical Almanac gives the proportional logarithm of the quotient of the first term of the above proportion, divided by the second term which is constant, viz., three hours. If the distance between the moon and a star increased or decreased uniformly, the Greenwich time corresponding to a given distance would be strictly correct; but an inspection of the columns of proportional logarithms in the ephemeris, will show that this is not the case. A correction for second differences, or for the irregularity in the lunar distances, must therefore be applied.

At page 602 of the Nautical Almanac for 1850 is given, besides the ordinary rule and an example under it, a full explanation of the method of employing a table contained in the Almanac for computing the correction on account of second differences in finding the Greenwich time. The theory of second differences has been given (Algebra, Art. 235). At the scientific meeting in New Haven, August, 1850, Prof. Chauvenet of the U. S. Naval Academy presented improvements in the formulæ and tables for lunars, which it is to be hoped will be perfected and published.

Let *m*, *s*, be the observed places of the moon and sun, or of the moon and a fixed star, and let M, S, be their true places. M will be above *m*, because the moon is depressed by parallax more than it is elevated by refraction; but S will be below *s*, because the sun is more elevated by refraction than it is depressed by parallax. Observation gives the apparent distance *ms*, and the apparent zenith distances Z*m*, Z*s* : by applying the proper corrections to these latter, we also deduce the true zenith distances ZM, ZS, and with these data we are to determine the true distance, MS, by computation.

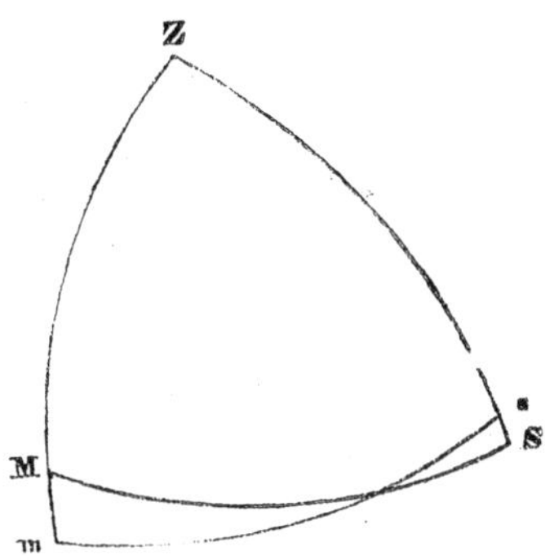

Put d for the apparent distance.*
D true distance.
a, a apparent altitudes.*
A, A′ true altitudes.

Then in the triangle MZS we have (Art. 82), R being 1,

$$\cos Z = \frac{\cos D - \sin A \sin A'}{\cos A \cos A'};\dagger$$

and in the triangle *mzs*

$$\cos Z = \frac{\cos d - \sin a \sin a'}{\cos a \cos a'};$$

hence, for the determination of D, we have this equation, viz.,

$$\frac{\cos D - \sin A \sin A'}{\cos A \cos A'} = \frac{\cos d - \sin a \sin a'}{\cos a \cos a'};$$

from which we immediately get

$$\cos D = (\cos d - \sin a \sin a') \frac{\cos A \cos A'}{\cos a \cos a'} + \sin A \sin A'$$

* In observing d with the sextant, it is the nearest point of the limb of the moon, which is made to coincide with the other heavenly body, and in observing a with the quadrant, it is the limb also which is made to coincide with the horizon; so that d and a must be corrected for the semidiameter of the moon; similar remarks apply to the sun, if he be the other heavenly body.

† Observe that A and A′ are the complements of ZM and ZS.

But $\cos a \cos a' - \sin a \sin a' = \cos (a + a')$ Art. 70; transposing $\cos a \cos a'$, and substituting the value of $- \sin a \sin a'$ thus obtained, we have

$$\cos \text{D} = \frac{\cos d + \cos (a + a') - \cos a \cos a'}{\cos a \cos a'} \cos \text{A} \cos \text{A}' + \sin \text{A} \sin \text{A}'$$

Dividing the last term of the numerator by the denominator, the quotient is -1; then observing that $-\cos \text{A} \cos \text{A}' + \sin \text{A} \sin \text{A}' = -\cos (\text{A} + \text{A}')$ and that $\cos d + \cos (a + a') = 2 \cos \frac{1}{2} (a + a' + d) \cos \frac{1}{2} (a + a' \sim d)$ Art. 83, we have

$$\cos \text{D} = \frac{2 \cos \frac{1}{2} (a + a' + d) \cos \frac{1}{2} (\overline{a + a'} \sim d) \cos \text{A} \cos \text{A}'}{\cos a \cos a'} - \cos(\text{A} + \text{A}') (1)$$

EXAMPLE.

1. Suppose the apparent distance between the centres of the sun and moon to be 83° 57′ 33″, the apparent altitude of the moon's centre 27° 34′ 5″, the apparent altitude of the sun's centre 48° 27′ 32″, the true altitude of the moon's centre 28° 20′ 48″, and the true altitude of the sun's centre 48° 26′ 49″; then we have

$$d = 83° \, 57' \, 33'', \; a = 27° \, 34' \, 5'', \; a' = 48° \, 27' \, 32''$$
$$\text{A} = 28° \, 20' \, 48'', \; \text{A}' = 48° \, 26'' \, 49';$$

and the computation for D, by formula (1), is as follows:

	d	83° 57′ 33″			
	a	27 34 5	ar. comp. cos	052339	
	a'	48 27 32	ar. comp. cos	178383	
		2)159 59 10	log. 2	301030	
½ sum		79 59 35	cos	9·239969	
½ sum ∼ d		3 57 58	cos	9·998959	
	A	28 20 48	cos	9·944527	
	A′	48 26 49	cos	9·821719	
		(Reject 40 from index)		$\overline{1}$·536926	= log. ·344292 +
	A + A′	76 47 37			nat. cos ·228460
		True distance 83° 20′ 54″			nat. cos ·115832

By glancing at the formula (1), we see that 30 must oe rejected from the sum of the above column of logarithms, to wit, 20 for the two ar.

comp^s. and 10 for R, which must be introduced into the denominator, in order to render the expression homogeneous, so that the logarithmic line resulting from the process is 9·536926. Now, as in the table of log. sines, log. cosines, &c., the radius is supposed to be 10^{10}, of which the log. is 10, and in the table of natural sines, cosines, &c., the rad. is 1, of which the log. is 0; it follows that when we wish to find, by help of a table of the logarithms of numbers, the natural trigonometrical line corresponding to any logarithmic one, we must diminish this latter by 10, and enter the table with the remainder. Hence the sum of the foregoing column of logarithms must be diminished by 40, and the remainder will be truly the logarithm of the natural number represented by the first term in the second number of the equation (1). If this natural number be less than nat. cos $(A + A')$, which is to be subtracted from it, the remainder will be negative, in which case D will be obtuse.

VARIATION OF THE COMPASS.

114. We shall conclude this part of our subject by briefly considering the methods of finding the variation of the compass, or the quantity by which the north point, as shown by the compass, varies easterly or westerly from the north point of the horizon.

The solution of this problem merely requires that we find by computation, or by some means independent of the compass, the *bearing* of a celestial object, that we observe the bearing by the compass, and then take the difference of the two. The problem resolves itself, therefore, into two cases, the object whose bearing is sought being either in the horizon or above it: in the one case we have to compute its *amplitude*, and in the other its *azimuth*.

The computation of the amplitude is simply determining the hypothenuse of a right angled triangle MSN, of which one side is given, viz. the declination NS of the object, as also the angle opposite to it, viz. the colatitude M. The computation of the azimuth requires the solution of an oblique spherical triangle, the three sides being given to find an angle; the three given sides are the colatitude PZ, the zenith distance of the object ZS, and its polar

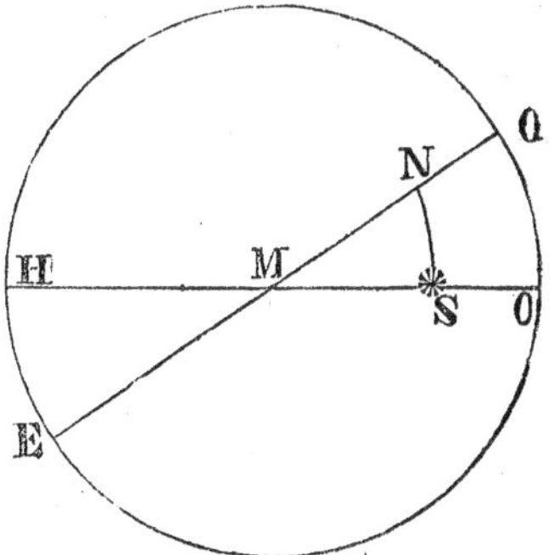

distance $\overset{\circ}{PS}$, and the azimuth being measured by the angle at the zenith z, opposite the polar distance, this is the angle sought. We shall give an example in each of these cases of the problem.

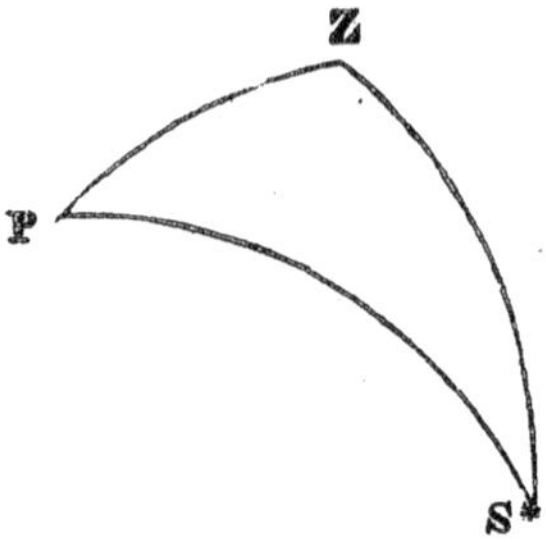

EXAMPLES.

1. In January, 1830, at latitude 27° 36′ N., the rising amplitude of Aldebaran was by the compass* E. 23° 30′ N.; required the variation.

From the Nautical Almanac, it appears that the declination of Aldebaran at the given time was 16° 9′ 37″ N., therefore since, by Napier's rule, Rad. × sin dec. = sin. amp. × cos lat., the computation is as follows:

sin declination	16°	9′	37″	9·44455
cos. latitude	27	36		9·94753
sin amplitude E.	18	18	17 N.	9·49702
Magnetic amplitude E.	23	30	0 N.	
Variation	5	11	43 E	

As the object is farther from the magnetic east than from the true east, the magnetic east has therefore advanced towards the south, and therefore the magnetic north towards the east; hence the variation is 5° 11′ 43″ E.

2. In latitude 48° 50′ north, the true altitude of the sun's centre was 22° 2′, the declination at the time was 10° 12′ S., and its magnetic bearing 161° 32′ East. Required the variation.

* The compass amplitude must be taken when the apparent altitude of the object is equal to the depression of the horizon.

☉'s polar distance	100°	12′		
sin zenith distance	67	58	ar. comp.	0·03294
sin colatitude	41	10	ar. comp.	0·18161
	2)209	20		
½ s.	104	40		
sin (½ s. — zen. dist.)	36	42	. . .	9·77643
sin (½ s. — colat.)	63	30	. . .	9·95179
				2)19·94277
sin ½ azim. 69° 25′ 40″			. . .	9·97138
		2		
☉'s true azimuth N.	138	51	20	E.
observed azimuth N.	161	32	0	E.
Variation	22	40	40	West.

The variation is west, because the sun's observed distance from the north, measured easterly, being greater than its true distance, intimates that the north point of the compass has approached towards the west.

3. In latitude 48° 20′ north, the star Rigel was observed to set 9° 50′ to the northward of the west point of the compass; required the variation, the declination of Rigel being 8° 25′ S.

Variation, 22° 33′ West.

APPENDIX TO PART V.

A VERY portable and accurate instrument for the measurement of altitudes of the heavenly bodies is

THE CIRCLE OF REFLECTION.*

This instrument is constructed on the same principles as the sextant, the only difference being that the circle, as its name imports, has a limb which is a complete circumference, measuring on the doubling principle of optics already explained 720° instead of 360°.

By having two verniers 180° apart, the instrument corrects its own eccentricity and by having three, as in Troughton's construction, for error of figure and division, to some extent also. By reversing the face of the instrument the angle may be taken on what is called the off arc, that is, on the other side of the zero. This, by taking the mean, corrects for index error, so that with three verniers six readings may be obtained for one angle.

Dolland's circle has an inner movable circle, with a vernier upon it, in consequence of which it admits of the repeating process explained for the theodolite, at p. 242.

The horizon glass and telescope are attached firmly to the inner movable circle, which has a clamp screw and screw of slow motion. The index glass is attached to an arm which moves freely around the centre, and is unconnected with the inner circle, telescope and horizon glass. This arm has a vernier and screw for clamping it to the outer circle, and a screw of slow motion.

The repeating process is conducted as follows: Place the zero of the vernier of the inner circle clamped accurately at 720° on the outer, and move the free index carrying the other vernier forward until the two objects are brought in contact, as in observing with the sextant. Leaving this index fast to the limb, unclamp the inner circle, which carries the telescope and horizon glass, and move it forward also, not merely by the same amount, which would bring back the horizon glass to parallelism again with the index glass, but move it twice the angular distance necessary for this purpose ; the horizon glass will now be inclined to the index glass, just as much as when the free index was first moved forward to produce the contact of the objects, but the inclination will be the other way. The contact may again be produced between the objects by the tangent screw of the inner circle, the telescope being

* Angles in any plane may be observed with the Circle of Reflection as with the Sextant.

presented to the other object if the face of the circle be continued one way, but to the same object if the face of the circle be reversed. The reading now of the vernier attached to the inner circle would be twice the angle between the objects. If now the free index be moved forward a distance equal to the angle between the objects, the horizon and index glasses will be parallel again ; and if it be moved forward still further by the same amount, the glasses will be inclined to each other, exactly as at first, and the contact of the objects may be made with the screw of slow motion attached to the free index, the face of the circle being as at first. Again, the inner circle is to be moved forward as before, over twice the angle between the objects, the face of the circle being inverted, the telescope directed always to one object, and the contact made with the screw of slow motion attached to the inner circle. The process above described is to be repeated until the vernier of the inner circle approaches near, or is a little past the 720 point again. The reading at which it stands, divided by twice the number of times that the inner circle has been moved forward, will give the angle subtended by the two objects corrected for all errors of division, centering and observation. If the angle between the objects be changing, as is often the case with celestial objects, the times of each contact of the object should be noted. The sum of the times, divided by the number of contacts, will be the mean time corresponding to the mean angle obtained, as already described. The Sextant and Reflecting Circle are used for taking altitudes on land, by the aid of a basin of mercury, called an artificial horizon. The telescope is presented to the reflected image of the sun or other heavenly body, seen in the mercury, and the angle between this and the sun in the heavens measured by moving the index forward. This angle will be double the altitude of the sun.

The following example of an observation of the altitude of the sun for time will illustrate the mode of using this instrument.

Observation with Repeating and Reflecting Circle, and Box Chronometer, of the sun's lower limb.

	Times		
	2^h 29^m 33^s		
	" 30 00•5		
	" 30 19		
	" 30 43•5		
	" 31 06.5		
Times of contacts.	" 31 34•5	117° 36′ 10″	Vernier reading.
	" 31 59•5	720°	
	" 32 15	10)837 36 10	
	" 32 36		
	" 32 55•5	2)83 45 37	
	10)313 03	41 52 48•5	
	2^h 31^m 18^s•3		

The mean of the angles being 41° 52′ 48″•5, and of the times, 2^h 31^m 18^s•3, the former is the apparent altitude at the instant expressed by the latter, with no error of excentricity or graduation, and a probable error of observation $\frac{1}{10}$ that which would have been obtained without the repeating process.

VARIOUS MODES OF DETERMINING LATITUDE.

LATITUDE BY A SINGLE ALTITUDE.

The data for this problem are the declination, the altitude, and the hour angle. We have thus three elements of the triangle SPZ (p. 296), viz., SP, SZ, and the angle P, known, to calculate a fourth. This method requires an accurate knowledge of the time.

If the latitude be known nearly, which it generally is, by means of the dead reckoning, it may be accurately found as follows. From (7) of Art. 72 we have

$$\cos \text{A} = 1 - 2 \sin^2 \tfrac{1}{2} \text{A} \qquad (1)$$

which substituted in the formula deduced at Art. 82, written thus

$$\cos a = \cos b \cos c + \sin b \sin c \cos \text{A} \qquad (2)$$

gives by (8) of Art. 70,

$$\cos a = \cos (b - c) - 2 \sin b \sin c \sin^2 \tfrac{1}{2} \text{A} \qquad (3)$$

substituting in (3) the sides and angles of ZPS, calling the polar dist. π, the zenith dist. ζ, and the colatitude λ, that equation becomes

$$\cos \zeta = \cos (\pi - \lambda) - 2 \sin \pi \sin \lambda \sin^2 \tfrac{1}{2} \text{P} \qquad (4)$$

But if ζ' denote the meridian zenith distance of the heavenly body

$$\zeta' = \pm (\pi - \lambda) \qquad (5)$$

Hence (4) becomes

$$\cos \zeta = \cos \zeta' - 2 \sin \pi \sin \lambda \sin^2 \tfrac{1}{2} \text{P}$$

or, by transposition,

$$\cos \zeta' = \cos \zeta + 2 \sin \pi \sin \lambda \sin^2 \tfrac{1}{2} \text{P} \qquad (6)$$

the formula for use in which

ζ' is meridian zenith dist.
ζ is observed zenith dist.
π is polar distance of the object observed.
λ is the approximate colatitude.
P is the hour angle.

The use of formula (6) is facilitated by Table XXIII., commencing p. 154 of Bowditch's Navigator, entitled log. rising, in which log. $2 \sin^2 \frac{1}{2}$ P is calculated for every value of the hour angle P. To this it is only necessary to add the logarithms of the sines of the polar distance and approximate colatitude, and we have the difference between the observed and meridian altitudes, or the correction to be applied to the former to obtain the latter, from which the latitude is calculated as at p. 280.

A formula may be derived from either of the forms (B) of Art. 86. Applied after clearing of fractions to the present triangle it becomes

$$\sin^2 \tfrac{1}{2} \text{P} \sin \pi \sin \lambda = \sin \tfrac{1}{2} (\zeta + \lambda - \pi) \sin \tfrac{1}{2} (\zeta + \pi - \lambda)$$

or from (5) above

$$\sin^2 \tfrac{1}{2} \text{P} \sin \pi \sin \lambda = \sin \tfrac{1}{2} (\zeta + \zeta') \sin \tfrac{1}{2} (\zeta - \zeta')$$

$$\sin \tfrac{1}{2} (\zeta - \zeta') = \sin^2 \tfrac{1}{2} \text{P} \sin \pi \sin \lambda \operatorname{cosec} \tfrac{1}{2} (\zeta + \zeta') \qquad (7)$$

which will serve to determine $\zeta - \zeta'$, the correction for the zenith distance, if in the second member the value of ζ' be used, which would be given by the approximate value of the latitude.

CIRCUM-MERIDIAN ALTITUDES.

If the heavenly body be near the meridian, P and $\zeta - \zeta'$ will be very small, and writing the small arcs in place of their sines, to which they are sensibly equal (7) becomes (considering $\zeta = \zeta'$ in the second member)

$$\tfrac{1}{2}(\zeta - \zeta') = \tfrac{1}{4}\,\mathrm{P}^2 \sin \pi \sin \lambda \operatorname{cosec} \zeta' \qquad (8)$$

in which the value of the first member is expressed in terms of the radius as unity. To express it in seconds of arc, its value, as well as that of P must be divided by the sine of 1″, which may be regarded as the length of 1″, in terms of radius as unity. (8) thus becomes, striking out at the same time the common factor $\frac{1}{2 \sin 1''}$

$$\zeta - \zeta' = \frac{\mathrm{P}^2}{2 \sin 1''} \sin \pi \sin \lambda \operatorname{cosec} \zeta' \qquad (9)$$

in which $\zeta - \zeta'$ is expressed in seconds of arc, as is also P the hour angle. If p denote the hour angle in time, $15p$ must be substituted for P, and (9) becomes

$$\zeta - \zeta' = \frac{225p^2}{2 \sin 1''} \sin \pi \sin \lambda \operatorname{cosec} \zeta' \qquad (10)$$

The value of $\zeta - \zeta'$ for the same station and star being proportional to p^2, if it were calculated for a value of $p = 1^m$, it might be found for any other value of p, by multiplying this by p^2 in minutes of time. Table XXXII. of Bowditch's Navigator contains values of $\zeta - \zeta'$ for $p = 1^m$ for all latitudes and all declinations less than 24°, so that entering this table with the declination of the star and proximate latitude of the station as arguments, the number taken from the table multiplied by the square of the hour angle, in minutes and decimals of time, which is given in Tab. XXXIII. of Bowditch, for every value of p up to 13^m, will produce the correction to be applied to the observed altitude, to obtain the meridian altitude.

$\zeta - \zeta'$ may be calculated more accurately by means of a table (Tab. XXXVI.), adapted to formula (9) above, in which $\frac{\mathrm{P}^2}{2}$ is equal to the versed sine of P, as may be seen by referring to (2) on p. 94, from which, using only two terms on account of the smallness of P, we have

$$\cos \mathrm{P} = 1 - \frac{\mathrm{P}^2}{2} \therefore \operatorname{vers} \mathrm{P} = 1 - \cos \mathrm{P} = \frac{\mathrm{P}^2}{2}$$

Table XXXVI. gives vers P and the arithmetical complement of the logarithm of the sin 1″ is 9·3144.

N. B. The correction $\zeta - \zeta'$ is subtractive from ζ the observed zen. dist. to obtain ζ' the merid. zen. dist. or it is additive to the observed altitude to obtain meridian altitude.

If several altitudes or zenith distances were observed near the meridian, and each reduced to the meridian by the above formula, the mean of the latitudes thence derived would be the true latitude more nearly in proportion to the number of observations.

But the mean of the values for $\zeta - \zeta'$, obtained from (10), since for each the quantities entering into (10) are the same except p^2, may be obtained by taking the mean of the values of p^2, and multiplying this by the constant factors. And if the mean of the values of $\zeta - \zeta'$ be subtracted from the mean of the values of ζ, the same latitude will result as if the latitude were calculated for each observed zenith distance, and the mean of all the latitudes taken, but with much less computation.

EXAMPLE.

Observed circum-meridian altitudes of ☉'s lower limb, at head of Upper Mistigougiche Lake, latitude about 48°, July 24th, 1841, with Repeating and Reflecting Circle, Artificial Horizon, and Box Chronometer.

SUN'S CENTRE ON THE MERIDIAN BY CHRONOMETER AT $11^h\ 12^m\ 48^s{\cdot}1$*, BAROMETER 28·9, THERMOMETER 69.

Times of obs.	Hour Angles, p.	p^2 Tab. XXXIII.	Tab. XXXVI.
11^h 09 55·5	$2^m\ 52^s{\cdot}6$	$8^m{\cdot}3$	78
10 31	2 17 ·1	5 ·2	50
10 47	2 1 ·1	4 ·1	39
11 09	1 39 ·1	2 ·7	26
11 30	1 18 ·1	1 ·7	16
11 51·5	0 56 ·6	0 ·9	8
12 13·5	0 34 ·6	0 ·3	3
12 36·5	0 11 ·6	0 ·0	0
12 53	0 4 ·9	0 ·0	0
13 11·5	0 23 ·4	0 ·1	1
13 24	0 35 ·9	0 ·4	3
13 44	0 55 ·9	0 ·9	8
		12)24 ·6	12)232
Vernier Reading 19° 26′ 20″		mean 2 ·05	19

$\zeta - \zeta'$ for $p = 1^m$ in lat. 48°, dec. 19°, Table XXXII. 2″·6

$\zeta - \zeta'$ for mean of hour angles = product 5″·3

The times in the first column above are the instants of contact of the images as observed with the reflecting circle, according to the method described at p. 300.

The numbers in the 2d column are obtained by subtracting those of the first from $11^h\ 12^m\ 48^s{\cdot}1$, the time at which the sun is on the meridian. The numbers in the 3d column are the squares of those in the 2d, expressed in minutes and tenths. The mean of the values of p^2 is $2^m{\cdot}05$, which, multiplied by 2″·6, the value of $\zeta - \zeta'$ lat. 48° and dec. 19°, gives 5″·3, the correction required, by which the mean of the observed altitudes is to be increased, to produce the meridian altitude.

The fourth column is for another mode of computation, the numbers in it being

* This of course depends on the equation of time, and the error of the chronometer.

taken from Tab. XXXVI.* The computation of formula (9) by the aid of this column is as follows:

Mean of vers.	24	log.	1·2787
Latitude,	48° 8′	log. cos	9·8243
Declination,	19 10	log. cos	9·9752
Zenith Dist.,	29 12	log. cosec	0·3116
Constant 1″		ar. co. log. sin	9·3144
Correction $\zeta'-\zeta$	5″·06	log.	0·7042

The reading of the vernier at the end of the observations 19° 26′ 20″ was after two complete revolutions of the circle; therefore the whole angle passed over is obtained by adding this to 1440° = twice 720°, and the double altitude is obtained by dividing this by twice the number of times that the inner circle has been moved forward, or by the whole number of contacts of images, in this case 12.

	19°	26′	20″
	1440		
	12)1459	26	20
Double altitude,	121	37	11·7
Altitude,	60	48	35·85
Reduction to Meridian,			5·06
Semidiameter,		15	46·4
	61	4	27·31
Refraction—Parallax,		—	25·40
	61	4	1·91
Declination,	19	10	47·3
Colatitude,	41	53	14·61
Latitude,	48	6	45·39

The following method of determining the latitude by means of three altitudes taken near the meridian, has been given by Mr. Littrow, of Vienna.

Let A be the first observed altitude corrected for dip, refraction, parallax, and semidiameter, and T the time.

A + a the second observed altitude, corrected also, and

T + t the corresponding time.

A + a' the third altitude, and T + t' the time.

Let A′ be the meridian altitude, and T + T′ the corresponding time. Then the variations of the altitude near the meridian being as the squares of the variations of the hour angle nearly, we have

$$A'-A : A'-a :: T'^2 : (T'-t)^2$$

$$\therefore \quad aT'^2 = (A'-A)(2T't-t^2) \qquad (1)$$

$$\text{Similarly } a'T'^2 = (A'-A)(2T't'-t'^2)$$

$$\text{By division } \frac{a}{a'} = \frac{2T't-t^2}{2T't'-t'^2} \text{ and } \therefore T' = \tfrac{1}{2}\,\frac{at'^2-a't^2}{at'-a't} \qquad (2)$$

$$\text{And from (1) } A'-A = \frac{aT'^2}{2Tt'-t^2} \qquad (3)$$

* For a table which gives the value of the whole fraction in (9) and (10), see Lee's Tables and Formulæ, p. 64, Part III.

From (2) may be obtained the value of T′, which added to T gives T + T′, the time when the object observed was on the meridian, and from (3) may be obtained the value of A′ — A, and by adding A, the value of A′ the meridian altitude becomes known, from which the latitude is to be computed as at Art. 111.

Determination of Latitude by an Altitude of the Pole Star out of the Meridian.

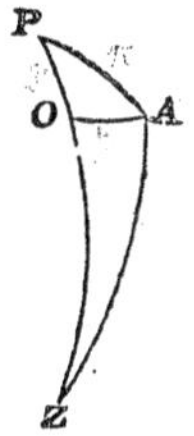

Let P be the pole, Z the zenith, and consequently PZ the meridian; A the place of the pole star at the time that its altitude a is observed. Denoting its polar distance PA by π, drawing the arc AO perpendicular to PZ, expressing PO by y, and the hour angle by p, in the right angled triangle PAO, which may be regarded as plane from being so small, we have

P O A Z

$$\text{AO} = \pi \sin p$$

In the right angled triangle ZAO, ZA and ZO are nearly equal; denoting their difference by x, we have $\text{ZO} = 90 - a - x$, and by Napier's rules,

$$\cos \text{ZA} = \cos \text{ZO} \cos \text{AO}$$

or,

$$\sin a = \sin (x + a) \cos (\pi \sin p) \qquad (1)$$

But

$$\sin (x + a) = \sin x \cos a + \cos x \sin a = \sin a + x \cos a \qquad (2)$$

since $\cos x = 1$, and $\sin x = x$ because x is so small. Also [p. 94 (2)]

$$\cos (\pi \sin p) = 1 - \tfrac{1}{2} \pi^2 \sin^2 p \qquad (3)$$

Uniting (2) and (3), (1) becomes

$$\sin a = (\sin a + x \cos a) (1 - \tfrac{1}{2} \pi^2 \sin^2 p)$$

Performing the multiplication indicated in the second member, and omitting the term $\frac{1}{2} x\pi^2 \cos a \sin p$ on account of the smallness of the quantities x, π, and p we deduce

$$x = \tfrac{1}{2} \pi^2 \tan a \sin^2 p$$

But in the right angled triangle PAO

$$\tan y = \tan \pi \cos p$$

And (p. 94, note),

$$\tan \pi = \pi + \tfrac{1}{3} \pi^3$$

Also, (p. 95, note),

$$y = \tan y - \tfrac{1}{3} \tan^3 y$$

$$\therefore y = (\pi + \tfrac{1}{3} \pi^3) \cos p - \tfrac{1}{3} \pi^3 \cos^3 p, \quad \text{or} \quad y = \pi \cos p + \tfrac{1}{3} \pi^3 \sin^2 p \cos p^*$$

omitting the powers of π higher than π^3.

* Since $\sin^2 p = 1 - \cos^2 p$.

Denoting the latitude required by λ, it is evident (see second note, p. 283), that

$$\lambda = a + x - y$$
$$\therefore \lambda = a - \pi \cos p + \tfrac{1}{2} \pi^2 \tan a \sin^2 p - \tfrac{1}{3} (\pi \cos p) (\pi \sin p)^2 \qquad (4)$$

To have λ in seconds of arc we must substitute for λ, $\lambda \sin 1''$, and for π, $\pi \sin 1''$. Thus (4) becomes, after dividing by $\sin 1''$

$$\lambda = a - \pi \cos p + \tfrac{1}{2} \sin 1'' \pi^2 \tan a \sin^2 p - \tfrac{1}{3} \sin^2 1'' (\pi \cos p) (\pi \sin p)^2 \qquad (5)$$
$$\log. \tfrac{1}{2} \sin 1'' = \bar{6}{\cdot}3845449$$
$$\log. \tfrac{1}{3} \sin^2 1'' = \overline{12}{\cdot}8940285$$

Formula (5) is that upon which the rule p. 619 of the Naut. Alm. of 1850 is founded. The argument for the first correction $- \pi \cos p$, in the formula, of the observed altitude, necessary to be applied to obtain the altitude of the pole equal to the latitude of the place, is the siderial time, upon which p or the hour angle evidently depends, the declination being regarded as constant. There will be two arguments of the second correction $\frac{1}{2} \pi^2 \tan a \sin^2 p - \frac{1}{3} (\pi \cos p) (\pi \sin p)^2$ to wit, the siderial time and the altitude. The third correction is the change in the value of the first, $- \pi \cos p$, which alone is of sufficient magnitude to be sensibly affected by the change in the right ascension and declination of the pole star. Denoting the changes by $d\alpha$ and $d\delta$, the change in $- \pi \cos p$ occasioned by the latter will evidently be

$$d\delta \cos p$$

and that occasioned by the former $d\alpha$ will be

$$- \pi (\cos (p - d\alpha) - \cos p) = - \pi \sin d\alpha \sin p = - \pi d\alpha \sin 1^s \sin p$$

as will be seen by developing $\cos (p - d\alpha)$, and making $\cos d\alpha = 1$ on account of the smallness of $d\alpha$. Or the above expression may be written

$$5380 \times 0{\cdot}000073\ d\alpha \sin p = 0{\cdot}4\ d\alpha \sin p$$

The third correction is sometimes positive, sometimes negative, but always less than 1′, and therefore

$$1' + \text{the third correction,}$$

which is the quantity given in the table in the Naut. Alm., is always positive, and hence the necessity of subtracting 1′ according to the rule given in that work.*

The instrument employed for measuring altitudes in a fixed observatory is

THE MURAL CIRCLE,

so called because it is sustained against a wall about four feet thick, and wide and

* The above method of finding the latitude is so convenient as to be worthy of particular attention. It is not confined to any precise hour, as is the case with meridian altitudes, but may be employed during the whole night, whenever the pole star is visible. An officer of the British Navy has, by means of it and a quadrant with a spirit level attached, the horizon being invisible, been able to run his frigate boldly up the English Channel, at the rate of eleven knots an hour, in a dark squally night, which allowed only occasional glimpses of the pole star between flying clouds.

Captain Porter, U.S.N., is in the habit of running his steamer along the Florida Reefs by the same means.

nigh enough to allow ample space for the circle, which is usually five or six feet in diameter. The graduation is not where it usually is, but upon the outer rim, the surface of which is normal to the plane of the circle. The degrees run from zero to 360. Exterior to the circle, and fastened against the wall, are six microscopes, pointing towards the centre of the circle for reading the graduated rim. They are placed at equal distances, viz. 60° apart. The circle turns round past these microscopes, which are stationary, upon a very strong axis, fastened solidly to one side of the circle at the centre, where the axis is about six inches thick. This axis passes entirely through the stone wall, tapering to about three inches or less at the other side of the wall. Against this small end of the axis, screws work both laterally and vertically, by means of which the circle is adjusted to the plane of the meridian. This adjustment is effected by the aid of what is called a ghost apparatus. Before describing this it will be necessary to mention that the telescope of the instrument is attached firmly to the outer face of the circle, in the direction of the diameter, to which it is equal in length, and turns with the circle on its axis. The ghost apparatus consists of two small microscopes, placed one at each end of the telescope, on the outside of its tube, and pointing horizontally and parallel to the plane of the circle, when the telescope is vertical. From a bracket at the top of the wall, moving outward and inward by a screw, is suspended a plumb line, which passes down directly before the object glasses of the microscopes, between them and a small mother of pearl disc, on which is a black spot, called a ghost, which is brought exactly on the line of vision of the microscopes, so as to be covered by the plumb line. This being done, if now the plumb line be moved out by means of the screw in the bracket, so as to clear everything, and the telescope be reversed by turning the circle 180° on its axis, then, if the plumb line, when brought back to cover one of the ghosts covers also the black spot in the other, the axis of the circle is horizontal. If not, half the correction must be made by the adjusting screws of the axis at the rear of the wall, and the other half by moving one of the ghosts. This latter movement is effected by turning on its axis the tube containing the mother of pearl disc, which tube is in the prolongation of the tube of the microscope, the connexion between them being broken, to permit the plumb line to pass in. The black spot of the ghost is at one side of the centre of the mother of pearl disc, so that as the tube containing the disc turns, the black spot is carried from side to side, through a small space, sufficient to bring it into coincidence with the plumb line, the latter remaining stationary, and covering the black spot of the other ghost.

The process above described must be repeated till the plumb line coincides with the black spot of the ghosts in both positions of the telescope.

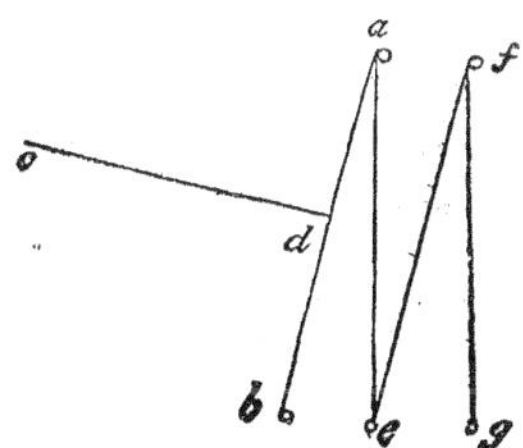

The rationale of this adjustment may be made evident by the following diagram.

Suppose the plane of the diagram to be a vertical plane through the centre of the mural circle, and perpendicular to its plane; *ab* its section with the plane of the circle, *cd* perpendicular to *ab*, the axis on which the circle turns, *ae* the first position of the plumb line coinciding with the black spots on the ghosts *a* and *e*. When the telescope is reversed by turning the circle on its axis *cd*, the ghost *e* will take the position *f*, and the ghost *a* will come to *b*, and the plumb line suspended from *f* will be in the direction *fg*. The lower ghost *b* will thus be the whole distance *bg* away from the plumb line *fg*. Half the correction necessary to bring it into coincidence with the plumb line, must therefore be made by lowering the end *c* of the axis, which is firmly fixed to the circle *ab*, till the point *b* comes to *e*,* which will render the axis *cd* horizontal, and the other half by moving *b*, now at *e*, to *g*, or the ghost *f*, together with the plumb line, to *a*. The axis *cd* is thus made horizontal, and the circle *ab* vertical. It being difficult in practice to lower the point *c* just enough to make half the correction which would render *cd* horizontal, the process has to be repeated. Each trial will bring the axis nearer to the horizontal position required, so long as only part of the correction necessary to bring the ghosts into alignment with the plumb line is made by the motion of the point *c* of the axis *cd*, by means of the screws which work against this point.

The axis being thus rendered horizontal, the instrument may be collimated by the method described at p. 161, and may be adjusted to the meridian, or its deviation from the meridian determined by the method of high and low stars, given at p. 157.

To measure the polar distance of a star with this instrument, the reading must be first taken as indicated by an index or pointer, fastened to the wall a little outside of the circle, when the telescope points to the pole of the heavens, and afterwards taken when the telescope points to the star, the circle having been moved on its axis past the index, which remains stationary. The difference between these two readings will be the polar distance of the star.

The first of the above mentioned readings is called the polar zero of the instrument. It may be found by taking the readings with the telescope pointing to a circumpolar star, at both its superior and inferior transits. The middle point between these readings or half their sum will be the polar zero.

In taking the observation the horizontal wire in the axis of the telescope is made to thread the star with great exactitude. This wire does not require collimating, but the vertical wires do, for the reason stated at p. 160.

Each degree of the graduated limb is divided into halves and quarters, or 15′; these again into 3 parts, or 5′ spaces. The reading of the degree is taken by the index or pointer above mentioned, the minutes and seconds with one of the microscopes, and the seconds with all six microscopes, the mean of the seconds given by the whole six being the number of seconds adopted. The construction and mode of using these microscopes must now be described. The wires of one of these microscopes, which are of the finest spider's web, cross each other at a very acute angle, with a horizontal line, and are placed in a frame in the tube of the microscope at the focus of its object glass. This frame is movable up and down, by means of a screw placed under the tube of the microscope, and working into it. A single turn of the screw moves the point of intersection of the wires over $\frac{1}{5}$ of one of the 5′ spaces, and the screw head is made large, and its circumference divided into 60 parts, so that the

* Or rather till *e* and *b* come together, the motion being about the point *d*, *a* moving half the distance *be* to the left, and *b* half the same distance to the right.

number of turns and fractions of a turn of the screw necessary to bring the wires to one of the dividing lines of the 5′ spaces will show how many minutes and seconds the intersection of the wires stood past this division. To save the trouble of counting the number of turns of the screw, a notched scale is placed vertically a little on one side, at the focus of the microscope, so as to be magnified by its eye-glass. A pin, which points horizontally past the scale, towards the intersection of the wires of the microscope, moves over one notch at each turn of the screw. The zero of the notched scale at which the pin ought to stand at the commencement of the observation, is marked by a hole at the middle of the scale.

To recapitulate, the reading of the degrees, minutes, and seconds will be taken as follows: the degrees by the index or pointer, then looking into the microscope, the degree nearest which the pointer stands will be recognised by a round indentation in the metal, near a long dividing line; the half degree is marked by a dividing line of the same length, without any indentation; the quarter degree by a shorter line, and the 5′ spaces, of which there are three in each quarter degree, by shorter lines still. If the intersection of the wires stand exactly upon one of these dividing lines, the reading will be so many degrees, halves, quarters, and five minutes; but if the intersection of the wires of the microscope be a little past one of the dividing lines on the limb, the intersection must be brought back to the dividing line by turning the screw which moves the frame containing the wires. The number of turns of the screw necessary for this purpose, indicated by the number of notches passed over on the scale by the pin within, will be so many additional minutes to be added to the reading as it now stands, and the seconds will be obtained from the screw head by noting at what numbers upon it its index stands.

The mural being used in the same observatory ordinarily with a transit instrument, by observing the time of transit of the star over the wires of the mural, and comparing the result with the transit observation corrected as explained under the head of that instrument, the hour angle of the star when it crosses the imaginary middle wire will be known; or it can be computed from a high and low star observed with the mural itself, as explained for the transit instrument. From this hour angle the error in the observed altitude of the star arising from the deviation of the instrument from the meridian, may be obtained as follows:

REDUCTION TO MERIDIAN OF AN OBSERVATION MADE WITH THE MURAL CIRCLE.

Let the full circle be the meridian of the station, s′ss″ the diurnal path described by the star under observation, *ms* the arc of a great circle of which the horizontal wire is a portion, s the place of the star when observed. Then in the triangle MSP, right angled at *m*, (since the meridian is a vertical circle)

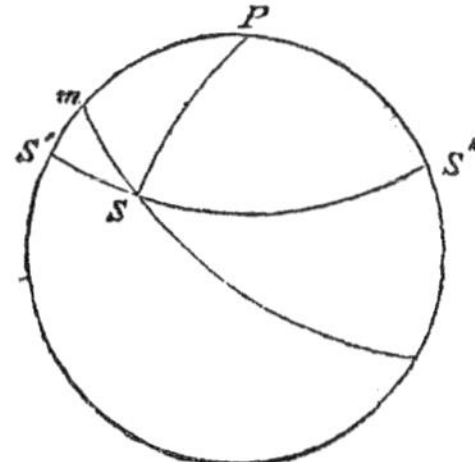

$$\cos \text{P} = \tan \text{P}m \cdot \cot. \text{PS} = \frac{\sin \text{P}m}{\cos \text{P}m} \cdot \frac{\cos \text{PS}}{\sin \text{PS}}$$

$$1 - \cos P = 1 - \frac{\sin Pm \cdot \cos PS}{\cos Pm \cdot \sin PS}$$

$$= \frac{\cos Pm \sin PS - \sin Pm \cos PS}{\cos Pm \sin PS} = \frac{\sin (PS - Pm)}{\cos Pm \sin PS}*$$

But $1 - \cos P = 2 \sin^2(\frac{1}{2} P)$, see (8) Art. 72.

Since $PS = PS'$, $PS = Pm$ very nearly, whence $PS - Pm = s'm$, and the hour angle SPS' is generally very small.

$$\therefore \quad 2 \sin^2 (\tfrac{1}{2} P) = 2 (\sin 1'')^2 \tfrac{1}{4}† P^2 = \frac{s'm \cdot \sin 1''}{\frac{1}{2} \sin 2 PS‡}$$

whence

$$s'm = \text{Reduction} = \tfrac{1}{4} \sin 2 PS, P^2 \sin 1''$$

which is expressed in arc. To express it in time make $P = 15\ p$, whence

$$\text{Reduction} = \frac{225}{4} \sin 2 PS\, p^2 \sin 1''\text{; its log} = 6{\cdot}4356974 + \log \sin 2 PS\, p^2$$

in which p is the hour angle in seconds of time, and PS the polar distance of the star. The correction or reduction does not become of any sensible magnitude, till the hour angle exceeds 5 seconds. The correction or reduction is always to be added to the apparent polar distance, if the star has a N.P. distance less than 90°, but subtracted if greater than 90°. This may be seen from the diagram, and still better on a globe; the great circle of which the horizontal wire is a portion, intersecting the meridian N. of the diurnal circle of the star, when its N.P.D. is less than 90°, and S. when it is greater.

Instead of the polar zero, a horizontal zero has been more commonly used. It is obtained by taking the reading with the horizontal wire bisecting the star, as seen direct on one night, and as seen by reflexion from mercury on the following night; half the difference of the two readings will be the meridian altitude of the star, from which and the latitude the polar dist. or declination may be obtained as explained at p. 130. Within a few years past a third zero, which may be called the nadir zero, has

* See (7) Art. 70.

† The sine of a very small arc differs insensibly in length from the arc itself, and its value may be found by multiplying the sin of 1″, taken from the tables, by the number of seconds in the arc. This serves to express the length of the arc in the same terms as the radius, sine, cosine, &c., are expressed, so that these quantities can enter the same formula. Sin 1″=0·000004848137; log. sin 1″=4·6855749.

‡ See form. (1) Art. 71.

§ Or both, the direct and reflected observation may be made on the same night, the star for one or both being a little off the meridian, and such observation reduced to the meridian by the formula above. A movable vertical micrometric wire serves to measure the distance of the star from the meridian. This may be still better done by observing the time of transit over vertical wires, and comparing this with the true time at meridian transit.

been employed. This is obtained by means of a collimating eye-piece and basin of mercury, placed under the object glass of the telescope, turned vertically downward, as described at p. 161, note. When the direct image of the horizontal wire coincides with that seen by reflexion, the reading will be the nadir zero, and the difference between this and the reading when the telescope points to a star crossing the meridian, will be the distance of the star from the nadir, which is the supplement of its zenith distance, from which the polar dist. or dec. may be obtained, as already explained.

The circle and transit instrument are combined in one, in the German observatories. The instrument which results is called a *transit circle* or *meridian circle*. Both observations, to wit, that for the right ascension and that for the declination of the object, are taken simultaneously.

TRIAL METHOD OF DETERMINING BOTH LATITUDE AND TIME.

Supposing neither the chronometer error nor the latitude to be exactly known, but the altitudes of two stars A and B, differing 90° in azimuth be observed, and assume successively two trial latitudes, computing the chronometer error by each latitude, and by the altitude of each of the stars. Suppose the first assumed latitude for example to be 45° 15′, and the resulting chronometer error by star A to be $46^s{\cdot}2$, and by star B, $50^s{\cdot}2$; the discordance is 4^s. Suppose the second assumed latitude to be 45° 25′, and the resulting chronometer error by A to be $53^s{\cdot}4$, by B $37^s{\cdot}4$; the discord now is 16^s the opposite way. Then 10′ of latitude has changed the discord 20^s; therefore a change of 2′ of latitude will remove the first discord of 4^s, and the latitude is therefore 45° 17′; and since 10′ altered the error by A $7^s{\cdot}2$, and by B $12^s{\cdot}8$, 2′ will alter the former by $1^s{\cdot}44$, and the latter by $2^s{\cdot}56$, and both agree in giving the error $47^s{\cdot}64$.

PART VI.

GEODESY.

PART VI.

GEODESY.

Geodesy is a higher kind of surveying, which takes into account the curvature of the earth's surface. It has for its object to determine, with the utmost possible accuracy, the geographical positions of points on the earth's surface by the process of triangulation already repeatedly described in this work, but requiring for the present purpose certain modifications, which it will be the object of the following pages to unfold.

The triangles composing the chain best fulfil their destination when the largest possible, and nearly equilateral. The sides are ordinarily from ten to fifty miles, and limited only by the want of distinct vision with the instruments, or interruptions from the nature of the ground. The primary chain being finished, a *secondary* chain of smaller triangles, having their vertices within the larger, is surveyed, and a still smaller chain of *tertiary* triangles. A great number of small bases and points of reference are thus determined, from which the surveys with the plane table or compass may originate, to complete the map in all its details. One of the chief problems, after the triangulation is finished, is the determination of the difference of latitude and longitude between the vertices of the triangles, so that when the absolute latitude and longitude of some of the vertices shall have been determined by astronomical observations, that of all the others may be known by *differentiation.* Previous to the explanation of the method employed for this purpose, it will be necessary to give some account of the mode of conducting the triangulation and, first, of the

MEASUREMENT OF BASES.

The measured base, from which the triangulation commences, should be selected upon ground which will admit of its extending several miles. Its length should be ascertained with the greatest care, and for this purpose it has been customary to use metallic rods, allowing for their expansion and contraction from changes of temperature, the amount of which had been previously determined by experiment, with a thermometer which was always observed when making the measurements.* For greater accuracy in placing the ends of the rods together, an optical contact has been employed. This is produced by placing horizontally upon tressels the rods, one a little above, and its end projecting over that of the next, a notch being cut out of the ends of the rods, across which a thread is horizontally stretched; a microscope supported on a stand, from which an arm holding the microscope projects over the ends of the rods so that the microscope can be placed vertically over the threads, looking down upon them; the rods are then moved by screws in the tressels, till the threads are seen to coincide in the microscope, or till each coincides with a mark on the stand below. The optical contact is then complete.

The best *base apparatus* now in existence, probably, is that employed upon the coast survey of the United States, and of this we shall attempt a more particular description. It is made self-adjusting under changes of temperature. The measuring rods consist each of two bars, the one above the other; the lower of brass and the upper of iron, which is less expansible. The two bars are connected firmly by a cross-piece at one end, but allowed each to expand freely, being unconnected at the other, at which, however, there is a short lever of the second order placed vertically, having its fulcrum or extremity at the end of the lower bar, on which it works as a hinge, and its point of resistance at the end of the upper bar, the lever continuing above this, and having the power applied horizontally to its upper end, through a steel rod, which projects horizontally from the next measuring rod, above which it is sustained by a short support. The contact between this steel rod and the upper end of the lever is that of a blunt knife edge against a plane of agate. The other end of the steel rod works freely against the lower end of a very short vertical lever of the first order, the upper end of which supports a spirit level. The end of the spirit level farthest from the steel rod has a tendency to fall, occasioned by a counterpoise weight, which projects from it, but this is prevented by pressure of the steel rod against the lower end of the short lever, on the top of which the spirit level rests. This delicate mode of contact, first suggested by Bessel, depends on the sensibility of the spirit level.† The tressels on which the rods rest, at two

* For each degree of the centigrade thermometer, platina expands 0·000008565 of its dimensions in every direction, iron 0·000010666, and brass 0·000017843. For 1° Fah. the expansion is for brass, 0·00001050903, iron 0·000006963535.

† The effect of this arrangement is evident; the whole rod, composed of the two bars, lengthens by the effect of heat, but the lower more than the upper bar, so that

points only, are strongly trussed, and their upper parts at least metallic, and admit, by means of screws, of the various motions required in placing the apparatus. In measuring the base line, the measuring rods need not be placed exactly in a horizontal position, but the measure they give can easily be reduced to a horizontal one, if only the inclination of the rod to the horizon be known*.

The contrivance to indicate this consists of a sector, the plane of which is vertical, attached to the rods and graduated; a brass radius of this sector, moving about its centre, and supporting a spirit level, stands at the zero of the sector when the rod and spirit level are both horizontal. When the rod is inclined, the number of degrees passed over on the sector, in making the spirit level horizontal, shows the inclination of the rod.

the upper end of the vertical lever, which makes the contact, is thrown back. The ratio of the length of the arms of the lever will depend on the ratio of expansibility of brass and iron.

* The formula would be evidently

$$B = l \cos a$$

B being the horizontal measure required, l the oblique measure given by the apparatus, and a its inclination shown by the sector. But a being very small, it is better to compute the correction $l - B$ to be subtracted from l to obtain B. It is

$$l\,(1 - \cos a) = 2\,l \sin^2 \tfrac{1}{2}\,a = \tfrac{1}{2}\,l\,a^2 \sin^2 1'.$$

or,

$$l - B = 0{\cdot}00000004231\;a^2\,l$$

or,

$$\log.\,(l - B) = 2{\cdot}626422 + 2\,\log.\,a + \log.\,l.$$

a being very small. In practice it is customary to tabulate this formula.

The base must next be reduced to the level of the neighboring sea. Let ρ be the radius of the earth (or better the normal) for the level of the sea; $\rho + h$ the radius for the level of the base, h being the mean height of the ground on which the base is measured above the level of the sea, and b the reduced base.

Then, since similar arcs are as their radii, we have

$$\frac{B}{b} = \frac{\rho + h}{\rho} \;\therefore\; B - b = \frac{Bh}{\rho + h} = \frac{\frac{Bh}{\rho}}{\left(1 + \frac{h}{\rho}\right)} = \frac{Bh}{\rho}\left(1 + \frac{h}{\rho}\right)^{-1}$$

Developing the last expression by the binominal formula

$$B - b = \frac{Bh}{\rho} - B\frac{h^2}{\rho^2} + B\frac{h^3}{\rho^3}\ \&c.$$

Which is the correction, always subtractive.

But ρ being very great in comparison of h, it is sufficient for all ordinary values of B to take

$$B - b = \frac{Bh}{\rho}$$

The horizontal alignment is made by means of a small transit, altitude-and-azimuth instrument, or theodolite, and pickets with cards of paste-board in their tops, placed along the line. The telescope of the instrument is directed to the distant extremity of the base, and then brought down on its horizontal or supporting axis, to indicate the proper position of each picket. The correctness of the ratio of the length of the arms of the vertical lever, to prevent changes in the distances between the contacts from changes of temperature, is tested by a pyrometer, invented by Mr. Saxton, of the Coast Survey. The rod is placed level upon two marble piers, sunk in the ground, which support its ends. The rod is then subjected to changes of temperature, artificially created, and being prevented from expanding in one direction by an upright stancheon, against which it abuts, its expansion, if any, in the opposite direction, acts against the vertical axis of a small plane mirror, giving the mirror an angular rotation about its vertical axis, the plane of the mirror always continuing vertical. At the opposite side of the room is a telescope placed horizontally on a pier, and directed to this mirror, and directly under the object glass of the telescope, is a horizontal scale of three feet in length, the divisions of which are $\frac{1}{4}$ of an inch. The movement of one of these divisions over the vertical wire of the telescope, occasioned by a motion of the small mirror in which it is reflected, corresponds to a change in length of the rod of $\frac{1}{25,000}$ of an inch. The distance of the piers, which is liable to change, by hygrometric changes, is tested by a standard bar at the temperature of freezing. The standard bar is compared with a bar from France, the only one in the country. Its length is an exact French metre, which is the ten millionth part of a quarter of the meridian, the value of which in units already in use has been found by means of two measured degrees in distant latitudes. (See Appendix VI. p. 368.)

A bar of brass and iron exposed to the same temperature will not heat equally in equal times ; this is well known to depend upon the different conducting powers of the two metals, their different specific heats, and the different powers of their surfaces to absorb heat. The bars, then, if of equal sections, when the temperature is rising or falling, will not have the same temperature, and the system is not compensating. By adapting the sections according to rules deduced, partly by theory and partly by experiment, a small residual quantity remains to be corrected, which is detected only by the delicate tests of the Saxton pyrometer, or the lever of contact and level of Bessel. This correction is made by applying a covering more absorbent of heat to one bar than to the other.

The rods are surrounded by a tin covering, and of about twenty feet (six metres) in length, the whole being easily transported by four men.

TO REDUCE A BROKEN BASE TO A STRAIGHT LINE.

Let a and b be the given sides, and c the included angle, which is nearly 180°. Put c $= 180° - \theta$.* The formula is

$$c = a + b - \overset{-1}{\log.} \; (2 \cdot 6264222 + \log. a + \log. b + \text{ar. co. } \log. (a + b) + 2 \log. \theta.)$$

The angles of the triangle of the great or primary chain are observed in England and this country with an instrument called

THE GREAT THEODOLITE.

That employed on the Coast Survey of the United States was made by Troughton and Simms, of London, under the direction of the late Mr. Hassler. It consists of a horizontal limb thirty inches in diameter, made narrow and light, with a vertical rim below, to strengthen it, supported by conical arms from beneath a central drum, upon which the telescope is mounted on pillars, as in the transit instrument. The telescope is of four feet focal length. The limb is graduated to 5′ spaces, and numbered to 360°. Three reading microscopes, reading to single seconds at intervals of 120°, are sustained above the limb, by horizontal arms projecting from the central drum. Three of the six horizontal arms which support the limb extend beyond the limb, and are provided with foot screws, upon which the instrument rests, on short pillars or legs, which fit each into one of three holes 120° apart, in a wooden frame strongly trussed.

The method of observing is as follows. The instrument is directed to the signal at one of the distant vertices of the triangle whose angles are to be measured, upon which the middle vertical wire is adjusted with great accuracy, and the reading taken by the three microscopes, the degrees for only one of them. The telescope is then, inverted by turning it on its horizontal or supporting axis, and the instrument turned on its vertical axis 180°, till the middle vertical wire again coincides with the signal, when the reading of the three microscopes is again taken. The legs

* θ being very small, the formula preceding (2) Art. 21, App. I., putting for sin ϕ its value in (1), becomes, putting sin $\frac{1}{2}\theta$ or $\frac{1}{2}\theta$ for its equal cos $\frac{1}{2}$ c, neglecting θ^4, &c.,

$$c = a + b - \tfrac{1}{2} \sin^2 1' \, \frac{ab\theta^2}{a + b}$$

$$= a + b - 0 \cdot 00000004231 \, \frac{ab}{a + b} \theta^2$$

Whence the formula in the text, in which θ is expressed in minutes

are then shifted in the holes of the wooden frame, which changes the position of the limb 120°, and the same operation gone through as before, and so on.* As there are three holes for the legs, the whole number of readings on a single signal will thus amount to 18, the indiscriminate mean of which will involve a compensation for all instrumental errors.†

SELECTION OF STATIONS AND SIGNALS.

Eminences are usually chosen, and, if possible, such as to permit the signals, which serve to mark the stations, being seen against the sky. A very small object is thus made visible at a very great distance.

Permanent monuments of masonry or pottery are sunk below the surface of the ground far enough to be undisturbed by ploughing, with an orifice in the top, in which to insert a signal staff. The top of this staff supports some object to which the telescope is directed. Spheres made of barrel hoops, covered with white muslin, have been found to answer well in mountainous regions, being visible fifty miles, but not so well in low grounds, and near the sea. Tin cones of an angle adapted to reflect advantageously the light of the morning and evening sun, were used by Mr. Hassler, who gives (Trans. Am. Phil. Soc., 1825), the mode of reducing in a simple manner the observation to the axis of the cone, a reduction depending on the relative position of the cone to the sun and the observer.‡ Steeples, circular or polygonal towers, windmills, &c., have been employed, and the methods of correcting the observations upon these are given by Puissant.§ At night, signals have been used formed of

* This is for the purpose of measuring the same angle upon different parts of the limb.

† The French employ a large repeating circle, with which the angles are observed, in oblique planes, passing through the objects and the eye. These require to be reduced to the horizon by methods given by Puissant (Traité de Geodesie). The theodolites employed on the Coast Survey, besides the 30 inch, are one of 24 inches, and one of 18 inches, by Troughton and Simms, and a number of 14, 12, 10, and 6 inch repeating circles by Troughton and Simms, and Gambey, of Paris.

‡ A formula easily deducible from Hasler's is

$$\text{Correction in seconds} = \pm \frac{r \cos \frac{1}{2} z}{D \sin 1''}$$

In which r = mean radius of signal cone,

z = diff. of azimuth between ⊙ and signal,

D = distance.

§ Traité de Geodesie, a standard work on this subject, to which we shall have frequent occasion to refer.

lamps, placed at the focus of a parabolic reflector, or behind a lens at the focus of parallel rays. The most perfect is the Drummond light, which may be seen at the distance of seventy miles.

The best signal when the sun shines is one employed at present on the Coast Survey of the United States, called a *heliotrope.* It consists of a common telescope, mounted upon a three-legged stand, horizontally. It is accompanied by a man called a heliotroper, who directs the telescope to the tent in which the great theodolite is placed. Upon the eye end of the telescope is supported a small plane mirror, which has motion round both a vertical and horizontal axis, so as to be capable of being placed in a position to reflect the sun in any direction, at pleasure. The heliotroper attends and turns the mirror continually, so as to reflect the sun in a direction parallel to the axis of the telescope, which he accomplishes by causing the rays to pass through two perforated discs, supported like the mirror, on the top of the telescope tube, one being near the object end, and the other between it and the mirror.* The signal pole is supported by a wooden tripod at least $\frac{1}{3}$ its height, and the heliotrope is placed at a short distance from it, in a line with the theodolite station. All the signals visible from the station at which the great theodolite is placed, are observed every day for several weeks. The instrument is then moved to a new station, and by this means all the angles of every triangle are repeatedly observed.

REDUCTION TO THE CENTRE OF THE STATION.

It sometimes happens from the nature of the signal employed, that the theodolite cannot be placed at the axis of the signal called the *centre of the station.* The process of determining what the observed angle would have been with the instrument so placed, from observation with the instrument placed at a short measured distance† from the proper point, is called *reducing to the centre of the station.*

Let C in the diagram be the centre of the station, O the place of the instrument. From the observed angle AOB required the angle ACB. Make $AOB = \omega$, $BC = g$, $AC = d$, $ACB = x$, $OC = r$, $COB = y$.

Then

$$AIB = \omega + IAO, \text{ and } AIB = x + CBO$$

* The heliotroper is on duty till 10 A.M. and after 3 P.M., the atmosphere in the middle of the day being too unsteady near the earth's surface for good observations.

† If the centre of the station be inaccessible, this distance must be calculated from measurements which can be made by methods which the student will easily devise for any given case.

21

Equating these two values of AIB we obtain

$$x - \omega = \text{IAO} - \text{CBO}$$

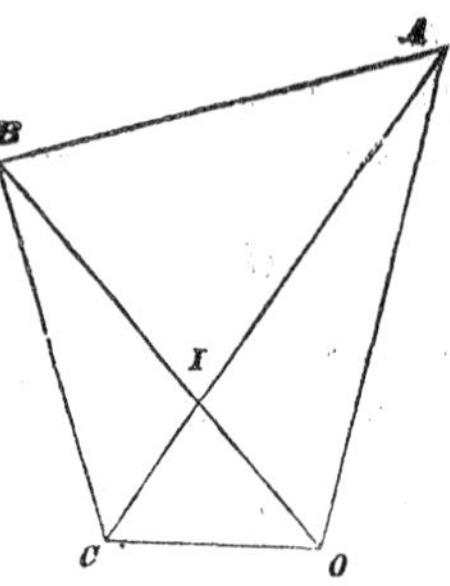

But,

$$\sin \text{CAO} = \frac{r \sin(\omega + y)}{d}, \ \sin \text{CBO} = \frac{r \sin y}{g}$$

Substituting these values of the sines of CAO, CBO, for the angles themselves, which are very small, we have

$$x - \omega = \frac{r \sin(\omega + y)}{d \sin 1''} - \frac{r \sin y}{g \sin 1''},$$

which is the formula for the correction to be applied to the observed angle ω, to obtain the required angle x.

The distance r being small, d and g are computed with the angle ω.

VERIFICATION OF THE OBSERVED ANGLES.

The excess of the sum of the angles of a spherical triangle over two right angles is technically called the *spherical excess.* One third of the spherical excess being subtracted from each of the angles of a spherical triangle occupying but a small portion of the surface of the sphere, a plane triangle may be formed with the resulting angles, and with rectilinear sides, equal in length to the curvilinear sides of the spherical triangle, and A, B, C being the angles, s the area of the triangle, and r the rad. of the earth (or better the rad. of curvature, see App. VI. p. 366),

$$\text{A} + \text{B} + \text{C} = 180^\circ + \frac{s}{r^2 \sin 1''} \; *$$

* This is Legendre's theorem, the demonstration of which, by Lagrange, is as follows:—The sides of a spherical triangle being a, b, and c, and the radius of the sphere r, the similar triangle on the sphere, whose radius is 1, will have for sides $\frac{a}{r}, \frac{b}{r}, \frac{c}{r}$ which put equal to α, β, γ, and by Art. 82,

$$\cos \text{A} = \frac{\cos \alpha - \cos \beta \cos \gamma}{\sin \beta \sin \gamma} \qquad (1)$$

But (p. 94) α and β being very small,

$$\cos \alpha = 1 - \frac{\alpha^2}{1 \cdot 2} + \frac{\alpha^4}{1 \cdot 2 \cdot 3 \cdot 4}, \ \sin \beta = \beta - \frac{\beta^3}{1 \cdot 2 \cdot 3}$$

and similar expressions obtain for $\cos \beta$, $\cos \gamma$, $\sin \gamma$ $\therefore$ (1) becomes

which is the formula of verification, the last term being expressed in seconds.

If the sum of the three observed angles exceed 180° by $\frac{s}{r^2 \sin 1''}$ the observations are correct.

As the spherical excess $\frac{s}{r^2}$ is expressed in terms of the area of the triangle, that must be computed, which may be done with sufficient accuracy by considering the spherical triangle as plane, and applying to it one of the formulas of Art. 19, App. I.

The angles of the plane triangle, whose sides are equal in length to those of the given spherical triangle, being found by means of the spherical excess, as above explained, and the length of one of the sides of the

$$\cos A = \frac{\frac{1}{2}(\beta^2 + \gamma^2 - a^2) + \frac{1}{24}(a^4 - \beta^4 - \gamma^4) - \frac{1}{4}\beta^2\gamma^2}{\beta\gamma(1 - \frac{1}{6}\beta^2 - \frac{1}{6}\gamma^2)} \qquad (2)$$

Transferring $(1 - \frac{1}{6}\beta^2 - \frac{1}{6}\gamma^2)$ to the numerator, by giving it the exponent -1, and developing as far as to terms of the fourth degree inclusive, (2) becomes

$$\cos A = \frac{\beta^2 + \gamma^2 - a^2}{2\beta\gamma} + \frac{a^4 + \beta^4 + \gamma^4 - 2a^2\beta^2 - 2a^2\gamma^2 - 2\beta^2\gamma^2}{24\beta\gamma} \qquad (3)$$

Replacing the values of a, β, γ, (3) may be expressed as follows:—

$$\cos A = \frac{M}{2bc} + \frac{N}{24bcr^2} \qquad (4)$$

If the same lengths, a, b, c, be sides of a plane triangle, and A' be the angle opposite a, by Art. 69,

$$\cos A' = \frac{b^2 + c^2 - a^2}{2bc} = \frac{M}{2bc} \qquad (5)$$

Raising both members of (5) to the square, and substituting $1 - \sin^2 A'$ for $\cos^2 A'$

$$-4\,b^2c^2\sin^2 A' = a^4 + b^4 + c^4 - 2a^2b^2 - 2a^2c^2 - 2b^2c^2 = N$$

Equation (4) thus reduces to

$$\cos A = \cos A' - \frac{bc}{6r^2}\sin^2 A' \qquad (6)$$

Let $A = A' + x$, x being the difference between the spherical and plane angle,

$$\cos A = \cos A' \cos x - \sin A' \sin x = \cos A' \sqrt{1 - \sin^2 x} - \sin A' \sin x$$

Putting x, which is very small, for $\sin x$, and rejecting the second power of x,

$$\cos A = \cos A' - x \sin A' \qquad (7)$$

Combining (6) and (7), which have the same first members

$$x = \frac{bc}{6r^2}\sin A' \text{ and since } A = A' + x$$

spherical triangle being known, that of the others may be obtained by the solution of the plane triangle.

Between the latitudes 45° and 25° the spherical excess amounts to about 1″ for an area of 75·5 square miles. To find the spherical excess in seconds of space therefore divide the area in square miles by 75·5.

The logarithm of the mean radius of the earth in yards is 6·8427917, of r^2 is 13·6855834.

The following example shows the form* in which the above rules are applied in practice on the U. S. Coast Survey.

$$A = A' + \frac{bc}{6r^2} \sin A' \tag{8}$$

But [Art. 19, (1) App. I.], $\frac{1}{2}\, b\, c$, sin A′ is the area of the plane triangle of which a, b, c are the sides, which area does not differ sensibly from the proposed spherical triangle. If s denote the area of either of these (8) becomes

$$A' = A - \frac{s}{3r^2}$$

In a similar manner may be found

$$B' = B - \frac{s}{3r^2}$$

$$C' = C - \frac{s}{3r^2}$$

$$\therefore A' + B' + C' = A + B + C - \frac{s}{r^2} \tag{9}$$

But $A' + B' + C' = 180° \therefore A + B + C = 180° + \frac{s}{r^2}$

And this last is the formula of verification. The same theorem has been extended to a spheroidal triangle, the difference between the spheroidal excess and spherical excess being less than $\frac{1}{20}$ of a second in the largest triangle ever measured on the surface of the earth. To express $\frac{s}{r^2}$ in seconds, it must be divided by sin 1″.†

* In the form given the 1st, 3d, and 4th columns explain themselves; the 2d column contains the names of the stations at the vertices of the triangle, the 7th the spherical excess 5·67, calculated by the formula on p. 323, the 5th the difference 0·15 between the excess of the sum of the observed angles over 180°, and the spherical excess, which difference ought to be zero. This error 0·15 is equally distributed between the three angles; the 6th column contains the observed angles thus corrected; the 8th column contains the angles of a plane triangle whose sides are of the same length with the spherical one, each determined by subtracting $\frac{1}{3}$ the spheri-

† A still more accurate formula, deduced rigorously from the spheroid, is Excess $= s\, \frac{1 + e^2 \cos 2\,L}{a^2}$, in which L = mean latitude, and a = equatorial radius. This form would only become important in carrying forward azimuths in a long chain.

No.	Denomination.	No. of Series.	Observed angles.	Distribution and Error.	Spherical angles.	Spherical excess.	Plane angles and distances.	Logarithms.
	Manomet	36	66 34 04·80	−0″·05	04″·75	1·89	66 34 02·86	0·0373802
37	Copecut	35	64 08 37·78	−0 ·05	37 ·73	1·89	64 08 35·84	9·9541886
	Bluehill	36	49 17 23·24	−0 ·05	23 ·19	1·89	49 17 21·30	9·8796760
				−0 ·15		5·67		
				Bluehill to Copecut,			54695·61	4·7379524
				Manomet to Bluehill,			53644·00	4·7295212
				Manomet to Copecut,			45186·49	4·6550086

DETERMINATION OF THE LATITUDES, LONGITUDES AND AZIMUTHS OF THE STATIONS.

The latitude and longitude of a few of the stations of a chain of triangles, selected at different parts of the whole, being determined by astronomical observations, the latitudes and longitudes of the other stations may be found *geodetically*, as it is termed, by methods which we now proceed to explain.

The problem to resolve is the following. Given the latitude and the longitude of the point S in the diagram, and the azimuth of the point S′ upon the horizon of S*, to find the latitude and longitude of this second point, and the azimuth of S upon the horizon of S′.

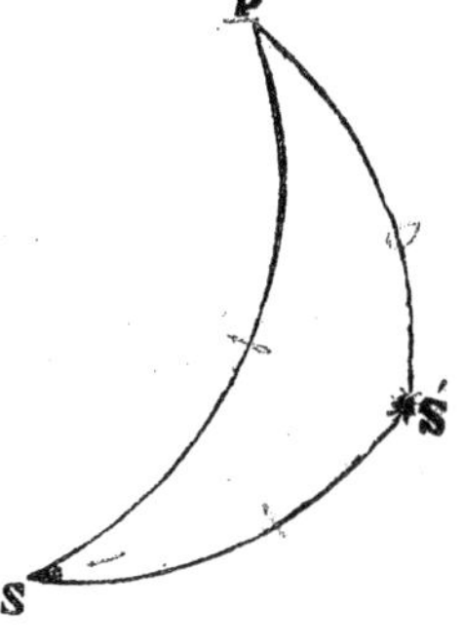

If L denote the given latitude, dL the difference of latitude between the two stations to be applied as a correction to the known latitude, in order to find the required latitude; M the longitude, dM the difference of longitude of the two stations, Z the azimuth, dZ the difference of azimuth; then the following will be the

FORMULAS FOR COMPUTATION OF L, M, Z OF PRIMARY TRIANGLES.

For the difference of latitude

$$-d\text{L} = \text{KB}\cos\text{Z} + \text{K}^2\,\text{C}\,\sin^2\text{Z} + (d\text{L})^2\,\text{D} - h\,\text{K}^2\,\text{E}\,\sin^2\text{Z}\dagger$$

cal excess, or 1·89 from the corresponding spherical angles; this column also contains the sides of the plane triangle, the last two of which are computed from the first, and the angles by the sine proportion, p. 62, the logarithms for which purpose are contained in the last column.

* Observed astronomically by methods to be described in the sequel.

† The following is the demonstration of this formula:—There are known in the triangle PSS′ the colatitude PS = 90° − L of the point S, the angle PSS′ = the azimuth

In which K = dist. between the two stations (in metres)

$$B = \frac{1}{R \text{ arc } 1''} = \frac{(1 - e^2 \sin^2 L)^{\frac{3}{2}}}{a(1 - e^2)\sin 1''} \text{ since } R^* \ (= \text{rad. of curvature}) = \frac{a(1 - e^2)}{(1 - e^2 \sin^2 L)^{\frac{3}{2}}}$$

of S′ from S = Z, and the side SS′ = K, the geodetic line or measured distance between S and S′. That is to say two sides and the included angle, to compute PS′, the colatitude, and PS′S = 180° — Z′ the azimuth of S from S′, and P = dM, the diff. of long. required.

The determination of the latitude, especially, by this method, would be attended with considerable error. We shall deduce the formula given by Delambre, for the difference of latitude between the two stations. The formula of Art. 82, applied to the present triangle, gives

$$\cos PS' = \cos S \sin PS \sin SS' + \cos PS \cos SS'$$

or, since $L + dL$ = the latitude of S′, of which PS′ is the complement

$$\sin(L + dL) = \cos Z \cos L \sin K + \sin L \cos K$$

or [Art. 70, (3)],

$$\sin L \cos dL + \cos L \sin dL = \cos Z \cos L \sin K + \sin L \cos K$$

or [Art. 72 (8), and Art. 71 (3)],

$$\sin L(1 - 2\sin^2 \tfrac{1}{2} dL) + 2\cos L \cos \tfrac{1}{2} dL \sin \tfrac{1}{2} dL = \cos Z \cos L \sin K + \sin L (1 - 2\sin^2 \tfrac{1}{2} K)$$

Whence, reducing

$$2\sin L \sin^2 \tfrac{1}{2} dL + 2\cos L \cos \tfrac{1}{2} dL \sin \tfrac{1}{2} dL = \cos Z \cos L \sin K - 2\sin L \sin^2 \tfrac{1}{2} K$$

Dividing by 2 cos L this becomes

$$-\tan L \sin^2 \tfrac{1}{2} dL + \cos \tfrac{1}{2} dL \sin \tfrac{1}{2} dL = \tfrac{1}{2}(\cos Z \sin K - 2\tan L \sin^2 \tfrac{1}{2} K)$$

Representing the second member by p, and — tan L by q, and dividing all the terms by $\cos^2 \frac{1}{2} dL$, we have

$$q \tan^2 \tfrac{1}{2} dL + \tan \tfrac{1}{2} dL = \frac{p}{\cos^2 \frac{1}{2} dL} = p(1 + \tan^2 \tfrac{1}{2} dL)$$

or,

$$(q - p)\tan^2 \tfrac{1}{2} dL + \tan \tfrac{1}{2} dL = p$$

Resolving this quadratic we have

$$\tan \tfrac{1}{2} dL = -\frac{1}{2(q-p)} + \frac{1}{2(q-p)}[1 + 4p(q-p)]^{\frac{1}{2}}$$

Developing the radical part by the binomial theorem,

$$\tan \tfrac{1}{2} dL = \frac{1}{2(q-p)}[2(q-p)p - 2(q-p)^2 p^2 + 4 \quad (q-p)^3 p^3 \ \&c.]$$

Or performing the operation indicated in the second member, and rejecting the terms beyond p^3,

* Values of R and N for every latitude are furnished by a table, p. 44, **Part I.**, of Lee's Tables and Formulas. See also (4), p. 366 and p 368 App. VI.

$$C = \frac{\tan L}{2 N R \text{ arc } 1''} = \frac{\tan L (1 - e^2 \sin^2 L)^2}{a^2 (1 - e^2) 2 \sin 1''}, N \text{ being} = \frac{a}{(1 - e^2 \sin^2 L)^{\frac{1}{2}}}$$

$$D = \frac{\frac{3}{2} e^2 \sin L \cos L \text{ arc } 1''}{(1 - e^2 \sin^2 L)^{\frac{3}{2}}}, E = \frac{1 + 3 \tan^2 L}{6 N^2} = \frac{(1 + 3 \tan^2 L)(1 - e^2 \sin^2 L)}{6 a^2}$$

$$\tan \tfrac{1}{2} dL = p - qp^2 + (1 + 2q^2) p^3$$

But (see note p. 95),

$$\tfrac{1}{2} dL = \tan \tfrac{1}{2} dL - \tfrac{1}{3} \tan^3 \tfrac{1}{2} dL$$

Substituting in the second member of this the value of $\tan \frac{1}{2} dL$, given by the preceding it becomes

$$\tfrac{1}{2} dL = p - q p^2 + (1 + 2q^2) p^3 - \tfrac{1}{3} p^3$$

rejecting the higher powers of p. Or,

$$dL = 2p - 2qp^2 + \tfrac{4}{3} p^3 (1 + 3q^2)$$

But,

$$2 p = \cos Z \sin K - 2 \tan L \sin^2 \tfrac{1}{2} K$$

$$2 q p^2 = - \tfrac{1}{2} \cos^2 Z \sin^2 K \tan L + 2 \cos Z \sin K \sin^2 \tfrac{1}{2} K \tan^2 L$$

$\frac{4}{3} p^3 = \frac{1}{6} \cos^3 Z \sin^3 K$, rejecting terms containing higher powers of $\sin K$ than the third.

But [App. I., p. 94 (1)],

$$\sin K = K - \tfrac{1}{6} K^3$$

Whence the first term in the value of $2p$ becomes

$$K \cos Z - \tfrac{1}{6} K^3 \cos Z \qquad (m)$$

and the value of $\frac{4}{3} p^3$ may be put under the form

$\frac{1}{6} K^3 \cos^2 Z \cos Z$, rejecting higher powers of K than K^3

This last, added to the second term of (m), gives

$$- \tfrac{1}{6} K^3 \cos Z (1 - \cos^2 Z) = - \tfrac{1}{6} K^3 \cos Z \sin^2 Z$$

so that (m) thus increased becomes

$$K \cos Z - \tfrac{1}{6} K^3 \sin^2 Z \cos Z$$

Again, putting $\frac{1}{2} K$ for its sine, being a small arc, the second term in the value of $2p$ becomes

$$- \tfrac{1}{2} K^2 \tan L$$

and the first term of the value of $-2qp^2$ becomes

$$+ \tfrac{1}{2} K^2 \cos^2 Z \tan L$$

These last two being added together produce

$$- \tfrac{1}{2} K^2 \tan L \sin^2 Z$$

Thus the expression for the difference of latitude reduces to

$$dL = K \cos Z - \tfrac{1}{2} K^2 \sin^2 Z \tan L - \tfrac{1}{6} K^3 \sin^2 Z \cos Z (1 + 3 \tan^2 L) \&c.$$

Delambre observes that the meridional arcs, computed on the supposition that the earth is a sphere differ insensibly from those computed on the spheroidal hypo-

a = equatorial semidiameter of the earth = 6377397·15 metres, log. a = 6·8046434637, h = 1st term K·B cos Z.

e = 0·0816967, log. e = 8·9122052271.

Subjoined is part of a table, from which B, C, D, E are to be taken.

Argum. Latitude.	Log. B.	Diff. 10″	Log. C.	Diff. 10″	Log. D.	Log. E.	Diff. 10″
		—		+			+
40° 00′	8·5108910·6		1·32843·1		2·3801·9	6·1044·4	
1	898·1		868·6		02·6	48·6	
2	885·6		894·1		03·4	52·7	
3	873·1		919·6		04·1	56·9	
4	860·6		945·1		04·9	61·0	
5	848·1	2·08	970·5	4·25	05·6	65·2	0·69
6	835·6		996·0		06·4	69·4	
7	823·1		1·33021·5		07·1	73·5	
8	810·6		047·0		07·9	77·7	
9	798·1		072·5		08·6	81,8	
10	8·5108785·6		1·33098·0		2·3809·4	6·1086·0	

For an example, let us make K = 100 miles = 160900 metres, L =

thesis. The consideration of the spheroidal figure is only of consequence, in converting the terrestrial arcs, measured in metres, into seconds. This may be done by dividing such arcs by their radii of curvature,[1] and this quotient by the length of 1″. Our formula is deduced by considering the normal N terminating at the polar axis as the radius of curvature of the geodetic arc K, which it is very nearly; then if K and N be both expressed in metres,

$$\frac{K}{N}$$

will be the length of K in terms of N as unity. If therefore

$$\frac{K}{N}$$

be substituted for K in the last value of dL, we have

$$dL = \frac{K \cos Z}{N} - \frac{1}{2}\frac{K^2 \sin^2 Z \tan L}{N^2} - \frac{1}{6}\frac{K^3 \sin^2 Z \cos Z\,(1 + 3\tan^2 L)}{N^3} \qquad (g)$$

in which dL is expressed in terms of N the radius of K as unity.

In order that it may be expressed in terms of its own radius as unity, which we will call R,[2] this value of dL must be multiplied by

$$\frac{N}{R}$$

and if the result thus obtained be divided by the length of 1″ in terms of radius unity, the value of dL will be expressed in seconds.

Multiplying therefore the second member of (g) throughout by $\frac{N}{R}$ dividing it by arc 1″, and estimating Z from S round by W, from 0° to 360°, which will be the supplement of the Z used in the diagram, it becomes

$$-dL = +\frac{K \cos Z}{R \text{ arc } 1''} + \frac{K^2 \sin^2 Z \tan L}{2NR \text{ arc } 1''} - \frac{K^3 \sin^2 Z \cos Z}{6\,N^2 R \text{ arc } 1''}(1 + 3\tan^2 L) \qquad (a)$$

[1] The radius of curvature at any point of a curve is the radius of a circle having the same curvature as the curve in that part of it.

[2] For the demonstration of a formula for the radius of curvature of an elliptical meridian, at any point of that meridian, in terms of the latitude of that point, see the Appendix to Part VI. p. 366.

40°, z = 54° ; the computation by means of the preceding table is as follows :

K log.	5·2065560	K² log.	10·41311		
z log. cos	9·7692187	z log. sin²	9·81592	$(dL)^2$* log.	6·9835
B log.	8·5108911	C log.	1·32843	D log.	2·3802
α log.	3·4866658	β log.	1·55746		9·3637

h log.	3·4867	1st term	3066″·661
K² sin² z log.	0·2290	2d "	+ 36 ·096
E log	6·1044	3d "	0 ·231
	9·8201		3102 ·988
		4th "	0 ·661
			3102·327

The 1st and 2d terms should always be used. The third term should be used whenever log. α is over 2·310. When K is less than 100,000 metres, or log. K not over 5·00, α^2 may be written in the 3d term for $(dL)^2$ for all z* less than 35°, or wherever β is not over 0·876.

$$\text{where } R = \frac{a\,(1-e^2)}{(1-e^2\sin^2 L)^{\frac{3}{2}}}{}^{1}\quad N = \frac{a}{(1-e^2\sin^2 L)^{\frac{1}{2}}}$$

The results are better if the radius of curvature midway between the two latitudes is used ; make $\frac{1}{2}\,dL = \lambda$; $L - \lambda = L_m$ the latitude of the middle point between L and L′, and the radius of curvature at $L_m = R_m$; then should the formula (a) be multiplied by $\frac{R}{R_m}$ if we would refer the arc dL to R_m. Then $dL\,\frac{R}{R_m} - dL = \frac{R - R_m}{R_m}\,dL$ is the correction to be added to (a) to make the required reduction.

$$\text{Now is } R - R_m = a\,(1-e^2)\left[\frac{1}{(1-e^2\sin^2 L)^{\frac{3}{2}}} - \frac{1}{(1-e^2\sin^2 L_m)^{\frac{3}{2}}}\right] = a\,(1-e^2)$$

$$\frac{1-\frac{3}{2}e^2\sin^2 L_m - 1 + \frac{3}{2}e^2\sin^2 L}{(1-e^2\sin^2 L)^{\frac{3}{2}}\,(1-e^2\sin^2 L_m)^{\frac{3}{2}}} = a\,(1-e^2)\,\frac{\frac{3}{2}e^2(\sin^2 L - \sin^2 L_m)}{(1-e^2\sin^2 L)^{\frac{3}{2}}\,(1-e^2\sin^2 L_m)^{\frac{3}{2}}}$$

But since (See. 63 p. 103), $\sin^2 L - \sin^2 L_m = \sin(L - L_m)\,\sin(L + L_m) = \sin\lambda\,\sin(2L - \lambda) = dL\sin L\cos L$ very nearly, because $\frac{1}{2}\sin 2L = \sin L\cos L$. The quantity neglected here is quite insensible in practice.

$$\text{We have then } \frac{R - R_m}{R_m} = \frac{a\,(1-e^2)\,\frac{3}{2}e^2\,dL\sin L\cos L}{(1-e^2\sin^2 L)^{\frac{3}{2}}\,(1-e^2\sin^2 L_m)^{\frac{3}{2}}} \times \frac{(1-e^2\sin^2 L_m)^{\frac{3}{2}}}{a\,(1-e^2)}$$

$$= \frac{\frac{3}{2}e^2\,dL\sin L\cos L}{(1-e^2\sin^2 L)^{\frac{3}{2}}} \text{ and } \frac{R - R_m}{R_m}\,dL = (dL)^2\,\frac{\frac{3}{2}e^2\sin L\cos L}{(1-e^2\sin^2 L)^{\frac{3}{2}}} \qquad (c)$$

As this quantity never amounts to $\frac{1}{10000}$ of dL, the third term of dL in (a) **need not**

* This dL is the sum of the first two terms α + β.

[1] See Appendix VI. p. 366.

For secondary work the 4th term $h\text{K}^2 \sin^2 \text{Z}.\text{E}$ may always be omitted. The 3d term very frequently is of no sensible value, and α^2 may *always* be written in the place of $d\text{L}^2$, when K does not exceed 86,500 metres (54 miles), or log. K = 4•937, which comprise the vast majority of cases. When K is less than 34000 metres, two terms are sufficient. The best rule for the omission of the third term is that it need not be used unless log. α is greater than 2•31 . . ., log. D (which scarcely varies), being about 2•38. . ., we shall, in that case, have log α^2 D = 7•00 . . = log. of 0″•001.

It appears that there are hardly any cases in which the second term may be omitted.

The 1st term gives the distance on the meridian of the point of departure from that point to the foot of the perpendicular from the second point, the second term gives the reduction to the parallel. It is only at a very small azimuth then, that the 2d term may be neglected even for a very short line.

The 4th term may be omitted between latitude 45° and 40°, when K is not over 17000 metres, or log. K = 4•2304. Between latitude 40° and 35°, when K is not over 18500 metres, or log. K = 4•2671, and between latitude 35° and 30°, when K is less than 20,000 metres, or log. K 4•301.

In computing carry log. B to 7 places,

" " " C to 5 places.

" " " D and E to 4 places.

The formula for difference of longitude is

$$d\text{M} = \frac{\text{A}'\text{K} \sin \text{Z}}{\cos \text{L}'} * \qquad (\text{G})$$

be used in making the substitution of $d\text{L}$ in (c), and the second term only when it is over 18°. If in (c) we introduce $d\text{L}$ expressed in seconds obtained by (*a*), we must of course multiply by arc 1″, and we have, finally,

$$-d\text{L} = \frac{\text{K} \cos \text{Z}}{\text{R arc } 1''} + \frac{\text{K}^2 \sin^2 \text{Z} \tan \text{L}}{2\,\text{N}\,\text{R arc } 1''} - \frac{\text{K}^3 \sin^2 \text{Z} \cos \text{Z}}{6\,\text{N}^2\,\text{R arc } 1''}(1 + 3\tan^2 \text{L}) + (d\text{L}^2)$$

$$\frac{\frac{3}{2} e^2 \sin \text{L} \cos \text{L arc } 1''}{(1 - e^2 \sin^2 \text{L})^{\frac{3}{2}}} \qquad (\text{A})$$

Making $\frac{1}{\text{R arc } 1''} = \text{B}$, $\frac{\tan \text{L}}{2\,\text{NR arc } 1''} = \text{C}$, $\frac{\frac{3}{2} e^2 \sin \text{L} \cos \text{L arc } 1''}{(1 - e^2 \sin^2 \text{L})^{\frac{3}{2}}} = \text{D}$, $\frac{1 + 3\tan^2 \text{L}}{6\,\text{N}^2} = \text{E}$,

and call the first term h, we may write $-d\text{L} = + \text{K} \cos \text{Z}\cdot\text{B} + \text{K}^2 \sin^2 \text{Z}\cdot\text{C} + (d\text{L})^2 \text{D} - h\,\text{K}^2 \sin^2 \text{Z}\cdot\text{E}$, in which E may be taken out at the same time and from the same page as B and C; h could be copied from the bottom, or sum of the logs. of the 1st term, and $\text{K}^2 \sin^2 \text{Z}$, by taking the sum of the first two logs. of the 2d term.

* The formula for the difference of longitude is obtained in an obvious manner, by applying the sine proportion (Art. 81), to the spherical triangle PSS′, which gives, writing $d\text{M}$ for sin $d\text{M}$ = sin P and K for sin K,

In which

$$A' = \frac{1}{N \text{ arc } 1''} = \frac{(1 - e^2 \sin^2 L')^{\frac{1}{2}}}{a \sin 1''}$$

L' = new latitude, computed from the formula for $-dL$.

$$dM = \frac{K \sin z}{\cos L'}$$

And the value of dM in seconds of arc is obtained by converting K into seconds, by dividing K in metres by $N \sin 1''$, N being the normal, and the length of the radius used at that part of the earth in metres. The above formula thus becomes the one already given (G). Lee's tables and formulæ gives a table for log. N, log. $\frac{1}{N \sin 1''}$ and log. $(1 + e^2 \cos^2 L)$ for any latitude between 20 and 50 degrees.

(G) is founded on the supposition that $\cos L' : \sin z :: K : dM$, whereas, in reality, $\cos L' : \sin z :: \sin \frac{K}{N} : \sin dM$. The error committed by the former supposition is expressed by $\frac{K^3}{N^3\, 6 \cos L' \text{ arc } 1''}\left(\frac{\sin^3 z}{\cos^2 L'} - \sin z\right)$ [see (1) p. 94], or for $L' = 45°$, $\frac{K^3}{3\sqrt{2}\; N^3 \text{ arc } 1''}(2 \sin^3 z - \sin z)$. This is a maximum when $z = 24° \; 06'$, and if we substitute this z in the latter expression, and make it equal to 0·001″, we find the corresponding log. K to be 4·4315 = log. of 27000. For any line over 27000 metres, then a correction ought to be applied to dM, or if we will allow an error of 0·002, for any line over 34000 metres = about 21 miles.

In the annexed table, the column headed dM contains the log. of the seconds in a given arc; the column headed diff. contains the diff. between the log. of that arc and the log. of its sine (to the seventh place); the column headed K containing the log. of the length of that arc in metres. To apply the correction in question after having first computed dM by the formula (G), enter the table with the given log. K, and take out the corresponding diff.; again enter the table with the computed log. dM, and take out the corresponding diff., and lastly, subtract the difference between the two quantities thus obtained from log. dM, the result will be the corrected log. dM.[1]

K	diff.	dM	diff.
contains log. K in metres.	contains diff. between log. arc and log. sin to seven places of decimals.	contains log. dM in seconds of arc.	contains diff. between log. of arc and log. sine to seven places of decimals.

[1] For denoting the difference between the log. arc and log. sin by δ, the formula (G) should be after the application of logarithms,

$\log. dM + \delta \log. dM = \log. \frac{K}{N} + \delta \log. \frac{K}{N} + \log. \frac{\sin z}{\cos L}$. Whence the rule is obvious.

Log. A′ should be carried to eight places. Seven places of logarithms should be used for dM.

For azimuth we have

$$-dz = \frac{d\text{M} \sin \lambda}{\cos \frac{1}{2}\, d\text{L}} \qquad (\text{D})^*$$

$$\lambda = \tfrac{1}{2} (\text{L} + \text{L}')$$

$$z' = 180^\circ + z - \frac{d\text{M} \sin \lambda}{\cos \frac{1}{2}\, d\text{L}}$$

For any line less than 340000 metres (21 miles) cos $\frac{1}{2}$ dL may be omitted, being regarded as 1.

In computing dz, sin $[\lambda = \frac{1}{2} (\text{L} + \text{L}')]$ is taken out to five places for main chain of triangles, and to four for the others, carrying forward dz in tenths of seconds in the first, and in whole seconds in the second.

* The formula for the difference of azimuth is deduced as follows:—In the triangle PSS′ we have, by Napier's analogies, calling π, π' the polar distance of S, S′,

$$\tan \tfrac{1}{2} (s' + s) = \frac{\cot \frac{1}{2} \text{P} \cos \frac{1}{2} (\pi - \pi')}{\cos \frac{1}{2} (\pi + \pi')}$$

Or recollecting that $\tan = \frac{1}{\cot}$ (Art. 37).

$$\cot \tfrac{1}{2} (s' + s) = \frac{\tan \frac{1}{2} \text{P} \cos \frac{1}{2} (\pi + \pi')}{\text{os} \frac{1}{2} (\pi - \pi')} = \frac{\tan \frac{1}{2}\, d\text{M} \sin \frac{1}{2} (\text{L} + \text{L}')}{\cos \frac{1}{2}\, d\text{L}} \qquad (n)$$

But $s' = 180^\circ - z'$, and $s = z$, and $\cot \frac{1}{2} (s' + s) = \tan [90^\circ - \frac{1}{2} (s' + s)]$ ∴ n becomes

$$\tan \tfrac{1}{2} (z' - z) = \frac{\tan \frac{1}{2}\, d\text{M} \sin \lambda}{\cos \frac{1}{2}\, d\text{L}}$$

which is the formula (D) above, if we write $\frac{1}{2}$ dz, for tan $\frac{1}{2}$ $(z' - z)$ and $\frac{1}{2}$ dM for tan $\frac{1}{2}$ dM.

The formula for dz requires some amendment within the same limits, within which we obtain dL and dM; we have

$$\tan \tfrac{1}{2} (z' - z) = \tan \tfrac{1}{2}\, d\text{M} \frac{\sin \lambda}{\cos \frac{1}{2}\, d\text{L}} \qquad (1)$$

for which we have hitherto used

$$dz = d\text{M} \frac{\sin \lambda}{\cos \frac{1}{2}\, d\text{L}}$$

By transformation of (1) we get (see note p. 94, and make cos² and cos³ of $\frac{1}{2}$ $d\text{L} = 1$)

$$dz = d\text{M} \frac{\sin \lambda}{\cos \frac{1}{2}\, d\text{L}} + \tfrac{1}{12}\, d\text{M}^3 \sin \lambda \cos^2 \lambda \sin^2 1''$$

We write the second term thus, $+ d\text{M}^3$ F where log. F is to be taken from the tables, into which it can easily be inserted, as only one value will be required for every half degree of L. It is 7·8324 for 25°, and 7·8404 for 45°; diff. for 30′ = 0·0002. The term $d\text{M}^3$ F can never exceed 0″·1.

Whenever the log. of any term is not over 7·00 . . the corresponding number need not be taken out.

Azimuths are reckoned from south round by west, and from 0° to 360°, the signs of sin z and cos z varying accordingly.

The following form, filled up with an example, is that at present used on the Coast Survey of the United States for the computation of the above formulæ for difference of latitude, longitude, and azimuth.

				°	′	″
z	A	to	B	101	23	16·757
∠	B	and	C	83	36	43·243
z	A	to	C	185	00	00·000
−dz				+	05	47·413
180						
z′	C	to	A	5	05	47·413

	°	′	″			°	′	″
L	45	00	00·000	A	M	70	31	50·000
−dL	1	04	32·264		d M	—	08	06·748
L′	46	04	32·264	C	M′	70	23	43·252

K	5·0791812·5	K^2	0·15836			h	3·5880
cos z	9·9983442·2	$\sin^2 z$	7·88059	δL^2	7·1760	$K^2 \sin^2 z$	8·0389
B	8·5105124·1	C	1·40411	D	2·3872	E	6·2132
h	3·5880379		9·44306		9·5632		7·8401

1st term	3872·914 —	3d term	0·366				
2d term	0·277 +	4th term	0·007				
	3872·637 —				— 249		
3d & 4th terms	0·373 +			A′	8·5090285	Arg.	
−dL	3872·264 —	d M	2·6873039	K	5·0791812	K	— 255
λ	45° 32′ 16″	sin λ	9·8535235	sin z	8·9402960	$d M_u$	+ 6
½ dL	32 16	cos ½dL ar. co.	191	cos L′ ar. co.	0·1588231		— 249
			2·5408465		2·6873039		
		−d z	347″·413	d M	486″·748		

* In this form the first horizontal line expresses the azimuth of the line joining the two stations A and B ; the second the angle formed by a line from A to a third station C, with AB ; the third is found by the addition of these, and is the azimuth of AC ; the fourth the excess of the difference of azimuth between AC and CA over 180°, computed below at the bottom of the form ; the fifth the azimuth of CA required, formed by the addition of the two above, and 180°. The sixth horizontal line contains the latitude L and longitude M of A ; the seventh the difference of latitude and longitude of A

PROJECTION OF MAPS.

The geographical positions of the vertices of the triangles having been determined by calculation, as above explained, blank maps are prepared with lines upon them representing meridians and parallels of latitude, upon which these points are accurately put down in their true positions, and the maps thus prepared being placed in the hands of the plane table parties, are filled up with the details of the ground which they represent, in the manner described at p. 235 et seq., the points marked upon them, and identified upon the ground by the sunk masonry or pottery of the signals employed in the triangulation becoming the base points or points of departure for the operations of the plane table.

The mode of preparing these maps in practice, it will be now proper to explain.

A spherical or spheroidal surface like that of the earth not being developable, it is impossible to represent upon a plane the positions of places without changing more or less their distances from one another.* When a small portion of the earth's surface is to be represented, the best mode is to conceive the earth to be enveloped by a tangent cone, the

and C, computed below; the eighth the latitude L′ and longitude M′ of C, found by taking the algebraic sum of the two above. The next four horizontal lines of the form contain the computation of the difference of latitude dL between A and C, the first column being the computation of the logarithm of the first term, the second that of the second term, and so on, of the formula dL, at p. 325. The next two lines contain the four terms themselves,[1] and the next two their combination to form — dL. The first two columns of the remainder of the form contain the computation of — dz; the third column that of the difference of longitude of A and C, viz. dM, and the fourth the correction of this, which is sometimes employed. Applied here the log. dM becomes 2·6873039, and dM 486·748, differing only 0″·012 from what it was without the correction. A correction is also sometimes applied to dz, as has been already stated at p. 332, the formula for which is FdM³, in which F $= \frac{1}{12}$ sin λ cos² λ sin² 1″. The computation of this correction in the present example would be as follows:—

$$
\begin{aligned}
dM^3 &= 8·0619 \\
F &= 7·8404 \\
\hline
& \ 5·9023
\end{aligned}
$$

In which F may be taken from a table previously prepared. The last number is the logarithm of the correction to be applied to — dz.

* For the ordinary modes of projecting the hemisphere, see "spherical projections" in Davies' Descriptive Geometry, and for the analytical investigations of the same, see Francœur (Geodésie, 309, et seq.)

[1] z being between 90° and 270°, cos z is negative, and ∴ h is negative.

circle of contact being the middle parallel of the region to be embraced, and to suppose the surface of this cone to coincide with that of the earth over the whole extent between the northern and southern parallels of the map. This cone, when developed, becomes the sector of a circle, the portion of which between the two extreme parallels which we have supposed to embrace the surface of contact, will represent the surface of the map.

Supposing the earth to be spherical, which may always be done in the projection of maps, its oblateness being so small, and representing the latitude of the middle parallel of the map by λ, and the number of degrees of longitude to be contained in the map by D, it is evident that the absolute length of the middle parallel of the map will be expressed by (see 1st note, p. 153)

$$\frac{D}{180^\circ}\pi\cos\lambda \qquad (1)$$

In the above expression the radius of the earth is unity, and this being the case, the slant height or length of the element of the cone from the vertex to the circle of contact will evidently be the cotangent of the latitude. The arc of the sector, which is expressed by (1), divided by its radius $\cot\lambda$, gives the length of the arc which measures the angle of the sector to radius unity. The result is

$$\frac{D}{180^\circ}\pi\sin\lambda$$

and this, which is the absolute length of the arc, must be multiplied by $\frac{180^\circ}{\pi}$* to have its value, or the measure of the angle of the sector in degrees,

$$D\sin\lambda \qquad (2)$$

then will be the formula for this angle, and the construction of the map will be very simple. It will only be necessary to draw two lines forming the angle expressed by (2), and with a radius equal to $\cos\lambda$ and the vertex of the angle as a centre, the arc representing the mean parallel may be described. If the map is to contain d degrees of latitude, then $\frac{\pi d}{180^\circ}$ will express the distance between the extreme parallels, and by describing arcs from the vertex of the sector with radii greater and less than

* $\frac{180^\circ}{\pi} = 59^\circ, 29573 = 3437', 74677 = 206264'', 80625.$

cot λ by the half of this expression, the extreme parallels of the map will be constructed. The distance between the parallels is then divided into any number of equal parts at pleasure, and arcs described with the vertex as a centre, and passing through the points of division. As to the meridians, they are drawn as straight lines through the vertex, and through points of division equally distant from one another upon the arc of the middle parallel.

This construction is so simple, that it is generally preferred to any other, and the greater part of maps of kingdoms and states are drawn upon this system.

For greater precision, the cone, instead of being taken tangent to the sphere, is partially inscribed in it by making it pass through the two extreme circles of latitude, so that these circles shall be sections of the cone perpendicular to its axis. Imagine a meridian section of the cone and sphere, the angle α formed by the element of this section with the axis will be measured by half the difference of the arcs included between its sides (Geom. Ex. 30, p. 48). Supposing a and a' to be the points in which the element intersects the meridian section, and λ and λ′ their latitudes, N being the place of the north pole, and S the south, the expression for the measure of the above angle will be

$$\alpha = \tfrac{1}{2}\,(\text{S}a - \text{N}a')$$

$$\text{But S}a = 90^\circ + \lambda, \text{ and N}a' = 90^\circ - \lambda' \quad \therefore \quad \alpha = \tfrac{1}{2}\,(\lambda + \lambda')$$

Now in the right angled triangle formed by the element of the cone, the axis and the radius of the parallel, which last is equal to cos λ, we have for the length of the element terminating at a

$$s = \frac{\cos\lambda}{\sin\frac{1}{2}(\lambda + \lambda')}$$

and for the length of the element terminating at a',

$$s = \frac{\cos\lambda'}{\sin\frac{1}{2}(\lambda + \lambda')}$$

The lengths of the elements of the developed sector being thus known, the rest is as above.

Still better, the cone may be made to pass through two parallels, situated at half distance between the middle parallel and the extremes; the cone would then be partly internal and partly external to the sphere.*

* It was in this way that Delisle constructed the great map of Russia.

PROJECTION OF FLAMSTEED.

This consists in drawing a straight line vertically to represent the central meridian of the map, laying off upon it equal distances say 1°, and through the points of division drawing perpendiculars to this meridian line, which represent parallels of latitude; then laying off upon these parallels distances bearing the same proportion to the distances on the meridian as the cosine of each latitude does to radius unity; finally, drawing through the points of the same graduation, thus determined, curved lines which will represent the other meridians.

The oblateness of the earth may be taken into the account in this method, by laying off in the central meridian not equal distances, but increasing towards the poles in the same proportion as the degrees of the meridian increase. For the demonstration of the formula see App. VI., p. 367. The formula itself is

$$\delta = \frac{\pi a}{180^\circ}(1 - \tfrac{1}{2}\omega - \tfrac{3}{2}\omega\cos 2\lambda)^*$$

In which

$a = 6377397{\cdot}15$ metres, $\log = 6{\cdot}8046434637$; $\log\omega = 7{\cdot}5233789824$;
$\lambda =$ latitude.

The objection to the method of Flamsteed is that it distorts somewhat the regions distant from the central meridian.

METHOD OF THE FRENCH DÉPÔT DE LA GUERRE.

This is a modification of the conic projection already given, and is that now in use on the coast survey of the United States. The radii of the arcs of circles representing the parallels upon the map being too long to be conveniently described from a centre, they are determined by points. Let there be drawn in the middle of the sheet the perpendiculars CA, NN′; NAN′ represents the middle parallel of the map. Then is known the radius $r = \text{CA} = \text{R} \cot\lambda$, R being the radius of the earth. Suppose that the map is to

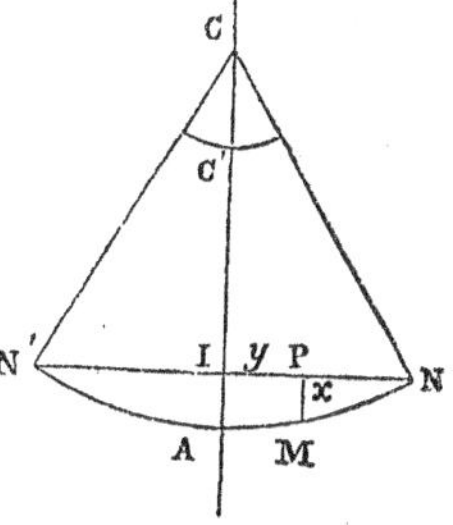

* For a table which gives the length of a meridional arc in any latitude in yards and a table which gives the length of a parallel, see Lee's Tables and Formulæ, Part II., p. 84.

embrace D degrees of longitude, the angle C is then known $= D \sin \lambda$. Representing half the chord NN′ by α, CI by β, we have in the triangle CNI

$$\alpha = r \sin \tfrac{1}{2} C, \quad \beta = r \cos \tfrac{1}{2} C, \quad AI = r\,(1 - \cos \tfrac{1}{2} C)$$
$$= 2r \sin^2 \tfrac{1}{4} C \text{ [see (7) p. 100].}$$

The extreme points N and N′ of the arc to be described NN′, are thus determined, and the point A, in which it intersects the meridian. Now for other points, such as M, a distance IP $= y$ is laid off from I, and a perpendicular PM is drawn in length equal to x, the value of x being expressed by the following formula

$$x = \sqrt{(r+y)(r-y)} - \beta^*$$

* The demonstration of this formula, which requires a knowledge of Analytical Geometry, is as follows:—The equation of the circle, the origin of co-ordinates being at C, is $x^2 + y^2 = r^2$. Transferring the origin to I, the formula for transformation will be $x = x + \beta$, and the equation of the circle becomes $(x + \beta)^2 = r^2 - y^2$

$$\therefore x = \sqrt{(r+y)\ (r-y)} - \beta$$

The formula in the text.

The above method does not take into account the earth's oblateness; the following is the generalization of the theory. Let C be the centre of the projection, AK the middle parallel, the latitude of which represent by l; BM another parallel, whose latitude is λ; M the point in question, whose co-ordinates are AP $= x$, PM $= y$, AX being tangent at A, and perpendicular to the principal meridian CA. We have AB $= s$, the distance in latitude between the two parallels, this length s being known by equation (5) p. 367, App. VI. The radius CA $= r$ is also known, being equal to KM in the diagram on p. 365, which, in the right angled triangle KMN, where MN is the normal N, has for its value $r = N \cot l$. Representing the angle ACM by θ, and CM by ρ, we have

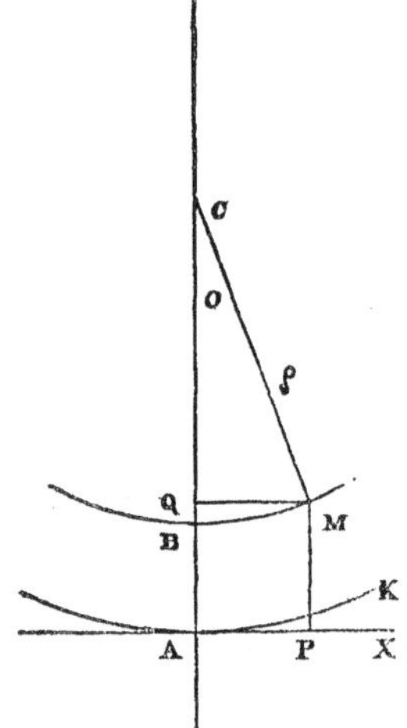

$$QM = x = \rho \sin \theta, \quad CQ = \rho \cos \theta$$
$$y = PM = BQ + s = s + BC - CQ = s + \rho - \rho \cos \theta = s + \rho\,(1 - \cos \theta)$$
$$= s + 2\,\rho \sin^2 \tfrac{1}{2}\,\theta \text{ [see (8) Art. 72].}$$

We may eliminate ρ from this last by means of the first $x = \rho \sin \theta$. It becomes

$$y = s + x\,\frac{1 - \cos \theta}{\sin \theta} = s + x \tan \tfrac{1}{2}\,\theta \text{ [see App. I., (74) p. 103.]}$$

Dividing therefore N into equal parts, and for each point of division finding the corresponding value of x from the above formula, so many points in the arc NN′ will be determined.

ρ is known since $\rho = r - s$. It remains only to find θ in order to have for each point like M the values of the co-ordinates x and y, viz:

$$x = \rho \sin \theta, \; y = s + x \tan \tfrac{1}{2} \theta$$

N. B.—That s must be taken negative when $\lambda < l$.

The longitude of M estimated from the central meridian suppose to be Λ. This will also be the number of degrees in the arc of the parallel.

But N being the normal at the point M, terminating at the polar axis, the radius of this parallel will be (see diagram, p. 365, App. VI.),

$$N \cos \lambda$$

Moreover, the arc BM of the projection is of the same length with the arc of the parallel, but the number of degrees in two arcs of the same length will be in the inverse ratio of their radii

$$\therefore \Lambda : \theta : : \rho : N \cos \lambda$$

$$\theta = \Lambda \frac{N \cos \lambda}{\rho}$$

which formula serves to determine θ in the same denominations that Λ is given. N is known in terms of λ from formula

$$N = \frac{a}{(1 - e^2 \sin^2 \lambda)^{\frac{1}{2}}}$$

(see App. VI., p. 368), in which $e = 0{\cdot}0816967$, log. $e = 8{\cdot}9122052271$.

It is easy to perceive now how a map would be drawn according to the projection under consideration. Two lines AC and AX are first drawn at right angles to each other, intersecting at the middle of the sheet A. Setting out from A, we lay off above and below distances such as AB, respectively equal to the values of s, that is to say to arcs of the meridian corresponding to 1°, 2°, 3°, . . . of distance from A, arcs which go on increasing towards the pole.[1] Next we compute the values of the normals N, N′, . . . from degree to degree, the radii ρ of the projected parallels, and finally the amplitudes of the angles θ, which correspond to values of Λ and λ, varying also by degrees, whence result the co-ordinates x and y of the vertices of quadrilaterals in which meridians and parallels of latitude distant from each other, respectively the space of 1° intersect. It remains only to lay off these co-ordinates by a scale of equal parts. The sides of the quadrilaterals joining these vertices thus determined may be drawn without sensible error as straight lines.

The territory to be represented by the map is ordinarily too extended to be placed

[1] For their values see p. 367, App. VI., also Lee's Tables and Formulas, p. 84, Part II.

LATITUDE BY ASTRONOMIC OBSERVATIONS.

OBSERVATIONS FOR LATITUDE WITH ZENITH SECTOR.

The zenith sector employed on the coast survey of the United States for determining latitude astronomically, is the same as the mural circle already described, p. 306, except that only two small portions of the limb, the one above, the other below the centre, are retained, the rest being conceived to be cut away, to render the instrument more portable. The limb and telescope, instead of being sustained by a wall, are attached to a vertical flat beam of iron, which is capable of reversal about a vertical axis, and also end for end. Long spirit levels can be attached to the

upon a single sheet. It is customary to form the map by the union, border to border, of a series of sheets, the dimensions of which are 8 decimetres by 5. To find the positions of the vertices of the quadrilaterals upon these sheets, the origin of co-ordinates is transferred to one of the corners of the sheet, an operation which consists simply in adding or subtracting 1, 2, 3, . . . times 8 decimetres in the direction of the X^s, and as many times 5 decimetres in the direction of the Y^s, according to the place which the sheet ought to occupy in the assemblage. The order of the sheets is marked upon them. Thus the sheet $\overset{2}{\square}3$ is the one which is second in the horizontal direction, and third in the vertical, estimating from A the intersection of the middle meridian and parallel.

As to the inverse problem, to find the latitude and longitude of a point given upon the map, it will be sufficient to draw through the point lines parallel to the sides of the quadrilateral within which it falls, and to determine upon the scale of equal parts, the values of the fractions which the lines represent.

The following formulas are used on the United States Coast Survey, when the extent of the map is not more than 4° of latitude and longitude.

$$\delta p = (n')\ p \sin \tfrac{1}{2}\,\mathrm{Z}$$
$$\delta m = (n')\ p \cos \tfrac{1}{2}\,\mathrm{Z}$$

In which δp is the ordinate $y = \mathrm{BQ}$.
" δm " abscissa $x = \mathrm{QM}$.
" $(n')\,p$ " length of the parallel.
" $\sin \frac{1}{2}\,\mathrm{Z} = \dfrac{(n')\ p}{2\mathrm{T}}$
" $\mathrm{T} = \mathrm{N} \cot \mathrm{L}$.
" $\mathrm{N} = \dfrac{a}{(1 - e^2 \sin^2 \mathrm{L})\,\frac{1}{2}}$
" $\mathrm{L} =$ latitude differentiated from.

Here the cone, instead of being assumed tangent to one of the parallels of the map, is supposed successively tangent to each, that it may be required to draw upon

back of this bar, in addition to the ghost apparatus in front*. Zenith telescopes are also employed, of similar but less elaborate construction. The practice on the coast survey with these instruments is to observe two stars near the zenith, one north of it, the other south, and differing so little in zenith distance that the difference may be measured with a micrometer.†

The following is a very full exposition of the theory of this method.

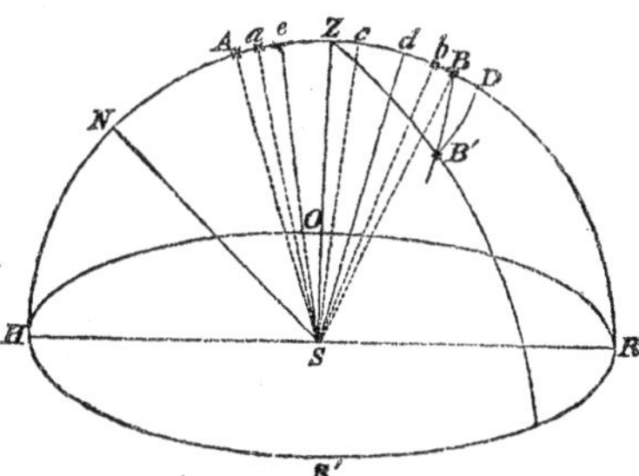

In the above figure let S represent the station occupied, Z the Zenith, N the Pole, HORS′ the Horizon.

it. The map thus becomes the developement of the surfaces of several successive cones.

To make the projection, a central meridian is drawn upon the map, along which the lengths of the required minutes are laid off; perpendicular lines are drawn at each of these points, and the values of δp and δm are laid off successively, along and from each of these lines.

Lee's Tables give the values of δp and δm for parallels 30′ apart. The manuscript tables in use on the Coast Survey are computed to every minute. In the diagram, MB, which is very small, is regarded as a straight line, and the angle QMB $= c$ is $\frac{1}{2}$ Z; CM is equal to MK $=$ T in the diagram on p. 365, App. VI., N $=$ MN, and L $=$ MNV in that diagram. With these explanations the student will readily deduce the above formulas for δp and δm.

* The mode of observing for latitude is similar to that employed with the mural, except that the readings of three levels, one above the other, at the back of the bar, are taken, and the observation is repeated upon the same star in reversed positions of the instrument. The correction for the state of the levels and the reduction to the meridian are made on the principles indicated at pp. 343, 344.

† For description of micrometer see p. 362, App. VI. In Silliman's Journal of Sept., 1852, Prof. Bache says, "The chief modifications of the instrument since its introduction in the Survey, have been in securing stability by a brass arc* instead of a rod; in increasing the facility of reaching the zenith, by raising the central

* The brass arc is attached to the bottom of the stand, and the eye end of the telescope slides upon it.

In the following investigation let

FOR STAR NORTH OF ZENITH.	FOR STAR SOUTH OF ZENITH.
Δ^n = North Polar Distance.	Δ^s = North Polar Distance.
z^n = Zenith Distance.	z^s = Zenith Distance.
N^n = Reading of north end of Level Scale.	N^s = North End of Level Reading.
S^n = Reading of south end of Level Scale.	S^s = South End of Level Reading.
M^n = Reduction to Meridian.	M^s = Reduction to Meridian.
r^n = Refraction for Star.	r^s = Refraction for Star.

λ = Latitude.

Now if the observation of a star were not affected by refraction, and it were observed at the moment it passed the meridian, and the instrument at the same time were perfect as to level, then the latitude resulting from the observation of a star *north* of the zenith would be expressed by

$$\lambda = 90^\circ - (\Delta^n + z^n) \qquad (1)$$

and for a star south of the zenith by

$$\lambda = 90^\circ - (\Delta^s - z^s) \qquad (2)$$

But every observation on a star is affected more or less by refraction, according to its distance from the zenith, and the instrument is constantly changing (as indicated by the level) during the observations. Suppose a star to be observed *north* of the zenith, and its north polar distance to be equal to NA in the diagram. If there were no refraction, the star would be observed at A, and the zenith distance would be AZ. But by the effect of refraction, which elevates an object, the star is seen and observed at *a*, consequently the *observed* zenith distance of the star is equal to *az*, which is *too small*, since NA is the true N. P. D. of the star. The measured Z. D. must therefore be *increased* by A*a*, or the amount of refraction.

Hence we have, as a result for latitude by observing a star north of the zenith,

$$\lambda = 90^\circ - (\Delta^n + z^n) - r^n \qquad (3)$$

Having observed the star north of the zenith, the telescope is turned

column and somewhat diminishing the diameter of the azimuth circle; in substituting a single for a double micrometer; in providing a parallactic eye-piece; in illuminating by a lamp not resting on the instrument; in bringing the divisions of the level and micrometer into just relations; in an adjustment for verticality of the axis (adapted by Mr. Simms, of London); and in providing stops to set the instrument in azimuth."

in azimuth 180°, for the purpose of observing the star south of the zenith, the N. P. D. of which is equal to NB.

On account of refraction, the star is observed at *b*, and the measured zenith distance is *zb*, which is evidently *too small*, and must be increased by B*b*, the amount of refraction.

For a star south of the zenith we have, therefore,

$$\lambda = 90^\circ - (\Delta^s - z^s) + r^s \qquad (4)$$

If a star *north* of the zenith be observed at *a*, while the instrument is perfectly level, but by a sudden change in the temperature of the atmosphere or any other cause, the instrument is thrown out of level, and the vertical axis takes the direction of the line SC; inclining the vertical axis towards the *south*, the *north* end of the level will become *elevated*, and the *south* end *depressed;* and therefore the north end of the level scale will read *greater* than the south end. Suppose another star of the same north polar distance as the one just observed, to come into the field of the telescope, it will be seen at *a*, and consequently the distance *ac* must be measured with the micrometer, thereby making the measured Z. D. greater than the true by the quantity *ae* = *zc*.

Since this distance *zc* is also *measured* by *half* the difference (in arc) of the readings of the level scale (see p. 155), it follows that the level correction will always equal the difference between the *measured* Z. D., and the *true* Z. D. of the star.

Hence we have for latitude, by observation of a star north of the zenith,

$$\lambda = 90^\circ - (\Delta^n + z^n) - r^n + \left(\frac{N^n - S^n}{2}\right) \qquad (5)$$

The telescope is next turned in azimuth 180°, for the purpose of observing a star south of the zenith. The vertical axis still being in the line *sc*, the telescope will take the line *sb*, but the star will be seen at *d*, therefore the *measured* Z. D. will be *too small* by the quantity *bd* = *zc*. The distance *zc* being measured (as I have before stated), by *half* the difference of the north and south readings of the level scale, we have for latitude by observing a star south of the zenith,

$$\lambda = 90^\circ - (\Delta^s - z^s) + r^s + \left(\frac{N^s - S^s}{2}\right) \qquad (6)$$

If a star be observed before it reaches, or after it has passed the meridian, the observation will require a third correction, called the "Reduction to Meridian."*

In the figure suppose the star seen at B to be observed on the meridian, and after it has passed the meridian, to be again observed at B', then the difference between ZB' and ZB = BD = "Reduction to Meridian."

If the vertical wire is in the meridian, and the star is observed before or after culmination, then the correction is

$$m = -\frac{H^2}{4} \sin 2\,\Delta$$

in which m is the correction, H the hour angle, and Δ the polar distance of the star.

It is evident, without demonstration, that the zenith distance of *any* star will be the *smallest* when it is on the meridian (the telescope being moved in azimuth), therefore the algebraic sign of the correction for "Reduction to Meridian" to the latitude resulting from an observation of a star *north* of the zenith will be +, and for the latitude resulting from the observation of a star *south* of the zenith, the algebraic sign of the correction will be —. Hence for a star *north* of zenith

$$\lambda = 90^\circ - (\Delta^n + z^n) - r^n + \left(\frac{N^n - S^n}{2}\right) + M^n \qquad (7)$$

and for a star *south* of the zenith

$$\lambda = 90^\circ - (\Delta^s - z^s) + r^s + \left(\frac{N^s - S^s}{2}\right) - M^s \qquad (8)$$

By adding (7) and (8) we have for twice the latitude,

$$2\lambda = 180^\circ - (\Delta^n + \Delta^s) - (z^n - z^s) - (r^n - r^s) + \left(\frac{N^s - S^s}{2}\right) + \left(\frac{N^n - S^n}{2}\right) + M^n - M^s$$

or,

$$\lambda = \frac{180^\circ - (\Delta^n + \Delta^s) - (z^n - z^s)\ a}{2} + \frac{(N^n + N^s) - (S^n + S^s)}{4}\,b + \frac{(M^n - M^s) + (r^s - r^n)}{2}$$

* A single observation on the meridian has, in the experience of the Coast Survey, been found preferable to several circum-meridian observations.

When there is a recorder to assist the observer, he calls out the time for setting the instrument for each pair of stars and when each star enters the field; after that, every ten seconds, the observer in the mean time following the star with the horizontal wire and moving the instrument in azimuth, if necessary, as the instant of culmination approaches, in order to have it take place in the centre of the field. At ten seconds before the culmination, the recorder calls each second till the instant of culmination previously computed. The level and micrometer are then read and recorded, and the instrument turned 180° to observe the opposite star of the pair.

in which a represents the arc value of one division of micrometer, and b the arc value of one division of the level scale.

The value of the micrometer measures is obtained by turning it at right angles to its ordinary position and noticing the number of divisions passed over by polaris in a given time near its culmination or elongation; in the latter case, preserving the ordinary position: when a theodolite is at hand, by the apparent diameter of a distant object measured by the two instruments.

From these observations, or a mean of many, a table is made, which, by simple inspection, shows the angular value of any number of turns of the screw and parts of a turn. By suitably selecting pairs of stars, any effect of inaccuracy in this determination may be avoided, by making the sum of the zenith distances of all the pairs, N and S of the zenith, zero, as nearly as may be.

The value of the level divisions is found by fixing the telescope on a distant mark, or, better, on a collimating telescope, moving the instrument till the bubble traverses the whole length of the level tube, and measuring the distance passed over by the micrometer. The value of the level divisions is then converted into arc, and a table made which shows the correction of twice the latitude for the difference between the sum of N and sum of S end readings of the level. One of the great advantages of Talcott's method is, that the correction for refraction is very small, being for the difference merely of the two refractions on each side the zenith. The correction for variation of temperature and pressure of the air from the mean state is insignificant, amounting for 25° zenith distance and a difference of 20′ of Z. D. in a variation of 2 inches of the barometer and 50° of the thermometer, to only 0″·02. The correction for refraction may be obtained by the formula

$$\log.\ \text{correction} = \log \frac{\text{M} \sin 1'' \text{ diff. zen. dist.}}{\cos^2 (\text{less zen. dist.})},$$

for demonstration of which, see App. VI., p. 372. A table may be computed from this, or by differences from ordinary refraction tables.

The following directions are given by Prof. Bache:

1. The latitude of the place is assumed to within 2′ or 3′ of arc.

2. The zenith distances should be as small as possible, and not extended beyond 25°.

3. The difference of zenith distance should be small, and in no case exceed a convenient range of the micrometer, in the instruments used on the Coast Survey say 10′, including about 13 turns of the micrometer screw.

4. The interval of time between the culmination of the stars should be not less than 1^m, so as to give time to read the micrometer and to turn the instrument in azimuth for the second observation, and should not exceed 20^m, to avoid changes in the instruments.

EXAMPLE.

SURVEY OF THE COAST

Sec. I. Latitude, Station Mt. Independence, Cumberland Co., Me.

Date.	No. B. A. C.	N. or S.	Micrometer.		Diff Z. D.		Polar distances	Twice Approx. Lat'de.	Levels.	
			Turns.	Divisi's.	By Microm.	In arc.			N.	S.
						′ ″	° ′ ″			
1849. Oct. 13	819	N.	3	32•0			37 07 13•52		60•0	43•2
	877	S.	19	62•8			55 33 51•71	87° ′ ″	44•0	59•5
					+16 30•8	+12 14•18	92 41 05•23	30 68•95	104•0	102•7
							87 18 54•77			
14	819	N.	3	37•0			37 07 13•27		55•0	49•5
	877	S.	19	66•6			55 33 51•55		49•5	55•0
					+16 29•6	+12 13•64	92 41 04•82	68•82	104•5	104•5
							87 18 55•18			
" 15	819	N.	4	06•0			37 07 13•01		51•0	48•5
	877	S.	20	34•6			55 33 51•39		46•5	53•5
					+16 28•6	+12 13•20	92 41 04•40	68•80	97•5	102•0
							87 18 55•60			
" 18	819	N.	3	10•4			37 07 12•24		42•0	55•2
	877	S.	19	41•2			55 33 50•90		55•0	42•5
					+16 30•8	+12 14•19	92 41 03•14	71•05	97•0	97•7
							87 18 56•86			
" 19	819	N.	2	06•2			37 07 11•99		55•0	47•5
	877	S.	18	32•6			55 33 50•74		49•0	53•6
					+16 26•4	+12 12•20	92 41 02•73	69•47	104•0	101•1
							87 18 57•27			
" 20	819	N.	3	15•0			37 07 11•73		55•0	50•0
	877	S.	19	40•2			55 33 50•58		51•3	53•8
					+16 25•2	+12 11•66	92 41 02•31	69•35	106•3	103•8
							87 18 57•69			

OF THE UNITED STATES.

Observations witn Zenith Telescope, No. 3, U. S. C. S.

State of Level.	Meridian distance.	Corrections for twice the Latitude.			Twice Lat'de.	Latitude	Remarks.
N.—S.		Level.	Merid'n.	Refract.			
	m. s.	"	"	"	87° ′ "	° ′ "	
+1·3		+0·58		+0·21	30 69·74	43 45 34·87	
+0·0		±0·00		+0·21	69·03	34·51	Approx. Latitude= ° ′ " 43 45 30 cos =9·85870 N.P.D. 37 07 14 sin =9·78067 Z.D. 9 07 16 ar. co. sin=0·79991 x=2·75=0·43928
	0 24						Mn=0·31 × 2·75=0·86.
—4·5		—2·02	+0·86	+0·21	67·85	33·92	
—0·7		—0·32		+0·21	70·94	35·47	
+2·9		+1·30		+0·21	70·98	35·49	
+2·5		+1·12		+0·21	70·68	35·34	
						Mean=34·93	

In the preceding example the 1st column contains the date of the observation, the 2d column the numbers of the stars observed in the British Association Catalogue, the 3d column indicates whether the star is north or south of the zenith; the 4th and 5th columns give the number of turns and fractions of a turn of the micrometer screw, necessary to bring the wire from zero to coincide with the star; the 6th column gives the difference of the micrometer reading, the 7th the value of the same in arc depending, of course, on the value of one turn of the micrometer screw;* the 8th column the polar distances of two stars observed on each day, their sum $\Delta^n + \Delta^s$, and $180^\circ - (\Delta^n + \Delta^s)$, according the formula, from which subtracting† the number in the 7th column, which is the difference of their zenith distances in arc, or $z^n - z^s$, according to the formula, p. 345, the remainder will be by the formula equal to twice the approximate latitude which is written in the 9th column. The 10th and 11th columns contain the level readings at the north and south ends of the scale, in both positions of the instrument, together with the values of $N^n + N^s$, and $S^n + S^s$, the 12th column shows the difference of these results, or the value of $(N^n + N^s) - (S^n + S^s)$, according to the formula; the 13th column contains the hour angle of the star when not observed exactly on the meridian in minutes and seconds of time; the 14th column contains the correction for error of level, which is obtained by dividing the result in the 12th by 4, and multiplying by the value of one division of the level scale, according to the formula; the 15th column contains the result obtained by the computation in the 19th column, of the correction for the star's not being observed exactly upon the meridian by a method similar to that at top of p. 304, using a more accurate table, in which the constant sin 1″ is incorporated; the 16th column contains the correction for refraction; the 17th column, the double latitude after the corrections in the 16th and 14th have been applied to the 9th; the 18th column, the latitude which is half the result contained in the 17th; the 19th column is for miscellaneous purposes, used in this example for the computation already mentioned.

LONGITUDE BY CELESTIAL OBSERVATIONS.

The best mode of determining longitude ordinarily is by means of moon culminations. The Nautical Almanac gives p. 504 et seq. in the edition of 1850, the apparent R. A. of the bright limb of the moon at the instant of its transit at Greenwich, both for the upper culmination marked U

* A good way of finding the value of one division of the screw head of the micrometer is to note the time by chronometer of the transit of Polaris over the movable wire placed vertically, and set successively to every division of the screw head. Representing by x the angular distance from the meridian at which any reading was taken, by p the hour angle, and by Δ the polar distance of the star, we have

$$\sin x = \sin \Delta \sin p$$

The value of x being computed for each reading, the difference of these values, divided by the difference of the corresponding micrometer readings, gives the value of one division.

† Really adding in this example, because z^n is less than z^s.

in the almanac, and for the lower marked L. If now the siderial time of transit be observed at any other station, this will be the ☽'s R. A. at the instant of observation (see p. 151), and the difference will be her variation in R. A. during the interval between the two transits, viz. that over the meridian of Greenwich and that over the meridian of the station. The meridian of the station (supposing it to be W. of Greenwich), has in this interval of time revolved by the diurnal rotation through an angular space equal to the longitude of the station from Greenwich, plus the distance which the moon has moved in R. A. towards the east. To know this angular space, we have only to compute the time occupied by the moon in changing her right ascension by the difference above mentioned. This may be done by means of the variation of the moon's R. A. for one hour, given at the same page of the Almanac* by proportion.

EXAMPLE.

Oct. 8th, 1840, sid. time transit ☽'s I. limb,	$23^h\ 1^m\ 9^s{\cdot}2$
Error of clock, too slow,	$7{\cdot}75$
True time of transit,	$23\ \ 1\ \ 16{\cdot}95$
R. A. ☽'s I. limb (Nautical Almanac, ☽ culm. stars),	$23\ \ 1\ \ 23{\cdot}31$
Difference = var. in R. A.,	$6{\cdot}36$

Nautical Almanac gives ☽'s var. in R. A. in 1^h, 122·59,

$$\therefore\quad 122^s{\cdot}59 : 1^h :: 6^s{\cdot}36 : 3^m\ 6^s{\cdot}8$$

which last term is the time occupied by the meridian of the station in revolving to that of Greenwich and $6^s{\cdot}36$ further, the last being the angular motion of the ☽ in R. A., since it made its transit at Greenwich,

$$\therefore\quad 3^m\ 6^s{\cdot}8 - 6^s{\cdot}36 = 3^m\ 0^s{\cdot}44$$

is the longitude of the place of observation.

The above method requires an exact knowledge of the siderial time. To obviate this necessity, the Almanac also gives the right ascensions of some stars which make their transit nearly at the same time with the moon, and differ little in declination from her, so as to be conveniently observed

* If the distance of the station in long. from Greenwich be great, the variation in R. A. corresponding to the middle interval between the two transits should be used, which may be obtained by interpolation. The numbers in this column of the Almanac include the change of the semidiameter of the limb.

in connexion with the moon. If the moon had no motion the difference of her right ascension from that of the star would be constant at all meridians; but in the interval of her transit over two different meridians, her right ascension will have varied, and the difference between the two compared differences will exhibit the amount of this variation,* which added to the difference of the meridians shows the angle through which the westerly meridian must revolve before it comes up with the moon. This angle, as before, will be the time in which the moon is undergoing the observed variation in R. A., which may be computed by means of her hourly variation in R. A. given in the Almanac. The variation of R. A. being subtracted from this result, the remainder will be the difference of longitude required.

EXAMPLE.

Oct. 8th, 1840, were observed the transits,

Of the ☽'s I. limb,	$23^h\ 1^m\ 9^s{\cdot}2$	R.A. ☽'s I. limb (N. Al.)	$23^h\ 1^m\ 23^s{\cdot}31$
Of the star ϰ Piscium,	$23\ 18\ 27{\cdot}6$	R.A. ϰ Piscium (do.)	$23\ 18\ 47{\cdot}98$
Difference,	$17\ 18{\cdot}4$	Difference,	$17\ 24{\cdot}67$
			$17\ 18{\cdot}\ 4$

The diff. of the two diffs. = ☽'s var. in R. A. = $6{\cdot}27$

By proportion as before,

$$122^s{\cdot}29 : 1^h :: 6^s{\cdot}27 : 3^m\ 4^s$$

$\therefore$ Long. required $= 3^m\ 4^s - 6^s{\cdot}27 = 2^m\ 57^s{\cdot}73$.

When the meridian to be determined is distant from Greenwich, a very simple and unexceptionable way of proceeding is to assume the longitude which is supposed to be known approximately, and from the culminations of the moon's limb, as given in the Nautical Almanac, to find by interpolation the time of culmination of the limb at the assumed meridian. The difference between this and the observed time of culmination will be the interval of time occupied by the moon's limb in passing from the assumed meridian to the true meridian of the station. The motion of the limb in

* For the determination of this variation with great accuracy, observations should be taken simultaneously at the different meridians to be compared. Errors in the computed places of the moon or stars are thereby avoided. The results given in the Almanac may be considered as a very near approximation to what would have been the indication of the Greenwich instruments, had the observations actually been made with them. The traveller has thus the opportunity of rendering his observation immediately available for determining his longitude with considerable accuracy.

right ascension during this interval must be computed by first determining the hourly motion in right ascension, by interpolation, for the instant of passing the assumed meridian, and proceeding by proportion, as in the examples above. The result thus obtained being subtracted from the interval, the remainder will be the difference of longitude between the assumed meridian and the meridian of the station.

The formula for interpolation is

$$y = \text{A} + \frac{m}{n}\,\delta + \tfrac{1}{2}\,\frac{m}{n}\left(\frac{m}{n} - 1\right)\delta_2 + \tfrac{1}{6}\,\frac{m}{n}\left(\frac{m^2}{n^2} - \frac{3m}{n} + 2\right)\delta_3 + \text{\&c.}$$

In which A is the element for the noon, midnight, or complete hour preceding the given instant,

y is the element required for the given time,

m the given number of hours since noon or midnight, or minutes since the even hour (the long. in time of the assumed meridian above).

n is 12 hours, 24 hours, or 60 minutes, the interval between the times, for which the element is given in the Nautical Alm.

δ the difference between two consecutive elements in the Naut. Alm.

δ_2 the difference between the successive values of δ,

δ_3 " " " " " " " δ_2, &c.

For a convenient mode of proceeding, and an example under it where the meridian is distant from Greenwich, see Lee's Tables and Formulæ, pp. 69—78, Part III.

LONGITUDE BY ECLIPSES OF JUPITER'S SATELLITES.

The eclipses of Jupiter's Satellites, especially the first, afford the readiest mode of obtaining the longitude, both from the frequent occurrence of the phenomena, and the simplicity of the calculation.

All that is necessary to be known is the exact time of observation; the difference between this time and the time at Greenwich* shows the difference of longitude, and is *east* or *west* of Greenwich, according as the time of observation is *greater* or *less* than the Greenwich time.

EXAMPLE.

Suppose the emersion of Jupiter's first satellite to be observed August 8th, 1850, at Paris, and the time of observation there to be $14^h\ 30^m$

* This is given at p. XX. of the Nautical Almanac for each month. At p. 605 of the edition of 1850 is a full description of the page and its use.

$17^s{\cdot}3$ mean time. The emersion takes place at Greenwich (Naut. Alm., p. XX.), at $14^h\ 20^m\ 55^s{\cdot}8$ Greenwich mean time; the difference $9^m\ 21^s{\cdot}5$ is the difference of longitude between Greenwich and Paris. And because the time at Paris is greater than that at Greenwich, the former is east of the latter.

ASTRONOMICAL DETERMINATION OF AZIMUTHS.

In the previous pages the methods of determining difference of azimuths geodetically, or from the triangulation, have been given. But the usefulness of these methods depends on the implied ability to obtain by astronomic observation the azimuths of certain lines from which the others are differentiated.

The method of proceeding is to determine by observation the difference of azimuth between the sun or a star, and the line whose azimuth is to be determined, then to find by calculation the azimuth of the sun or star; the sum or difference of these results will be the azimuth required. The difference of azimuth between the sun or star and the line whose azimuth is to be observed is obtained with an altitude and azimuth instrument, or theodolite. The middle vertical wire is made to bisect the star, or to touch the limb of the sun, and the siderial time is observed at the same instant; the reading is then taken on the horizontal limb of the instrument, which is afterwards turned to a signal (bearing a lamp, if at night), which is placed upon one of the sides of the triangulation, or upon any other convenient line, the horizontal angle between which, and the line whose azimuth is required, can be subsequently measured, and the reading of the horizontal limb again taken. The difference of the two readings will be the difference of azimuth between the sun's limb, or star and the signal, at the instant of siderial time above mentioned. With the altitude and azimuth instrument, the transit of both limbs of the sun, or the transit of the star, may be taken over all the wires of the instrument, and the mean of the times taken as the time at which the azimuthal position of the sun's centre, or the star, corresponded to the reading of the horizontal limb.

AZIMUTH OF THE SUN OR A STAR.

The determination of this requires merely the solution of the triangle ZPS, in which PZ the colatitude of the place of observation, PS the polar distance of the sun or star, and P the hour angle, equal to the difference between the right ascension of the object and the siderial time of observation are given to compute the angle z, which is the azimuth required. Where the object is the sun, of course the value of the semidiameter at the instant must be computed and applied to the reading for the sun's limb to obtain that for his centre. If the altitude of the object is also observed at the same instant, or immediately before or after, and reduced to the instant by interpolation, one of the above data, either the hour angle, or the latitude, may be replaced by the zenith, distance zs in the triangle.

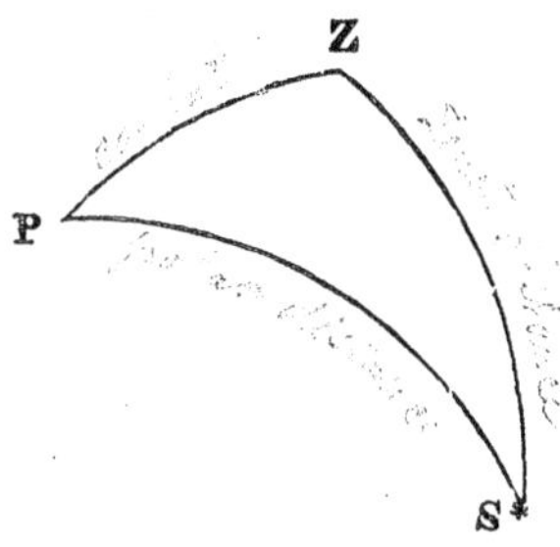

The formulæ will be

$$\tan \tfrac{1}{2} (z + s) = \cot \tfrac{1}{2} P \frac{\cos \tfrac{1}{2} (\pi - \lambda)}{\cos \tfrac{1}{2} (\pi + \lambda)}$$

$$\tan \tfrac{1}{2} (z - s) = \cot \tfrac{1}{2} P \frac{\sin \tfrac{1}{2} (\pi - \lambda)}{\sin \tfrac{1}{2} (\pi + \lambda)}$$

$$z = \tfrac{1}{2} (z + s) + \tfrac{1}{2} (z - s)$$

In which

z = azimuth required.
P = hour angle.
π = polar distance of object.
λ = colatitude of station.

The formula, if the siderial time be unknown, and the altitude observed is

$$\cos \tfrac{1}{2} z = \sqrt{\frac{\sin \tfrac{1}{2} s \sin (\tfrac{1}{2} s - \pi)}{\sin \zeta \sin \lambda}}$$

$$s = \zeta + \pi + \lambda$$

In which

ζ = observed zenith distance.

AZIMUTH BY POLARIS.

The best mode of obtaining the azimuth of a line upon the surface of the earth is by means of the pole star when at its greatest eastern or western elongation. With a telescope as powerful as that of the great theodolite, the necessary observations may be conducted in the day time, the star being distinctly visible. The mode of proceeding is to commence about 15 minutes before the time of greatest elongation, and place the middle vertical wire alternately upon the star, and upon a signal nearly in the direction of the meridian, a mile or two distant, illuminated if the observation be at night. The readings are taken by the micrometer microscope, on the horizontal limb, both when the middle wire is upon the star and upon the signal, the difference of azimuth of which will be indicated by the difference of the reading, so that when the azimuth of Polaris, at the instant of each observation upon it, is known, the azimuth of the signal becomes known; the mean of all the results is taken as the true azimuth, and thus a line whose azimuth is fixed becomes determined on the ground, from which other azimuths may be differentiated.

The following is the mode of determining, at any instant, the

AZIMUTH OF POLARIS.

If we suppose a spherical triangle having for its three vertices the zenith, the pole, and the star; this triangle, at the time of the star's greatest elongation, will be right angled at the star; for if a cone be conceived having its vertex at the eye of the observer, and for its base the diurnal circle of the star, the tangent plane to this cone, passing through the star, is perpendicular to the declination circle through the star, which is a meridian plane of the cone; the visual or tangent plane through the star at its greatest elongation being a vertical plane, passes through the zenith, and, also passing through the star, determines on the celestial sphere a side ZS of the spherical triangle ZSP, so that the angle at S is therefore a right angle. In this right angled triangle are known ZP, the colatitude of the station, and PS, the polar distance of the star, to find the hour angle P, and the azimuth Z, at the time of greatest elongation. The former, applied to the time of the star's meridian transit or R. A. will give the time of greatest elongation. The formulas are

$$\text{For the hour angle} \cos P = \tan \pi \cot \lambda$$
$$\text{For the azimuth,} \sin Z = \sin \pi \operatorname{cosec} \lambda$$

In which π = polar distance, λ = colatitude.

If the star be observed within 45^m of the time of the greatest elongation, the observation may be reduced by the formula

$$c = \frac{225}{2} t^2 \sin 1'' \tan Z$$

in which c is the correction of the azimuth, t the siderial time from elongation, and z the greatest azimuth. The correction is deduced in a manner similar to that on p. 302. Table XXXVI. may be made available as explained at the bottom of that page, or the constant log. 112·5 sin 1″ = 6·7367274 may be used with the logs. of t^2 and tan z. This correction being applied subtractively to the azimuth at the time of greatest elongation, computed as above, will give the azimuth at the time of observation.

If the axis of the telescope be not horizontal, the correction for azimuth is, d being the value of one division of the level scale,

$$d\,\frac{(\omega + \omega') \sim (e + e')}{4}\tan *^{s}\text{ alt.}$$

TRIGONOMETRIC LEVELLING.

This consists in observing the zenith distances of two stations, and applying the corrections for curvature and refractions, to obtain their difference of level. The theory is simple, and the necessary formulas and table are found at pp. 50 to 54, Part I. of Lee Tables and Formulas.*

The usual mode of observing zenith distances is as follows: the instrument is carefully levelled, *i. e.*, the vertical axis is placed truly vertical; the horizontal wire of the telescope is then pointed at the object, and the vertical circle read off; next the instrument is revolved 180° in azimuth, and the telescope being then moved through the double zenith distance of the object, is pointed again. If we now read off, the difference between the two readings will be 2 Z. D.; the operation is, however, repeated (generally six times) if the vertical limb has the repeating motion, before it is read off again. The instrument should be levelled for each set of observations.

MAGNETIC OBSERVATIONS.

These usually accompany the operations of a Geodetic survey. They have for their object to determine, 1. The angle which the magnetic meridian makes with the astronomic meridian, commonly called the variation of the needle, but more properly the *Declination*. 2. The angle under which a needle suspended by a perfectly flexible thread at its centre of gravity, would be inclined to the horizon, commonly called the dip, but more properly the *inclination;* and 3. The *intensity* of the magnetic

* Immediately following (p. 55) are formulæ and tables for the barometric measurement of heights.

force at any place; with the daily and other periodical variations in these three elements.

The instrument for observing the declination is called a *declinometer* or *declination magnetometer*. Where only the variation of the declination is to be observed, the instrument consists of a horizontal telescope, firmly supported, pointing towards a magnetic needle bearing a mirror so adjusted as to reflect a horizontal scale placed directly under the object glass of the telescope. The least change in the direction of the needle will be indicated by a change in the reading of the scale marked by the middle vertical wire of the telescope.

The best form of instrument for the measurement of absolute declination is a theodolite, or altitude and azimuth instrument, in front of which is suspended a collimator magnet, by fibres of untwisted silk, resting horizontally in a stirrup of gun metal. The collimator magnet is a hollow cylindrical magnet, with a small object glass like a telescope, and a horizontal scale at its focus.

The adjustments of this instrument consist in bringing the collimator magnet into the magnetic meridian without torsion of the thread; in determining the zero division of the scale corresponding to the magnetic axis of the collimator magnet; and in bringing the line of collimation of the theodolite telescope into the magnetic meridian, its vertical wire coinciding with this division. These adjustments are all made at once, by putting in a bar first, equal in weight to the collimating magnet, and adjusting the stirrup approximately; then, after restoring the collimating magnet by repeated trials, making half the necessary correction by moving the theodolite in azimuth, and half by turning the torsion screw at the top of the thread, till the same division of the scale is read, with the collimator in two positions, the second position being produced by turning the collimator over, so that it shall have revolved 180° about its optical axis. There is then no torsion of the thread, the axis of the collimator magnet and of the theodolite are both in the magnetic meridian, and the division read is the zero of the scale.

If in this position the verniers of the azimuth circle of the theodolite be read, and if its telescope then be turned in the direction of some object, whose azimuth is known or can be afterwards determined, the difference of the reading, added to or subtracted from the azimuth of the object, will give the absolute declination. The angular value of one division of the scale is determined by measuring with the theodolite the horizontal angle subtended by a certain number of the divisions, the magnet being temporarily fixed.

If a denote the angular value of one division of the scale, and $\frac{H}{F}$ the ratio of the torsion and magnetic forces, the true declination changes are deduced by multiplying the observed differences of reading by $a\left(1+\frac{H}{F}\right)$. The value of $\frac{H}{F}$ is determined by turning the torsion through two large angles, and noting the corresponding differences of reading. If ω denotes the angular value of the former, and u that of the latter,

$$\frac{H}{F}=\frac{\omega}{\omega-u}$$

ABSOLUTE HORIZONTAL INTENSITY

Requires for its determination, 1, experiments of *deflexion*, 2, of *vibration.* The former give the *ratio* of the magnetic moment of the deflecting magnet to the horizontal intensity, the latter the *product* of the same quantities, and their separate value is obtained by algebraic elimination.

Experiments of deflection consist in placing a magnetic bar, called a deflector, at one side of a freely suspended magnet, in a line drawn horizontally through the centre of the suspended magnet, perpendicularly to the magnetic meridian, its axis coinciding with this line. The deflector should be placed at three different distances from the suspended magnet on this line, in direct and reversed positions, or turned end for end, at each.

Experiments of vibration consist in suspending the same magnet which was used as a deflector, and noting the times at which some central division of the scale passes across the vertical wire of the telescope, at the beginning and end of at least 300 horizontal vibrations of the magnet, the magnet vibrating steadily in a very small arc.

As the time of vibration depends on the form and weight of the suspended mass as well as upon the product of the magnetic moment and horizontal intensity, its moment of inertia must be ascertained by means of a series of vibrations with two cylindrical weights of equal dimensions, whose moment of inertia is known, at opposite ends of the magnet.

If m denote the magnetic moment of the deflecting magnet, X the horizontal intensity, the formulas are

$$\frac{m}{X}=\tfrac{1}{2}\,r^3\tan u$$

$$mX = \frac{\pi^2 K}{T^2}$$

In the first of which

r = dist. between centres of deflecting and suspended magnets in feet and decimals.

u = angle of deflection obtained by multiplying half the mean of each partial result by the coefficient (see above), $a\ (1 + \frac{H}{F})$

In the second

$\pi = 3{\cdot}1416$

$K = \frac{T^2}{T'^2 - T^2} K'$

T' = time of vibration with weights.

T = " " without "

The moment of inertion of the weights is

$$K' = (\tfrac{1}{2}\, l^2 + 2r'^2)\, p$$

In which l = interval of the points of suspension.

" r' = radius of the cylinders in decimal of a foot.

" $2p$ = their mass in grains.

THE INCLINATION

is found directly by the dipping needle, which consists of a magnetic needle, suspended at the centre of a graduated vertical circle. The mean must be taken of results with several needles, reversed on their magnetic axes, and reversed as to their poles by remagnetizing. Observations should be made at different azimuths to test the limb of the instrument, which is often magnetic, in which use the formula

$$\tan \theta = \tan \eta \operatorname{cosec} a$$

In which θ = inclination sought.

" η = " observed.

" a = azimuth of the vertical circle.

The inclination may also be found by means of the horizontal and vertical components of the intensity, as it would be determined by the direction of their resultant. The vertical component is observed by means of a vertical force magnetometer, which is a needle suspended like the dipping needle, but placed in a plane perpendicular to the magnetic meridian, and made to vibrate in this plane.

On the other hand the vertical component may be deduced from the inclination and the horizontal component.

For further information on this subject see Lee's Tables and Formulæ, and Riddell's Magnetical Instructions. For the theory of magnetism as applicable, see the papers of Gauss, and a late elementary work of Prof. Lamonte, of Munich. Translations of some of the papers of Gauss, Lamonte, and Weber have been published in Taylor's Scientific Memoirs, Parts 5, 6, 11, and 12.

APPENDIX TO PART VI.

INSTRUMENTS FOR EXTRA MERIDIAN OBSERVATIONS.

THE principal of these are the *equatorial,* and the *altitude and azimuth instrument.*

THE EQUATORIAL

is a telescope usually of large size, upon an equatorial mounting. The latter consists, 1, of a strong metallic axis, placed in a position parallel to the axis of the earth, so as to point to the pole of the heavens, the lower end of this axis, which is called the polar axis, being enlarged into a circle called the hour circle, the plane of which is parallel to the equator, and the circumference of which is divided into hours and fractions of an hour. 2. Of another axis crossing the upper end of the former at right angles, called the equatorial axis, one end of which is enlarged into a circle called the declination circle, divided into degrees and fractions of a degree, and firmly fastened to the other end of which, at right angles, near the middle of its tube, is the telescope. The instrument must be so adjusted that when the optical axis of the telescope describes the meridian as the instrument moves upon the equatorial axis alone, the index of the hour circle is at the zero, and when the optical axis points to a star in the equator, the index of the declination circle is at zero. Then if the instrument be turned on its equatorial axis till the index or vernier of the declination circle points to the declination of any celestial object as given by the Nautical Almanac or by catalogue, and on its polar axis till the index of the hour circle points to the hour angle, which is the difference between the right ascension and the time by the siderial clock, the object will be seen in the centre of the field of view of the telescope. As it passes out of the field of view by the rotation of the earth on which the instrument stands, the telescope is made to follow it by a rotation of the instrument on its polar axis alone. Attached to this axis is a clamp and screw of slow motion for the purpose. Sometimes the polar axis is made to move by clockwork, the velocity being regulated by friction, and the motion becoming uniform when the friction is equal to the accelerating force of the clock-weights. In the Fraunhofer* mounting, a hollow inverted frustum of a cone contains balls, supported at the ends of a flexible bar at right angles to the axis of the frustum, about which it revolves, carrying the balls which rub against the sides of the frustum. The velocity should be different for the sun, moon, each of the planets, and

* So called, from the inventor and first manufacturer, Fraunhofer, of Munich.

for the fixed stars. If the bar be lowered in the frustum, less velocity will make the friction equal to the accelerating force. If raised, more velocity will be required. For each kind of heavenly body the requisite velocity is determined by experiment, and a permanent mark made where an attached index stands.

Approximate adjustment is sufficient for this instrument,[1] which is ordinarily used as a differential instrument, by means of an appendage which we proceed to describe, called

THE POSITION MICROMETER.

This is an eye-piece which screws on in place of the ordinary eye-piece of the telescope, and consists of a circle of brass about four inches in diameter, the plane of which is perpendicular to the optical axis, which passes through its centre. It is graduated on the outer rim, the graduation being numbered to 360°. A rectangular box, about one inch by four, and the eighth of an inch in thickness, is fitted to the circle in the position of a diameter, at the ends of which are micrometer screws, which move each one of two parallel wires along a notched scale, the wires and scale being seen (when the eye is applied to the telescope) at the focus of the object glass, where also the image of the heavenly body is formed. The circle carrying the box has also a motion round the optical axis, by means of a screw projecting perpendicularly to the plane of the circle, which acts as a pinion by cogs, in a cog-wheel of less diameter than the circle, attached to the piece which screws into the telescope to which two verniers, 90° apart, marked A and B, are firmly fixed.

To determine the right ascension and declination of a new heavenly body, as a comet, for instance, with this instrument in any part of the visible heavens, let the object be brought into the field of view at the same time with some fixed star, one whose place is given by catalogue, if possible. Bring the star to one of the movable micrometer wires, and turn the micrometer in position, *i. e.* round the optical axis till the wire threads the star in its motion along its diurnal path. The wire is then parallel to the equator. Let the two wires now be separated by turning the micrometer screws till one of them passes through or bisects the star, and the other bisects the comet; the number of turns of the screw shown by the notched scale, and the fractions of a turn by the screw-head, will indicate the difference in declination between the comet and the star.* Let the micrometer now be turned in position 90°, and the transits of the comet and star across the two wires be observed by the siderial clock. The difference in the times of transit will be the difference of right ascension of the comet and star. The absolute right ascension and declination of the comet thus becomes known, if that of the *star of comparison* be known from catalogue. If this be not the case, the star must be brought to the centre of the field of view indicated by the point at which a third wire at right angles to the other two crosses them when they are made to coincide at the zero of the notched scale, and the approximate right ascension and declination of the star must be noted by the declination and hour circles and clock, with sufficient accuracy to identify it, in

* It will be found convenient to make the wires coincide before commencing the operation with the screwhead of one of them at the zero, and let this be the only one moved, if possible, and read by its screw.

[1] For methods of exact adjustment, see Lond. Ast. Soc. Memoirs, vol. IV. p. 495.

order that its place may be more exactly determined by observation with the meridian instruments, the transit and mural, at some subsequent time.

The micrometer screw head is divided into 100 parts. The value of a single turn of the screw in arc is determined by measuring the diameter of a planet, given by the Nautical Almanac or the known distance apart of a pair of stars, and then by the proportion, as the number of turns and hundredths of a turn of the micrometer screw is to the known distance measured, so is 1 to the value of one turn.

MEASUREMENT OF ANGLES OF POSITION AND DISTANCE OF DOUBLE STARS.

The angle of position of a pair of stars is the angle which the visual plane passing through both the stars makes with the plane of the declination circle passing through the larger star. It is estimated from the s. round by the w. to 360°. The following is Capt. Smythe's method of observing position and distance.

Bring the wires coinciding at the zero of the scale, with the index of one screw-head at the zero, upon the line of the two stars, so as to bisect both, and read one of the verniers; next turn the instrument 90° in position, and measure the distance of the stars apart; finally turn in position till one of the stars runs along either of the wires, and read one of the verniers again, the difference between the first and last vernier reading, will give the angle which the visual plane of the two stars makes with the equator, from which the angle of position may be obtained in an obvious manner. In the transit instrument and instruments of that class the wires are made visible at night by a lamp placed at one end of the supporting axis, which is left open for the purpose, with a piece of glass over it; the light is received by a small plane mirror in the axis of the telescope, and reflected down the tube to the wires. In the equatorial instrument the horizontal tube bearing the lens (colored red) of a small lamp is inserted in the tube of the telescope, near the wires of the micrometer, and a reflector so arranged as to throw the light on the wires.

When the object to be observed is so faint as not to bear illumination, a ring micrometer is used. This is a black circle on a piece of plane glass in the focus of the object glass, with which differences of right ascension and declination are obtained by noting the times occupied by the two objects to be compared in crossing the circle. Half the sum of the times of either object's making the transit of the circumference on opposite sides will be the time of its passing the middle diameter, and the difference of the time of passing the middle diameter by the two objects will be their difference of right ascension.

For declination it is necessary to ascertain, by experiment, the time of an equatorial star's passing over a diameter of the ring, by observing the time of any other star, and multiplying by the cosine of the declination. Then the ratio of the time occupied by a star in passing over a chord of the ring to the time which it would occupy in passing over the diameter is the cosine of an angle, the sine of which to the radius of the ring is the difference of declination between the centre of the ring and the star. (For the whole theory see Ast. Nach., Vol. 8.)

THE ALTITUDE AND AZIMUTH INSTRUMENT.

This is in effect a large theodolite, with two micrometer microscopes, 180° apart, on both the horizontal and vertical limb. It may be used as a theodolite, also as a transit instrument. It may be used like the zenith sector, for determining latitude by a star nearly on the meridian, the instrument having a spirit level parallel to the plane of the vertical circle.

The following is a good form.

No. of observation.	Date.	Object.	Approx. zen. dist.	North or South.	Direct or reflex.	Face E. or W.	READINGS.							Error of time keeper.	Barometer.	Thermom.	REMARKS.
							Time Keeper.	Level.	Microscopes.								
									A		B						
									Reading.	Corr. for run.*	Reading.	Corr. for run.	Mean.				
			° '				h. m. s.		° ' "	"	"	"	° ' "	s			

There are five vertical and five horizontal wires, the latter of which are convenient for observing single altitudes, or equal altitudes of the sun for either time or latitude. The mean of the times of the two limbs passing the five horizontal wires is taken as the time of the altitude shown on the vertical limb.

A very accurate mode of determining the true time and error of a time keeper is by equal altitudes, morning and afternoon. If the sun did not change his declination in the interval between the two observations, half the interval in time added to the time of the morning observation would express the hour by the time keeper, when the sun was on the meridian. But as the declination does change, a correction of the half interval must be made, the formula for which is

$$d \tfrac{1}{2} p = d\delta \, (\tan \delta \cot \tfrac{1}{2} p - \tan \lambda \operatorname{cosec} \tfrac{1}{2} p)$$

In which

$d \tfrac{1}{2} p =$ the correction of the half interval,

$d\delta =$ the change of declination in the half interval,

$\lambda =$ the latitude (— if south).

The correction is + if the declination is increasing, and — if decreasing.

The time of the sun's being on the meridian being corrected for the equation of time will give the time of mean noon by the watch, which will show the error of the watch.

If a star be used instead of the sun, no correction is requisite for change of declination, the mean between the two times of observation must be compared with the computed mean time at which the star culminates, in order to have the error of the time keeper.

If the readings be taken on the horizontal circle at the two times of observation,

* This is for error in the divisions of the limb, tested by running the microscope over them.

the reading midway will correspond to the direction of the meridian. This also, in the case of the sun, requires a correction for change of declination in the interval, the formula for which is

$$dz = \frac{\cos \delta}{\sin z \cos \lambda \cos a}$$

In which

dz = correction of azimuth.
a = observed altitude.

CONVERSION OF ASTRONOMIC AND GEOCENTRIC LATITUDE.

From the nature of the astronomic instruments, the zenith point being determined by a plumb line, basin of mercury, or spirit level, it follows, by the law of gravitation, that the line from the station to the zenith is a normal to the elliptical meridian, and the angle which this line makes with the major axis or equatorial diameter will be the astronomic latitude, or latitude deduced from observation. This will be the angle MBA, in the diagram.

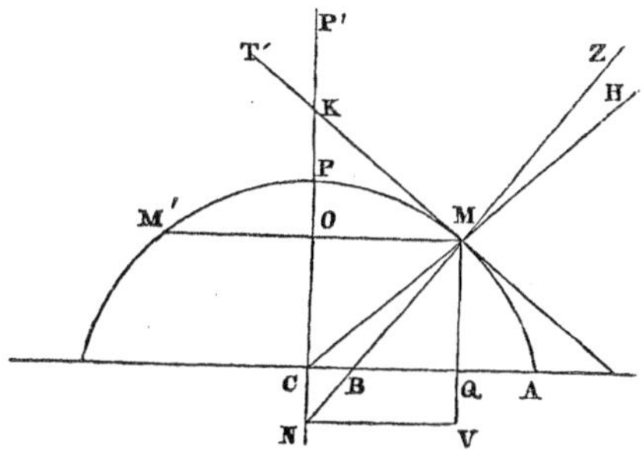

The expression for the subnormal BQ is

$$\frac{B^2 x}{A^2}$$

and the ratio of this to CQ $= x$ is

$$\frac{B^2}{A^2}$$

But from the diagram we have the proportion

$$CQ : BQ :: \tan CMQ : \tan BMQ$$
$$\therefore \quad A^2 : B^2 :: \cot MCQ : \cot MBQ$$

But if the ratio of A to B be taken as 305 to 304, then

$$\frac{B^2}{A^2} = \cdot 9934$$

and the formula for converting astronomic into geocentric latitude will be

$$\tan \lambda' = \cdot 9934 \tan \lambda$$

λ = astronomic latitude,
λ' = geocentric latitude.

RADIUS OF CURVATURE IN TERMS OF THE LATITUDE.

We have had occasion to use an expression for the radius of curvature* of the meridian considered as an ellipse, in terms of the latitude of the point of the meridian, under consideration, in various places in the part of this volume devoted to Geodesy. The following is the mode of deriving it.

The ordinary expression for the radius of curvature of the ellipse found in elementary mathematical works is

$$\rho = \frac{(a^4 y^2 + b^4 x^2)^{\frac{3}{2}}}{a^4 b^4} \qquad (1)$$

in which a and b denote the semi-axes of the ellipse x and y, the co-ordinates of the point at which ρ is the radius of curvature. If λ denote the latitude of this point, since it is the angle which the normal makes with the major axis, we have

$$\tan\lambda = \frac{a^2 y}{b^2 x} \quad \therefore \quad \tan^2\lambda = \frac{a^4 y^2}{b^4 x^2} \quad \therefore \quad \sec^2\lambda = \frac{a^4 y^2 + b^4 x^2}{b^4 x^2}$$

whence,

$$\frac{\tan^2\lambda}{\sec^2\lambda} = \frac{a^4 y^2}{a^4 y^2 + b^4 x^2} = \sin^2\lambda$$

But (e denoting the excentricity of the ellipse),

$$e^2 = \frac{a^2 - b^2}{a^2} \quad (2) \quad \therefore \quad e^2 \sin^2\lambda = \frac{a^2 (a^2 - b^2) y^2}{a^4 y^2 + b^4 x^2}$$

$$1 - e^2 \sin^2\lambda = \frac{b^4 x^2 + a^2 b^2 y^2}{a^4 y^2 + b^4 x^2} = \frac{b^2 (b^2 x^2 + a^2 y^2)}{a^4 y^2 + b^4 x^2} = \frac{a^2 b^4}{a^4 y^2 + b^4 x^2} \qquad (m)$$

since the part of the numerator in parenthesis is, by the equation of the ellipse, equal to $a^2 b^2$. From the last equation we obtain

$$(a^4 y^2 + b^4 x^2)^{\frac{3}{2}} = \frac{a^3 b^6}{(1 - e^2 \sin^2\lambda)^{\frac{3}{2}}}$$

Substituting the second member of the last result for the numerator of (1) that formula becomes

$$\rho = \frac{b^2}{a} \quad \frac{1}{(1 - e^2 \sin^2\lambda)^{\frac{3}{2}}} \qquad (3)$$

But from (2) $b^2 = a^2 (1 - e^2)$, therefore (3) becomes

$$\rho = a \frac{1 - e^2}{(1 - e^2 \sin^2\lambda)^{\frac{3}{2}}} \qquad (4)$$

DETERMINATION OF THE FIGURE AND DIMENSIONS OF THE EARTH FROM THE MEASUREMENT OF TWO DEGREES OF THE MERIDIAN AT TWO DISTANT LATITUDES.

The deviation of an oblate spheroid from a sphere is expressed by what is termed

* The radius of curvature of a curve at any point is the radius of a circle having the same curvature as the curve at that point.

its compression or oblateness. This is the ratio of the difference between its axis to the major axis in symbols, ω representing the oblateness,

$$\omega = \frac{a - b}{a} \tag{1}$$

$$\therefore \quad b = (1 - \omega)\, a$$

But (2) p. 366,

$$e^2 = \frac{a^2 - b^2}{a^2} = \frac{a^2 - (1 - \omega)^2 a^2}{a^2} = 1 - (1 - \omega)^2 = 2\omega - \omega^2$$

omitting ω^2, which is a very small fraction, in consequence of the smallness of ω, we may write

$$e^2 = 2\omega \tag{2}$$

But from (4) p. 366, applying either the binominal or McClaurin's theorem to the second member, we have

$$\rho = a\,(1 - e^2 + \tfrac{3}{2}\, e^2 \sin^2 \lambda + \text{terms too small to affect the result}) \tag{3}$$

By formula (5) p. 100, $\cos 2\lambda = 1 - 2 \sin^2 \lambda$,

$$\therefore \quad \frac{\sin^2 \lambda}{2} = \frac{1 - \cos 2\lambda}{4}$$

substituting the second member of this last in place of the first in (3), that equation becomes

$$\rho = a\,(1 - \tfrac{1}{4}\, e^2 - \tfrac{3}{4}\, e^2 \cos 2\lambda + \&c.)$$

or by (2),

$$\rho = a\,(1 - \tfrac{1}{2}\,\omega - \tfrac{3}{2}\,\omega \cos 2\lambda) \tag{4}$$

If now δ denote the length of a degree measured in the latitude λ, since ρ is the radius of the arc of the meridian in that latitude,

$$\delta = \frac{2\pi\rho}{360} = \frac{\pi\rho}{180}$$

hence substituting the value of ρ given by (4)

$$\delta = \frac{\pi a}{180}\,(1 - \tfrac{1}{2}\,\omega - \tfrac{3}{2}\,\omega \cos 2\lambda) \tag{5}$$

If δ' denote the length of a degree measured in another latitude λ', in a similar manner

$$\delta' = \frac{\pi a}{180}\,(1 - \tfrac{1}{2}\,\omega - \tfrac{3}{2}\,\omega \cos 2\lambda')$$

$$\frac{\delta}{\delta'} = \frac{1 - \frac{1}{2}\,\omega\,(1 + 3 \cos 2\lambda)}{1 - \frac{1}{2}\,\omega\,(1 + 3 \cos 2\lambda')}$$

Performing the division in the second member, and neglecting the squares and higher powers of ω we have

$$\frac{\delta}{\delta'} = 1 + \tfrac{3}{2}\,\omega\,(\cos 2\lambda' - \cos 2\lambda)$$

Therefore

$$\omega = \tfrac{2}{3}\,\frac{1}{\cos 2\lambda' - \cos 2\lambda}\,\frac{\delta - \delta'}{\delta'} \qquad (6)$$

Hence this *rule.*

1. Form a fraction which shall be the ratio of a degree in one latitude to its excess over a degree in another latitude.
2. Form another fraction, which shall be the ratio of unity to the difference between the cosines of the doubles of each latitude.
3. Take $\frac{2}{3}$ of the product of these two fractions.

The value of ω being known, that of a may be found from (5).

EXAMPLE.

The length of a degree at the equator is $\delta' = 56{\cdot}753$ toises.
" " " at 45° $\delta = 57{\cdot}008$ "

$$\therefore \quad \cos 2\lambda = 0$$

$$\cos 2\lambda' = 1$$

$$\frac{\delta - \delta'}{\delta} = \frac{\cdot 255}{57{\cdot}008}$$

$$\omega = \frac{2}{3}\cdot\frac{\cdot 255}{56{\cdot}753} = \frac{\cdot 510}{170{\cdot}259} = \frac{\cdot 255}{85{\cdot}129} = \cdot 00299.$$

We have had occasion to use the expression

$$N = \frac{a}{(1 - e^2 \sin^2 \lambda)^{\frac{1}{2}}}$$

in which N denoted the y normal, and λ the latitude.

This formula may be deduced as follows:—The expression for the y normal in the ellipse is

$$y \text{ normal} = \left(\frac{a^4\, y^2 + b^4\, x^2}{b^4}\right)^{\frac{1}{2}}$$

But we have seen (m) p. 366, that

$$\frac{a^4\, y^2 + b^4\, x^2}{a^2\, b^4} = \frac{1}{1 - e^2 \sin^2 \lambda}$$

whence the formula required.

PRIME VERTICAL TRANSIT.

A transit instrument, mounted in the prime vertical, or at right angles to the meridian, affords a very accurate method of determining latitude or declination when either is known, by observing the times of transit of the same star over the prime vertical on both sides of the zenith. Stars near the zenith are the best for this purpose, as the interval between the two transits is shortest for them, and there is less opportunity for instrumental changes between the two observations. The triangle PZS, which we have so often used in the preceding pages, which must, for our present purpose, be considered right angled at Z, and in which P = the half interval between the transits, will produce the requisite formulæ in a very simple manner. They are as follows:

cos of ½ interval reduced to arc × cot dec. = cot lat.

$$\sin \text{alt.} = \frac{\sin \text{dec.}}{\sin \text{lat.}} \qquad \cos. \text{hour ang.} = \frac{\cot \text{lat.}}{\cot. \text{dec.}}$$

The first is for computing the latitude of the station when the declination of the star observed is known, or vice versâ. The other two are for the purpose of determining at what altitude to set the instrument, and at what time to look for the transit of any given star. In the latter two an approximate value of the latitude is to be used.

For the description of a large transit instrument, contrived for rapid reversal in the prime vertical, and having the telescope at one end of the axis, so that the striding level need never be removed from the supporting axis, see Struve's account of the Pulkova instrument, in 468 of the Astronomische Nachrichten of Schumacher. See also the Washington Astronomical Observations of 1845, introduction p. li. and p. 131. In these instruments there are 16 wires, 7 on each side of the middle one. The transits are taken over seven, and the instrument being quickly reversed, the transits are taken over the same seven in the reverse order.

The following is an example of one of Struve's observations. The 2d column reads upward.

January 15th, 1842, o Draconis.

Wires.	East Vertical.	West Vertical.
	Telescope S.	Telescope S.
	h m s	h m s
I.	17 54 30·75	19 42 51·4
II.	55 8·65	42 13·65
III.	55 44·4	41 38·0
IV.	56 22·25	40 59·85
V.	57 0·6	40 21·7
VI.	57 40·9	39 41·4
VII.	17 58 19·5	19 39 2·7
	Telescope N.	Telescope N.
VII.	18 1 4·0	19 36 17·85
VI.	1 45·5	35 37
V.	2 29·8	34 52·35
IV.	3 12·7	34 9·3
III.	3 57·6	33 24·7
II.	4 39·8	32 42·1
I.	18 5 26·35	19 31 55·6
	$i = 0''·687$	$i' = 0'·923$

Time of meridian transit not corrected for azimuth error of the instrument,

N.	18^h	48^m	41^s·13
S.			41 ·05
Mean	18	48	41 ·09

A knowledge of the distance of each wire from the optical axis is unnecessary; for if this distance be denoted by c plus when the wire is N. of the optical axis, and minus when it is south, we have, t and t' being the corresponding hour angles, δ the declination, and ϕ the latitude,

$$-\sin c = \cos t \cos \delta \sin \phi - \sin \delta \cos \phi$$
$$+\sin c = \cos t' \cos \delta \sin \phi - \sin \delta \cos \phi$$
$$\therefore \quad o = (\cos t' + \cos t) \cos \delta \sin \phi - 2 \sin \delta \cos \phi$$
$$2 \sin c = (\cos t' - \cos t) \cos \delta \sin \phi$$

If we make $\frac{1}{2}(t' + t) = s$, and $\frac{1}{2}(t' - t) = u$, we have

$$\tan \delta = \tan \phi \cos s \cos u \qquad (1)$$
$$\sin c = \sin s \sin u \cos \delta \sin \phi$$

Formula (1) gives the declination, c being eliminated.
" (2) " distance of the wire from the optical axis.
The following is the application of (1) to the example above.

Wires.	I.	II	III.	IV.	V.	VI.	VII.	
	h m s	m s	m s	m s	m s	m s	m s	
$W. - E. = 2t'$	1 48 20·79	47 5 ·09	45 53·69	44 37·69	43 21·19	42 0·59	40 43·29	Telescope S.
$= 2t$	1 26 29·34	23 2·39	29 27·19	30 56·69	32 22·64	33 51·59	35 13·94	" N.
$s = \frac{1}{2}(t + t')$	48 42·53	48 46·87	48 50·22	48 53·60	48 55·96	48 58·05	48 59·31	
$u = \frac{1}{2}(t' - t)$	5 27·86	4 45·67	4 6 ·62	3 25·25	2 44·64	2 2·25	1 22·33	
s log. cos	9·9901167	00871	00642	00411	00250	00107	00020	
u log. cos	9·9998765	063	301	516	688	828	23	Mean.
ϕ log. tan	10·2345728	2345728	2345728	2345728	2345728	2345728	2345728	
δ log. tan	10·2245660	662	671	655	666	663	670	·22456638
δ	59° 11′ 39″	39″·04	39″·23	38″·90	39″·12	39″·06	39″·21	59° 11′ 39″·071

If the inclination of the axis be denoted by i, which is the mean of the two inclinations, telescope N. and telescope S., then $\phi + i$ should be used in place of ϕ in the above formulas, or the correction for the declination should be

$$d\delta = \frac{\sin 2\delta}{\sin 2\phi} i$$

In the example above $\delta =$	59° 11′ 39″·071
Correction for inclination of axis $d\delta =$	0 ·814
Observed declination,	59° 11′ 39 ·885

The declination thus found is exact only on the hypothesis that the azimuth of the axis of rotation is zero. If there be an azimuth a we have $\pi = \frac{a}{\sin \phi}$ for the angle at the pole between the true meridian and the meridian of the instrument, or circle of declination perpendicular to the circle described by the optical axis of the instrument. The instant of transit of the star over the meridian of the instrument is the half sum of the times of corresponding transits E. and W. Thus for the star o Draconis above, we have

Wires.	Telescope S.	Telescope N.
	h m s	h m s
I.	18 48 41·10	18 48 40·93
II.	41·15	41·25
III.	41·20	41·07
IV.	41·05	41
V.	41·15	41.15
VI.	41·15	40·95
VII.	41·10	40·97
Mean	18 48 41·13	41·05

Mean $18^h\ 48^m\ 41^s{\cdot}09$ time of meridian passage.

The instant of meridian passage p requires a small correction for the difference of inclinations of the axis in the two verticals E. and W. Denoting the former by i, and the latter by i'

$$\delta p = \frac{i - i'}{30\sqrt{\sin(\phi + \delta)\sin(\phi - \delta)}}\ \frac{\sin\delta}{\sin\phi}$$

In our example,

$$i = +\,0''{\cdot}687,\quad i' = +\,0''{\cdot}923$$

$$\therefore\quad i - i' = -\,0''{\cdot}236,\ \therefore\ dp = -\,0''{\cdot}08$$

and hence the true time of meridian passage by the instrument instead of $18^h\ 48^m\ 41^s{\cdot}09$, as above, is $p' = 18\ 48\ 41{\cdot}01$.

If α denote the right ascension of the star, and e the error of the clock, let $\alpha' = \alpha - e$ denote the time of passage of the star over the true meridian. Then, for the angle of the two meridians

$$\pi = p' - \alpha' \text{ in time}$$

and for the azimuth of the axis of rotation reckoned from the south round by the west,

$$a = 15\pi\ \sin\varphi, \text{ in arc}$$

With this the correction of the observed declination for the axis of rotation becomes

$$d\delta = \tfrac{1}{4}\,(15\pi)^2 \sin 1'' \sin 2\delta$$

For stars near the zenith ϕ may be used instead of δ, and the formula becomes

$$d\delta = \tfrac{1}{4}\,(15\pi)^2\ \sin 1''\ \sin 2\,\phi$$

The clock error in the above example on 15th January, $18^h\ 48^m$ was $e =$ $8^s{\cdot}31$
The apparent right ascension of o Draconis $\alpha =$ $18^h\ 48^m\ 50^s{\cdot}17$
$\therefore\ \alpha' =$ $18^h\ 48^m\ 41^s{\cdot}86$

$$\therefore\ \pi = -\,0^s{\cdot}85 \text{ in time, and } a = -\,11''{\cdot}0 \text{ in arc}$$

Finally the correction of the declination is

$$d\delta = 0''{\cdot}00017$$

too small to notice.

NOTE.

The formula for refraction, given at p. 345, depends on the well-known law of atmospheric refraction, viz., that it is nearly proportional to the tangent of the zenith distance, and therefore for very small differences of zenith distance, proportional to the differential of the tangent. But

$$d \tan zs = \frac{dzs}{\cos^2 zs}$$

zs being the zenith distance. Applying logarithms and introducing the constant of refraction M, the formula in the text is obtained.

CONCLUDING NOTE.

The author had designed giving the theory of eclipses and occultations, with their application to the determination of longitude, and also Bessel's method of measuring an arc of the meridian; but as longitude by moon culminations is the better mode, and as measurements of the meridian are not at present being carried on or immediately contemplated in this country, it was thought expedient not to increase the size of a work intended for very general use. As, however, the method by occultations requires only a common telescope and a good timepiece, the reader is referred to the Appendix of the Nautical Almanac for 1836, pp. 134 and 145, for the necessary formulas, and an example of the computation of longitude by an occultation. (See also Lee's Tables and Formulas, p. 78, Part III.)

TABLE I.

Difference of Latitude and Departure for ¼ Point.

N. ¼E.			N. ¼W.			S. ¼E.			S. ¼W.					
Dist.	Lat.	Dep.	Dist.	Lat.	Dep.	Dist.	Lat.	Dep.	Dist.	Lat.	Dep.	Dist.	Lat.	Dep.
1	01.0	00.0	61	60.9	03.0	121	120.9	05.9	181	180.8	08.9	241	240.7	11.8
2	02.0	00.1	62	61.9	03.0	22	121.9	06.0	82	181.8	08.9	42	241.7	11.9
3	03.0	00.1	63	62.9	03.1	23	122.9	06.0	83	182.8	09.0	43	242.7	11.9
4	04.0	00.2	64	63.9	03.1	24	123.9	06.1	84	183.8	09.0	44	243.7	12.0
5	05.0	00.2	65	64.9	03.2	25	124.8	06.1	85	184.8	09.1	45	244.7	12.0
6	06.0	00.3	66	65.9	03.2	26	125.8	06.2	86	185.8	09.1	46	245.7	12.1
7	07.0	00.3	67	66.9	03.3	27	126.8	06.2	87	186.8	09.2	47	246.7	12.1
8	08.0	00.4	68	67.9	03.3	28	127.8	06.3	88	187.8	09.2	48	247.7	12.2
9	09.0	00.4	69	68.9	03.4	29	128.8	06.3	89	188.8	09.3	49	248.7	12.2
10	10.0	00.5	70	69.9	03.4	30	129.8	06.4	90	189.8	09.3	50	249.7	12.3
11	11.0	00.5	71	70.9	03.5	131	130.8	06.4	191	190.8	09.4	251	250.7	12.3
12	12.0	00.6	72	71.9	03.5	32	131.8	06.5	92	191.8	09.4	52	251.7	12.4
13	13.0	00.6	73	72.9	03.6	33	132.8	06.5	93	192.8	09.5	53	252.7	12.4
14	14.0	00.7	74	73.9	03.6	34	133.8	06.6	94	193.8	09.5	54	253.7	12.5
15	15.0	00.7	75	74.9	03.7	35	134.8	06.6	95	194.8	09.6	55	254.7	12.5
16	16.0	00.8	76	75.9	03.7	36	135.8	06.7	96	195.8	09.6	56	255.7	12.6
17	17.0	00.8	77	76.9	03.8	37	136.8	06.7	97	196.8	09.7	57	256.7	12.6
18	18.0	00.9	78	77.9	03.8	38	137.8	06.8	98	197.8	09.7	58	257.7	12.7
19	19.0	00.9	79	78.9	03.9	39	138.8	06.8	99	198.8	09.8	59	258.7	12.7
20	20.0	01.0	80	79.9	03.9	40	139.8	06.9	200	199.8	09.8	60	259.7	12.8
21	21.0	01.0	81	80.9	04.0	141	140.8	06.9	201	200.8	09.9	261	260.7	12.8
22	22.0	01.1	82	81.9	04.0	42	141.8	07.0	02	201.8	09.9	62	261.7	12.9
23	23.0	01.1	83	82.9	04.1	43	142.8	07.0	03	202.8	10.0	63	262.7	12.9
24	24.0	01.2	84	83.9	04.1	44	143.8	07.1	04	203.8	10.0	64	263.7	13.0
25	25.0	01.2	85	84.9	04.2	45	144.8	07.1	05	204.8	10.1	65	264.7	13.0
26	26.0	01.3	86	85.9	04.2	46	145.8	07.2	06	205.8	10.1	66	265.7	13.1
27	27.0	01.3	87	86.9	04.3	47	146.8	07.2	07	206.8	10.2	67	266.7	13.1
28	28.0	01.4	88	87.9	04.3	48	147.8	07.3	08	207.7	10.2	68	267.7	13.2
29	29.0	01.4	89	88.9	04.4	49	148.8	07.3	09	208.7	10.3	69	268.7	13.2
30	30.0	01.5	90	89.9	04.4	50	149.8	07.4	10	209.7	10.3	70	269.7	13.2
31	31.0	01.5	91	90.9	04.5	151	150.8	07.4	211	210.7	10.4	271	270.7	13.3
32	32.0	01.6	92	91.9	04.5	52	151.8	07.5	12	211.7	10.4	72	271.7	13.3
33	33.0	01.6	93	92.9	04.6	53	152.8	07.5	13	212.7	10.5	73	272.7	13.4
34	34.0	01.7	94	93.9	04.6	54	153.8	07.6	14	213.7	10.5	74	273.7	13.4
35	35.0	01.7	95	94.9	04.7	55	154.8	07.6	15	214.7	10.5	75	274.7	13.5
36	36.0	01.8	96	95.9	04.7	56	155.8	07.7	16	215.7	10.6	76	275.7	13.5
37	37.0	01.8	97	96.9	04.8	57	156.8	07.7	17	216.7	10.6	77	276.7	13.6
38	38.0	01.9	98	97.9	04.8	58	157.8	07.8	18	217.7	10.7	78	277.7	13.6
39	39.0	01.9	99	98.9	04.9	59	158.8	07.8	19	218.7	10.7	79	278.7	13.7
40	40.0	02.0	100	99.9	04.9	60	159.8	07.9	20	219.7	10.8	80	279.7	13.7
41	41.0	02.0	101	100.9	05.0	161	160.8	07.9	221	220.7	10.8	281	280.7	13.8
42	41.9	02.1	02	101.9	05.0	62	161.8	07.9	22	221.7	10.9	82	281.7	13.8
43	42.9	02.1	03	102.9	05.1	63	162.8	08.0	23	222.7	10.9	83	282.7	13.9
44	43.9	02.2	04	103.9	05.1	64	163.8	08.0	24	223.7	11.0	84	283.7	13.9
45	44.9	02.2	05	104.9	05.2	65	164.8	08.1	25	224.7	11.0	85	284.7	14.0
46	45.9	02.3	06	105.9	05.2	66	165.8	08.1	26	225.7	11.1	86	285.7	14.0
47	46.9	02.3	07	106.9	05.3	67	166.8	08.2	27	226.7	11.1	87	286.7	14.1
48	47.9	02.4	08	107.9	05.3	68	167.8	08.2	28	227.7	11.2	88	287.7	14.1
49	48.9	02.4	09	108.9	05.3	69	168.8	08.3	29	228.7	11.2	89	288.7	14.2
50	49.9	02.5	10	109.9	05.4	70	169.8	08.3	30	229.7	11.3	90	289.7	14.2
51	50.9	02.5	111	110.9	05.4	171	170.8	08.4	231	230.7	11.3	291	290.6	14.3
52	51.9	02.6	12	111.9	05.5	72	171.8	08.4	32	231.7	11.4	92	291.6	14.3
53	52.9	02.6	13	112.9	05.5	73	172.8	08.5	33	232.7	11.4	93	292.6	14.4
54	53.9	02.6	14	113.9	05.6	74	173.8	08.5	34	233.7	11.5	94	293.6	14.4
55	54.9	02.7	15	114.9	05.6	75	174.8	08.6	35	234.7	11.5	95	294.6	14.5
56	55.9	02.7	16	115.9	05.7	76	175.8	08.6	36	235.7	11.6	96	295.6	14.5
57	56.9	02.8	17	116.9	05.7	77	176.8	08.7	37	236.7	11.6	97	296.6	14.6
58	57.9	02.8	18	117.9	05.8	78	177.8	08.7	38	237.7	11.7	98	297.6	14.6
59	58.9	02.9	19	118.9	05.8	79	178.8	08.8	39	238.7	11.7	99	298.6	14.7
60	59.9	02.9	20	119.9	05.9	80	179.8	08.8	40	239.7	11.8	300	299.6	14.7
Dist.	Dep.	Lat.	Dist.	Dep.	Lat.	Dist.	Dep.	Lat.	Dist.	Dep.	Lat.	Dist.	Dep.	Lat.
E. ¼N.			E. ¼S.			W. ¼N.			W. ¼S.			[For 7¾ Points.		

TABLE I.

Difference of Latitude and Departure for ½ Point.

N.½ E. N.½ W. S.½ E. S.½ W.

Dist.	Lat.	Dep.	Dist.	Lat.	Dep.	Dist.	Lat.	Dep.	Dist.	Lat.	Dep.	Dist.	Lat.	Dep.
1	01.0	00.1	61	60.7	06.0	121	120.4	11.9	181	180.1	17.7	241	239.8	23.6
2	02.0	00.2	62	61.7	06.1	22	121.4	12.0	82	181.1	17.8	42	240.8	23.7
3	03.0	00.3	63	62.7	06.2	23	122.4	12.1	83	182.1	17.9	43	241.8	23.8
4	04.0	00.4	64	63.7	06.3	24	123.4	12.2	84	183.1	18.0	44	242.8	23.9
5	05.0	00.5	65	64.7	06.4	25	124.4	12.3	85	184.1	18.1	45	243.8	24.0
6	06.0	00.6	66	65.7	06.5	26	125.4	12.4	86	185.1	18.2	46	244.8	24.1
7	07.0	00.7	67	66.7	06.6	27	126.4	12.4	87	186.1	18.3	47	245.8	24.2
8	08.0	00.8	68	67.7	06.7	28	127.4	12.5	88	187.1	18.4	48	246.8	24.3
9	09.0	00.9	69	68.7	06.8	29	128.4	12.6	89	188.1	18.5	49	247.8	24.4
10	10.0	01.0	70	69.7	06.9	30	129.4	12.7	90	189.1	18.6	50	248.8	24.5
11	10.9	01.1	71	70.7	07.0	131	130.4	12.8	191	190.1	18.7	251	249.8	24.6
12	11.9	01.2	72	71.7	07.1	32	131.4	12.9	92	191.1	18.8	52	250.8	24.7
13	12.9	01.3	73	72.6	07.2	33	132.4	13.0	93	192.1	18.9	53	251.8	24.8
14	13.9	01.4	74	73.6	07.3	34	133.4	13.1	94	193.1	19.0	54	252.8	24.9
15	14.9	01.5	75	74.6	07.4	35	134.3	13.2	95	194.1	19.1	55	253.8	25.0
16	15.9	01.6	76	75.6	07.4	36	135.3	13.3	96	195.1	19.2	56	254.8	25.1
17	16.9	01.7	77	76.6	07.5	37	136.3	13.4	97	196.1	19.3	57	255.8	25.2
18	17.9	01.8	78	77.6	07.6	38	137.3	13.5	98	197.0	19.4	58	256.8	25.3
19	18.9	01.9	79	78.6	07.7	39	138.3	13.6	99	198.0	19.5	59	257.8	25.4
20	19.9	02.0	80	79.6	07.8	40	139.3	13.7	200	199.0	19.6	60	258.7	25.5
21	20.9	02.1	81	80.6	07.9	141	140.3	13.8	201	200.0	19.7	261	259.7	25.6
22	21.9	02.2	82	81.6	08.0	42	141.3	13.9	02	201.0	19.8	62	260.7	25.7
23	22.9	02.3	83	82.6	08.1	43	142.3	14.0	03	202.0	19.9	63	261.7	25.8
24	23.9	02.4	84	83.6	08.2	44	143.3	14.1	04	203.0	20.0	64	262.7	25.9
25	24.9	02.5	85	84.6	08.3	45	144.3	14.2	05	204.0	20.1	65	263.7	26.0
26	25.9	02.5	86	85.6	08.4	46	145.3	14.3	06	205.0	20.2	66	264.7	26.1
27	26.9	02.6	87	86.6	08.5	47	146.3	14.4	07	206.0	20.3	67	265.7	26.2
28	27.9	02.7	88	87.6	08.6	48	147.3	14.5	08	207.0	20.4	68	266.7	26.3
29	28.9	02.8	89	88.6	08.7	49	148.3	14.6	09	208.0	20.5	69	267.7	26.4
30	29.9	02.9	90	89.6	08.8	50	149.3	14.7	10	209.0	20.6	70	268.7	26.5
31	30.9	03.0	91	90.6	08.9	151	150.3	14.8	211	210.0	20.7	271	269.7	26.6
32	31.8	03.1	92	91.6	09.0	52	151.3	14.9	12	211.0	20.8	72	270.7	26.7
33	32.8	03.2	93	92.6	09.1	53	152.3	15.0	13	212.0	20.9	73	271.7	26.8
34	33.8	03.3	94	93.5	09.2	54	153.3	15.1	14	213.0	21.0	74	272.7	26.9
35	34.8	03.4	95	94.5	09.3	55	154.3	15.2	15	214.0	21.1	75	273.7	27.0
36	35.8	03.5	96	95.5	09.4	56	155.2	15.3	16	215.0	21.2	76	274.7	27.1
37	36.8	03.6	97	96.5	09.5	57	156.2	15.4	17	216.0	21.3	77	275.7	27.2
38	37.8	03.7	98	97.5	09.6	58	157.2	15.5	18	217.0	21.4	78	276.7	27.2
39	38.8	03.8	99	98.5	09.7	59	158.2	15.6	19	217.9	21.5	79	277.7	27.3
40	39.8	03.9	100	99.5	09.8	60	159.2	15.7	20	218.9	21.6	80	278.7	27.4
41	40.8	04.0	101	100.5	09.9	161	160.2	15.8	221	219.9	21.7	281	279.6	27.5
42	41.8	04.1	02	101.5	10.0	62	161.2	15.9	22	220.9	21.8	82	280.6	27.6
43	42.8	04.2	03	102.5	10.1	63	162.2	16.0	23	221.9	21.9	83	281.6	27.7
44	43.8	04.3	04	103.5	10.2	64	163.2	16.1	24	222.9	22.0	84	282.6	27.8
45	44.8	04.4	05	104.5	10.3	65	164.2	16.2	25	223.9	22.1	85	283.6	27.9
46	45.8	04.5	06	105.5	10.4	66	165.2	16.3	26	224.9	22.2	86	284.6	28.0
47	46.8	04.6	07	106.5	10.5	67	166.2	16.4	27	225.9	22.2	87	285.6	28.1
48	47.8	04.7	08	107.5	10.6	68	167.2	16.5	28	226.9	22.3	88	286.6	28.2
49	48.8	04.8	09	108.5	10.7	69	168.2	16.6	29	227.9	22.4	89	287.6	28.3
50	49.8	04.9	10	109.5	10.8	70	169.2	16.7	30	228.9	22.5	90	288.6	28.4
51	50.8	05.0	111	110.5	10.9	171	170.2	16.8	231	229.9	22.6	291	289.6	28.5
52	51.7	05.1	12	111.5	11.0	72	171.2	16.9	32	230.9	22.7	92	290.6	28.6
53	52.7	05.2	13	112.5	11.1	73	172.2	17.0	33	231.9	22.8	93	291.6	28.7
54	53.7	05.3	14	113.5	11.2	74	173.2	17.1	34	232.9	22.9	94	292.6	28.8
55	54.7	05.4	15	114.4	11.3	75	174.2	17.2	35	233.9	23.0	95	293.6	28.9
56	55.7	05.5	16	115.4	11.4	76	175.2	17.3	36	234.9	23.1	96	294.6	29.0
57	56.7	05.6	17	116.4	11.5	77	176.1	17.3	37	235.9	23.2	97	295.6	29.1
58	57.7	05.7	18	117.4	11.6	78	177.1	17.4	38	236.9	23.3	98	296.6	29.2
59	58.7	05.8	19	118.4	11.7	79	178.1	17.5	39	237.8	23.4	99	297.6	29.3
60	59.7	05.9	20	119.4	11.8	80	179.1	17.6	40	238.8	23.5	300	298.6	29.4
Dist.	Dep.	Lat.	Dist.	Dep.	Lat.	Dist.	Dep.	Lat.	Dist.	Dep.	Lat.	Dist.	Dep.	Lat.

E.½ N. E.½ S. W.½ N. W.½ S. [For 7½ Points.

TABLE I.

Difference of Latitude and Departure for ¾ Point.

N.¾ E.			N.¾ W.			S.¾ E.			S.¾ W.					
Dist.	Lat.	Dep.	Dist.	Lat.	Dep.	Dist.	Lat.	Dep.	Dist.	Lat.	Dep.	Dist.	Lat.	Dep.
1	01.0	00.1	61	60.3	09.0	121	119.7	17.8	181	179.0	26.6	241	238.4	35.4
2	02.0	00.3	62	61.3	09.1	22	120.7	17.9	82	180.0	26.7	42	239.4	35.5
3	03.0	00.4	63	62.3	09.2	23	121.7	18.0	83	181.0	26.9	43	240.4	35.7
4	04.0	00.6	64	63.3	09.4	24	122.7	18.2	84	182.0	27.0	44	241.4	35.8
5	04.9	00.7	65	64.3	09.5	25	123.6	18.3	85	183.0	27.1	45	242.3	35.9
6	05.9	00.9	66	65.3	09.7	26	124.6	18.5	86	184.0	27.3	46	243.3	36.1
7	06.9	01.0	67	66.3	09.8	27	125.6	18.6	87	185.0	27.4	47	244.3	36.2
8	07.9	01.2	68	67.3	10.0	28	126.6	18.8	88	186.0	27.6	48	245.3	36.4
9	08.9	01.3	69	68.3	10.1	29	127.6	18.9	89	187.0	27.7	49	246.3	36.5
10	09.9	01.5	70	69.2	10.3	30	128.6	19.1	90	187.9	27.9	50	247.3	36.7
11	10.9	01.6	71	70.2	10.4	131	129.6	19.2	191	188.9	28.0	251	248.3	36.8
12	11.9	01.8	72	71.2	10.6	32	130.6	19.4	92	189.9	28.2	52	249.3	37.0
13	12.9	01.9	73	72.2	10.7	33	131.6	19.5	93	190.9	28.3	53	250.3	37.1
14	13.8	02.1	74	73.2	10.9	34	132.5	19.7	94	191.9	28.5	54	251.3	37.3
15	14.8	02.2	75	74.2	11.0	35	133.5	19.8	95	192.9	28.6	55	252.2	37.4
16	15.8	02.3	76	75.2	11.2	36	134.5	20.0	96	193.9	28.8	56	253.2	37.6
17	16.8	02.5	77	76.2	11.3	37	135.5	20.1	97	194.9	28.9	57	254.2	37.7
18	17.8	02.6	78	77.2	11.4	38	136.5	20.2	98	195.9	29.1	58	255.2	37.9
19	18.8	02.8	79	78.1	11.6	39	137.5	20.4	99	196.8	29.2	59	256.2	38.0
20	19.8	02.9	80	79.1	11.7	40	138.5	20.5	200	197.8	29.3	60	257.2	38.1
21	20.8	03.1	81	80.1	11.9	141	139.5	20.7	201	198.8	29.5	261	258.2	38.3
22	21.8	03.2	82	81.1	12.0	42	140.5	20.8	02	199.8	29.6	62	259.2	38.4
23	22.8	03.4	83	82.1	12.2	43	141.5	21.0	03	200.8	29.8	63	260.2	38.6
24	23.7	03.5	84	83.1	12.3	44	142.4	21.1	04	201.8	29.9	64	261.1	38.7
25	24.7	03.7	85	84.1	12.5	45	143.4	21.3	05	202.8	30.1	65	262.1	38.9
26	25.7	03.8	86	85.1	12.6	46	144.4	21.4	06	203.8	30.2	66	263.1	39.0
27	26.7	04.0	87	86.1	12.8	47	145.4	21.6	07	204.8	30.4	67	264.1	39.2
28	27.7	04.1	88	87.0	12.9	48	146.4	21.7	08	205.7	30.5	68	265.1	39.3
29	28.7	04.3	89	88.0	13.1	49	147.4	21.9	09	206.7	30.7	69	266.1	39.5
30	29.7	04.4	90	89.0	13.2	50	148.4	22.0	10	207.7	30.8	70	267.1	39.6
31	30.7	04.5	91	90.0	13.4	151	149.4	22.2	211	208.7	31.0	271	268.1	39.8
32	31.7	04.7	92	91.0	13.5	52	150.4	22.3	12	209.7	31.1	72	269.1	39.9
33	32.6	04.8	93	92.0	13.6	53	151.3	22.4	13	210.7	31.3	73	270.0	40.1
34	33.6	05.0	94	93.0	13.8	54	152.3	22.6	14	211.7	31.4	74	271.0	40.2
35	34.6	05.1	95	94.0	13.9	55	153.3	22.7	15	212.7	31.5	75	272.0	40.4
36	35.6	05.3	96	95.0	14.1	56	154.3	22.9	16	213.7	31.7	76	273.0	40.5
37	36.6	05.4	97	96.0	14.2	57	155.3	23.0	17	214.7	31.8	77	274.0	40.6
38	37.6	05.6	98	96.9	14.4	58	156.3	23.2	18	215.6	32.0	78	275.0	40.8
39	38.6	05.7	99	97.9	14.5	59	157.3	23.3	19	216.6	32.1	79	276.0	40.9
40	39.6	05.9	100	98.9	14.7	60	158.3	23.5	20	217.6	32.3	80	277.0	41.1
41	40.6	06.0	101	99.9	14.8	161	159.3	23.6	221	218.6	32.4	281	278.0	41.2
42	41.5	06.2	02	100.9	15.0	62	160.2	23.8	22	219.6	32.6	82	278.9	41.4
43	42.5	06.3	03	101.9	15.1	63	161.2	23.9	23	220.6	32.7	83	279.9	41.5
44	43.5	06.5	04	102.9	15.3	64	162.2	24.1	24	221.6	32.9	84	280.9	41.7
45	44.5	06.6	05	103.9	15.4	65	163.2	24.2	25	222.6	33.0	85	281.9	41.8
46	45.5	06.7	06	104.9	15.6	66	164.2	24.4	26	223.6	33.2	86	282.9	42.0
47	46.5	06.9	07	105.8	15.7	67	165.2	24.5	27	224.5	33.3	87	283.9	42.1
48	47.5	07.0	08	106.8	15.8	68	166.2	24.7	28	225.5	33.5	88	284.9	42.3
49	48.5	07.2	09	107.8	16.0	69	167.2	24.8	29	226.5	33.6	89	285.9	42.4
50	49.5	07.3	10	108.8	16.1	70	168.2	24.9	30	227.5	33.7	90	286.9	42.6
51	50.4	07.5	111	109.8	16.3	171	169.1	25.1	231	228.5	33.9	291	287.9	42.7
52	51.4	07.6	12	110.8	16.4	72	170.1	25.2	32	229.5	34.0	92	288.8	42.8
53	52.4	07.8	13	111.8	16.6	73	171.1	25.4	33	230.5	34.2	93	289.8	43.0
54	53.4	07.9	14	112.8	16.7	74	172.1	25.5	34	231.5	34.3	94	290.8	43.1
55	54.4	08.1	15	113.8	16.9	75	173.1	25.7	35	232.5	34.5	95	291.8	43.3
56	55.4	08.2	16	114.7	17.0	76	174.1	25.8	36	233.4	34.6	96	292.8	43.4
57	56.4	08.4	17	115.7	17.2	77	175.1	26.0	37	234.4	34.8	97	293.8	43.6
58	57.4	08.5	18	116.7	17.3	78	176.1	26.1	38	235.4	34.9	98	294.8	43.7
59	58.4	08.7	19	117.7	17.5	79	177.1	26.3	39	236.4	35.1	99	295.8	43.9
60	59.4	08.8	20	118.7	17.6	80	178.1	26.4	40	237.4	35.2	300	296.8	44.0
Dist.	Dep.	Lat.	Dist.	Dep.	Lat.	Dist.	Dep.	Lat.	Dist.	Dep.	Lat.	Dist.	Dep.	Lat.
E.¾ N.			E.¾ S.			W.¾ N.			W.¾ S.			[For 7¼ Points.		

TABLE I.

Difference of Latitude and Departure for 1 Point.

N byE.			N.byW.			S.byE.			S.byW.					
Dist.	Lat.	Dep.	Dist.	Lat.	Dep.	Dist.	Lat.	Dep.	Dist.	Lat.	Dep.	Dist.	Lat.	Dep.
1	01.0	00.2	61	59.8	11.9	121	118.7	23.6	181	177.5	35.3	241	236.4	47.0
2	02.0	00.4	62	60.8	12.1	22	119.7	23.8	82	178.5	35.5	42	237.4	47.2
3	02.9	00.6	63	61.8	12.3	23	120.6	24.0	83	179.5	35.7	43	238.3	47.4
4	03.9	00.8	64	62.8	12.5	24	121.6	24.2	84	180.5	35.9	44	239.3	47.6
5	04.9	01.0	65	63.8	12.7	25	122.6	24.4	85	181.4	36.1	45	240.3	47.8
6	05.9	01.2	66	64.7	12.9	26	123.6	24.6	86	182.4	36.3	46	241.3	48.0
7	06.9	01.4	67	65.7	13.1	27	124.6	24.8	87	183.4	36.5	47	242.3	48.2
8	07.8	01.6	68	66.7	13.3	28	125.5	25.0	88	184.4	36.7	48	243.2	48.4
9	08.8	01.8	69	67.7	13.5	29	126.5	25.2	89	185.4	36.9	49	244.2	48.6
10	09.8	02.0	70	68.7	13.7	30	127.5	25.4	90	186.3	37.1	50	245.2	48.8
11	10.8	02.1	71	69.6	13.9	131	128.5	25.6	191	187.3	37.3	251	246.2	49.0
12	11.8	02.3	72	70.6	14.0	32	129.5	25.8	92	188.3	37.5	52	247.2	49.2
13	12.8	02.5	73	71.6	14.2	33	130.4	25.9	93	189.3	37.7	53	248.1	49.4
14	13.7	02.7	74	72.6	14.4	34	131.4	26.1	94	190.3	37.8	54	249.1	49.6
15	14.7	02.9	75	73.6	14.6	35	132.4	26.3	95	191.3	38.0	55	250.1	49.7
16	15.7	03.1	76	74.5	14.8	36	133.4	26.5	96	192.2	38.2	56	251.1	49.9
17	16.7	03.3	77	75.5	15.0	37	134.4	26.7	97	193.2	38.4	57	252.1	50.1
18	17.7	03.5	78	76.5	15.2	38	135.3	26.9	98	194.2	38 6	58	253.0	50.3
19	18.6	03.7	79	77.5	15.4	39	136.3	27.1	99	195.2	38.8	59	254.0	50.5
20	19.6	03.9	80	78.5	15.6	40	137.3	27.3	200	196.2	39.0	60	255.0	50.7
21	20.6	04.1	81	79.4	15.8	141	138.3	27.5	201	197.1	39.2	261	256.0	50.9
22	21.6	04.3	82	80.4	16.0	42	139.3	27.7	02	198.1	39.4	62	257.0	51.1
23	22.6	04.5	83	81.4	16.2	43	140.3	27.9	03	199.1	39.6	63	257.9	51.3
24	23.5	04.7	84	82.4	16.4	44	141.2	28.1	04	200.1	39.8	64	258.9	51.5
25	24.5	04.9	85	83.4	16.6	45	142.2	28.3	05	201.1	40.0	65	259.9	51.7
26	25.5	05.1	86	84.3	16.8	46	143.2	28.5	06	202.0	40.2	66	260.9	51.9
27	26.5	05.3	87	85.3	17.0	47	144.2	28.7	07	203.0	40.4	67	261.9	52.1
28	27.5	05.5	88	86.3	17.2	48	145.2	28.9	08	204.0	40.6	68	262.9	52.3
29	28.4	05.7	89	87.3	17.4	49	146.1	29.1	09	205.0	40.8	69	263.8	52.5
30	29.4	05.9	90	88.3	17.6	50	147.1	29.3	10	206.0	41.0	70	264.8	52.7
31	30.4	06.0	91	89.3	17.8	151	148.1	29.5	211	206.9	41.2	271	265.8	52.9
32	31.4	06.2	92	90.2	17.9	52	149.1	29.7	12	207.9	41.4	72	266.8	53.1
33	32.4	06.4	93	91.2	18.1	53	150.1	29.8	13	208.9	41.6	73	267.8	53.3
34	33.3	06.6	94	92.2	18.3	54	151.0	30.0	14	209.9	41.7	74	268.7	53.5
35	34.3	06.8	95	93.2	18.5	55	152.0	30.2	15	210.9	41.9	75	269.7	53.6
36	35.3	07.0	96	94.2	18.7	56	153.0	30.4	16	211.8	42.1	76	270.7	53.8
37	36.3	07.2	97	95.1	18.9	57	154.0	30.6	17	212.8	42.3	77	271.7	54.0
38	37.3	07.4	98	96.1	19.1	58	155.0	30.8	18	213.8	42.5	78	272.7	54.2
39	38.3	07.6	99	97.1	19.3	59	155.9	31.0	19	214.8	42.7	79	273.6	54.4
40	39.2	07.8	100	98.1	19.5	60	156.9	31.2	20	215.8	42.9	80	274.6	54.6
41	40.2	08.0	101	99.1	19.7	161	157.9	31.4	221	216.8	43.1	281	275.6	54.8
42	41.2	08.2	02	100.0	19.9	62	158.9	31.6	22	217.7	43.3	82	276.6	55.0
43	42.2	08.4	03	101.0	20.1	63	159.9	31.8	23	218.7	43.5	83	277.6	55.2
44	43.2	08.6	04	102.0	20.3	64	160.8	32.0	24	219.7	43.7	84	278.5	55.4
45	44.1	08.8	05	103.0	20.5	65	161.8	32.2	25	220.7	43.9	85	279.5	55.6
46	45.1	09.0	06	104.0	20.7	66	162.8	32.4	26	221.7	44.1	86	280.5	55.8
47	46.1	09.2	07	104.9	20.9	67	163.8	32.6	27	222.6	44.3	87	281.5	56.0
48	47.1	09.4	08	105.9	21.1	68	164.8	32.8	28	223.6	44.5	88	282.5	56.2
49	48.1	09.6	09	106.9	21.3	69	165.8	33.0	29	224.6	44.7	89	283.4	56.4
50	49.0	09.8	10	107.9	21.5	70	166.7	33.2	30	225.6	44.9	90	284.4	56.6
51	50.0	09.9	111	108.9	21.7	171	167.7	33.4	231	226.6	45.1	291	285.4	56.8
52	51.0	10.1	12	109.8	21.9	72	168.7	33.6	32	227.5	45.3	92	286.4	57.0
53	52.0	10.3	13	110.8	22.0	73	169.7	33.8	33	228.5	45.5	93	287.4	57.2
54	53.0	10.5	14	111.8	22.2	74	170.7	33.9	34	229.5	45.7	94	288.4	57.4
55	53.9	10.7	15	112.8	22.4	75	171.6	34.1	35	230.5	45.8	95	289.3	57.6
56	54.9	10.9	16	113.8	22.6	76	172.6	34.3	36	231.5	46.0	96	290.3	57.7
57	55.9	11.1	17	114.8	22.8	77	173.6	34.5	37	232.4	46.2	97	291.3	57.9
58	56.9	11.3	18	115.7	23.0	78	174.6	34.7	38	233.4	46.4	98	292.3	58.1
59	57.9	11.5	19	116.7	23.2	79	175.6	34.9	39	234.4	46.6	99	293.3	58.3
60	58.8	11.7	20	117.7	23.4	80	176.5	35.1	40	235.4	46.8	300	294.2	58.5
Dist.	Dep.	Lat.	Dist.	Dep.	Lat.	Dist.	Dep.	Lat.	Dist.	Dep.	Lat.	Dist.	Dep.	Lat.
E.byN.			E.byS.			W.byN.			W.byS.			[For 7 Points.		

TABLE I.

Difference of Latitude and Departure for 1¼ Points.

N.byE.¼E. N.byW.¼W. S.byE.¼E. S byW.¼W.

Dist.	Lat.	Dep.	Dist.	Lat.	Dep.	Dist.	Lat.	Dep.	Dist.	Lat.	Dep.	Dist.	Lat.	Dep.
1	01.0	00.2	61	59.2	14.8	121	117.4	29.4	181	175.6	44.0	241	233.8	58.6
2	01.9	00.5	62	60.1	15.1	22	118.3	29.6	82	176.5	44.2	42	234.7	58.8
3	02.9	00.7	63	61.1	15.3	23	119.3	29.9	83	177.5	44.5	43	235.7	59.0
4	03.9	01.0	64	62.1	15.6	24	120.3	30.1	84	178.5	44.7	44	236.7	59.3
5	04.9	01.2	65	63.1	15.8	25	121.3	30.4	85	179.5	45.0	45	237.7	59.5
6	05.8	01.5	66	64.0	16.0	26	122.2	30.6	86	180.4	45.2	46	238.6	59.8
7	06.8	01.7	67	65.0	16.3	27	123.2	30.9	87	181.4	45.4	47	239.6	60.0
8	07.8	01.9	68	66.0	16.5	28	124.2	31.1	88	182.4	45.7	48	240.6	60.3
9	08.7	02.2	69	66.9	16.8	29	125.1	31.3	89	183.3	45.9	49	241.5	60.5
10	09.7	02.4	70	67.9	17.0	30	126.1	31.6	90	184.3	46.2	50	242.5	60.7
11	10.7	02.7	71	68.9	17.3	131	127.1	31.8	191	185.3	46.4	251	243.5	61.0
12	11.6	02.9	72	69.8	17.5	32	128.0	32.1	92	186.2	46.7	52	244.4	61.2
13	12.6	03.2	73	70.8	17.7	33	129.0	32.3	93	187.2	46.9	53	245.4	61.5
14	13.6	03.4	74	71.8	18.0	34	130.0	32.6	94	188.2	47.1	54	246.4	61.7
15	14.6	03.6	75	72.8	18.2	35	131.0	32.8	95	189.2	47.4	55	247.4	62.0
16	15.5	03.9	76	73.7	18.5	36	131.9	33.0	96	190.1	47.6	56	248.3	62.2
17	16.5	04.1	77	74.7	18.7	37	132.9	33.3	97	191.1	47.9	57	249.3	62.4
18	17.5	04.4	78	75.7	19.0	38	133.9	33.5	98	192.1	48.1	58	250.3	62.7
19	18.4	04.6	79	76.6	19.2	39	134.8	33.8	99	193.0	48.4	59	251.2	62.9
20	19.4	04.9	80	77.6	19.4	40	135.8	34.0	200	194.0	48.6	60	252.2	63.2
21	20.4	05.1	81	78.6	19.7	141	136.8	34.3	201	195.0	48.8	261	253.2	63.4
22	21.3	05.3	82	79.5	19.9	42	137.7	34.5	02	195.9	49.1	62	254.1	63.7
23	22.3	05.6	83	80.5	20.2	43	138.7	34.7	03	196.9	49.3	63	255.1	63.9
24	23.3	05.8	84	81.5	20.4	44	139.7	35.0	04	197.9	49.6	64	256.1	64.1
25	24.3	06.1	85	82.5	20.7	45	140.7	35.2	05	198.9	49.8	65	257.1	64.4
26	25.2	06.3	86	83.4	20.9	46	141.6	35.5	06	199.8	50.1	66	258.0	64.6
27	26.2	06.6	87	84.4	21.1	47	142.6	35.7	07	200.8	50.3	67	259.0	64.9
28	27.2	06.8	88	85.4	21.4	48	143.6	36.0	08	201.8	50.5	68	260.0	65.1
29	28.1	07.0	89	86.3	21.6	49	144.5	36.2	09	202.7	50.8	69	260.9	65.4
30	29.1	07.3	90	87.3	21.9	50	145.5	36.4	10	203.7	51.0	70	261.9	65.6
31	30.1	07.5	91	88.3	22.1	151	146.5	36.7	211	204.7	51.3	271	262.9	65.8
32	31.0	07.8	92	89.2	22.4	52	147.4	36.9	12	205.6	51.5	72	263.8	66.1
33	32.0	08.0	93	90.2	22.6	53	148.4	37.2	13	206.6	51.8	73	264.8	66.3
34	33.0	08.3	94	91.2	22.8	54	149.4	37.4	14	207.6	52.0	74	265.8	66.6
35	34.0	08.5	95	92.2	23.1	55	150.4	37.7	15	208.6	52.2	75	266.8	66.8
36	34.9	08.7	96	93.1	23.3	56	151.3	37.9	16	209.5	52.5	76	267.7	67.1
37	35.9	09.0	97	94.1	23.6	57	152.3	38.1	17	210.5	52.7	77	268.7	67.3
38	36.9	09.2	98	95.1	23.8	58	153.3	38.4	18	211.5	53.0	78	269.7	67.5
39	37.8	09.5	99	96.0	24.1	59	154.2	38.6	19	212.4	53.2	79	270.6	67.8
40	38.8	09.7	100	97.0	24.3	60	155.2	38.9	20	213.4	53.5	80	271.6	68.0
41	39.8	10.0	101	98.0	24.5	161	156.2	39.1	221	214.4	53.7	281	272.6	68.3
42	40.7	10.2	02	98.9	24.8	62	157.1	39.4	22	215.3	53.9	82	273.5	68.5
43	41.7	10.4	03	99.9	25.0	63	158.1	39.6	23	216.3	54.2	83	274.5	68.8
44	42.7	10.7	04	100.9	25.3	64	159.1	39.8	24	217.3	54.4	84	275.5	69.0
45	43.7	10.9	05	101.9	25.5	65	160.1	40.1	25	218.3	54.7	85	276.5	69.2
46	44.6	11.2	06	102.8	25.8	66	161.0	40.3	26	219.2	54.9	86	277.4	69.5
47	45.6	11.4	07	103.8	26.0	67	162.0	40.6	27	220.2	55.2	87	278.4	69.7
48	46.6	11.7	08	104.8	26.2	68	163.0	40.8	28	221.2	55.4	88	279.4	70.0
49	47.5	11.9	09	105.7	26.5	69	163.9	41.1	29	222.1	55.6	89	280.3	70.2
50	48.5	12.1	10	106.7	26.7	70	164.9	41.3	30	223.1	55.9	90	281.3	70.5
51	49.5	12.4	111	107.7	27.0	171	165.9	41.5	231	224.1	56.1	291	282.3	70.7
52	50.4	12.6	12	108.6	27.2	72	166.8	41.8	32	225.0	56.4	92	283.2	71.0
53	51.4	12.9	13	109.6	27.5	73	167.8	42.0	33	226.0	56.6	93	284.2	71.2
54	52.4	13.1	14	110.6	27.7	74	168.8	42.3	34	227.0	56.9	94	285.2	71.4
55	53.4	13.4	15	111.6	27.9	75	169.8	42.5	35	228.0	57.1	95	286.2	71.7
56	54.3	13.6	16	112.5	28.2	76	170.7	42.8	36	228.9	57.3	96	287.1	71.9
57	55.3	13.8	17	113.5	28.4	77	171.7	43.0	37	229.9	57.6	97	288.1	72.2
58	56.3	14.1	18	114.5	28.7	78	172.7	43.3	38	230.9	57.8	98	289.1	72.4
59	57.2	14.3	19	115.4	28.9	79	173.6	43.5	39	231.8	58.1	99	290.0	72.7
60	58.2	14.6	20	116.4	29.2	80	174.6	43.7	40	232.8	58.3	300	291.0	72.9
Dist.	Dep.	Lat.	Dist.	Dep.	Lat.	Dist.	Dep.	Lat.	Dist.	Dep.	Lat.	Dist.	Dep.	Lat.

E.N.E.¾E. E.S.E.¾E. W.N.W.¾W. W.S.W.¾W. [For 6¾ Points.

TABLE I.

Difference of Latitude and Departure for 1½ Points.

N.byE.½E.			N.byW.½W.			S.byE.½E			S.byW.½W.					
Dist.	Lat.	Dep.	Dist.	Lat.	Dep.	Dist.	Lat.	Dep.	Dist.	Lat.	Dep.	Dist.	Lat.	Dep.
1	01.0	00.3	61	58.4	17.7	121	115.8	35.1	181	173.2	52.5	241	230.6	70.0
2	01.9	00.6	62	59.3	18.0	22	116.7	35.4	82	174.2	52.8	42	231.6	70.2
3	02.9	00.9	63	60.3	18.3	23	117.7	35.7	83	175.1	53.1	43	232.5	70.5
4	03.8	01.2	64	61.2	18.6	24	118.7	36.0	84	176.1	53.4	44	233.5	70.8
5	04.8	01.5	65	62.2	18.9	25	119.6	36.3	85	177.0	53.7	45	234.5	71.1
6	05.7	01.7	66	63.2	19.2	26	120.6	36.6	86	178.0	54.0	46	235.4	71.4
7	06.7	02.0	67	64.1	19.4	27	121.5	36.9	87	178.9	54.3	47	236.4	71.7
8	07.7	02.3	68	65.1	19.7	28	122.5	37.2	88	179.9	54.6	48	237.3	72.0
9	08.6	02.6	69	66.0	20.0	29	123.4	37.4	89	180.9	54.9	49	238.3	72.3
10	09.6	02.9	70	67.0	20.3	30	124.4	37.7	90	181.8	55.2	50	239.2	72.6
11	10.5	03.2	71	67.9	20.6	131	125.4	38.0	191	182.8	55.4	251	240.2	72.9
12	11.5	03.5	72	68.9	20.9	32	126.3	38.3	92	183.7	55.7	52	241.1	73.2
13	12.4	03.8	73	69.9	21.2	33	127.3	38.6	93	184.7	56.0	53	242.1	73.4
14	13.4	04.1	74	70.8	21.5	34	128.2	38.9	94	185.6	56.3	54	243.1	73.7
15	14.4	04.4	75	71.8	21.8	35	129.2	39.2	95	186.6	56.6	55	244.0	74.0
16	15.3	04.6	76	72.7	22.1	36	130.1	39.5	96	187.6	56.9	56	245.0	74.3
17	16.3	04.9	77	73.7	22.4	37	131.1	39.8	97	188.5	57.2	57	245.9	74.6
18	17.2	05.2	78	74.6	22.6	38	132.1	40.1	98	189.5	57.5	58	246.9	74.9
19	18.2	05.5	79	75.6	22.9	39	133.0	40.3	99	190.4	57.8	59	247.8	75.2
20	19.1	05.8	80	76.6	23.2	40	134.0	40.6	200	191.4	58.1	60	248.8	75.5
21	20.1	06.1	81	77.5	23.5	141	134.9	40.9	201	192.3	58.3	261	249.8	75.8
22	21.1	06.4	82	78.5	23.8	42	135.9	41.2	02	193.3	58.6	62	250.7	76.1
23	22.0	06.7	83	79.4	24.1	43	136.8	41.5	03	194.3	58.9	63	251.7	76.3
24	23.0	07.0	84	80.4	24.4	44	137.8	41.8	04	195.2	59.2	64	252.6	76.6
25	23.9	07.3	85	81.3	24.7	45	138.8	42.1	05	196.2	59.5	65	253.6	76.9
26	24.9	07.5	86	82.3	25.0	46	139.7	42.4	06	197.1	59.8	66	254.5	77.2
27	25.8	07.8	87	83.3	25.3	47	140.7	42.7	07	198.1	60.1	67	255.5	77.5
28	26.8	08.1	88	84.2	25.5	48	141.6	43.0	08	199.0	60.4	68	256.5	77.8
29	27.8	08.4	89	85.2	25.8	49	142.6	43.3	09	200.0	60.7	69	257.4	78.1
30	28.7	08.7	90	86.1	26.1	50	143.5	43.5	10	201.0	61.0	70	258.4	78.4
31	29.7	09.0	91	87.1	26.4	151	144.5	43.8	211	201.9	61.3	271	259.3	78.7
32	30.6	09.3	92	88.0	26.7	52	145.5	44.1	12	202.9	61.5	72	260.3	79.0
33	31.6	09.6	93	89.0	27.0	53	146.4	44.4	13	203.8	61.8	73	261.2	79.2
34	32.5	09.9	94	90.0	27.3	54	147.4	44.7	14	204.8	62.1	74	262.2	79.5
35	33.5	10.2	95	90.9	27.6	55	148.3	45.0	15	205.7	62.4	75	263.2	79.8
36	34.4	10.5	96	91.9	27.9	56	149.3	45.3	16	206.7	62.7	76	264.1	80.1
37	35.4	10.7	97	92.8	28.2	57	150.2	45.6	17	207.7	63.0	77	265.1	80.4
38	36.4	11.0	98	93.8	28.4	58	151.2	45.9	18	208.6	63.3	78	266.0	80.7
39	37.3	11.3	99	94.7	28.7	59	152.2	46.2	19	209.6	63.6	79	267.0	81.0
40	38.3	11.6	100	95.7	29.0	60	153.1	46.4	20	210.5	63.9	80	267.9	81.3
41	39.2	11.9	101	96.7	29.3	161	154.1	46.7	221	211.5	64.2	281	268.9	81.6
42	40.2	12.2	02	97.6	29.6	62	155.0	47.0	22	212.4	64.4	82	269.9	81.9
43	41.1	12.5	03	98.6	29.9	63	156.0	47.3	23	213.4	64.7	83	270.8	82.2
44	42.1	12.8	04	99.5	30.2	64	156.9	47.6	24	214.4	65.0	84	271.8	82.4
45	43.1	13.1	05	100.5	30.5	65	157.9	47.9	25	215.3	65.3	85	272.7	82.7
46	44.0	13.4	06	101.4	30.8	66	158.9	48.2	26	216.3	65.6	86	273.7	83.0
47	45.0	13.6	07	102.4	31.1	67	159.8	48.5	27	217.2	65.9	87	274.6	83.3
48	45.9	13.9	08	103.3	31.4	68	160.8	48.8	28	218.2	66.2	88	275.6	83.6
49	46.9	14.2	09	104.3	31.6	69	161.7	49.1	29	219.1	66.5	89	276.6	83.9
50	47.8	14.5	10	105.3	31.9	70	162.7	49.3	30	220.1	66.8	90	277.5	84.2
51	48.8	14.8	111	106.2	32.2	171	163.6	49.6	231	221.1	67.1	291	278.5	84.5
52	49.8	15.1	12	107.2	32.5	72	164.6	49.9	32	222.0	67.3	92	279.4	84.8
53	50.7	15.4	13	108.1	32.8	73	165.6	50.2	33	223.0	67.6	93	280.4	85.1
54	51.7	15.7	14	109.1	33.1	74	166.5	50.5	34	223.9	67.9	94	281.3	85.3
55	52.6	16.0	15	110.0	33.4	75	167.5	50.8	35	224.9	68.2	95	282.3	85.6
56	53.6	16.3	16	111.0	33.7	76	168.4	51.1	36	225.8	68.5	96	283.3	85.9
57	54.5	16.5	17	112.0	34.0	77	169.4	51.4	37	226.8	68.8	97	284.2	86.2
58	55.5	16.8	18	112.9	34.3	78	170.3	51.7	38	227.8	69.1	98	285.2	86.5
59	56.5	17.1	19	113.9	34.5	79	171.3	52.0	39	228.7	69.4	99	286.1	86.8
60	57.4	17.4	20	114.8	34.8	80	172.2	52.3	40	229.7	69.7	300	287.1	87.1
Dis.	Dep.	Lat.	Dist.	Dep.	Lat.	Dist.	Dep.	Lat.	Dist.	Dep.	Lat.	Dist.	Dep.	Lat.
E.N.E.½E.			E.S.E.½E.			W.N.W.½W.			W.S.W.½W.			[For 6½ Points.		

TABLE I.

Difference of Latitude and Departure for 1¾ Points.

	N.by E.¾E.			N.by W.¾W.			S.by E.¾E.			S.by W.¾W.				
Dist.	Lat.	Dep.	Dist.	Lat.	Dep.	Dist.	Lat.	Dep.	Dist.	Lat.	Dep.	Dist.	Lat.	Dep.
1	00.9	00.3	61	57.4	20.6	121	113.9	40.8	181	170.4	61.0	241	226.9	81.2
2	01.9	00.7	62	58.4	20.9	22	114.9	41.1	82	171.4	61.3	42	227.9	81.5
3	02.8	01.0	63	59.3	21.2	23	115.8	41.4	83	172.3	61.7	43	228.8	81.9
4	03.8	01.3	64	60.3	21.6	24	116.8	41.8	84	173.2	62.0	44	229.7	82.2
5	04.7	01.7	65	61.2	21.9	25	117.7	42.1	85	174.2	62.3	45	230.7	82.5
6	05.6	02.0	66	62.1	22.2	26	118.6	42.4	86	175.1	62.7	46	231.6	82.9
7	06.6	02.4	67	63.1	22.6	27	119.6	42.8	87	176.1	63.0	47	232.6	83.2
8	07.5	02.7	68	64.0	22.9	28	120.5	43.1	88	177.0	63.3	48	233.5	83.5
9	08.5	03.0	69	65.0	23.2	29	121.5	43.5	89	178.0	63.7	49	234.4	83.9
10	09.4	03.4	70	65.9	23.6	30	122.4	43.8	90	178.9	64.0	50	235.4	84.2
11	10.4	03.7	71	66.8	23.9	131	123.3	44.1	191	179.8	64.3	251	236.3	84 6
12	11.3	04.0	72	67.8	24.3	32	124.3	44.5	92	180.8	64.7	52	237.3	84.9
13	12.2	04.4	73	68.7	24.6	33	125.2	44.8	93	181.7	65.0	53	238.2	85.2
14	13.2	04.7	74	69.7	24.9	34	126.2	45.1	94	182.7	65.4	54	239.2	85.6
15	14.1	05.1	75	70.6	25.3	35	127.1	45.5	95	183.6	65.7	55	240.1	85.9
16	15.1	05.4	76	71.6	25.6	36	128.0	45.8	96	184.5	66.0	56	241.0	86.2
17	16.0	05.7	77	72.5	25.9	37	129.0	46.2	97	185.5	66.4	57	242.0	86.6
18	16.9	06.1	78	73.4	26.3	38	129.9	46.5	98	186.4	66.7	58	242.9	86.9
19	17.9	06.4	79	74.4	26.6	39	130.9	46.8	99	187.4	67.0	59	243.9	87.3
20	18.8	06.7	80	75.3	27.0	40	131.8	47.2	200	188.3	67.4	60	244.8	87.6
21	19.8	07.1	81	76.3	27.3	141	132.8	47.5	201	189.3	67.7	261	245.7	87.9
22	20.7	07.4	82	77.2	27.6	42	133.7	47.8	02	190.2	68.1	62	246.7	88.3
23	21.7	07.7	83	78.1	28.0	43	134.6	48.2	03	191.1	68.4	63	247.6	88.6
24	22.6	08.1	84	79.1	28.3	44	135.6	48.5	04	192.1	68.7	64	248.6	88.9
25	23.5	08.4	85	80.0	28.6	45	136.5	48.8	05	193.0	69.1	65	249.5	89.3
26	24.5	08.8	86	81.0	29.0	46	137.5	49.2	06	194.0	69.4	66	250.5	89.6
27	25.4	09.1	87	81.9	29.3	47	138.4	49.5	07	194.9	69.7	67	251.4	89.9
28	26.4	09.4	88	82.9	29.6	48	139.3	49.9	08	195.8	70.1	68	252.3	90.3
29	27.3	09.8	89	83.8	30.0	49	140.3	50.2	09	196.8	70.4	69	253.3	90.6
30	28.2	10.1	90	84.7	30.3	50	141.2	50.5	10	197.7	70.7	70	254.2	91.0
31	29.2	10.4	91	85.7	30.7	151	142.2	50.9	211	198.7	71.1	271	255.2	91.3
32	30.1	10.8	92	86.6	31.0	52	143.1	51.2	12	199.6	71.4	72	256.1	91.6
33	31.1	11.1	93	87.6	31.3	53	144.1	51.5	13	200.5	71.8	73	257.0	92.0
34	32.0	11.5	94	88.5	31.7	54	145.0	51.9	14	201.5	72.1	74	258.0	92.3
35	33.0	11.8	95	89.4	32.0	55	145.9	52.2	15	202.4	72.4	75	258.9	92.6
36	33.9	12.1	96	90.4	32.3	56	146.9	52.6	16	203.4	72.8	76	259.9	93.0
37	34.8	12.5	97	91.3	32.7	57	147.8	52.9	17	204.3	73.1	77	260.8	93.3
38	35.8	12.8	98	92.3	33.0	58	148.8	53.2	18	205.3	73.4	78	261.7	93.7
39	36.7	13.1	99	93.2	33.4	59	149.7	53.6	19	206.2	73.8	79	262.7	94.0
40	37.7	13.5	100	94.2	33.7	60	150.6	53.9	20	207.1	74.1	80	263.6	94.3
41	38.6	13.8	101	95.1	34.0	161	151.6	54.2	221	208.1	74.5	281	264.6	94.7
42	39.5	14.1	02	96.0	34.4	62	152.5	54.6	22	209.0	74.8	82	265.5	95.0
43	40.5	14.5	03	97.0	34.7	63	153.5	54.9	23	210.0	75.1	83	266.5	95.3
44	41.4	14.8	04	97.9	35.0	64	154.4	55.2	24	210.9	75.5	84	267.4	95.7
45	42.4	15.2	05	98.9	35.4	65	155.4	55.6	25	211.8	75.8	85	268.3	96.0
46	43.3	15.5	06	99.8	35.7	66	156.3	55.9	26	212.8	76.1	86	269.3	96.4
47	44.3	15.8	07	100.7	36.0	67	157.2	56.3	27	213.7	76.5	87	270.2	96.7
48	45.2	16.2	08	101.7	36.4	68	158.2	56.6	28	214.7	76.8	88	271.2	97.0
49	46.1	16.5	09	102.6	36.7	69	159.1	56.9	29	215.6	77.1	89	272.1	97.4
50	47.1	16.8	10	103.6	37.1	70	160.1	57.3	30	216.6	77.5	90	273.0	97.7
51	48.0	17.2	111	104.5	37.4	171	161.0	57.6	231	217.5	77.8	291	274.0	98.0
52	49.0	17.5	12	105.5	37.7	72	161.9	57.9	32	218.4	78.2	92	274.9	98.4
53	49.9	17.9	13	106.4	38.1	73	162.9	58.3	33	219.4	78.5	93	275.9	98.7
54	50.8	18.2	14	107.3	38.4	74	163.8	58.6	34	220.3	78.8	94	276.8	99.0
55	51.8	18.5	15	108.3	38.7	75	164.8	59.0	35	221.3	79.2	95	277.8	99.4
56	52.7	18.9	16	109.2	39.1	76	165.7	59.3	36	222.2	79.5	96	278.7	99.7
57	53.7	19.2	17	110.2	39.4	77	166.7	59.6	37	223.1	79.8	97	279.6	100.1
58	54.6	19.5	18	111.1	39.8	78	167.6	60.0	38	224.1	80.2	98	280.6	100.4
59	55.6	19.9	19	112.0	40.1	79	168.5	60.3	39	225.0	80.5	99	281.5	100.7
60	56.5	20.2	20	113.0	40.4	80	169.5	60.6	40	226.0	80.9	300	282.5	101.1
Dist.	Dep.	Lat.	Dist.	Dep.	Lat.	Dist.	Dep.	Lat.	Dist.	Dep.	Lat.	Dist.	Dep.	Lat.
	E.N.E.¼E.			E.S.E.¼E.			W.N.W.¼W.			W.S.W.¼W.			[For 6¼ Points.	

TABLE I.

Difference of Latitude and Departure for 2 Points.

	N.N.E.			N.N.W.			S.S.E.			S.S.W.				
Dist.	Lat.	Dep.	Dist.	Lat.	Dep.	Dist.	Lat.	Dep.	Dist.	Lat.	Dep.	Dist.	Lat.	Dep.
1	00.9	00.4	61	56.4	23.3	121	111.8	46.3	181	167.2	69.3	241	222.7	92.2
2	01.8	00.8	62	57.3	23.7	22	112.7	46.7	82	168.1	69.6	42	223.6	92.6
3	02.8	01.1	63	58.2	24.1	23	113.6	47.1	83	169.1	70.0	43	224.5	93.0
4	03.7	01.5	64	59.1	24.5	24	114.6	47.5	84	170.0	70.4	44	225.4	93.4
5	04.6	01.9	65	60.1	24.9	25	115.5	47.8	85	170.9	70.8	45	226.4	93.8
6	05.5	02.3	66	61.0	25.3	26	116.4	48.2	86	171.8	71.2	46	227.3	94.1
7	06.5	02.7	67	61.9	25.6	27	117.3	48.6	87	172.8	71.6	47	228.2	94.5
8	07.4	03.1	68	62.8	26.0	28	118.3	49.0	88	173.7	71.9	48	229.1	94.9
9	08.3	03.4	69	63.7	26.4	29	119.2	49.4	89	174.6	72.3	49	230.0	95.3
10	09.2	03.8	70	64.7	26.8	30	120.1	49.7	90	175.5	72.7	50	231.0	95.7
11	10.2	04.2	71	65.6	27.2	131	121.0	50.1	191	176.5	73.1	251	231.9	96.1
12	11.1	04.6	72	66.5	27.6	32	122.0	50.5	92	177.4	73.5	52	232.8	96.4
13	12.0	05.0	73	67.4	27.9	33	122.9	50.9	93	178.3	73.9	53	233.7	96.8
14	12.9	05.4	74	68.4	28.3	34	123.8	51.3	94	179.2	74.2	54	234.7	97.2
15	13.9	05.7	75	69.3	28.7	35	124.7	51.7	95	180.2	74.6	55	235.6	97.6
16	14.8	06.1	76	70.2	29.1	36	125.6	52.0	96	181.1	75.0	56	236.5	98.0
17	15.7	06.5	77	71.1	29.5	37	126.6	52.4	97	182.0	75.4	57	237.4	98.3
18	16.6	06.9	78	72.1	29.8	38	127.5	52.8	98	182.9	75.8	58	238.4	98.7
19	17.6	07.3	79	73.0	30.2	39	128.4	53.2	99	183.9	76.2	59	239.3	99.1
20	18.5	07.7	80	73.9	30.6	40	129.3	53.6	200	184.8	76.5	60	240.2	99.5
21	19.4	08.0	81	74.8	31.0	141	130.3	54.0	201	185.7	76.9	261	241.1	99.9
22	20.3	08.4	82	75.8	31.4	42	131.2	54.3	02	186.6	77.3	62	242.1	100.3
23	21.2	08.8	83	76.7	31.8	43	132.1	54.7	03	187.5	77.7	63	243.0	100.6
24	22.2	09.2	84	77.6	32.1	44	133.0	55.1	04	188.5	78.1	64	243.9	101.0
25	23.1	09.6	85	78.5	32.5	45	134.0	55.5	05	189.4	78.5	65	244.8	101.4
26	24.0	09.9	86	79.5	32.9	46	134.9	55.9	06	190.3	78.8	66	245.8	101.8
27	24.9	10.3	87	80.4	33.3	47	135.8	56.3	07	191.2	79.2	67	246.7	102.2
28	25.9	10.7	88	81.3	33.7	48	136.7	56.6	08	192.2	79.6	68	247.6	102.6
29	26.8	11.1	89	82.2	34.1	49	137.7	57.0	09	193.1	80.0	69	248.5	102.9
30	27.7	11.5	90	83.1	34.4	50	138.6	57.4	10	194.0	80.4	70	249.4	103.3
31	28.6	11.9	91	84.1	34.8	151	139.5	57.8	211	194.9	80.7	271	250.4	103.7
32	29.6	12.2	92	85.0	35.2	52	140.4	58.2	12	195.9	81.1	72	251.3	104.1
33	30.5	12.6	93	85.9	35.6	53	141.4	58.6	13	196.8	81.5	73	252.2	104.5
34	31.4	13.0	94	86.8	36.0	54	142.3	58.9	14	197.7	81.9	74	253.1	104.9
35	32.3	13.4	95	87.8	36.4	55	143.2	59.3	15	198.6	82.3	75	254.1	105.2
36	33.3	13.8	96	88.7	36.7	56	144.1	59.7	16	199.6	82.7	76	255.0	105.6
37	34.2	14.2	97	89.6	37.1	57	145.0	60.1	17	200.5	83.0	77	255.9	106.0
38	35.1	14.5	98	90.5	37.5	58	146.0	60.5	18	201.4	83.4	78	256.8	106.4
39	36.0	14.9	99	91.5	37.9	59	146.9	60.8	19	202.3	83.8	79	257.8	106.8
40	37.0	15.3	100	92.4	38.3	60	147.8	61.2	20	203.3	84.2	80	258.7	107.2
41	37.9	15.7	101	93.3	38.7	161	148.7	61.6	221	204.2	84.6	281	259.6	107.5
42	38.8	16.1	02	94.2	39.0	62	149.7	62.0	22	205.1	85.0	82	260.5	107.9
43	39.7	16.5	03	95.2	39.4	63	150.6	62.4	23	206.0	85.3	83	261.5	108.3
44	40.7	16.8	04	96.1	39.8	64	151.5	62.8	24	206.9	85.7	84	262.4	108.7
45	41.6	17.2	05	97.0	40.2	65	152.4	63.1	25	207.9	86.1	85	263.3	109.1
46	42.5	17.6	06	97.9	40.6	66	153.4	63.5	26	208.8	86.5	86	264.2	109.4
47	43.4	18.0	07	98.9	40.9	67	154.3	63.9	27	209.7	86.9	87	265.2	109.8
48	44.3	18.4	08	99.8	41.3	68	155.2	64.3	28	210.6	87.3	88	266.1	110.2
49	45.3	18.8	09	100.7	41.7	69	156.1	64.7	29	211.6	87.6	89	267.0	110.6
50	46.2	19.1	10	101.6	42.1	70	157.1	65.1	30	212.5	88.0	90	267.9	111.0
51	47.1	19.5	111	102.6	42.5	171	158.0	65.4	231	213.4	88.4	291	268.8	111.4
52	48.0	19.9	12	103.5	42.9	72	158.9	65.8	32	214.3	88.8	92	269.8	111.7
53	49.0	20.3	13	104.4	43.2	73	159.8	66.2	33	215.3	89.2	93	270.7	112.1
54	49.9	20.7	14	105.3	43.6	74	160.8	66.6	34	216.2	89.5	94	271.6	112.5
55	50.8	21.0	15	106.2	44.0	75	161.7	67.0	35	217.1	89.9	95	272.5	112.9
56	51.7	21.4	16	107.2	44.4	76	162.6	67.4	36	218.0	90.3	96	273.5	113.3
57	52.7	21.8	17	108.1	44.8	77	163.5	67.7	37	219.0	90.7	97	274.4	113.7
58	53.6	22.2	18	109.0	45.2	78	164.5	68.1	38	219.9	91.1	98	275.3	114.0
59	54.5	22.6	19	109.9	45.5	79	165.4	68.5	39	220.8	91.5	99	276.2	114.4
60	55.4	23.0	20	110.9	45.9	80	166.3	68.9	40	221.7	91.8	300	277.2	114.8
Dist.	Dep.	Lat.	Dist.	Dep.	Lat.	Dist.	Dep.	Lat.	Dist.	Dep.	Lat.	Dist.	Dep.	Lat.
	E.N.E.			E.S.E.			W.N.W.			W.S.W.			[For 6 Points.	

TABLE I.

Difference of Latitude and Departure for 2¼ Points.

N.N.E.¼E.			N.N.W.¼W.						S.S.E.¼E.			S.S.W.¼W.		
Dist.	Lat.	Dep.	Dist.	Lat.	Dep.	Dist.	Lat.	Dep.	Dist.	Lat.	Dep.	Dist.	Lat.	Dep.
1	00.9	00.4	61	55.1	26.1	121	109.4	51.7	181	163.6	77.4	241	217.9	103.0
2	01.8	00.9	62	56.0	26.5	22	110.3	52.2	82	164.5	77.8	42	218.8	103.5
3	02.7	01.3	63	57.0	26.9	23	111.2	52.6	83	165.4	78.2	43	219.7	103.9
4	03.6	01.7	64	57.9	27.4	24	112.1	53.0	84	166.3	78.7	44	220.6	104.3
5	04.5	02.1	65	58.8	27.8	25	113.0	53.4	85	167.2	79.1	45	221.5	104.8
6	05.4	02.6	66	59.7	28.2	26	113.9	53.9	86	168.1	79.5	46	222.4	105.2
7	06.3	03.0	67	60.6	28.6	27	114.8	54.3	87	169.0	80.0	47	223.3	105.6
8	07.2	03.4	68	61.5	29.1	28	115.7	54.7	88	169.9	80.4	48	224.2	106.0
9	08.1	03.8	69	62.4	29.5	29	116.6	55.2	89	170.9	80.8	49	225.1	106.5
10	09.0	04.3	70	63.3	29.9	30	117.5	55.6	90	171.8	81.2	50	226.0	106.9
11	09.9	04.7	71	64.2	30.4	131	118.4	56.0	191	172.7	81.7	251	226.9	107.3
12	10.8	05.1	72	65.1	30.8	32	119.3	56.4	92	173.6	82.1	52	227.8	107.7
13	11.8	05.6	73	66.0	31.2	33	120.2	56.9	93	174.5	82.5	53	228.7	108.2
14	12.7	06.0	74	66.9	31.6	34	121.1	57.3	94	175.4	82.9	54	229.6	108.6
15	13.6	06.4	75	67.8	32.1	35	122.0	57.7	95	176.3	83.4	55	230.5	109.0
16	14.5	06.8	76	68.7	32.5	36	122.9	58.1	96	177.2	83.8	56	231.4	109.5
17	15.4	07.3	77	69.6	32.9	37	123.8	58.6	97	178.1	84.2	57	232.3	109.9
18	16.3	07.7	78	70.5	33.3	38	124.8	59.0	98	179.0	84.7	58	233.2	110.3
19	17.2	08.1	79	71.4	33.8	39	125.7	59.4	99	179.9	85.1	59	234.1	110.7
20	18.1	08.6	80	72.3	34.2	40	126.6	59.9	200	180.8	85.5	60	235.0	111.2
21	19.0	09.0	81	73.2	34.6	141	127.5	60.3	201	181.7	85.9	261	235.9	111.6
22	19.9	09.4	82	74.1	35.1	42	128.4	60.7	02	182.6	86.4	62	236.8	112.0
23	20.8	09.8	83	75.0	35.5	43	129.3	61.1	03	183.5	86.8	63	237.7	112.4
24	21.7	10.3	84	75.9	35.9	44	130.2	61.6	04	184.4	87.2	64	238.7	112.9
25	22.6	10.7	85	76.8	36.3	45	131.1	62.0	05	185.3	87.6	65	239.6	113.3
26	23.5	11.1	86	77.7	36.8	46	132.0	62.4	06	186.2	88.1	66	240.5	113.7
27	24.4	11.5	87	78.6	37.2	47	132.9	62.9	07	187.1	88.5	67	241.4	114.2
28	25.3	12.0	88	79.6	37.6	48	133.8	63.3	08	188.0	88.9	68	242.3	114.6
29	26.2	12.4	89	80.5	38.1	49	134.7	63.7	09	188.9	89.4	69	243.2	115.0
30	27.1	12.8	90	81.4	38.5	50	135.6	64.1	10	189.8	89.8	70	244.1	115.4
31	28.0	13.3	91	82.3	38.9	151	136.5	64.6	211	190.7	90.2	271	245.0	115.9
32	28.9	13.7	92	83.2	39.3	52	137.4	65.0	12	191.6	90.6	72	245.9	116.3
33	29.8	14.1	93	84.1	39.8	53	138.3	65.4	13	192.5	91.1	73	246.8	116.7
34	30.7	14.5	94	85.0	40.2	54	139.2	65.8	14	193.5	91.5	74	247.7	117.2
35	31.6	15.0	95	85.9	40.6	55	140.1	66.3	15	194.4	91.9	75	248.6	117.6
36	32.5	15.4	96	86.8	41.0	56	141.0	66.7	16	195.3	92.4	76	249.5	118.0
37	33.4	15.8	97	87.7	41.5	57	141.9	67.1	17	196.2	92.8	77	250.4	118.4
38	34.4	16.2	98	88.6	41.9	58	142.8	67.6	18	197.1	93.2	78	251.3	118.9
39	35.3	16.7	99	89.5	42.3	59	143.7	68.0	19	198.0	93.6	79	252.2	119.3
40	36.2	17.1	100	90.4	42.8	60	144.6	68.4	20	198.9	94.1	80	253.1	119.7
41	37.1	17.5	101	91.3	43.2	161	145.5	68.8	221	199.8	94.5	281	254.0	120.1
42	38.0	18.0	02	92.2	43.6	62	146.4	69.3	22	200.7	94.9	82	254.9	120.6
43	38.9	18.4	03	93.1	44.0	63	147.4	69.7	23	201.6	95.3	83	255.8	121.0
44	39.8	18.8	04	94.0	44.5	64	148.3	70.1	24	202.5	95.8	84	256.7	121.4
45	40.7	19.2	05	94.9	44.9	65	149.2	70.5	25	203.4	96.2	85	257.6	121.9
46	41.6	19.7	06	95.8	45.3	66	150.1	71.0	26	204.3	96.6	86	258.5	122.3
47	42.5	20.1	07	96.7	45.7	67	151.0	71.4	27	205.2	97.1	87	259.4	122.7
48	43.4	20.5	08	97.6	46.2	68	151.9	71.8	28	206.1	97.5	88	260.3	123.1
49	44.3	21.0	09	98.5	46.6	69	152.8	72.3	29	207.0	97.9	89	261.3	123.6
50	45.2	21.4	10	99.4	47.0	70	153.7	72.7	30	207.9	98.3	90	262.2	124.0
51	46.1	21.8	111	100.3	47.5	171	154.6	73.1	231	208.8	98.8	291	263.1	124.4
52	47.0	22.2	12	101.2	47.9	72	155.5	73.5	32	209.7	99.2	92	264.0	124.8
53	47.9	22.7	13	102.2	48.3	73	156.4	74.0	33	210.6	99.6	93	264.9	125.3
54	48.8	23.1	14	103.1	48.7	74	157.3	74.4	34	211.5	100.0	94	265.8	125.7
55	49.7	23.5	15	104.0	49.2	75	158.2	74.8	35	212.4	100.5	95	266.7	126.1
56	50.6	23.9	16	104.9	49.6	76	159.1	75.2	36	213.3	100.9	96	267.6	126.6
57	51.5	24.4	17	105.8	50.0	77	160.0	75.7	37	214.2	101.3	97	268.5	127.0
58	52.4	24.8	18	106.7	50.5	78	160.9	76.1	38	215.1	101.8	98	269.4	127.4
59	53.3	25.2	19	107.6	50.9	79	161.8	76.5	39	216.1	102.2	99	270.3	127.8
60	54.2	25.7	20	108.5	51.3	80	162.7	77.0	40	217.0	102.6	300	271.2	128.3
Dist.	Dep.	Lat.	Dist.	Dep.	Lat.	Dist.	Dep.	Lat.	Dist.	Dep.	Lat.	Dist.	Dep.	Lat.
N.E.byE.¾E.			S.E.byE.¾E.			N.W.byW.¾W.			S.W.byW.¾W.			[For 5¾ Points.		

TABLE I.

Difference of Latitude and Departure for 2½ Points.

N.N.E.½E. N.N.W.½W. S.S.E.½E. S.S.W.½W.

Dist.	Lat.	Dep.	Dist.	Lat.	Dep.	Dist.	Lat.	Dep.	Dist.	Lat.	Dep.	Dist.	Lat.	Dep.
1	00.9	00.5	61	53.8	28.8	121	106.7	57.0	181	159.6	85.3	241	212.5	113.6
2	01.8	00.9	62	54.7	29.2	22	107.6	57.5	82	160.5	85.8	42	213.4	114.1
3	02.6	01.4	63	55.6	29.7	23	108.5	58.0	83	161.4	86.3	43	214.3	114.5
4	03.5	01.9	64	56.4	30.2	24	109.4	58.5	84	162.3	86.7	44	215.2	115.0
5	04.4	02.4	65	57.3	30.6	25	110.2	58.9	85	163.2	87.2	45	216.1	115.5
6	05.3	02.8	66	58.2	31.1	26	111.1	59.4	86	164.0	87.7	46	217.0	116.0
7	06.2	03.3	67	59.1	31.6	27	112.0	59.9	87	164.9	88.2	47	217.8	116.4
8	07.1	03.8	68	60.0	32.1	28	112.9	60.3	88	165.8	88.6	48	218.7	116.9
9	07.9	04.2	69	60.9	32.5	29	113.8	60.8	89	166.7	89.1	49	219.6	117.4
10	08.8	04.7	70	61.7	33.0	30	114.6	61.3	90	167.6	89.6	50	220.5	117.8
11	09.7	05.2	71	62.6	33.5	131	115.5	61.8	191	168.4	90.0	251	221.4	118.3
12	10.6	05.7	72	63.5	33.9	32	116.4	62.2	92	169.3	90.5	52	222.2	118.8
13	11.5	06.1	73	64.4	34.4	33	117.3	62.7	93	170.2	91.0	53	223.1	119.3
14	12.3	06.6	74	65.3	34.9	34	118.2	63.2	94	171.1	91.5	54	224.0	119.7
15	13.2	07.1	75	66.1	35.4	35	119.1	63.6	95	172.0	91.9	55	224.9	120.2
16	14.1	07.5	76	67.0	35.8	36	119.9	64.1	96	172.9	92.4	56	225.8	120.7
17	15.0	08.0	77	67.9	36.3	37	120.8	64.6	97	173.7	92.9	57	226.7	121.1
18	15.9	08.5	78	68.8	36.8	38	121.7	65.1	98	174.6	93.3	58	227.5	121.6
19	16.8	09.0	79	69.7	37.2	39	122.6	65.5	99	175.5	93.8	59	228.4	122.1
20	17.6	09.4	80	70.6	37.7	40	123.5	66.0	200	176.4	94.3	60	229.3	122.6
21	18.5	09.9	81	71.4	38.2	141	124.4	66.5	201	177.3	94.8	261	230.2	123.0
22	19.4	10.4	82	72.3	38.7	42	125.2	66.9	02	178.1	95.2	62	231.1	123.5
23	20.3	10.8	83	73.2	39.1	43	126.1	67.4	03	179.0	95.7	63	231.9	124.0
24	21.2	11.3	84	74.1	39.6	44	127.0	67.9	04	179.9	96.2	64	232.8	124.4
25	22.0	11.8	85	75.0	40.1	45	127.9	68.4	05	180.8	96.6	65	233.7	124.9
26	22.9	12.3	86	75.8	40.5	46	128.8	68.8	06	181.7	97.1	66	234.6	125.4
27	23.8	12.7	87	76.7	41.0	47	129.6	69.3	07	182.6	97.6	67	235.5	125.9
28	24.7	13.2	88	77.6	41.5	48	130.5	69.8	08	183.4	98.1	68	236.4	126.3
29	25.6	13.7	89	78.5	42.0	49	131.4	70.2	09	184.3	98.5	69	237.2	126.8
30	26.5	14.1	90	79.4	42.4	50	132.3	70.7	10	185.2	99.0	70	238.1	127.3
31	27.3	14.6	91	80.3	42.9	151	133.2	71.2	211	186.1	99.5	271	239.0	127.7
32	28.2	15.1	92	81.1	43.4	52	134.1	71.7	12	187.0	99.9	72	239.9	128.2
33	29.1	15.6	93	82.0	43.8	53	134.9	72.1	13	187.8	100.4	73	240.8	128.7
34	30.0	16.0	94	82.9	44.3	54	135.8	72.6	14	188.7	100.9	74	241.6	129.2
35	30.9	16.5	95	83.8	44.8	55	136.7	73.1	15	189.6	101.4	75	242.5	129.6
36	31.7	17.0	96	84.7	45.3	56	137.6	73.5	16	190.5	101.8	76	243.4	130.1
37	32.6	17.4	97	85.5	45.7	57	138.5	74.0	17	191.4	102.3	77	244.3	130.6
38	33.5	17.9	98	86.4	46.2	58	139.3	74.5	18	192.3	102.8	78	245.2	131.0
39	34.4	18.4	99	87.3	46.7	59	140.2	75.0	19	193.1	103.2	79	246.1	131.5
40	35.3	18.9	100	88.2	47.1	60	141.1	75.4	20	194.0	103.7	80	246.9	132.0
41	36.2	19.3	101	89.1	47.6	161	142.0	75.9	221	194.9	104.2	281	247.8	132.5
42	37.0	19.8	02	90.0	48.1	62	142.9	76.4	22	195.8	104.7	82	248.7	132.9
43	37.9	20.3	03	90.8	48.6	63	143.8	76.8	23	196.7	105.1	83	249.6	133.4
44	38.8	20.7	04	91.7	49.0	64	144.6	77.3	24	197.6	105.6	84	250.5	133.9
45	39.7	21.2	05	92.6	49.5	65	145.5	77.8	25	198.4	106.1	85	251.3	134.3
46	40.6	21.7	06	93.5	50.0	66	146.4	78.3	26	199.3	106.5	86	252.2	134.8
47	41.5	22.2	07	94.4	50.4	67	147.3	78.7	27	200.2	107.0	87	253.1	135.3
48	42.3	22.6	08	95.2	50.9	68	148.2	79.2	28	201.1	107.5	88	254.0	135.8
49	43.2	23.1	09	96.1	51.4	69	149.0	79.7	29	202.0	107.9	89	254.9	136.2
50	44.1	23.6	10	97.0	51.9	70	149.9	80.1	30	202.8	108.4	90	255.8	136.7
51	45.0	24.0	111	97.9	52.3	171	150.8	80.6	231	203.7	108.9	291	256.6	137.2
52	45.9	24.5	12	98.8	52.8	72	151.7	81.1	32	204.6	109.4	92	257.5	137.6
53	46.7	25.0	13	99.7	53.3	73	152.6	81.6	33	205.5	109.8	93	258.4	138.1
54	47.6	25.5	14	100.5	53.7	74	153.5	82.0	34	206.4	110.3	94	259.3	138.6
55	48.5	25.9	15	101.4	54.2	75	154.3	82.5	35	207.3	110.8	95	260.2	139.1
56	49.4	26.4	16	102.3	54.7	76	155.2	83.0	36	208.1	111.2	96	261.0	139.5
57	50.3	26.9	17	103.2	55.2	77	156.1	83.4	37	209.0	111.7	97	261.9	140.0
58	51.2	27.3	18	104.1	55.6	78	157.0	83.9	38	209.9	112.2	98	262.8	140.5
59	52.0	27.8	19	104.9	56.1	79	157.9	84.4	39	210.8	112.7	99	263.7	140.9
60	52.9	28.3	20	105.8	56.6	80	158.7	84.9	40	211.7	113.1	300	264.6	141.4
Dist.	Dep.	Lat.	Dist.	Dep.	Lat.	Dist.	Dep.	Lat.	Dist.	Dep.	Lat.	Dist.	Dep.	Lat.

N.E.byE.½E. S.E.byE.½E. N.W.byW.½W. S.W.byW.½W. [For 5½ Points.

TABLE I.

Difference of Latitude and Departure for 2¾ Points.

N.N.E.¾E.			N.N.W.¾W.			S.S.E.¾E.			S.S.W.¾W.					
Dist.	Lat.	Dep.	Dist.	Lat.	Dep.	Dist.	Lat.	Dep.	Dist.	Lat.	Dep.	Dist.	Lat.	Dep.
1	00.9	00.5	61	52.3	31.4	121	103.8	62.2	181	155.2	93.1	241	206.7	123.9
2	01.7	01.0	62	53.2	31.9	22	104.6	62.7	82	156.1	93.6	42	207.6	124.4
3	02.6	01.5	63	54.0	32.4	23	105.5	63.2	83	157.0	94.1	43	208.4	124.9
4	03.4	02.1	64	54.9	32.9	24	106.4	63.7	84	157.8	94.6	44	209.3	125.4
5	04.3	02.6	65	55.8	33.4	25	107.2	64.3	85	158.7	95.1	45	210.1	126.0
6	05.1	03.1	66	56.6	33.9	26	108.1	64.8	86	159.5	95.6	46	211.0	126.5
7	06.0	03.6	67	57.5	34.4	27	108.9	65.3	87	160.4	96.1	47	211.9	127.0
8	06.9	04.1	68	58.3	35.0	28	109.8	65.8	88	161.3	96.7	48	212.7	127.5
9	07.7	04.6	69	59.2	35.5	29	110.6	66.3	89	162.1	97.2	49	213.6	128.0
10	08.6	05.1	70	60.0	36.0	30	111.5	66.8	90	163.0	97.7	50	214.4	128.5
11	09.4	05.7	71	60.9	36.5	131	112.4	67.3	191	163.8	98.2	251	215.3	129.0
12	10.3	06.2	72	61.8	37.0	32	113.2	67.9	92	164.7	98.7	52	216.1	129.6
13	11.2	06.7	73	62.6	37.5	33	114.1	68.4	93	165.5	99.2	53	217.0	130.1
14	12.0	07.2	74	63.5	38.0	34	114.9	68.9	94	166.4	99.7	54	217.9	130.6
15	12.9	07.7	75	64.3	38.6	35	115.8	69.4	95	167.3	100.3	55	218.7	131.1
16	13.7	08.2	76	65.2	39.1	36	116.7	69.9	96	168.1	100.8	56	219.6	131.6
17	14.6	08.7	77	66.0	39.6	37	117.5	70.4	97	169.0	101.3	57	220.4	132.1
18	15.4	09.3	78	66.9	40.1	38	118.4	70.9	98	169.8	101.8	58	221.3	132.6
19	16.3	09.8	79	67.8	40.6	39	119.2	71.5	99	170.7	102.3	59	222.2	133.2
20	17.2	10.3	80	68.6	41.1	40	120.1	72.0	200	171.5	102.8	60	223.0	133.7
21	18.0	10.8	81	69.5	41.6	141	120.9	72.5	201	172.4	103.3	261	223.9	134.2
22	18.9	11.3	82	70.3	42.2	42	121.8	73.0	02	173.3	103.8	62	224.7	134.7
23	19.7	11.8	83	71.2	42.7	43	122.7	73.5	03	174.1	104.4	63	225.6	135.2
24	20.6	12.3	84	72.0	43.2	44	123.5	74.0	04	175.0	104.9	64	226.4	135.7
25	21.4	12.9	85	72.9	43.7	45	124.4	74.5	05	175.8	105.4	65	227.3	136.2
26	22.3	13.4	86	73.8	44.2	46	125.2	75.1	06	176.7	105.9	66	228.2	136.8
27	23.2	13.9	87	74.6	44.7	47	126.1	75.6	07	177.5	106.4	67	229.0	137.3
28	24.0	14.4	88	75.5	45.2	48	126.9	76.1	08	178.4	106.9	68	229.9	137.8
29	24.9	14.9	89	76.3	45.8	49	127.8	76.6	09	179.3	107.4	69	230.7	138.3
30	25.7	15.4	90	77.2	46.3	50	128.7	77.1	10	180.1	108.0	70	231.6	138.8
31	26.6	15.9	91	78.1	46.8	151	129.5	77.6	211	181.0	108.5	271	232.4	139.3
32	27.4	16.5	92	78.9	47.3	52	130.4	78.1	12	181.8	109.0	72	233.3	139.8
33	28.3	17.0	93	79.8	47.8	53	131.2	78.7	13	182.7	109.5	73	234.2	140.4
34	29.2	17.5	94	80.6	48.3	54	132.1	79.2	14	183.6	110.0	74	235.0	140.9
35	30.0	18.0	95	81.5	48.8	55	132.9	79.7	15	184.4	110.5	75	235.9	141.4
36	30.9	18.5	96	82.3	49.4	56	133.8	80.2	16	185.3	111.0	76	236.7	141.9
37	31.7	19.0	97	83.2	49.9	57	134.7	80.7	17	186.1	111.6	77	237.6	142.4
38	32.6	19.5	98	84.1	50.4	58	135.5	81.2	18	187.0	112.1	78	238.4	142.9
39	33.5	20.1	99	84.9	50.9	59	136.4	81.7	19	187.8	112.6	79	239.3	143.4
40	34.3	20.6	100	85.8	51.4	60	137.2	82.3	20	188.7	113.1	80	240.2	143.9
41	35.2	21.1	101	86.6	51.9	161	138.1	82.8	221	189.6	113.6	281	241.0	144.5
42	36.0	21.6	02	87.5	52.4	62	139.0	83.3	22	190.4	114.1	82	241.9	145.0
43	36.9	22.1	03	88.3	53.0	63	139.8	83.8	23	191.3	114.6	83	242.7	145.5
44	37.7	22.6	04	89.2	53.5	64	140.7	84.3	24	192.1	115.2	84	243.6	146.0
45	38.6	23.1	05	90.1	54.0	65	141.5	84.8	25	193.0	115.7	85	244.5	146.5
46	39.5	23.6	06	90.9	54.5	66	142.4	85.3	26	193.8	116.2	86	245.3	147.0
47	40.3	24.2	07	91.8	55.0	67	143.2	85.9	27	194.7	116.7	87	246.2	147.5
48	41.2	24.7	08	92.6	55.5	68	144.1	86.4	28	195.6	117.2	88	247.0	148.1
49	42.0	25.2	09	93.5	56.0	69	145.0	86.9	29	196.4	117.7	89	247.9	148.6
50	42.9	25.7	10	94.4	56.6	70	145.8	87.4	30	197.3	118.2	90	248.7	149.1
51	43.7	26.2	111	95.2	57.1	171	146.7	87.9	231	198.1	118.8	291	249.6	149.6
52	44.6	26.7	12	96.1	57.6	72	147.5	88.4	32	199.0	119.3	92	250.5	150.1
53	45.5	27.2	13	96.9	58.1	73	148.4	88.9	33	199.9	119.8	93	251.3	150.6
54	46.3	27.8	14	97.8	58.6	74	149.2	89.5	34	200.7	120.3	94	252.2	151.1
55	47.2	28.3	15	98.6	59.1	75	150.1	90.0	35	201 6	120.8	95	253.0	151.7
56	48.0	28.8	16	99.5	59.6	76	151.0	90.5	36	202.4	121.3	96	253.9	152.2
57	48.9	29.3	17	100.4	60.2	77	151.8	91.0	37	203.3	121.8	97	254.7	152.7
58	49.7	29.8	18	101.2	60.7	78	152.7	91.5	38	204.1	122.4	98	255.6	153.2
59	50.6	30.3	19	102.1	61.2	79	153.5	92.0	39	205.0	122.9	99	256.5	153.7
60	51.5	30.8	20	102.9	61.7	80	154.4	92.5	40	205.9	123.4	300	257.3	154.2
Dist.	Dep.	Lat.	Dist.	Dep.	Lat.	Dist.	Dep.	Lat.	Dist.	Dep.	Lat.	Dist.	Dep.	Lat.
N.E.byE.¼E.			S.E.byE.¼E.			N.W.byW.¼W.			S.W.byW.¼W.			[For 5¼ Points.		

TABLE I.

Difference of Latitude and Departure for 3 Points.

	N.E.byN.			N.W.byN.			S.E.byS.			S.W.byS.				
Dist.	Lat.	Dep.	Dist.	Lat.	Dep.	Dist.	Lat.	Dep.	Dist.	Lat.	Dep.	Dist.	Lat.	Dep.
1	00.8	00.6	61	50.7	33.9	121	100.6	67.2	181	150.5	100.6	241	200.4	133.9
2	01.7	01.1	62	51.6	34.4	22	101.4	67.8	82	151.3	101.1	42	201.2	134.4
3	02.5	01.7	63	52.4	35.0	23	102.3	68.3	83	152.2	101.7	43	202.0	135.0
4	03.3	02.2	64	53.2	35.6	24	103.1	68.9	84	153.0	102.2	44	202.9	135 6
5	04.2	02.8	65	54.0	36.1	25	103.9	69.4	85	153.8	102.8	45	203.7	136.1
6	05.0	03.3	66	54.9	36.7	26	104.8	70.0	86	154.7	103.3	46	204.5	136.7
7	05.8	03.9	67	55.7	37.2	27	105.6	70.6	87	155.5	103.9	47	205.4	137.2
8	06.7	04.4	68	56.5	37.8	28	106.4	71.1	88	156.3	104.4	48	206.2	137.8
9	07.5	05.0	69	57.4	38.3	29	107.3	71.7	89	157.1	105.0	49	207.0	138.3
10	08.3	05.6	70	58.2	38.9	30	108.1	72.2	90	158.0	105.6	50	207.9	138.9
11	09.1	06.1	71	59.0	39.4	131	108.9	72.8	191	158.8	106.1	251	208.7	139.4
12	10.0	06.7	72	59.9	40.0	32	109.8	73.3	92	159.6	106.7	52	209.5	140.0
13	10.8	07.2	73	60.7	40.6	33	110.6	73.9	93	160.5	107.2	53	210.4	140.6
14	11.6	07.8	74	61.5	41.1	34	111.4	74.4	94	161.3	107.8	54	211.2	141.1
15	12.5	08.3	75	62.4	41.7	35	112.2	75.0	95	162.1	108.3	55	212.0	141.7
16	13.3	08.9	76	63.2	42.2	36	113.1	75.6	96	163.0	108.9	56	212.9	142.2
17	14.1	09.4	77	64.0	42.8	37	113.9	76.1	97	163.8	109.4	57	213.7	142.8
18	15.0	10.0	78	64.9	43.3	38	114.7	76.7	98	164.6	110.0	58	214.5	143.3
19	15.8	10.6	79	65.7	43.9	39	115.6	77.2	99	165.5	110.6	59	215.4	143.9
20	16.6	11.1	80	66.5	44.4	40	116.4	77.8	200	166.3	111.1	60	216.2	144.4
21	17.5	11.7	81	67.3	45.0	141	117.2	78.3	201	167.1	111.7	261	217.0	145.0
22	18.3	12.2	82	68.2	45.6	42	118.1	78.9	02	168.0	112.2	62	217.8	145.6
23	19.1	12.8	83	69.0	46.1	43	118.9	79.4	03	168.8	112.8	63	218.7	146.1
24	20.0	13.3	84	69.8	46.7	44	119.7	80.0	04	169.6	113.3	64	219.5	146.7
25	20.8	13.9	85	70.7	47.2	45	120.6	80.6	05	170.5	113.9	65	220.3	147.2
26	21.6	14.4	86	71.5	47.8	46	121.4	81.1	06	171.3	114.4	66	221.2	147.8
27	22.4	15.0	87	72.3	48.3	47	122.2	81.7	07	172.1	115.0	67	222.0	148.3
28	23.3	15.6	88	73.2	48.9	43	123.1	82.2	08	172.9	115.6	68	222.8	148.9
29	24.1	16.1	89	74.0	49.4	49	123.9	82.8	09	173.8	116.1	69	223.7	149.4
30	24.9	16.7	90	74.8	50.0	50	124.7	83.3	10	174.6	116.7	70	224.5	150.0
31	25.8	17.2	91	75.7	50.6	151	125.6	83.9	211	175.4	117.2	271	225.3	150.6
32	26.6	17.8	92	76.5	51.1	52	126.4	84.4	12	176.3	117.8	72	226.2	151.1
33	27.4	18.3	93	77.3	51.7	53	127.2	85.0	13	177.1	118.3	73	227.0	151.7
34	28.3	18.9	94	78.2	52.2	54	128.0	85.6	14	177.9	118.9	74	227.8	152.2
35	29.1	19.4	95	79.0	52.8	55	128.9	86.1	15	178.8	119.4	75	228.7	152.8
36	29.9	20.0	96	79.8	53.3	56	129.7	86.7	16	179.6	120.0	76	229.5	153.3
37	30.8	20.6	97	80.7	53.9	57	130.5	87.2	17	180.4	120.6	77	230.3	153.9
38	31.6	21.1	98	81.5	54.4	58	131.4	87.8	18	181.3	121.1	78	231.1	154.4
39	32.4	21.7	99	82.3	55.0	59	132.2	88.3	19	182.1	121.7	79	232.0	155.0
40	33.3	22.2	100	83.1	55.6	60	133.0	88.9	20	182.9	122.2	80	232.8	155.6
41	34.1	22.8	101	84.0	56.1	161	133.9	89.4	221	183.8	122.8	281	233.6	156.1
42	34.9	23.3	02	84.8	56.7	62	134.7	90.0	22	184.6	123.3	82	234.5	156.7
43	35.8	23.9	03	85.6	57.2	63	135.5	90.6	23	185.4	123.9	83	235.3	157.2
44	36.6	24.4	04	86.5	57.8	64	136.4	91.1	24	186.2	124.4	84	236.1	157 8
45	37.4	25.0	05	87.3	58.3	65	137.2	91.7	25	187.1	125.0	85	237.0	158.3
46	38.2	25.6	06	88.1	58.9	66	138.0	92.2	26	187.9	125.6	86	237.8	158.9
47	39.1	26.1	07	89.0	59.4	67	138.9	92.8	27	188.7	126.1	87	238.6	159.4
48	39.9	26.7	08	89.8	60.0	68	139.7	93.3	28	189.6	126.7	88	239.5	160.0
49	40.7	27.2	09	90.6	60.6	69	140.5	93.9	29	190.4	127.2	89	240.3	160.6
50	41.6	27.8	10	91.5	61.1	70	141.3	94.4	30	191.2	127.8	90	241.1	161.1
51	42.4	28.3	111	92.3	61.7	171	142.2	95.0	231	192.1	128.3	291	242.0	161.7
52	43.2	28.9	12	93.1	62.2	72	143.0	95.6	32	192.9	128.9	92	242.8	162.2
53	44.1	29.4	13	94.0	62.8	73	143.8	96.1	33	193.7	129.4	93	243.6	162.8
54	44.9	30.0	14	94.8	63.3	74	144.7	96.7	34	194.6	130.0	94	244.5	163.3
55	45.7	30.6	15	95.6	63.9	75	145.5	97.2	35	195.4	130.6	95	245.3	163.9
56	46.6	31.1	16	96.5	64.4	76	146.3	97.8	36	196.2	131.1	96	246.1	164.4
57	47.4	31.7	17	97.3	65.0	77	147.2	98.3	37	197.1	131.7	97	246.9	165.0
58	48.2	32.2	18	98.1	65.6	78	148.0	98.9	38	197.9	132.2	98	247.8	165.6
59	49.1	32.8	19	98.9	66.1	79	148.8	99.4	39	198.7	132.8	99	248.6	166.1
60	49.9	33.3	20	99.8	66.7	80	149.7	100.0	40	199.6	133.3	300	249.4	166.7
Dist.	Dep.	Lat.	Dist.	Dep.	Lat.	Dist.	Dep.	Lat.	Dist.	Dep.	Lat.	Dist.	Dep.	Lat.
	N.E.byE.			S.E.byE.			N.W.byW.			S.W.byW.			[For 5 Points.	

TABLE I.

Difference of Latitude and Departure for 3¼ Points.

N.E.¾N.			N.W.¾N.			S.E.¾S.			S.W.¾S.					
Dist.	Lat.	Dep.	Dist.	Lat.	Dep.	Dist.	Lat.	Dep.	Dist.	Lat.	Dep.	Dist.	Lat.	Dep.
1	00.8	00.6	61	49.0	36.3	121	97.2	72.1	181	145.4	107.8	241	193.6	143.6
2	01.6	01.2	62	49.8	36.9	22	98.0	72.7	82	146.2	108.4	42	194.4	144.2
3	02.4	01.8	63	50.6	37.5	23	98.8	73.3	83	147.0	109.0	43	195.2	144.8
4	03.2	02.4	64	51.4	38.1	24	99.6	73.9	84	147.8	109.6	44	196.0	145.4
5	04.0	03.0	65	52.2	38.7	25	100.4	74.5	85	148.6	110.2	45	196.8	145.9
6	04.8	03.6	66	53.0	39.3	26	101.2	75.1	86	149.4	110.8	46	197.6	146.5
7	05.6	04.2	67	53.8	39.9	27	102.0	75.7	87	150.2	111.4	47	198.4	147.1
8	06.4	04.8	68	54.6	40.5	28	102.8	76.2	88	151.0	112.0	48	199.2	147.7
9	07.2	05.4	69	55.4	41.1	29	103.6	76.8	89	151.8	112.6	49	200.0	148.3
10	08.0	06.0	70	56.2	41.7	30	104.4	77.4	90	152.6	113.2	50	200.8	148.9
11	08.8	06.6	71	57.0	42.3	131	105.2	78.0	191	153.4	113.8	251	201.6	149.5
12	09.6	07.1	72	57.8	42.9	32	106.0	78.6	92	154.2	114.4	52	202.4	150.1
13	10.4	07.7	73	58.6	43.5	33	106.8	79.2	93	155.0	115.0	53	203.2	150.7
14	11.2	08.3	74	59.4	44.1	34	107.6	79.8	94	155.8	115.6	54	204.0	151.3
15	12.0	08.9	75	60.2	44.7	35	108.4	80.4	95	156.6	116.2	55	204.8	151.9
16	12.9	09.5	76	61.0	45.3	36	109.2	81.0	96	157.4	116.8	56	205.6	152.5
17	13.7	10.1	77	61.8	45.9	37	110.0	81.6	97	158.2	117.4	57	206.4	153.1
18	14.5	10.7	78	62.7	46.5	38	110.8	82.2	98	159.0	117.9	58	207.2	153.7
19	15.3	11.3	79	63.5	47.1	39	111.6	82.8	99	159.8	118.5	59	208.0	154.3
20	16.1	11.9	80	64.3	47.7	40	112.4	83.4	200	160.6	119.1	60	208.8	154.9
21	16.9	12.5	81	65.1	48.3	141	113.3	84.0	201	161.4	119.7	261	209.6	155.5
22	17.7	13.1	82	65.9	48.8	42	114.1	84.6	02	162.2	120.3	62	210.4	156.1
23	18.5	13.7	83	66.7	49.4	43	114.9	85.2	03	163.1	120.9	63	211.2	156.7
24	19.3	14.3	84	67.5	50.0	44	115.7	85.8	04	163.9	121.5	64	212.0	157.3
25	20.1	14.9	85	68.3	50.6	45	116.5	86.4	05	164.7	122.1	65	212.8	157.9
26	20.9	15.5	86	69.1	51.2	46	117.3	87.0	06	165.5	122.7	66	213.7	158.5
27	21.7	16.1	87	69.9	51.8	47	118.1	87.6	07	166.3	123.3	67	214.5	159.1
28	22.5	16.7	88	70.7	52.4	48	118.9	88.2	08	167.1	123.9	68	215.3	159.6
29	23.3	17.3	89	71.5	53.0	49	119.7	88.8	09	167.9	124.5	69	216.1	160.2
30	24.1	17.9	90	72.3	53.6	50	120.5	89.4	10	168.7	125.1	70	216.9	160.8
31	24.9	18.5	91	73.1	54.2	151	121.3	90.0	211	169.5	125.7	271	217.7	161.4
32	25.7	19.1	92	73.9	54.8	52	122.1	90.5	12	170.3	126.3	72	218.5	162.0
33	26.5	19.7	93	74.7	55.4	53	122.9	91.1	13	171.1	126.9	73	219.3	162.6
34	27.3	20.3	94	75.5	56.0	54	123.7	91.7	14	171.9	127.5	74	220.1	163.2
35	28.1	20.8	95	76.3	56.6	55	124.5	92.3	15	172.7	128.1	75	220.9	163.8
36	28.9	21.4	96	77.1	57.2	56	125.3	92.9	16	173.5	128.7	76	221.7	164.4
37	29.7	22.0	97	77.9	57.8	57	126.1	93.5	17	174.3	129.3	77	222.5	165.0
38	30.5	22.6	98	78.7	58.4	58	126.9	94.1	18	175.1	129.9	78	223.3	165.6
39	31.3	23.2	99	79.5	59.0	59	127.7	94.7	19	175.9	130.5	79	224.1	166.2
40	32.1	23.8	100	80.3	59.6	60	128.5	95.3	20	176.7	131.1	80	224.9	166.8
41	32.9	24.4	101	81.1	60.2	161	129.3	95.9	221	177.5	131.6	281	225.7	167.4
42	33.7	25.0	02	81.9	60.8	62	130.1	96.5	22	178.3	132.2	82	226.5	168.0
43	34.5	25.6	03	82.7	61.4	63	130.9	97.1	23	179.1	132.8	83	227.3	168.6
44	35.3	26.2	04	83.5	62.0	64	131.7	97.7	24	179.9	133.4	84	228.1	169.2
45	36.1	26.8	05	84.3	62.5	65	132.5	98.3	25	180.7	134.0	85	228.9	169.8
46	36.9	27.4	06	85.1	63.1	66	133.3	98.9	26	181.5	134.6	86	229.7	170.4
47	37.8	28.0	07	85.9	63.7	67	134.1	99.5	27	182.3	135.2	87	230.5	171.0
48	38.6	28.6	08	86.7	64.3	68	134.9	100.1	28	183.1	135.8	88	231.3	171.6
49	39.4	29.2	09	87.5	64.9	69	135.7	100.7	29	183.9	136.4	89	232.1	172.2
50	40.2	29.8	10	88.4	65.5	70	136.5	101.3	30	184.7	137.0	90	232.9	172.8
51	41.0	30.4	111	89.2	66.1	171	137.3	101.9	231	185.5	137.6	291	233.7	173.3
52	41.8	31.0	12	90.0	66.7	72	138.2	102.5	32	186.3	138.2	92	234.5	173.9
53	42.6	31.6	13	90.8	67.3	73	139.0	103.1	33	187.1	138.8	93	235.3	174.5
54	43.4	32.2	14	91.6	67.9	74	139.8	103.7	34	188.0	139.4	94	236.1	175.1
55	44.2	32.8	15	92.4	68.5	75	140.6	104.2	35	188.8	140.0	95	236.9	175.7
56	45.0	33.4	16	93.2	69.1	76	141.4	104.8	36	189.6	140.6	96	237.7	176.3
57	45.8	34.0	17	94.0	69.7	77	142.2	105.4	37	190.4	141.2	97	238.6	176.9
58	46.6	34.6	18	94.8	70.3	78	143.0	106.0	38	191.2	141.8	98	239.4	177.5
59	47.4	35.1	19	95.6	70.9	79	143.8	106.6	39	192.0	142.4	99	240.2	178.1
60	48.2	35.7	20	96.4	71.5	80	144.6	107.2	40	192.8	143.0	300	241.0	178.7
Dist.	Dep.	Lat.	Dist.	Dep.	Lat.	Dist.	Dep.	Lat.	Dist.	Dep.	Lat.	Dist.	Dep.	Lat.
N.E.¾E.			S.E.¾E.			N.W.¾W.			S.W.¾W.			[For 4¾ Points.		

TABLE I.

Difference of Latitude and Departure for 3½ Points.

N.E ½N.			N.W.½N.			S.E.½S.			S.W.½S.					
Dist.	Lat.	Dep.	Dist.	Lat.	Dep.	Dist.	Lat.	Dep.	Dist.	Lat.	Dep.	Dist.	Lat.	Dep.
1	00.8	00.6	61	47.2	38.7	121	93.5	76.8	181	139.9	114.8	241	186.3	152.9
2	01.5	01.3	62	47.9	39.3	22	94.3	77.4	82	140.7	115.5	42	187.1	153.5
3	02.3	01.9	63	48.7	40.0	23	95.1	78.0	83	141.5	116.1	43	187.8	154.2
4	03.1	02.5	64	49.5	40.6	24	95.9	78.7	84	142.2	116.7	44	188.6	154.8
5	03.9	03.2	65	50.2	41.2	25	96.6	79.3	85	143.0	117.4	45	189.4	155.4
6	04.6	03.8	66	51.0	41.9	26	97.4	79.9	86	143.8	118.0	46	190.2	156.1
7	05.4	04.4	67	51.8	42.5	27	98.2	80.6	87	144.6	118.6	47	190.9	156.7
8	06.2	05.1	68	52.6	43.1	28	98.9	81.2	88	145.3	119.3	48	191.7	157.3
9	07.0	05.7	69	53.3	43.8	29	99.7	81.8	89	146.1	119.9	49	192.5	158.0
10	07.7	06.3	70	54.1	44.4	30	100.5	82.5	90	146.9	120.5	50	193.3	158.6
11	08.5	07.0	71	54.9	45.0	131	101.3	83.1	191	147.6	121.2	251	194.0	159.2
12	09.3	07.6	72	55.7	45.7	32	102.0	83.7	92	148.4	121.8	52	194.8	159.9
13	10.0	08.2	73	56.4	46.3	33	102.8	84.4	93	149.2	122.4	53	195.6	160.5
14	10.8	08.9	74	57.2	46.9	34	103.6	85.0	94	150.0	123.1	54	196.3	161.1
15	11.6	09.5	75	58.0	47.6	35	104.4	85.6	95	150.7	123.7	55	197.1	161.8
16	12.4	10.2	76	58.7	48.2	36	105.1	86.3	96	151.5	124.3	56	197.9	162.4
17	13.1	10.8	77	59.5	48.8	37	105.9	86.9	97	152.3	125.0	57	198.7	163.0
18	13.9	11.4	78	60.3	49.5	38	106.7	87.5	98	153.1	125.6	58	199.4	163.7
19	14.7	12.1	79	61.1	50.1	39	107.4	88.2	99	153.8	126.2	59	200.2	164.3
20	15.5	12.7	80	61.8	50.8	40	108.2	88.8	200	154.6	126.9	60	201.0	164.9
21	16.2	13.3	81	62.6	51.4	141	109.0	89.4	201	155.4	127.5	261	201.8	165.6
22	17.0	14.0	82	63.4	52.0	42	109.8	90.1	02	156.1	128.1	62	202.5	166.2
23	17.8	14.6	83	64.2	52.7	43	110.5	90.7	03	156.9	128.8	63	203.3	166.8
24	18.6	15.2	84	64.9	53.3	44	111.3	91.4	04	157.7	129.4	64	204.1	167.5
25	19.3	15.9	85	65.7	53.9	45	112.1	92.0	05	158.5	130.1	65	204.8	168.1
26	20.1	16.5	86	66.5	54.6	46	112.9	92.6	06	159.2	130.7	66	205.6	168.7
27	20.9	17.1	87	67.3	55.2	47	113.6	93.3	07	160.0	131.3	67	206.4	169.4
28	21.6	17.8	88	68.0	55.8	48	114.4	93.9	08	160.8	132.0	68	207.2	170.0
29	22.4	18.4	89	68.8	56.5	49	115.2	94.5	09	161.6	132.6	69	207.9	170.7
30	23.2	19.0	90	69.6	57.1	50	116.0	95.2	10	162.3	133.2	70	208.7	171.3
31	24.0	19.7	91	70.3	57.7	151	116.7	95.8	211	163.1	133.9	271	209.5	171.9
32	24.7	20.3	92	71.1	58.4	52	117.5	96.4	12	163.9	134.5	72	210.3	172.6
33	25.5	20.9	93	71.9	59.0	53	118.3	97.1	13	164.7	135.1	73	211.0	173.2
34	26.3	21.6	94	72.7	59.6	54	119.0	97.7	14	165.4	135.8	74	211.8	173.8
35	27.1	22.2	95	73.4	60.3	55	119.8	98.3	15	166.2	136.4	75	212.6	174.5
36	27.8	22.8	96	74.2	60.9	56	120.6	99.0	16	167.0	137.0	76	213.4	175.1
37	28.6	23.5	97	75.0	61.5	57	121.4	99.6	17	167.7	137.7	77	214.1	175.7
38	29.4	24.1	98	75.8	62.2	58	122.1	100.2	18	168.5	138.3	78	214.9	176.4
39	30.1	24.7	99	76.5	62.8	59	122.9	100.9	19	169.3	138.9	79	215.7	177.0
40	30.9	25.4	100	77.3	63.4	60	123.7	101.5	20	170.1	139.6	80	216.4	177.6
41	31.7	26.0	101	78.1	64.1	161	124.5	102.1	221	170.8	140.2	281	217.2	178.3
42	32.5	26.6	02	78.8	64.7	62	125.2	102.8	22	171.6	140.8	82	218.0	178.9
43	33.2	27.3	03	79.6	65.3	63	126.0	103.4	23	172.4	141.5	83	218.8	179.5
44	34.0	27.9	04	80.4	66.0	64	126.8	104.0	24	173.2	142.1	84	219.5	180.2
45	34.8	28.5	05	81.2	66.6	65	127.5	104.7	25	173.9	142.7	85	220.3	180.8
46	35.6	29.2	06	81.9	67.2	66	128.3	105.3	26	174.7	143.4	86	221.1	181.4
47	36.3	29.8	07	82.7	67.9	67	129.1	105.9	27	175.5	144.0	87	221.9	182.1
48	37.1	30.5	08	83.5	68.5	68	129.9	106.6	28	176.2	144.6	88	222.6	182.7
49	37.9	31.1	09	84.3	69.1	69	130.6	107.2	29	177.0	145.3	89	223.4	183.3
50	38.7	31.7	10	85.0	69.8	70	131.4	107.8	30	177.8	145.9	90	224.2	184.0
51	39.4	32.4	111	85.8	70.4	171	132.2	108.5	231	178.6	146.5	291	224.9	184.6
52	40.2	33.0	12	86.6	71.1	72	133.0	109.1	32	179.3	147.2	92	225.7	185.2
53	41.0	33.6	13	87.4	71.7	73	133.7	109.8	33	180.1	147.8	93	226.5	185.9
54	41.7	34.3	14	88.1	72.3	74	134.5	110.4	34	180.9	148.4	94	227.3	186.5
55	42.5	34.9	15	88.9	73.0	75	135.3	111.0	35	181 7	149.1	95	228.0	187.1
56	43.3	35.5	16	89.7	73.6	76	136.0	111.7	36	182.4	149.7	96	228.8	187.8
57	44.1	36.2	17	90.4	74.2	77	136.8	112.3	37	183.2	150.4	97	229.6	188.4
58	44.8	36.8	18	91.2	74.9	78	137.6	112.9	38	184.0	151.0	98	230.4	189.0
59	45.6	37.4	19	92.0	75.5	79	138.4	113.6	39	184.7	151.6	99	231.1	189.7
60	46.4	38.1	20	92.8	76.1	80	139.1	114.2	40	185.5	152.3	300	231.9	190.3
Dist.	Dep.	Lat.	Dist.	Dep.	Lat.	Dist.	Dep.	Lat.	Dist.	Dep.	Lat.	Dist.	Dep.	Lat.
N.E.½E.			S.E.½E.			N.W.½W.			S.W.½W.					

[For 4½ Points.

TABLE I.

Difference of Latitude and Departure for 3¾ Points.

N.E.¼N. N.W.¼N. S.E.¼S. S.W.¼S.

Dist.	Lat.	Dep.	Dist.	Lat.	Dep.	Dist.	Lat.	Dep.	Dist.	Lat.	Dep.	Dist.	Lat.	Dep.
1	00.7	00.7	61	45.2	41.0	121	89.7	81.3	181	134.1	121.6	241	178.6	161.8
2	01.5	01.3	62	45.9	41.6	22	90.4	81.9	82	134.9	122.2	42	179.3	162.5
3	02.2	02.0	63	46.7	42.3	23	91.1	82.6	83	135.6	122.9	43	180.1	163.2
4	03.0	02.7	64	47.4	43.0	24	91.9	83.3	84	136.3	123.6	44	180.8	163.9
5	03.7	03.4	65	48.2	43.7	25	92.6	83.9	85	137.1	124.2	45	181.5	164.5
6	04.4	04.0	66	48.9	44.3	26	93.4	84.6	86	137.8	124.9	46	182.3	165.2
7	05.2	04.7	67	49.6	45.0	27	94.1	85.3	87	138.6	125.6	47	183.0	165.9
8	05.9	05.4	68	50.4	45.7	28	94.8	86.0	88	139.3	126.3	48	183.8	166.5
9	06.7	06.0	69	51.1	46.3	29	95.6	86.6	89	140.0	126.9	49	184.5	167.2
10	07.4	06.7	70	51.9	47.0	30	96.3	87.3	90	140.8	127.6	50	185.2	167.9
11	08.2	07.4	71	52.6	47.7	131	97.1	88.0	191	141.5	128.3	251	186.0	168.6
12	08.9	08.1	72	53.3	48.4	32	97.8	88.6	92	142.3	128.9	52	186.7	169.2
13	09.6	08.7	73	54.1	49.0	33	98.5	89.3	93	143.0	129.6	53	187.5	169.9
14	10.4	09.4	74	54.8	49.7	34	99.3	90.0	94	143.7	130.3	54	188.2	170.6
15	11.1	10.1	75	55.6	50.4	35	100.0	90.7	95	144.5	131.0	55	188.9	171.2
16	11.9	10.7	76	56.3	51.0	36	100.8	91.3	96	145.2	131.6	56	189.7	171.9
17	12.6	11.4	77	57.1	51.7	37	101.5	92.0	97	146.0	132.3	57	190.4	172.6
18	13.3	12.1	78	57.8	52.4	38	102.3	92.7	98	146.7	133.0	58	191.2	173.3
19	14.1	12.8	79	58.5	53.1	39	103.0	93.3	99	147.4	133.6	59	191.9	173.9
20	14.8	13.4	80	59.3	53.7	40	103.7	94.0	200	148.2	134.3	60	192.6	174.6
21	15.6	14.1	81	60.0	54.4	141	104.5	94.7	201	148.9	135.0	261	193.4	175.3
22	16.3	14.8	82	60.8	55.1	42	105.2	95.4	02	149.7	135.7	62	194.1	175.9
23	17.0	15.4	83	61.5	55.7	43	106.0	96.0	03	150.4	136.3	63	194.9	176.6
24	17.8	16.1	84	62.2	56.4	44	106.7	96.7	04	151.2	137.0	64	195.6	177.3
25	18.5	16.8	85	63.0	57.1	45	107.4	97.4	05	151.9	137.7	65	196.4	178.0
26	19.3	17.5	86	63.7	57.8	46	108.2	98.0	06	152.6	138.3	66	197.1	178.6
27	20.0	18.1	87	64.5	58.4	47	108.9	98.7	07	153.4	139.0	67	197.8	179.3
28	20.7	18.8	88	65.2	59.1	48	109.7	99.4	08	154.1	139.7	68	198.6	180.0
29	21.5	19.5	89	65.9	59.8	49	110.4	100.1	09	154.9	140.4	69	199.3	180.6
30	22.2	20.1	90	66.7	60.4	50	111.1	100.7	10	155.6	141.0	70	200.1	181.3
31	23.0	20.8	91	67.4	61.1	151	111.9	101.4	211	156.3	141.7	271	200.8	182.0
32	23.7	21.5	92	68.2	61.8	52	112.6	102.1	12	157.1	142.4	72	201.5	182.7
33	24.5	22.2	93	68.9	62.5	53	113.4	102.7	13	157.8	143.0	73	202.3	183.3
34	25.2	22.8	94	69.6	63.1	54	114.1	103.4	14	158.6	143.7	74	203.0	184.0
35	25.9	23.5	95	70.4	63.8	55	114.8	104.1	15	159.3	144.4	75	203.8	184.7
36	26.7	24.2	96	71.1	64.5	56	115.6	104.8	16	160.0	145.1	76	204.5	185.4
37	27.4	24.8	97	71.9	65.1	57	116.3	105.4	17	160.8	145.7	77	205.2	186.0
38	28.2	25.5	98	72.6	65.8	58	117.1	106.1	18	161.5	146.4	78	206.0	186.7
39	28.9	26.2	99	73.4	66.5	59	117.8	106.8	19	162.3	147.1	79	206.7	187.4
40	29.6	26.9	100	74.1	67.2	60	118.6	107.4	20	163.0	147.7	80	207.5	188.0
41	30.4	27.5	101	74.8	67.8	161	119.3	108.1	221	163.8	148.4	281	208.2	188.7
42	31.1	28.2	02	75.6	68.5	62	120.0	108.8	22	164.5	149.1	82	208.9	189.4
43	31.9	28.9	03	76.3	69.2	63	120.8	109.5	23	165.2	149.8	83	209.7	190.1
44	32.6	29.5	04	77.1	69.8	64	121.5	110.1	24	166.0	150.4	84	210.4	190.7
45	33.3	30.2	05	77.8	70.5	65	122.3	110.8	25	166.7	151.1	85	211.2	191.4
46	34.1	30.9	06	78.5	71.2	66	123.0	111.5	26	167.5	151.8	86	211.9	192.1
47	34.8	31.6	07	79.3	71.9	67	123.7	112.2	27	168.2	152.4	87	212.7	192.7
48	35.6	32.2	08	80.0	72.5	68	124.5	112.8	28	168.9	153.1	88	213.4	193.4
49	36.3	32.9	09	80.8	73.2	69	125.2	113.5	29	169.7	153.8	89	214.1	194.1
50	37.0	33.6	10	81.5	73.9	70	126.0	114.2	30	170.4	154.5	90	214.9	194.8
51	37.8	34.2	111	82.2	74.5	171	126.7	114.8	231	171.2	155.1	291	215.6	195.4
52	38.5	34.9	12	83.0	75.2	72	127.4	115.5	32	171.9	155.8	92	216.4	196.1
53	39.3	35.6	13	83.7	75.9	73	128.2	116.2	33	172.6	156.5	93	217.1	196.8
54	40.0	36.3	14	84.5	76.6	74	128.9	116.9	34	173.4	157.1	94	217.8	197.4
55	40.8	36.9	15	85.2	77.2	75	129.7	117.5	35	174.1	157.8	95	218.6	198.1
56	41.5	37.6	16	86.0	77.9	76	130.4	118.2	36	174.9	158.5	96	219.3	198.8
57	42.2	38.3	17	86.7	78.6	77	131.1	118.9	37	175.6	159.2	97	220.1	199.5
58	43.0	39.0	18	87.4	79.2	78	131.9	119.5	38	176.3	159.8	98	220.8	200.1
59	43.7	39.6	19	88.2	79.9	79	132.6	120.2	39	177.1	160.5	99	221.5	200.8
60	44.5	40.3	20	88.9	80.6	80	133.4	120.9	40	177.8	161.2	300	222.3	201.5
Dist.	Dep.	Lat.	Dist.	Dep.	Lat.	Dist.	Dep.	Lat.	Dist.	Dep.	Lat.	Dist.	Dep.	Lat.

N.E.¼E. S.E.¼E. N.W.¼W. S.W.¼W.

[For 4¼ Points.

TABLE I.

Difference of Latitude and Departure for 4 Points.

N.E.			N.W.			S.E.			S.W.					
Dist.	Lat.	Dep.	Dist.	Lat.	Dep.	Dist.	Lat.	Dep.	Dist.	Lat.	Dep.	Dist.	Lat.	Dep.
1	00.7	00.7	61	43.1	43.1	121	85.6	85.6	181	128.0	128.0	241	170.4	170.4
2	01.4	01.4	62	43.8	43.8	22	86.3	86.3	82	128.7	128.7	42	171.1	171.1
3	02.1	02.1	63	44.5	44.5	23	87.0	87.0	83	129.4	129.4	43	171.8	171.8
4	02.8	02.8	64	45.3	45.3	24	87.7	87.7	84	130.1	130.1	44	172.5	172.5
5	03.5	03.5	65	46.0	46.0	25	88.4	88.4	85	130.8	130.8	45	173.2	173.2
6	04.2	04.2	66	46.7	46.7	26	89.1	89.1	86	131.5	131.5	46	173.9	173.9
7	04.9	04.9	67	47.4	47.4	27	89.8	89.8	87	132.2	132.2	47	174.7	174.7
8	05.7	05.7	68	48.1	48.1	28	90.5	90.5	88	132.9	132.9	48	175.4	175.4
9	06.4	06.4	69	48.8	48.8	29	91.2	91.2	89	133.6	133.6	49	176.1	176.1
10	07.1	07.1	70	49.5	49.5	30	91.9	91.9	90	134.4	134.4	50	176.8	176.8
11	07.8	07.8	71	50.2	50.2	131	92.6	92.6	191	135.1	135.1	251	177.5	177.5
12	08.5	08.5	72	50.9	50.9	32	93.3	93.3	92	135.8	135.8	52	178.2	178.2
13	09.2	09.2	73	51.6	51.6	33	94.0	94.0	93	136.5	136.5	53	178.9	178.9
14	09.9	09.9	74	52.3	52.3	34	94.8	94.8	94	137.2	137.2	54	179.6	179.6
15	10.6	10.6	75	53.0	53.0	35	95.5	95.5	95	137.9	137.9	55	180.3	180.3
16	11.3	11.3	76	53.7	53.7	36	96.2	96.2	96	138.6	138.6	56	181.0	181.0
17	12.0	12.0	77	54.4	54.4	37	96.9	96.9	97	139.3	139.3	57	181.7	181.7
18	12.7	12.7	78	55.2	55.2	38	97.6	97.6	98	140.0	140.0	58	182.4	182.4
19	13.4	13.4	79	55.9	55.9	39	98.3	98.3	99	140.7	140.7	59	183.1	183.1
20	14.1	14.1	80	56.6	56.6	40	99.0	99.0	200	141.4	141.4	60	183.8	183.8
21	14.8	14.8	81	57.3	57.3	141	99.7	99.7	201	142.1	142.1	261	184.6	184.6
22	15.6	15.6	82	58.0	58.0	42	100.4	100.4	02	142.8	142.8	62	185.3	185.3
23	16.3	16.3	83	58.7	58.7	43	101.1	101.1	03	143.5	143.5	63	186.0	186.0
24	17.0	17.0	84	59.4	59.4	44	101.8	101.8	04	144.2	144.2	64	186.7	186.7
25	17.7	17.7	85	60.1	60.1	45	102.5	102.5	05	145.0	145.0	65	187.4	187.4
26	18.4	18.4	86	60.8	60.8	46	103.2	103.2	06	145.7	145.7	66	188.1	188.1
27	19.1	19.1	87	61.5	61.5	47	103.9	103.9	07	146.4	146.4	67	188.8	188.8
28	19.8	19.8	88	62.2	62.2	48	104.7	104.7	08	147.1	147.1	68	189.5	189.5
29	20.5	20.5	89	62.9	62.9	49	105.4	105.4	09	147.8	147.8	69	190.2	190.2
30	21.2	21.2	90	63.6	63.6	50	106.1	106.1	10	148.5	148.5	70	190.9	190.9
31	21.9	21.9	91	64.3	64.3	151	106.8	106.8	211	149.2	149.2	271	191.6	191.6
32	22.6	22.6	92	65.1	65.1	52	107.5	107.5	12	149.9	149.9	72	192.3	192.3
33	23.3	23.3	93	65.8	65.8	53	108.2	108.2	13	150.6	150.6	73	193.0	193.0
34	24.0	24.0	94	66.5	66.5	54	108.9	108.9	14	151.3	151.3	74	193.7	193.7
35	24.7	24.7	95	67.2	67.2	55	109.6	109.6	15	152.0	152.0	75	194.5	194.5
36	25.5	25.5	96	67.9	67.9	56	110.3	110.3	16	152.7	152.7	76	195.2	195.2
37	26.2	26.2	97	68.6	68.6	57	111.0	111.0	17	153.4	153.4	77	195.9	195.9
38	26.9	26.9	98	69.3	69.3	58	111.7	111.7	18	154.1	154.1	78	196.6	196.6
39	27.6	27.6	99	70.0	70.0	59	112.4	112.4	19	154.9	154.9	79	197.3	197.3
40	28.3	28.3	100	70.7	70.7	60	113.1	113.1	20	155.6	155.6	80	198.0	198.0
41	29.0	29.0	101	71.4	71.4	161	113.8	113.8	221	156.3	156.3	281	198.7	198.7
42	29.7	29.7	02	72.1	72.1	62	114.6	114.6	22	157.0	157.0	82	199.4	199.4
43	30.4	30.4	03	72.8	72.8	63	115.3	115.3	23	157.7	157.7	83	200.1	200.1
44	31.1	31.1	04	73.5	73.5	64	116.0	116.0	24	158.4	158.4	84	200.8	200.8
45	31.8	31.8	05	74.2	74.2	65	116.7	116.7	25	159.1	159.1	85	201.5	201.5
46	32.5	32.5	06	75.0	75.0	66	117.4	117.4	26	159.8	159.8	86	202.2	202.2
47	33.2	33.2	07	75.7	75.7	67	118.1	118.1	27	160.5	160.5	87	202.9	202.9
48	33.9	33.9	08	76.4	76.4	68	118.8	118.8	28	161.2	161.2	88	203.6	203.6
49	34.6	34.6	09	77.1	77.1	69	119.5	119.5	29	161.9	161.9	89	204.4	204.4
50	35.4	35.4	10	77.8	77.8	70	120.2	120.2	30	162.6	162.6	90	205.1	205.1
51	36.1	36.1	111	78.5	78.5	171	120.9	120.9	231	163.3	163.3	291	205.8	205.8
52	36.8	36.8	12	79.2	79.2	72	121.6	121.6	32	164.0	164.0	92	206.5	206.5
53	37.5	37.5	13	79.9	79.9	73	122.3	122.3	33	164.8	164.8	93	207.2	207.2
54	38.2	38.2	14	80.6	80.6	74	123.0	123.0	34	165.5	165.5	94	207.9	207.9
55	38.9	38.9	15	81.3	81.3	75	123.7	123.7	35	166.2	166.2	95	208.6	208.6
56	39.6	39.6	16	82.0	82.0	76	124.5	124.5	36	166.9	166.9	96	209.3	209.3
57	40.3	40.3	17	82.7	82.7	77	125.2	125.2	37	167.6	167.6	97	210.0	210.0
58	41.0	41.0	18	83.4	83.4	78	125.9	125.9	38	168.3	168.3	98	210.7	210.7
59	41.7	41.7	19	84.1	84.1	79	126.6	126.6	39	169.0	169.0	99	211.4	211.4
60	42.4	42.4	20	84.9	84.9	80	127.3	127.3	40	169.7	169.7	300	212.1	212.1
Dist.	Dep.	Lat.	Dist.	Dep.	Lat.	Dist.	Dep.	Lat.	Dist.	Dep.	Lat.	Dist.	Dep.	Lat.
N.E.			N.W.			S.E.			S.W.			[For 4 Points.		

TABLE III.

Meridional Parts.

M.	0°	1°	2°	3°	4°	5°	6°	7°	8°	9°	10°	11°	12°	13°	M.
0	0	60	120	180	240	300	361	421	482	542	603	664	725	787	0
1	1	61	121	181	241	301	362	422	483	543	604	665	726	788	1
2	2	62	122	182	242	302	363	423	484	544	605	666	727	789	2
3	3	63	123	183	243	303	364	424	485	545	606	667	728	790	3
4	4	64	124	184	244	304	365	425	486	546	607	668	729	791	4
5	5	65	125	185	245	305	366	426	487	547	608	669	730	792	5
6	6	66	126	186	246	306	367	427	488	548	609	670	731	793	6
7	7	67	127	187	247	307	368	428	489	549	610	671	732	794	7
8	8	68	128	188	248	308	369	429	490	550	611	672	734	795	8
9	9	69	129	189	249	309	370	430	491	551	612	673	735	796	9
10	10	70	130	190	250	310	371	431	492	552	613	674	736	797	10
11	11	71	131	191	251	311	372	432	493	553	614	675	737	798	11
12	12	72	132	192	252	312	373	433	494	554	615	676	738	799	12
13	13	73	133	193	253	313	374	434	495	555	616	677	739	800	13
14	14	74	134	194	254	314	375	435	496	556	617	678	740	801	14
15	15	75	135	195	255	315	376	436	497	557	618	679	741	802	15
16	16	76	136	196	256	316	377	437	498	558	619	680	742	803	16
17	17	77	137	197	257	317	378	438	499	559	620	681	743	804	17
18	18	78	138	198	258	318	379	439	500	560	621	682	744	805	18
19	19	79	139	199	259	319	380	440	501	561	622	683	745	806	19
20	20	80	140	200	260	320	381	441	502	562	623	684	746	807	20
21	21	81	141	201	261	321	382	442	503	564	624	685	747	808	21
22	22	82	142	202	262	322	383	443	504	565	625	687	748	809	22
23	23	83	143	203	263	323	384	444	505	566	626	688	749	810	23
24	24	84	144	204	264	324	385	445	506	567	627	689	750	811	24
25	25	85	145	205	265	325	386	446	507	568	628	690	751	812	25
26	26	86	146	206	266	326	387	447	508	569	629	691	752	813	26
27	27	87	147	207	267	327	388	448	509	570	631	692	753	815	27
28	28	88	148	208	268	328	389	449	510	571	632	693	754	816	28
29	29	89	149	209	269	330	390	450	511	572	633	694	755	817	29
30	30	90	150	210	270	331	391	451	512	573	634	695	756	818	30
31	31	91	151	211	271	332	392	452	513	574	635	696	757	819	31
32	32	92	152	212	272	333	393	453	514	575	636	697	758	820	32
33	33	93	153	213	273	334	394	454	515	576	637	698	759	821	33
34	34	94	154	214	274	335	395	455	516	577	638	699	760	822	34
35	35	95	155	215	275	336	396	456	517	578	639	700	761	823	35
36	36	96	156	216	276	337	397	457	518	579	640	701	762	824	36
37	37	97	157	217	277	338	398	458	519	580	641	702	763	825	37
38	38	98	158	218	278	339	399	459	520	581	642	703	764	826	38
39	39	99	159	219	279	340	400	460	521	582	643	704	765	827	39
40	40	100	160	220	280	341	401	461	522	583	644	705	766	828	40
41	41	101	161	221	281	342	402	462	523	584	645	706	767	829	41
42	42	102	162	222	282	343	403	463	524	585	646	707	768	830	42
43	43	103	163	223	283	344	404	464	525	586	647	708	769	831	43
44	44	104	164	224	284	345	405	465	526	587	648	709	770	832	44
45	45	105	165	225	285	346	406	466	527	588	649	710	771	833	45
46	46	106	166	226	286	347	407	467	528	589	650	711	772	834	46
47	47	107	167	227	287	348	408	468	529	590	651	712	773	835	47
48	48	108	168	228	288	349	409	469	530	591	652	713	774	836	48
49	49	109	169	229	289	350	410	470	531	592	653	714	775	837	49
50	50	110	170	230	290	351	411	471	532	593	654	715	777	838	50
51	51	111	171	231	291	352	412	472	533	594	655	716	778	839	51
52	52	112	172	232	292	353	413	473	534	595	656	717	779	840	52
53	53	113	173	233	293	354	414	474	535	596	657	718	780	841	53
54	54	114	174	234	294	355	415	476	536	597	658	719	781	842	54
55	55	115	175	235	295	356	416	477	537	598	659	720	782	843	55
56	56	116	176	236	296	357	417	478	538	599	660	721	783	844	56
57	57	117	177	237	297	358	418	479	539	600	661	722	784	845	57
58	58	118	178	238	298	359	419	480	540	601	662	723	785	846	58
59	59	119	179	239	299	360	420	481	541	602	663	724	786	847	59
M.	0°	1°	2°	3°	4°	5°	6°	7°	8°	9°	10°	11°	12°	13°	M.

TABLE III.

Meridional Parts.

M.	14°	15°	16°	17°	18°	19°	20°	21°	22°	23°	24°	25°	26°	27°	M.
0	848	910	973	1035	1098	1161	1225	1289	1354	1419	1484	1550	1616	1684	0
1	850	911	974	36	99	63	26	90	55	20	85	51	18	85	1
2	851	913	975	37	1100	64	27	91	56	21	86	52	19	86	2
3	852	914	976	38	01	65	28	92	57	22	87	53	20	87	3
4	853	915	977	39	02	66	29	93	58	23	88	54	21	88	4
5	854	916	978	1041	1103	1167	1230	1295	1359	1424	1490	1556	1622	1689	5
6	855	917	979	42	05	68	32	96	60	25	91	57	23	90	6
7	856	918	980	43	06	69	33	97	61	26	92	58	24	91	7
8	857	919	981	44	07	70	34	98	62	27	93	59	25	93	8
9	858	920	982	45	08	71	35	99	63	28	94	60	26	94	9
10	859	921	983	1046	1109	1172	1236	1300	1364	1430	1495	1561	1628	1695	10
11	860	922	984	47	10	73	37	01	66	31	96	62	29	96	11
12	861	923	985	48	11	74	38	02	67	32	97	63	30	97	12
13	862	924	986	49	12	75	39	03	68	33	98	64	31	98	13
14	863	925	987	50	13	76	40	04	69	34	99	65	32	99	14
15	864	926	988	1051	1114	1177	1241	1305	1370	1435	1500	1567	1633	1700	15
16	865	927	989	52	15	78	42	06	71	36	02	68	34	01	16
17	866	928	990	53	16	79	43	07	72	37	03	69	35	03	17
18	867	929	991	54	17	81	44	08	73	38	04	70	37	04	18
19	868	930	993	55	18	82	45	10	74	39	05	71	38	05	19
20	869	931	994	1056	1119	1183	1246	1311	1375	1440	1506	1572	1639	1706	20
21	870	932	995	57	20	84	48	12	76	41	07	73	40	07	21
22	871	933	996	58	21	85	49	13	77	43	08	74	41	08	22
23	872	934	997	59	22	86	50	14	79	44	09	75	42	09	23
24	873	935	998	60	23	87	51	15	80	45	10	77	43	11	24
25	874	936	999	1061	1125	1188	1252	1316	1381	1446	1511	1578	1644	1712	25
26	875	937	1000	63	26	89	53	17	82	47	13	79	45	13	26
27	876	938	01	64	27	90	54	18	83	48	14	80	47	14	27
28	877	939	02	65	28	91	55	19	84	49	15	81	48	15	28
29	878	941	03	66	29	92	56	20	85	50	16	82	49	16	29
30	879	942	1004	1067	1130	1193	1257	1321	1386	1451	1517	1583	1650	1717	30
31	880	943	05	68	31	94	58	22	87	52	18	84	51	18	31
32	882	944	06	69	32	95	59	24	88	53	19	85	52	20	32
33	883	945	07	70	33	96	60	25	89	55	20	86	53	21	33
34	884	946	08	71	34	98	61	26	90	56	21	88	54	22	34
35	885	947	1009	1072	1135	1199	1262	1327	1392	1457	1522	1589	1656	1723	35
36	886	948	10	73	36	1200	64	28	93	58	24	90	57	24	36
37	887	949	11	74	37	01	65	29	94	59	25	91	58	25	37
38	888	950	12	75	38	02	66	30	95	60	26	92	59	26	38
39	889	951	13	76	39	03	67	31	96	61	27	93	60	27	39
40	890	952	1014	1077	1140	1204	1268	1332	1397	1462	1528	1594	1661	1729	40
41	891	953	15	78	41	05	69	33	98	63	29	95	62	30	41
42	892	954	16	79	42	06	70	34	99	64	30	96	63	31	42
43	893	955	18	80	44	07	71	35	1400	65	31	98	64	32	43
44	894	956	19	81	45	08	72	36	01	67	32	99	66	33	44
45	895	957	1020	1082	1146	1209	1273	1338	1402	1468	1533	1600	1667	1734	45
46	896	958	21	84	47	10	74	39	03	69	35	01	68	35	46
47	897	959	22	85	48	11	75	40	05	70	36	02	69	36	47
48	898	960	23	86	49	12	76	41	06	71	37	03	70	38	48
49	899	961	24	87	50	13	77	42	07	72	38	04	71	39	49
50	900	962	1025	1088	1151	1215	1278	1343	1408	1473	1539	1605	1672	1740	50
51	901	963	26	89	52	16	80	44	09	74	40	06	73	41	51
52	902	964	27	90	53	17	81	45	10	75	41	08	75	42	52
53	903	965	28	91	54	18	82	46	11	76	42	09	76	43	53
54	904	966	29	92	55	19	83	47	12	77	43	10	77	44	54
55	905	968	1030	1093	1156	1220	1284	1348	1413	1479	1544	1611	1678	1746	55
56	906	969	31	94	57	21	85	49	14	80	46	12	79	47	56
57	907	970	32	95	58	22	86	50	15	81	47	13	80	48	57
58	908	971	33	96	59	23	87	52	16	82	48	14	81	49	58
59	909	972	34	97	60	24	88	53	18	83	49	15	82	50	59
M.	14°	15°	16°	17°	18°	19°	20°	21°	22°	23°	24°	25°	26°	27°	M.

TABLE III

Meridional Parts.

M.	28°	29°	30°	31°	32°	33°	34°	35°	36°	37°	38°	39°	40°	41°	M.
0	1751	1819	1888	1958	2028	2100	2171	2244	2318	2393	2468	2545	2623	2702	0
1	52	21	90	59	30	01	73	46	19	94	70	46	24	03	1
2	53	22	91	60	31	02	74	47	20	95	71	48	25	04	2
3	55	23	92	62	32	03	75	48	22	96	72	49	27	06	3
4	56	24	93	63	33	04	76	49	23	98	73	50	28	07	4
5	1757	1825	1894	1964	2034	2105	2178	2250	2324	2399	2475	2551	2629	2708	5
6	58	26	95	65	35	07	79	52	25	2400	76	53	31	10	6
7	59	27	96	66	37	08	80	53	27	01	77	54	32	11	7
8	60	29	98	67	38	09	81	54	28	03	78	55	33	12	8
9	61	30	99	69	39	10	82	55	29	04	80	57	34	14	9
10	1762	1831	1900	1970	2040	2111	2184	2257	2330	2405	2481	2558	2636	2715	10
11	64	32	01	71	41	13	85	58	32	06	82	59	37	16	11
12	65	33	02	72	43	14	86	59	33	08	84	60	38	18	12
13	66	34	03	73	44	15	87	60	34	09	85	62	40	19	13
14	67	35	05	74	45	16	88	61	35	10	86	63	41	20	14
15	1768	1837	1906	1976	2046	2117	2190	2263	2337	2411	2487	2564	2642	2722	15
16	69	38	07	77	47	19	91	64	38	13	89	66	44	23	16
17	70	39	08	78	48	20	92	65	39	14	90	67	45	24	17
18	72	40	09	79	50	21	93	66	40	15	91	68	46	26	18
19	73	41	10	80	51	22	94	68	42	16	92	69	48	27	19
20	1774	1842	1912	1981	2052	2123	2196	2269	2343	2418	2494	2571	2649	2728	20
21	75	43	13	83	53	25	97	70	44	19	95	72	50	29	21
22	76	45	14	84	54	26	98	71	45	20	96	73	51	31	22
23	77	46	15	85	56	27	99	72	46	22	98	75	53	32	23
24	78	47	16	86	57	28	2200	74	48	23	99	76	54	33	24
25	1780	1848	1917	1987	2058	2129	2202	2275	2349	2424	2500	2577	2655	2735	25
26	81	49	18	88	59	31	03	76	50	25	01	78	57	36	26
27	82	50	20	90	60	32	04	77	51	27	03	80	58	37	27
28	83	52	21	91	61	33	05	79	53	28	04	81	59	39	28
29	84	53	22	92	63	34	07	80	54	29	05	82	61	40	29
30	1785	1854	1923	1993	2064	2135	2208	2281	2355	2430	2506	2584	2662	2742	30
31	86	55	24	94	65	37	09	82	56	32	08	85	63	43	31
32	87	56	25	95	66	38	10	83	58	33	09	86	65	44	32
33	89	57	27	97	67	39	11	85	59	34	10	88	66	46	33
34	90	58	28	98	69	40	13	86	60	35	12	89	67	47	34
35	1791	1860	1929	1999	2070	2141	2214	2287	2361	2437	2513	2590	2669	2748	35
36	92	61	30	2000	71	43	15	88	63	38	14	91	70	50	36
37	93	62	31	01	72	44	16	90	64	39	15	93	71	51	37
38	94	63	32	02	73	45	17	91	65	40	17	94	73	52	38
39	95	64	34	04	75	46	19	92	66	42	18	95	74	54	39
40	1797	1865	1935	2005	2076	2147	2220	2293	2368	2443	2519	2597	2675	2755	40
41	98	66	36	06	77	49	21	95	69	44	21	98	76	56	41
42	99	68	37	07	78	50	22	96	70	45	22	99	78	58	42
43	1800	69	38	08	79	51	24	97	71	47	23	2601	79	59	43
44	01	70	39	10	80	52	25	98	73	48	24	02	80	60	44
45	1802	1871	1941	2011	2082	2153	2226	2299	2374	2449	2526	2603	2682	2762	45
46	03	72	42	12	83	55	27	2301	75	51	27	04	83	63	46
47	05	73	43	13	84	56	28	02	76	52	28	06	84	64	47
48	06	75	44	14	85	57	30	03	78	53	30	07	86	66	48
49	07	76	45	15	86	58	31	04	79	54	31	08	87	67	49
50	1808	1877	1946	2017	2088	2159	2232	2306	2380	2456	2532	2610	2688	2768	50
51	09	78	48	18	89	61	33	07	81	57	33	11	90	70	51
52	10	79	49	19	90	62	35	08	83	58	35	12	91	71	52
53	11	80	50	20	91	63	36	09	84	59	36	14	92	72	53
54	13	81	51	21	92	64	37	11	85	61	37	15	94	74	54
55	1814	1883	1952	2022	2094	2165	2238	2312	2386	2462	2538	2616	2695	2775	55
56	15	84	53	24	95	67	39	13	88	63	40	17	96	76	56
57	16	85	55	25	96	68	41	14	89	64	41	19	98	78	57
58	17	86	56	26	97	69	42	16	90	66	42	20	99	79	58
59	18	87	57	27	98	70	43	17	91	67	44	21	2700	80	59
M.	28°	29°	30°	31°	32°	33°	34°	35°	36°	37°	38°	39°	40°	41°	M.

TABLE III.

Meridional Parts.

M.	42°	43°	44°	45°	46°	47°	48°	49°	50°	51°	52°	53°	54°	55°	M.
0	2782	2863	2946	3030	3116	3203	3292	3382	3474	3569	3665	3764	3865	3968	0
1	83	64	47	31	17	04	93	84	76	70	67	65	66	70	1
2	84	66	49	33	18	06	95	85	78	72	68	67	68	71	2
3	86	67	50	34	20	07	96	87	79	74	70	69	70	73	3
4	87	69	51	36	21	09	98	88	81	75	72	70	71	75	4
5	2788	2870	2953	3037	3123	3210	3299	3390	3482	3577	3673	3772	3873	3977	5
6	90	71	54	38	24	12	3301	91	84	78	75	74	75	78	6
7	91	73	56	40	26	13	02	93	85	80	77	75	77	80	7
8	92	74	57	41	27	14	03	94	87	82	78	77	78	82	8
9	94	75	58	43	29	16	05	96	88	83	80	79	80	84	9
10	2795	2877	2960	3044	3130	3217	3306	3397	3490	3585	3681	3780	3882	3985	10
11	97	78	61	46	31	19	08	99	92	86	83	82	83	87	11
12	98	80	63	47	33	20	09	3400	93	88	85	84	85	89	12
13	99	81	64	48	34	22	11	02	95	90	86	85	87	91	13
14	2801	82	65	50	36	23	12	03	96	91	88	87	89	92	14
15	2802	2884	2967	3051	3137	3225	3314	3405	3498	3593	3690	3789	3890	3994	15
16	03	85	68	53	39	26	16	07	99	94	91	90	92	96	16
17	05	86	70	54	40	28	17	08	3501	96	93	92	94	98	17
18	06	88	71	55	42	29	19	10	03	98	95	94	95	99	18
19	07	89	72	57	43	31	20	11	04	99	96	95	97	4001	19
20	2809	2891	2974	3058	3144	3232	3322	3413	3506	3601	3698	3797	3899	4003	20
21	10	92	75	60	46	34	23	14	07	02	99	99	3901	05	21
22	11	93	76	61	47	35	25	16	09	04	3701	3800	02	06	22
23	13	95	78	63	49	37	26	17	10	06	03	02	04	08	23
24	14	96	79	64	50	38	28	19	12	07	04	04	06	10	24
25	2815	2897	2981	3065	3152	3240	3329	3420	3514	3609	3706	3806	3907	4012	25
26	17	99	82	67	53	41	31	22	15	10	08	07	09	14	26
27	18	2900	83	68	55	42	32	23	17	12	09	09	11	15	27
28	20	02	85	70	56	44	34	25	18	14	11	11	13	17	28
29	21	03	86	71	57	45	35	27	20	15	13	12	14	19	29
30	2822	2904	2988	3073	3159	3247	3337	3428	3521	3617	3714	3814	3916	4021	30
31	24	06	89	74	60	48	38	30	23	18	16	16	18	22	31
32	25	07	91	75	62	50	40	31	25	20	17	17	19	24	32
33	26	08	92	77	63	51	41	33	26	22	19	19	21	26	33
34	28	10	93	78	65	53	43	34	28	23	21	21	23	28	34
35	2829	2911	2995	3080	3166	3254	3344	3436	3529	3625	3722	3822	3925	4029	35
36	30	13	96	81	68	56	46	37	31	26	24	24	26	31	36
37	32	14	98	83	69	57	47	39	32	28	26	26	28	33	37
38	33	15	99	84	71	59	49	40	34	30	27	27	30	35	38
39	34	17	3000	85	72	60	50	42	36	31	29	29	32	37	39
40	2836	2918	3002	3087	3173	3262	3352	3443	3537	3633	3731	3831	3933	4038	40
41	37	19	03	88	75	63	53	45	39	34	32	32	35	40	41
42	39	21	05	90	76	65	55	47	40	36	34	34	37	42	42
43	40	22	06	91	78	66	56	48	42	38	36	36	38	44	43
44	41	24	07	93	79	68	58	50	43	39	37	38	40	45	44
45	2843	2925	3009	3094	3181	3269	3359	3451	3545	3641	3739	3839	3942	4047	45
46	44	26	10	95	82	71	61	53	47	43	41	41	44	49	46
47	45	28	12	97	84	72	62	54	48	44	42	43	45	51	47
48	47	29	13	98	85	74	64	56	50	46	44	44	47	52	48
49	48	31	14	3100	87	75	65	57	51	47	46	46	49	54	49
50	2849	2932	3016	3101	3188	3277	3367	3459	3553	3649	3747	3848	3951	4056	50
51	51	33	17	03	90	78	68	60	55	51	49	49	52	58	51
52	52	35	19	04	91	80	70	62	56	52	50	51	54	60	52
53	54	36	20	05	92	81	71	64	58	54	52	53	56	61	53
54	55	37	21	07	94	83	73	65	59	55	54	54	58	63	54
55	2856	2939	3023	3108	3195	3284	3374	3467	3561	3657	3755	3856	3959	4065	55
56	58	40	24	10	97	86	76	68	62	59	57	58	61	67	56
57	59	42	26	11	98	87	78	70	64	60	59	60	63	69	57
58	60	43	27	13	3200	89	79	71	66	62	60	61	64	70	58
59	62	44	29	14	01	90	81	73	67	64	62	63	66	72	59
M.	42°	43°	44°	45°	46°	47°	48°	49°	50°	51°	52°	53°	54°	55°	M.

TABLE III.

Meridional Parts.

M.	56°	57°	58°	59°	60°	61°	62°	63°	64°	65°	66°	67°	68°	69°	M.
0	4074	4183	4294	4409	4527	4649	4775	4905	5039	5179	5324	5474	5631	5795	0
1	76	84	96	11	29	51	77	07	42	81	26	77	33	97	1
2	77	86	98	13	31	53	79	09	44	84	28	79	36	5800	2
3	79	88	4300	15	33	55	81	12	46	86	31	82	39	03	3
4	81	90	02	17	35	57	84	14	49	88	33	84	42	06	4
5	4083	4192	4304	4419	4537	4660	4786	4916	5051	5191	5336	5487	5644	5809	5
6	85	94	06	21	39	62	88	18	53	93	38	89	47	11	6
7	86	95	08	23	41	64	90	20	55	95	41	92	50	14	7
8	88	97	09	25	43	66	92	23	58	98	43	95	52	17	8
9	90	99	11	27	45	68	94	25	60	5200	46	97	55	20	9
10	4092	4201	4313	4429	4547	4670	4796	4927	5062	5203	5348	5500	5658	5823	10
11	94	03	15	31	49	72	98	29	65	05	51	02	60	25	11
12	95	05	17	33	51	74	4801	31	67	07	53	05	63	28	12
13	97	07	19	34	53	76	03	34	69	10	56	07	66	31	13
14	99	08	21	36	55	78	05	36	71	12	58	10	68	34	14
15	4101	4210	4323	4438	4557	4680	4807	4938	5074	5214	5361	5513	5671	5837	15
16	03	12	25	40	59	82	09	40	76	17	63	15	74	39	16
17	04	14	27	42	62	84	11	43	78	19	66	18	76	42	17
18	06	16	28	44	64	87	14	45	81	22	68	20	79	45	18
19	08	18	30	46	66	89	16	47	83	24	71	23	82	48	19
20	4110	4220	4332	4448	4568	4691	4818	4949	5085	5226	5373	5526	5685	5851	20
21	12	21	34	50	70	93	20	51	88	29	76	28	87	54	21
22	13	23	36	52	72	95	22	54	90	31	78	31	90	56	22
23	15	25	38	54	74	97	24	56	92	34	80	33	93	59	23
24	17	27	40	56	76	99	26	58	95	36	83	36	95	62	24
25	4119	4229	4342	4458	4578	4701	4829	4960	5097	5238	5385	5539	5698	5865	25
26	21	31	44	60	80	03	31	63	99	41	88	41	5701	68	26
27	22	32	46	62	82	05	33	65	5102	43	90	44	04	71	27
28	24	34	47	64	84	07	35	67	04	46	93	46	06	74	28
29	26	36	49	66	86	10	37	69	06	48	95	49	09	76	29
30	4128	4238	4351	4468	4588	4712	4839	4972	5108	5250	5398	5552	5712	5879	30
31	30	40	53	70	90	14	42	74	11	53	5401	54	15	82	31
32	32	42	55	72	92	16	44	76	13	55	03	57	17	85	32
33	33	44	57	74	94	18	46	78	15	58	06	59	20	88	33
34	35	46	59	76	96	20	48	81	18	60	08	62	23	91	34
35	4137	4247	4361	4478	4598	4722	4850	4983	5120	5263	5411	5565	5725	5894	35
36	39	49	63	80	4600	24	52	85	22	65	13	67	28	96	36
37	41	51	65	82	02	26	55	87	25	67	16	70	31	99	37
38	42	53	67	84	04	28	57	90	27	70	18	73	34	5902	38
39	44	55	69	86	06	31	59	92	29	72	21	75	36	05	39
40	4146	4257	4370	4488	4608	4733	4861	4994	5132	5275	5423	5578	5739	5908	40
41	48	59	72	90	10	35	63	96	34	77	26	80	42	11	41
42	50	60	74	92	12	37	65	99	36	80	28	83	45	14	42
43	52	62	76	94	14	39	68	5001	39	82	31	86	47	17	43
44	53	64	78	95	16	41	70	03	41	84	33	88	50	19	44
45	4155	4266	4380	4497	4618	4743	4872	5005	5143	5287	5436	5591	5753	5922	45
46	57	68	82	99	20	45	74	08	46	89	38	94	56	25	46
47	59	70	84	4501	23	47	76	10	48	92	41	96	58	28	47
48	61	72	86	03	25	50	79	12	51	94	43	99	61	31	48
49	62	74	88	05	27	52	81	14	53	97	46	5602	64	34	49
50	4164	4275	4390	4507	4629	4754	4883	5017	5155	5299	5448	5604	5767	5937	50
51	66	77	92	09	31	56	85	19	58	5301	51	07	70	40	51
52	68	79	94	11	33	58	87	21	60	04	54	10	72	43	52
53	70	81	96	13	35	60	90	23	62	06	56	12	75	46	53
54	72	83	98	15	37	62	92	26	65	09	59	15	78	48	54
55	4173	4285	4399	4517	4639	4764	4894	5028	5167	5311	5461	5617	5781	5951	55
56	75	87	4401	19	41	66	96	30	69	14	64	20	83	54	56
57	77	89	03	21	43	69	98	33	72	16	66	23	86	57	57
58	79	91	05	23	45	71	4901	35	74	19	69	25	89	60	58
59	81	92	07	25	47	73	03	37	76	21	71	28	92	63	59
M.	56°	57°	58°	59°	60°	61°	62°	63°	64°	65°	66°	67°	68°	69°	M.

TABLE III.

Meridional Parts.

M.	70°	71°	72°	73°	74°	75°	76°	77°	78°	79°	80°	81°	82°	83°	M.
0	5966	6146	6335	6534	6746	6970	7210	7467	7745	8046	8375	8739	9145	9606	0
1	69	49	38	38	49	74	14	72	49	51	81	45	53	14	1
2	72	52	41	41	53	78	18	76	54	56	87	52	60	22	2
3	75	55	45	45	57	82	22	81	59	61	93	58	67	31	3
4	78	58	48	48	60	86	27	85	64	67	98	65	74	39	4
5	5981	6161	6351	6552	6764	6990	7231	7490	7769	8072	8404	8771	9182	9647	5
6	84	64	54	55	68	94	35	94	74	77	10	78	89	55	6
7	86	67	58	58	71	97	39	98	78	83	16	84	96	64	7
8	89	70	61	62	75	7001	43	7503	83	88	22	91	9203	72	8
9	92	73	64	65	79	05	47	07	88	93	27	97	11	80	9
10	5995	6177	6367	6569	6782	7009	7252	7512	7793	8099	8433	8804	9218	9689	10
11	98	80	71	72	86	13	56	16	98	8104	39	10	25	97	11
12	6001	83	74	76	90	17	60	21	7803	09	45	17	33	9706	12
13	04	86	77	79	93	21	64	25	08	15	51	23	40	14	13
14	07	89	80	83	97	25	68	30	13	20	57	30	48	23	14
15	6010	6192	6384	6586	6801	7029	7273	7535	7817	8125	8463	8836	9255	9731	15
16	13	95	87	90	04	33	77	39	22	31	69	43	62	40	16
17	16	98	90	93	08	37	81	44	27	36	74	49	70	48	17
18	19	6201	94	97	12	41	85	48	32	41	80	56	77	57	18
19	22	05	97	6600	15	45	89	53	37	47	86	63	85	65	19
20	6025	6208	6400	6603	6819	7048	7294	7557	7842	8152	8492	8869	9292	9774	20
21	28	11	03	07	23	52	98	62	47	58	98	76	9300	83	21
22	31	14	07	10	26	56	7302	66	52	63	8504	83	07	91	22
23	34	17	10	14	30	60	06	71	57	68	10	89	15	9800	23
24	37	20	13	17	34	64	11	76	62	74	16	96	22	09	24
25	6040	6223	6417	6621	6838	7068	7315	7580	7867	8179	8522	8903	9330	9817	25
26	43	26	20	24	41	72	19	85	72	85	28	09	37	26	26
27	46	30	23	28	45	76	23	89	77	90	34	16	45	35	27
28	49	33	27	31	49	80	28	94	82	96	40	23	53	44	28
29	52	36	30	35	53	84	32	99	87	8201	46	30	60	52	29
30	6055	6239	6433	6639	6856	7088	7336	7603	7892	8207	8552	8936	9368	9861	30
31	58	42	37	42	60	92	41	08	97	12	58	43	76	70	31
32	61	45	40	46	64	96	45	12	7902	18	65	50	83	79	32
33	64	49	43	49	68	7100	49	17	07	23	71	57	91	88	33
34	67	52	47	53	71	04	53	22	12	29	77	63	99	97	34
35	6070	6255	6450	6656	6875	7108	7358	7626	7917	8234	8583	8970	9407	9906	35
36	73	58	53	60	79	12	62	31	22	40	89	77	14	15	36
37	76	61	57	63	83	16	66	36	27	45	95	84	22	24	37
38	79	64	60	67	86	20	71	40	32	51	8601	91	30	33	38
39	82	68	63	70	90	24	75	45	37	56	07	98	38	42	39
40	6085	6271	6467	6674	6894	7128	7379	7650	7942	8262	8614	9005	9445	9951	40
41	88	74	70	77	98	32	84	54	48	67	20	12	53	60	41
42	91	77	73	81	6901	36	88	59	53	73	26	18	61	69	42
43	94	80	77	85	05	40	92	64	58	79	32	25	69	78	43
44	97	83	80	88	09	45	97	68	63	84	38	32	77	87	44
45	6100	6287	6483	6692	6913	7149	7401	7673	7968	8290	8644	9039	9485	9996	45
46	03	90	87	95	17	53	06	78	73	95	51	46	93	10005	46
47	06	93	90	99	20	57	10	83	78	8301	57	53	9501	10015	47
48	09	96	94	6702	24	61	14	87	83	07	63	60	09	10024	48
49	12	99	97	06	28	65	19	92	89	12	69	67	17	10033	49
50	6115	6303	6500	6710	6932	7169	7423	7697	7994	8318	8676	9074	9525	10043	50
51	18	06	04	13	36	73	27	7702	99	24	82	81	33	10052	51
52	21	09	07	17	40	77	32	06	8004	29	88	88	41	10061	52
53	24	12	11	20	43	81	36	11	09	35	95	96	49	10071	53
54	27	15	14	24	47	85	41	16	14	41	8701	9103	57	10080	54
55	6130	6319	6517	6728	6951	7189	7445	7721	8020	8347	8707	9110	9565	10089	55
56	33	22	21	31	55	94	49	25	25	52	14	17	73	10099	56
57	36	25	24	35	59	98	54	30	30	58	20	24	81	10108	57
58	40	28	28	38	63	7202	58	35	35	64	26	31	89	10118	58
59	43	32	31	42	66	06	63	40	40	69	33	38	98	10127	59
M.	70°	71°	72°	73°	74°	75°	76°	77°	78°	79°	80°	81°	82°	83°	M.

TABLE XXI.

For turning Degrees and Minutes into Time, and the contrary.

D.	H. M.	D.	H. M.	D.	H. M.	D.	H. M.	D.	H. M.	D.	H. M.
M.	M. S.	M.	M. S.	M.	M. S.	M.	M. S.	M.	M. S.	M.	M. S.
1	0. 4	61	4. 4	121	8. 4	181	12. 4	241	16. 4	301	20. 4
2	0. 8	62	4. 8	122	8. 8	182	12. 8	242	16. 8	302	20. 8
3	0.12	63	4.12	123	8.12	183	12.12	243	16.12	303	20.12
4	0.16	64	4.16	124	8.16	184	12.16	244	16.16	304	20.16
5	0.20	65	4.20	125	8.20	185	12.20	245	16.20	305	20.20
6	0.24	66	4.24	126	8.24	186	12.24	246	16.24	306	20.24
7	0.28	67	4.28	127	8.28	187	12.28	247	16.28	307	20.28
8	0.32	68	4.32	128	8.32	188	12.32	248	16.32	308	20.32
9	0.36	69	4.36	129	8.36	189	12.36	249	16.36	309	20.36
10	0.40	70	4.40	130	8.40	190	12.40	250	16.40	310	20.40
11	0.44	71	4.44	131	8.44	191	12.44	251	16.44	311	20.44
12	0.48	72	4.48	132	8.48	192	12.48	252	16.48	312	20.48
13	0.52	73	4.52	133	8.52	193	12.52	253	16.52	313	20.52
14	0.56	74	4.56	134	8.56	194	12.56	254	16.56	314	20.56
15	1. 0	75	5. 0	135	9. 0	195	13. 0	255	17. 0	315	21. 0
16	1. 4	76	5. 4	136	9. 4	196	13. 4	256	17. 4	316	21. 4
17	1. 8	77	5. 8	137	9. 8	197	13. 8	257	17. 8	317	21. 8
18	1.12	78	5.12	138	9.12	198	13.12	258	17.12	318	21.12
19	1.16	79	5.16	139	9.16	199	13.16	259	17.16	319	21.16
20	1.20	80	5.20	140	9.20	200	13.20	260	17.20	320	21.20
21	1.24	81	5.24	141	9.24	201	13.24	261	17.24	321	21.24
22	1.28	82	5.28	142	9.28	202	13.28	262	17.28	322	21.28
23	1.32	83	5.32	143	9.32	203	13.32	263	17.32	323	21.32
24	1.36	84	5.36	144	9.36	204	13.36	264	17.36	324	21.36
25	1.40	85	5.40	145	9.40	205	13.40	265	17.40	325	21.40
26	1.44	86	5.44	146	9.44	206	13.44	266	17.44	326	21.44
27	1.48	87	5.48	147	9.48	207	13.48	267	17.48	327	21.48
28	1.52	88	5.52	148	9.52	208	13.52	268	17.52	328	21.52
29	1.56	89	5.56	149	9.56	209	13.56	269	17.56	329	21.56
30	2. 0	90	6. 0	150	10. 0	210	14. 0	270	18. 0	330	22. 0
31	2. 4	91	6. 4	151	10. 4	211	14. 4	271	18. 4	331	22. 4
32	2. 8	92	6. 8	152	10. 8	212	14. 8	272	18. 8	332	22. 8
33	2.12	93	6.12	153	10.12	213	14.12	273	18.12	333	22.12
34	2.16	94	6.16	154	10.16	214	14.16	274	18.16	334	22.16
35	2.20	95	6.20	155	10.20	215	14.20	275	18.20	335	22.20
36	2.24	96	6.24	156	10.24	216	14.24	276	18.24	336	22.24
37	2.28	97	6.28	157	10.28	217	14.28	277	18.28	337	22.28
38	2.32	98	6.32	158	10.32	218	14.32	278	18.32	338	22.32
39	2.36	99	6.36	159	10.36	219	14.36	279	18.36	339	22.36
40	2.40	100	6.40	160	10.40	220	14.40	280	18.40	340	22.40
41	2.44	101	6.44	161	10.44	221	14.44	281	18.44	341	22.44
42	2.48	102	6.48	162	10.48	222	14.48	282	18.48	342	22.48
43	2.52	103	6.52	163	10.52	223	14.52	283	18.52	343	22.52
44	2.56	104	6.56	164	10.56	224	14.56	284	18.56	344	22.56
45	3. 0	105	7. 0	165	11. 0	225	15. 0	285	19. 0	345	23. 0
46	3. 4	106	7. 4	166	11. 4	226	15. 4	286	19. 4	346	23. 4
47	3. 8	107	7. 8	167	11. 8	227	15. 8	287	19. 8	347	23. 8
48	3.12	108	7.12	168	11.12	228	15.12	288	19.12	348	23.12
49	3.16	109	7.16	169	11.16	229	15.16	289	19.16	349	23.16
50	3.20	110	7.20	170	11.20	230	15.20	290	19.20	350	23.20
51	3.24	111	7.24	171	11.24	231	15.24	291	19.24	351	23.24
52	3.28	112	7.28	172	11.28	232	15.28	292	19.28	352	23.28
53	3.32	113	7.32	173	11.32	233	15.32	293	19.32	353	23.32
54	3.36	114	7.36	174	11.36	234	15.36	294	19.36	354	23.36
55	3.40	115	7.40	175	11.40	235	15.40	295	19.40	355	23.40
56	3.44	116	7.44	176	11.44	236	15.44	296	19.44	356	23.44
57	3.48	117	7.48	177	11.48	237	15.48	297	19.48	357	23.48
58	3.52	118	7.52	178	11.52	238	15.52	298	19.52	358	23.52
59	3.56	119	7.56	179	11.56	239	15.56	299	19.56	359	23.56
60	4. 0	120	8. 0	180	12. 0	240	16. 0	300	20. 0	360	24. 0

TABLE XXII.

Proportional Logarithms.

S.	h m 0° 0′	h m 0° 1′	h m 0° 2′	h m 0° 3′	h m 0° 4′	h m 0° 5′	h m 0° 6′	h m 0° 7′	h m 0° 8′	S.
0		2.2553	1.9542	1.7782	1.6532	1.5563	1.4771	1.4102	1.3522	0
1	4.0334	2481	9506	7757	6514	5549	4759	4091	3513	1
2	3.7324	2410	9471	7734	6496	5534	4747	4081	3504	2
3	5563	2341	9435	7710	6478	5520	4735	4071	3495	3
4	4314	2272	9400	7686	6460	5506	4723	4061	3486	4
5	3.3345	2.2205	1.9365	1.7663	1.6443	1.5491	1.4711	1.4050	1.3477	5
6	2553	2139	9331	7639	6425	5477	4699	4040	3468	6
7	1883	2073	9296	7616	6407	5463	4688	4030	3459	7
8	1303	2009	9262	7593	6390	5449	4676	4020	3450	8
9	0792	1946	9228	7570	6372	5435	4664	4010	3441	9
10	3.0334	2.1883	1.9195	1.7547	1.6355	1.5421	1.4652	1.4000	1.3432	10
11	2.9920	1822	9162	7524	6338	5407	4640	3989	3423	11
12	9542	1761	9128	7501	6320	5393	4629	3979	3415	12
13	9195	1701	9096	7479	6303	5379	4617	3969	3406	13
14	8873	1642	9063	7456	6286	5365	4606	3959	3397	14
15	2.8573	2.1584	1.9031	1.7434	1.6269	1.5351	1.4594	1.3949	1.3388	15
16	8293	1526	8999	7412	6252	5337	4582	3939	3379	16
17	8030	1469	8967	7390	6235	5324	4571	3929	3371	17
18	7782	1413	8935	7368	6218	5310	4559	3919	3362	18
19	7547	1358	8904	7346	6201	5296	4548	3910	3353	19
20	2.7324	2.1303	1.8873	1.7324	1.6185	1.5283	1.4536	1.3900	1.3345	20
21	7112	1249	8842	7302	6168	5269	4525	3890	3336	21
22	6910	1196	8811	7281	6151	5256	4514	3880	3327	22
23	6717	1143	8781	7259	6135	5242	4502	3870	3319	23
24	6532	1091	8751	7238	6118	5229	4491	3860	3310	24
25	2.6355	2.1040	1.8721	1.7217	1.6102	1.5215	1.4480	1.3851	1.3301	25
26	6185	0989	8691	7196	6085	5202	4468	3841	3293	26
27	6021	0939	8661	7175	6069	5189	4457	3831	3284	27
28	5863	0889	8632	7154	6053	5175	4446	3821	3276	28
29	5710	0840	8602	7133	6037	5162	4435	3812	3267	29
30	2.5563	2.0792	1.8573	1.7112	1.6021	1.5149	1.4424	1.3802	1.3259	30
31	5421	0744	8544	7091	6005	5136	4412	3792	3250	31
32	5283	0696	8516	7071	5989	5123	4401	3783	3242	32
33	5149	0649	8487	7050	5973	5110	4390	3773	3233	33
34	5019	0603	8459	7030	5957	5097	4379	3764	3225	34
35	2.4894	2.0557	1.8431	1.7010	1.5941	1.5084	1.4368	1.3754	1.3216	35
36	4771	0512	8403	6990	5925	5071	4357	3745	3208	36
37	4652	0467	8375	6970	5909	5058	4346	3735	3199	37
38	4536	0422	8348	6950	5894	5045	4335	3726	3191	38
39	4424	0378	8320	6930	5878	5032	4325	3716	3183	39
40	2.4314	2.0334	1.8293	1.6910	1.5863	1.5019	1.4314	1.3707	1.3174	40
41	4206	0291	8266	6890	5847	5007	4303	3697	3166	41
42	4102	0248	8239	6871	5832	4994	4292	3688	3158	42
43	4000	0206	8212	6851	5816	4981	4281	3678	3149	43
44	3900	0164	8186	6832	5801	4969	4270	3669	3141	44
45	2.3802	2.0122	1.8159	1.6812	1.5786	1.4956	1.4260	1.3660	1.3133	45
46	3707	0081	8133	6793	5771	4943	4249	3650	3124	46
47	3613	0040	8107	6774	5755	4931	4238	3641	3116	47
48	3522	0000	8081	6755	5740	4918	4228	3632	3108	48
49	3432	1.9960	8055	6736	5725	4906	4217	3623	3100	49
50	2.3345	1.9920	1.8030	1.6717	1.5710	1.4894	1.4206	1.3613	1.3091	50
51	3259	9881	8004	6698	5695	4881	4196	3604	3083	51
52	3174	9842	7979	6679	5680	4869	4185	3595	3075	52
53	3091	9803	7954	6661	5666	4856	4175	3586	3067	53
54	3010	9765	7929	6642	5651	4844	4164	3576	3059	54
55	2 2931	1.9727	1.7904	1.6624	1.5636	1.4832	1.4154	1.3567	1.3051	55
56	2852	9690	7879	6605	5621	4820	4143	3558	3043	56
57	2775	9652	7855	6587	5607	4808	4133	3549	3034	57
58	2700	9615	7830	6568	5592	4795	4122	3540	3026	58
59	2626	9579	7806	6550	5578	4783	4112	3531	3018	59
S.	0° 0′	0° 1′	0° 2′	0° 3′	0° 4′	0° 5′	0° 6′	0° 7′	0° 8′	S.

TABLE XXII.

Proportional Logarithms.

S.	h m 0° 9′	h m 0° 10′	h m 0° 11′	h m 0° 12′	h m 0° 13′	h m 0° 14′	h m 0° 15′	h m 0° 16′	h m 0° 17′	S.
0	1.3010	1.2553	1.2139	1.1761	1.1413	1.1091	1.0792	1.0512	1.0248	0
1	3002	2545	2132	1755	1408	1086	0787	0507	0244	1
2	2994	2538	2126	1749	1402	1081	0782	0502	0240	2
3	2986	2531	2119	1743	1397	1076	0777	0498	0235	3
4	2978	2524	2113	1737	1391	1071	0773	0493	0231	4
5	1.2970	1.2517	1.2106	1.1731	1.1386	1.1066	1.0768	1.0489	1.0227	5
6	2962	2510	2099	1725	1380	1061	0763	0484	0223	6
7	2954	2502	2093	1719	1374	1055	0758	0480	0219	7
8	2946	2495	2086	1713	1369	1050	0753	0475	0214	8
9	2939	2488	2080	1707	1363	1045	0749	0471	0210	9
10	1.2931	1.2481	1.2073	1.1701	1.1358	1.1040	1.0744	1.0467	1.0206	10
11	2923	2474	2067	1695	1352	1035	0739	0462	0202	11
12	2915	2467	2061	1689	1347	1030	0734	0458	0197	12
13	2907	2460	2054	1683	1342	1025	0730	0453	0193	13
14	2899	2453	2048	1677	1336	1020	0725	0449	0189	14
15	1.2891	1.2445	1.2041	1.1671	1.1331	1.1015	1.0720	1.0444	1.0185	15
16	2883	2438	2035	1665	1325	1009	0715	0440	0181	16
17	2876	2431	2028	1660	1320	1004	0711	0435	0176	17
18	2868	2424	2022	1654	1314	0999	0706	0431	0172	18
19	2860	2417	2016	1648	1309	0994	0701	0426	0168	19
20	1.2852	1.2410	1.2009	1.1642	1.1303	1.0989	1.0696	1.0422	1.0164	20
21	2845	2403	2003	1636	1298	0984	0692	0418	0160	21
22	2837	2396	1996	1630	1292	0979	0687	0413	0156	22
23	2829	2389	1990	1624	1287	0974	0682	0409	0151	23
24	2821	2382	1984	1619	1282	0969	0678	0404	0147	24
25	1.2814	1.2375	1.1977	1.1613	1.1276	1.0964	1.0673	1.0400	1.0143	25
26	2806	2368	1971	1607	1271	0959	0668	0395	0139	26
27	2798	2362	1965	1601	1266	0954	0663	0391	0135	27
28	2791	2355	1958	1595	1260	0949	0659	0387	0131	28
29	2783	2348	1952	1589	1255	0944	0654	0382	0126	29
30	1.2775	1.2341	1.1946	1.1584	1.1249	1.0939	1.0649	1.0378	1.0122	30
31	2768	2334	1939	1578	1244	0934	0645	0374	0118	31
32	2760	2327	1933	1572	1239	0929	0640	0369	0114	32
33	2753	2320	1927	1566	1233	0924	0635	0365	0110	33
34	2745	2313	1921	1561	1228	0919	0631	0360	0106	34
35	1.2738	1.2307	1.1914	1.1555	1.1223	1.0914	1.0626	1.0356	1.0102	35
36	2730	2300	1908	1549	1217	0909	0621	0352	0098	36
37	2722	2293	1902	1543	1212	0904	0617	0347	0093	37
38	2715	2286	1896	1538	1207	0899	0612	0343	0089	38
39	2707	2279	1889	1532	1201	0894	0608	0339	0085	39
40	1.2700	1.2272	1.1883	1.1526	1.1196	1.0889	1.0603	1.0334	1.0081	40
41	2692	2266	1877	1520	1191	0884	0598	0330	0077	41
42	2685	2259	1871	1515	1186	0880	0594	0326	0073	42
43	2678	2252	1865	1509	1180	0875	0589	0321	0069	43
44	2670	2245	1859	1503	1175	0870	0585	0317	0065	44
45	1.2663	1.2239	1.1852	1.1498	1.1170	1.0865	1.0580	1.0313	1.0061	45
46	2655	2232	1846	1492	1164	0860	0575	0308	0057	46
47	2648	2225	1840	1486	1159	0855	0571	0304	0053	47
48	2640	2218	1834	1481	1154	0850	0566	0300	0049	48
49	2633	2212	1828	1475	1149	0845	0562	0295	0044	49
50	1.2626	1.2205	1.1822	1.1469	1.1143	1.0840	1.0557	1.0291	1.0040	50
51	2618	2198	1816	1464	1138	0835	0552	0287	0036	51
52	2611	2192	1809	1458	1133	0831	0548	0282	0032	52
53	2604	2185	1803	1452	1128	0826	0543	0278	0028	53
54	2596	2178	1797	1447	1123	0821	0539	0274	0024	54
55	1.2589	1.2172	1.1791	1.1441	1.1117	1.0816	1.0534	1.0270	1.0020	55
56	2582	2165	1785	1436	1112	0811	0530	0265	0016	56
57	2574	2159	1779	1430	1107	0806	0525	0261	0012	57
58	2567	2152	1773	1424	1102	0801	0521	0257	0008	58
59	2560	2145	1767	1419	1097	0797	0516	0252	0004	59
S.	0° 9′	0° 10′	0° 11′	0° 12′	0° 13′	0° 14′	0° 15′	0° 16′	0° 17′	S.

TABLE XXII.

Proportional Logarithms.

S.	*h m* 0° 18′	*h m* 0° 19′	*h m* 0° 20′	*h m* 0° 21′	*h m* 0° 22′	*h m* 0° 23′	*h m* 0° 24′	*h m* 0° 25′	*h m* 0° 26′	*h m* 0° 27′	*h m* 0° 28′	*h m* 0° 29′	S.
0	10000	9765	9542	9331	9128	8935	8751	8573	8403	8239	8081	7929	0
1	9996	9761	9539	9327	9125	8932	8748	8570	8400	8236	8079	7926	1
2	9992	9758	9535	9324	9122	8929	8745	8568	8397	8234	8076	7924	2
3	9988	9754	9532	9320	9119	8926	8742	8565	8395	8231	8073	7921	3
4	9984	9750	9528	9317	9115	8923	8739	8562	8392	8228	8071	7919	4
5	9980	9746	9524	9313	9112	8920	8736	8559	8389	8226	8068	7916	5
6	9976	9742	9521	9310	9109	8917	8733	8556	8386	8223	8066	7914	6
7	9972	9739	9517	9306	9106	8913	8730	8553	8384	8220	8063	7911	7
8	9968	9735	9514	9303	9102	8910	8727	8550	8381	8218	8061	7909	8
9	9964	9731	9510	9300	9099	8907	8724	8547	8378	8215	8058	7906	9
10	9960	9727	9506	9296	9096	8904	8721	8544	8375	8212	8055	7904	10
11	9956	9723	9503	9293	9092	8901	8718	8542	8372	8210	8053	7901	11
12	9952	9720	9499	9289	9089	8898	8715	8539	8370	8207	8050	7899	12
13	9948	9716	9496	9286	9086	8895	8712	8536	8367	8204	8048	7896	13
14	9944	9712	9492	9283	9083	8892	8709	8533	8364	8202	8045	7894	14
15	9940	9708	9488	9279	9079	8888	8706	8530	8361	8199	8043	7891	15
16	9936	9705	9485	9276	9076	8885	8703	8527	8359	8196	8040	7889	16
17	9932	9701	9481	9272	9073	8882	8700	8524	8356	8194	8037	7887	17
18	9928	9697	9478	9269	9070	8879	8697	8522	8353	8191	8035	7884	18
19	9924	9693	9474	9266	9066	8876	8694	8519	8350	8188	8032	7882	19
20	9920	9690	9471	9262	9063	8873	8691	8516	8348	8186	8030	7879	20
21	9916	9686	9467	9259	9060	8870	8688	8513	8345	8183	8027	7877	21
22	9912	9682	9464	9255	9057	8867	8685	8510	8342	8181	8025	7874	22
23	9908	9678	9460	9252	9053	8864	8682	8507	8339	8178	8022	7872	23
24	9905	9675	9456	9249	9050	8861	8679	8504	8337	8175	8020	7869	24
25	9901	9671	9453	9245	9047	8857	8676	8502	8334	8173	8017	7867	25
26	9897	9667	9449	9242	9044	8854	8673	8499	8331	8170	8014	7864	26
27	9893	9664	9446	9238	9041	8851	8670	8496	8328	8167	8012	7862	27
28	9889	9660	9442	9235	9037	8848	8667	8493	8326	8165	8009	7859	28
29	9885	9656	9439	9232	9034	8845	8664	8490	8323	8162	8007	7857	29
30	9881	9652	9435	9228	9031	8842	8661	8487	8320	8159	8004	7855	30
31	9877	9649	9432	9225	9028	8839	8658	8484	8318	8157	8002	7852	31
32	9873	9645	9428	9222	9024	8836	8655	8482	8315	8154	7999	7850	32
33	9869	9641	9425	9218	9021	8833	8652	8479	8312	8152	7997	7847	33
34	9865	9638	9421	9215	9018	8830	8649	8476	8309	8149	7994	7845	34
35	9861	9634	9418	9212	9015	8827	8646	8473	8307	8146	7992	7842	35
36	9858	9630	9414	9208	9012	8824	8643	8470	8304	8144	7989	7840	36
37	9854	9626	9411	9205	9008	8821	8640	8467	8301	8141	7987	7837	37
38	9850	9623	9407	9201	9005	8817	8637	8465	8298	8138	7984	7835	38
39	9846	9619	9404	9198	9002	8814	8635	8462	8296	8136	7981	7832	39
40	9842	9615	9400	9195	8999	8811	8632	8459	8293	8133	7979	7830	40
41	9838	9612	9397	9191	8996	8808	8629	8456	8290	8131	7976	7828	41
42	9834	9608	9393	9188	8992	8805	8626	8453	8288	8128	7974	7825	42
43	9830	9604	9390	9185	8989	8802	8623	8451	8285	8125	7971	7823	43
44	9827	9601	9386	9181	8986	8799	8620	8448	8282	8123	7969	7820	44
45	9823	9597	9383	9178	8983	8796	8617	8445	8279	8120	7966	7818	45
46	9819	9593	9379	9175	8980	8793	8614	8442	8277	8117	7964	7815	46
47	9815	9590	9376	9171	8977	8790	8611	8439	8274	8115	7961	7813	47
48	9811	9586	9372	9168	8973	8787	8608	8437	8271	8112	7959	7811	48
49	9807	9582	9369	9165	8970	8784	8605	8434	8269	8110	7956	7808	49
50	9803	9579	9365	9162	8967	8781	8602	8431	8266	8107	7954	7806	50
51	9800	9575	9362	9158	8964	8778	8599	8428	8263	8104	7951	7803	51
52	9796	9571	9358	9155	8961	8775	8597	8425	8261	8102	7949	7801	52
53	9792	9568	9355	9152	8958	8772	8594	8423	8258	8099	7946	7798	53
54	9788	9564	9351	9148	8954	8769	8591	8420	8255	8097	7944	7796	54
55	9784	9561	9348	9145	8951	8766	8588	8417	8253	8094	7941	7794	55
56	9780	9557	9344	9142	8948	8763	8585	8414	8250	8091	7939	7791	56
57	9777	9553	9341	9138	8945	8760	8582	8411	8247	8089	7936	7789	57
58	9773	9550	9337	9 35	8942	8757	8579	8409	8244	8086	7934	7786	58
59	9769	9546	9334	9132	8939	8754	8576	8406	8242	8084	7931	7784	59
S.	0° 18′	0° 19′	0° 20′	0° 21′	0° 22′	0° 23′	0° 24′	0° 25′	0° 26′	0° 27′	0° 28′	0° 29′	S.

TABLE XXII.

Proportional Logarithms.

S.	*h m* 0° 30′	*h m* 0° 31′	*h m* 0° 32′	*h m* 0° 33′	*h m* 0° 34′	*h m* 0° 35′	*h m* 0° 36′	*h m* 0° 37′	*h m* 0° 38′	*h m* 0° 39′	*h m* 0° 40′	*h m* 0° 41′	S.
0	7782	7639	7501	7368	7238	7112	6990	6871	6755	6642	6532	6425	0
1	7779	7637	7499	7365	7236	7110	6988	6869	6753	6640	6530	6423	1
2	7777	7634	7497	7363	7234	7108	6986	6867	6751	6638	6529	6421	2
3	7774	7632	7494	7361	7232	7106	6984	6865	6749	6637	6527	6420	3
4	7772	7630	7492	7359	7229	7104	6982	6863	6747	6635	6525	6418	4
5	7769	7627	7490	7357	7227	7102	6980	6861	6745	6633	6523	6416	5
6	7767	7625	7488	7354	7225	7100	6978	6859	6743	6631	6521	6414	6
7	7765	7623	7485	7352	7223	7098	6976	6857	6742	6629	6519	6413	7
8	7762	7620	7483	7350	7221	7096	6974	6855	6740	6627	6518	6411	8
9	7760	7618	7481	7348	7219	7093	6972	6853	6738	6625	6516	6409	9
10	7757	7616	7479	7346	7217	7091	6970	6851	6736	6624	6514	6407	10
11	7755	7613	7476	7344	7215	7089	6968	6849	6734	6622	6512	6406	11
12	7753	7611	7474	7341	7212	7087	6966	6847	6732	6620	6510	6404	12
13	7750	7609	7472	7339	7210	7085	6964	6845	6730	6618	6509	6402	13
14	7748	7607	7470	7337	7208	7083	6962	6843	6728	6616	6507	6400	14
15	7745	7604	7467	7335	7206	7081	6960	6841	6726	6614	6505	6398	15
16	7743	7602	7465	7333	7204	7079	6958	6840	6725	6612	6503	6397	16
17	7741	7600	7463	7330	7202	7077	6956	6838	6723	6611	6501	6395	17
18	7738	7597	7461	7328	7200	7075	6954	6836	6721	6609	6500	6393	18
19	7736	7595	7458	7326	7198	7073	6952	6834	6719	6607	6498	6391	19
20	7734	7593	7456	7324	7196	7071	6950	6832	6717	6605	6496	6390	20
21	7731	7590	7454	7322	7193	7069	6948	6830	6715	6603	6494	6388	21
22	7729	7588	7452	7320	7191	7067	6946	6828	6713	6601	6492	6386	22
23	7726	7586	7450	7317	7189	7065	6944	6826	6711	6600	6491	6384	23
24	7724	7583	7447	7315	7187	7063	6942	6824	6709	6598	6489	6383	24
25	7722	7581	7445	7313	7185	7061	6940	6822	6708	6596	6487	6381	25
26	7719	7579	7443	7311	7183	7059	6938	6820	6706	6594	6485	6379	26
27	7717	7577	7441	7309	7181	7057	6936	6818	6704	6592	6484	6377	27
28	7714	7574	7438	7307	7179	7055	6934	6816	6702	6590	6482	6376	28
29	7712	7572	7436	7304	7177	7052	6932	6814	6700	6589	6480	6374	29
30	7710	7570	7434	7302	7175	7050	6930	6812	6698	6587	6478	6372	30
31	7707	7567	7432	7300	7172	7048	6928	6810	6696	6585	6476	6371	31
32	7705	7565	7429	7298	7170	7046	6926	6809	6694	6583	6475	6369	32
33	7703	7563	7427	7296	7168	7044	6924	6807	6692	6581	6473	6367	33
34	7700	7560	7425	7294	7166	7042	6922	6805	6691	6579	6471	6365	34
35	7698	7558	7423	7291	7164	7040	6920	6803	6689	6578	6469	6364	35
36	7696	7556	7421	7289	7162	7038	6918	6801	6687	6576	6467	6362	36
37	7693	7554	7418	7287	7160	7036	6916	6799	6685	6574	6466	6360	37
38	7691	7551	7416	7285	7158	7034	6914	6797	6683	6572	6464	6358	38
39	7688	7549	7414	7283	7156	7032	6912	6795	6681	6570	6462	6357	39
40	7686	7547	7412	7281	7154	7030	6910	6793	6679	6568	6460	6355	40
41	7684	7544	7409	7279	7152	7028	6908	6791	6677	6567	6459	6353	41
42	7681	7542	7407	7276	7149	7026	6906	6789	6676	6565	6457	6351	42
43	7679	7540	7405	7274	7147	7024	6904	6787	6674	6563	6455	6350	43
44	7677	7538	7403	7272	7145	7022	6902	6785	6672	6561	6453	6348	44
45	7674	7535	7401	7270	7143	7020	6900	6784	6670	6559	6451	6346	45
46	7672	7533	7398	7268	7141	7018	6898	6782	6668	6558	6450	6344	46
47	7670	7531	7396	7266	7139	7016	6896	6780	6666	6556	6448	6343	47
48	7667	7528	7394	7264	7137	7014	6894	6778	6664	6554	6446	6341	48
49	7665	7526	7392	7261	7135	7012	6892	6776	6663	6552	6444	6339	49
50	7663	7524	7390	7259	7133	7010	6890	6774	6661	6550	6443	6338	50
51	7660	7522	7387	7257	7131	7008	6888	6772	6659	6548	6441	6336	51
52	7658	7519	7385	7255	7129	7006	6886	6770	6657	6547	6439	6334	52
53	7655	7517	7383	7253	7127	7004	6884	6768	6655	6545	6437	6332	53
54	7653	7515	7381	7251	7124	7002	6882	6766	6653	6543	6435	6331	54
55	7651	7513	7379	7249	7122	7000	6881	6764	6651	6541	6434	6329	55
56	7648	7510	7376	7246	7120	6998	6879	6763	6650	6539	6432	6327	56
57	7646	7508	7374	7244	7118	6996	6877	6761	6648	6538	6430	6325	57
58	7644	7506	7372	7242	7116	6994	6875	6759	6646	6536	6428	6324	58
59	7641	7503	7370	7240	7114	6992	6873	6757	6644	6534	6427	6322	59
S.	0° 30′	0° 31′	0° 32′	0° 33′	0° 34′	0° 35′	0° 36′	0° 37′	0° 38′	0° 39′	0° 40′	0° 41′	S.

TABLE XXII.

Proportional Logarithms.

S.	h m 0° 42′	h m 0° 43′	h m 0° 44′	h m 0° 45′	h m 0° 46′	h m 0° 47′	h m 0° 48′	h m 0° 49′	h m 0° 50	h m 0° 51′	h m 0° 52′	h m 0° 53′	S.
0	6320	6218	6118	6021	5925	5832	5740	5651	5563	5477	5393	5310	0
1	6319	6216	6117	6019	5924	5830	5739	5649	5562	5476	5391	5309	1
2	6317	6215	6115	6017	5922	5829	5737	5648	5560	5474	5390	5307	2
3	6315	6213	6113	6016	5920	5827	5736	5646	5559	5473	5389	5306	3
4	6313	6211	6112	6014	5919	5826	5734	5645	5557	5471	5387	5305	4
5	6312	6210	6110	6013	5917	5824	5733	5643	5556	5470	5386	5303	5
6	6310	6208	6108	6011	5916	5823	5731	5642	5554	5469	5384	5302	6
7	6308	6206	6107	6009	5914	5821	5730	5640	5553	5467	5383	5300	7
8	6306	6205	6105	6008	5913	5819	5728	5639	5551	5466	5382	5299	8
9	6305	6203	6103	6006	5911	5818	5727	5637	5550	5464	5380	5298	9
10	6303	6201	6102	6005	5909	5816	5725	5636	5549	5463	5379	5296	10
11	6301	6200	6100	6003	5908	5815	5724	5635	5547	5461	5377	5295	11
12	6300	6198	6099	6001	5906	5813	5722	5633	5546	5460	5376	5294	12
13	6298	6196	6097	6000	5905	5812	5721	5632	5544	5459	5375	5292	13
14	6296	6195	6095	5998	5903	5810	5719	5630	5543	5457	5373	5291	14
15	6294	6193	6094	5997	5902	5809	5718	5629	5541	5456	5372	5290	15
16	6293	6191	6092	5995	5900	5807	5716	5627	5540	5454	5370	5288	16
17	6291	6190	6090	5993	5898	5806	5715	5626	5538	5453	5369	5287	17
18	6289	6188	6089	5992	5897	5804	5713	5624	5537	5452	5368	5285	18
19	6288	6186	6087	5990	5895	5803	5712	5623	5536	5450	5366	5284	19
20	6286	6185	6085	5989	5894	5801	5710	5621	5534	5449	5365	5283	20
21	6284	6183	6084	5987	5892	5800	5709	5620	5533	5447	5364	5281	21
22	6282	6181	6082	5985	5891	5798	5707	5618	5531	5446	5362	5280	22
23	6281	6179	6081	5984	5889	5796	5706	5617	5530	5445	5361	5279	23
24	6279	6178	6079	5982	5888	5795	5704	5615	5528	5443	5359	5277	24
25	6277	6176	6077	5981	5886	5793	5703	5614	5527	5442	5358	5276	25
26	6276	6174	6076	5979	5884	5792	5701	5613	5526	5440	5357	5275	26
27	6274	6173	6074	5977	5883	5790	5700	5611	5524	5439	5355	5273	27
28	6272	6171	6072	5976	5881	5789	5698	5610	5523	5437	5354	5272	28
29	6271	6169	6071	5974	5880	5787	5697	5608	5521	5436	5353	5271	29
30	6269	6168	6069	5973	5878	5786	5695	5607	5520	5435	5351	5269	30
31	6267	6166	6067	5971	5877	5784	5694	5605	5518	5433	5350	5268	31
32	6265	6165	6066	5969	5875	5783	5692	5604	5517	5432	5348	5266	32
33	6264	6163	6064	5968	5874	5781	5691	5602	5516	5430	5347	5265	33
34	6262	6161	6063	5966	5872	5780	5689	5601	5514	5429	5346	5264	34
35	6260	6160	6061	5965	5870	5778	5688	5599	5513	5428	5344	5262	35
36	6259	6158	6059	5963	5869	5777	5686	5598	5511	5426	5343	5261	36
37	6257	6156	6058	5961	5867	5775	5685	5596	5510	5425	5341	5260	37
38	6255	6155	6056	5960	5866	5774	5683	5595	5508	5423	5340	5258	38
39	6254	6153	6055	5958	5864	5772	5682	5594	5507	5422	5339	5257	39
40	6252	6151	6053	5957	5863	5771	5680	5592	5506	5421	5337	5256	40
41	6250	6150	6051	5955	5861	5769	5679	5591	5504	5419	5336	5254	41
42	6248	6148	6050	5954	5860	5768	5677	5589	5503	5418	5335	5253	42
43	6247	6146	6048	5952	5858	5766	5676	5588	5501	5416	5333	5252	43
44	6245	6145	6046	5950	5856	5765	5674	5586	5500	5415	5332	5250	44
45	6243	6143	6045	5949	5855	5763	5673	5585	5498	5414	5331	5249	45
46	6242	6141	6043	5947	5853	5761	5671	5583	5497	5412	5329	5248	46
47	6240	6140	6042	5946	5852	5760	5670	5582	5496	5411	5328	5246	47
48	6238	6138	6040	5944	5850	5758	5669	5580	5494	5409	5326	5245	48
49	6237	6136	6038	5942	5849	5757	5667	5579	5493	5408	5325	5244	49
50	6235	6135	6037	5941	5847	5755	5666	5578	5491	5407	5324	5242	50
51	6233	6133	6035	5939	5846	5754	5664	5576	5490	5405	5322	5241	51
52	6232	6131	6033	5938	5844	5752	5663	5575	5488	5404	5321	5240	52
53	6230	6130	6032	5936	5843	5751	5661	5573	5487	5402	5320	5238	53
54	6228	6128	6030	5935	5841	5749	5660	5572	5486	5401	5318	5237	54
55	6226	6126	6029	5933	5839	5748	5658	5570	5484	5400	5317	5235	55
56	6225	6125	6027	5931	5838	5746	5657	5569	5483	5398	5315	5234	56
57	6223	6123	6025	5930	5836	5745	5655	5567	5481	5397	5314	5233	57
58	6221	6121	6024	5928	5835	5743	5654	5566	5480	5395	5313	5231	58
59	6220	6120	6022	5927	5833	5742	5652	5564	5478	5394	5311	5230	59
S.	0° 42′	0° 43′	0° 44′	0° 45′	0° 46′	0° 47′	0° 48′	0° 49′	0° 50′	0° 51′	0° 52′	0° 53′	S.

TABLE XXII.

Proportional Logarithms.

S.	h m 0° 54′	h m 0° 55′	h m 0° 56′	h m 0° 57′	h m 0° 58′	h m 0° 59′	h m 1° 0′	h m 1° 1′	h m 1° 2′	h m 1° 3′	h m 1° 4′	h m 1° 5′	S.
0	5229	5149	5071	4994	4918	4844	4771	4699	4629	4559	4491	4424	0
1	5227	5148	5070	4993	4917	4843	4770	4698	4628	4558	4490	4422	1
2	5226	5146	5068	4991	4916	4842	4769	4697	4626	4557	4489	4421	2
3	5225	5145	5067	4990	4915	4841	4768	4696	4625	4556	4488	4420	3
4	5223	5144	5066	4989	4913	4839	4766	4695	4624	4555	4486	4419	4
5	5222	5143	5064	4988	4912	4838	4765	4693	4623	4554	4485	4418	5
6	5221	5141	5063	4986	4911	4837	4764	4692	4622	4552	4484	4417	6
7	5219	5140	5062	4985	4910	4836	4763	4691	4621	4551	4483	4416	7
8	5218	5139	5061	4984	4908	4834	4762	4690	4619	4550	4482	4415	8
9	5217	5137	5059	4983	4907	4833	4760	4689	4618	4549	4481	4414	9
10	5215	5136	5058	4981	4906	4832	4759	4688	4617	4548	4480	4412	10
11	5214	5135	5057	4980	4905	4831	4758	4686	4616	4547	4479	4411	11
12	5213	5133	5055	4979	4903	4830	4757	4685	4615	4546	4477	4410	12
13	5211	5132	5054	4977	4902	4828	4756	4684	4614	4544	4476	4409	13
14	5210	5131	5053	4976	4901	4827	4754	4683	4612	4543	4475	4408	14
15	5209	5129	5051	4975	4900	4826	4753	4682	4611	4542	4474	4407	15
16	5207	5128	5050	4974	4899	4825	4752	4680	4610	4541	4473	4406	16
17	5206	5127	5049	4972	4897	4823	4751	4679	4609	4540	4472	4405	17
18	5205	5125	5048	4971	4896	4822	4750	4678	4608	4539	4471	4404	18
19	5203	5124	5046	4970	4895	4821	4748	4677	4607	4538	4469	4402	19
20	5202	5123	5045	4969	4894	4820	4747	4676	4606	4536	4468	4401	20
21	5201	5122	5044	4967	4892	4819	4746	4675	4604	4535	4467	4400	21
22	5199	5120	5043	4966	4891	4817	4745	4673	4603	4534	4466	4399	22
23	5198	5119	5041	4965	4890	4816	4744	4672	4602	4533	4465	4398	23
24	5197	5118	5040	4964	4889	4815	4742	4671	4601	4532	4464	4397	24
25	5195	5116	5039	4962	4887	4814	4741	4670	4600	4531	4463	4396	25
26	5194	5115	5037	4961	4886	4812	4740	4669	4599	4530	4462	4395	26
27	5193	5114	5036	4960	4885	4811	4739	4668	4597	4528	4460	4394	27
28	5191	5112	5035	4959	4884	4810	4738	4666	4596	4527	4459	4393	28
29	5190	5111	5034	4957	4882	4809	4736	4665	4595	4526	4458	4391	29
30	5189	5110	5032	4956	4881	4808	4735	4664	4594	4525	4457	4390	30
31	5187	5108	5031	4955	4880	4806	4734	4663	4593	4524	4456	4389	31
32	5186	5107	5030	4954	4879	4805	4733	4662	4592	4523	4455	4388	32
33	5185	5106	5028	4952	4877	4804	4732	4660	4590	4522	4454	4387	33
34	5183	5105	5027	4951	4876	4803	4730	4659	4589	4520	4453	4386	34
35	5182	5103	5026	4950	4875	4801	4729	4658	4588	4519	4452	4385	35
36	5181	5102	5025	4949	4874	4800	4728	4657	4587	4518	4450	4384	36
37	5179	5101	5023	4947	4873	4799	4727	4656	4586	4517	4449	4383	37
38	5178	5099	5022	4946	4871	4798	4726	4655	4585	4516	4448	4381	38
39	5177	5098	5021	4945	4870	4797	4724	4653	4584	4515	4447	4380	39
40	5175	5097	5019	4943	4869	4795	4723	4652	4582	4514	4446	4379	40
41	5174	5095	5018	4942	4868	4794	4722	4651	4581	4512	4445	4378	41
42	5173	5094	5017	4941	4866	4793	4721	4650	4580	4511	4444	4377	42
43	5172	5093	5016	4940	4865	4792	4720	4649	4579	4510	4443	4376	43
44	5170	5092	5014	4938	4864	4791	4718	4648	4578	4509	4441	4375	44
45	5169	5090	5013	4937	4863	4789	4717	4646	4577	4508	4440	4374	45
46	5168	5089	5012	4936	4861	4788	4716	4645	4575	4507	4439	4373	46
47	5166	5088	5011	4935	4860	4787	4715	4644	4574	4506	4438	4372	47
48	5165	5086	5009	4933	4859	4786	4714	4643	4573	4505	4437	4370	48
49	5164	5085	5008	4932	4858	4785	4712	4642	4572	4503	4436	4369	49
50	5162	5084	5007	4931	4856	4783	4711	4640	4571	4502	4435	4368	50
51	5161	5082	5005	4930	4855	4782	4710	4639	4570	4501	4434	4367	51
52	5160	5081	5004	4928	4854	4781	4709	4638	4569	4500	4433	4366	52
53	5158	5080	5003	4927	4853	4780	4708	4637	4567	4499	4431	4365	53
54	5157	5079	5002	4926	4852	4778	4707	4636	4566	4498	4430	4364	54
55	5156	5077	5000	4925	4850	4777	4705	4635	4565	4497	4429	4363	55
56	5154	5076	4999	4923	4849	4776	4704	4633	4564	4495	4428	4362	56
57	5153	5075	4998	4922	4848	4775	4703	4632	4563	4494	4427	4361	57
58	5152	5073	4997	4921	4847	4774	4702	4631	4562	4493	4426	4359	58
59	5150	5072	4995	4920	4845	4772	4701	4630	4560	4492	4425	4358	59
S.	0° 54′	0° 55′	0° 56′	0° 57′	0° 58′	0° 59′	1° 0′	1° 1′	1° 2′	1° 3′	1° 4′	1° 5′	S.

TABLE XXII.

Proportional Logarithms.

S.	h m 1° 6′	h m 1° 7′	h m 1° 8′	h m 1° 9′	h m 1° 10′	h m 1° 11′	h m 1° 12′	h m 1° 13′	h m 1° 14′	h m 1° 15′	h m 1° 16′	h m 1° 17′	S.
0	4357	4292	4228	4164	4102	4040	3979	3919	3860	3802	3745	3688	0
1	4356	4291	4227	4163	4101	4039	3978	3919	3859	3801	3744	3687	1
2	4355	4290	4226	4162	4100	4038	3977	3918	3858	3800	3743	3686	2
3	4354	4289	4224	4161	4099	4037	3976	3917	3857	3799	3742	3685	3
4	4353	4288	4223	4160	4098	4036	3975	3916	3856	3798	3741	3684	4
5	4352	4287	4222	4159	4097	4035	3974	3915	3856	3797	3740	3683	5
6	4351	4285	4221	4158	4096	4034	3973	3914	3855	3796	3739	3682	6
7	4350	4284	4220	4157	4095	4033	3972	3913	3854	3795	3738	3681	7
8	4349	4283	4219	4156	4093	4032	3971	3912	3853	3794	3737	3680	8
9	4347	4282	4218	4155	4092	4031	3970	3911	3852	3793	3736	3679	9
10	4346	4281	4217	4154	4091	4030	3969	3910	3851	3792	3735	3678	10
11	4345	4280	4216	4153	4090	4029	3968	3909	3850	3792	3734	3677	11
12	4344	4279	4215	4152	4089	4028	3967	3908	3849	3791	3733	3677	12
13	4343	4278	4214	4151	4088	4027	3966	3907	3848	3790	3732	3676	13
14	4342	4277	4213	4150	4087	4026	3965	3906	3847	3789	3731	3675	14
15	4341	4276	4212	4149	4086	4025	3964	3905	3846	3788	3730	3674	15
16	4340	4275	4211	4147	4085	4024	3963	3904	3845	3787	3729	3673	16
17	4339	4274	4210	4146	4084	4023	3962	3903	3844	3786	3728	3672	17
18	4338	4273	4209	4145	4083	4022	3961	3902	3843	3785	3727	3671	18
19	4336	4271	4207	4144	4082	4021	3960	3901	3842	3784	3727	3670	19
20	4335	4270	4206	4143	4081	4020	3959	3900	3841	3783	3726	3669	20
21	4334	4269	4205	4142	4080	4019	3958	3899	3840	3782	3725	3668	21
22	4333	4268	4204	4141	4079	4018	3957	3898	3839	3781	3724	3667	22
23	4332	4267	4203	4140	4078	4017	3956	3897	3838	3780	3723	3666	23
24	4331	4266	4202	4139	4077	4016	3955	3896	3837	3779	3722	3665	24
25	4330	4265	4201	4138	4076	4015	3954	3895	3836	3778	3721	3664	25
26	4329	4264	4200	4137	4075	4014	3953	3894	3835	3777	3720	3663	26
27	4328	4263	4199	4136	4074	4013	3952	3893	3834	3776	3719	3663	27
28	4327	4262	4198	4135	4073	4012	3951	3892	3833	3775	3718	3662	28
29	4326	4261	4197	4134	4072	4011	3950	3891	3832	3774	3717	3661	29
30	4325	4260	4196	4133	4071	4010	3949	3890	3831	3773	3716	3660	30
31	4323	4259	4195	4132	4070	4009	3948	3889	3830	3772	3715	3659	31
32	4322	4258	4194	4131	4069	4008	3947	3888	3829	3771	3714	3658	32
33	4321	4256	4193	4130	4068	4007	3946	3887	3828	3770	3713	3657	33
34	4320	4255	4192	4129	4067	4006	3945	3886	3827	3769	3712	3656	34
35	4319	4254	4191	4128	4066	4005	3944	3885	3826	3768	3711	3655	35
36	4318	4253	4189	4127	4065	4004	3943	3884	3825	3768	3710	3654	36
37	4317	4252	4188	4126	4064	4003	3942	3883	3824	3767	3709	3653	37
38	4316	4251	4187	4125	4063	4002	3941	3882	3823	3766	3709	3652	38
39	4315	4250	4186	4124	4062	4001	3940	3881	3822	3765	3708	3651	39
40	4314	4249	4185	4122	4061	4000	3939	3880	3821	3764	3707	3650	40
41	4313	4248	4184	4121	4060	3999	3938	3879	3820	3763	3706	3649	41
42	4311	4247	4183	4120	4059	3998	3937	3878	3820	3762	3705	3649	42
43	4310	4246	4182	4119	4058	3997	3936	3877	3819	3761	3704	3648	43
44	4309	4245	4181	4118	4056	3996	3935	3876	3818	3760	3703	3647	44
45	4308	4244	4180	4117	4055	3995	3934	3875	3817	3759	3702	3646	45
46	4307	4243	4179	4116	4054	3993	3933	3874	3816	3758	3701	3645	46
47	4306	4241	4178	4115	4053	3992	3932	3873	3815	3757	3700	3644	47
48	4305	4240	4177	4114	4052	3991	3931	3872	3814	3756	3699	3643	48
49	4304	4239	4176	4113	4051	3990	3930	3871	3813	3755	3698	3642	49
50	4303	4238	4175	4112	4050	3989	3929	3870	3812	3754	3697	3641	50
51	4302	4237	4174	4111	4049	3988	3928	3869	3811	3753	3696	3640	51
52	4301	4236	4173	4110	4048	3987	3927	3868	3810	3752	3695	3639	52
53	4300	4235	4172	4109	4047	3986	3926	3867	3809	3751	3694	3638	53
54	4298	4234	4171	4108	4046	3985	3925	3866	3808	3750	3693	3637	54
55	4297	4233	4169	4107	4045	3984	3924	3865	3807	3749	3693	3636	55
56	4296	4232	4168	4106	4044	3983	3923	3864	3806	3748	3692	3635	56
57	4295	4231	4167	4105	4043	3982	3922	3863	3805	3747	3691	3635	57
58	4294	4230	4166	4104	4042	3981	3921	3862	3804	3746	3690	3634	58
59	4293	4229	4165	4103	4041	3980	3920	3861	3803	3746	3689	3633	59
S.	1° 6′	1° 7′	1° 8′	1° 9′	1° 10′	1° 11′	1° 12′	1° 13′	1° 14′	1 15′	1° 16′	1° 17′	S.

TABLE XXII.

Proportional Logarithms.

S.	*h m* 1° 18′	*h m* 1° 19′	*h m* 1° 20′	*h m* 1° 21′	*h m* 1° 22′	*h m* 1° 23′	*h m* 1° 24′	*h m* 1° 25′	*h m* 1° 26′	*h m* 1° 27′	*h m* 1° 28′	*h m* 1° 29′	S.
0	3632	3576	3522	3468	3415	3362	3310	3259	3208	3158	3108	3059	0
1	3631	3576	3521	3467	3414	3361	3309	3258	3207	3157	3107	3058	1
2	3630	3575	3520	3466	3413	3360	3308	3257	3206	3156	3106	3057	2
3	3629	3574	3519	3465	3412	3359	3307	3256	3205	3155	3105	3056	3
4	3628	3573	3518	3464	3411	3358	3306	3255	3204	3154	3105	3056	4
5	3627	3572	3517	3463	3410	3358	3306	3254	3204	3153	3104	3055	5
6	3626	3571	3516	3463	3409	3357	3305	3253	3203	3153	3103	3054	6
7	3625	3570	3515	3462	3408	3356	3304	3253	3202	3152	3102	3053	7
8	3624	3569	3515	3461	3408	3355	3303	3252	3201	3151	3101	3052	8
9	3623	3568	3514	3460	3407	3354	3302	3251	3200	3150	3101	3052	9
10	3623	3567	3513	3459	3406	3353	3301	3250	3199	3149	3100	3051	10
11	3622	3566	3512	3458	3405	3352	3300	3249	3198	3148	3099	3050	11
12	3621	3565	3511	3457	3404	3351	3300	3248	3198	3148	3098	3049	12
13	3620	3565	3510	3456	3403	3351	3299	3247	3197	3147	3097	3048	13
14	3619	3564	3509	3455	3402	3350	3298	3247	3196	3146	3096	3047	14
15	3618	3563	3508	3454	3401	3349	3297	3246	3195	3145	3096	3047	15
16	3617	3562	3507	3454	3400	3348	3296	3245	3194	3144	3095	3046	16
17	3616	3561	3506	3453	3400	3347	3295	3244	3193	3143	3094	3045	17
18	3615	3560	3506	3452	3399	3346	3294	3243	3193	3143	3093	3044	18
19	3614	3559	3505	3451	3398	3345	3294	3242	3192	3142	3092	3043	19
20	3613	3558	3504	3450	3397	3345	3293	3242	3191	3141	3091	3043	20
21	3612	3557	3503	3449	3396	3344	3292	3241	3190	3140	3091	3042	21
22	3611	3556	3502	3448	3395	3343	3291	3240	3189	3139	3090	3041	22
23	3610	3555	3501	3447	3394	3342	3290	3239	3188	3138	3089	3040	23
24	3610	3555	3500	3446	3393	3341	3289	3238	3188	3138	3088	3039	24
25	3609	3554	3499	3446	3393	3340	3288	3237	3187	3137	3087	3039	25
26	3608	3553	3498	3445	3392	3339	3288	3236	3186	3136	3087	3038	26
27	3607	3552	3497	3444	3391	3338	3287	3236	3185	3135	3086	3037	27
28	3606	3551	3497	3443	3390	3338	3286	3235	3184	3134	3085	3036	28
29	3605	3550	3496	3442	3389	3337	3285	3234	3183	3133	3084	3035	29
30	3604	3549	3495	3441	3388	3336	3284	3233	3183	3133	3083	3034	30
31	3603	3548	3494	3440	3387	3335	3283	3232	3182	3132	3082	3034	31
32	3602	3547	3493	3439	3386	3334	3282	3231	3181	3131	3082	3033	32
33	3601	3546	3492	3438	3386	3333	3282	3231	3180	3130	3081	3032	33
34	3600	3545	3491	3438	3385	3332	3281	3230	3179	3129	3080	3031	34
35	3599	3545	3490	3437	3384	3332	3280	3229	3178	3129	3079	3030	35
36	3598	3544	3489	3436	3383	3331	3279	3228	3178	3128	3078	3030	36
37	3598	3543	3488	3435	3382	3330	3278	3227	3177	3127	3078	3029	37
38	3597	3542	3488	3434	3381	3329	3277	3226	3176	3126	3077	3028	38
39	3596	3541	3487	3433	3380	3328	3276	3225	3175	3125	3076	3027	39
40	3595	3540	3486	3432	3379	3327	3276	3225	3174	3124	3075	3026	40
41	3594	3539	3485	3431	3379	3326	3275	3224	3173	3124	3074	3026	41
42	3593	3538	3484	3431	3378	3325	3274	3223	3173	3123	3073	3025	42
43	3592	3537	3483	3430	3377	3325	3273	3222	3172	3122	3073	3024	43
44	3591	3536	3482	3429	3376	3324	3272	3221	3171	3121	3072	3023	44
45	3590	3535	3481	3428	3375	3323	3271	3220	3170	3120	3071	3022	45
46	3589	3535	3480	3427	3374	3322	3270	3220	3169	3119	3070	3022	46
47	3588	3534	3480	3426	3373	3321	3270	3219	3168	3119	3069	3021	47
48	3587	3533	3479	3425	3372	3320	3269	3218	3168	3118	3069	3020	48
49	3587	3532	3478	3424	3372	3319	3268	3217	3167	3117	3068	3019	49
50	3586	3531	3477	3423	3371	3319	3267	3216	3166	3116	3067	3018	50
51	3585	3530	3476	3423	3370	3318	3266	3215	3165	3115	3066	3018	51
52	3584	3529	3475	3422	3369	3317	3265	3214	3164	3114	3065	3017	52
53	3583	3528	3474	3421	3368	3316	3265	3214	3163	3114	3065	3016	53
54	3582	3527	3473	3420	3367	3315	3264	3213	3163	3113	3064	3015	54
55	3581	3526	3472	3419	3366	3314	3263	3212	3162	3112	3063	3014	55
56	3580	3525	3471	3418	3365	3313	3262	3211	3161	3111	3062	3014	56
57	3579	3525	3471	3417	3365	3313	3261	3210	3160	3110	3061	3013	57
58	3578	3524	3470	3416	3364	3312	3260	3209	3159	3110	3060	3012	58
59	3577	3523	3469	3415	3363	3311	3259	3209	3158	3109	3060	3011	59
S.	1° 18′	1° 19′	1° 20′	1° 21′	1° 22′	1° 23′	1° 24′	1° 25′	1° 26′	1° 27′	1° 28′	1° 29′	S.

TABLE XXII.

Proportional Logarithms.

S.	h m 1° 30′	h m 1° 31′	h m 1° 32′	h m 1° 33′	h m 1° 34′	h m 1° 35′	h m 1° 36′	h m 1° 37′	h m 1° 38′	h m 1° 39′	h m 1° 40′	h m 1° 41′	S.
0	3010	2962	2915	2868	2821	2775	2730	2685	2640	2596	2553	2510	0
1	3009	2962	2914	2867	2821	2775	2729	2684	2640	2596	2552	2509	1
2	3009	2961	2913	2866	2820	2774	2729	2684	2639	2595	2551	2508	2
3	3008	2960	2912	2866	2819	2773	2728	2683	2638	2594	2551	2507	3
4	3007	2959	2912	2865	2818	2772	2727	2682	2638	2593	2550	2507	4
5	3006	2958	2911	2864	2818	2772	2726	2681	2637	2593	2549	2506	5
6	3005	2958	2910	2863	2817	2771	2725	2681	2636	2592	2548	2505	6
7	3005	2957	2909	2862	2816	2770	2725	2680	2635	2591	2548	2504	7
8	3004	2956	2909	2862	2815	2769	2724	2679	2635	2591	2547	2504	8
9	3003	2955	2908	2861	2815	2769	2723	2678	2634	2590	2546	2503	9
10	3002	2954	2907	2860	2814	2768	2722	2678	2633	2589	2545	2502	10
11	3001	2954	2906	2859	2813	2767	2722	2677	2632	2588	2545	2502	11
12	3001	2953	2905	2859	2812	2766	2721	2676	2632	2588	2544	2501	12
13	3000	2952	2905	2858	2811	2766	2720	2675	2631	2587	2543	2500	13
14	2999	2951	2904	2857	2811	2765	2719	2675	2630	2586	2543	2499	14
15	2998	2950	2903	2856	2810	2764	2719	2674	2629	2585	2542	2499	15
16	2997	2950	2902	2855	2809	2763	2718	2673	2629	2585	2541	2498	16
17	2997	2949	2901	2855	2808	2763	2717	2672	2628	2584	2540	2497	17
18	2996	2948	2901	2854	2808	2762	2716	2672	2627	2583	2540	2497	18
19	2995	2947	2900	2853	2807	2761	2716	2671	2626	2583	2539	2496	19
20	2994	2946	2899	2852	2806	2760	2715	2670	2626	2582	2538	2495	20
21	2993	2946	2898	2852	2805	2760	2714	2669	2625	2581	2538	2494	21
22	2993	2945	2898	2851	2805	2759	2713	2669	2624	2580	2537	2494	22
23	2992	2944	2897	2850	2804	2758	2713	2668	2624	2580	2536	2493	23
24	2991	2943	2896	2849	2803	2757	2712	2667	2623	2579	2535	2492	24
25	2990	2942	2895	2848	2802	2756	2711	2666	2622	2578	2535	2492	25
26	2989	2942	2894	2848	2801	2756	2710	2666	2621	2577	2534	2491	26
27	2989	2941	2894	2847	2801	2755	2710	2665	2621	2577	2533	2490	27
28	2988	2940	2893	2846	2800	2754	2709	2664	2620	2576	2533	2489	28
29	2987	2939	2892	2845	2799	2753	2708	2663	2619	2575	2532	2489	29
30	2986	2939	2891	2845	2798	2753	2707	2663	2618	2574	2531	2488	30
31	2985	2938	2891	2844	2798	2752	2707	2662	2618	2574	2530	2487	31
32	2985	2937	2890	2843	2797	2751	2706	2661	2617	2573	2530	2487	32
33	2984	2936	2889	2842	2796	2750	2705	2660	2616	2572	2529	2486	33
34	2983	2935	2888	2842	2795	2750	2704	2660	2615	2572	2528	2485	34
35	2982	2935	2887	2841	2795	2749	2704	2659	2615	2571	2527	2485	35
36	2981	2934	2887	2840	2794	2748	2703	2658	2614	2570	2527	2484	36
37	2981	2933	2886	2839	2793	2747	2702	2657	2613	2569	2526	2483	37
38	2980	2932	2885	2838	2792	2747	2701	2657	2612	2569	2525	2482	38
39	2979	2931	2884	2838	2792	2746	2701	2656	2612	2568	2525	2482	39
40	2978	2931	2883	2837	2791	2745	2700	2655	2611	2567	2524	2481	40
41	2977	2930	2883	2836	2790	2744	2699	2655	2610	2566	2523	2480	41
42	2977	2929	2882	2835	2789	2744	2698	2654	2610	2566	2522	2480	42
43	2976	2928	2881	2835	2788	2743	2698	2653	2609	2565	2522	2479	43
44	2975	2927	2880	2834	2788	2742	2697	2652	2608	2564	2521	2478	44
45	2974	2927	2880	2833	2787	2741	2696	2652	2607	2564	2520	2477	45
46	2973	2926	2879	2832	2786	2741	2695	2651	2607	2563	2520	2477	46
47	2973	2925	2878	2831	2785	2740	2695	2650	2606	2562	2519	2476	47
48	2972	2924	2877	2831	2785	2739	2694	2649	2605	2561	2518	2475	48
49	2971	2924	2876	2830	2784	2738	2693	2649	2604	2561	2517	2475	49
50	2970	2923	2876	2829	2783	2738	2692	2648	2604	2560	2517	2474	50
51	2969	2922	2875	2828	2782	2737	2692	2647	2603	2559	2516	2473	51
52	2969	2921	2874	2828	2782	2736	2691	2646	2602	2559	2515	2472	52
53	2968	2920	2873	2827	2781	2735	2690	2646	2601	2558	2515	2472	53
54	2967	2920	2873	2826	2780	2735	2689	2645	2601	2557	2514	2471	54
55	2966	2919	2872	2825	2779	2734	2689	2644	2600	2556	2513	2470	55
56	2965	2918	2871	2825	2779	2733	2688	2643	2599	2556	2512	2470	56
57	2965	2917	2870	2824	2778	2732	2687	2643	2599	2555	2512	2469	57
58	2964	2916	2869	2823	2777	2732	2687	2642	2598	2554	2511	2468	58
59	2963	2916	2869	2822	2776	2731	2686	2641	2597	2553	2510	2467	59
S.	1° 30′	1° 31′	1° 32′	1° 33′	1° 34′	1° 35′	1° 36′	1° 37′	1° 38′	1° 39′	1° 40′	1° 41′	S.

TABLE XXII.

Proportional Logarithms.

S.	h m 1° 42′	h m 1° 43′	h m 1° 44′	h m 1° 45′	h m 1° 46′	h m 1° 47′	h m 1° 48′	h m 1° 49′	h m 1° 50′	h m 1° 51′	h m 1° 52′	h m 1° 53′	S.
0	2467	2424	2382	2341	2300	2259	2218	2178	2139	2099	2061	2022	0
1	2466	2424	2382	2340	2299	2258	2218	2178	2138	2099	2060	2021	1
2	2465	2423	2381	2339	2298	2258	2217	2177	2137	2098	2059	2021	2
3	2465	2422	2380	2339	2298	2257	2216	2176	2137	2098	2059	2020	3
4	2464	2422	2380	2338	2297	2256	2216	2176	2136	2097	2058	2019	4
5	2463	2421	2379	2337	2296	2256	2215	2175	2136	2096	2057	2019	5
6	2462	2420	2378	2337	2296	2255	2214	2174	2135	2096	2057	2018	6
7	2462	2419	2378	2336	2295	2254	2214	2174	2134	2095	2056	2017	7
8	2461	2419	2377	2335	2294	2253	2213	2173	2134	2094	2055	2017	8
9	2460	2418	2376	2335	2294	2253	2212	2172	2133	2094	2055	2016	9
10	2460	2417	2375	2334	2293	2252	2212	2172	2132	2093	2054	2016	10
11	2459	2417	2375	2333	2292	2251	2211	2171	2132	2092	2053	2015	11
12	2458	2416	2374	2333	2291	2251	2210	2170	2131	2092	2053	2014	12
13	2458	2415	2373	2332	2291	2250	2210	2170	2130	2091	2052	2014	13
14	2457	2415	2373	2331	2290	2249	2209	2169	2130	2090	2052	2013	14
15	2456	2414	2372	2331	2289	2249	2208	2169	2129	2090	2051	2012	15
16	2455	2413	2371	2330	2289	2248	2208	2168	2128	2089	2050	2012	16
17	2455	2412	2371	2329	2288	2247	2207	2167	2128	2088	2050	2011	17
18	2454	2412	2370	2328	2287	2247	2206	2167	2127	2088	2049	2010	18
19	2453	2411	2369	2328	2287	2246	2206	2166	2126	2087	2048	2010	19
20	2453	2410	2368	2327	2286	2245	2205	2165	2126	2086	2048	2009	20
21	2452	2410	2368	2326	2285	2245	2204	2165	2125	2086	2047	2009	21
22	2451	2409	2367	2326	2285	2244	2204	2164	2124	2085	2046	2008	22
23	2450	2408	2366	2325	2284	2243	2203	2163	2124	2085	2046	2007	23
24	2450	2408	2366	2324	2283	2243	2202	2163	2123	2084	2045	2007	24
25	2449	2407	2365	2324	2283	2242	2202	2162	2122	2083	2044	2006	25
26	2448	2406	2364	2323	2282	2241	2201	2161	2122	2083	2044	2005	26
27	2448	2405	2364	2322	2281	2241	2200	2161	2121	2082	2043	2005	27
28	2447	2405	2363	2322	2281	2240	2200	2160	2120	2081	2042	2004	28
29	2446	2404	2362	2321	2280	2239	2199	2159	2120	2081	2042	2003	29
30	2445	2403	2362	2320	2279	2239	2198	2159	2119	2080	2041	2003	30
31	2445	2403	2361	2320	2279	2238	2198	2158	2118	2079	2041	2002	31
32	2444	2402	2360	2319	2278	2237	2197	2157	2118	2079	2040	2001	32
33	2443	2401	2359	2318	2277	2237	2196	2157	2117	2078	2039	2001	33
34	2443	2401	2359	2317	2277	2236	2196	2156	2116	2077	2039	2000	34
35	2442	2400	2358	2317	2276	2235	2195	2155	2116	2077	2038	2000	35
36	2441	2399	2357	2316	2275	2235	2194	2155	2115	2076	2037	1999	36
37	2441	2398	2357	2315	2274	2234	2194	2154	2115	2075	2037	1998	37
38	2440	2398	2356	2315	2274	2233	2193	2153	2114	2075	2036	1998	38
39	2439	2397	2355	2314	2273	2233	2192	2153	2113	2074	2035	1997	39
40	2438	2396	2355	2313	2272	2232	2192	2152	2113	2073	2035	1996	40
41	2438	2396	2354	2313	2272	2231	2191	2151	2112	2073	2034	1996	41
42	2437	2395	2353	2312	2271	2231	2190	2151	2111	2072	2033	1995	42
43	2436	2394	2353	2311	2270	2230	2190	2150	2111	2072	2033	1994	43
44	2436	2394	2352	2311	2270	2229	2189	2149	2110	2071	2032	1994	44
45	2435	2393	2351	2310	2269	2229	2188	2149	2109	2070	2032	1993	45
46	2434	2392	2350	2309	2268	2228	2188	2148	2109	2070	2031	1993	46
47	2433	2391	2350	2309	2268	2227	2187	2147	2108	2069	2030	1992	47
48	2433	2391	2349	2308	2267	2227	2186	2147	2107	2068	2030	1991	48
49	2432	2390	2348	2307	2266	2226	2186	2146	2107	2068	2029	1991	49
50	2431	2389	2348	2307	2266	2225	2185	2145	2106	2067	2028	1990	50
51	2431	2389	2347	2306	2265	2225	2184	2145	2105	2066	2028	1989	51
52	2430	2388	2346	2305	2264	2224	2184	2144	2105	2066	2027	1989	52
53	2429	2387	2346	2304	2264	2223	2183	2143	2104	2065	2026	1988	53
54	2429	2387	2345	2304	2263	2223	2182	2143	2103	2064	2026	1987	54
55	2428	2386	2344	2303	2262	2222	2182	2142	2103	2064	2025	1987	55
56	2427	2385	2344	2302	2262	2221	2181	2141	2102	2063	2025	1986	56
57	2426	2384	2343	2302	2261	2220	2180	2141	2101	2062	2024	1986	57
58	2426	2384	2342	2301	2260	2220	2180	2140	2101	2062	2023	1985	58
59	2425	2383	2342	2300	2260	2219	2179	2139	2100	2061	2023	1984	59
S.	1° 42′	1° 43′	1° 44′	1° 45′	1° 46′	1° 47′	1° 48′	1° 49′	1° 50′	1° 51′	1° 52′	1° 53′	S.

TABLE XXII.

Proportional Logarithms.

S.	h m 1° 54′	h m 1° 55′	h m 1° 56′	h m 1° 57′	h m 1° 58′	h m 1° 59′	h m 2° 0′	h m 2° 1′	h m 2° 2′	h m 2° 3′	h m 2° 4′	S.
0	1984	1946	1908	1871	1834	1797	1761	1725	1689	1654	1619	0
1	1983	1945	1908	1870	1833	1797	1760	1724	1689	1653	1618	1
2	1982	1944	1907	1870	1833	1796	1760	1724	1688	1652	1617	2
3	1982	1944	1906	1869	1832	1795	1759	1723	1687	1652	1617	3
4	1981	1943	1906	1868	1831	1795	1759	1722	1687	1651	1616	4
5	1981	1943	1905	1868	1831	1794	1758	1722	1686	1651	1616	5
6	1980	1942	1904	1867	1830	1794	1757	1721	1686	1650	1615	6
7	1979	1941	1904	1867	1830	1793	1757	1721	1685	1650	1614	7
8	1979	1941	1903	1866	1829	1792	1756	1720	1684	1649	1614	8
9	1978	1940	1903	1865	1828	1792	1755	1719	1684	1648	1613	9
10	1977	1939	1902	1865	1828	1791	1755	1719	1683	1648	1613	10
11	1977	1939	1901	1864	1827	1791	1754	1718	1683	1647	1612	11
12	1976	1938	1901	1863	1827	1790	1754	1718	1682	1647	1612	12
13	1975	1938	1900	1863	1826	1789	1753	1717	1681	1646	1611	13
14	1975	1937	1899	1862	1825	1789	1752	1717	1681	1645	1610	14
15	1974	1936	1899	1862	1825	1788	1752	1716	1680	1645	1610	15
16	1974	1936	1898	1861	1824	1788	1751	1715	1680	1644	1609	16
17	1973	1935	1898	1860	1823	1787	1751	1715	1679	1644	1609	17
18	1972	1934	1897	1860	1823	1786	1750	1714	1678	1643	1608	18
19	1972	1934	1896	1859	1822	1786	1749	1714	1678	1643	1607	19
20	1971	1933	1896	1859	1822	1785	1749	1713	1677	1642	1607	20
21	1970	1933	1895	1858	1821	1785	1748	1712	1677	1641	1606	21
22	1970	1932	1894	1857	1820	1784	1748	1712	1676	1641	1606	22
23	1969	1931	1894	1857	1820	1783	1747	1711	1676	1640	1605	23
24	1968	1931	1893	1856	1819	1783	1746	1711	1675	1640	1605	24
25	1968	1930	1893	1855	1819	1782	1746	1710	1674	1639	1604	25
26	1967	1929	1892	1855	1818	1781	1745	1709	1674	1638	1603	26
27	1967	1929	1891	1854	1817	1781	1745	1709	1673	1638	1603	27
28	1966	1928	1891	1854	1817	1780	1744	1708	1673	1637	1602	28
29	1965	1928	1890	1853	1816	1780	1743	1708	1672	1637	1602	29
30	1965	1927	1889	1852	1816	1779	1743	1707	1671	1636	1601	30
31	1964	1926	1889	1852	1815	1778	1742	1706	1671	1635	1600	31
32	1963	1926	1888	1851	1814	1778	1742	1706	1670	1635	1600	32
33	1963	1925	1888	1850	1814	1777	1741	1705	1670	1634	1599	33
34	1962	1924	1887	1850	1813	1777	1740	1705	1669	1634	1599	34
35	1962	1924	1886	1849	1812	1776	1740	1704	1668	1633	1598	35
36	1961	1923	1886	1849	1812	1775	1739	1703	1668	1633	1598	36
37	1960	1923	1885	1848	1811	1775	1739	1703	1667	1632	1597	37
38	1960	1922	1884	1847	1811	1774	1738	1702	1667	1631	1596	38
39	1959	1921	1884	1847	1810	1774	1737	1702	1666	1631	1596	39
40	1958	1921	1883	1846	1809	1773	1737	1701	1665	1630	1595	40
41	1958	1920	1883	1846	1809	1772	1736	1700	1665	1630	1595	41
42	1957	1919	1882	1845	1808	1772	1736	1700	1664	1629	1594	42
43	1956	1919	1881	1844	1808	1771	1735	1699	1664	1628	1593	43
44	1956	1918	1881	1844	1807	1771	1734	1699	1663	1628	1593	44
45	1955	1918	1880	1843	1806	1770	1734	1698	1663	1627	1592	45
46	1955	1917	1880	1843	1806	1769	1733	1697	1662	1627	1592	46
47	1954	1916	1879	1842	1805	1769	1733	1697	1661	1626	1591	47
48	1953	1916	1878	1841	1805	1768	1732	1696	1661	1626	1591	48
49	1953	1915	1878	1841	1804	1768	1731	1696	1660	1625	1590	49
50	1952	1914	1877	1840	1803	1767	1731	1695	1660	1624	1589	50
51	1951	1914	1876	1839	1803	1766	1730	1694	1659	1624	1589	51
52	1951	1913	1876	1839	1802	1766	1730	1694	1658	1623	1588	52
53	1950	1913	1875	1838	1802	1765	1729	1693	1658	1623	1588	53
54	1950	1912	1875	1838	1801	1765	1728	1693	1657	1622	1587	54
55	1949	1911	1874	1837	1800	1764	1728	1692	1657	1621	1587	55
56	1948	1911	1873	1836	1800	1763	1727	1692	1656	1621	1586	56
57	1948	1910	1873	1836	1799	1763	1727	1691	1655	1620	1585	57
58	1947	1909	1872	1835	1798	1762	1726	1690	1655	1620	1585	58
59	1946	1909	1871	1835	1798	1762	1725	1690	1654	1619	1584	59
S.	1° 54′	1° 55′	1° 56′	1° 57′	1° 58′	1° 59′	2° 0′	2° 1′	2° 2′	2° 3′	2° 4′	S.

TABLE XXII.

Proportional Logarithms.

S.	h m 2° 5′	h m 2° 6′	h m 2° 7′	h m 2° 8′	h m 2° 9′	h m 2° 10′	h m 2° 11′	h m 2° 12′	h m 2° 13′	h m 2° 14′	h m 2° 15′	S.
0	1584	1549	1515	1481	1447	1413	1380	1347	1314	1282	1249	0
1	1583	1548	1514	1480	1446	1413	1379	1346	1314	1281	1249	1
2	1582	1548	1514	1479	1446	1412	1379	1346	1313	1281	1248	2
3	1582	1547	1513	1479	1445	1412	1378	1345	1313	1280	1248	3
4	1581	1547	1512	1478	1445	1411	1378	1345	1312	1280	1247	4
5	1581	1546	1512	1478	1444	1411	1377	1344	1311	1279	1247	5
6	1580	1546	1511	1477	1443	1410	1377	1344	1311	1278	1246	6
7	1580	1545	1511	1477	1443	1409	1376	1343	1310	1278	1246	7
8	1579	1544	1510	1476	1442	1409	1376	1343	1310	1277	1245	8
9	1578	1544	1510	1476	1442	1408	1375	1342	1309	1277	1245	9
10	1578	1543	1509	1475	1441	1408	1374	1342	1309	1276	1244	10
11	1577	1543	1508	1474	1441	1407	1374	1341	1308	1276	1243	11
12	1577	1542	1508	1474	1440	1407	1373	1340	1308	1275	1243	12
13	1576	1542	1507	1473	1440	1406	1373	1340	1307	1275	1242	13
14	1576	1541	1507	1473	1439	1406	1372	1339	1307	1274	1242	14
15	1575	1540	1506	1472	1438	1405	1372	1339	1306	1274	1241	15
16	1574	1540	1506	1472	1438	1404	1371	1338	1306	1273	1241	16
17	1574	1539	1505	1471	1437	1404	1371	1338	1305	1273	1240	17
18	1573	1539	1504	1470	1437	1403	1370	1337	1304	1272	1240	18
19	1573	1538	1504	1470	1436	1403	1370	1337	1304	1271	1239	19
20	1572	1538	1503	1469	1436	1402	1369	1336	1303	1271	1239	20
21	1571	1537	1503	1469	1435	1402	1368	1335	1303	1270	1238	21
22	1571	1536	1502	1468	1435	1401	1368	1335	1302	1270	1238	22
23	1570	1536	1502	1468	1434	1401	1367	1334	1302	1269	1237	23
24	1570	1535	1501	1467	1433	1400	1367	1334	1301	1269	1237	24
25	1569	1535	1500	1467	1433	1399	1366	1333	1301	1268	1236	25
26	1569	1534	1500	1466	1432	1399	1366	1333	1300	1268	1235	26
27	1568	1534	1499	1465	1432	1398	1365	1332	1300	1267	1235	27
28	1567	1533	1499	1465	1431	1398	1365	1332	1299	1267	1234	28
29	1567	1532	1498	1464	1431	1397	1364	1331	1298	1266	1234	29
30	1566	1532	1498	1464	1430	1397	1363	1331	1298	1266	1233	30
31	1566	1531	1497	1463	1429	1396	1363	1330	1297	1265	1233	31
32	1565	1531	1496	1463	1429	1396	1362	1329	1297	1264	1232	32
33	1565	1530	1496	1462	1428	1395	1362	1329	1296	1264	1232	33
34	1564	1530	1495	1461	1428	1394	1361	1328	1296	1263	1231	34
35	1563	1529	1495	1461	1427	1394	1361	1328	1295	1263	1231	35
36	1563	1528	1494	1460	1427	1393	1360	1327	1295	1262	1230	36
37	1562	1528	1494	1460	1426	1393	1360	1327	1294	1262	1230	37
38	1562	1527	1493	1459	1426	1392	1359	1326	1294	1261	1229	38
39	1561	1527	1493	1459	1425	1392	1359	1326	1293	1261	1229	39
40	1561	1526	1492	1458	1424	1391	1358	1325	1292	1260	1228	40
41	1560	1526	1491	1458	1424	1391	1357	1325	1292	1260	1227	41
42	1559	1525	1491	1457	1423	1390	1357	1324	1291	1259	1227	42
43	1559	1524	1490	1456	1423	1389	1356	1323	1291	1259	1226	43
44	1558	1524	1490	1456	1422	1389	1356	1323	1290	1258	1226	44
45	1558	1523	1489	1455	1422	1388	1355	1322	1290	1257	1225	45
46	1557	1523	1489	1455	1421	1388	1355	1322	1289	1257	1225	46
47	1556	1522	1488	1454	1421	1387	1354	1321	1289	1256	1224	47
48	1556	1522	1487	1454	1420	1387	1354	1321	1288	1256	1224	48
49	1555	1521	1487	1453	1419	1386	1353	1320	1288	1255	1223	49
50	1555	1520	1486	1452	1419	1386	1352	1320	1287	1255	1223	50
51	1554	1520	1486	1452	1418	1385	1352	1319	1287	1254	1222	51
52	1554	1519	1485	1451	1418	1384	1351	1319	1286	1254	1222	52
53	1553	1519	1485	1451	1417	1384	1351	1318	1285	1253	1221	53
54	1552	1518	1484	1450	1417	1383	1350	1317	1285	1253	1221	54
55	1552	1518	1483	1450	1416	1383	1350	1317	1284	1252	1220	55
56	1551	1517	1483	1449	1416	1382	1349	1316	1284	1252	1219	56
57	1551	1516	1482	1449	1415	1382	1349	1316	1283	1251	1219	57
58	1550	1516	1482	1448	1414	1381	1348	1315	1283	1250	1218	58
59	1550	1515	1481	1447	1414	1381	1348	1315	1282	1250	1218	59
S.	2° 5′	2° 6′	2° 7′	2° 8′	2° 9′	2° 10′	2° 11′	2° 12′	2° 13′	2° 14′	2° 15′	S.

TABLE XXII.

Proportional Logarithms.

S.	h m 2° 16′	h m 2° 17′	h m 2° 18′	h m 2° 19′	h m 2° 20′	h m 2° 21′	h m 2° 22′	h m 2° 23′	h m 2° 24′	h m 2° 25′	h m 2° 26′	S.
0	1217	1186	1154	1123	1091	1061	1030	0999	0969	0939	0909	0
1	1217	1185	1153	1122	1091	1060	1029	0999	0969	0939	0909	1
2	1216	1184	1153	1122	1090	1060	1029	0998	0968	0938	0908	2
3	1216	1184	1152	1121	1090	1059	1028	0998	0968	0938	0908	3
4	1215	1183	1152	1120	1089	1058	1028	0997	0967	0937	0907	4
5	1215	1183	1151	1120	1089	1058	1027	0997	0967	0937	0907	5
6	1214	1182	1151	1119	1088	1057	1027	0996	0966	0936	0906	6
7	1214	1182	1150	1119	1088	1057	1026	0996	0966	0936	0906	7
8	1213	1181	1150	1118	1087	1056	1026	0995	0965	0935	0905	8
9	1213	1181	1149	1118	1087	1056	1025	0995	0965	0935	0905	9
10	1212	1180	1149	1117	1086	1055	1025	0994	0964	0934	0904	10
11	1211	1180	1148	1117	1086	1055	1024	0994	0964	0934	0904	11
12	1211	1179	1148	1116	1085	1054	1024	0993	0963	0933	0903	12
13	1210	1179	1147	1116	1085	1054	1023	0993	0963	0933	0903	13
14	1210	1178	1147	1115	1084	1053	1023	0992	0962	0932	0902	14
15	1209	1178	1146	1115	1084	1053	1022	0992	0962	0932	0902	15
16	1209	1177	1146	1114	1083	1052	1022	0991	0961	0931	0901	16
17	1208	1177	1145	1114	1083	1052	1021	0991	0961	0931	0901	17
18	1208	1176	1145	1113	1082	1051	1021	0990	0960	0930	0900	18
19	1207	1175	1144	1113	1082	1051	1020	0990	0960	0930	0900	19
20	1207	1175	1143	1112	1081	1050	1020	0989	0959	0929	0899	20
21	1206	1174	1143	1112	1081	1050	1019	0989	0959	0929	0899	21
22	1206	1174	1142	1111	1080	1049	1019	0988	0958	0928	0898	22
23	1205	1173	1142	1111	1080	1049	1018	0988	0958	0928	0898	23
24	1205	1173	1141	1110	1079	1048	1018	0987	0957	0927	0897	24
25	1204	1172	1141	1110	1079	1048	1017	0987	0957	0927	0897	25
26	1204	1172	1140	1109	1078	1047	1017	0986	0956	0926	0896	26
27	1203	1171	1140	1109	1078	1047	1016	0986	0956	0926	0896	27
28	1202	1171	1139	1108	1077	1046	1016	0985	0955	0925	0895	28
29	1202	1170	1139	1108	1076	1046	1015	0985	0955	0925	0895	29
30	1201	1170	1138	1107	1076	1045	1015	0984	0954	0924	0894	30
31	1201	1169	1138	1106	1075	1045	1014	0984	0954	0924	0894	31
32	1200	1169	1137	1106	1075	1044	1014	0983	0953	0923	0893	32
33	1200	1168	1137	1105	1074	1044	1013	0983	0953	0923	0893	33
34	1199	1168	1136	1105	1074	1043	1013	0982	0952	0922	0892	34
35	1199	1167	1136	1104	1073	1043	1012	0982	0952	0922	0892	35
36	1198	1167	1135	1104	1073	1042	1012	0981	0951	0921	0891	36
37	1198	1166	1135	1103	1072	1042	1011	0981	0951	0921	0891	37
38	1197	1165	1134	1103	1072	1041	1011	0980	0950	0920	0890	38
39	1197	1165	1134	1102	1071	1041	1010	0980	0950	0920	0890	39
40	1196	1164	1133	1102	1071	1040	1009	0979	0949	0919	0889	40
41	1196	1164	1132	1101	1070	1040	1009	0979	0949	0919	0889	41
42	1195	1163	1132	1101	1070	1039	1008	0978	0948	0918	0888	42
43	1195	1163	1131	1100	1069	1039	1008	0978	0948	0918	0888	43
44	1194	1162	1131	1100	1069	1038	1007	0977	0947	0917	0887	44
45	1193	1162	1130	1099	1068	1037	1007	0977	0947	0917	0887	45
46	1193	1161	1130	1099	1068	1037	1006	0976	0946	0916	0886	46
47	1192	1161	1129	1098	1067	1036	1006	0976	0946	0916	0886	47
48	1192	1160	1129	1098	1067	1036	1005	0975	0945	0915	0885	48
49	1191	1160	1128	1097	1066	1035	1005	0975	0945	0915	0885	49
50	1191	1159	1128	1097	1066	1035	1004	0974	0944	0914	0884	50
51	1190	1159	1127	1096	1065	1034	1004	0974	0944	0914	0884	51
52	1190	1158	1127	1096	1065	1034	1003	0973	0943	0913	0883	52
53	1189	1158	1126	1095	1064	1033	1003	0973	0943	0913	0883	53
54	1189	1157	1126	1095	1064	1033	1002	0972	0942	0912	0883	54
55	1188	1157	1125	1094	1063	1032	1002	0972	0942	0912	0882	55
56	1188	1156	1125	1094	1063	1032	1001	0971	0941	0911	0882	56
57	1187	1156	1124	1093	1062	1031	1001	0971	0941	0911	0881	57
58	1187	1155	1124	1092	1062	1031	1000	0970	0940	0910	0881	58
59	1186	1154	1123	1092	1061	1030	1000	0970	0940	0910	0880	59
S.	2° 16′	2° 17′	2° 18′	2° 19′	2° 20′	2° 21′	2° 22′	2° 23′	2° 24′	2° 25′	2° 26′	S.

TABLE XXII.

Proportional Logarithms.

S.	h m 2° 27′	h m 2° 28′	h m 2° 29′	h m 2° 30′	h m 2° 31′	h m 2° 32′	h m 2° 33′	h m 2° 34′	h m 2° 35′	h m 2° 36′	h m 2° 37′	S.
0	0880	0850	0821	0792	0763	0734	0706	0678	0649	0621	0594	0
1	0879	0850	0820	0791	0762	0734	0705	0677	0649	0621	0593	1
2	0879	0849	0820	0791	0762	0733	0705	0677	0648	0621	0593	2
3	0878	0849	0819	0790	0762	0733	0704	0676	0648	0620	0592	3
4	0878	0848	0819	0790	0761	0732	0704	0676	0648	0620	0592	4
5	0877	0848	0818	0789	0761	0732	0703	0675	0647	0619	0591	5
6	0877	0847	0818	0789	0760	0731	0703	0675	0647	0619	0591	6
7	0876	0847	0817	0788	0760	0731	0703	0674	0646	0618	0591	7
8	0876	0846	0817	0788	0759	0730	0702	0674	0646	0618	0590	8
9	0875	0846	0816	0787	0759	0730	0702	0673	0645	0617	0590	9
10	0875	0845	0816	0787	0758	0730	0701	0673	0645	0617	0589	10
11	0874	0845	0816	0787	0758	0729	0701	0672	0644	0616	0589	11
12	0874	0844	0815	0786	0757	0729	0700	0672	0644	0616	0588	12
13	0873	0844	0815	0786	0757	0728	0700	0671	0643	0615	0588	13
14	0873	0843	0814	0785	0756	0728	0699	0671	0643	0615	0587	14
15	0872	0843	0814	0785	0756	0727	0699	0670	0642	0615	0587	15
16	0872	0842	0813	0784	0755	0727	0698	0670	0642	0614	0586	16
17	0871	0842	0813	0784	0755	0726	0698	0670	0641	0614	0586	17
18	0871	0841	0812	0783	0754	0726	0697	0669	0641	0613	0585	18
19	0870	0841	0812	0783	0754	0725	0697	0669	0641	0613	0585	19
20	0870	0840	0811	0782	0753	0725	0696	0668	0640	0612	0585	20
21	0869	0840	0811	0782	0753	0724	0696	0668	0640	0612	0584	21
22	0869	0839	0810	0781	0752	0724	0695	0667	0639	0611	0584	22
23	0868	0839	0810	0781	0752	0723	0695	0667	0639	0611	0583	23
24	0868	0838	0809	0780	0751	0723	0694	0666	0638	0610	0583	24
25	0867	0838	0809	0780	0751	0722	0694	0666	0638	0610	0582	25
26	0867	0837	0808	0779	0751	0722	0694	0665	0637	0609	0582	26
27	0866	0837	0808	0779	0750	0721	0693	0665	0637	0609	0581	27
28	0866	0836	0807	0778	0750	0721	0693	0664	0636	0609	0581	28
29	0865	0836	0807	0778	0749	0721	0692	0664	0636	0608	0580	29
30	0865	0835	0806	0777	0749	0720	0692	0663	0635	0608	0580	30
31	0864	0835	0806	0777	0748	0720	0691	0663	0635	0607	0579	31
32	0864	0834	0805	0776	0748	0719	0691	0663	0634	0607	0579	32
33	0863	0834	0805	0776	0747	0719	0690	0662	0634	0606	0579	33
34	0863	0834	0804	0775	0747	0718	0690	0662	0634	0606	0578	34
35	0862	0833	0804	0775	0746	0718	0689	0661	0633	0605	0578	35
36	0862	0833	0803	0774	0746	0717	0689	0661	0633	0605	0577	36
37	0861	0832	0803	0774	0745	0717	0688	0660	0632	0604	0577	37
38	0861	0832	0802	0774	0745	0716	0688	0660	0632	0604	0576	38
39	0860	0831	0802	0773	0744	0716	0687	0659	0631	0603	0576	39
40	0860	0831	0801	0773	0744	0715	0687	0659	0631	0603	0575	40
41	0859	0830	0801	0772	0743	0715	0686	0658	0630	0602	0575	41
42	0859	0830	0801	0772	0743	0714	0686	0658	0630	0602	0574	42
43	0858	0829	0800	0771	0742	0714	0686	0657	0629	0602	0574	43
44	0858	0829	0800	0771	0742	0713	0685	0657	0629	0601	0573	44
45	0857	0828	0799	0770	0741	0713	0685	0656	0628	0601	0573	45
46	0857	0828	0799	0770	0741	0712	0684	0656	0628	0600	0573	46
47	0856	0827	0798	0769	0740	0712	0684	0655	0628	0600	0572	47
48	0856	0827	0798	0769	0740	0711	0683	0655	0627	0599	0572	48
49	0855	0826	0797	0768	0740	0711	0683	0655	0627	0599	0571	49
50	0855	0826	0797	0768	0739	0711	0682	0654	0626	0598	0571	50
51	0855	0825	0796	0767	0739	0710	0682	0654	0626	0598	0570	51
52	0854	0825	0796	0767	0738	0710	0681	0653	0625	0597	0570	52
53	0854	0824	0795	0766	0738	0709	0681	0653	0625	0597	0569	53
54	0853	0824	0795	0766	0737	0709	0680	0652	0624	0596	0569	54
55	0853	0823	0794	0765	0737	0708	0680	0652	0624	0596	0568	55
56	0852	0823	0794	0765	0736	0708	0679	0651	0623	0596	0568	56
57	0852	0822	0793	0764	0736	0707	0679	0651	0623	0595	0568	57
58	0851	0822	0793	0764	0735	0707	0678	0650	0622	0595	0567	58
59	0851	0821	0792	0763	0735	0706	0678	0650	0622	0594	0567	59
S.	2° 27′	2° 28′	2° 29′	2° 30′	2° 31′	2° 32′	2° 33′	2° 34′	2° 35′	2° 36′	2° 37′	S.

TABLE XXII.

Proportional Logarithms.

S.	h m 2° 38′	h m 2° 39′	h m 2° 40′	h m 2° 41′	h m 2° 42′	h m 2° 43′	h m 2° 44′	h m 2° 45′	h m 2° 46′	h m 2° 47′	h m 2° 48′	S.
0	0566	0539	0512	0484	0458	0431	0404	0378	0352	0326	0300	0
1	0566	0538	0511	0484	0457	0430	0404	0377	0351	0325	0299	1
2	0565	0538	0511	0484	0457	0430	0403	0377	0351	0325	0299	2
3	0565	0537	0510	0483	0456	0430	0403	0377	0350	0324	0298	3
4	0564	0537	0510	0483	0456	0429	0403	0376	0350	0324	0298	4
5	0564	0536	0509	0482	0455	0429	0402	0376	0349	0323	0297	5
6	0563	0536	0509	0482	0455	0428	0402	0375	0349	0323	0297	6
7	0563	0536	0508	0481	0454	0428	0401	0375	0349	0323	0297	7
8	0562	0535	0508	0481	0454	0427	0401	0374	0348	0322	0296	8
9	0562	0535	0507	0480	0454	0427	0400	0374	0348	0322	0296	9
10	0562	0534	0507	0480	0453	0426	0400	0374	0347	0321	0295	10
11	0561	0534	0507	0480	0453	0426	0399	0373	0347	0321	0295	11
12	0561	0533	0506	0479	0452	0426	0399	0373	0346	0320	0294	12
13	0560	0533	0506	0479	0452	0425	0399	0372	0346	0320	0294	13
14	0560	0532	0505	0478	0451	0425	0398	0372	0346	0319	0294	14
15	0559	0532	0505	0478	0451	0424	0398	0371	0345	0319	0293	15
16	0559	0531	0504	0477	0450	0424	0397	0371	0345	0319	0293	16
17	0558	0531	0504	0477	0450	0423	0397	0370	0344	0318	0292	17
18	0558	0531	0503	0476	0450	0423	0396	0370	0344	0318	0292	18
19	0557	0530	0503	0476	0449	0422	0396	0370	0343	0317	0291	19
20	0557	0530	0502	0475	0449	0422	0395	0369	0343	0317	0291	20
21	0557	0529	0502	0475	0448	0422	0395	0369	0342	0316	0291	21
22	0556	0529	0502	0475	0448	0421	0395	0368	0342	0316	0290	22
23	0556	0528	0501	0474	0447	0421	0394	0368	0342	0316	0290	23
24	0555	0528	0501	0474	0447	0420	0394	0367	0341	0315	0289	24
25	0555	0527	0500	0473	0446	0420	0393	0367	0341	0315	0289	25
26	0554	0527	0500	0473	0446	0419	0393	0366	0340	0314	0288	26
27	0554	0526	0499	0472	0446	0419	0392	0366	0340	0314	0288	27
28	0553	0526	0499	0472	0445	0418	0392	0366	0339	0313	0288	28
29	0553	0526	0498	0471	0445	0418	0392	0365	0339	0313	0287	29
30	0552	0525	0498	0471	0444	0418	0391	0365	0339	0313	0287	30
31	0552	0525	0498	0471	0444	0417	0391	0364	0338	0312	0286	31
32	0552	0524	0497	0470	0443	0417	0390	0364	0338	0312	0286	32
33	0551	0524	0497	0470	0443	0416	0390	0363	0337	0311	0285	33
34	0551	0523	0496	0469	0442	0416	0389	0363	0337	0311	0285	34
35	0550	0523	0496	0469	0442	0415	0389	0363	0336	0310	0285	35
36	0550	0522	0495	0468	0442	0415	0388	0362	0336	0310	0284	36
37	0549	0522	0495	0468	0441	0414	0388	0362	0336	0310	0284	37
38	0549	0521	0494	0467	0441	0414	0388	0361	0335	0309	0283	38
39	0548	0521	0494	0467	0440	0414	0387	0361	0335	0309	0283	39
40	0548	0521	0493	0467	0440	0413	0387	0360	0334	0308	0282	40
41	0547	0520	0493	0466	0439	0413	0386	0360	0334	0308	0282	41
42	0547	0520	0493	0466	0439	0412	0386	0359	0333	0307	0282	42
43	0546	0519	0492	0465	0438	0412	0385	0359	0333	0307	0281	43
44	0546	0519	0492	0465	0438	0411	0385	0359	0333	0307	0281	44
45	0546	0518	0491	0464	0438	0411	0384	0358	0332	0306	0280	45
46	0545	0518	0491	0464	0437	0410	0384	0358	0332	0306	0280	46
47	0545	0517	0490	0463	0437	0410	0384	0357	0331	0305	0279	47
48	0544	0517	0490	0463	0436	0410	0383	0357	0331	0305	0279	48
49	0544	0517	0489	0462	0436	0409	0383	0356	0330	0304	0279	49
50	0543	0516	0489	0462	0435	0409	0382	0356	0330	0304	0278	50
51	0543	0516	0489	0462	0435	0408	0382	0356	0329	0304	0278	51
52	0542	0515	0488	0461	0434	0408	0381	0355	0329	0303	0277	52
53	0542	0515	0488	0461	0434	0407	0381	0355	0329	0303	0277	53
54	0541	0514	0487	0460	0434	0407	0381	0354	0328	0302	0276	54
55	0541	0514	0487	0460	0433	0406	0380	0354	0328	0302	0276	55
56	0541	0513	0486	0459	0433	0406	0380	0353	0327	0301	0276	56
57	0540	0513	0486	0459	0432	0406	0379	0353	0327	0301	0275	57
58	0540	0512	0485	0458	0432	0405	0379	0353	0326	0300	0275	58
59	0539	0512	0485	0458	0431	0405	0378	0352	0326	0300	0274	59
S.	2° 38′	2° 39′	2° 40′	2° 41′	2° 42′	2° 43′	2° 44′	2° 45′	2° 46′	2° 47′	2° 48′	S.

TABLE XXII.

Proportional Logarithms.

S.	*h m* 2° 49′	*h m* 2° 50′	*h m* 2° 51′	*h m* 2° 52′	*h m* 2° 53′	*h m* 2° 54′	*h m* 2° 55′	*h m* 2° 56′	*h m* 2° 57′	*h m* 2° 58′	*h m* 2° 59′	S.
0	0274	0248	0223	0197	0172	0147	0122	0098	0073	0049	0024	0
1	0273	0248	0222	0197	0172	0147	0122	0097	0073	0048	0024	1
2	0273	0247	0222	0197	0171	0146	0122	0097	0072	0048	0023	2
3	0273	0247	0221	0196	0171	0146	0121	0096	0072	0047	0023	3
4	0272	0247	0221	0196	0171	0146	0121	0096	0071	0047	0023	4
5	0272	0246	0221	0195	0170	0145	0120	0096	0071	0046	0022	5
6	0271	0246	0220	0195	0170	0145	0120	0095	0071	0046	0022	6
7	0271	0245	0220	0194	0169	0144	0119	0095	0070	0046	0021	7
8	0270	0245	0219	0194	0169	0144	0119	0094	0070	0045	0021	8
9	0270	0244	0219	0194	0169	0143	0119	0094	0069	0045	0021	9
10	0270	0244	0219	0193	0168	0143	0118	0093	0069	0044	0020	10
11	0269	0244	0218	0193	0168	0143	0118	0093	0068	0044	0020	11
12	0269	0243	0218	0192	0167	0142	0117	0093	0068	0044	0019	12
13	0268	0243	0217	0192	0167	0142	0117	0092	0068	0043	0019	13
14	0268	0242	0217	0192	0166	0141	0117	0092	0067	0043	0019	14
15	0267	0242	0216	0191	0166	0141	0116	0091	0067	0042	0018	15
16	0267	0241	0216	0191	0166	0141	0116	0091	0066	0042	0018	16
17	0267	0241	0216	0190	0165	0140	0115	0091	0066	0042	0017	17
18	0266	0241	0215	0190	0165	0140	0115	0090	0066	0041	0017	18
19	0266	0240	0215	0189	0164	0139	0114	0090	0065	0041	0017	19
20	0265	0240	0214	0189	0164	0139	0114	0089	0065	0040	0016	20
21	0265	0239	0214	0189	0163	0139	0114	0089	0064	0040	0016	21
22	0264	0239	0213	0188	0163	0138	0113	0089	0064	0040	0015	22
23	0264	0238	0213	0188	0163	0138	0113	0088	0064	0039	0015	23
24	0264	0238	0213	0187	0162	0137	0112	0088	0063	0039	0015	24
25	0263	0238	0212	0187	0162	0137	0112	0087	0063	0038	0014	25
26	0263	0237	0212	0187	0161	0136	0112	0087	0062	0038	0014	26
27	0262	0237	0211	0186	0161	0136	0111	0087	0062	0038	0013	27
28	0262	0236	0211	0186	0161	0136	0111	0086	0062	0037	0013	28
29	0261	0236	0211	0185	0160	0135	0110	0086	0061	0037	0012	29
30	0261	0235	0210	0185	0160	0135	0110	0085	0061	0036	0012	30
31	0261	0235	0210	0184	0159	0134	0110	0085	0060	0036	0012	31
32	0260	0235	0209	0184	0159	0134	0109	0084	0060	0036	0011	32
33	0260	0234	0209	0184	0158	0134	0109	0084	0060	0035	0011	33
34	0259	0234	0208	0183	0158	0133	0108	0084	0059	0035	0010	34
35	0259	0233	0208	0183	0158	0133	0108	0083	0059	0034	0010	35
36	0258	0233	0208	0182	0157	0132	0107	0083	0058	0034	0010	36
37	0258	0233	0207	0182	0157	0132	0107	0082	0058	0034	0009	37
38	0258	0232	0207	0181	0156	0131	0107	0082	0057	0033	0009	38
39	0257	0232	0206	0181	0156	0131	0106	0082	0057	0033	0008	39
40	0257	0231	0206	0181	0156	0131	0106	0081	0057	0032	0008	40
41	0256	0231	0205	0180	0155	0130	0105	0081	0056	0032	0008	41
42	0256	0230	0205	0180	0155	0130	0105	0080	0056	0031	0007	42
43	0255	0230	0205	0179	0154	0129	0105	0080	0055	0031	0007	43
44	0255	0230	0204	0179	0154	0129	0104	0080	0055	0031	0006	44
45	0255	0229	0204	0179	0153	0129	0104	0079	0055	0030	0006	45
46	0254	0229	0203	0178	0153	0128	0103	0079	0054	0030	0006	46
47	0254	0228	0203	0178	0153	0128	0103	0078	0054	0029	0005	47
48	0253	0228	0202	0177	0152	0127	0103	0078	0053	0029	0005	48
49	0253	0227	0202	0177	0152	0127	0102	0077	0053	0029	0004	49
50	0252	0227	0202	0176	0151	0126	0102	0077	0053	0028	0004	50
51	0252	0227	0201	0176	0151	0126	0101	0077	0052	0028	0004	51
52	0252	0226	0201	0176	0151	0126	0101	0076	0052	0027	0003	52
53	0251	0226	0200	0175	0150	0125	0100	0076	0051	0027	0003	53
54	0251	0225	0200	0175	0150	0125	0100	0075	0051	0027	0002	54
55	0250	0225	0200	0174	0149	0124	0100	0075	0051	0026	0002	55
56	0250	0224	0199	0174	0149	0124	0099	0075	0050	0026	0002	56
57	0250	0224	0199	0174	0148	0124	0099	0074	0050	0025	0001	57
58	0249	0224	0198	0173	0148	0123	0098	0074	0049	0025	0001	58
59	0249	0223	0198	0173	0148	0123	0098	0073	0049	0025	0000	59
S.	2° 49′	2° 50′	2° 51′	2° 52′	2° 53′	2° 54′	2° 55′	2° 56′	2° 57′	2° 58′	2° 59′	S.

TABLES

TABLE XXIV.

Of Natural Sines.

Prop. parts		0°		1°		2°		3°		4°			Prop. parts
29	M	N. sine.	N. cos.	N. sine.	N. cos.	N. sine.	N. cos.	N. sine.	N. cos.	N. sine.	N. cos.		2
0	0	00000	100000	01745	99985	03490	99939	05234	99863	06976	99756	60	2
0	1	00029	100000	01774	99984	03519	99938	05263	99861	07005	99754	59	2
1	2	00058	100000	01803	99984	03548	99937	05292	99860	07034	99752	58	2
1	3	00087	100000	01832	99983	03577	99936	05321	99858	07063	99750	57	2
2	4	00116	100000	01862	99983	03606	99935	05350	99857	07092	99748	56	2
2	5	00145	100000	01891	99982	03635	99934	05379	99855	07121	99746	55	2
3	6	00175	100000	01920	99982	03664	99933	05408	99854	07150	99744	54	2
3	7	00204	100000	01949	99981	03693	99932	05437	99852	07179	99742	53	2
4	8	00233	100000	01978	99980	03723	99931	05466	99851	07208	99740	52	2
4	9	00262	100000	02007	99980	03752	99930	05495	99849	07237	99738	51	2
5	10	00291	100000	02036	99979	03781	99929	05524	99847	07266	99736	50	2
5	11	00320	99999	02065	99979	03810	99927	05553	99846	07295	99734	49	2
6	12	00349	99999	02094	99978	03839	99926	05582	99844	07324	99731	48	2
6	13	00378	99999	02123	99977	03868	99925	05611	99842	07353	99729	47	2
7	14	00407	99999	02152	99977	03897	99924	05640	99841	07382	99727	46	2
7	15	00436	99999	02181	99976	03926	99923	05669	99839	07411	99725	45	2
8	16	00465	99999	02211	99976	03955	99922	05698	99838	07440	99723	44	1
8	17	00495	99999	02240	99975	03984	99921	05727	99836	07469	99721	43	1
9	18	00524	99999	02269	99974	04013	99919	05756	99834	07498	99719	42	1
9	19	00553	99998	02298	99974	04042	99918	05785	99833	07527	99716	41	1
10	20	00582	99998	02327	99973	04071	99917	05814	99831	07556	99714	40	1
10	21	00611	99998	02356	99972	04100	99916	05844	99829	07585	99712	39	1
11	22	00640	99998	02385	99972	04129	99915	05873	99827	07614	99710	38	1
11	23	00669	99998	02414	99971	04159	99913	05902	99826	07643	99708	37	1
12	24	00698	99998	02443	99970	04188	99912	05931	99824	07672	99705	36	1
12	25	00727	99997	02472	99969	04217	99911	05960	99822	07701	99703	35	1
13	26	00756	99997	02501	99969	04246	99910	05989	99821	07730	99701	34	1
13	27	00785	99997	02530	99968	04275	99909	06018	99819	07759	99699	33	1
14	28	00814	99997	02560	99967	04304	99907	06047	99817	07788	99696	32	1
14	29	00844	99996	02589	99966	04333	99906	06076	99815	07817	99694	31	1
15	30	00873	99996	02618	99966	04362	99905	06105	99813	07846	99692	30	1
15	31	00902	99996	02647	99965	04391	99904	06134	99812	07875	99689	29	1
15	32	00931	99996	02676	99964	04420	99902	06163	99810	07904	99687	28	1
16	33	00960	99995	02705	99963	04449	99901	06192	99808	07933	99685	27	1
16	34	00989	99995	02734	99963	04478	99900	06221	99806	07962	99683	26	1
17	35	01018	99995	02763	99962	04507	99898	06250	99804	07991	99680	25	1
17	36	01047	99995	02792	99961	04536	99897	06279	99803	08020	99678	24	1
18	37	01076	99994	02821	99960	04565	99896	06308	99801	08049	99676	23	1
18	38	01105	99994	02850	99959	04594	99894	06337	99799	08078	99673	22	1
19	39	01134	99994	02879	99959	04623	99893	06366	99797	08107	99671	21	1
19	40	01164	99993	02908	99958	04653	99892	06395	99795	08136	99668	20	1
20	41	01193	99993	02938	99957	04682	99890	06424	99793	08165	99666	19	1
20	42	01222	99993	02967	99956	04711	99889	06453	99792	08194	99664	18	1
21	43	01251	99992	02996	99955	04740	99888	06482	99790	08223	99661	17	1
21	44	01280	99992	03025	99954	04769	99886	06511	99788	08252	99659	16	1
22	45	01309	99991	03054	99953	04798	99885	06540	99786	08281	99657	15	1
22	46	01338	99991	03083	99952	04827	99883	06569	99784	08310	99654	14	0
23	47	01367	99991	03112	99952	04856	99882	06598	99782	08339	99652	13	0
23	48	01396	99990	03141	99951	04885	99881	06627	99780	08368	99649	12	0
24	49	01425	99990	03170	99950	04914	99879	06656	99778	08397	99647	11	0
24	50	01454	99989	03199	99949	04943	99878	06685	99776	08426	99644	10	0
25	51	01483	99989	03228	99948	04972	99876	06714	99774	08455	99642	9	0
25	52	01513	99989	03257	99947	05001	99875	06743	99772	08484	99639	8	0
26	53	01542	99988	03286	99946	05030	99873	06773	99770	08513	99637	7	0
26	54	01571	99988	03316	99945	05059	99872	06802	99768	08542	99635	6	0
27	55	01600	99987	03345	99944	05088	99870	06831	99766	08571	99632	5	0
27	56	01629	99987	03374	99943	05117	99869	06860	99764	08600	99630	4	0
28	57	01658	99986	03403	99942	05146	99867	06889	99762	08629	99627	3	0
28	58	01687	99986	03432	99941	05175	99866	06918	99760	08658	99625	2	0
29	59	01716	99985	03461	99940	05205	99864	06947	99758	08687	99622	1	0
29	60	01745	99985	03490	99939	05234	99863	06976	99756	08716	99619	0	0
		N. cos.	N. sine.	N. cos.	N. sine.	N. cos.	N. sine.	N. cos.	N. sine.	N. cos.	N. sine.	M	
		89°		88°		87°		86°		85°			

TABLE XXIV.

Of Natural Sines.

Prop. parts		5°		6°		7°		8°		9°			Prop. parts
29	M	N. sine.	N. cos.	N. sine.	N. cos.	N. sine.	N. cos.	N. sine.	N. cos.	N. sine.	N. cos.		4
0	0	08716	99619	10453	99452	12187	99255	13917	99027	15643	98769	60	4
0	1	08745	99617	10482	99449	12216	99251	13946	99023	15672	98764	59	4
1	2	08774	99614	10511	99446	12245	99248	13975	99019	15701	98760	58	4
1	3	08803	99612	10540	99443	12274	99244	14004	99015	15730	98755	57	4
2	4	08831	99609	10569	99440	12302	99240	14033	99011	15758	98751	56	4
2	5	08860	99607	10597	99437	12331	99237	14061	99006	15787	98746	55	4
3	6	08889	99604	10626	99434	12360	99233	14090	99002	15816	98741	54	4
3	7	08918	99602	10655	99431	12389	99230	14119	98998	15845	98737	53	4
4	8	08947	99599	10684	99428	12418	99226	14148	98994	15873	98732	52	3
4	9	08976	99596	10713	99424	12447	99222	14177	98990	15902	98728	51	3
5	10	09005	99594	10742	99421	12476	99219	14205	98986	15931	98723	50	3
5	11	09034	99591	10771	99418	12504	99215	14234	98982	15959	98718	49	3
6	12	09063	99588	10800	99415	12533	99211	14263	98978	15988	98714	48	3
6	13	09092	99586	10829	99412	12562	99208	14292	98973	16017	98709	47	3
7	14	09121	99583	10858	99409	12591	99204	14320	98969	16046	98704	46	3
7	15	09150	99580	10887	99406	12620	99200	14349	98965	16074	98700	45	3
8	16	09179	99578	10916	99402	12649	99197	14378	98961	16103	98695	44	3
8	17	09208	99575	10945	99399	12678	99193	14407	98957	16132	98690	43	3
9	18	09237	99572	10973	99396	12706	99189	14436	98953	16160	98686	42	3
9	19	09266	99570	11002	99393	12735	99186	14464	98948	16189	98681	41	3
10	20	09295	99567	11031	99390	12764	99182	14493	98944	16218	98676	40	3
10	21	09324	99564	11060	99386	12793	99178	14522	98940	16246	98671	39	3
11	22	09353	99562	11089	99383	12822	99175	14551	98936	16275	98667	38	3
11	23	09382	99559	11118	99380	12851	99171	14580	98931	16304	98662	37	2
12	24	09411	99556	11147	99377	12880	99167	14608	98927	16333	98657	36	2
12	25	09440	99553	11176	99374	12908	99163	14637	98923	16361	98652	35	2
13	26	09469	99551	11205	99370	12937	99160	14666	98919	16390	98648	34	2
13	27	09498	99548	11234	99367	12966	99156	14695	98914	16419	98643	33	2
14	28	09527	99545	11263	99364	12995	99152	14723	98910	16447	98638	32	2
14	29	09556	99542	11291	99360	13024	99148	14752	98906	16476	98633	31	2
15	30	09585	99540	11320	99357	13053	99144	14781	98902	16505	98629	30	2
15	31	09614	99537	11349	99354	13081	99141	14810	98897	16533	98624	29	2
15	32	09642	99534	11378	99351	13110	99137	14838	98893	16562	98619	28	2
16	33	09671	99531	11407	99347	13139	99133	14867	98889	16591	98614	27	2
16	34	09700	99528	11436	99344	13168	99129	14896	98884	16620	98609	26	2
17	35	09729	99526	11465	99341	13197	99125	14925	98880	16648	98604	25	2
17	36	09758	99523	11494	99337	13226	99122	14954	98876	16677	98600	24	2
18	37	09787	99520	11523	99334	13254	99118	14982	98871	16706	98595	23	2
18	38	09816	99517	11552	99331	13283	99114	15011	98867	16734	98590	22	1
19	39	09845	99514	11580	99327	13312	99110	15040	98863	16763	98585	21	1
19	40	09874	99511	11609	99324	13341	99106	15069	98858	16792	98580	20	1
20	41	09903	99508	11638	99320	13370	99102	15097	98854	16820	98575	19	1
20	42	09932	99506	11667	99317	13399	99098	15126	98849	16849	98570	18	1
21	43	09961	99503	11696	99314	13427	99094	15155	98845	16878	98565	17	1
21	44	09990	99500	11725	99310	13456	99091	15184	98841	16906	98561	16	1
22	45	10019	99497	11754	99307	13485	99087	15212	98836	16935	98556	15	1
22	46	10048	99494	11783	99303	13514	99083	15241	98832	16964	98551	14	1
23	47	10077	99491	11812	99300	13543	99079	15270	98827	16992	98546	13	1
23	48	10106	99488	11840	99297	13572	99075	15299	98823	17021	98541	12	1
24	49	10135	99485	11869	99293	13600	99071	15327	98818	17050	98536	11	1
24	50	10164	99482	11898	99290	13629	99067	15356	98814	17078	98531	10	1
25	51	10192	99479	11927	99286	13658	99063	15385	98809	17107	98526	9	1
25	52	10221	99476	11956	99283	13687	99059	15414	98805	17136	98521	8	1
26	53	10250	99473	11985	99279	13716	99055	15442	98800	17164	98516	7	0
26	54	10279	99470	12014	99276	13744	99051	15471	98796	17193	98511	6	0
27	55	10308	99467	12043	99272	13773	99047	15500	98791	17222	98506	5	0
27	56	10337	99464	12071	99269	13802	99043	15529	98787	17250	98501	4	0
28	57	10366	99461	12100	99265	13831	99039	15557	98782	17279	98496	3	0
28	58	10395	99458	12129	99262	13860	99035	15586	98778	17308	98491	2	0
29	59	10424	99455	12158	99258	13889	99031	15615	98773	17336	98486	1	0
29	60	10453	99452	12187	99255	13917	99027	15643	98769	17365	98481	0	0
		N. cos.	N. sine.	N. cos.	N. sine.	N. cos.	N. sine.	N. cos.	N. sine.	N. cos.	N. sine.	M	
		84°		83°		82°		81°		80°			

TABLE XXIV.

Of Natural Sines.

Prop. parts		10°		11°		12°		13°		14°			Prop. parts
28	M	N. sine.	N. cos.	N. sine.	N. cos.	N. sine.	N. cos.	N. sine.	N. cos.	N. sine.	N. cos.		6
0	0	17365	98481	19081	98163	20791	97815	22495	97437	24192	97030	60	6
0	1	17393	98476	19109	98157	20820	97809	22523	97430	24220	97023	59	6
1	2	17422	98471	19138	98152	20848	97803	22552	97424	24249	97015	58	6
1	3	17451	98466	19167	98146	20877	97797	22580	97417	24277	97008	57	6
2	4	17479	98461	19195	98140	20905	97791	22608	97411	24305	97001	56	6
2	5	17508	98455	19224	98135	20933	97784	22637	97404	24333	96994	55	6
3	6	17537	98450	19252	98129	20962	97778	22665	97398	24362	96987	54	5
3	7	17565	98445	19281	98124	20990	97772	22693	97391	24390	96980	53	5
4	8	17594	98440	19309	98118	21019	97766	22722	97384	24418	96973	52	5
4	9	17623	98435	19338	98112	21047	97760	22750	97378	24446	96966	51	5
5	10	17651	98430	19366	98107	21076	97754	22778	97371	24474	96959	50	5
5	11	17680	98425	19395	98101	21104	97748	22807	97365	24503	96952	49	5
6	12	17708	98420	19423	98096	21132	97742	22835	97358	24531	96945	48	5
6	13	17737	98414	19452	98090	21161	97735	22863	97351	24559	96937	47	5
7	14	17766	98409	19481	98084	21189	97729	22892	97345	24587	96930	46	5
7	15	17794	98404	19509	98079	21218	97723	22920	97338	24615	96923	45	5
7	16	17823	98399	19538	98073	21246	97717	22948	97331	24644	96916	44	4
8	17	17852	98394	19566	98067	21275	97711	22977	97325	24672	96909	43	4
8	18	17880	98389	19595	98061	21303	97705	23005	97318	24700	96902	42	4
9	19	17909	98383	19623	98056	21331	97698	23033	97311	24728	96894	41	4
9	20	17937	98378	19652	98050	21360	97692	23062	97304	24756	96887	40	4
10	21	17966	98373	19680	98044	21388	97686	23090	97298	24784	96880	39	4
10	22	17995	98368	19709	98039	21417	97680	23118	97291	24813	96873	38	4
11	23	18023	98362	19737	98033	21445	97673	23146	97284	24841	96866	37	4
11	24	18052	98357	19766	98027	21474	97667	23175	97278	24869	96858	36	4
12	25	18081	98352	19794	98021	21502	97661	23203	97271	24897	96851	35	4
12	26	18109	98347	19823	98016	21530	97655	23231	97264	24925	96844	34	3
13	27	18138	98341	19851	98010	21559	97648	23260	97257	24954	96837	33	3
13	28	18166	98336	19880	98004	21587	97642	23288	97251	24982	96829	32	3
14	29	18195	98331	19908	97998	21616	97636	23316	97244	25010	96822	31	3
14	30	18224	98325	19937	97992	21644	97630	23345	97237	25038	96815	30	3
14	31	18252	98320	19965	97987	21672	97623	23373	97230	25066	96807	29	3
15	32	18281	98315	19994	97981	21701	97617	23401	97223	25094	96800	28	3
15	33	18309	98310	20022	97975	21729	97611	23429	97217	25122	96793	27	3
16	34	18338	98304	20051	97969	21758	97604	23458	97210	25151	96786	26	3
16	35	18367	98299	20079	97963	21786	97598	23486	97203	25179	96778	25	3
17	36	18395	98294	20108	97958	21814	97592	23514	97196	25207	96771	24	2
17	37	18424	98288	20136	97952	21843	97585	23542	97189	25235	96764	23	2
18	38	18452	98283	20165	97946	21871	97579	23571	97182	25263	96756	22	2
18	39	18481	98277	20193	97940	21899	97573	23599	97176	25291	96749	21	2
19	40	18509	98272	20222	97934	21928	97566	23627	97169	25320	96742	20	2
19	41	18538	98267	20250	97928	21956	97560	23656	97162	25348	96734	19	2
20	42	18567	98261	20279	97922	21985	97553	23684	97155	25376	96727	18	2
20	43	18595	98256	20307	97916	22013	97547	23712	97148	25404	96719	17	2
21	44	18624	98250	20336	97910	22041	97541	23740	97141	25432	96712	16	2
21	45	18652	98245	20364	97905	22070	97534	23769	97134	25460	96705	15	2
21	46	18681	98240	20393	97899	22098	97528	23797	97127	25488	96697	14	1
22	47	18710	98234	20421	97893	22126	97521	23825	97120	25516	96690	13	1
22	48	18738	98229	20450	97887	22155	97515	23853	97113	25545	96682	12	1
23	49	18767	98223	20478	97881	22183	97508	23882	97106	25573	96675	11	1
23	50	18795	98218	20507	97875	22212	97502	23910	97100	25601	96667	10	1
24	51	18824	98212	20535	97869	22240	97496	23938	97093	25629	96660	9	1
24	52	18852	98207	20563	97863	22268	97489	23966	97086	25657	96653	8	1
25	53	18881	98201	20592	97857	22297	97483	23995	97079	25685	96645	7	1
25	54	18910	98196	20620	97851	22325	97476	24023	97072	25713	96638	6	1
26	55	18938	98190	20649	97845	22353	97470	24051	97065	25741	96630	5	1
26	56	18967	98185	20677	97839	22382	97463	24079	97058	25769	96623	4	0
27	57	18995	98179	20706	97833	22410	97457	24108	97051	25798	96615	3	0
27	58	19024	98174	20734	97827	22438	97450	24136	97044	25826	96608	2	0
28	59	19052	98168	20763	97821	22467	97444	24164	97037	25854	96600	1	0
28	60	19081	98163	20791	97815	22495	97437	24192	97030	25882	96593	0	0
		N. cos.	N. sine.	N. cos.	N. sine.	N. cos.	N. sine.	N. cos.	N. sine.	N. cos.	N. sine.	M	
		79°		78°		77°		76°		75°			

TABLE XXIV.

Of Natural Sines.

Prop. parts 27	M	15° N. sine.	15° N. cos.	16° N. sine.	16° N. cos.	17° N. sine.	17° N. cos.	18° N. sine.	18° N. cos.	19° N. sine.	19° N. cos.		Prop. parts 9
0	0	25882	96593	27564	96126	29237	95630	30902	95106	32557	94552	60	9
0	1	25910	96585	27592	96118	29265	95622	30929	95097	32584	94542	59	9
1	2	25938	96578	27620	96110	29293	95613	30957	95088	32612	94533	58	9
1	3	25966	96570	27648	96102	29321	95605	30985	95079	32639	94523	57	9
2	4	25994	96562	27676	96094	29348	95596	31012	95070	32667	94514	56	8
2	5	26022	96555	27704	96086	29376	95588	31040	95061	32694	94504	55	8
3	6	26050	96547	27731	96078	29404	95579	31068	95052	32722	94495	54	8
3	7	26079	96540	27759	96070	29432	95571	31095	95043	32749	94485	53	8
4	8	26107	96532	27787	96062	29460	95562	31123	95033	32777	94476	52	8
4	9	26135	96524	27815	96054	29487	95554	31151	95024	32804	94466	51	8
5	10	26163	96517	27843	96046	29515	95545	31178	95015	32832	94457	50	8
5	11	26191	96509	27871	96037	29543	95536	31206	95006	32859	94447	49	7
5	12	26219	96502	27899	96029	29571	95528	31233	94997	32887	94438	48	7
6	13	26247	96494	27927	96021	29599	95519	31261	94988	32914	94428	47	7
6	14	26275	96486	27955	96013	29626	95511	31289	94979	32942	94418	46	7
7	15	26303	96479	27983	96005	29654	95502	31316	94970	32969	94409	45	7
7	16	26331	96471	28011	95997	29682	95493	31344	94961	32997	94399	44	7
8	17	26359	96463	28039	95989	29710	95485	31372	94952	33024	94390	43	6
8	18	26387	96456	28067	95981	29737	95476	31399	94943	33051	94380	42	6
9	19	26415	96448	28095	95972	29765	95467	31427	94933	33079	94370	41	6
9	20	26443	96440	28123	95964	29793	95459	31454	94924	33106	94361	40	6
9	21	26471	96433	28150	95956	29821	95450	31482	94915	33134	94351	39	6
10	22	26500	96425	28178	95948	29849	95441	31510	94906	33161	94342	38	6
10	23	26528	96417	28206	95940	29876	95433	31537	94897	33189	94332	37	6
11	24	26556	96410	28234	95931	29904	95424	31565	94888	33216	94322	36	5
11	25	26584	96402	28262	95923	29932	95415	31593	94878	33244	94313	35	5
12	26	26612	96394	28290	95915	29960	95407	31620	94869	33271	94303	34	5
12	27	26640	96386	28318	95907	29987	95398	31648	94860	33298	94293	33	5
13	28	26668	96379	28346	95898	30015	95389	31675	94851	33326	94284	32	5
13	29	26696	96371	28374	95890	30043	95380	31703	94842	33353	94274	31	5
14	30	26724	96363	28402	95882	30071	95372	31730	94832	33381	94264	30	5
14	31	26752	96355	28429	95874	30098	95363	31758	94823	33408	94254	29	4
14	32	26780	96347	28457	95865	30126	95354	31786	94814	33436	94245	28	4
15	33	26808	96340	28485	95857	30154	95345	31813	94805	33463	94235	27	4
15	34	26836	96332	28513	95849	30182	95337	31841	94795	33490	94225	26	4
16	35	26864	96324	28541	95841	30209	95328	31868	94786	33518	94215	25	4
16	36	26892	96316	28569	95832	30237	95319	31896	94777	33545	94206	24	4
17	37	26920	96308	28597	95824	30265	95310	31923	94768	33573	94196	23	3
17	38	26948	96301	28625	95816	30292	95301	31951	94758	33600	94186	22	3
18	39	26976	96293	28652	95807	30320	95293	31979	94749	33627	94176	21	3
18	40	27004	96285	28680	95799	30348	95284	32006	94740	33655	94167	20	3
18	41	27032	96277	28708	95791	30376	95275	32034	94730	33682	94157	19	3
19	42	27060	96269	28736	95782	30403	95266	32061	94721	33710	94147	18	3
19	43	27088	96261	28764	95774	30431	95257	32089	94712	33737	94137	17	3
20	44	27116	96253	28792	95766	30459	95248	32116	94702	33764	94127	16	2
20	45	27144	96246	28820	95757	30486	95240	32144	94693	33792	94118	15	2
21	46	27172	96238	28847	95749	30514	95231	32171	94684	33819	94108	14	2
21	47	27200	96230	28875	95740	30542	95222	32199	94674	33846	94098	13	2
22	48	27228	96222	28903	95732	30570	95213	32227	94665	33874	94088	12	2
22	49	27256	96214	28931	95724	30597	95204	32254	94656	33901	94078	11	2
23	50	27284	96206	28959	95715	30625	95195	32282	94646	33929	94068	10	2
23	51	27312	96198	28987	95707	30653	95186	32309	94637	33956	94058	9	1
23	52	27340	96190	29015	95698	30680	95177	32337	94627	33983	94049	8	1
24	53	27368	96182	29042	95690	30708	95168	32364	94618	34011	94039	7	1
24	54	27396	96174	29070	95681	30736	95159	32392	94609	34038	94029	6	1
25	55	27424	96166	29098	95673	30763	95150	32419	94599	34065	94019	5	1
25	56	27452	96158	29126	95664	30791	95142	32447	94590	34093	94009	4	1
26	57	27480	96150	29154	95656	30819	95133	32474	94580	34120	93999	3	0
26	58	27508	96142	29182	95647	30846	95124	32502	94571	34147	93989	2	0
27	59	27536	96134	29209	95639	30874	95115	32529	94561	34175	93979	1	0
27	60	27564	96126	29237	95630	30902	95106	32557	94552	34202	93969	0	0
		N. cos.	N. sine.	N. cos.	N. sine.	N. cos.	N. sine.	N. cos.	N. sine.	N. cos.	N. sine.	M	
		74°		73°		72°		71°		70°			

TABLE XXIV.

Of Natural Sines.

Prop. parts		20°		21°		22°		23°		24°			Prop. parts
27	M	N. sine.	N. cos.	N. sine.	N. cos.	N. sine.	N. cos.	N. sine.	N. cos.	N. sine.	N. cos.		11
0	0	34202	93969	35837	93358	37461	92718	39073	92050	40674	91355	60	11
0	1	34229	93959	35864	93348	37488	92707	39100	92039	40700	91343	59	11
1	2	34257	93949	35891	93337	37515	92697	39127	92028	40727	91331	58	11
1	3	34284	93939	35918	93327	37542	92686	39153	92016	40753	91319	57	10
2	4	34311	93929	35945	93316	37569	92675	39180	92005	40780	91307	56	10
2	5	34339	93919	35973	93306	37595	92664	39207	91994	40806	91295	55	10
3	6	34366	93909	36000	93295	37622	92653	39234	91982	40833	91283	54	10
3	7	34393	93899	36027	93285	37649	92642	39260	91971	40860	91272	53	10
4	8	34421	93889	36054	93274	37676	92631	39287	91959	40886	91260	52	10
4	9	34448	93879	36081	93264	37703	92620	39314	91948	40913	91248	51	9
5	10	34475	93869	36108	93253	37730	92609	39341	91936	40939	91236	50	9
5	11	34503	93859	36135	93243	37757	92598	39367	91925	40966	91224	49	9
5	12	34530	93849	36162	93232	37784	92587	39394	91914	40992	91212	48	9
6	13	34557	93839	36190	93222	37811	92576	39421	91902	41019	91200	47	9
6	14	34584	93829	36217	93211	37838	92565	39448	91891	41045	91188	46	8
7	15	34612	93819	36244	93201	37865	92554	39474	91879	41072	91176	45	8
7	16	34639	93809	36271	93190	37892	92543	39501	91868	41098	91164	44	8
8	17	34666	93799	36298	93180	37919	92532	39528	91856	41125	91152	43	8
8	18	34694	93789	36325	93169	37946	92521	39555	91845	41151	91140	42	8
9	19	34721	93779	36352	93159	37973	92510	39581	91833	41178	91128	41	8
9	20	34748	93769	36379	93148	37999	92499	39608	91822	41204	91116	40	7
9	21	34775	93759	36406	93137	38026	92488	39635	91810	41231	91104	39	7
10	22	34803	93748	36434	93127	38053	92477	39661	91799	41257	91092	38	7
10	23	34830	93738	36461	93116	38080	92466	39688	91787	41284	91080	37	7
11	24	34857	93728	36488	93106	38107	92455	39715	91775	41310	91068	36	7
11	25	34884	93718	36515	93095	38134	92444	39741	91764	41337	91056	35	6
12	26	34912	93708	36542	93084	38161	92432	39768	91752	41363	91044	34	6
12	27	34939	93698	36569	93074	38188	92421	39795	91741	41390	91032	33	6
13	28	34966	93688	36596	93063	38215	92410	39822	91729	41416	91020	32	6
13	29	34993	93677	36623	93052	38241	92399	39848	91718	41443	91008	31	6
14	30	35021	93667	36650	93042	38268	92388	39875	91706	41469	90996	30	6
14	31	35048	93657	36677	93031	38295	92377	39902	91694	41496	90984	29	5
14	32	35075	93647	36704	93020	38322	92366	39928	91683	41522	90972	28	5
15	33	35102	93637	36731	93010	38349	92355	39955	91671	41549	90960	27	5
15	34	35130	93626	36758	92999	38376	92343	39982	91660	41575	90948	26	5
16	35	35157	93616	36785	92988	38403	92332	40008	91648	41602	90936	25	5
16	36	35184	93606	36812	92978	38430	92321	40035	91636	41628	90924	24	4
17	37	35211	93596	36839	92967	38456	92310	40062	91625	41655	90911	23	4
17	38	35239	93585	36867	92956	38483	92299	40088	91613	41681	90899	22	4
18	39	35266	93575	36894	92945	38510	92287	40115	91601	41707	90887	21	4
18	40	35293	93565	36921	92935	38537	92276	40141	91590	41734	90875	20	4
18	41	35320	93555	36948	92924	38564	92265	40168	91578	41760	90863	19	3
19	42	35347	93544	36975	92913	38591	92254	40195	91566	41787	90851	18	3
19	43	35375	93534	37002	92902	38617	92243	40221	91555	41813	90839	17	3
20	44	35402	93524	37029	92892	38644	92231	40248	91543	41840	90826	16	3
20	45	35429	93514	37056	92881	38671	92220	40275	91531	41866	90814	15	3
21	46	35456	93503	37083	92870	38698	92209	40301	91519	41892	90802	14	3
21	47	35484	93493	37110	92859	38725	92198	40328	91508	41919	90790	13	2
22	48	35511	93483	37137	92849	38752	92186	40355	91496	41945	90778	12	2
22	49	35538	93472	37164	92838	38778	92175	40381	91484	41972	90766	11	2
23	50	35565	93462	37191	92827	38805	92164	40408	91472	41998	90753	10	2
23	51	35592	93452	37218	92816	38832	92152	40434	91461	42024	90741	9	2
23	52	35619	93441	37245	92805	38859	92141	40461	91449	42051	90729	8	1
24	53	35647	93431	37272	92794	38886	92130	40488	91437	42077	90717	7	1
24	54	35674	93420	37299	92784	38912	92119	40514	91425	42104	90704	6	1
25	55	35701	93410	37326	92773	38939	92107	40541	91414	42130	90692	5	1
25	56	35728	93400	37353	92762	38966	92096	40567	91402	42156	90680	4	1
26	57	35755	93389	37380	92751	38993	92085	40594	91390	42183	90668	3	1
26	58	35782	93379	37407	92740	39020	92073	40621	91378	42209	90655	2	0
27	59	35810	93368	37434	92729	39046	92062	40647	91366	42235	90643	1	0
27	60	35837	93358	37461	92718	39073	92050	40674	91355	42262	90631	0	0
		N. cos.	N. sine.	N. cos.	N. sine.	N. cos.	N. sine.	N. cos.	N. sine.	N. cos.	N. sine.	M	
		69°		68°		67°		66°		65°			

TABLE XXIV.

Of Natural Sines.

Prop. parts 26	M	25° N. sine.	25° N. cos.	26° N. sine.	26° N. cos.	27° N. sine.	27° N. cos.	28° N. sine.	28° N. cos.	29° N. sine.	29° N. cos.		Prop. parts 14
0	0	42262	90631	43837	89879	45399	89101	46947	88295	48481	87462	60	14
0	1	42288	90618	43863	89867	45425	89087	46973	88281	48506	87448	59	14
1	2	42315	90606	43889	89854	45451	89074	46999	88267	48532	87434	58	14
1	3	42341	90594	43916	89841	45477	89061	47024	88254	48557	87420	57	13
2	4	42367	90582	43942	89828	45503	89048	47050	88240	48583	87406	56	13
2	5	42394	90569	43968	89816	45529	89035	47076	88226	48608	87391	55	13
3	6	42420	90557	43994	89803	45554	89021	47101	88213	48634	87377	54	13
3	7	42446	90545	44020	89790	45580	89008	47127	88199	48659	87363	53	12
3	8	42473	90532	44046	89777	45606	88995	47153	88185	48684	87349	52	12
4	9	42499	90520	44072	89764	45632	88981	47178	88172	48710	87335	51	12
4	10	42525	90507	44098	89752	45658	88968	47204	88158	48735	87321	50	12
5	11	42552	90495	44124	89739	45684	88955	47229	88144	48761	87306	49	11
5	12	42578	90483	44151	89726	45710	88942	47255	88130	48786	87292	48	11
6	13	42604	90470	44177	89713	45736	88928	47281	88117	48811	87278	47	11
6	14	42631	90458	44203	89700	45762	88915	47306	88103	48837	87264	46	11
7	15	42657	90446	44229	89687	45787	88902	47332	88089	48862	87250	45	11
7	16	42683	90433	44255	89674	45813	88888	47358	88075	48888	87235	44	10
7	17	42709	90421	44281	89662	45839	88875	47383	88062	48913	87221	43	10
8	18	42736	90408	44307	89649	45865	88862	47409	88048	48938	87207	42	10
8	19	42762	90396	44333	89636	45891	88848	47434	88034	48964	87193	41	10
9	20	42788	90383	44359	89623	45917	88835	47460	88020	48989	87178	40	9
9	21	42815	90371	44385	89610	45942	88822	47486	88006	49014	87164	39	9
10	22	42841	90358	44411	89597	45968	88808	47511	87993	49040	87150	38	9
10	23	42867	90346	44437	89584	45994	88795	47537	87979	49065	87136	37	9
10	24	42894	90334	44464	89571	46020	88782	47562	87965	49090	87121	36	8
11	25	42920	90321	44490	89558	46046	88768	47588	87951	49116	87107	35	8
11	26	42946	90309	44516	89545	46072	88755	47614	87937	49141	87093	34	8
12	27	42972	90296	44542	89532	46097	88741	47639	87923	49166	87079	33	8
12	28	42999	90284	44568	89519	46123	88728	47665	87909	49192	87064	32	7
13	29	43025	90271	44594	89506	46149	88715	47690	87896	49217	87050	31	7
13	30	43051	90259	44620	89493	46175	88701	47716	87882	49242	87036	30	7
13	31	43077	90246	44646	89480	46201	88688	47741	87868	49268	87021	29	7
14	32	43104	90233	44672	89467	46226	88674	47767	87854	49293	87007	28	7
14	33	43130	90221	44698	89454	46252	88661	47793	87840	49318	86993	27	6
15	34	43156	90208	44724	89441	46278	88647	47818	87826	49344	86978	26	6
15	35	43182	90196	44750	89428	46304	88634	47844	87812	49369	86964	25	6
16	36	43209	90183	44776	89415	46330	88620	47869	87798	49394	86949	24	6
16	37	43235	90171	44802	89402	46355	88607	47895	87784	49419	86935	23	5
16	38	43261	90158	44828	89389	46381	88593	47920	87770	49445	86921	22	5
17	39	43287	90146	44854	89376	46407	88580	47946	87756	49470	86906	21	5
17	40	43313	90133	44880	89363	46433	88566	47971	87743	49495	86892	20	5
18	41	43340	90120	44906	89350	46458	88553	47997	87729	49521	86878	19	4
18	42	43366	90108	44932	89337	46484	88539	48022	87715	49546	86863	18	4
19	43	43392	90095	44958	89324	46510	88526	48048	87701	49571	86849	17	4
19	44	43418	90082	44984	89311	46536	88512	48073	87687	49596	86834	16	4
20	45	43445	90070	45010	89298	46561	88499	48099	87673	49622	86820	15	4
20	46	43471	90057	45036	89285	46587	88485	48124	87659	49647	86805	14	3
20	47	43497	90045	45062	89272	46613	88472	48150	87645	49672	86791	13	3
21	48	43523	90032	45088	89259	46639	88458	48175	87631	49697	86777	12	3
21	49	43549	90019	45114	89245	46664	88445	48201	87617	49723	86762	11	3
22	50	43575	90007	45140	89232	46690	88431	48226	87603	49748	86748	10	2
22	51	43602	89994	45166	89219	46716	88417	48252	87589	49773	86733	9	2
23	52	43628	89981	45192	89206	46742	88404	48277	87575	49798	86719	8	2
23	53	43654	89968	45218	89193	46767	88390	48303	87561	49824	86704	7	2
23	54	43680	89956	45243	89180	46793	88377	48328	87546	49849	86690	6	1
24	55	43706	89943	45269	89167	46819	88363	48354	87532	49874	86675	5	1
24	56	43733	89930	45295	89153	46844	88349	48379	87518	49899	86661	4	1
25	57	43759	89918	45321	89140	46870	88336	48405	87504	49924	86646	3	1
25	58	43785	89905	45347	89127	46896	88322	48430	87490	49950	86632	2	0
26	59	43811	89892	45373	89114	46921	88308	48456	87476	49975	86617	1	0
26	60	43837	89879	45399	89101	46947	88295	48481	87462	50000	86603	0	0
		N. cos.	N. sine.	N. cos.	N. sine.	N. cos.	N. sine.	N. cos.	N. sine.	N. cos.	N. sine.	M	
		64°		63°		62°		61°		60°			

TABLE XXIV.

Of Natural Sines.

Prop. parts		30°		31°		32°		33°		34°			Prop. parts
25	M	N. sine.	N. cos.	N. sine.	N. cos.	N. sine.	N. cos.	N. sine.	N. cos.	N. sine.	N. cos.		16
0	0	50000	86603	51504	85717	52992	84805	54464	83867	55919	82904	60	16
0	1	50025	86588	51529	85702	53017	84789	54488	83851	55943	82887	59	16
1	2	50050	86573	51554	85687	53041	84774	54513	83835	55968	82871	58	15
1	3	50076	86559	51579	85672	53066	84759	54537	83819	55992	82855	57	15
2	4	50101	86544	51604	85657	53091	84743	54561	83804	56016	82839	56	15
2	5	50126	86530	51628	85642	53115	84728	54586	83788	56040	82822	55	15
3	6	50151	86515	51653	85627	53140	84712	54610	83772	56064	82806	54	14
3	7	50176	86501	51678	85612	53164	84697	54635	83756	56088	82790	53	14
3	8	50201	86486	51703	85597	53189	84681	54659	83740	56112	82773	52	14
4	9	50227	86471	51728	85582	53214	84666	54683	83724	56136	82757	51	14
4	10	50252	86457	51753	85567	53238	84650	54708	83708	56160	82741	50	13
5	11	50277	86442	51778	85551	53263	84635	54732	83692	56184	82724	49	13
5	12	50302	86427	51803	85536	53288	84619	54756	83676	56208	82708	48	13
5	13	50327	86413	51828	85521	53312	84604	54781	83660	56232	82692	47	13
6	14	50352	86398	51852	85506	53337	84588	54805	83645	56256	82675	46	12
6	15	50377	86384	51877	85491	53361	84573	54829	83629	56280	82659	45	12
7	16	50403	86369	51902	85476	53386	84557	54854	83613	56305	82643	44	12
7	17	50428	86354	51927	85461	53411	84542	54878	83597	56329	82626	43	11
8	18	50453	86340	51952	85446	53435	84526	54902	83581	56353	82610	42	11
8	19	50478	86325	51977	85431	53460	84511	54927	83565	56377	82593	41	11
8	20	50503	86310	52002	85416	53484	84495	54951	83549	56401	82577	40	11
9	21	50528	86295	52026	85401	53509	84480	54975	83533	56425	82561	39	10
9	22	50553	86281	52051	85385	53534	84464	54999	83517	56449	82544	38	10
10	23	50578	86266	52076	85370	53558	84448	55024	83501	56473	82528	37	10
10	24	50603	86251	52101	85355	53583	84433	55048	83485	56497	82511	36	10
10	25	50628	86237	52126	85340	53607	84417	55072	83469	56521	82495	35	9
11	26	50654	86222	52151	85325	53632	84402	55097	83453	56545	82478	34	9
11	27	50679	86207	52175	85310	53656	84386	55121	83437	56569	82462	33	9
12	28	50704	86192	52200	85294	53681	84370	55145	83421	56593	82446	32	9
12	29	50729	86178	52225	85279	53705	84355	55169	83405	56617	82429	31	8
13	30	50754	86163	52250	85264	53730	84339	55194	83389	56641	82413	30	8
13	31	50779	86148	52275	85249	53754	84324	55218	83373	56665	82396	29	8
13	32	50804	86133	52299	85234	53779	84308	55242	83356	56689	82380	28	7
14	33	50829	86119	52324	85218	53804	84292	55266	83340	56713	82363	27	7
14	34	50854	86104	52349	85203	53828	84277	55291	83324	56736	82347	26	7
15	35	50879	86089	52374	85188	53853	84261	55315	83308	56760	82330	25	7
15	36	50904	86074	52399	85173	53877	84245	55339	83292	56784	82314	24	6
15	37	50929	86059	52423	85157	53902	84230	55363	83276	56808	82297	23	6
16	38	50954	86045	52448	85142	53926	84214	55388	83260	56832	82281	22	6
16	39	50979	86030	52473	85127	53951	84198	55412	83244	56856	82264	21	6
17	40	51004	86015	52498	85112	53975	84182	55436	83228	56880	82248	20	5
17	41	51029	86000	52522	85096	54000	84167	55460	83212	56904	82231	19	5
18	42	51054	85985	52547	85081	54024	84151	55484	83195	56928	82214	18	5
18	43	51079	85970	52572	85066	54049	84135	55509	83179	56952	82198	17	5
18	44	51104	85956	52597	85051	54073	84120	55533	83163	56976	82181	16	4
19	45	51129	85941	52621	85035	54097	84104	55557	83147	57000	82165	15	4
19	46	51154	85926	52646	85020	54122	84088	55581	83131	57024	82148	14	4
20	47	51179	85911	52671	85005	54146	84072	55605	83115	57047	82132	13	3
20	48	51204	85896	52696	84989	54171	84057	55630	83098	57071	82115	12	3
20	49	51229	85881	52720	84974	54195	84041	55654	83082	57095	82098	11	3
21	50	51254	85866	52745	84959	54220	84025	55678	83066	57119	82082	10	3
21	51	51279	85851	52770	84943	54244	84009	55702	83050	57143	82065	9	2
22	52	51304	85836	52794	84928	54269	83994	55726	83034	57167	82048	8	2
22	53	51329	85821	52819	84913	54293	83978	55750	83017	57191	82032	7	2
23	54	51354	85806	52844	84897	54317	83962	55775	83001	57215	82015	6	2
23	55	51379	85792	52869	84882	54342	83946	55799	82985	57238	81999	5	1
23	56	51404	85777	52893	84866	54366	83930	55823	82969	57262	81982	4	1
24	57	51429	85762	52918	84851	54391	83915	55847	82953	57286	81965	3	1
24	58	51454	85747	52943	84836	54415	83899	55871	82936	57310	81949	2	1
25	59	51479	85732	52967	84820	54440	83883	55895	82920	57334	81932	1	0
25	60	51504	85717	52992	84805	54464	83867	55919	82904	0	0
		N. cos.	N. sine.	N. cos.	N. sine.	N. cos.	N. sine.	N. cos.	N. sine.	N. cos.	N. sine.	M	
		59°		58°		57°		56°		55°			

TABLE XXIV.

Of Natural Sines.

Prop. parts	′	35°		36°		37°		38°		39°		′	Prop. parts
23	M	N. sine.	N. cos.	N. sine.	N. cos.	N. sine.	N. cos.	N. sine.	N. cos.	N. sine.	N. cos.		18
0	0	57358	81915	58779	80902	60182	79864	61566	78801	62932	77715	60	18
0	1	57381	81899	58802	80885	60205	79846	61589	78783	62955	77696	59	18
1	2	57405	81882	58826	80867	60228	79829	61612	78765	62977	77678	58	17
1	3	57429	81865	58849	80850	60251	79811	61635	78747	63000	77660	57	17
2	4	57453	81848	58873	80833	60274	79793	61658	78729	63022	77641	56	17
2	5	57477	81832	58896	80816	60298	79776	61681	78711	63045	77623	55	17
2	6	57501	81815	58920	80799	60321	79758	61704	78694	63068	77605	54	16
3	7	57524	81798	58943	80782	60344	79741	61726	78676	63090	77586	53	16
3	8	57548	81782	58967	80765	60367	79723	61749	78658	63113	77568	52	16
3	9	57572	81765	58990	80748	60390	79706	61772	78640	63135	77550	51	15
4	10	57596	81748	59014	80730	60414	79688	61795	78622	63158	77531	50	15
4	11	57619	81731	59037	80713	60437	79671	61818	78604	63180	77513	49	15
5	12	57643	81714	59061	80696	60460	79653	61841	78586	63203	77494	48	14
5	13	57667	81698	59084	80679	60483	79635	61864	78568	63225	77476	47	14
5	14	57691	81681	59108	80662	60506	79618	61887	78550	63248	77458	46	14
6	15	57715	81664	59131	80644	60529	79600	61909	78532	63271	77439	45	14
6	16	57738	81647	59154	80627	60553	79583	61932	78514	63293	77421	44	13
7	17	57762	81631	59178	80610	60576	79565	61955	78496	63316	77402	43	13
7	18	57786	81614	59201	80593	60599	79547	61978	78478	63338	77384	42	13
7	19	57810	81597	59225	80576	60622	79530	62001	78460	63361	77366	41	12
8	20	57833	81580	59248	80558	60645	79512	62024	78442	63383	77347	40	12
8	21	57857	81563	59272	80541	60668	79494	62046	78424	63406	77329	39	12
8	22	57881	81546	59295	80524	60691	79477	62069	78405	63428	77310	38	11
9	23	57904	81530	59318	80507	60714	79459	62092	78387	63451	77292	37	11
9	24	57928	81513	59342	80489	60738	79441	62115	78369	63473	77273	36	11
10	25	57952	81496	59365	80472	60761	79424	62138	78351	63496	77255	35	11
10	26	57976	81479	59389	80455	60784	79406	62160	78333	63518	77236	34	10
10	27	57999	81462	59412	80438	60807	79388	62183	78315	63540	77218	33	10
11	28	58023	81445	59436	80420	60830	79371	62206	78297	63563	77199	32	10
11	29	58047	81428	59459	80403	60853	79353	62229	78279	63585	77181	31	9
12	30	58070	81412	59482	80386	60876	79335	62251	78261	63608	77162	30	9
12	31	58094	81395	59506	80368	60899	79318	62274	78243	63630	77144	29	9
12	32	58118	81378	59529	80351	60922	79300	62297	78225	63653	77125	28	8
13	33	58141	81361	59552	80334	60945	79282	62320	78206	63675	77107	27	8
13	34	58165	81344	59576	80316	60968	79264	62342	78188	63698	77088	26	8
13	35	58189	81327	59599	80299	60991	79247	62365	78170	63720	77070	25	8
14	36	58212	81310	59622	80282	61015	79229	62388	78152	63742	77051	24	7
14	37	58236	81293	59646	80264	61038	79211	62411	78134	63765	77033	23	7
15	38	58260	81276	59669	80247	61061	79193	62433	78116	63787	77014	22	7
15	39	58283	81259	59693	80230	61084	79176	62456	78098	63810	76996	21	6
15	40	58307	81242	59716	80212	61107	79158	62479	78079	63832	76977	20	6
16	41	58330	81225	59739	80195	61130	79140	62502	78061	63854	76959	19	6
16	42	58354	81208	59763	80178	61153	79122	62524	78043	63877	76940	18	5
16	43	58378	81191	59786	80160	61176	79105	62547	78025	63899	76921	17	5
17	44	58401	81174	59809	80143	61199	79087	62570	78007	63922	76903	16	5
17	45	58425	81157	59832	80125	61222	79069	62592	77988	63944	76884	15	5
18	46	58449	81140	59856	80108	61245	79051	62615	77970	63966	76866	14	4
18	47	58472	81123	59879	80091	61268	79033	62638	77952	63989	76847	13	4
18	48	58496	81106	59902	80073	61291	79016	62660	77934	64011	76828	12	4
19	49	58519	81089	59926	80056	61314	78998	62683	77916	64033	76810	11	3
19	50	58543	81072	59949	80038	61337	78980	62706	77897	64056	76791	10	3
20	51	58567	81055	59972	80021	61360	78962	62728	77879	64078	76772	9	3
20	52	58590	81038	59995	80003	61383	78944	62751	77861	64100	76754	8	2
20	53	58614	81021	60019	79986	61406	78926	62774	77843	64123	76735	7	2
21	54	58637	81004	60042	79968	61429	78908	62796	77824	64145	76717	6	2
21	55	58661	80987	60065	79951	61451	78891	62819	77806	64167	76698	5	2
21	56	58684	80970	60089	79934	61474	78873	62842	77788	64190	76679	4	1
22	57	58708	80953	60112	79916	61497	78855	62864	77769	64212	76661	3	1
22	58	58731	80936	60135	79899	61520	78837	62887	77751	64234	76642	2	1
23	59	58755	80919	60158	79881	61543	78819	62909	77733	64256	76623	1	0
23	60	58779	80902	60182	79864	61566	78801	62932	77715	64279	76604	0	0
		N. cos.	N. sine.	N. cos.	N. sine.	N. cos.	N. sine.	N. cos.	N. sine.	N. cos.	N. sine.	M	
		54°		53°		52°		51°		50°			

TABLE XXIV.

Of Natural Sines.

Prop. parts		40°		41°		42°		43°		44°			Prop. parts
22	M	N. sine.	N. cos.	N. sine.	N. cos.	N. sine.	N. cos.	N. sine.	N. cos.	N. sine.	N. cos.		19
0	0	64279	76604	65606	75471	66913	74314	68200	73135	69466	71934	60	19
0	1	64301	76586	65628	75452	66935	74295	68221	73116	69487	71914	59	19
1	2	64323	76567	65650	75433	66956	74276	68242	73096	69508	71894	58	18
1	3	64346	76548	65672	75414	66978	74256	68264	73076	69529	71873	57	18
1	4	64368	76530	65694	75395	66999	74237	68285	73056	69549	71853	56	18
2	5	64390	76511	65716	75375	67021	74217	68306	73036	69570	71833	55	17
2	6	64412	76492	65738	75356	67043	74198	68327	73016	69591	71813	54	17
3	7	64435	76473	65759	75337	67064	74178	68349	72996	69612	71792	53	17
3	8	64457	76455	65781	75318	67086	74159	68370	72976	69633	71772	52	16
3	9	64479	76436	65803	75299	67107	74139	68391	72957	69654	71752	51	16
4	10	64501	76417	65825	75280	67129	74120	68412	72937	69675	71732	50	16
4	11	64524	76398	65847	75261	67151	74100	68434	72917	69696	71711	49	16
4	12	64546	76380	65869	75241	67172	74080	68455	72897	69717	71691	48	15
5	13	64568	76361	65891	75222	67194	74061	68476	72877	69737	71671	47	15
5	14	64590	76342	65913	75203	67215	74041	68497	72857	69758	71650	46	15
6	15	64612	76323	65935	75184	67237	74022	68518	72837	69779	71630	45	14
6	16	64635	76304	65956	75165	67258	74002	68539	72817	69800	71610	44	14
6	17	64657	76286	65978	75146	67280	73983	68561	72797	69821	71590	43	14
7	18	64679	76267	66000	75126	67301	73963	68582	72777	69842	71569	42	13
7	19	64701	76248	66022	75107	67323	73944	68603	72757	69862	71549	41	13
7	20	64723	76229	66044	75088	67344	73924	68624	72737	69883	71529	40	13
8	21	64746	76210	66066	75069	67366	73904	68645	72717	69904	71508	39	12
8	22	64768	76192	66088	75050	67387	73885	68666	72697	69925	71488	38	12
8	23	64790	76173	66109	75030	67409	73865	68688	72677	69946	71468	37	12
9	24	64812	76154	66131	75011	67430	73846	68709	72657	69966	71447	36	11
9	25	64834	76135	66153	74992	67452	73826	68730	72637	69987	71427	35	11
10	26	64856	76116	66175	74973	67473	73806	68751	72617	70008	71407	34	11
10	27	64878	76097	66197	74953	67495	73787	68772	72597	70029	71386	33	10
10	28	64901	76078	66218	74934	67516	73767	68793	72577	70049	71366	32	10
11	29	64923	76059	66240	74915	67538	73747	68814	72557	70070	71345	31	10
11	30	64945	76041	66262	74896	67559	73728	68835	72537	70091	71325	30	10
11	31	64967	76022	66284	74876	67580	73708	68857	72517	70112	71305	29	9
12	32	64989	76003	66306	74857	67602	73688	68878	72497	70132	71284	28	9
12	33	65011	75984	66327	74838	67623	73669	68899	72477	70153	71264	27	9
12	34	65033	75965	66349	74818	67645	73649	68920	72457	70174	71243	26	8
13	35	65055	75946	66371	74799	67666	73629	68941	72437	70195	71223	25	8
13	36	65077	75927	66393	74780	67688	73610	68962	72417	70215	71203	24	8
14	37	65100	75908	66414	74760	67709	73590	68983	72397	70236	71182	23	7
14	38	65122	75889	66436	74741	67730	73570	69004	72377	70257	71162	22	7
14	39	65144	75870	66458	74722	67752	73551	69025	72357	70277	71141	21	7
15	40	65166	75851	66480	74703	67773	73531	69046	72337	70298	71121	20	6
15	41	65188	75832	66501	74683	67795	73511	69067	72317	70319	71100	19	6
15	42	65210	75813	66523	74664	67816	73491	69088	72297	70339	71080	18	6
16	43	65232	75794	66545	74644	67837	73472	69109	72277	70360	71059	17	5
16	44	65254	75775	66566	74625	67859	73452	69130	72257	70381	71039	16	5
17	45	65276	75756	66588	74606	67880	73432	69151	72236	70401	71019	15	5
17	46	65298	75738	66610	74586	67901	73413	69172	72216	70422	70998	14	4
17	47	65320	75719	66632	74567	67923	73393	69193	72196	70443	70978	13	4
18	48	65342	75700	66653	74548	67944	73373	69214	72176	70463	70957	12	4
18	49	65364	75680	66675	74528	67965	73353	69235	72156	70484	70937	11	3
18	50	65386	75661	66697	74509	67987	73333	69256	72136	70505	70916	10	3
19	51	65408	75642	66718	74489	68008	73314	69277	72116	70525	70896	9	3
19	52	65430	75623	66740	74470	68029	73294	69298	72095	70546	70875	8	3
19	53	65452	75604	66762	74451	68051	73274	69319	72075	70567	70855	7	2
20	54	65474	75585	66783	74431	68072	73254	69340	72055	70587	70834	6	2
20	55	65496	75566	66805	74412	68093	73234	69361	72035	70608	70813	5	2
21	56	65518	75547	66827	74392	68115	73215	69382	72015	70628	70793	4	1
21	57	65540	75528	66848	74373	68136	73195	69403	71995	70649	70772	3	1
21	58	65562	75509	66870	74353	68157	73175	69424	71974	70670	70752	2	1
22	59	65584	75490	66891	74334	68179	73155	69445	71954	70690	70731	1	0
22	60	65606	75471	66913	74314	68200	73135	69466	71934	70711	70711	0	0
		N. cos.	N. sine.	N. cos.	N. sine.	N. cos.	N. sine.	N. cos.	N. sine.	N. cos.	N. sine.	M	
		49°		48°		47°		46°		45°			

TABLE XXVI.

Logarithms of Numbers.

No. 100——1600. Log. 00000——20412.

No.	0	1	2	3	4	5	6	7	8	9
100	00000	00043	00087	00130	00173	00217	00260	00303	00346	00389
101	00432	00475	00518	00561	00604	00647	00689	00732	00775	00817
102	00860	00903	00945	00988	01030	01072	01115	01157	01199	01242
103	01284	01326	01368	01410	01452	01494	01536	01578	01620	01662
104	01703	01745	01787	01828	01870	01912	01953	01995	02036	02078
105	02119	02160	02202	02243	02284	02325	02366	02407	02449	02490
106	02531	02572	02612	02653	02694	02735	02776	02816	02857	02898
107	02938	02979	03019	03060	03100	03141	03181	03222	03262	03302
108	03342	03383	03423	03463	03503	03543	03583	03623	03663	03703
109	03743	03782	03822	03862	03902	03941	03981	04021	04060	04100
110	04139	04179	04218	04258	04297	04336	04376	04415	04454	04493
111	04532	04571	04610	04650	04689	04727	04766	04805	04844	04883
112	04922	04961	04999	05038	05077	05115	05154	05192	05231	05269
113	05308	05346	05385	05423	05461	05500	05538	05576	05614	05652
114	05690	05729	05767	05805	05843	05881	05918	05956	05994	06032
115	06070	06108	06145	06183	06221	06258	06296	06333	06371	06408
116	06446	06483	06521	06558	06595	06633	06670	06707	06744	06781
117	06819	06856	06893	06930	06967	07004	07041	07078	07115	07151
118	07188	07225	07262	07298	07335	07372	07408	07445	07482	07518
119	07555	07591	07628	07664	07700	07737	07773	07809	07846	07882
120	07918	07954	07990	08027	08063	08099	08135	08171	08207	08243
121	08279	08314	08350	08386	08422	08458	08493	08529	08565	08600
122	08636	08672	08707	08743	08778	08814	08849	08884	08920	08955
123	08991	09026	09061	09096	09132	09167	09202	09237	09272	09307
124	09342	09377	09412	09447	09482	09517	09552	09587	09621	09656
125	09691	09726	09760	09795	09830	09864	09899	09934	09968	10003
126	10037	10072	10106	10140	10175	10209	10243	10278	10312	10346
127	10380	10415	10449	10483	10517	10551	10585	10619	10653	10687
128	10721	10755	10789	10823	10857	10890	10924	10958	10992	11025
129	11059	11093	11126	11160	11193	11227	11261	11294	11327	11361
130	11394	11428	11461	11494	11528	11561	11594	11628	11661	11694
131	11727	11760	11793	11826	11860	11893	11926	11959	11992	12024
132	12057	12090	12123	12156	12189	12222	12254	12287	12320	12352
133	12385	12418	12450	12483	12516	12548	12581	12613	12646	12678
134	12710	12743	12775	12808	12840	12872	12905	12937	12969	13001
135	13033	13066	13098	13130	13162	13194	13226	13258	13290	13322
136	13354	13386	13418	13450	13481	13513	13545	13577	13609	13640
137	13672	13704	13735	13767	13799	13830	13862	13893	13925	13956
138	13988	14019	14051	14082	14114	14145	14176	14208	14239	14270
139	14301	14333	14364	14395	14426	14457	14489	14520	14551	14582
140	14613	14644	14675	14706	14737	14768	14799	14829	14860	14891
141	14922	14953	14983	15014	15045	15076	15106	15137	15168	15198
142	15229	15259	15290	15320	15351	15381	15412	15442	15473	15503
143	15534	15564	15594	15625	15655	15685	15715	15746	15776	15806
144	15836	15866	15897	15927	15957	15987	16017	16047	16077	16107
145	16137	16167	16197	16227	16256	16286	16316	16346	16376	16406
146	16435	16465	16495	16524	16554	16584	16613	16643	16673	16702
147	16732	16761	16791	16820	16850	16879	16909	16938	16967	16997
148	17026	17056	17085	17114	17143	17173	17202	17231	17260	17289
149	17319	17348	17377	17406	17435	17464	17493	17522	17551	17580
150	17609	17638	17667	17696	17725	17754	17782	17811	17840	17869
151	17898	17926	17955	17984	18013	18041	18070	18099	18127	18156
152	18184	18213	18241	18270	18298	18327	18355	18384	18412	18441
153	18469	18498	18526	18554	18583	18611	18639	18667	18696	18724
154	18752	18780	18808	18837	18865	18893	18921	18949	18977	19005
155	19033	19061	19089	19117	19145	19173	19201	19229	19257	19285
156	19312	19340	19368	19396	19424	19451	19479	19507	19535	19562
157	19590	19618	19645	19673	19700	19728	19756	19783	19811	19838
158	19866	19893	19921	19948	19976	20003	20030	20058	20085	20112
159	20140	20167	20194	20222	20249	20276	20303	20330	20358	20385
No.	0	1	2	3	4	5	6	7	8	9

	43	42
1	4	4
2	9	8
3	13	13
4	17	17
5	22	21
6	26	25
7	30	29
8	34	34
9	39	38

	41	40
1	4	4
2	8	8
3	12	12
4	16	16
5	21	20
6	25	24
7	29	28
8	33	32
9	37	36

	39	38
1	4	4
2	8	8
3	12	11
4	16	15
5	20	19
6	23	23
7	27	27
8	31	30
9	35	34

	37	36
1	4	4
2	7	7
3	11	11
4	15	14
5	19	18
6	22	22
7	26	25
8	30	29
9	33	32

	35	34
1	4	3
2	7	7
3	11	10
4	14	14
5	18	17
6	21	20
7	25	24
8	28	27
9	32	31

	33	32
1	3	3
2	7	6
3	10	10
4	13	13
5	17	16
6	20	19
7	23	22
8	26	26
9	30	29

TABLE XXVI.

Logarithms of Numbers.

No. 1600——2200. Log. 20412——34242.

No.	0	1	2	3	4	5	6	7	8	9
160	20412	20439	20466	20493	20520	20548	20575	20602	20629	20656
161	20683	20710	20737	20763	20790	20817	20844	20871	20898	20925
162	20952	20978	21005	21032	21059	21085	21112	21139	21165	21192
163	21219	21245	21272	21299	21325	21352	21378	21405	21431	21458
164	21484	21511	21537	21564	21590	21617	21643	21669	21696	21722
165	21748	21775	21801	21827	21854	21880	21906	21932	21958	21985
166	22011	22037	22063	22089	22115	22141	22167	22194	22220	22246
167	22272	22298	22324	22350	22376	22401	22427	22453	22479	22505
168	22531	22557	22583	22608	22634	22660	22686	22712	22737	22763
169	22789	22814	22840	22866	22891	22917	22943	22968	22994	23019
170	23045	23070	23096	23121	23147	23172	23198	23223	23249	23274
171	23300	23325	23350	23376	23401	23426	23452	23477	23502	23528
172	23553	23578	23603	23629	23654	23679	23704	23729	23754	23779
173	23805	23830	23855	23880	23905	23930	23955	23980	24005	24030
174	24055	24080	24105	24130	24155	24180	24204	24229	24254	24279
175	24304	24329	24353	24378	24403	24428	24452	24477	24502	24527
176	24551	24576	24601	24625	24650	24674	24699	24724	24748	24773
177	24797	24822	24846	24871	24895	24920	24944	24969	24993	25018
178	25042	25066	25091	25115	25139	25164	25188	25212	25237	25261
179	25285	25310	25334	25358	25382	25406	25431	25455	25479	25503
180	25527	25551	25575	25600	25624	25648	25672	25696	25720	25744
181	25768	25792	25816	25840	25864	25888	25912	25935	25959	25983
182	26007	26031	26055	26079	26102	26126	26150	26174	26198	26221
183	26245	26269	26293	26316	26340	26364	26387	26411	26435	26458
184	26482	26505	26529	26553	26576	26600	26623	26647	26670	26694
185	26717	26741	26764	26788	26811	26834	26858	26881	26905	26928
186	26951	26975	26998	27021	27045	27068	27091	27114	27138	27161
187	27184	27207	27231	27254	27277	27300	27323	27346	27370	27393
188	27416	27439	27462	27485	27508	27531	27554	27577	27600	27623
189	27646	27669	27692	27715	27738	27761	27784	27807	27830	27852
190	27875	27898	27921	27944	27967	27989	28012	28035	28058	28081
191	28103	28126	28149	28171	28194	28217	28240	28262	28285	28307
192	28330	28353	28375	28398	28421	28443	28466	28488	28511	28533
193	28556	28578	28601	28623	28646	28668	28691	28713	28735	28758
194	28780	28803	28825	28847	28870	28892	28914	28937	28959	28981
195	29003	29026	29048	29070	29092	29115	29137	29159	29181	29203
196	29226	29248	29270	29292	29314	29336	29358	29380	29403	29425
197	29447	29469	29491	29513	29535	29557	29579	29601	29623	29645
198	29667	29688	29710	29732	29754	29776	29798	29820	29842	29863
199	29885	29907	29929	29951	29973	29994	30016	30038	30060	30081
200	30103	30125	30146	30168	30190	30211	30233	30255	30276	30298
201	30320	30341	30363	30384	30406	30428	30449	30471	30492	30514
202	30535	30557	30578	30600	30621	30643	30664	30685	30707	30728
203	30750	30771	30792	30814	30835	30856	30878	30899	30920	30942
204	30963	30984	31006	31027	31048	31069	31091	31112	31133	31154
205	31175	31197	31218	31239	31260	31281	31302	31323	31345	31366
206	31387	31408	31429	31450	31471	31492	31513	31534	31555	31576
207	31597	31618	31639	31660	31681	31702	31723	31744	31765	31785
208	31806	31827	31848	31869	31890	31911	31931	31952	31973	31994
209	32015	32035	32056	32077	32098	32118	32139	32160	32181	32201
210	32222	32243	32263	32284	32305	32325	32346	32366	32387	32408
211	32428	32449	32469	32490	32510	32531	32552	32572	32593	32613
212	32634	32654	32675	32695	32715	32736	32756	32777	32797	32818
213	32838	32858	32879	32899	32919	32940	32960	32980	33001	33021
214	33041	33062	33082	33102	33122	33143	33163	33183	33203	33224
215	33244	33264	33284	33304	33325	33345	33365	33385	33405	33425
216	33445	33465	33486	33506	33526	33546	33566	33586	33606	33626
217	33646	33666	33686	33706	33726	33746	33766	33786	33806	33826
218	33846	33866	33885	33905	33925	33945	33965	33985	34005	34025
219	34044	34064	34084	34104	34124	34143	34163	34183	34203	34223
No.	0	1	2	3	4	5	6	7	8	9

	31	30	29	28	27	26	25	24	23	22	21	20
1	3	3	3	3	3	3	3	2	2	2	2	2
2	6	6	6	6	5	5	5	5	5	4	4	4
3	9	9	9	8	8	8	8	7	7	7	6	6
4	12	12	12	11	11	10	10	10	9	9	8	8
5	16	15	15	14	14	13	13	12	12	11	11	10
6	19	18	17	17	16	16	15	14	14	13	13	12
7	22	21	20	20	19	18	18	17	16	15	15	14
8	25	24	23	22	22	21	20	19	18	18	17	16
9	28	27	26	25	24	23	23	22	21	20	19	18

TABLE XXVI.

Logarithms of Numbers.

No. 2200——2800. Log. 34242——44716.

No.	0	1	2	3	4	5	6	7	8	9
220	34242	34262	34282	34301	34321	34341	34361	34380	34400	34420
221	34439	34459	34479	34498	34518	34537	34557	34577	34596	34616
222	34635	34655	34674	34694	34713	34733	34753	34772	34792	34811
223	34830	34850	34869	34889	34908	34928	34947	34967	34986	35005
224	35025	35044	35064	35083	35102	35122	35141	35160	35180	35199
225	35218	35238	35257	35276	35295	35315	35334	35353	35372	35392
226	35411	35430	35449	35468	35488	35507	35526	35545	35564	35583
227	35603	35622	35641	35660	35679	35698	35717	35736	35755	35774
228	35793	35813	35832	35851	35870	35889	35908	35927	35946	35965
229	35984	36003	36021	36040	36059	36078	36097	36116	36135	36154
230	36173	36192	36211	36229	36248	36267	36286	36305	36324	36342
231	36361	36380	36399	36418	36436	36455	36474	36493	36511	36530
232	36549	36568	36586	36605	36624	36642	36661	36680	36698	36717
233	36736	36754	36773	36791	36810	36829	36847	36866	36884	36903
234	36922	36940	36959	36977	36996	37014	37033	37051	37070	37088
235	37107	37125	37144	37162	37181	37199	37218	37236	37254	37273
236	37291	37310	37328	37346	37365	37383	37401	37420	37438	37457
237	37475	37493	37511	37530	37548	37566	37585	37603	37621	37639
238	37658	37676	37694	37712	37731	37749	37767	37785	37803	37822
239	37840	37858	37876	37894	37912	37931	37949	37967	37985	38003
240	38021	38039	38057	38075	38093	38112	38130	38148	38166	38184
241	38202	38220	38238	38256	38274	38292	38310	38328	38346	38364
242	38382	38399	38417	38435	38453	38471	38489	38507	38525	38543
243	38561	38578	38596	38614	38632	38650	38668	38686	38703	38721
244	38739	38757	38775	38792	38810	38828	38846	38863	38881	38899
245	38917	38934	38952	38970	38987	39005	39023	39041	39058	39076
246	39094	39111	39129	39146	39164	39182	39199	39217	39235	39252
247	39270	39287	39305	39322	39340	39358	39375	39393	39410	39428
248	39445	39463	39480	39498	39515	39533	39550	39568	39585	39602
249	39620	39637	39655	39672	39690	39707	39724	39742	39759	39777
250	39794	39811	39829	39846	39863	39881	39898	39915	39933	39950
251	39967	39985	40002	40019	40037	40054	40071	40088	40106	40123
252	40140	40157	40175	40192	40209	40226	40243	40261	40278	40295
253	40312	40329	40346	40364	40381	40398	40415	40432	40449	40466
254	40483	40500	40518	40535	40552	40569	40586	40603	40620	40637
255	40654	40671	40688	40705	40722	40739	40756	40773	40790	40807
256	40824	40841	40858	40875	40892	40909	40926	40943	40960	40976
257	40993	41010	41027	41044	41061	41078	41095	41111	41128	41145
258	41162	41179	41196	41212	41229	41246	41263	41280	41296	41313
259	41330	41347	41363	41380	41397	41414	41430	41447	41464	41481
260	41497	41514	41531	41547	41564	41581	41597	41614	41631	41647
261	41664	41681	41697	41714	41731	41747	41764	41780	41797	41814
262	41830	41847	41863	41880	41896	41913	41929	41946	41963	41979
263	41996	42012	42029	42045	42062	42078	42095	42111	42127	42144
264	42160	42177	42193	42210	42226	42243	42259	42275	42292	42308
265	42325	42341	42357	42374	42390	42406	42423	42439	42455	42472
266	42488	42504	42521	42537	42553	42570	42586	42602	42619	42635
267	42651	42667	42684	42700	42716	42732	42749	42765	42781	42797
268	42813	42830	42846	42862	42878	42894	42911	42927	42943	42959
269	42975	42991	43008	43024	43040	43056	43072	43088	43104	43120
270	43136	43152	43169	43185	43201	43217	43233	43249	43265	43281
271	43297	43313	43329	43345	43361	43377	43393	43409	43425	43441
272	43457	43473	43489	43505	43521	43537	43553	43569	43584	43600
273	43616	43632	43648	43664	43680	43696	43712	43727	43743	43759
274	43775	43791	43807	43823	43838	43854	43870	43886	43902	43917
275	43933	43949	43965	43981	43996	44012	44028	44044	44059	44075
276	44091	44107	44122	44138	44154	44170	44185	44201	44217	44232
277	44248	44264	44279	44295	44311	44326	44342	44358	44373	44389
278	44404	44420	44436	44451	44467	44483	44498	44514	44529	44545
279	44560	44576	44592	44607	44623	44638	44654	44669	44685	44700
No.	0	1	2	3	4	5	6	7	8	9

	20	19	18	17	16	15
1	2	2	2	2	2	2
2	4	4	4	3	3	3
3	6	6	5	5	5	5
4	8	8	7	7	6	6
5	10	10	9	9	8	8
6	12	11	11	10	10	9
7	14	13	13	12	11	11
8	16	15	14	14	13	12
9	18	17	16	15	14	14

TABLE XXVI.

Logarithms of Numbers.

No. 2800——3400. Log. 44716——53148.

No.	0	1	2	3	4	5	6	7	8	9
280	44716	44731	44747	44762	44778	44793	44809	44824	44840	44855
281	44871	44886	44902	44917	44932	44948	44963	44979	44994	45010
282	45025	45040	45056	45071	45086	45102	45117	45133	45148	45163
283	45179	45194	45209	45225	45240	45255	45271	45286	45301	45317
284	45332	45347	45362	45378	45393	45408	45423	45439	45454	45469
285	45484	45500	45515	45530	45545	45561	45576	45591	45606	45621
286	45637	45652	45667	45682	45697	45712	45728	45743	45758	45773
287	45788	45803	45818	45834	45849	45864	45879	45894	45909	45924
288	45939	45954	45969	45984	46000	46015	46030	46045	46060	46075
289	46090	46105	46120	46135	46150	46165	46180	46195	46210	46225
290	46240	46255	46270	46285	46300	46315	46330	46345	46359	46374
291	46389	46404	46419	46434	46449	46464	46479	46494	46509	46523
292	46538	46553	46568	46583	46598	46613	46627	46642	46657	46672
293	46687	46702	46716	46731	46746	46761	46776	46790	46805	46820
294	46835	46850	46864	46879	46894	46909	46923	46938	46953	46967
295	46982	46997	47012	47026	47041	47056	47070	47085	47100	47114
296	47129	47144	47159	47173	47188	47202	47217	47232	47246	47261
297	47276	47290	47305	47319	47334	47349	47363	47378	47392	47407
298	47422	47436	47451	47465	47480	47494	47509	47524	47538	47553
299	47567	47582	47596	47611	47625	47640	47654	47669	47683	47698
300	47712	47727	47741	47756	47770	47784	47799	47813	47828	47842
301	47857	47871	47885	47900	47914	47929	47943	47958	47972	47986
302	48001	48015	48029	48044	48058	48073	48087	48101	48116	48130
303	48144	48159	48173	48187	48202	48216	48230	48244	48259	48273
304	48287	48302	48316	48330	48344	48359	48373	48387	48401	48416
305	48430	48444	48458	48473	48487	48501	48515	48530	48544	48558
306	48572	48586	48601	48615	48629	48643	48657	48671	48686	48700
307	48714	48728	48742	48756	48770	48785	48799	48813	48827	48841
308	48855	48869	48883	48897	48911	48926	48940	48954	48968	48982
309	48996	49010	49024	49038	49052	49066	49080	49094	49108	49122
310	49136	49150	49164	49178	49192	49206	49220	49234	49248	49262
311	49276	49290	49304	49318	49332	49346	49360	49374	49388	49402
312	49415	49429	49443	49457	49471	49485	49499	49513	49527	49541
313	49554	49568	49582	49596	49610	49624	49638	49651	49665	49679
314	49693	49707	49721	49734	49748	49762	49776	49790	49803	49817
315	49831	49845	49859	49872	49886	49900	49914	49927	49941	49955
316	49969	49982	49996	50010	50024	50037	50051	50065	50079	50092
317	50106	50120	50133	50147	50161	50174	50188	50202	50215	50229
318	50243	50256	50270	50284	50297	50311	50325	50338	50352	50365
319	50379	50393	50406	50420	50433	50447	50461	50474	50488	50501
320	50515	50529	50542	50556	50569	50583	50596	50610	50623	50637
321	50651	50664	50678	50691	50705	50718	50732	50745	50759	50772
322	50786	50799	50813	50826	50840	50853	50866	50880	50893	50907
323	50920	50934	50947	50961	50974	50987	51001	51014	51028	51041
324	51055	51068	51081	51095	51108	51121	51135	51148	51162	51175
325	51188	51202	51215	51228	51242	51255	51268	51282	51295	51308
326	51322	51335	51348	51362	51375	51388	51402	51415	51428	51441
327	51455	51468	51481	51495	51508	51521	51534	51548	51561	51574
328	51587	51601	51614	51627	51640	51654	51667	51680	51693	51706
329	51720	51733	51746	51759	51772	51786	51799	51812	51825	51838
330	51851	51865	51878	51891	51904	51917	51930	51943	51957	51970
331	51983	51996	52009	52022	52035	52048	52061	52075	52088	52101
332	52114	52127	52140	52153	52166	52179	52192	52205	52218	52231
333	52244	52257	52270	52284	52297	52310	52323	52336	52349	52362
334	52375	52388	52401	52414	52427	52440	52453	52466	52479	52492
335	52504	52517	52530	52543	52556	52569	52582	52595	52608	52621
336	52634	52647	52660	52673	52686	52699	52711	52724	52737	52750
337	52763	52776	52789	52802	52815	52827	52840	52853	52866	52879
338	52892	52905	52917	52930	52943	52956	52969	52982	52994	53007
339	53020	53033	53046	53058	53071	53084	53097	53110	53122	53135
No.	0	1	2	3	4	5	6	7	8	9

16	
1	2
2	3
3	5
4	6
5	8
6	10
7	11
8	13
9	14

15	
1	2
2	3
3	5
4	6
5	8
6	9
7	11
8	12
9	14

14	
1	1
2	3
3	4
4	6
5	7
6	8
7	10
8	11
9	13

13	
1	1
2	3
3	4
4	5
5	7
6	8
7	9
8	10
9	12

12	
1	1
2	2
3	4
4	5
5	6
6	7
7	8
8	10
9	11

TABLE XXVI.

Logarithms of Numbers.

No. 4600——5200. Log. 66276——71600.

No.	0	1	2	3	4	5	6	7	8	9
460	66276	66285	66295	66304	66314	66323	66332	66342	66351	66361
461	66370	66380	66389	66398	66408	66417	66427	66436	66445	66455
462	66464	66474	66483	66492	66502	66511	66521	66530	66539	66549
463	66558	66567	66577	66586	66596	66605	66614	66624	66633	66642
464	66652	66661	66671	66680	66689	66699	66708	66717	66727	66736
465	66745	66755	66764	66773	66783	66792	66801	66811	66820	66829
466	66839	66848	66857	66867	66876	66885	66894	66904	66913	66922
467	66932	66941	66950	66960	66969	66978	66987	66997	67006	67015
468	67025	67034	67043	67052	67062	67071	67080	67089	67099	67108
469	67117	67127	67136	67145	67154	67164	67173	67182	67191	67201
470	67210	67219	67228	67237	67247	67256	67265	67274	67284	67293
471	67302	67311	67321	67330	67339	67348	67357	67367	67376	67385
472	67394	67403	67413	67422	67431	67440	67449	67459	67468	67477
473	67486	67495	67504	67514	67523	67532	67541	67550	67560	67569
474	67578	67587	67596	67605	67614	67624	67633	67642	67651	67660
475	67669	67679	67688	67697	67706	67715	67724	67733	67742	67752
476	67761	67770	67779	67788	67797	67806	67815	67825	67834	67843
477	67852	67861	67870	67879	67888	67897	67906	67916	67925	67934
478	67943	67952	67961	67970	67979	67988	67997	68006	68015	68024
479	68034	68043	68052	68061	68070	68079	68088	68097	68106	68115
480	68124	68133	68142	68151	68160	68169	68178	68187	68196	68205
481	68215	68224	68233	68242	68251	68260	68269	68278	68287	68296
482	68305	68314	68323	68332	68341	68350	68359	68368	68377	68386
483	68395	68404	68413	68422	68431	68440	68449	68458	68467	68476
484	68485	68494	68502	68511	68520	68529	68538	68547	68556	68565
485	68574	68583	68592	68601	68610	68619	68628	68637	68646	68655
486	68664	68673	68681	68690	68699	68708	68717	68726	68735	68744
487	68753	68762	68771	68780	68789	68797	68806	68815	68824	68833
488	68842	68851	68860	68869	68878	68886	68895	68904	68913	68922
489	68931	68940	68949	68958	68966	68975	68984	68993	69002	69011
490	69020	69028	69037	69046	69055	69064	69073	69082	69090	69099
491	69108	69117	69126	69135	69144	69152	69161	69170	69179	69188
492	69197	69205	69214	69223	69232	69241	69249	69258	69267	69276
493	69285	69294	69302	69311	69320	69329	69338	69346	69355	69364
494	69373	69381	69390	69399	69408	69417	69425	69434	69443	69452
495	69461	69469	69478	69487	69496	69504	69513	69522	69531	69539
496	69548	69557	69566	69574	69583	69592	69601	69609	69618	69627
497	69636	69644	69653	69662	69671	69679	69688	69697	69705	69714
498	69723	69732	69740	69749	69758	69767	69775	69784	69793	69801
499	69810	69819	69827	69836	69845	69854	69862	69871	69880	69888
500	69897	69906	69914	69923	69932	69940	69949	69958	69966	69975
501	69984	69992	70001	70010	70018	70027	70036	70044	70053	70062
502	70070	70079	70088	70096	70105	70114	70122	70131	70140	70148
503	70157	70165	70174	70183	70191	70200	70209	70217	70226	70234
504	70243	70252	70260	70269	70278	70286	70295	70303	70312	70321
505	70329	70338	70346	70355	70364	70372	70381	70389	70398	70406
506	70415	70424	70432	70441	70449	70458	70467	70475	70484	70492
507	70501	70509	70518	70526	70535	70544	70552	70561	70569	70578
508	70586	70595	70603	70612	70621	70629	70638	70646	70655	70663
509	70672	70680	70689	70697	70706	70714	70723	70731	70740	70749
510	70757	70766	70774	70783	70791	70800	70808	70817	70825	70834
511	70842	70851	70859	70868	70876	70885	70893	70902	70910	70919
512	70927	70935	70944	70952	70961	70969	70978	70986	70995	71003
513	71012	71020	71029	71037	71046	71054	71063	71071	71079	71088
514	71096	71105	71113	71122	71130	71139	71147	71155	71164	71172
515	71181	71189	71198	71206	71214	71223	71231	71240	71248	71257
516	71265	71273	71282	71290	71299	71307	71315	71324	71332	71341
517	71349	71357	71366	71374	71383	71391	71399	71408	71416	71425
518	71433	71441	71450	71458	71466	71475	71483	71492	71500	71508
519	71517	71525	71533	71542	71550	71559	71567	71575	71584	71592
No.	0	1	2	3	4	5	6	7	8	9

10	
1	1
2	2
3	3
4	4
5	5
6	6
7	7
8	8
9	9

9	
1	1
2	2
3	3
4	4
5	5
6	5
7	6
8	7
9	8

8	
1	1
2	2
3	2
4	3
5	4
6	5
7	6
8	6
9	7

TABLE XXVI.

Logarithms of Numbers.

No. 5200——5800. Log. 71600——76343.

No.	0	1	2	3	4	5	6	7	8	9
520	71600	71609	71617	71625	71634	71642	71650	71659	71667	71675
521	71684	71692	71700	71709	71717	71725	71734	71742	71750	71759
522	71767	71775	71784	71792	71800	71809	71817	71825	71834	71842
523	71850	71858	71867	71875	71883	71892	71900	71908	71917	71925
524	71933	71941	71950	71958	71966	71975	71983	71991	71999	72008
525	72016	72024	72032	72041	72049	72057	72066	72074	72082	72090
526	72099	72107	72115	72123	72132	72140	72148	72156	72165	72173
527	72181	72189	72198	72206	72214	72222	72230	72239	72247	72255
528	72263	72272	72280	72288	72296	72304	72313	72321	72329	72337
529	72346	72354	72362	72370	72378	72387	72395	72403	72411	72419
530	72428	72436	72444	72452	72460	72469	72477	72485	72493	72501
531	72509	72518	72526	72534	72542	72550	72558	72567	72575	72583
532	72591	72599	72607	72616	72624	72632	-2640	72648	72656	72665
533	72673	72681	72689	72697	72705	72713	72722	72730	72738	72746
534	72754	72762	72770	72779	72787	72795	72803	72811	72819	72827
535	72835	72843	72852	72860	72868	72876	72884	72892	72900	72908
536	72916	72925	72933	72941	72949	72957	72965	72973	72981	72989
537	72997	73006	73014	73022	73030	73038	73046	73054	73062	73070
538	73078	73086	73094	73102	73111	73119	73127	73135	73143	73151
539	73159	73167	73175	73183	73191	73199	73207	73215	73223	73231
540	73239	73247	73255	73263	73272	73280	73288	73296	73304	73312
541	73320	73328	73336	73344	73352	73360	73368	73376	73384	73392
542	73400	73408	73416	73424	73432	73440	73448	73456	73464	73472
543	73480	73488	73496	73504	73512	73520	73528	73536	73544	73552
544	73560	73568	73576	73584	73592	73600	73608	73616	73624	73632
545	73640	73648	73656	73664	73672	73679	73687	73695	73703	73711
546	73719	73727	73735	73743	73751	73759	73767	73775	73783	73791
547	73799	73807	73815	73823	73830	73838	73846	73854	73862	73870
548	73878	73886	73894	73902	73910	73918	73926	73933	73941	73949
549	73957	73965	73973	73981	73989	73997	74005	74013	74020	74028
550	74036	74044	74052	74060	74068	74076	74084	74092	74099	74107
551	74115	74123	74131	74139	74147	74155	74162	74170	74178	74186
552	74194	74202	74210	74218	74225	74233	74241	74249	74257	74265
553	74273	74280	74288	74296	74304	74312	74320	74327	74335	74343
554	74351	74359	74367	74374	74382	74390	74398	74406	74414	74421
555	74429	74437	74445	74453	74461	74468	74476	74484	74492	74500
556	74507	74515	74523	74531	74539	74547	74554	74562	74570	74578
557	74586	74593	74601	74609	74617	74624	74632	74640	74648	74656
558	74663	74671	74679	74687	74695	74702	74710	74718	74726	74733
559	74741	74749	74757	74764	74772	74780	74788	74796	74803	74811
560	74819	74827	74834	74842	74850	74858	74865	74873	74881	74889
561	74896	74904	74912	74920	74927	74935	74943	74950	74958	74966
562	74974	74981	74989	74997	75005	75012	75020	75028	75035	75043
563	75051	75059	75066	75074	75082	75089	75097	75105	75113	75120
564	75128	75136	75143	75151	75159	75166	75174	75182	75189	75197
565	75205	75213	75220	75228	75236	75243	75251	75259	75266	75274
566	75282	75289	75297	75305	75312	75320	75328	75335	75343	75351
567	75358	75366	75374	75381	75389	75397	75404	75412	75420	75427
568	75435	75442	75450	75458	75465	75473	75481	75488	75496	75504
569	75511	75519	75526	75534	75542	75549	75557	75565	75572	75580
570	75587	75595	75603	75610	75618	75626	75633	75641	75648	75656
571	75664	75671	75679	75686	75694	75702	75709	75717	75724	75732
572	75740	75747	75755	75762	75770	75778	75785	75793	75800	75808
573	75815	75823	75831	75838	75846	75853	75861	75868	75876	75884
574	75891	75899	75906	75914	75921	75929	75937	75944	75952	75959
575	75967	75974	75982	75989	75997	76005	76012	76020	76027	76035
576	76042	76050	76057	76065	76072	76080	76087	76095	76103	76110
577	76118	76125	76133	76140	76148	76155	76163	76170	76178	76185
578	76193	76200	76208	76215	76223	76230	76238	76245	76253	76260
579	76268	76275	76283	76290	76298	76305	76313	76320	76328	76335
No.	0	1	2	3	4	5	6	7	8	9

9	
1	1
2	2
3	3
4	4
5	5
6	5
7	6
8	7
9	8

8	
1	1
2	2
3	2
4	3
5	4
6	5
7	6
8	6
9	7

7	
1	1
2	1
3	2
4	3
5	4
6	4
7	5
8	6
9	6

TABLE XXVI.

Logarithms of Numbers.

No. 5800——6400. Log. 76343——80618.

No.	0	1	2	3	4	5	6	7	8	9
580	76343	76350	76358	76365	76373	76380	76388	76395	76403	76410
581	76418	76425	76433	76440	76448	76455	76462	76470	76477	76485
582	76492	76500	76507	76515	76522	76530	76537	76545	76552	76559
583	76567	76574	76582	76589	76597	76604	76612	76619	76626	76634
584	76641	76649	76656	76664	76671	76678	76686	76693	76701	76708
585	76716	76723	76730	76738	76745	76753	76760	76768	76775	76782
586	76790	76797	76805	76812	76819	76827	76834	76842	76849	76856
587	76864	76871	76879	76886	76893	76901	76908	76916	76923	76930
588	76938	76945	76953	76960	76967	76975	76982	76989	76997	77004
589	77012	77019	77026	77034	77041	77048	77056	77063	77070	77078
590	77085	77093	77100	77107	77115	77122	77129	77137	77144	77151
591	77159	77166	77173	77181	77188	77195	77203	77210	77217	77225
592	77232	77240	77247	77254	77262	77269	77276	77283	77291	77298
593	77305	77313	77320	77327	77335	77342	77349	77357	77364	77371
594	77379	77386	77393	77401	77408	77415	77422	77430	77437	77444
595	77452	77459	77466	77474	77481	77488	77495	77503	77510	77517
596	77525	77532	77539	77546	77554	77561	77568	77576	77583	77590
597	77597	77605	77612	77619	77627	77634	77641	77648	77656	77663
598	77670	77677	77685	77692	77699	77706	77714	77721	77728	77735
599	77743	77750	77757	77764	77772	77779	77786	77793	77801	77808
600	77815	77822	77830	77837	77844	77851	77859	77866	77873	77880
601	77887	77895	77902	77909	77916	77924	77931	77938	77945	77952
602	77960	77967	77974	77981	77988	77996	78003	78010	78017	78025
603	78032	78039	78046	78053	78061	78068	78075	78082	78089	78097
604	78104	78111	78118	78125	78132	78140	78147	78154	78161	78168
605	78176	78183	78190	78197	78204	78211	78219	78226	78233	78240
606	78247	78254	78262	78269	78276	78283	78290	78297	78305	78312
607	78319	78326	78333	78340	78347	78355	78362	78369	78376	78383
608	78390	78398	78405	78412	78419	78426	78433	78440	78447	78455
609	78462	78469	78476	78483	78490	78497	78504	78512	78519	78526
610	78533	78540	78547	78554	78561	78569	78576	78583	78590	78597
611	78604	78611	78618	78625	78633	78640	78647	78654	78661	78668
612	78675	78682	78689	78696	78704	78711	78718	78725	78732	78739
613	78746	78753	78760	78767	78774	78781	78789	78796	78803	78810
614	78817	78824	78831	78838	78845	78852	78859	78866	78873	78880
615	78888	78895	78902	78909	78916	78923	78930	78937	78944	78951
616	78958	78965	78972	78979	78986	78993	79000	79007	79014	79021
617	79029	79036	79043	79050	79057	79064	79071	79078	79085	79092
618	79099	79106	79113	79120	79127	79134	79141	79148	79155	79162
619	79169	79176	79183	79190	79197	79204	79211	79218	79225	79232
620	79239	79246	79253	79260	79267	79274	79281	79288	79295	79302
621	79309	79316	79323	79330	79337	79344	79351	79358	79365	79372
622	79379	79386	79393	79400	79407	79414	79421	79428	79435	79442
623	79449	79456	79463	79470	79477	79484	79491	79498	79505	79511
624	79518	79525	79532	79539	79546	79553	79560	79567	79574	79581
625	79588	79595	79602	79609	79616	79623	79630	79637	79644	79650
626	79657	79664	79671	79678	79685	79692	79699	79706	79713	79720
627	79727	79734	79741	79748	79754	79761	79768	79775	79782	79789
628	79796	79803	79810	79817	79824	79831	79837	79844	79851	79858
629	79865	79872	79879	79886	79893	79900	79906	79913	79920	79927
630	79934	79941	79948	79955	79962	79969	79975	79982	79989	79996
631	80003	80010	80017	80024	80030	80037	80044	80051	80058	80065
632	80072	80079	80085	80092	80099	80106	80113	80120	80127	80134
633	80140	80147	80154	80161	80168	80175	80182	80188	80195	80202
634	80209	80216	80223	80229	80236	80243	80250	80257	80264	80271
635	80277	80284	80291	80298	80305	80312	80318	80325	80332	80339
636	80346	80353	80359	80366	80373	80380	80387	80393	80400	80407
637	80414	80421	80428	80434	80441	80448	80455	80462	80468	80475
638	80482	80489	80496	80502	80509	80516	80523	80530	80536	80543
639	80550	80557	80564	80570	80577	80584	80591	80598	80604	80611
No.	0	1	2	3	4	5	6	7	8	9

8	
1	1
2	2
3	2
4	3
5	4
6	5
7	6
8	6
9	7

7	
1	1
2	1
3	2
4	3
5	4
6	4
7	5
8	6
9	6

6	
1	1
2	1
3	2
4	2
5	3
6	4
7	4
8	5
9	5

TABLE XXVI.

Logarithms of Numbers.

No. 6400——7000. Log. 80618——84510.

No.	0	1	2	3	4	5	6	7	8	9
640	80618	80625	80632	80638	80645	80652	80659	80665	80672	80679
641	80686	80693	80699	80706	80713	80720	80726	80733	80740	80747
642	80754	80760	80767	80774	80781	80787	80794	80801	80808	80814
643	80821	80828	80835	80841	80848	80855	80862	80868	80875	80882
644	80889	80895	80902	80909	80916	80922	80929	80936	80943	80949
645	80956	80963	80969	80976	80983	80990	80996	81003	81010	81017
646	81023	81030	81037	81043	81050	81057	81064	81070	81077	81084
647	81090	81097	81104	81111	81117	81124	81131	81137	81144	81151
648	81158	81164	81171	81178	81184	81191	81198	81204	81211	81218
649	81224	81231	81238	81245	81251	81258	81265	81271	81278	81285
650	81291	81298	81305	81311	81318	81325	81331	81338	81345	81351
651	81358	81365	81371	81378	81385	81391	81398	81405	81411	81418
652	81425	81431	81438	81445	81451	81458	81465	81471	81478	81485
653	81491	81498	81505	81511	81518	81525	81531	81538	81544	81551
654	81558	81564	81571	81578	81584	81591	81598	81604	81611	81617
655	81624	81631	81637	81644	81651	81657	81664	81671	81677	81684
656	81690	81697	81704	81710	81717	81723	81730	81737	81743	81750
657	81757	81763	81770	81776	81783	81790	81796	81803	81809	81816
658	81823	81829	81836	81842	81849	81856	81862	81869	81875	81882
659	81889	81895	81902	81908	81915	81921	81928	81935	81941	81948
660	81954	81961	81968	81974	81981	81987	81994	82000	82007	82014
661	82020	82027	82033	82040	82046	82053	82060	82066	82073	82079
662	82086	82092	82099	82105	82112	82119	82125	82132	82138	82145
663	82151	82158	82164	82171	82178	82184	82191	82197	82204	82210
664	82217	82223	82230	82236	82243	82249	82256	82263	82269	82276
665	82282	82289	82295	82302	82308	82315	82321	82328	82334	82341
666	82347	82354	82360	82367	82373	82380	82387	82393	82400	82406
667	82413	82419	82426	82432	82439	82445	82452	82458	82465	82471
668	82478	82484	82491	82497	82504	82510	82517	82523	82530	82536
669	82543	82549	82556	82562	82569	82575	82582	82588	82595	82601
670	82607	82614	82620	82627	82633	82640	82646	82653	82659	82666
671	82672	82679	82685	82692	82698	82705	82711	82718	82724	82730
672	82737	82743	82750	82756	82763	82769	82776	82782	82789	82795
673	82802	82808	82814	82821	82827	82834	82840	82847	82853	82860
674	82866	82872	82879	82885	82892	82898	82905	82911	82918	82924
675	82930	82937	82943	82950	82956	82963	82969	82975	82982	82988
676	82995	83001	83008	83014	83020	83027	83033	83040	83046	83052
677	83059	83065	83072	83078	83085	83091	83097	83104	83110	83117
678	83123	83129	83136	83142	83149	83155	83161	83168	83174	83181
679	83187	83193	83200	83206	83213	83219	83225	83232	83238	83245
680	83251	83257	83264	83270	83276	83283	83289	83296	83302	83308
681	83315	83321	83327	83334	83340	83347	83353	83359	83366	83372
682	83378	83385	83391	83398	83404	83410	83417	83423	83429	83436
683	83442	83448	83455	83461	83467	83474	83480	83487	83493	83499
684	83506	83512	83518	83525	83531	83537	83544	83550	83556	83563
685	83569	83575	83582	83588	83594	83601	83607	83613	83620	83626
686	83632	83639	83645	83651	83658	83664	83670	83677	83683	83689
687	83696	83702	83708	83715	83721	83727	83734	83740	83746	83753
688	83759	83765	83771	83778	83784	83790	83797	83803	83809	83816
689	83822	83828	83835	83841	83847	83853	83860	83866	83872	83879
690	83885	83891	83897	83904	83910	83916	83923	83929	83935	83942
691	83948	83954	83960	83967	83973	83979	83985	83992	83998	84004
692	84011	84017	84023	84029	84036	84042	84048	84055	84061	84067
693	84073	84080	84086	84092	84098	84105	84111	84117	84123	84130
694	84136	84142	84148	84155	84161	84167	84173	84180	84186	84192
695	84198	84205	84211	84217	84223	84230	84236	84242	84248	84255
696	84261	84267	84273	84280	84286	84292	84298	84305	84311	84317
697	84323	84330	84336	84342	84348	84354	84361	84367	84373	84379
698	84386	84392	84398	84404	84410	84417	84423	84429	84435	84442
699	84448	84454	84460	84466	84473	84479	84485	84491	84497	84504
No.	0	1	2	3	4	5	6	7	8	9

7	
1	1
2	1
3	2
4	3
5	4
6	4
7	5
8	6
9	6

6	
1	1
2	1
3	2
4	2
5	3
6	4
7	4
8	5
9	5

TABLE XXVI.

Logarithms of Numbers.

No. 7000——7600. Log. 84510——88081.

No.	0	1	2	3	4	5	6	7	8	9
700	84510	84516	84522	84528	84535	84541	84547	84553	84559	84566
701	84572	84578	84584	84590	84597	84603	84609	84615	84621	84628
702	84634	84640	84646	84652	84658	84665	84671	84677	84683	84689
703	84696	84702	84708	84714	84720	84726	84733	84739	84745	84751
704	84757	84763	84770	84776	84782	84788	84794	84800	84807	84813
705	84819	84825	84831	84837	84844	84850	84856	84862	84868	84874
706	84880	84887	84893	84899	84905	84911	84917	84924	84930	84936
707	84942	84948	84954	84960	84967	84973	84979	84985	84991	84997
708	85003	85009	85016	85022	85028	85034	85040	85046	85052	85058
709	85065	85071	85077	85083	85089	85095	85101	85107	85114	85120
710	85126	85132	85138	85144	85150	85156	85163	85169	85175	85181
711	85187	85193	85199	85205	85211	85217	85224	85230	85236	85242
712	85248	85254	85260	85266	85272	85278	85285	85291	85297	85303
713	85309	85315	85321	85327	85333	85339	85345	85352	85358	85364
714	85370	85376	85382	85388	85394	85400	85406	85412	85418	85425
715	85431	85437	85443	85449	85455	85461	85467	85473	85479	85485
716	85491	85497	85503	85509	85516	85522	85528	85534	85540	85546
717	85552	85558	85564	85570	85576	85582	85588	85594	85600	85606
718	85612	85618	85625	85631	85637	85643	85649	85655	85661	85667
719	85673	85679	85685	85691	85697	85703	85709	85715	85721	85727
720	85733	85739	85745	85751	85757	85763	85769	85775	85781	85788
721	85794	85800	85806	85812	85818	85824	85830	85836	85842	85848
722	85854	85860	85866	85872	85878	85884	85890	85896	85902	85908
723	85914	85920	85926	85932	85938	85944	85950	85956	85962	85968
724	85974	85980	85986	85992	85998	86004	86010	86016	86022	86028
725	86034	86040	86046	86052	86058	86064	86070	86076	86082	86088
726	86094	86100	86106	86112	86118	86124	86130	86136	86141	86147
727	86153	86159	86165	86171	86177	86183	86189	86195	86201	86207
728	86213	86219	86225	86231	86237	86243	86249	86255	86261	86267
729	86273	86279	86285	86291	86297	86303	86308	86314	86320	86326
730	86332	86338	86344	86350	86356	86362	86368	86374	86380	86386
731	86392	86398	86404	86410	86415	86421	86427	86433	86439	86445
732	86451	86457	86463	86469	86475	86481	86487	86493	86499	86504
733	86510	86516	86522	86528	86534	86540	86546	86552	86558	86564
734	86570	86576	86581	86587	86593	86599	86605	86611	86617	86623
735	86629	86635	86641	86646	86652	86658	86664	86670	86676	86682
736	86688	86694	86700	86705	86711	86717	86723	86729	86735	86741
737	86747	86753	86759	86764	86770	86776	86782	86788	86794	86800
738	86806	86812	86817	86823	86829	86835	86841	86847	86853	86859
739	86864	86870	86876	86882	86888	86894	86900	86906	86911	86917
740	86923	86929	86935	86941	86947	86953	86958	86964	86970	86976
741	86982	86988	86994	86999	87005	87011	87017	87023	87029	87035
742	87040	87046	87052	87058	87064	87070	87075	87081	87087	87093
743	87099	87105	87111	87116	87122	87128	87134	87140	87146	87151
744	87157	87163	87169	87175	87181	87186	87192	87198	87204	87210
745	87216	87221	87227	87233	87239	87245	87251	87256	87262	87268
746	87274	87280	87286	87291	87297	87303	87309	87315	87320	87326
747	87332	87338	87344	87349	87355	87361	87367	87373	87379	87384
748	87390	87396	87402	87408	87413	87419	87425	87431	87437	87442
749	87448	87454	87460	87466	87471	87477	87483	87489	87495	87500
750	87506	87512	87518	87523	87529	87535	87541	87547	87552	87558
751	87564	87570	87576	87581	87587	87593	87599	87604	87610	87616
752	87622	87628	87633	87639	87645	87651	87656	87662	87668	87674
753	87679	87685	87691	87697	87703	87708	87714	87720	87726	87731
754	87737	87743	87749	87754	87760	87766	87772	87777	87783	87789
755	87795	87800	87806	87812	87818	87823	87829	87835	87841	87846
756	87852	87858	87864	87869	87875	87881	87887	87892	87898	87904
757	87910	87915	87921	87927	87933	87938	87944	87950	87955	87961
758	87967	87973	87978	87984	87990	87996	88001	88007	88013	88018
759	88024	88030	88036	88041	88047	88053	88058	88064	88070	88076
No.	0	1	2	3	4	5	6	7	8	9

7	
1	1
2	1
3	2
4	3
5	4
6	4
7	5
8	6
9	6

6	
1	1
2	1
3	2
4	2
5	3
6	4
7	4
8	5
9	5

5	
1	1
2	1
3	2
4	2
5	3
6	3
7	4
8	4
9	5

TABLE XXVI.

Logarithms of Numbers.

No. 7600——8200. Log. 88081——91381.

No.	0	1	2	3	4	5	6	7	8	9
760	88081	88087	88093	88098	88104	88110	88116	88121	88127	88133
761	88138	88144	88150	88156	88161	88167	88173	88178	88184	88190
762	88195	88201	88207	88213	88218	88224	88230	88235	88241	88247
763	88252	88258	88264	88270	88275	88281	88287	88292	88298	88304
764	88309	88315	88321	88326	88332	88338	88343	88349	88355	88360
765	88366	88372	88377	88383	88389	88395	88400	88406	88412	88417
766	88423	88429	88434	88440	88446	88451	88457	88463	88468	88474
767	88480	88485	88491	88497	88502	88508	88513	88519	88525	88530
768	88536	88542	88547	88553	88559	88564	88570	88576	88581	88587
769	88593	88598	88604	88610	88615	88621	88627	88632	88638	88643
770	88649	88655	88660	88666	88672	88677	88683	88689	88694	88700
771	88705	88711	88717	88722	88728	88734	88739	88745	88750	88756
772	88762	88767	88773	88779	88784	88790	88795	88801	88807	88812
773	88818	88824	88829	88835	88840	88846	88852	88857	88863	88868
774	88874	88880	88885	88891	88897	88902	88908	88913	88919	88925
775	88930	88936	88941	88947	88953	88958	88964	88969	88975	88981
776	88986	88992	88997	89003	89009	89014	89020	89025	89031	89037
777	89042	89048	89053	89059	89064	89070	89076	89081	89087	89092
778	89098	89104	89109	89115	89120	89126	89131	89137	89143	89148
779	89154	89159	89165	89170	89176	89182	89187	89193	89198	89204
780	89209	89215	89221	89226	89232	89237	89243	89248	89254	89260
781	89265	89271	89276	89282	89287	89293	89298	89304	89310	89315
782	89321	89326	89332	89337	89343	89348	89354	89360	89365	89371
783	89376	89382	89387	89393	89398	89404	89409	89415	89421	89426
784	89432	89437	89443	89448	89454	89459	89465	89470	89476	89481
785	89487	89492	89498	89504	89509	89515	89520	89526	89531	89537
786	89542	89548	89553	89559	89564	89570	89575	89581	89586	89592
787	89597	89603	89609	89614	89620	89625	89631	89636	89642	89647
788	89653	89658	89664	89669	89675	89680	89686	89691	89697	89702
789	89708	89713	89719	89724	89730	89735	89741	89746	89752	89757
790	89763	89768	89774	89779	89785	89790	89796	89801	89807	89812
791	89818	89823	89829	89834	89840	89845	89851	89856	89862	89867
792	89873	89878	89883	89889	89894	89900	89905	89911	89916	89922
793	89927	89933	89938	89944	89949	89955	89960	89966	89971	89977
794	89982	89988	89993	89998	90004	90009	90015	90020	90026	90031
795	90037	90042	90048	90053	90059	90064	90069	90075	90080	90086
796	90091	90097	90102	90108	90113	90119	90124	90129	90135	90140
797	90146	90151	90157	90162	90168	90173	90179	90184	90189	90195
798	90200	90206	90211	90217	90222	90227	90233	90238	90244	90249
799	90255	90260	90266	90271	90276	90282	90287	90293	90298	90304
800	90309	90314	90320	90325	90331	90336	90342	90347	90352	90358
801	90363	90369	90374	90380	90385	90390	90396	90401	90407	90412
802	90417	90423	90428	90434	90439	90445	90450	90455	90461	90466
803	90472	90477	90482	90488	90493	90499	90504	90509	90515	90520
804	90526	90531	90536	90542	90547	90553	90558	90563	90569	90574
805	90580	90585	90590	90596	90601	90607	90612	90617	90623	90628
806	90634	90639	90644	90650	90655	90660	90666	90671	90677	90682
807	90687	90693	90698	90703	90709	90714	90720	90725	90730	90736
808	90741	90747	90752	90757	90763	90768	90773	90779	90784	90789
809	90795	90800	90806	90811	90816	90822	90827	90832	90838	90843
810	90849	90854	90859	90865	90870	90875	90881	90886	90891	90897
811	90902	90907	90913	90918	90924	90929	90934	90940	90945	90950
812	90956	90961	90966	90972	90977	90982	90988	90993	90998	91004
813	91009	91014	91020	91025	91030	91036	91041	91046	91052	91057
814	91062	91068	91073	91078	91084	91089	91094	91100	91105	91110
815	91116	91121	91126	91132	91137	91142	91148	91153	91158	91164
816	91169	91174	91180	91185	91190	91196	91201	91206	91212	91217
817	91222	91228	91233	91238	91243	91249	91254	91259	91265	91270
818	91275	91281	91286	91291	91297	91302	91307	91312	91318	91323
819	91328	91334	91339	91344	91350	91355	91360	91365	91371	91376
No.	0	1	2	3	4	5	6	7	8	9

6	
1	1
2	1
3	2
4	2
5	3
6	4
7	4
8	5
9	5

5	
1	1
2	1
3	2
4	2
5	3
6	3
7	4
8	4
9	5

TABLE XXVI.

Logarithms of Numbers.

No. 8200——8800. Log. 91381——94448.

No.	0	1	2	3	4	5	6	7	8	9
820	91381	91387	91392	91397	91403	91408	91413	91418	91424	91429
821	91434	91440	91445	91450	91455	91461	91466	91471	91477	91482
822	91487	91492	91498	91503	91508	91514	91519	91524	91529	91535
823	91540	91545	91551	91556	91561	91566	91572	91577	91582	91587
824	91593	91598	91603	91609	91614	91619	91624	91630	91635	91640
825	91645	91651	91656	91661	91666	91672	91677	91682	91687	91693
826	91698	91703	91709	91714	91719	91724	91730	91735	91740	91745
827	91751	91756	91761	91766	91772	91777	91782	91787	91793	91798
828	91803	91808	91814	91819	91824	91829	91834	91840	91845	91850
829	91855	91861	91866	91871	91876	91882	91887	91892	91897	91903
830	91908	91913	91918	91924	91929	91934	91939	91944	91950	91955
831	91960	91965	91971	91976	91981	91986	91991	91997	92002	92007
832	92012	92018	92023	92028	92033	92038	92044	92049	92054	92059
833	92065	92070	92075	92080	92085	92091	92096	92101	92106	92111
834	92117	92122	92127	92132	92137	92143	92148	92153	92158	92163
835	92169	92174	92179	92184	92189	92195	92200	92205	92210	92215
836	92221	92226	92231	92236	92241	92247	92252	92257	92262	92267
837	92273	92278	92283	92288	92293	92298	92304	92309	92314	92319
838	92324	92330	92335	92340	92345	92350	92355	92361	92366	92371
839	92376	92381	92387	92392	92397	92402	92407	92412	92418	92423
840	92428	92433	92438	92443	92449	92454	92459	92464	92469	92474
841	92480	92485	92490	92495	92500	92505	92511	92516	92521	92526
842	92531	92536	92542	92547	92552	92557	92562	92567	92572	92578
843	92583	92588	92593	92598	92603	92609	92614	92619	92624	92629
844	92634	92639	92645	92650	92655	92660	92665	92670	92675	92681
845	92686	92691	92696	92701	92706	92711	92716	92722	92727	92732
846	92737	92742	92747	92752	92758	92763	92768	92773	92778	92783
847	92788	92793	92799	92804	92809	92814	92819	92824	92829	92834
848	92840	92845	92850	92855	92860	92865	92870	92875	92881	92886
849	92891	92896	92901	92906	92911	92916	92921	92927	92932	92937
850	92942	92947	92952	92957	92962	92967	92973	92978	92983	92988
851	92993	92998	93003	93008	93013	93018	93024	93029	93034	93039
852	93044	93049	93054	93059	93064	93069	93075	93080	93085	93090
853	93095	93100	93105	93110	93115	93120	93125	93131	93136	93141
854	93146	93151	93156	93161	93166	93171	93176	93181	93186	93192
855	93197	93202	93207	93212	93217	93222	93227	93232	93237	93242
856	93247	93252	93258	93263	93268	93273	93278	93283	93288	93293
857	93298	93303	93308	93313	93318	93323	93328	93334	93339	93344
858	93349	93354	93359	93364	93369	93374	93379	93384	93389	93394
859	93399	93404	93409	93414	93420	93425	93430	93435	93440	93445
860	93450	93455	93460	93465	93470	93475	93480	93485	93490	93495
861	93500	93505	93510	93515	93520	93526	93531	93536	93541	93546
862	93551	93556	93561	93566	93571	93576	93581	93586	93591	93596
863	93601	93606	93611	93616	93621	93626	93631	93636	93641	93646
864	93651	93656	93661	93666	93671	93676	93682	93687	93692	93697
865	93702	93707	93712	93717	93722	93727	93732	93737	93742	93747
866	93752	93757	93762	93767	93772	93777	93782	93787	93792	93797
867	93802	93807	93812	93817	93822	93827	93832	93837	93842	93847
868	93852	93857	93862	93867	93872	93877	93882	93887	93892	93897
869	93902	93907	93912	93917	93922	93927	93932	93937	93942	93947
870	93952	93957	93962	93967	93972	93977	93982	93987	93992	93997
871	94002	94007	94012	94017	94022	94027	94032	94037	94042	94047
872	94052	94057	94062	94067	94072	94077	94082	94086	94091	94096
873	94101	94106	94111	94116	94121	94126	94131	94136	94141	94146
874	94151	94156	94161	94166	94171	94176	94181	94186	94191	94196
875	94201	94206	94211	94216	94221	94226	94231	94236	94240	94245
876	94250	94255	94260	94265	94270	94275	94280	94285	94290	94295
877	94300	94305	94310	94315	94320	94325	94330	94335	94340	94345
878	94349	94354	94359	94364	94369	94374	94379	94384	94389	94394
879	94399	94404	94409	94414	94419	94424	94429	94433	94438	94443
No.	0	1	2	3	4	5	6	7	8	9

6	
1	1
2	1
3	2
4	2
5	3
6	4
7	4
8	5
9	5

5	
1	1
2	1
3	2
4	2
5	3
6	3
7	4
8	4
9	5

4	
1	0
2	1
3	1
4	2
5	2
6	2
7	3
8	3
9	4

TABLE XXVI.

Logarithms of Numbers.

No. 8800——9400. Log. 94448——97313.

No.	0	1	2	3	4	5	6	7	8	9
880	94448	94453	94458	94463	94468	94473	94478	94483	94488	94493
881	94498	94503	94507	94512	94517	94522	94527	94532	94537	94542
882	94547	94552	94557	94562	94567	94571	94576	94581	94586	94591
883	94596	94601	94606	94611	94616	94621	94626	94630	94635	94640
884	94645	94650	94655	94660	94665	94670	94675	94680	94685	94689
885	94694	94699	94704	94709	94714	94719	94724	94729	94734	94738
886	94743	94748	94753	94758	94763	94768	94773	94778	94783	94787
887	94792	94797	94802	94807	94812	94817	94822	94827	94832	94836
888	94841	94846	94851	94856	94861	94866	94871	94876	94880	94885
889	94890	94895	94900	94905	94910	94915	94919	94924	94929	94934
890	94939	94944	94949	94954	94959	94963	94968	94973	94978	94983
891	94988	94993	94998	95002	95007	95012	95017	95022	95027	95032
892	95036	95041	95046	95051	95056	95061	95066	95071	95075	95080
893	95085	95090	95095	95100	95105	95109	95114	95119	95124	95129
894	95134	95139	95143	95148	95153	95158	95163	95168	95173	95177
895	95182	95187	95192	95197	95202	95207	95211	95216	95221	95226
896	95231	95236	95240	95245	95250	95255	95260	95265	95270	95274
897	95279	95284	95289	95294	95299	95303	95308	95313	95318	95323
898	95328	95332	95337	95342	95347	95352	95357	95361	95366	95371
899	95376	95381	95386	95390	95395	95400	95405	95410	95415	95419
900	95424	95429	95434	95439	95444	95448	95453	95458	95463	95468
901	95472	95477	95482	95487	95492	95497	95501	95506	95511	95516
902	95521	95525	95530	95535	95540	95545	95550	95554	95559	95564
903	95569	95574	95578	95583	95588	95593	95598	95602	95607	95612
904	95617	95622	95626	95631	95636	95641	95646	95650	95655	95660
905	95665	95670	95674	95679	95684	95689	95694	95698	95703	95708
906	95713	95718	95722	95727	95732	95737	95742	95746	95751	95756
907	95761	95766	95770	95775	95780	95785	95789	95794	95799	95804
908	95809	95813	95818	95823	95828	95832	95837	95842	95847	95852
909	95856	95861	95866	95871	95875	95880	95885	95890	95895	95899
910	95904	95909	95914	95918	95923	95928	95933	95938	95942	95947
911	95952	95957	95961	95966	95971	95976	95980	95985	95990	95995
912	95999	96004	96009	96014	96019	96023	96028	96033	96038	96042
913	96047	96052	96057	96061	96066	96071	96076	96080	96085	96090
914	96095	96099	96104	96109	96114	96118	96123	96128	96133	96137
915	96142	96147	96152	96156	96161	96166	96171	96175	96180	96185
916	96190	96194	96199	96204	96209	96213	96218	96223	96227	96232
917	96237	96242	96246	96251	96256	96261	96265	96270	96275	96280
918	96284	96289	96294	96298	96303	96308	96313	96317	96322	96327
919	96332	96336	96341	96346	96350	96355	96360	96365	96369	96374
920	96379	96384	96388	96393	96398	96402	96407	96412	96417	96421
921	96426	96431	96435	96440	96445	96450	96454	96459	96464	96468
922	96473	96478	96483	96487	96492	96497	96501	96506	96511	96515
923	96520	96525	96530	96534	96539	96544	96548	96553	96558	96562
924	96567	96572	96577	96581	96586	96591	96595	96600	96605	96609
925	96614	96619	96624	96628	96633	96638	96642	96647	96652	96656
926	96661	96666	96670	96675	96680	96685	96689	96694	96699	96703
927	96708	96713	96717	96722	96727	96731	96736	96741	96745	96750
928	96755	96759	96764	96769	96774	96778	96783	96788	96792	96797
929	96802	96806	96811	96816	96820	96825	96830	96834	96839	96844
930	96848	96853	96858	96862	96867	96872	96876	96881	96886	96890
931	96895	96900	96904	96909	96914	96918	96923	96928	96932	96937
932	96942	96946	96951	96956	96960	96965	96970	96974	96979	96984
933	96988	96993	96997	97002	97007	97011	97016	97021	97025	97030
934	97035	97039	97044	97049	97053	97058	97063	97067	97072	97077
935	97081	97086	97090	97095	97100	97104	97109	97114	97118	97123
936	97128	97132	97137	97142	97146	97151	97155	97160	97165	97169
937	97174	97179	97183	97188	97192	97197	97202	97206	97211	97216
938	97220	97225	97230	97234	97239	97243	97248	97253	97257	97262
939	97267	97271	97276	97280	97285	97290	97294	97299	97304	97308
No.	0	1	2	3	4	5	6	7	8	9

5	
1	1
2	1
3	2
4	2
5	3
6	3
7	4
8	4
9	5

4	
1	0
2	1
3	1
4	2
5	2
5	2
7	3
8	3
9	4

TABLE XXVI.

Logarithms of Numbers.

No. 9400——10000. Log. 97313——99996.

No.	0	1	2	3	4	5	6	7	8	9
940	97313	97317	97322	97327	97331	97336	97340	97345	97350	97354
941	97359	97364	97368	97373	97377	97382	97387	97391	97396	97400
942	97405	97410	97414	97419	97424	97428	97433	97437	97442	97447
943	97451	97456	97460	97465	97470	97474	97479	97483	97488	97493
944	97497	97502	97506	97511	97516	97520	97525	97529	97534	97539
945	97543	97548	97552	97557	97562	97566	97571	97575	97580	97585
946	97589	97594	97598	97603	97607	97612	97617	97621	97626	97630
947	97635	97640	97644	97649	97653	97658	97663	97667	97672	97676
948	97681	97685	97690	97695	97699	97704	97708	97713	97717	97722
949	97727	97731	97736	97740	97745	97749	97754	97759	97763	97768
950	97772	97777	97782	97786	97791	97795	97800	97804	97809	97813
951	97818	97823	97827	97832	97836	97841	97845	97850	97855	97859
952	97864	97868	97873	97877	97882	97886	97891	97896	97900	97905
953	97909	97914	97918	97923	97928	97932	97937	97941	97946	97950
954	97955	97959	97964	97968	97973	97978	97982	97987	97991	97996
955	98000	98005	98009	98014	98019	98023	98028	98032	98037	98041
956	98046	98050	98055	98059	98064	98068	98073	98078	98082	98087
957	98091	98096	98100	98105	98109	98114	98118	98123	98127	98132
958	98137	98141	98146	98150	98155	98159	98164	98168	98173	98177
959	98182	98186	98191	98195	98200	98204	98209	98214	98218	98223
960	98227	98232	98236	98241	98245	98250	98254	98259	98263	98268
961	98272	98277	98281	98286	98290	98295	98299	98304	98308	98313
962	98318	98322	98327	98331	98336	98340	98345	98349	98354	98358
963	98363	98367	98372	98376	98381	98385	98390	98394	98399	98403
964	98408	98412	98417	98421	98426	98430	98435	98439	98444	98448
965	98453	98457	98462	98466	98471	98475	98480	98484	98489	98493
966	98498	98502	98507	98511	98516	98520	98525	98529	98534	98538
967	98543	98547	98552	98556	98561	98565	98570	98574	98579	98583
968	98588	98592	98597	98601	98605	98610	98614	98619	98623	98628
969	98632	98637	98641	98646	98650	98655	98659	98664	98668	98673
970	98677	98682	98686	98691	98695	98700	98704	98709	98713	98717
971	98722	98726	98731	98735	98740	98744	98749	98753	98758	98762
972	98767	98771	98776	98780	98784	98789	98793	98798	98802	98807
973	98811	98816	98820	98825	98829	98834	98838	98843	98847	98851
974	98856	98860	98865	98869	98874	98878	98883	98887	98892	98896
975	98900	98905	98909	98914	98918	98923	98927	98932	98936	98941
976	98945	98949	98954	98958	98963	98967	98972	98976	98981	98985
977	98989	98994	98998	99003	99007	99012	99016	99021	99025	99029
978	99034	99038	99043	99047	99052	99056	99061	99065	99069	99074
979	99078	99083	99087	99092	99096	99100	99105	99109	99114	99118
980	99123	99127	99131	99136	99140	99145	99149	99154	99158	99162
981	99167	99171	99176	99180	99185	99189	99193	99198	99202	99207
982	99211	99216	99220	99224	99229	99233	99238	99242	99247	99251
983	99255	99260	99264	99269	99273	99277	99282	99286	99291	99295
984	99300	99304	99308	99313	99317	99322	99326	99330	99335	99339
985	99344	99348	99352	99357	99361	99366	99370	99374	99379	99383
986	99388	99392	99396	99401	99405	99410	99414	99419	99423	99427
987	99432	99436	99441	99445	99449	99454	99458	99463	99467	99471
988	99476	99480	99484	99489	99493	99498	99502	99506	99511	99515
989	99520	99524	99528	99533	99537	99542	99546	99550	99555	99559
990	99564	99568	99572	99577	99581	99585	99590	99594	99599	99603
991	99607	99612	99616	99621	99625	99629	99634	99638	99642	99647
992	99651	99656	99660	99664	99669	99673	99677	99682	99686	99691
993	99695	99699	99704	99708	99712	99717	99721	99726	99730	99734
994	99739	99743	99747	99752	99756	99760	99765	99769	99774	99778
995	99782	99787	99791	99795	99800	99804	99808	99813	99817	99822
996	99826	99830	99835	99839	99843	99848	99852	99856	99861	99865
997	99870	99874	99878	99883	99887	99891	99896	99900	99904	99909
998	99913	99917	99922	99926	99930	99935	99939	99944	99948	99952
999	99957	99961	99965	99970	99974	99978	99983	99987	99991	99996
No.	0	1	2	3	4	5	6	7	8	9

5	
1	1
2	1
3	2
4	2
5	3
6	3
7	4
8	4
9	5

4	
1	0
2	1
3	1
4	2
5	2
6	2
7	3
8	3
9	4

TABLE XXVII.

Log. Sines, Tangents, and Secants.

0° 179°

M	Hour A.M.	Hour P.M.	Sine.	Diff. 1'	Cosecant.	Tangent.	Diff. 1'	Cotangent	Secant.	Cosine.	M
0	12 0 0	0 0 0	Inf. Neg.		Infinite.	Inf. Neg.		Infinite.	10.00000	10.00000	60
1	11 59 52	0 8	6.46373	30103	13.53627	6.46373	30103	13.53627	00000	00000	59
2	59 44	0 16	76476	17609	23524	76476	17609	23524	00000	00000	58
3	59 36	0 24	94085	12494	05915	94085	12494	05915	00000	00000	57
4	59 28	0 32	7.06579	9691	12.93421	7.06579	9691	12.93421	00000	00000	56
5	11 59 20	0 0 40	7.16270	7918	12.83730	7.16270	7918	12.83730	10.00000	10.00000	55
6	59 12	0 48	24188	6694	75812	24188	6694	75812	00000	00000	54
7	59 4	0 56	30882	5800	69118	30882	5800	69118	00000	00000	53
8	58 56	1 4	36682	5115	63318	36682	5115	63318	00000	00000	52
9	58 48	1 12	41797	4576	58203	41797	4576	58203	00000	00000	51
10	11 58 40	0 1 20	7.46373	4139	12.53627	7.46373	4139	12.53627	10.00000	10.00000	50
11	58 32	1 28	50512	3779	49488	50512	3779	49488	00000	00000	49
12	58 24	1 36	54291	3476	45709	54291	3476	45709	00000	00000	48
13	58 16	1 44	57767	3218	42233	57767	3219	42233	00000	00000	47
14	58 8	1 52	60985	2997	39015	60986	2996	39014	00000	00000	46
15	11 58 0	0 2 0	7.63982	2802	12.36018	7.63982	2803	12.36018	10.00000	10.00000	45
16	57 52	2 8	66784	2633	33216	66785	2633	33215	00000	00000	44
17	57 44	2 16	69417	2483	30583	69418	2482	30582	00001	9.99999	43
18	57 36	2 24	71900	2348	28100	71900	2348	28100	00001	99999	42
19	57 28	2 32	74248	2227	25752	74248	2228	25752	00001	99999	41
20	11 57 20	0 2 40	7.76475	2119	12.23525	7.76476	2119	12.23524	10.00001	9.99999	40
21	57 12	2 48	78594	2021	21406	78595	2020	21405	00001	99999	39
22	57 4	2 56	80615	1930	19385	80615	1931	19385	00001	99999	38
23	56 56	3 4	82545	1848	17455	82546	1848	17454	00001	99999	37
24	56 48	3 12	84393	1773	15607	84394	1773	15606	00001	99999	36
25	11 56 40	0 3 20	7.86166	1704	12.13834	7.86167	1704	12.13833	10.00001	9.99999	35
26	56 32	3 28	87870	1639	12130	87871	1639	12129	00001	99999	34
27	56 24	3 36	89509	1579	10491	89510	1579	10490	00001	99999	33
28	56 16	3 44	91088	1524	08912	91089	1524	08911	00001	99999	32
29	56 8	3 52	92612	1472	07388	92613	1473	07387	00002	99998	31
30	11 56 0	0 4 0	7.94084	1424	12.05916	7.94086	1424	12.05914	10.00002	9.99998	30
31	55 52	4 8	95508	1379	04492	95510	1379	04490	00002	99998	29
32	55 44	4 16	96887	1336	03113	96889	1336	03111	00002	99998	28
33	55 36	4 24	98223	1297	01777	98225	1297	01775	00002	99998	27
34	55 28	4 32	99520	1259	00480	99522	1259	00478	00002	99998	26
35	11 55 20	0 4 40	8.00779	1223	11.99221	8.00781	1223	11.99219	10.00002	9.99998	25
36	55 12	4 48	02002	1190	97998	02004	1190	97996	00002	99998	24
37	55 4	4 56	03192	1158	96808	03194	1159	96806	00003	99997	23
38	54 56	5 4	04350	1128	95650	04353	1128	95647	00003	99997	22
39	54 48	5 12	05478	1100	94522	05481	1100	94519	00003	99997	21
40	11 54 40	0 5 20	8.06578	1072	11.93422	8.06581	1072	11.93419	10.00003	9.99997	20
41	54 32	5 28	07650	1046	92350	07653	1047	92347	00003	99997	19
42	54 24	5 36	08696	1022	91304	08700	1022	91300	00003	99997	18
43	54 16	5 44	09718	999	90282	09722	998	90278	00003	99997	17
44	54 8	5 52	10717	976	89283	10720	976	89280	00004	99996	16
45	11 54 0	0 6 0	8.11693	954	11.88307	8.11696	955	11.88304	10.00004	9.99996	15
46	53 52	6 8	12647	934	87353	12651	934	87349	00004	99996	14
47	53 44	6 16	13581	914	86419	13585	915	86415	00004	99996	13
48	53 36	6 24	14495	896	85505	14500	895	85500	00004	99996	12
49	53 28	6 32	15391	877	84609	15395	878	84605	00004	99996	11
50	11 53 20	0 6 40	8.16268	860	11.83732	8.16273	860	11.83727	10.00005	9.99995	10
51	53 12	6 48	17128	843	82872	17133	843	82867	00005	99995	9
52	53 4	6 56	17971	827	82029	17976	828	82024	00005	99995	8
53	52 56	7 4	18798	812	81202	18804	812	81196	00005	99995	7
54	52 48	7 12	19610	797	80390	19616	797	80384	00005	99995	6
55	11 52 40	0 7 20	8.20407	782	11.79593	8.20413	782	11.79587	10.00006	9.99994	5
56	52 32	7 28	21189	769	78811	21195	769	78805	00006	99994	4
57	52 24	7 36	21958	755	78042	21964	756	78036	00006	99994	3
58	52 16	7 44	22713	743	77287	22720	742	77280	00006	99994	2
59	52 8	7 52	23456	730	76544	23462	730	76538	00006	99994	1
60	52 0	8 0	24186	717	75814	24192	718	75808	00007	99993	0
M	Hour P.M.	Hour A.M.	Cosine.	Diff. 1'	Secant.	Cotangent	Diff. 1'	Tangent.	Cosecant.	Sine.	M

90° 89°

TABLE XXVII.

Log. Sines, Tangents, and Secants.

1° 178°

M	Hour A.M.	Hour P.M.	Sine.	Diff.1'	Cosecant.	Tangent.	Diff.1'	Cotangent	Secant.	Cosine.	M
0	11 52 0	0 8 0	8.24186	717	11.75814	8.24192	718	11.75808	10.00007	9.99993	60
1	51 52	8 8	24903	706	75097	24910	706	75090	00007	99993	59
2	51 44	8 16	25609	695	74391	25616	696	74384	00007	99993	58
3	51 36	8 24	26304	684	73696	26312	684	73688	00007	99993	57
4	51 28	8 32	26988	673	73012	26996	673	73004	00008	99992	56
5	11 51 20	0 8 40	8.27661	663	11.72339	8.27669	663	11.72331	10.00008	9.99992	55
6	51 12	8 48	28324	653	71676	28332	654	71668	00008	99992	54
7	51 4	8 56	28977	644	71023	28986	643	71014	00008	99992	53
8	50 56	9 4	29621	634	70379	29629	634	70371	00008	99992	52
9	50 48	9 12	30255	624	69745	30263	625	69737	00009	99991	51
10	11 50 40	0 9 20	8.30879	616	11.69121	8.30888	617	11.69112	10.00009	9.99991	50
11	50 32	9 28	31495	608	68505	31505	607	68495	00009	99991	49
12	50 24	9 36	32103	599	67897	32112	599	67888	00010	99990	48
13	50 16	9 44	32702	590	67298	32711	591	67289	00010	99990	47
14	50 8	9 52	33292	583	66708	33302	584	66698	00010	99990	46
15	11 50 0	0 10 0	8.33875	575	11.66125	8.33886	575	11.66114	10.00010	9.99990	45
16	49 52	10 8	34450	568	65550	34461	568	65539	00011	99989	44
17	49 44	10 16	35018	560	64982	35029	561	64971	00011	99989	43
18	49 36	10 24	35578	553	64422	35590	553	64410	00011	99989	42
19	49 28	10 32	36131	547	63869	36143	546	63857	00011	99989	41
20	11 49 20	0 10 40	8.36678	539	11.63322	8.36689	540	11.63311	10.00012	9.99988	40
21	49 12	10 48	37217	533	62783	37229	533	62771	00012	99988	39
22	49 4	10 56	37750	526	62250	37762	527	62238	00012	99988	38
23	48 56	11 4	38276	520	61724	38289	520	61711	00013	99987	37
24	48 48	11 12	38796	514	61204	38809	514	61191	00013	99987	36
25	11 48 40	0 11 20	8.39310	508	11.60690	8.39323	509	11.60677	10.00013	9.99987	35
26	48 32	11 28	39818	502	60182	39832	502	60168	00014	99986	34
27	48 24	11 36	40320	496	59680	40334	496	59666	00014	99986	33
28	48 16	11 44	40816	491	59184	40830	491	59170	00014	99986	32
29	48 8	11 52	41307	485	58693	41321	486	58679	00015	99985	31
30	11 48 0	0 12 0	8.41792	480	11.58208	8.41807	480	11.58193	10.00015	9.99985	30
31	47 52	12 8	42272	474	57728	42287	475	57713	00015	99985	29
32	47 44	12 16	42746	470	57254	42762	470	57238	00016	99984	28
33	47 36	12 24	43216	464	56784	43232	464	56768	00016	99984	27
34	47 28	12 32	43680	459	56320	43696	460	56304	00016	99984	26
35	11 47 20	0 12 40	8.44139	455	11.55861	8.44156	455	11.55844	10.00017	9.99983	25
36	47 12	12 48	44594	450	55406	44611	450	55389	00017	99983	24
37	47 4	12 56	45044	445	54956	45061	446	54939	00017	99983	23
38	46 56	13 4	45489	441	54511	45507	441	54493	00018	99982	22
39	46 48	13 12	45930	436	54070	45948	437	54052	00018	99982	21
40	11 46 40	0 13 20	8.46366	433	11.53634	8.46385	432	11.53615	10.00018	9.99982	20
41	46 32	13 28	46799	427	53201	46817	428	53183	00019	99981	19
42	46 24	13 36	47226	424	52774	47245	424	52755	00019	99981	18
43	46 16	13 44	47650	419	52350	47669	420	52331	00019	99981	17
44	46 8	13 52	48069	416	51931	48089	416	51911	00020	99980	16
45	11 46 0	0 14 0	8.48485	411	11.51515	8.48505	412	11.51495	10.00020	9.99980	15
46	45 52	14 8	48896	408	51104	48917	408	51083	00021	99979	14
47	45 44	14 16	49304	404	50696	49325	404	50675	00021	99979	13
48	45 36	14 24	49708	400	50292	49729	401	50271	00021	99979	12
49	45 28	14 32	50108	396	49892	50130	397	49870	00022	99978	11
50	11 45 20	0 14 40	8.50504	393	11.49496	8.50527	393	11.49473	10.00022	9.99978	10
51	45 12	14 48	50897	390	49103	50920	390	49080	00023	99977	9
52	45 4	14 56	51287	386	48713	51310	386	48690	00023	99977	8
53	44 56	15 4	51673	382	48327	51696	383	48304	00023	99977	7
54	44 48	15 12	52055	379	47945	52079	380	47921	00024	99976	6
55	11 44 40	0 15 20	8.52434	376	11.47566	8.52459	376	11.47541	10.00024	9.99976	5
56	44 32	15 28	52810	373	47190	52835	373	47165	00025	99975	4
57	44 24	15 36	53183	369	46817	53208	370	46792	00025	99975	3
58	44 16	15 44	53552	367	46448	53578	367	46422	00026	99974	2
59	44 8	15 52	53919	363	46081	53945	363	46055	00026	99974	1
60	44 0	16 0	54282	360	45718	54308	361	45692	00026	99974	0
M	Hour P.M.	Hour A.M.	Cosine.	Diff.1'	Secant.	Cotangent	Diff.1'	Tangent.	Cosecant.	Sine.	M

91° 88°

TABLE XXVII.

Log. Sines, Tangents, and Secants.

2° 177°

M	Hour A.M.	Hour P.M.	Sine.	Diff. 1′	Cosecant.	Tangent.	Diff. 1′	Cotangent	Secant.	Cosine.	M
0	11 44 0	0 16 0	8.54282	360	11.45718	8.54308	361	11.45692	10.00026	9.99974	60
1	43 52	16 8	54642	357	45358	54669	358	45331	00027	99973	59
2	43 44	16 16	54999	355	45001	55027	355	44973	00027	99973	58
3	43 36	16 24	55354	351	44646	55382	352	44618	00028	99972	57
4	43 28	16 32	55705	349	44295	55734	349	44266	00028	99972	56
5	11 43 20	0 16 40	8.56054	346	11.43946	8.56083	346	11.43917	10.00029	9.99971	55
6	43 12	16 48	56400	343	43600	56429	344	43571	00029	99971	54
7	43 4	16 56	56743	341	43257	56773	341	43227	00030	99970	53
8	42 56	17 4	57084	337	42916	57114	338	42886	00030	99970	52
9	42 48	17 12	57421	336	42579	57452	336	42548	00031	99969	51
10	11 42 40	0 17 20	8.57757	332	11.42243	8.57788	333	11.42212	10.00031	9.99969	50
11	42 32	17 28	58089	330	41911	58121	330	41879	00032	99968	49
12	42 24	17 36	58419	328	41581	58451	328	41549	00032	99968	48
13	42 16	17 44	58747	325	41253	58779	326	41221	00033	99967	47
14	42 8	17 52	59072	323	40928	59105	323	40895	00033	99967	46
15	11 42 0	0 18 0	8.59395	320	11.40605	8.59428	321	11.40572	10.00033	9.99967	45
16	41 52	18 8	59715	318	40285	59749	319	40251	00034	99966	44
17	41 44	18 16	60033	316	39967	60068	316	39932	00034	99966	43
18	41 36	18 24	60349	313	39651	60384	314	39616	00035	99965	42
19	41 28	18 32	60662	311	39338	60698	311	39302	00036	99964	41
20	11 41 20	0 18 40	8.60973	309	11.39027	8.61009	310	11.38991	10.00036	9.99964	40
21	41 12	18 48	61282	307	38718	61319	307	38681	00037	99963	39
22	41 4	18 56	61589	305	38411	61626	305	38374	00037	99963	38
23	40 56	19 4	61894	302	38106	61931	303	38069	00038	99962	37
24	40 48	19 12	62196	301	37804	62234	301	37766	00038	99962	36
25	11 40 40	0 19 20	8.62497	298	11.37503	8.62535	299	11.37465	10.00039	9.99961	35
26	40 32	19 28	62795	296	37205	62834	297	37166	00039	99961	34
27	40 24	19 36	63091	294	36909	63131	295	36869	00040	99960	33
28	40 16	19 44	63385	293	36615	63426	292	36574	00040	99960	32
29	40 8	19 52	63678	290	36322	63718	291	36282	00041	99959	31
30	11 40 0	0 20 0	8.63968	288	11.36032	8.64009	289	11.35991	10.00041	9.99959	30
31	39 52	20 8	64256	287	35744	64298	287	35702	00042	99958	29
32	39 44	20 16	64543	284	35457	64585	285	35415	00042	99958	28
33	39 36	20 24	64827	283	35173	64870	284	35130	00043	99957	27
34	39 28	20 32	65110	281	34890	65154	281	34846	00044	99956	26
35	11 39 20	0 20 40	8.65391	279	11.34609	8.65435	280	11.34565	10.00044	9.99956	25
36	39 12	20 48	65670	277	34330	65715	278	34285	00045	99955	24
37	39 4	20 56	65947	276	34053	65993	276	34007	00045	99955	23
38	38 56	21 4	66223	274	33777	66269	274	33731	00046	99954	22
39	38 48	21 12	66497	272	33503	66543	273	33457	00046	99954	21
40	11 38 40	0 21 20	8.66769	270	11.33231	8.66816	271	11.33184	10.00047	9.99953	20
41	38 32	21 28	67039	269	32961	67087	269	32913	00048	99952	19
42	38 24	21 36	67308	267	32692	67356	268	32644	00048	99952	18
43	38 16	21 44	67575	266	32425	67624	266	32376	00049	99951	17
44	38 8	21 52	67841	263	32159	67890	264	32110	00049	99951	16
45	11 38 0	0 22 0	8.68104	263	11.31896	8.68154	263	11.31846	10.00050	9.99950	15
46	37 52	22 8	68367	260	31633	68417	261	31583	00051	99949	14
47	37 44	22 16	68627	259	31373	68678	260	31322	00051	99949	13
48	37 36	22 24	68886	258	31114	68938	258	31062	00052	99948	12
49	37 28	22 32	69144	256	30856	69196	257	30804	00052	99948	11
50	11 37 20	0 22 40	8.69400	254	11.30600	8.69453	255	11.30547	10.00053	9.99947	10
51	37 12	22 48	69654	253	30346	69708	254	30292	00054	99946	9
52	37 4	22 56	69907	252	30093	69962	252	30038	00054	99946	8
53	36 56	23 4	70159	250	29841	70214	251	29786	00055	99945	7
54	36 48	23 12	70409	249	29591	70465	249	29535	00056	99944	6
55	11 36 40	0 23 20	8.70658	247	11.29342	8.70714	248	11.29286	10.00056	9.99944	5
56	36 32	23 28	70905	246	29095	70962	246	29038	00057	99943	4
57	36 24	23 36	71151	244	28849	71208	245	28792	00058	99942	3
58	36 16	23 44	71395	243	28605	71453	244	28547	00058	99942	2
59	36 8	23 52	71638	242	28362	71697	243	28303	00059	99941	1
60	36 0	24 0	71880	240	28120	71940	241	28060	00060	99940	0
M	Hour P.M.	Hour A.M.	Cosine.	Diff. 1′	Secant.	Cotangent	Diff. 1′	Tangent.	Cosecant.	Sine.	M

92° 87°

TABLE XXVII.

Log. Sines, Tangents, and Secants.

3° 176°

M	Hour A.M.	Hour P.M.	Sine.	Diff. 1'	Cosecant.	Tangent.	Diff. 1'	Cotangent	Secant.	Cosine.	M
0	11 36 0	0 24 0	8.71880	240	11.28120	8.71940	241	11.28060	10.00060	9.99940	60
1	35 52	24 8	72120	239	27880	72181	239	27819	00060	99940	59
2	35 44	24 16	72359	238	27641	72420	239	27580	00061	99939	58
3	35 36	24 24	72597	237	27403	72659	237	27341	00062	99938	57
4	35 28	24 32	72834	235	27166	72896	236	27104	00062	99938	56
5	11 35 20	0 24 40	8.73069	234	11.26931	8.73132	234	11.26868	10.00063	9.99937	55
6	35 12	24 48	73303	232	26697	73366	234	26634	00064	99936	54
7	35 4	24 56	73535	232	26465	73600	232	26400	00064	99936	53
8	34 56	25 4	73767	230	26233	73832	231	26168	00065	99935	52
9	34 48	25 12	73997	229	26003	74063	229	25937	00066	99934	51
10	11 34 40	0 25 20	8.74226	228	11.25774	8.74292	229	11.25708	10.00066	9.99934	50
11	34 32	25 28	74454	226	25546	74521	227	25479	00067	99933	49
12	34 24	25 36	74680	226	25320	74748	226	25252	00068	99932	48
13	34 16	25 44	74906	224	25094	74974	225	25026	00068	99932	47
14	34 8	25 52	75130	223	24870	75199	224	24801	00069	99931	46
15	11 34 0	0 26 0	8.75353	222	11.24647	8.75423	222	11.24577	10.00070	9.99930	45
16	33 52	26 8	75575	220	24425	75645	222	24355	00071	99929	44
17	33 44	26 16	75795	220	24205	75867	220	24133	00071	99929	43
18	33 36	26 24	76015	219	23985	76087	219	23913	00072	99928	42
19	33 28	26 32	76234	217	23766	76306	219	23694	00073	99927	41
20	11 33 20	0 26 40	8.76451	216	11.23549	8.76525	217	11.23475	10.00074	9.99926	40
21	33 12	26 48	76667	216	23333	76742	216	23258	00074	99926	39
22	33 4	26 56	76883	214	23117	76958	215	23042	00075	99925	38
23	32 56	27 4	77097	213	22903	77173	214	22827	00076	99924	37
24	32 48	27 12	77310	212	22690	77387	213	22613	00077	99923	36
25	11 32 40	0 27 20	8.77522	211	11.22478	8.77600	211	11.22400	10.00077	9.99923	35
26	32 32	27 28	77733	210	22267	77811	211	22189	00078	99922	34
27	32 24	27 36	77943	209	22057	78022	210	21978	00079	99921	33
28	32 16	27 44	78152	208	21848	78232	209	21768	00080	99920	32
29	32 8	27 52	78360	208	21640	78441	208	21559	00080	99920	31
30	11 32 0	0 28 0	8.78568	206	11.21432	8.78649	206	11.21351	10.00081	9.99919	30
31	31 52	28 8	78774	205	21226	78855	206	21145	00082	99918	29
32	31 44	28 16	78979	204	21021	79061	205	20939	00083	99917	28
33	31 36	28 24	79183	203	20817	79266	204	20734	00083	99917	27
34	31 28	28 32	79386	202	20614	79470	203	20530	00084	99916	26
35	11 31 20	0 28 40	8.79588	201	11.20412	8.79673	202	11.20327	10.00085	9.99915	25
36	31 12	28 48	79789	201	20211	79875	201	20125	00086	99914	24
37	31 4	28 56	79990	199	20010	80076	201	19924	00087	99913	23
38	30 56	29 4	80189	199	19811	80277	199	19723	00087	99913	22
39	30 48	29 12	80388	197	19612	80476	198	19524	00088	99912	21
40	11 30 40	0 29 20	8.80585	197	11.19415	8.80674	198	11.19326	10.00089	9.99911	20
41	30 32	29 28	80782	196	19218	80872	196	19128	00090	99910	19
42	30 24	29 36	80978	195	19022	81068	196	18932	00091	99909	18
43	30 16	29 44	81173	194	18827	81264	195	18736	00091	99909	17
44	30 8	29 52	81367	193	18633	81459	194	18541	00092	99908	16
45	11 30 0	0 30 0	8.81560	192	11.18440	8.81653	193	11.18347	10.00093	9.99907	15
46	29 52	30 8	81752	192	18248	81846	192	18154	00094	99906	14
47	29 44	30 16	81944	190	18056	82038	192	17962	00095	99905	13
48	29 36	30 24	82134	190	17866	82230	190	17770	00096	99904	12
49	29 28	30 32	82324	189	17676	82420	190	17580	00096	99904	11
50	11 29 20	0 30 40	8.82513	188	11.17487	8.82610	189	11.17390	10.00097	9.99903	10
51	29 12	30 48	82701	187	17299	82799	188	17201	00098	99902	9
52	29 4	30 56	82888	187	17112	82987	188	17013	00099	99901	8
53	28 56	31 4	83075	186	16925	83175	186	16825	00100	99900	7
54	28 48	31 12	83261	185	16739	83361	186	16639	00101	99899	6
55	11 28 40	0 31 20	8.83446	184	11.16554	8.83547	185	11.16453	10.00102	9.99898	5
56	28 32	31 28	83630	183	16370	83732	184	16268	00102	99898	4
57	28 24	31 36	83813	183	16187	83916	184	16084	00103	99897	3
58	28 16	31 44	83996	181	16004	84100	182	15900	00104	99896	2
59	28 8	31 52	84177	181	15823	84282	182	15718	00105	99895	1
60	28 0	32 0	84358	181	15642	84464	182	15536	00106	99894	0
M	Hour P.M.	Hour A.M.	Cosine.	Diff. 1'	Secant.	Cotangent	Diff. 1'	Tangent.	Cosecant.	Sine.	M

93° 86°

TABLE XXVII.

Log. Sines, Tangents, and Secants.

4° 175°

M	Hour A.M.	Hour P.M.	Sine.	Diff. 1′	Cosecant.	Tangent.	Diff. 1′	Cotangent	Secant.	Cosine.	M
0	11 28 0	0 32 0	8.84358	181	11.15642	8.84464	182	11.15536	10.00106	9.99894	60
1	27 52	32 8	84539	179	15461	84646	180	15354	00107	99893	59
2	27 44	32 16	84718	179	15282	84826	180	15174	00108	99892	58
3	27 36	32 24	84897	178	15103	85006	179	14994	00109	99891	57
4	27 28	32 32	85075	177	14925	85185	178	14815	00109	99891	56
5	11 27 20	0 32 40	8.85252	177	11.14748	8.85363	177	11.14637	10.00110	9.99890	55
6	27 12	32 48	85429	176	14571	85540	177	14460	00111	99889	54
7	27 4	32 56	85605	175	14395	85717	176	14283	00112	99888	53
8	26 56	33 4	85780	175	14220	85893	176	14107	00113	99887	52
9	26 48	33 12	85955	173	14045	86069	174	13931	00114	99886	51
10	11 26 40	0 33 20	8.86128	173	11.13872	8.86243	174	11.13757	10.00115	9.99885	50
11	26 32	33 28	86301	173	13699	86417	174	13583	00116	99884	49
12	26 24	33 36	86474	171	13526	86591	172	13409	00117	99883	48
13	26 16	33 44	86645	171	13355	86763	172	13237	00118	99882	47
14	26 8	33 52	86816	171	13184	86935	171	13065	00119	99881	46
15	11 26 0	0 34 0	8.86987	169	11.13013	8.87106	171	11.12894	10.00120	9.99880	45
16	25 52	34 8	87156	169	12844	87277	170	12723	00121	99879	44
17	25 44	34 16	87325	169	12675	87447	169	12553	00121	99879	43
18	25 36	34 24	87494	167	12506	87616	169	12384	00122	99878	42
19	25 28	34 32	87661	168	12339	87785	168	12215	00123	99877	41
20	11 25 20	0 34 40	8.87829	166	11.12171	8.87953	167	11.12047	10.00124	9.99876	40
21	25 12	34 48	87995	166	12005	88120	167	11880	00125	99875	39
22	25 4	34 56	88161	165	11839	88287	166	11713	00126	99874	38
23	24 56	35 4	88326	164	11674	88453	165	11547	00127	99873	37
24	24 48	35 12	88490	164	11510	88618	165	11382	00128	99872	36
25	11 24 40	0 35 20	8.88654	163	11.11346	8.88783	165	11.11217	10.00129	9.99871	35
26	24 32	35 28	88817	163	11183	88948	163	11052	00130	99870	34
27	24 24	35 36	88980	162	11020	89111	163	10889	00131	99869	33
28	24 16	35 44	89142	162	10858	89274	163	10726	00132	99868	32
29	24 8	35 52	89304	160	10696	89437	161	10563	00133	99867	31
30	11 24 0	0 36 0	8.89464	161	11.10536	8.89598	162	11.10402	10.00134	9.99866	30
31	23 52	36 8	89625	159	10375	89760	160	10240	00135	99865	29
32	23 44	36 16	89784	159	10216	89920	160	10080	00136	99864	28
33	23 36	36 24	89943	159	10057	90080	160	09920	00137	99863	27
34	23 28	36 32	90102	158	09898	90240	159	09760	00138	99862	26
35	11 23 20	0 36 40	8.90260	157	11.09740	8.90399	158	11.09601	10.00139	9.99861	25
36	23 12	36 48	90417	157	09583	90557	158	09443	00140	99860	24
37	23 4	36 56	90574	156	09426	90715	157	09285	00141	99859	23
38	22 56	37 4	90730	155	09270	90872	157	09128	00142	99858	22
39	22 48	37 12	90885	155	09115	91029	156	08971	00143	99857	21
40	11 22 40	0 37 20	8.91040	155	11.08960	8.91185	155	11.08815	10.00144	9.99856	20
41	22 32	37 28	91195	154	08805	91340	155	08660	00145	99855	19
42	22 24	37 36	91349	153	08651	91495	155	08505	00146	99854	18
43	22 16	37 44	91502	153	08498	91650	153	08350	00147	99853	17
44	22 8	37 52	91655	152	08345	91803	154	08197	00148	99852	16
45	11 22 0	0 38 0	8.91807	152	11.08193	8.91957	153	11.08043	10.00149	9.99851	15
46	21 52	38 8	91959	151	08041	92110	152	07890	00150	99850	14
47	21 44	38 16	92110	151	07890	92262	152	07738	00152	99848	13
48	21 36	38 24	92261	150	07739	92414	151	07586	00153	99847	12
49	21 28	38 32	92411	150	07589	92565	151	07435	00154	99846	11
50	11 21 20	0 38 40	8.92561	149	11.07439	8.92716	150	11.07284	10.00155	9.99845	10
51	21 12	38 48	92710	149	07290	92866	150	07134	00156	99844	9
52	21 4	38 56	92859	148	07141	93016	149	06984	00157	99843	8
53	20 56	39 4	93007	147	06993	93165	148	06835	00158	99842	7
54	20 48	39 12	93154	147	06846	93313	149	06687	00159	99841	6
55	11 20 40	0 39 20	8.93301	147	11.06699	8.93462	147	11.06538	10.00160	9.99840	5
56	20 32	39 28	93448	146	06552	93609	147	06391	00161	99839	4
57	20 24	39 36	93594	146	06406	93756	147	06244	00162	99838	3
58	20 16	39 44	93740	145	06260	93903	146	06097	00163	99837	2
59	20 8	39 52	93885	145	06115	94049	146	05951	00164	99836	1
60	20 0	40 0	94030	144	05970	94195	145	05805	00166	99834	0
M	Hour P.M.	Hour A.M.	Cosine.	Diff. 1′	Secant.	Cotangent	Diff. 1′	Tangent.	Cosecant.	Sine.	M

94° 85°

TABLE XXVII.

S' | Log. Sines, Tangents, and Secants. | G'.

5°			A		A	B		B	C		C	174°
M	Hour A.M.	Hour P.M.	Sine.	Diff.	Cosecant.	Tangent.	Diff.	Cotangent	Secant.	Diff.	Cosine.	M
0	11 20 00	0 40 0	8.94030	0	11.05970	8.94195	0	11.05805	10.00166	0	9.99834	60
1	19 52	40 8	94174	2	05826	94340	2	05660	00167	0	99833	59
2	19 44	40 16	94317	4	05683	94485	4	05515	00168	0	99832	58
3	19 36	40 24	94461	7	05539	94630	7	05370	00169	0	99831	57
4	19 28	40 32	94603	9	05397	94773	9	05227	00170	0	99830	56
5	11 19 20	0 40 40	8.94746	11	11.05254	8.94917	11	11.05083	10.00171	0	9.99829	55
6	19 12	40 48	94887	13	05113	95060	13	04940	00172	0	99828	54
7	19 4	40 56	95029	15	04971	95202	15	04798	00173	0	99827	53
8	18 56	41 4	95170	18	04830	95344	18	04656	00175	0	99825	52
9	18 48	41 12	95310	20	04690	95486	20	04514	00176	0	99824	51
10	11 18 40	0 41 20	8.95450	22	11.04550	8.95627	22	11.04373	10.00177	0	9.99823	50
11	18 32	41 28	95589	24	04411	95767	24	04233	00178	0	99822	49
12	18 24	41 36	95728	26	04272	95908	27	04092	00179	0	99821	48
13	18 16	41 44	95867	29	04133	96047	29	03953	00180	0	99820	47
14	18 8	41 52	96005	31	03995	96187	31	03813	00181	0	99819	46
15	11 18 0	0 42 0	8.96143	33	11.03857	8.96325	33	11.03675	10.00183	0	9.99817	45
16	17 52	42 8	96280	35	03720	96464	35	03536	00184	0	99816	44
17	17 44	42 16	96417	37	03583	96602	38	03398	00185	0	99815	43
18	17 36	42 24	96553	39	03447	96739	40	03261	00186	0	99814	42
19	17 28	42 32	96689	42	03311	96877	42	03123	00187	0	99813	41
20	11 17 20	0 42 40	8.96825	44	11.03175	8.97013	44	11.02987	10.00188	0	9.99812	40
21	17 12	42 48	96960	46	03040	97150	46	02850	00190	0	99810	39
22	17 4	42 56	97095	48	02905	97285	49	02715	00191	0	99809	38
23	16 56	43 4	97229	50	02771	97421	51	02579	00192	0	99808	37
24	16 48	43 12	97363	53	02637	97556	53	02444	00193	0	99807	36
25	11 16 40	0 43 20	8.97496	55	11.02504	8.97691	55	11.02309	10.00194	1	9.99806	35
26	16 32	43 28	97629	57	02371	97825	58	02175	00196	1	99804	34
27	16 24	43 36	97762	59	02238	97959	60	02041	00197	1	99803	33
28	16 16	43 44	97894	61	02106	98092	62	01908	00198	1	99802	32
29	16 8	43 52	98026	64	01974	98225	64	01775	00199	1	99801	31
30	11 16 0	0 44 0	8.98157	66	11.01843	8.98358	66	11.01642	10.00200	1	9.99800	30
31	15 52	44 8	98288	68	01712	98490	69	01510	00202	1	99798	29
32	15 44	44 16	98419	70	01581	98622	71	01378	00203	1	99797	28
33	15 36	44 24	98549	72	01451	98753	73	01247	00204	1	99796	27
34	15 28	44 32	98679	75	01321	98884	75	01116	00205	1	99795	26
35	11 15 20	0 44 40	8.98808	77	11.01192	8.99015	77	11.00985	10.00207	1	9.99793	25
36	15 12	44 48	98937	79	01063	99145	80	00855	00208	1	99792	24
37	15 4	44 56	99066	81	00934	99275	82	00725	00209	1	99791	23
38	14 56	45 4	99194	83	00806	99405	84	00595	00210	1	99790	22
39	14 48	45 12	99322	86	00678	99534	86	00466	00212	1	99788	21
40	11 14 40	0 45 20	8.99450	88	11.00550	8.99662	89	11.00338	10.00213	1	9.99787	20
41	14 32	45 28	99577	90	00423	99791	91	00209	00214	1	99786	19
42	14 24	45 36	99704	92	00296	99919	93	00081	00215	1	99785	18
43	14 16	45 44	99830	94	00170	9.00046	95	10.99954	00217	1	99783	17
44	14 8	45 52	99956	96	00044	00174	97	99826	00218	1	99782	16
45	11 14 0	0 46 0	9.00082	99	10.99918	9.00301	100	10.99699	10.00219	1	9.99781	15
46	13 52	46 8	00207	101	99793	00427	102	99573	00220	1	99780	14
47	13 44	46 16	00332	103	99668	00553	104	99447	00222	1	99778	13
48	13 36	46 24	00456	105	99544	00679	106	99321	00223	1	99777	12
49	13 28	46 32	00581	107	99419	00805	108	99195	00224	1	99776	11
50	11 13 20	0 46 40	9.00704	110	10.99296	9.00930	111	10.99070	10.00225	1	9.99775	10
51	13 12	46 48	00828	112	99172	01055	113	98945	00227	1	99773	9
52	13 4	46 56	00951	114	99049	01179	115	98821	00228	1	99772	8
53	12 56	47 4	01074	116	98926	01303	117	98697	00229	1	99771	7
54	12 48	47 12	01196	118	98804	01427	120	98573	00231	1	99769	6
55	11 12 40	0 47 20	9.01318	121	10.98682	9.01550	122	10.98450	10.00232	1	9.99768	5
56	12 32	47 28	01440	123	98560	01673	124	98327	00233	1	99767	4
57	12 24	47 36	01561	125	98439	01796	126	98204	00235	1	99765	3
58	12 16	47 44	01682	127	98318	01918	128	98082	00236	1	99764	2
59	12 8	47 52	01803	129	98197	02040	131	97960	00237	1	99763	1
60	12 0	48 0	01923	132	98077	02162	133	97838	00239	1	99761	0
M	Hour P.M.	Hour A.M.	Cosine.	Diff.	Secant.	Cotangent	Diff.	Tangent.	Cosecant.	Diff.	Sine.	M
95°			A		A	B		B	C		C	84°

Seconds of time		1s	2s	3s	4s	5s	6s	7s
Prop. parts of cols.	A	16	33	49	66	82	99	115
	B	17	33	50	66	83	100	116
	C	0	0	0	1	1	1	1

TABLE XXVII.

S'. G'.

Log. Sines, Tangents, and Secants.

6° 173°

M	Hour A.M.	Hour P.M.	Sine.	Diff.	Cosecant.	Tangent.	Diff.	Cotangent	Secant.	Diff.	Cosine.	M
			A		A	B		B	C		C	
0	11 12 0	0 48 0	9.01923	0	10.98077	9.02162	0	10.97838	10.00239	0	9.99761	60
1	11 52	48 8	02043	2	97957	02283	2	97717	00240	0	99760	59
2	11 44	48 16	02163	4	97837	02404	4	97596	00241	0	99759	58
3	11 36	48 24	02283	6	97717	02525	6	97475	00243	0	99757	57
4	11 28	48 32	02402	7	97598	02645	8	97355	00244	0	99756	56
5	11 11 20	0 48 40	9.02520	9	10.97480	9.02766	9	10.97234	10.00245	0	9.99755	55
6	11 12	48 48	02639	11	97361	02885	11	97115	00247	0	99753	54
7	11 4	48 56	02757	13	97243	03005	13	96995	00248	0	99752	53
8	10 56	49 4	02874	15	97126	03124	15	96876	00249	0	99751	52
9	10 48	49 12	02992	17	97008	03242	17	96758	00251	0	99749	51
10	11 10 40	0 49 20	9.03109	19	10.96891	9.03361	19	10.96639	10.00252	0	9.99748	50
11	10 32	49 28	03226	20	96774	03479	21	96521	00253	0	99747	49
12	10 24	49 36	03342	22	96658	03597	23	96403	00255	0	99745	48
13	10 16	49 44	03458	24	96542	03714	24	96286	00256	0	99744	47
14	10 8	49 52	03574	26	96426	03832	26	96168	00258	0	99742	46
15	11 10 0	0 50 0	9.03690	28	10.96310	9.03948	28	10.96052	10.00259	0	9.99741	45
16	9 52	50 8	03805	30	96195	04065	30	95935	00260	0	99740	44
17	9 44	50 16	03920	31	96080	04181	32	95819	00262	0	99738	43
18	9 36	50 24	04034	33	95966	04297	34	95703	00263	0	99737	42
19	9 28	50 32	04149	35	95851	04413	36	95587	00264	0	99736	41
20	11 9 20	0 50 40	9.04262	37	10.95738	9.04528	38	10.95472	10.00266	0	9.99734	40
21	9 12	50 48	04376	39	95624	04643	39	95357	00267	1	99733	39
22	9 4	50 56	04490	41	95510	04758	41	95242	00269	1	99731	38
23	8 56	51 4	04603	43	95397	04873	43	95127	00270	1	99730	37
24	8 48	51 12	04715	44	95285	04987	45	95013	00272	1	99728	36
25	11 8 40	0 51 20	9.04828	46	10.95172	9.05101	47	10.94899	10.00273	1	9.99727	35
26	8 32	51 28	04940	48	95060	05214	49	94786	00274	1	99726	34
27	8 24	51 36	05052	50	94948	05328	51	94672	00276	1	99724	33
28	8 16	51 44	05164	52	94836	05441	53	94559	00277	1	99723	32
29	8 8	51 52	05275	54	94725	05553	54	94447	00279	1	99721	31
30	11 8 0	0 52 0	9.05386	56	10.94614	9.05666	56	10.94334	10.00280	1	9.99720	30
31	7 52	52 8	05497	57	94503	05778	58	94222	00282	1	99718	29
32	7 44	52 16	05607	59	94393	05890	60	94110	00283	1	99717	28
33	7 36	52 24	05717	61	94283	06002	62	93998	00284	1	99716	27
34	7 28	52 32	05827	63	94173	06113	64	93887	00286	1	99714	26
35	11 7 20	0 52 40	9.05937	65	10.94063	9.06224	66	10.93776	10.00287	1	9.99713	25
36	7 12	52 48	06046	67	93954	06335	68	93665	00289	1	99711	24
37	7 4	52 56	06155	69	93845	06445	69	93555	00290	1	99710	23
38	6 56	53 4	06264	70	93736	06556	71	93444	00292	1	99708	22
39	6 48	53 12	06372	72	93628	06666	73	93334	00293	1	99707	21
40	11 6 40	0 53 20	9.06481	74	10.93519	9.06775	75	10.93225	10.00295	1	9.99705	20
41	6 32	53 28	06589	76	93411	06885	77	93115	00296	1	99704	19
42	6 24	53 36	06696	78	93304	06994	79	93006	00298	1	99702	18
43	6 16	53 44	06804	80	93196	07103	81	92897	00299	1	99701	17
44	6 8	53 52	06911	81	93089	07211	83	92789	00301	1	99699	16
45	11 6 0	0 54 0	9.07018	83	10.92982	9.07320	84	10.92680	10.00302	1	9.99698	15
46	5 52	54 8	07124	85	92876	07428	86	92572	00304	1	99696	14
47	5 44	54 16	07231	87	92769	07536	88	92464	00305	1	99695	13
48	5 36	54 24	07337	89	92663	07643	90	92357	00307	1	99693	12
49	5 28	54 32	07442	91	92558	07751	92	92249	00308	1	99692	11
50	11 5 20	0 54 40	9.07548	93	10.92452	9.07858	94	10.92142	10.00310	1	9.99690	10
51	5 12	54 48	07653	94	92347	07964	96	92036	00311	1	99689	9
52	5 4	54 56	07758	96	92242	08071	98	91929	00313	1	99687	8
53	4 56	55 4	07863	98	92137	08177	99	91823	00314	1	99686	7
54	4 48	55 12	07968	100	92032	08283	101	91717	00316	1	99684	6
55	11 4 40	0 55 20	9.08072	102	10.91928	9.08389	103	10.91611	10.00317	1	9.99683	5
56	4 32	55 28	08176	104	91824	08495	105	91505	00319	1	99681	4
57	4 24	55 36	08280	106	91720	08600	107	91400	00320	1	99680	3
58	4 16	55 44	08383	107	91617	08705	109	91295	00322	1	99678	2
59	4 8	55 52	08486	109	91514	08810	111	91190	00323	1	99677	1
60	4 0	56 0	08589	111	91411	08914	113	91086	00325	1	99675	0
M	Hour P.M.	Hour A.M.	Cosine.	Diff.	Secant.	Cotangent	Diff.	Tangent.	Cosecant.	Diff.	Sine	M
			A		A	B		B	C		C	

96° 83°

Seconds of time		1s	2s	3s	4s	5s	6s	7s
Prop. parts of cols.	A	14	28	42	56	69	83	97
	B	14	28	42	56	70	84	98
	C	0	0	1	1	1	1	1

TABLE XXVII.

S'.   **Log. Sines, Tangents, and Secants.**   G'.

7°			A		A	B		B	C		C	172°
M	Hour A.M.	Hour P.M.	Sine.	Diff.	Cosecant.	Tangent.	Diff.	Cotangent	Secant.	Diff.	Cosine.	M
0	11 4 0	0 56 0	9.08589	0	10.91411	9.08914	0	10.91086	10.00325	0	9.99675	60
1	3 52	56 8	08692	2	91308	09019	2	90981	00326	0	99674	59
2	3 44	56 16	08795	3	91205	09123	3	90877	00328	0	99672	58
3	3 36	56 24	08897	5	91103	09227	5	90773	00330	0	99670	57
4	3 28	56 32	08999	6	91001	09330	7	90670	00331	0	99669	56
5	11 3 20	0 56 40	9.09101	8	10.90899	9.09434	8	10.90566	10.00333	0	9.99667	55
6	3 12	56 48	09202	10	90798	09537	10	90463	00334	0	99666	54
7	3 4	56 56	09304	11	90696	09640	11	90360	00336	0	99664	53
8	2 56	57 4	09405	13	90595	09742	13	90258	00337	0	99663	52
9	2 48	57 12	09506	14	90494	09845	15	90155	00339	0	99661	51
10	11 2 40	0 57 20	9.09606	16	10.90394	9.09947	16	10.90053	10.00341	0	9.99659	50
11	2 32	57 28	09707	18	90293	10049	18	89951	00342	0	99658	49
12	2 24	57 36	09807	19	90193	10150	20	89850	00344	0	99656	48
13	2 16	57 44	09907	21	90093	10252	21	89748	00345	0	99655	47
14	2 8	57 52	10006	22	89994	10353	23	89647	00347	0	99653	46
15	11 2 0	0 58 0	9.10106	24	10.89894	9.10454	24	10.89546	10.00349	0	9.99651	45
16	1 52	58 8	10205	26	89795	10555	26	89445	00350	0	99650	44
17	1 44	58 16	10304	27	89696	10656	28	89344	00352	0	99648	43
18	1 36	58 24	10402	29	89598	10756	29	89244	00353	1	99647	42
19	1 28	58 32	10501	30	89499	10856	31	89144	00355	1	99645	41
20	11 1 20	0 58 40	9.10599	32	10.89401	9.10956	33	10.89044	10.00357	1	9.99643	40
21	1 12	58 48	10697	34	89303	11056	34	88944	00358	1	99642	39
22	1 4	58 56	10795	35	89205	11155	36	88845	00360	1	99640	38
23	0 56	59 4	10893	37	89107	11254	37	88746	00362	1	99638	37
24	0 48	59 12	10990	38	89010	11353	39	88647	00363	1	99637	36
25	11 0 40	0 59 20	9.11087	40	10.88913	9.11452	41	10.88548	10.00365	1	9.99635	35
26	0 32	59 28	11184	42	88816	11551	42	88449	00367	1	99633	34
27	0 24	59 36	11281	43	88719	11649	44	88351	00368	1	99632	33
28	0 16	59 44	11377	45	88623	11747	46	88253	00370	1	99630	32
29	0 8	59 52	11474	46	88526	11845	47	88155	00371	1	99629	31
30	11 0 0	1 0 0	9.11570	48	10.88430	9.11943	49	10.88057	10.00373	1	9.99627	30
31	10 59 52	0 8	11666	50	88334	12040	51	87960	00375	1	99625	29
32	59 44	0 16	11761	51	88239	12138	52	87862	00376	1	99624	28
33	59 36	0 24	11857	53	88143	12235	54	87765	00378	1	99622	27
34	59 28	0 32	11952	54	88048	12332	55	87668	00380	1	99620	26
35	10 59 20	1 0 40	9.12047	56	10.87953	9.12428	57	10.87572	10.00382	1	9.99618	25
36	59 12	0 48	12142	58	87858	12525	59	87475	00383	1	99617	24
37	59 4	0 56	12236	59	87764	12621	60	87379	00385	1	99615	23
38	58 56	1 4	12331	61	87669	12717	62	87283	00387	1	99613	22
39	58 48	1 12	12425	62	87575	12813	64	87187	00388	1	99612	21
40	10 58 40	1 1 20	9.12519	64	10.87481	9.12909	65	10.87091	10.00390	1	9.99610	20
41	58 32	1 28	12612	66	87388	13004	67	86996	00392	1	99608	19
42	58 24	1 36	12706	67	87294	13099	68	86901	00393	1	99607	18
43	58 16	1 44	12799	69	87201	13194	70	86806	00395	1	99605	17
44	58 8	1 52	12892	70	87108	13289	72	86711	00397	1	99603	16
45	10 58 0	1 2 0	9.12985	72	10.87015	9.13384	73	10.86616	10.00399	1	9.99601	15
46	57 52	2 8	13078	74	86922	13478	75	86522	00400	1	99600	14
47	57 44	2 16	13171	75	86829	13573	77	86427	00402	1	99598	13
48	57 36	2 24	13263	77	86737	13667	78	86333	00404	1	99596	12
49	57 28	2 32	13355	78	86645	13761	80	86239	00405	1	99595	11
50	10 57 20	1 2 40	9.13447	80	10.86553	9.13854	81	10.86146	10.00407	1	9.99593	10
51	57 12	2 48	13539	82	86461	13948	83	86052	00409	1	99591	9
52	57 4	2 56	13630	83	86370	14041	85	85959	00411	1	99589	8
53	56 56	3 4	13722	85	86278	14134	86	85866	00412	1	99588	7
54	56 48	3 12	13813	87	86187	14227	88	85773	00414	2	99586	6
55	10 56 40	1 3 20	9.13904	88	10.86096	9.14320	90	10.85680	10.00416	2	9.99584	5
56	56 32	3 28	13994	90	86006	14412	91	85588	00418	2	99582	4
57	56 24	3 36	14085	91	85915	14504	93	85496	00419	2	99581	3
58	56 16	3 44	14175	93	85825	14597	95	85403	00421	2	99579	2
59	56 8	3 52	14266	95	85734	14688	96	85312	00423	2	99577	1
60	56 0	4 0	14356	96	85644	14780	98	85220	00425	2	99575	0
M	Hour P.M.	Hour A.M.	Cosine.	Diff.	Secant.	Cotangent	Diff.	Tangent.	Cosecant.	Diff.	Sine.	M
97°			A		A	B		B	C		C	82°

Seconds of time		1s	2s	3s	4s	5s	6s	7s
Prop. parts of cols.	A	12	24	36	48	60	72	84
	B	12	24	37	49	61	73	86
	C	0	0	1	1	1	1	1

TABLE XXVII.

Log. Sines, Tangents, and Secants.

S′. G′.

8°			A		A	B		B	C		C 171°	
M	Hour A.M.	Hour P.M.	Sine.	Diff.	Cosecant.	Tangent.	Diff.	Cotangent	Secant.	Diff.	Cosine.	M
0	10 56 0	1 4 0	9.14356	0	10.85644	9.14780	0	10.85220	10.00425	0	9.99575	60
1	55 52	4 8	14445	1	85555	14872	1	85128	00426	0	99574	59
2	55 44	4 16	14535	3	85465	14963	3	85037	00428	0	99572	58
3	55 36	4 24	14624	4	85376	15054	4	84946	00430	0	99570	57
4	55 28	4 32	14714	6	85286	15145	6	84855	00432	0	99568	56
5	10 55 20	1 4 40	9.14803	7	10.85197	9.15236	7	10.84764	10.00434	0	9.99566	55
6	55 12	4 48	14891	8	85109	15327	9	84673	00435	0	99565	54
7	55 4	4 56	14980	10	85020	15417	10	84583	00437	0	99563	53
8	54 56	5 4	15069	11	84931	15508	12	84492	00439	0	99561	52
9	54 48	5 12	15157	13	84843	15598	13	84402	00441	0	99559	51
10	10 54 40	1 5 20	9.15245	14	10.84755	9.15688	14	10.84312	10.00443	0	9.99557	50
11	54 32	5 28	15333	16	84667	15777	16	84223	00444	0	99556	49
12	54 24	5 36	15421	17	84579	15867	17	84133	00446	0	99554	48
13	54 16	5 44	15508	18	84492	15956	19	84044	00448	0	99552	47
14	54 8	5 52	15596	20	84404	16046	20	83954	00450	0	99550	46
15	10 54 0	1 6 0	9.15683	21	10.84317	9.16135	22	10.83865	10.00452	0	9.99548	45
16	53 52	6 8	15770	23	84230	16224	23	83776	00454	1	99546	44
17	53 44	6 16	15857	24	84143	16312	25	83688	00455	1	99545	43
18	53 36	6 24	15944	25	84056	16401	26	83599	00457	1	99543	42
19	53 28	6 32	16030	27	83970	16489	27	83511	00459	1	99541	41
20	10 53 20	1 6 40	9.16116	28	10.83884	9.16577	29	10.83423	10.00461	1	9.99539	40
21	53 12	6 48	16203	30	83797	16665	30	83335	00463	1	99537	39
22	53 4	6 56	16289	31	83711	16753	32	83247	00465	1	99535	38
23	52 56	7 4	16374	32	83626	16841	33	83159	00467	1	99533	37
24	52 48	7 12	16460	34	83540	16928	35	83072	00468	1	99532	36
25	10 52 40	1 7 20	9.16545	35	10.83455	9.17016	36	10.82984	10.00470	1	9.99530	35
26	52 32	7 28	16631	37	83369	17103	37	82897	00472	1	99528	34
27	52 24	7 36	16716	38	83284	17190	39	82810	00474	1	99526	33
28	52 16	7 44	16801	39	83199	17277	40	82723	00476	1	99524	32
29	52 8	7 52	16886	41	83114	17363	42	82637	00478	1	99522	31
30	10 52 0	1 8 0	9.16970	42	10.83030	9.17450	43	10.82550	10.00480	1	9.99520	30
31	51 52	8 8	17055	44	82945	17536	45	82464	00482	1	99518	29
32	51 44	8 16	17139	45	82861	17622	46	82378	00483	1	99517	28
33	51 36	8 24	17223	47	82777	17708	48	82292	00485	1	99515	27
34	51 28	8 32	17307	48	82693	17794	49	82206	00487	1	99513	26
35	10 51 20	1 8 40	9.17391	49	10.82609	9.17880	50	10.82120	10.00489	1	9.99511	25
36	51 12	8 48	17474	51	82526	17965	52	82035	00491	1	99509	24
37	51 4	8 56	17558	52	82442	18051	53	81949	00493	1	99507	23
38	50 56	9 4	17641	54	82359	18136	55	81864	00495	1	99505	22
39	50 48	9 12	17724	55	82276	18221	56	81779	00497	1	99503	21
40	10 50 40	1 9 20	9.17807	56	10.82193	9.18306	58	10.81694	10.00499	1	9.99501	20
41	50 32	9 28	17890	58	82110	18391	59	81609	00501	1	99499	19
42	50 24	9 36	17973	59	82027	18475	61	81525	00503	1	99497	18
43	50 16	9 44	18055	61	81945	18560	62	81440	00505	1	99495	17
44	50 8	9 52	18137	62	81863	18644	63	81356	00506	1	99494	16
45	10 50 0	1 10 0	9.18220	63	10.81780	9.18728	65	10.81272	10.00508	1	9.99492	15
46	49 52	10 8	18302	65	81698	18812	66	81188	00510	1	99490	14
47	49 44	10 16	18383	66	81617	18896	68	81104	00512	1	99488	13
48	49 36	10 24	18465	68	81535	18979	69	81021	00514	2	99486	12
49	49 28	10 32	18547	69	81453	19063	71	80937	00516	2	99484	11
50	10 49 20	1 10 40	9.18628	71	10.81372	9.19146	72	10.80854	10.00518	2	9.99482	10
51	49 12	10 48	18709	72	81291	19229	74	80771	00520	2	99480	9
52	49 4	10 56	18790	73	81210	19312	75	80688	00522	2	99478	8
53	48 56	11 4	18871	75	81129	19395	76	80605	00524	2	99476	7
54	48 48	11 12	18952	76	81048	19478	78	80522	00526	2	99474	6
55	10 48 40	1 11 20	9.19033	78	10.80967	9.19561	79	10.80439	10.00528	2	9.99472	5
56	48 32	11 28	19113	79	80887	19643	81	80357	00530	2	99470	4
57	48 24	11 36	19193	80	80807	19725	82	80275	00532	2	99468	3
58	48 16	11 44	19273	82	80727	19807	84	80193	00534	2	99466	2
59	48 8	11 52	19353	83	80647	19889	85	80111	00536	2	99464	1
60	48 0	12 0	19433	85	80567	19971	87	80029	00538	2	99462	0
M	Hour P.M.	Hour A.M.	Cosine.	Diff.	Secant.	Cotangent	Diff.	Tangent.	Cosecant.	Diff.	Sine.	M
98°			A		A	B		B	C		C 81°	

Seconds of time		1s	2s	3s	4s	5s	6s	7s
Prop parts of cols.	A	11	21	32	42	53	63	74
	B	11	22	32	43	54	65	76
	C	0	0	1	1	1	1	2

TABLE XXVII.

S′. Log. Sines, Tangents, and Secants. G′.

9°			A		A	B		B	C		C	170°
M	Hour A.M.	Hour P.M.	Sine.	Diff.	Cosecant.	Tangent.	Diff.	Cotangent	Secant.	Diff.	Cosine.	M
0	10 48 0	1 12 0	9.19433	0	10.80567	9.19971	0	10.80029	10.00538	0	9.99462	60
1	47 52	12 8	19513	1	80487	20053	1	79947	00540	0	99460	59
2	47 44	12 16	19592	3	80408	20134	3	79866	00542	0	99458	58
3	47 36	12 24	19672	4	80328	20216	4	79784	00544	0	99456	57
4	47 28	12 32	19751	5	80249	20297	5	79703	00546	0	99454	56
5	10 47 20	1 12 40	9.19830	6	10.80170	9.20378	6	10.79622	10.00548	0	9.99452	55
6	47 12	12 48	19909	8	80091	20459	8	79541	00550	0	99450	54
7	47 4	12 56	19988	9	80012	20540	9	79460	00552	0	99448	53
8	46 56	13 4	20067	10	79933	20621	10	79379	00554	0	99446	52
9	46 48	13 12	20145	11	79855	20701	12	79299	00556	0	99444	51
10	10 46 40	1 13 20	9.20223	13	10.79777	9.20782	13	10.79218	10.00558	0	9.99442	50
11	46 32	13 28	20302	14	79698	20862	14	79138	00560	0	99440	49
12	46 24	13 36	20380	15	79620	20942	16	79058	00562	0	99438	48
13	46 16	13 44	20458	16	79542	21022	17	78978	00564	0	99436	47
14	46 8	13 52	20535	18	79465	21102	18	78898	00566	0	99434	46
15	10 46 0	1 14 0	9.20613	19	10.79387	9.21182	19	10.78818	10.00568	1	9.99432	45
16	45 52	14 8	20691	20	79309	21261	21	78739	00571	1	99429	44
17	45 44	14 16	20768	21	79232	21341	22	78659	00573	1	99427	43
18	45 36	14 24	20845	23	79155	21420	23	78580	00575	1	99425	42
19	45 28	14 32	20922	24	79078	21499	25	78501	00577	1	99423	41
20	10 45 20	1 14 40	9.20999	25	10.79001	9.21578	26	10.78422	10.00579	1	9.99421	40
21	45 12	14 48	21076	26	78924	21657	27	78343	00581	1	99419	39
22	45 4	14 56	21153	28	78847	21736	28	78264	00583	1	99417	38
23	44 56	15 4	21229	29	78771	21814	30	78186	00585	1	99415	37
24	44 48	15 12	21306	30	78694	21893	31	78107	00587	1	99413	36
25	10 44 40	1 15 20	9.21382	31	10.78618	9.21971	32	10.78029	10.00589	1	9.99411	35
26	44 32	15 28	21458	33	78542	22049	34	77951	00591	1	99409	34
27	44 24	15 36	21534	34	78466	22127	35	77873	00593	1	99407	33
28	44 16	15 44	21610	35	78390	22205	36	77795	00596	1	99404	32
29	44 8	15 52	21685	37	78315	22283	38	77717	00598	1	99402	31
30	10 44 0	1 16 0	9.21761	38	10.78239	9.22361	39	10.77639	10.00600	1	9.99400	30
31	43 52	16 8	21836	39	78164	22438	40	77562	00602	1	99398	29
32	43 44	16 16	21912	40	78088	22516	41	77484	00604	1	99396	28
33	43 36	16 24	21987	42	78013	22593	43	77407	00606	1	99394	27
34	43 28	16 32	22062	43	77938	22670	44	77330	00608	1	99392	26
35	10 43 20	1 16 40	9.22137	44	10.77863	9.22747	45	10.77253	10.00610	1	9.99390	25
36	43 12	16 48	22211	45	77789	22824	47	77176	00612	1	99388	24
37	43 4	16 56	22286	47	77714	22901	48	77099	00615	1	99385	23
38	42 56	17 4	22361	48	77639	22977	49	77023	00617	1	99383	22
39	42 48	17 12	22435	49	77565	23054	50	76946	00619	1	99381	21
40	10 42 40	1 17 20	9.22509	50	10.77491	9.23130	52	10.76870	10.00621	1	9.99379	20
41	42 32	17 28	22583	52	77417	23206	53	76794	00623	1	99377	19
42	42 24	17 36	22657	53	77343	23283	54	76717	00625	1	99375	18
43	42 16	17 44	22731	54	77269	23359	56	76641	00628	2	99372	17
44	42 8	17 52	22805	55	77195	23435	57	76565	00630	2	99370	16
45	10 42 0	1 18 0	9.22878	57	10.77122	9.23510	58	10.76490	10.00632	2	9.99368	15
46	41 52	18 8	22952	58	77048	23586	60	76414	00634	2	99366	14
47	41 44	18 16	23025	59	76975	23661	61	76339	00636	2	99364	13
48	41 36	18 24	23098	60	76902	23737	62	76263	00638	2	99362	12
49	41 28	18 32	23171	62	76829	23812	63	76188	00641	2	99359	11
50	10 41 20	1 18 40	9.23244	63	10.76756	9.23887	65	10.76113	10.00643	2	9.99357	10
51	41 12	18 48	23317	64	76683	23962	66	76038	00645	2	99355	9
52	41 4	18 56	23390	65	76610	24037	67	75963	00647	2	99353	8
53	40 56	19 4	23462	67	76538	24112	69	75888	00649	2	99351	7
54	40 48	19 12	23535	68	76465	24186	70	75814	00652	2	99348	6
55	10 40 40	1 19 20	9.23607	69	10.76393	9.24261	71	10.75739	10.00654	2	9.99346	5
56	40 32	19 28	23679	71	76321	24335	73	75665	00656	2	99344	4
57	40 24	19 36	23752	72	76248	24410	74	75590	00658	2	99342	3
58	40 16	19 44	23823	73	76177	24484	75	75516	00660	2	99340	2
59	40 8	19 52	23895	74	76105	24558	76	75442	00663	2	99337	1
60	40 0	20 0	23967	76	76033	24632	78	75368	00665	2	99335	0
M	Hour P.M.	Hour A.M.	Cosine.	Diff.	Secant.	Cotangent	Diff.	Tangent.	Cosecant.	Diff.	Sine.	M
99°			A		A	B		B	C		C	80°

Seconds of time		1s	2s	3s	4s	5s	6s	7s
Prop. parts of cols.	A	9	19	28	38	47	57	66
	B	10	19	29	39	49	58	68
	C	0	1	1	1	1	2	2

TABLE XXVII.

S′. **Log. Sines, Tangents, and Secants.** G′.

10°			A		A	B		B	C		C	169°
M	Hour A.M.	Hour P.M.	Sine.	Diff.	Cosecant.	Tangent.	Diff.	Cotangent	Secant.	Diff.	Cosine.	M
0	10 40 0	1 20 0	9.23967	0	10.76033	9.24632	0	10.75368	10.00665	0	9.99335	60
1	39 52	20 8	24039	1	75961	24706	1	75294	00667	0	99333	59
2	39 44	20 16	24110	2	75890	24779	2	75221	00669	0	99331	58
3	39 36	20 24	24181	3	75819	24853	4	75147	00672	0	99328	57
4	39 28	20 32	24253	5	75747	24926	5	75074	00674	0	99326	56
5	10 39 20	1 20 40	9.24324	6	10.75676	9.25000	6	10.75000	10.00676	0	9.99324	55
6	39 12	20 48	24395	7	75605	25073	7	74927	00678	0	99322	54
7	39 4	20 56	24466	8	75534	25146	8	74854	00681	0	99319	53
8	38 56	21 4	24536	9	75464	25219	9	74781	00683	0	99317	52
9	38 48	21 12	24607	10	75393	25292	11	74708	00685	0	99315	51
10	10 38 40	1 21 20	9.24677	11	10.75323	9.25365	12	10.74635	10.00687	0	9.99313	50
11	38 32	21 28	24748	13	75252	25437	13	74563	00690	0	99310	49
12	38 24	21 36	24818	14	75182	25510	14	74490	00692	0	99308	48
13	38 16	21 44	24888	15	75112	25582	15	74418	00694	1	99306	47
14	38 8	21 52	24958	16	75042	25655	16	74345	00696	1	99304	46
15	10 38 0	1 22 0	9.25028	17	10.74972	9.25727	18	10.74273	10.00699	1	9.99301	45
16	37 52	22 8	25098	18	74902	25799	19	74201	00701	1	99299	44
17	37 44	22 16	25168	19	74832	25871	20	74129	00703	1	99297	43
18	37 36	22 24	25237	20	74763	25943	21	74057	00706	1	99294	42
19	37 28	22 32	25307	22	74693	26015	22	73985	00708	1	99292	41
20	10 37 20	1 22 40	9.25376	23	10.74624	9.26086	24	10.73914	10.00710	1	9.99290	40
21	37 12	22 48	25445	24	74555	26158	25	73842	00712	1	99288	39
22	37 4	22 56	25514	25	74486	26229	26	73771	00715	1	99285	38
23	36 56	23 4	25583	26	74417	26301	27	73699	00717	1	99283	37
24	36 48	23 12	25652	27	74348	26372	28	73628	00719	1	99281	36
25	10 36 40	1 23 20	9.25721	28	10.74279	9.26443	29	10.73557	10.00722	1	9.99278	35
26	36 32	23 28	25790	30	74210	26514	31	73486	00724	1	99276	34
27	36 24	23 36	25858	31	74142	26585	32	73415	00726	1	99274	33
28	36 16	23 44	25927	32	74073	26655	33	73345	00729	1	99271	32
29	36 8	23 52	25995	33	74005	26726	34	73274	00731	1	99269	31
30	10 36 0	1 24 0	9.26063	34	10.73937	9.26797	35	10.73203	10.00733	1	9.99267	30
31	35 52	24 8	26131	35	73869	26867	36	73133	00736	1	99264	29
32	35 44	24 16	26199	36	73801	26937	38	73063	00738	1	99262	28
33	35 36	24 24	26267	38	73733	27008	39	72992	00740	1	99260	27
34	35 28	24 32	26335	39	73665	27078	40	72922	00743	1	99257	26
35	10 35 20	1 24 40	9.26403	40	10.73597	9.27148	41	10.72852	10.00745	1	9.99255	25
36	35 12	24 48	26470	41	73530	27218	42	72782	00748	1	99252	24
37	35 4	24 56	26538	42	73462	27288	44	72712	00750	1	99250	23
38	34 56	25 4	26605	43	73395	27357	45	72643	00752	1	99248	22
39	34 48	25 12	26672	44	73328	27427	46	72573	00755	2	99245	21
40	10 34 40	1 25 20	9.26739	45	10.73261	9.27496	47	10.72504	10.00757	2	9.99243	20
41	34 32	25 28	26806	47	73194	27566	48	72434	00759	2	99241	19
42	34 24	25 36	26873	48	73127	27635	49	72365	00762	2	99238	18
43	34 16	25 44	26940	49	73060	27704	51	72296	00764	2	99236	17
44	34 8	25 52	27007	50	72993	27773	52	72227	00767	2	99233	16
45	10 34 0	1 26 0	9.27073	51	10.72927	9.27842	53	10.72158	10.00769	2	9.99231	15
46	33 52	26 8	27140	52	72860	27911	54	72089	00771	2	99229	14
47	33 44	26 16	27206	53	72794	27980	55	72020	00774	2	99226	13
48	33 36	26 24	27273	55	72727	28049	56	71951	00776	2	99224	12
49	33 28	26 32	27339	56	72661	28117	58	71883	00779	2	99221	11
50	10 33 20	1 26 40	9.27405	57	10.72595	9.28186	59	10.71814	10.00781	2	9.99219	10
51	33 12	26 48	27471	58	72529	28254	60	71746	00783	2	99217	9
52	33 4	26 56	27537	59	72463	28323	61	71677	00786	2	99214	8
53	32 56	27 4	27602	60	72398	28391	62	71609	00788	2	99212	7
54	32 48	27 12	27668	61	72332	28459	63	71541	00791	2	99209	6
55	10 32 40	1 27 20	9.27734	63	10.72266	9.28527	65	10.71473	10.00793	2	9.99207	5
56	32 32	27 28	27799	64	72201	28595	66	71405	00796	2	99204	4
57	32 24	27 36	27864	65	72136	28662	67	71338	00798	2	99202	3
58	32 16	27 44	27930	66	72070	28730	68	71270	00800	2	99200	2
59	32 8	27 52	27995	67	72005	28798	69	71202	00803	2	99197	1
60	32 0	28 0	28060	68	71940	28865	71	71135	00805	2	99195	0
M	Hour P.M.	Hour A.M.	Cosine.	Diff.	Secant.	Cotangent	Diff.	Tangent.	Cosecant.	Diff.	Sine.	M
100°			A		A	B		B	C		C	79°

Seconds of time		1ˢ	2ˢ	3ˢ	4ˢ	5ˢ	6ˢ	7ˢ
Prop. parts of cols.	A	9	17	26	34	43	51	60
	B	9	18	26	35	44	53	62
	C	0	1	1	1	1	2	2

TABLE XXVII.

Log. Sines, Tangents, and Secants.

$S^{\prime}$. $G^{\prime}$.

11ᵇ | A | A | B | B | C | C 168°

M	Hour A.M.	Hour P.M.	Sine.	Diff.	Cosecant.	Tangent.	Diff.	Cotangent	Secant.	Diff.	Cosine.	M
0	10 32 0	1 28 0	9.28060	0	10.71940	9.28865	0	10.71135	10.00805	0	9.99195	60
1	31 52	28 8	28125	1	71875	28933	1	71067	00808	0	99192	59
2	31 44	28 16	28190	2	71810	29000	2	71000	00810	0	99190	58
3	31 36	28 24	28254	3	71746	29067	3	70933	00813	0	99187	57
4	31 28	28 32	28319	4	71681	29134	4	70866	00815	0	99185	56
5	10 31 20	1 28 40	9.28384	5	10.71616	9.29201	5	10.70799	10.00818	0	9.99182	55
6	31 12	28 48	28448	6	71552	29268	6	70732	00820	0	99180	54
7	31 4	28 56	28512	7	71488	29335	8	70665	00823	0	99177	53
8	30 56	29 4	28577	8	71423	29402	9	70598	00825	0	99175	52
9	30 48	29 12	28641	9	71359	29468	10	70532	00828	0	99172	51
10	10 30 40	1 29 20	9.28705	10	10.71295	9.29535	11	10.70465	10.00830	0	9.99170	50
11	30 32	29 28	28769	11	71231	29601	12	70399	00833	0	99167	49
12	30 24	29 36	28833	12	71167	29668	13	70332	00835	1	99165	48
13	30 16	29 44	28896	13	71104	29734	14	70266	00838	1	99162	47
14	30 8	29 52	28960	14	71040	29800	15	70200	00840	1	99160	46
15	10 30 0	1 30 0	9.29024	16	10.70976	9.29866	16	10.70134	10.00843	1	9.99157	45
16	29 52	30 8	29087	17	70913	29932	17	70068	00845	1	99155	44
17	29 44	30 16	29150	18	70850	29998	18	70002	00848	1	99152	43
18	29 36	30 24	29214	19	70786	30064	19	69936	00850	1	99150	42
19	29 28	30 32	29277	20	70723	30130	20	69870	00853	1	99147	41
20	10 29 20	1 30 40	9.29340	21	10.70660	9.30195	22	10.69805	10.00855	1	9.99145	40
21	29 12	30 48	29403	22	70597	30261	23	69739	00858	1	99142	39
22	29 4	30 56	29466	23	70534	30326	24	69674	00860	1	99140	38
23	28 56	31 4	29529	24	70471	30391	25	69609	00863	1	99137	37
24	28 48	31 12	29591	25	70409	30457	26	69543	00865	1	99135	36
25	10 28 40	1 31 20	9.29654	26	10.70346	9.30522	27	10.69478	10.00868	1	9.99132	35
26	28 32	31 28	29716	27	70284	30587	28	69413	00870	1	99130	34
27	28 24	31 36	29779	28	70221	30652	29	69348	00873	1	99127	33
28	28 16	31 44	29841	29	70159	30717	30	69283	00876	1	99124	32
29	28 8	31 52	29903	30	70097	30782	31	69218	00878	1	99122	31
30	10 28 0	1 32 0	9.29966	31	10.70034	9.30846	32	10.69154	10.00881	1	9.99119	30
31	27 52	32 8	30028	32	69972	30911	33	69089	00883	1	99117	29
32	27 44	32 16	30090	33	69910	30975	35	69025	00886	1	99114	28
33	27 36	32 24	30151	34	69849	31040	36	68960	00888	1	99112	27
34	27 28	32 32	30213	35	69787	31104	37	68896	00891	1	99109	26
35	10 27 20	1 32 40	9.30275	36	10.69725	9.31168	38	10.68832	10.00894	2	9.99106	25
36	27 12	32 48	30336	37	69664	31233	39	68767	00896	2	99104	24
37	27 4	32 56	30398	38	69602	31297	40	68703	00899	2	99101	23
38	26 56	33 4	30459	39	69541	31361	41	68639	00901	2	99099	22
39	26 48	33 12	30521	40	69479	31425	42	68575	00904	2	99096	21
40	10 26 40	1 33 20	9.30582	41	10.69418	9.31489	43	10.68511	10.00907	2	9.99093	20
41	26 32	33 28	30643	42	69357	31552	44	68448	00909	2	99091	19
42	26 24	33 36	30704	43	69296	31616	45	68384	00912	2	99088	18
43	26 16	33 44	30765	45	69235	31679	46	68321	00914	2	99086	17
44	26 8	33 52	30826	46	69174	31743	47	68257	00917	2	99083	16
45	10 26 0	1 34 0	9.30887	47	10.69113	9.31806	49	10.68194	10.00920	2	9.99080	15
46	25 52	34 8	30947	48	69053	31870	50	68130	00922	2	99078	14
47	25 44	34 16	31008	49	68992	31933	51	68067	00925	2	99075	13
48	25 36	34 24	31068	50	68932	31996	52	68004	00928	2	99072	12
49	25 28	34 32	31129	51	68871	32059	53	67941	00930	2	99070	11
50	10 25 20	1 34 40	9.31189	52	10.68811	9.32122	54	10.67878	10.00933	2	9.99067	10
51	25 12	34 48	31250	53	68750	32185	55	67815	00936	2	99064	9
52	25 4	34 56	31310	54	68690	32248	56	67752	00938	2	99062	8
53	24 56	35 4	31370	55	68630	32311	57	67689	00941	2	99059	7
54	24 48	35 12	31430	56	68570	32373	58	67627	00944	2	99056	6
55	10 24 40	1 35 20	9.31490	57	10.68510	9.32436	59	10.67564	10.00946	2	9.99054	5
56	24 32	35 28	31549	58	68451	32498	60	67502	00949	2	99051	4
57	24 24	35 36	31609	59	68391	32561	61	67439	00952	2	99048	3
58	24 16	35 44	31669	60	68331	32623	63	67377	00954	2	99046	2
59	24 8	35 52	31728	61	68272	32685	64	67315	00957	3	99043	1
60	24 0	36 0	31788	62	68212	32747	65	67253	00960	3	99040	0
M	Hour P.M.	Hour A.M.	Cosine.	Diff.	Secant.	Cotangent	Diff.	Tangent.	Cosecant.	Diff.	Sine.	M

101° | A | A | B | B | C | C 78°

Seconds of time ……		1ˢ	2ˢ	3ˢ	4ˢ	5ˢ	6ˢ	7ˢ
Prop. parts of cols.	A	8	16	23	31	39	47	54
	B	8	16	24	32	40	49	57
	C	0	1	1	1	2	2	2

TABLE XXVII.

Log. Sines, Tangents, and Secants.

S'. 12° G'. 167°

M	Hour A.M.	Hour P.M.	Sine. (A)	Diff.	Cosecant. (A)	Tangent. (B)	Diff.	Cotangent (B)	Secant. (C)	Diff.	Cosine. (C)	M
0	10 24 0	1 36 0	9.31788	0	10.68212	9.32747	0	10.67253	10.00960	0	9.99040	60
1	23 52	36 8	31847	1	68153	32810	1	67190	00962	0	99038	59
2	23 44	36 16	31907	2	68093	32872	2	67128	00965	0	99035	58
3	23 36	36 24	31966	3	68034	32933	3	67067	00968	0	99032	57
4	23 28	36 32	32025	4	67975	32995	4	67005	00970	0	99030	56
5	10 23 20	1 36 40	9.32084	5	10.67916	9.33057	5	10.66943	10.00973	0	9.99027	55
6	23 12	36 48	32143	6	67857	33119	6	66881	00976	0	99024	54
7	23 4	36 56	32202	7	67798	33180	7	66820	00978	0	99022	53
8	22 56	37 4	32261	8	67739	33242	8	66758	00981	0	99019	52
9	22 48	37 12	32319	9	67681	33303	9	66697	00984	0	99016	51
10	10 22 40	1 37 20	9.32378	10	10.67622	9.33365	10	10.66635	10.00987	0	9.99013	50
11	22 32	37 28	32437	10	67563	33426	11	66574	00989	1	99011	49
12	22 24	37 36	32495	11	67505	33487	12	66513	00992	1	99008	48
13	22 16	37 44	32553	12	67447	33548	13	66452	00995	1	99005	47
14	22 8	37 52	32612	13	67388	33609	14	66391	00998	1	99002	46
15	10 22 0	1 38 0	9.32670	14	10.67330	9.33670	15	10.66330	10.01000	1	9.99000	45
16	21 52	38 8	32728	15	67272	33731	16	66269	01003	1	98997	44
17	21 44	38 16	32786	16	67214	33792	17	66208	01006	1	98994	43
18	21 36	38 24	32844	17	67156	33853	18	66147	01009	1	98991	42
19	21 28	38 32	32902	18	67098	33913	19	66087	01011	1	98989	41
20	10 21 20	1 38 40	9.32960	19	10.67040	9.33974	20	10.66026	10.01014	1	9.98986	40
21	21 12	38 48	33018	20	66982	34034	21	65966	01017	1	98983	39
22	21 4	38 56	33075	21	66925	34095	22	65905	01020	1	98980	38
23	20 56	39 4	33133	22	66867	34155	23	65845	01022	1	98978	37
24	20 48	39 12	33190	23	66810	34215	24	65785	01025	1	98975	36
25	10 20 40	1 39 20	9.33248	24	10.66752	9.34276	25	10.65724	10.01028	1	9.98972	35
26	20 32	39 28	33305	25	66695	34336	26	65664	01031	1	98969	34
27	20 24	39 36	33362	26	66638	34396	27	65604	01033	1	98967	33
28	20 16	39 44	33420	27	66580	34456	28	65544	01036	1	98964	32
29	20 8	39 52	33477	28	66523	34516	29	65484	01039	1	98961	31
30	10 20 0	1 40 0	9.33534	29	10.66466	9.34576	30	10.65424	10.01042	1	9.98958	30
31	19 52	40 8	33591	29	66409	34635	31	65365	01045	1	98955	29
32	19 44	40 16	33647	30	66353	34695	32	65305	01047	1	98953	28
33	19 36	40 24	33704	31	66296	34755	33	65245	01050	2	98950	27
34	19 28	40 32	33761	32	66239	34814	34	65186	01053	2	98947	26
35	10 19 20	1 40 40	9.33818	33	10.66182	9.34874	35	10.65126	10.01056	2	9.98944	25
36	19 12	40 48	33874	34	66126	34933	36	65067	01059	2	98941	24
37	19 4	40 56	33931	35	66069	34992	37	65008	01062	2	98938	23
38	18 56	41 4	33987	36	66013	35051	38	64949	01064	2	98936	22
39	18 48	41 12	34043	37	65957	35111	39	64889	01067	2	98933	21
40	10 18 40	1 41 20	9.34100	38	10.65900	9.35170	40	10.64830	10.01070	2	9.98930	20
41	18 32	41 28	34156	39	65844	35229	41	64771	01073	2	98927	19
42	18 24	41 36	34212	40	65788	35288	42	64712	01076	2	98924	18
43	18 16	41 44	34268	41	65732	35347	43	64653	01079	2	98921	17
44	18 8	41 52	34324	42	65676	35405	44	64595	01081	2	98919	16
45	10 18 0	1 42 0	9.34380	43	10.65620	9.35464	45	10.64536	10.01084	2	9.98916	15
46	17 52	42 8	34436	44	65564	35523	46	64477	01087	2	98913	14
47	17 44	42 16	34491	45	65509	35581	47	64419	01090	2	98910	13
48	17 36	42 24	34547	46	65453	35640	48	64360	01093	2	98907	12
49	17 28	42 32	34602	47	65398	35698	49	64302	01096	2	98904	11
50	10 17 20	1 42 40	9.34658	48	10.65342	9.35757	50	10.64243	10.01099	2	9.98901	10
51	17 12	42 48	34713	48	65287	35815	51	64185	01102	2	98898	9
52	17 4	42 56	34769	49	65231	35873	52	64127	01104	2	98896	8
53	16 56	43 4	34824	50	65176	35931	53	64069	01107	2	98893	7
54	16 48	43 12	34879	51	65121	35989	54	64011	01110	3	98890	6
55	10 16 40	1 43 20	9.34934	52	10.65066	9.36047	55	10.63953	10.01113	3	9.98887	5
56	16 32	43 28	34989	53	65011	36105	56	63895	01116	3	98884	4
57	16 24	43 36	35044	54	64956	36163	57	63837	01119	3	98881	3
58	16 16	43 44	35099	55	64901	36221	58	63779	01122	3	98878	2
59	16 8	43 52	35154	56	64846	36279	59	63721	01125	3	98875	1
60	16 0	44 0	35209	57	64791	36336	60	63664	01128	3	98872	0
M	Hour P.M.	Hour A.M.	Cosine. (A)	Diff.	Secant. (A)	Cotangent (B)	Diff.	Tangent. (B)	Cosecant. (C)	Diff.	Sine. (C)	M

102° 77°

Seconds of time		1s	2s	3s	4s	5s	6s	7s
Prop. parts of cols.	A	7	14	21	29	36	43	50
	B	7	15	22	30	37	45	52
	C	0	1	1	1	2	2	2

TABLE XXVII.

S'. G

Log. Sines, Tangents, and Secants.

13° A A B B C C 166°

M	Hour A.M.	Hour P.M.	Sine.	Diff.	Cosecant.	Tangent.	Diff.	Cotangent.	Secant.	Diff.	Cosine.	M
0	10 16 0	1 44 0	9.35209	0	10.64791	9.36336	0	10.63664	10.01128	0	9.98872	60
1	15 52	44 8	35263	1	64737	36394	1	63606	01131	0	98869	59
2	15 44	44 16	35318	2	64682	36452	2	63548	01133	0	98867	58
3	15 36	44 24	35373	3	64627	36509	3	63491	01136	0	98864	57
4	15 28	44 32	35427	4	64573	36566	4	63434	01139	0	98861	56
5	10 15 20	1 44 40	9.35481	4	10.64519	9.36624	5	10.63376	10.01142	0	9.98858	55
6	15 12	44 48	35536	5	64464	36681	6	63319	01145	0	98855	54
7	15 4	44 56	35590	6	64410	36738	6	63262	01148	0	98852	53
8	14 56	45 4	35644	7	64356	36795	7	63205	01151	0	98849	52
9	14 48	45 12	35698	8	64302	36852	8	63148	01154	0	98846	51
10	10 14 40	1 45 20	9.35752	9	10.64248	9.36909	9	10.63091	10.01157	1	9.98843	50
11	14 32	45 28	35806	10	64194	36966	10	63034	01160	1	98840	49
12	14 24	45 36	35860	11	64140	37023	11	62977	01163	1	98837	48
13	14 16	45 44	35914	11	64086	37080	12	62920	01166	1	98834	47
14	14 8	45 52	35968	12	64032	37137	13	62863	01169	1	98831	46
15	10 14 0	1 46 0	9.36022	13	10.63978	9.37193	14	10.62807	10.01172	1	9.98828	45
16	13 52	46 8	36075	14	63925	37250	15	62750	01175	1	98825	44
17	13 44	46 16	36129	15	63871	37306	16	62694	01178	1	98822	43
18	13 36	46 24	36182	16	63818	37363	17	62637	01181	1	98819	42
19	13 28	46 32	36236	17	63764	37419	18	62581	01184	1	98816	41
20	10 13 20	1 46 40	9.36289	18	10.63711	9.37476	19	10.62524	10.01187	1	9.98813	40
21	13 12	46 48	36342	18	63658	37532	19	62468	01190	1	98810	39
22	13 4	46 56	36395	19	63605	37588	20	62412	01193	1	98807	38
23	12 56	47 4	36449	20	63551	37644	21	62356	01196	1	98804	37
24	12 48	47 12	36502	21	63498	37700	22	62300	01199	1	98801	36
25	10 12 40	1 47 20	9.36555	22	10.63445	9.37756	23	10.62244	10.01202	1	9.98798	35
26	12 32	47 28	36608	23	63392	37812	24	62188	01205	1	98795	34
27	12 24	47 36	36660	24	63340	37868	25	62132	01208	1	98792	33
28	12 16	47 44	36713	25	63287	37924	26	62076	01211	1	98789	32
29	12 8	47 52	36766	25	63234	37980	27	62020	01214	1	98786	31
30	10 12 0	1 48 0	9.36819	26	10.63181	9.38035	28	10.61965	10.01217	2	9.98783	30
31	11 52	48 8	36871	27	63129	38091	29	61909	01220	2	98780	29
32	11 44	48 16	36924	28	63076	38147	30	61853	01223	2	98777	28
33	11 36	48 24	36976	29	63024	38202	31	61798	01226	2	98774	27
34	11 28	48 32	37028	30	62972	38257	32	61743	01229	2	98771	26
35	10 11 20	1 48 40	9.37081	31	10.62919	9.38313	32	10.61687	10.01232	2	9.98768	25
36	11 12	48 48	37133	32	62867	38368	33	61632	01235	2	98765	24
37	11 4	48 56	37185	32	62815	38423	34	61577	01238	2	98762	23
38	10 56	49 4	37237	33	62763	38479	35	61521	01241	2	98759	22
39	10 48	49 12	37289	34	62711	38534	36	61466	01244	2	98756	21
40	10 10 40	1 49 20	9.37341	35	10.62659	9.38589	37	10.61411	10.01247	2	9.98753	20
41	10 32	49 28	37393	36	62607	38644	38	61356	01250	2	98750	19
42	10 24	49 36	37445	37	62555	38699	39	61301	01254	2	98746	18
43	10 16	49 44	37497	38	62503	38754	40	61246	01257	2	98743	17
44	10 8	49 52	37549	39	62451	38808	41	61192	01260	2	98740	16
45	10 10 0	1 50 0	9.37600	39	10.62400	9.38863	42	10.61137	10.01263	2	9.98737	15
46	9 52	50 8	37652	40	62348	38918	43	61082	01266	2	98734	14
47	9 44	50 16	37703	41	62297	38972	44	61028	01269	2	98731	13
48	9 36	50 24	37755	42	62245	39027	45	60973	01272	2	98728	12
49	9 28	50 32	37806	43	62194	39082	45	60918	01275	2	98725	11
50	10 9 20	1 50 40	9.37858	44	10.62142	9.39136	46	10.60864	10.01278	3	9.98722	10
51	9 12	50 48	37909	45	62091	39190	47	60810	01281	3	98719	9
52	9 4	50 56	37960	46	62040	39245	48	60755	01285	3	98715	8
53	8 56	51 4	38011	47	61989	39299	49	60701	01288	3	98712	7
54	8 48	51 12	38062	47	61938	39353	50	60647	01291	3	98709	6
55	10 8 40	1 51 20	9.38113	48	10.61887	9.39407	51	10.60593	10.01294	3	9.98706	5
56	8 32	51 28	38164	49	61836	39461	52	60539	01297	3	98703	4
57	8 24	51 36	38215	50	61785	39515	53	60485	01300	3	98700	3
58	8 16	51 44	38266	51	61734	39569	54	60431	01303	3	98697	2
59	8 8	51 52	38317	52	61683	39623	55	60377	01306	3	98694	1
60	8 0	52 0	38368	53	61632	39677	56	60323	01310	3	98690	0
M	Hour P.M.	Hour A.M.	Cosine.	Diff.	Secant.	Cotangent	Diff.	Tangent.	Cosecant.	Diff.	Sine.	M

103° A A B B C C 76°

Seconds of time		1s	2s	3s	4s	5s	6s	7s
Prop. parts of cols.	A	7	13	20	26	33	39	46
	B	7	14	21	28	35	42	49
	C	0	1	1	2	2	2	3

TABLE XXVII.

Log. Sines, Tangents, and Secants.

S'. G'.

14° 165°

M	Hour A.M.	Hour P.M.	Sine. (A)	Diff.	Cosecant. (A)	Tangent. (B)	Diff.	Cotangent (B)	Secant. (C)	Diff.	Cosine. (C)	M
0	10 8 0	1 52 0	9.38368	0	10.61632	9.39677	0	10.60323	10.01310	0	9.98690	60
1	7 52	52 8	38418	1	61582	39731	1	60269	01313	0	98687	59
2	7 44	52 16	38469	2	61531	39785	2	60215	01316	0	98684	58
3	7 36	52 24	38519	2	61481	39838	3	60162	01319	0	98681	57
4	7 28	52 32	38570	3	61430	39892	3	60108	01322	0	98678	56
5	10 7 20	1 52 40	9.38620	4	10.61380	9.39945	4	10.60055	10.01325	0	9.98675	55
6	7 12	52 48	38670	5	61330	39999	5	60001	01329	0	98671	54
7	7 4	52 56	38721	6	61279	40052	6	59948	01332	0	98668	53
8	6 56	53 4	38771	7	61229	40106	7	59894	01335	0	98665	52
9	6 48	53 12	38821	7	61179	40159	8	59841	01338	0	98662	51
10	10 6 40	1 53 20	9.38871	8	10.61129	9.40212	9	10.59788	10.01341	1	9.98659	50
11	6 32	53 28	38921	9	61079	40266	10	59734	01344	1	98656	49
12	6 24	53 36	38971	10	61029	40319	10	59681	01348	1	98652	48
13	6 16	53 44	39021	11	60979	40372	11	59628	01351	1	98649	47
14	6 8	53 52	39071	11	60929	40425	12	59575	01354	1	98646	46
15	10 6 0	1 54 0	9.39121	12	10.60879	9.40478	13	10.59522	10.01357	1	9.98643	45
16	5 52	54 8	39170	13	60830	40531	14	59469	01360	1	98640	44
17	5 44	54 16	39220	14	60780	40584	15	59416	01364	1	98636	43
18	5 36	54 24	39270	15	60730	40636	16	59364	01367	1	98633	42
19	5 28	54 32	39319	15	60681	40689	17	59311	01370	1	98630	41
20	10 5 20	1 54 40	9.39369	16	10.60631	9.40742	17	10.59258	10.01373	1	9.98627	40
21	5 12	54 48	39418	17	60582	40795	18	59205	01377	1	98623	39
22	5 4	54 56	39467	18	60533	40847	19	59153	01380	1	98620	38
23	4 56	55 4	39517	19	60483	40900	20	59100	01383	1	98617	37
24	4 48	55 12	39566	20	60434	40952	21	59048	01386	1	98614	36
25	10 4 40	1 55 20	9.39615	20	10.60385	9.41005	22	10.58995	10.01390	1	9.98610	35
26	4 32	55 28	39664	21	60336	41057	23	58943	01393	1	98607	34
27	4 24	55 36	39713	22	60287	41109	23	58891	01396	1	98604	33
28	4 16	55 44	39762	23	60238	41161	24	58839	01399	2	98601	32
29	4 8	55 52	39811	24	60189	41214	25	58786	01403	2	98597	31
30	10 4 0	1 56 0	9.39860	24	10.60140	9.41266	26	10.58734	10.01406	2	9.98594	30
31	3 52	56 8	39909	25	60091	41318	27	58682	01409	2	98591	29
32	3 44	56 16	39958	26	60042	41370	28	58630	01412	2	98588	28
33	3 36	56 24	40006	27	59994	41422	29	58578	01416	2	98584	27
34	3 28	56 32	40055	28	59945	41474	30	58526	01419	2	98581	26
35	10 3 20	1 56 40	9.40103	29	10.59897	9.41526	30	10.58474	10.01422	2	9.98578	25
36	3 12	56 48	40152	29	59848	41578	31	58422	01426	2	98574	24
37	3 4	56 56	40200	30	59800	41629	32	58371	01429	2	98571	23
38	2 56	57 4	40249	31	59751	41681	33	58319	01432	2	98568	22
39	2 48	57 12	40297	32	59703	41733	34	58267	01435	2	98565	21
40	10 2 40	1 57 20	9.40346	33	10.59654	9.41784	35	10.58216	10.01439	2	9.98561	20
41	2 32	57 28	40394	33	59606	41836	36	58164	01442	2	98558	19
42	2 24	57 36	40442	34	59558	41887	36	58113	01445	2	98555	18
43	2 16	57 44	40490	35	59510	41939	37	58061	01449	2	98551	17
44	2 8	57 52	40538	36	59462	41990	38	58010	01452	2	98548	16
45	10 2 0	1 58 0	9.40586	37	10.59414	9.42041	39	10.57959	10.01455	2	9.98545	15
46	1 52	58 8	40634	37	59366	42093	40	57907	01459	3	98541	14
47	1 44	58 16	40682	38	59318	42144	41	57856	01462	3	98538	13
48	1 36	58 24	40730	39	59270	42195	42	57805	01465	3	98535	12
49	1 28	58 32	40778	40	59222	42246	43	57754	01469	3	98531	11
50	10 1 20	1 58 40	9.40825	41	10.59175	9.42297	43	10.57703	10.01472	3	9.98528	10
51	1 12	58 48	40873	42	59127	42348	44	57652	01475	3	98525	9
52	1 4	58 56	40921	42	59079	42399	45	57601	01479	3	98521	8
53	0 56	59 4	40968	43	59032	42450	46	57550	01482	3	98518	7
54	0 48	59 12	41016	44	58984	42501	47	57499	01485	3	98515	6
55	10 0 40	1 59 20	9.41063	45	10.58937	9.42552	48	10.57448	10.01489	3	9.98511	5
56	0 32	59 28	41111	46	58889	42603	49	57397	01492	3	98508	4
57	0 24	59 36	41158	46	58842	42653	50	57347	01495	3	98505	3
58	0 16	59 44	41205	47	58795	42704	50	57296	01499	3	98501	2
59	0 8	59 52	41252	48	58748	42755	51	57245	01502	3	98498	1
60	0 0	2 0 0	41300	49	58700	42805	52	57195	01506	3	98494	0
M	Hour P.M.	Hour A.M.	Cosine. (A)	Diff.	Secant. (A)	Cotangent (B)	Diff.	Tangent. (B)	Cosecant. (C)	Diff.	Sine. (C)	M

104° 75°

Seconds of time		1s	2s	3s	4s	5s	6s	7s
Prop. parts of cols.	A	6	12	18	24	31	37	43
	B	7	13	20	26	33	39	46
	C	0	1	1	2	2	2	3

TABLE XXVII.

S'. G.

Log. Sines, Tangents, and Secants.

15° A A B B C C 164°

M	Hour A.M.	Hour P.M.	Sine.	Diff.	Cosecant.	Tangent.	Diff.	Cotangent	Secant.	Diff.	Cosine.	M
0	10 0 0	2 0 0	9.41300	0	10.58700	9.42805	0	10.57195	10.01506	0	9.98494	60
1	9 59 52	0 8	41347	1	58653	42856	1	57144	01509	0	98491	59
2	59 44	0 16	41394	2	58606	42906	2	57094	01512	0	98488	58
3	59 36	0 24	41441	2	58559	42957	2	57043	01516	0	98484	57
4	59 28	0 32	41488	3	58512	43007	3	56993	01519	0	98481	56
5	9 59 20	2 0 40	9.41535	4	10.58465	9.43057	4	10.56943	10.01523	0	9.98477	55
6	59 12	0 48	41582	5	58418	43108	5	56892	01526	0	98474	54
7	59 4	0 56	41628	5	58372	43158	6	56842	01529	0	98471	53
8	58 56	1 4	41675	6	58325	43208	7	56792	01533	0	98467	52
9	58 48	1 12	41722	7	58278	43258	7	56742	01536	1	98464	51
10	9 58 40	2 1 20	9.41768	8	10.58232	9.43308	8	10.56692	10.01540	1	9.98460	50
11	58 32	1 28	41815	8	58185	43358	9	56642	01543	1	98457	49
12	58 24	1 36	41861	9	58139	43408	10	56592	01547	1	98453	48
13	58 16	1 44	41908	10	58092	43458	11	56542	01550	1	98450	47
14	58 8	1 52	41954	11	58046	43508	11	56492	01553	1	98447	46
15	9 58 0	2 2 0	9.42001	11	10.57999	9.43558	12	10.56442	10.01557	1	9.98443	45
16	57 52	2 8	42047	12	57953	43607	13	56393	01560	1	98440	44
17	57 44	2 16	42093	13	57907	43657	14	56343	01564	1	98436	43
18	57 36	2 24	42140	14	57860	43707	15	56293	01567	1	98433	42
19	57 28	2 32	42186	14	57814	43756	16	56244	01571	1	98429	41
20	9 57 20	2 2 40	9.42232	15	10.57768	9.43806	16	10.56194	10.01574	1	9.98426	40
21	57 12	2 48	42278	16	57722	43855	17	56145	01578	1	98422	39
22	57 4	2 56	42324	17	57676	43905	18	56095	01581	1	98419	38
23	56 56	3 4	42370	17	57630	43954	19	56046	01585	1	98415	37
24	56 48	3 12	42416	18	57584	44004	20	55996	01588	1	98412	36
25	9 56 40	2 3 20	9.42461	19	10.57539	9.44053	20	10.55947	10.01591	1	9.98409	35
26	56 32	3 28	42507	20	57493	44102	21	55898	01595	2	98405	34
27	56 24	3 36	42553	21	57447	44151	22	55849	01598	2	98402	33
28	56 16	3 44	42599	21	57401	44201	23	55799	01602	2	98398	32
29	56 8	3 52	42644	22	57356	44250	24	55750	01605	2	98395	31
30	9 56 0	2 4 0	9.42690	23	10.57310	9.44299	25	10.55701	10.01609	2	9.98391	30
31	55 52	4 8	42735	24	57265	44348	25	55652	01612	2	98388	29
32	55 44	4 16	42781	24	57219	44397	26	55603	01616	2	98384	28
33	55 36	4 24	42826	25	57174	44446	27	55554	01619	2	98381	27
34	55 28	4 32	42872	26	57128	44495	28	55505	01623	2	98377	26
35	9 55 20	2 4 40	9.42917	27	10.57083	9.44544	29	10.55456	10.01627	2	9.98373	25
36	55 12	4 48	42962	27	57038	44592	29	55408	01630	2	98370	24
37	55 4	4 56	43008	28	56992	44641	30	55359	01634	2	98366	23
38	54 56	5 4	43053	29	56947	44690	31	55310	01637	2	98363	22
39	54 48	5 12	43098	30	56902	44738	32	55262	01641	2	98359	21
40	9 54 40	2 5 20	9.43143	30	10.56857	9.44787	33	10.55213	10.01644	2	9.98356	20
41	54 32	5 28	43188	31	56812	44836	34	55164	01648	2	98352	19
42	54 24	5 36	43233	32	56767	44884	34	55116	01651	2	98349	18
43	54 16	5 44	43278	33	56722	44933	35	55067	01655	3	98345	17
44	54 8	5 52	43323	33	56677	44981	36	55019	01658	3	98342	16
45	9 54 0	2 6 0	9.43367	34	10.56633	9.45029	37	10.54971	10.01662	3	9.98338	15
46	53 52	6 8	43412	35	56588	45078	38	54922	01666	3	98334	14
47	53 44	6 16	43457	36	56543	45126	38	54874	01669	3	98331	13
48	53 36	6 24	43502	36	56498	45174	39	54826	01673	3	98327	12
49	53 28	6 32	43546	37	56454	45222	40	54778	01676	3	98324	11
50	9 53 20	2 6 40	9.43591	38	10.56409	9.45271	41	10.54729	10.01680	3	9.98320	10
51	53 12	6 48	43635	39	56365	45319	42	54681	01683	3	98317	9
52	53 4	6 56	43680	39	56320	45367	43	54633	01687	3	98313	8
53	52 56	7 4	43724	40	56276	45415	43	54585	01691	3	98309	7
54	52 48	7 12	43769	41	56231	45463	44	54537	01694	3	98306	6
55	9 52 40	2 7 20	9.43813	42	10.56187	9.45511	45	10.54489	10.01698	3	9.98302	5
56	52 32	7 28	43857	43	56143	45559	46	54441	01701	3	98299	4
57	52 24	7 36	43901	43	56099	45606	47	54394	01705	3	98295	3
58	52 16	7 44	43946	44	56054	45654	47	54346	01709	3	98291	2
59	52 8	7 52	43990	45	56010	45702	48	54298	01712	3	98288	1
60	52 0	8 0	44034	46	55966	45750	49	54250	01716	4	98284	0
M	Hour P.M.	Hour A.M.	Cosine.	Diff.	Secant.	Cotangent	Diff.	Tangent.	Cosecant.	Diff.	Sine.	M

105° A A B B C C 74°

Seconds of time		1s	2s	3s	4s	5s	6s	7s
Prop. parts of cols.	A	6	11	17	23	28	34	40
	B	6	12	18	25	31	37	43
	C	0	1	1	2	2	3	3

TABLE XXVII.

Log. Sines, Tangents, and Secants.

8^h G'.

16° A A B B C C 163°

M	Hour A.M.	Hour P.M.	Sine.	Diff.	Cosecant.	Tangent.	Diff.	Cotangent	Secant.	Diff.	Cosine.	M
0	9 52 0	2 8 0	9.44034	0	10.55966	9.45750	0	10.54250	10.01716	0	9.98284	60
1	51 52	8 8	44078	1	55922	45797	1	54203	01719	0	98281	59
2	51 44	8 16	44122	1	55878	45845	2	54155	01723	0	98277	58
3	51 36	8 24	44166	2	55834	45892	2	54108	01727	0	98273	57
4	51 28	8 32	44210	3	55790	45940	3	54060	01730	0	98270	56
5	9 51 20	2 8 40	9.44253	4	10.55747	9.45987	4	10.54013	10.01734	0	9.98266	55
6	51 12	8 48	44297	4	55703	46035	5	53965	01738	0	98262	54
7	51 4	8 56	44341	5	55659	46082	5	53918	01741	0	98259	53
8	50 56	9 4	44385	6	55615	46130	6	53870	01745	0	98255	52
9	50 48	9 12	44428	6	55572	46177	7	53823	01749	1	98251	51
10	9 50 40	2 9 20	9.44472	7	10.55528	9.46224	8	10.53776	10.01752	1	9.98248	50
11	50 32	9 28	44516	8	55484	46271	9	53729	01756	1	98244	49
12	50 24	9 36	44559	9	55441	46319	9	53681	01760	1	98240	48
13	50 16	9 44	44602	9	55398	46366	10	53634	01763	1	98237	47
14	50 8	9 52	44646	10	55354	46413	11	53587	01767	1	98233	46
15	9 50 0	2 10 0	9.44689	11	10.55311	9.46460	12	10.53540	10.01771	1	9.98229	45
16	49 52	10 8	44733	11	55267	46507	12	53493	01774	1	98226	44
17	49 44	10 16	44776	12	55224	46554	13	53446	01778	1	98222	43
18	49 36	10 24	44819	13	55181	46601	14	53399	01782	1	98218	42
19	49 28	10 32	44862	14	55138	46648	15	53352	01785	1	98215	41
20	9 49 20	2 10 40	9.44905	14	10.55095	9.46694	15	10.53306	10.01789	1	9.98211	40
21	49 12	10 48	44948	15	55052	46741	16	53259	01793	1	98207	39
22	49 4	10 56	44992	16	55008	46788	17	53212	01796	1	98204	38
23	48 56	11 4	45035	16	54965	46835	18	53165	01800	1	98200	37
24	48 48	11 12	45077	17	54923	46881	19	53119	01804	1	98196	36
25	9 48 40	2 11 20	9.45120	18	10.54880	9.46928	19	10.53072	10.01808	2	9.98192	35
26	48 32	11 28	45163	18	54837	46975	20	53025	01811	2	98189	34
27	48 24	11 36	45206	19	54794	47021	21	52979	01815	2	98185	33
28	48 16	11 44	45249	20	54751	47068	22	52932	01819	2	98181	32
29	48 8	11 52	45292	21	54708	47114	22	52886	01823	2	98177	31
30	9 48 0	2 12 0	9.45334	21	10.54666	9.47160	23	10.52840	10.01826	2	9.98174	30
31	47 52	12 8	45377	22	54623	47207	24	52793	01830	2	98170	29
32	47 44	12 16	45419	23	54581	47253	25	52747	01834	2	98166	28
33	47 36	12 24	45462	23	54538	47299	26	52701	01838	2	98162	27
34	47 28	12 32	45504	24	54496	47346	26	52654	01841	2	98159	26
35	9 47 20	2 12 40	9.45547	25	10.54453	9.47392	27	10.52608	10.01845	2	9.98155	25
36	47 12	12 48	45589	26	54411	47438	28	52562	01849	2	98151	24
37	47 4	12 56	45632	26	54368	47484	29	52516	01853	2	98147	23
38	46 56	13 4	45674	27	54326	47530	29	52470	01856	2	98144	22
39	46 48	13 12	45716	28	54284	47576	30	52424	01860	2	98140	21
40	9 46 40	2 13 20	9.45758	28	10.54242	9.47622	31	10.52378	10.01864	2	9.98136	20
41	46 32	13 28	45801	29	54199	47668	32	52332	01868	3	98132	19
42	46 24	13 36	45843	30	54157	47714	32	52286	01871	3	98129	18
43	46 16	13 44	45885	31	54115	47760	33	52240	01875	3	98125	17
44	46 8	13 52	45927	31	54073	47806	34	52194	01879	3	98121	16
45	9 46 0	2 14 0	9.45969	32	10.54031	9.47852	35	10.52148	10.01883	3	9.98117	15
46	45 52	14 8	46011	33	53989	47897	36	52103	01887	3	98113	14
47	45 44	14 16	46053	33	53947	47943	36	52057	01890	3	98110	13
48	45 36	14 24	46095	34	53905	47989	37	52011	01894	3	98106	12
49	45 28	14 32	46136	35	53864	48035	38	51965	01898	3	98102	11
50	9 45 20	2 14 40	9.46178	36	10.53822	9.48080	39	10.51920	10.01902	3	9.98098	10
51	45 12	14 48	46220	36	53780	48126	39	51874	01906	3	98094	9
52	45 4	14 56	46262	37	53738	48171	40	51829	01910	3	98090	8
53	44 56	15 4	46303	38	53697	48217	41	51783	01913	3	98087	7
54	44 48	15 12	46345	38	53655	48262	42	51738	01917	3	98083	6
55	9 44 40	2 15 20	9.46386	39	10.53614	9.48307	43	10.51693	10.01921	3	9.98079	5
56	44 32	15 28	46428	40	53572	48353	43	51647	01925	3	98075	4
57	44 24	15 36	46469	41	53531	48398	44	51602	01929	4	98071	3
58	44 16	15 44	46511	41	53489	48443	45	51557	01933	4	98067	2
59	44 8	15 52	46552	42	53448	48489	46	51511	01937	4	98063	1
60	44 0	16 0	46594	43	53406	48534	46	51466	01940	4	98060	0
M	Hour P.M.	Hour A.M.	Cosine.	Diff.	Secant.	Cotangent	Diff.	Tangent.	Cosecant.	Diff.	Sine.	M

106° A A B B C C 73°

Seconds of time		1ˢ	2ˢ	3ˢ	4ˢ	5ˢ	6ˢ	7ˢ
Prop. parts of cols.	A	5	11	16	21	27	32	37
	B	6	12	17	23	29	35	41
	C	0	1	1	2	2	3	3

TABLE XXVII.

S′. Log. Sines, Tangents, and Secants. *G′.*

17°			A		A	B		B	C		C	162°
M	Hour A.M.	Hour P.M.	Sine.	Diff.	Cosecant.	Tangent.	Diff.	Cotangent	Secant.	Diff.	Cosine.	M
0	9 44 0	2 16 0	9.46594	0	10.53406	9.48534	0	10.51466	10.01940	0	9.98060	60
1	43 52	16 8	46635	1	53365	48579	1	51421	01944	0	98056	59
2	43 44	16 16	46676	1	53324	48624	1	51376	01948	0	98052	58
3	43 36	16 24	46717	2	53283	48669	2	51331	01952	0	98048	57
4	43 28	16 32	46758	3	53242	48714	3	51286	01956	0	98044	56
5	9 43 20	2 16 40	9.46800	3	10.53200	9.48759	4	10.51241	10.01960	0	9.98040	55
6	43 12	16 48	46841	4	53159	48804	4	51196	01964	0	98036	54
7	43 4	16 56	46882	5	53118	48849	5	51151	01968	0	98032	53
8	42 56	17 4	46923	5	53077	48894	6	51106	01971	1	98029	52
9	42 48	17 12	46964	6	53036	48939	7	51061	01975	1	98025	51
10	9 42 40	2 17 20	9.47005	7	10.52995	9.48984	7	10.51016	10.01979	1	9.98021	50
11	42 32	17 28	47045	7	52955	49029	8	50971	01983	1	98017	49
12	42 24	17 36	47086	8	52914	49073	9	50927	01987	1	98013	48
13	42 16	17 44	47127	9	52873	49118	10	50882	01991	1	98009	47
14	42 8	17 52	47168	9	52832	49163	10	50837	01995	1	98005	46
15	9 42 0	2 18 0	9.47209	10	10.52791	9.49207	11	10.50793	10.01999	1	9.98001	45
16	41 52	18 8	47249	11	52751	49252	12	50748	02003	1	97997	44
17	41 44	18 16	47290	11	52710	49296	12	50704	02007	1	97993	43
18	41 36	18 24	47330	12	52670	49341	13	50659	02011	1	97989	42
19	41 28	18 32	47371	13	52629	49385	14	50615	02014	1	97986	41
20	9 41 20	2 18 40	9.47411	13	10.52589	9.49430	15	10.50570	10.02018	1	9.97982	40
21	41 12	18 48	47452	14	52548	49474	15	50526	02022	1	97978	39
22	41 4	18 56	47492	15	52508	49519	16	50481	02026	1	97974	38
23	40 56	19 4	47533	15	52467	49563	17	50437	02030	2	97970	37
24	40 48	19 12	47573	16	52427	49607	18	50393	02034	2	97966	36
25	9 40 40	2 19 20	9.47613	17	10.52387	9.49652	18	10.50348	10.02038	2	9.97962	35
26	40 32	19 28	47654	17	52346	49696	19	50304	02042	2	97958	34
27	40 24	19 36	47694	18	52306	49740	20	50260	02046	2	97954	33
28	40 16	19 44	47734	19	52266	49784	21	50216	02050	2	97950	32
29	40 8	19 52	47774	19	52226	49828	21	50172	02054	2	97946	31
30	9 40 0	2 20 0	9.47814	20	10.52186	9.49872	22	10.50128	10.02058	2	9.97942	30
31	39 52	20 8	47854	21	52146	49916	23	50084	02062	2	97938	29
32	39 44	20 16	47894	21	52106	49960	24	50040	02066	2	97934	28
33	39 36	20 24	47934	22	52066	50004	24	49996	02070	2	97930	27
34	39 28	20 32	47974	23	52026	50048	25	49952	02074	2	97926	26
35	9 39 20	2 20 40	9.48014	23	10.51986	9.50092	26	10.49908	10.02078	2	9.97922	25
36	39 12	20 48	48054	24	51946	50136	26	49864	02082	2	97918	24
37	39 4	20 56	48094	25	51906	50180	27	49820	02086	2	97914	23
38	38 56	21 4	48133	25	51867	50223	28	49777	02090	3	97910	22
39	38 48	21 12	48173	26	51827	50267	29	49733	02094	3	97906	21
40	9 38 40	2 21 20	9.48213	27	10.51787	9.50311	29	10.49689	10.02098	3	9.97902	20
41	38 32	21 28	48252	27	51748	50355	30	49645	02102	3	97898	19
42	38 24	21 36	48292	28	51708	50398	31	49602	02106	3	97894	18
43	38 16	21 44	48332	29	51668	50442	32	49558	02110	3	97890	17
44	38 8	21 52	48371	29	51629	50485	32	49515	02114	3	97886	16
45	9 38 0	2 22 0	9.48411	30	10.51589	9.50529	33	10.49471	10.02118	3	9.97882	15
46	37 52	22 8	48450	31	51550	50572	34	49428	02122	3	97878	14
47	37 44	22 16	48490	31	51510	50616	35	49384	02126	3	97874	13
48	37 36	22 24	48529	32	51471	50659	35	49341	02130	3	97870	12
49	37 28	22 32	48568	33	51432	50703	36	49297	02134	3	97866	11
50	9 37 20	2 22 40	9.48607	33	10.51393	9.50746	37	10.49254	10.02139	3	9.97861	10
51	37 12	22 48	48647	34	51353	50789	37	49211	02143	3	97857	9
52	37 4	22 56	48686	35	51314	50833	38	49167	02147	3	97853	8
53	36 56	23 4	48725	35	51275	50876	39	49124	02151	4	97849	7
54	36 48	23 12	48764	36	51236	50919	40	49081	02155	4	97845	6
55	9 36 40	2 23 20	9.48803	37	10.51197	9.50962	40	10.49038	10.02159	4	9.97841	5
56	36 32	23 28	48842	37	51158	51005	41	48995	02163	4	97837	4
57	36 24	23 36	48881	38	51119	51048	42	48952	02167	4	97833	3
58	36 16	23 44	48920	39	51080	51092	43	48908	02171	4	97829	2
59	36 8	23 52	48959	39	51041	51135	43	48865	02175	4	97825	1
60	36 0	24 0	48998	40	51002	51178	44	48822	02179	4	97821	0
M	Hour P.M.	Hour A.M.	Cosine.	Diff.	Secant.	Cotangent	Diff.	Tangent.	Cosecant.	Diff.	Sine.	M
107°			A		A	B		B	C		C	72°

Seconds of time		1s	2s	3s	4s	5s	6s	7s
Prop. parts of cols.	A	5	10	15	20	25	30	35
	B	6	11	17	22	28	33	39
	C	0	1	1	2	2	3	3

TABLE XXVII.

Log. Sines, Tangents, and Secants.

S′. 18° | A | A | B | B | C | C 161° G′.

M	Hour A.M.	Hour P.M.	Sine. (A)	Diff.	Cosecant. (A)	Tangent. (B)	Diff.	Cotangent (B)	Secant. (C)	Diff.	Cosine. (C)	M
0	9 36 0	2 24 0	9.48998	0	10.51002	9.51178	0	10.48822	10.02179	0	9.97821	60
1	35 52	24 8	49037	1	50963	51221	1	48779	02183	0	97817	59
2	35 44	24 16	49076	1	50924	51264	1	48736	02188	0	97812	58
3	35 36	24 24	49115	2	50885	51306	2	48694	02192	0	97808	57
4	35 28	24 32	49153	3	50847	51349	3	48651	02196	0	97804	56
5	9 35 20	2 24 40	9.49192	3	10.50808	9.51392	3	10.48608	10.02200	0	9.97800	55
6	35 12	24 48	49231	4	50769	51435	4	48565	02204	0	97796	54
7	35 4	24 56	49269	4	50731	51478	5	48522	02208	0	97792	53
8	34 56	25 4	49308	5	50692	51520	6	48480	02212	1	97788	52
9	34 48	25 12	49347	6	50653	51563	6	48437	02216	1	97784	51
10	9 34 40	2 25 20	9.49385	6	10.50615	9.51606	7	10.48394	10.02221	1	9.97779	50
11	34 32	25 28	49424	7	50576	51648	8	48352	02225	1	97775	49
12	34 24	25 36	49462	8	50538	51691	8	48309	02229	1	97771	48
13	34 16	25 44	49500	8	50500	51734	9	48266	02233	1	97767	47
14	34 8	25 52	49539	9	50461	51776	10	48224	02237	1	97763	46
15	9 34 0	2 26 0	9.49577	9	10.50423	9.51819	10	10.48181	10.02241	1	9.97759	45
16	33 52	26 8	49615	10	50385	51861	11	48139	02246	1	97754	44
17	33 44	26 16	49654	11	50346	51903	12	48097	02250	1	97750	43
18	33 36	26 24	49692	11	50308	51946	13	48054	02254	1	97746	42
19	33 28	26 32	49730	12	50270	51988	13	48012	02258	1	97742	41
20	9 33 20	2 26 40	9.49768	13	10.50232	9.52031	14	10.47969	10.02262	1	9.97738	40
21	33 12	26 48	49806	13	50194	52073	15	47927	02266	1	97734	39
22	33 4	26 56	49844	14	50156	52115	15	47885	02271	2	97729	38
23	32 56	27 4	49882	14	50118	52157	16	47843	02275	2	97725	37
24	32 48	27 12	49920	15	50080	52200	17	47800	02279	2	97721	36
25	9 32 40	2 27 20	9.49958	16	10.50042	9.52242	17	10.47758	10.02283	2	9.97717	35
26	32 32	27 28	49996	16	50004	52284	18	47716	02287	2	97713	34
27	32 24	27 36	50034	17	49966	52326	19	47674	02292	2	97708	33
28	32 16	27 44	50072	18	49928	52368	20	47632	02296	2	97704	32
29	32 8	27 52	50110	18	49890	52410	20	47590	02300	2	97700	31
30	9 32 0	2 28 0	9.50148	19	10.49852	9.52452	21	10.47548	10.02304	2	9.97696	30
31	31 52	28 8	50185	20	49815	52494	22	47506	02309	2	97691	29
32	31 44	28 16	50223	20	49777	52536	22	47464	02313	2	97687	28
33	31 36	28 24	50261	21	49739	52578	23	47422	02317	2	97683	27
34	31 28	28 32	50298	21	49702	52620	24	47380	02321	2	97679	26
35	9 31 20	2 28 40	9.50336	22	10.49664	9.52661	24	10.47339	10.02326	2	9.97674	25
36	31 12	28 48	50374	23	49626	52703	25	47297	02330	3	97670	24
37	31 4	28 56	50411	23	49589	52745	26	47255	02334	3	97666	23
38	30 56	29 4	50449	24	49551	52787	27	47213	02338	3	97662	22
39	30 48	29 12	50486	25	49514	52829	27	47171	02343	3	97657	21
40	9 30 40	2 29 20	9.50523	25	10.49477	9.52870	28	10.47130	10.02347	3	9.97653	20
41	30 32	29 28	50561	26	49439	52912	29	47088	02351	3	97649	19
42	30 24	29 36	50598	26	49402	52953	29	47047	02355	3	97645	18
43	30 16	29 44	50635	27	49365	52995	30	47005	02360	3	97640	17
44	30 8	29 52	50673	28	49327	53037	31	46963	02364	3	97636	16
45	9 30 0	2 30 0	9.50710	28	10.49290	9.53078	31	10.46922	10.02368	3	9.97632	15
46	29 52	30 8	50747	29	49253	53120	32	46880	02372	3	97628	14
47	29 44	30 16	50784	30	49216	53161	33	46839	02377	3	97623	13
48	29 36	30 24	50821	30	49179	53202	34	46798	02381	3	97619	12
49	29 28	30 32	50858	31	49142	53244	34	46756	02385	3	97615	11
50	9 29 20	2 30 40	9.50896	31	10.49104	9.53285	35	10.46715	10.02390	4	9.97610	10
51	29 12	30 48	50933	32	49067	53327	36	46673	02394	4	97606	9
52	29 4	30 56	50970	33	49030	53368	36	46632	02398	4	97602	8
53	28 56	31 4	51007	33	48993	53409	37	46591	02403	4	97597	7
54	28 48	31 12	51043	34	48957	53450	38	46550	02407	4	97593	6
55	9 28 40	2 31 20	9.51080	35	10.48920	9.53492	38	10.46508	10.02411	4	9.97589	5
56	28 32	31 28	51117	35	48883	53533	39	46467	02416	4	97584	4
57	28 24	31 36	51154	36	48846	53574	40	46426	02420	4	97580	3
58	28 16	31 44	51191	37	48809	53615	41	46385	02424	4	97576	2
59	28 8	31 52	51227	37	48773	53656	41	46344	02429	4	97571	1
60	28 0	32 0	51264	38	48736	53697	42	46303	02433	4	97567	0
M	Hour P.M.	Hour A.M.	Cosine.	Diff.	Secant.	Cotangent	Diff.	Tangent.	Cosecant.	Diff.	Sine.	M

108° | A | A | B | B | C | C 71°

Seconds of time		1s	2s	3s	4s	5s	6s	7s
Prop. parts of cols.	A	5	9	14	19	24	28	33
	B	5	10	16	21	26	31	37
	C	1	1	2	2	3	3	4

TABLE XXVII.

S′. Log. Sines, Tangents, and Secants. G′.

19°			A		A	B		B	C		C 160°	
M	Hour A.M.	Hour P.M.	Sine.	Diff.	Cosecant.	Tangent.	Diff.	Cotangent	Secant.	Diff.	Cosine.	M
0	9 28 0	2 32 0	9.51264	0	10.48736	9.53697	0	10.46303	10.02433	0	9.97567	60
1	27 52	32 8	51301	1	48699	53738	1	46262	02437	0	97563	59
2	27 44	32 61	51338	1	48662	53779	1	46221	02442	0	97558	58
3	27 36	32 24	51374	2	48626	53820	2	46180	02446	0	97554	57
4	27 28	32 32	51411	2	48589	53861	3	46139	02450	0	97550	56
5	9 27 20	2 32 40	9.51447	3	10.48553	9.53902	3	10.46098	10.02455	0	9.97545	55
6	27 12	32 48	51484	4	48516	53943	4	46057	02459	0	97541	54
7	27 4	32 56	51520	4	48480	53984	5	46016	02464	1	97536	53
8	26 56	33 4	51557	5	48443	54025	5	45975	02468	1	97532	52
9	26 48	33 12	51593	5	48407	54065	6	45935	02472	1	97528	51
10	9 26 40	2 33 20	9.51629	6	10.48371	9.54106	7	10.45894	10.02477	1	9.97523	50
11	26 32	33 28	51666	7	48334	54147	7	45853	02481	1	97519	49
12	26 24	33 36	51702	7	48298	54187	8	45813	02485	1	97515	48
13	26 16	33 44	51738	8	48262	54228	9	45772	02490	1	97510	47
14	26 8	33 52	51774	8	48226	54269	9	45731	02494	1	97506	46
15	9 26 0	2 34 0	9.51811	9	10.48189	9.54309	10	10.45691	10.02499	1	9.97501	45
16	25 52	34 8	51847	10	48153	54350	11	45650	02503	1	97497	44
17	25 44	34 16	51883	10	48117	54390	11	45610	02508	1	97492	43
18	25 36	34 24	51919	11	48081	54431	12	45569	02512	1	97488	42
19	25 28	34 32	51955	11	48045	54471	13	45529	02516	1	97484	41
20	9 25 20	2 34 40	9.51991	12	10.48009	9.54512	13	10.45488	10.02521	1	9.97479	40
21	25 12	34 48	52027	12	47973	54552	14	45448	02525	2	97475	39
22	25 4	34 56	52063	13	47937	54593	15	45407	02530	2	97470	38
23	24 56	35 4	52099	14	47901	54633	15	45367	02534	2	97466	37
24	24 48	35 12	52135	14	47865	54673	16	45327	02539	2	97461	36
25	9 24 40	2 35 20	9.52171	15	10.47829	9.54714	17	10.45286	10.02543	2	9.97457	35
26	24 32	35 28	52207	15	47793	54754	17	45246	02547	2	97453	34
27	24 24	35 36	52242	16	47758	54794	18	45206	02552	2	97448	33
28	24 16	35 44	52278	17	47722	54835	19	45165	02556	2	97444	32
29	24 8	35 52	52314	17	47686	54875	19	45125	02561	2	97439	31
30	9 24 0	2 36 0	9.52350	18	10.47650	9.54915	20	10.45085	10.02565	2	9.97435	30
31	23 52	36 8	52385	18	47615	54955	21	45045	02570	2	97430	29
32	23 44	36 16	52421	19	47579	54995	21	45005	02574	2	97426	28
33	23 36	36 24	52456	20	47544	55035	22	44965	02579	2	97421	27
34	23 28	36 32	52492	20	47508	55075	23	44925	02583	3	97417	26
35	9 23 20	2 36 40	9.52527	21	10.47473	9.55115	23	10.44885	10.02588	3	9.97412	25
36	23 12	36 48	52563	21	47437	55155	24	44845	02592	3	97408	24
37	23 4	36 56	52598	22	47402	55195	25	44805	02597	3	97403	23
38	22 56	37 4	52634	23	47366	55235	25	44765	02601	3	97399	22
39	22 48	37 12	52669	23	47331	55275	26	44725	02606	3	97394	21
40	9 22 40	2 37 20	9.52705	24	10.47295	9.55315	27	10.44685	10.02610	3	9.97390	20
41	22 32	37 28	52740	24	47260	55355	27	44645	02615	3	97385	19
42	22 24	37 36	52775	25	47225	55395	28	44605	02619	3	97381	18
43	22 16	37 44	52811	26	47189	55434	29	44566	02624	3	97376	17
44	22 8	37 52	52846	26	47154	55474	29	44526	02628	3	97372	16
45	9 22 0	2 38 0	9.52881	27	10.47119	9.55514	30	10.44486	10.02633	3	9.97367	15
46	21 52	38 8	52916	27	47084	55554	31	44446	02637	3	97363	14
47	21 44	38 16	52951	28	47049	55593	31	44407	02642	3	97358	13
48	21 36	38 24	52986	29	47014	55633	32	44367	02647	4	97353	12
49	21 28	38 32	53021	29	46979	55673	33	44327	02651	4	97349	11
50	9 21 20	2 38 40	9.53056	30	10.46944	9.55712	33	10.44288	10.02656	4	9.97344	10
51	21 12	38 48	53092	30	46908	55752	34	44248	02660	4	97340	9
52	21 4	38 56	53126	31	46874	55791	35	44209	02665	4	97335	8
53	20 56	39 4	53161	32	46839	55831	35	44169	02669	4	97331	7
54	20 48	39 12	53196	32	46804	55870	36	44130	02674	4	97326	6
55	9 20 40	2 39 20	9.53231	33	10.46769	9.55910	37	10.44090	10.02678	4	9.97322	5
56	20 32	39 28	53266	33	46734	55949	37	44051	02683	4	97317	4
57	20 24	39 36	53301	34	46699	55989	38	44011	02688	4	97312	3
58	20 16	39 44	53336	34	46664	56028	39	43972	02692	4	97308	2
59	20 8	39 52	53370	35	46630	56067	39	43933	02697	4	97303	1
60	20 0	40 0	53405	36	46595	56107	40	43893	02701	4	97299	0
M	Hour P.M.	Hour A.M.	Cosine.	Diff.	Secant.	Cotangent	Diff.	Tangent.	Cosecant.	Diff.	Sine.	M
109°			A		A	B		B	C		C 70°	

Seconds of time		1s	2s	3s	4s	5s	6s	7s
Prop. parts of cols.	A	4	9	13	18	22	27	31
	B	5	10	15	20	25	30	35
	C	1	1	2	2	3	3	4

TABLE XXVII.

Log. Sines, Tangents, and Secants.

S′. G′.

20° 159°

			A		A	B		B	C		C	
M	Hour A.M.	Hour P.M.	Sine.	Diff.	Cosecant.	Tangent.	Diff.	Cotangent	Secant.	Diff.	Cosine.	M
0	9 20 0	2 40 0	9.53405	0	10.46595	9.56107	0	10.43893	10.02701	0	9.97299	60
1	19 52	40 8	53440	1	46560	56146	1	43854	02706	0	97294	59
2	19 44	40 16	53475	1	46525	56185	1	43815	02711	0	97289	58
3	19 36	40 24	53509	2	46491	56224	2	43776	02715	0	97285	57
4	19 28	40 32	53544	2	46456	56264	3	43736	02720	0	97280	56
5	9 19 20	2 40 40	9.53578	3	10.46422	9.56303	3	10.43697	10.02724	0	9.97276	55
6	19 12	40 48	53613	3	46387	56342	4	43658	02729	0	97271	54
7	19 4	40 56	53647	4	46353	56381	4	43619	02734	1	97266	53
8	18 56	41 4	53682	5	46318	56420	5	43580	02738	1	97262	52
9	18 48	41 12	53716	5	46284	56459	6	43541	02743	1	97257	51
10	9 18 40	2 41 20	9.53751	6	10.46249	9.56498	6	10.43502	10.02748	1	9.97252	50
11	18 32	41 28	53785	6	46215	56537	7	43463	02752	1	97248	49
12	18 24	41 36	53819	7	46181	56576	8	43424	02757	1	97243	48
13	18 16	41 44	53854	7	46146	56615	8	43385	02762	1	97238	47
14	18 8	41 52	53888	8	46112	56654	9	43346	02766	1	97234	46
15	9 18 0	2 42 0	9.53922	8	10.46078	9.56693	10	10.43307	10.02771	1	9.97229	45
16	17 52	42 8	53957	9	46043	56732	10	43268	02776	1	97224	44
17	17 44	42 16	53991	10	46009	56771	11	43229	02780	1	97220	43
18	17 36	42 24	54025	10	45975	56810	12	43190	02785	1	97215	42
19	17 28	42 32	54059	11	45941	56849	12	43151	02790	1	97210	41
20	9 17 20	2 42 40	9.54093	11	10.45907	9.56887	13	10.43113	10.02794	2	9.97206	40
21	17 12	42 48	54127	12	45873	56926	13	43074	02799	2	97201	39
22	17 4	42 56	54161	12	45839	56965	14	43035	02804	2	97196	38
23	16 56	43 4	54195	13	45805	57004	15	42996	02808	2	97192	37
24	16 48	43 12	54229	14	45771	57042	15	42958	02813	2	97187	36
25	9 16 40	2 43 20	9.54263	14	10.45737	9.57081	16	10.42919	10.02818	2	9.97182	35
26	16 32	43 28	54297	15	45703	57120	17	42880	02822	2	97178	34
27	16 24	43 36	54331	15	45669	57158	17	42842	02827	2	97173	33
28	16 16	43 44	54365	16	45635	57197	18	42803	02832	2	97168	32
29	16 8	43 52	54399	16	45601	57235	19	42765	02837	2	97163	31
30	9 16 0	2 44 0	9.54433	17	10.45567	9.57274	19	10.42726	10.02841	2	9.97159	30
31	15 52	44 8	54466	17	45534	57312	20	42688	02846	2	97154	29
32	15 44	44 16	54500	18	45500	57351	21	42649	02851	3	97149	28
33	15 36	44 24	54534	19	45466	57389	21	42611	02855	3	97145	27
34	15 28	44 32	54567	19	45433	57428	22	42572	02860	3	97140	26
35	9 15 20	2 44 40	9.54601	20	10.45399	9.57466	22	10.42534	10.02865	3	9.97135	25
36	15 12	44 48	54635	20	45365	57504	23	42496	02870	3	97130	24
37	15 4	44 56	54668	21	45332	57543	24	42457	02874	3	97126	23
38	14 56	45 4	54702	21	45298	57581	24	42419	02879	3	97121	22
39	14 48	45 12	54735	22	45265	57619	25	42381	02884	3	97116	21
40	9 14 40	2 45 20	9.54769	23	10.45231	9.57658	26	10.42342	10.02889	3	9.97111	20
41	14 32	45 28	54802	23	45198	57696	26	42304	02893	3	97107	19
42	14 24	45 36	54836	24	45164	57734	27	42266	02898	3	97102	18
43	14 16	45 44	54869	24	45131	57772	28	42228	02903	3	97097	17
44	14 8	45 52	54903	25	45097	57810	28	42190	02908	3	97092	16
45	9 14 0	2 46 0	9.54936	25	10.45064	9.57849	29	10.42151	10.02913	4	9.97087	15
46	13 52	46 8	54969	26	45031	57887	30	42113	02917	4	97083	14
47	13 44	46 16	55003	26	44997	57925	30	42075	02922	4	97078	13
48	13 36	46 24	55036	27	44964	57963	31	42037	02927	4	97073	12
49	13 28	46 32	55069	28	44931	58001	31	41999	02932	4	97068	11
50	9 13 20	2 46 40	9.55102	28	10.44898	9.58039	32	10.41961	10.02937	4	9.97063	10
51	13 12	46 48	55136	29	44864	58077	33	41923	02941	4	97059	9
52	13 4	46 56	55169	29	44831	58115	33	41885	02946	4	97054	8
53	12 56	47 4	55202	30	44798	58153	34	41847	02951	4	97049	7
54	12 48	47 12	55235	30	44765	58191	35	41809	02956	4	97044	6
55	9 12 40	2 47 20	9.55268	31	10.44732	9.58229	35	10.41771	10.02961	4	9.97039	5
56	12 32	47 28	55301	32	44699	58267	36	41733	02965	4	97035	4
57	12 24	47 36	55334	32	44666	58304	37	41696	02970	4	97030	3
58	12 16	47 44	55367	33	44633	58342	37	41658	02975	5	97025	2
59	12 8	47 52	55400	33	44600	58380	38	41620	02980	5	97020	1
60	12 0	48 0	55433	34	44567	58418	39	41582	02985	5	97015	0
M	Hour P.M.	Hour A.M.	Cosine.	Diff.	Secant.	Cotangent	Diff.	Tangent.	Cosecant.	Diff.	Sine.	M
			A		A	B		B	C		C	

110° 69°

Seconds of time		1ˢ	2ˢ	3ˢ	4ˢ	5ˢ	6ˢ	7ˢ
Prop. parts of cols.	A	4	8	13	17	21	25	30
	B	5	10	14	19	24	29	34
	C	1	1	2	2	3	4	4

TABLE XXVII.

S′. Log. Sines, Tangents, and Secants. G′.

21°			A		A	B		B	C		C 158°	
M	Hour A.M.	Hour P.M.	Sine.	Diff.	Cosecant.	Tangent.	Diff.	Cotangent	Secant.	Diff.	Cosine.	M
0	9 12 0	2 48 0	9.55433	0	10.44567	9.58418	0	10.41582	10.02985	0	9.97015	60
1	11 52	48 8	55466	1	44534	58455	1	41545	02990	0	97010	59
2	11 44	48 16	55499	1	44501	58493	1	41507	02995	0	97005	58
3	11 36	48 24	55532	2	44468	58531	2	41469	02999	0	97001	57
4	11 28	48 32	55564	2	44436	58569	2	41431	03004	0	96996	56
5	9 11 20	2 48 40	9.55597	3	10.44403	9.58606	3	10.41394	10.03009	0	9.96991	55
6	11 12	48 48	55630	3	44370	58644	4	41356	03014	0	96986	54
7	11 4	48 56	55663	4	44337	58681	4	41319	03019	1	96981	53
8	10 56	49 4	55695	4	44305	58719	5	41281	03024	1	96976	52
9	10 48	49 12	55728	5	44272	58757	6	41243	03029	1	96971	51
10	9 10 40	2 49 20	9.55761	5	10.44239	9.58794	6	10.41206	10.03034	1	9.96966	50
11	10 32	49 28	55793	6	44207	58832	7	41168	03038	1	96962	49
12	10 24	49 36	55826	6	44174	58869	7	41131	03043	1	96957	48
13	10 16	49 44	55858	7	44142	58907	8	41093	03048	1	96952	47
14	10 8	49 52	55891	7	44109	58944	9	41056	03053	1	96947	46
15	9 10 0	2 50 0	9.55923	8	10.44077	9.58981	9	10.41019	10.03058	1	9.96942	45
16	9 52	50 8	55956	9	44044	59019	10	40981	03063	1	96937	44
17	9 44	50 16	55988	9	44012	59056	10	40944	03068	1	96932	43
18	9 36	50 24	56021	10	43979	59094	11	40906	03073	1	96927	42
19	9 28	50 32	56053	10	43947	59131	12	40869	03078	2	96922	41
20	9 9 20	2 50 40	9.56085	11	10.43915	9.59168	12	10.40832	10.03083	2	9.96917	40
21	9 12	50 48	56118	11	43882	59205	13	40795	03088	2	96912	39
22	9 4	50 56	56150	12	43850	59243	14	40757	03093	2	96907	38
23	8 56	51 4	56182	12	43818	59280	14	40720	03097	2	96903	37
24	8 48	51 12	56215	13	43785	59317	15	40683	03102	2	96898	36
25	9 8 40	2 51 20	9.56247	13	10.43753	9.59354	15	10.40646	10.03107	2	9.96893	35
26	8 32	51 28	56279	14	43721	59391	16	40609	03112	2	96888	34
27	8 24	51 36	56311	14	43689	59429	17	40571	03117	2	96883	33
28	8 16	51 44	56343	15	43657	59466	17	40534	03122	2	96878	32
29	8 8	51 52	56375	16	43625	59503	18	40497	03127	2	96873	31
30	9 8 0	2 52 0	9.56408	16	10.43592	9.59540	19	10.40460	10.03132	2	9.96868	30
31	7 52	52 8	56440	17	43560	59577	19	40423	03137	3	96863	29
32	7 44	52 16	56472	17	43528	59614	20	40386	03142	3	96858	28
33	7 36	52 24	56504	18	43496	59651	20	40349	03147	3	96853	27
34	7 28	52 32	56536	18	43464	59688	21	40312	03152	3	96848	26
35	9 7 20	2 52 40	9.56568	19	10.43432	9.59725	22	10.40275	10.03157	3	9.96843	25
36	7 12	52 48	56599	19	43401	59762	22	40238	03162	3	96838	24
37	7 4	52 56	56631	20	43369	59799	23	40201	03167	3	96833	23
38	6 56	53 4	56663	20	43337	59835	23	40165	03172	3	96828	22
39	6 48	53 12	56695	21	43305	59872	24	40128	03177	3	96823	21
40	9 6 40	2 53 20	9.56727	21	10.43273	9.59909	25	10.40091	10.03182	3	9.96818	20
41	6 32	53 28	56759	22	43241	59946	25	40054	03187	3	96813	19
42	6 24	53 36	56790	22	43210	59983	26	40017	03192	3	96808	18
43	6 16	53 44	56822	23	43178	60019	27	39981	03197	4	96803	17
44	6 8	53 52	56854	24	43146	60056	27	39944	03202	4	96798	16
45	9 6 0	2 54 0	9.56886	24	10.43114	9.60093	28	10.39907	10.03207	4	9.96793	15
46	5 52	54 8	56917	25	43083	60130	28	39870	03212	4	96788	14
47	5 44	54 16	56949	25	43051	60166	29	39834	03217	4	96783	13
48	5 36	54 24	56980	26	43020	60203	30	39797	03222	4	96778	12
49	5 28	54 32	57012	26	42988	60240	30	39760	03228	4	96772	11
50	9 5 20	2 54 40	9.57044	27	10.42956	9.60276	31	10.39724	10.03233	4	9.96767	10
51	5 12	54 48	57075	27	42925	60313	31	39687	03238	4	96762	9
52	5 4	54 56	57107	28	42893	60349	32	39651	03243	4	96757	8
53	4 56	55 4	57138	28	42862	60386	33	39614	03248	4	96752	7
54	4 48	55 12	57169	29	42831	60422	33	39578	03253	4	96747	6
55	9 4 40	2 55 20	9.57201	29	10.42799	9.60459	34	10.39541	10.03258	5	9.96742	5
56	4 32	55 28	57232	30	42768	60495	35	39505	03263	5	96737	4
57	4 24	55 36	57264	30	42736	60532	35	39468	03268	5	96732	3
58	4 16	55 44	57295	31	42705	60568	36	39432	03273	5	96727	2
59	4 8	55 52	57326	32	42674	60605	36	39395	03278	5	96722	1
60	4 0	56 0	57358	32	42642	60641	37	39359	03283	5	96717	0
M	Hour P.M.	Hour A.M.	Cosine.	Diff.	Secant.	Cotangent	Diff.	Tangent.	Cosecant.	Diff.	Sine.	M
111°			A		A	B		B	C		C	68°

Seconds of time		1ˢ	2ˢ	3ˢ	4ˢ	5ˢ	6ˢ	7ˢ
Prop. parts of cols.	A	4	8	12	16	20	24	28
	B	5	9	14	19	23	28	32
	C	1	1	2	2	3	4	4

TABLE XXVII.

S′. Log. Sines, Tangents, and Secants. G′.

22° A A B B C C 157°

M	Hour A.M.	Hour P.M.	Sine. A	Diff.	Cosecant. A	Tangent. B	Diff.	Cotangent B	Secant. C	Diff.	Cosine. C	M
0	9 4 0	2 56 0	9.57358	0	10.42642	9.60641	0	10.39359	10.03283	0	9.96717	60
1	3 52	56 8	57389	1	42611	60677	1	39323	03289	0	96711	59
2	3 44	56 16	57420	1	42580	60714	1	39286	03294	0	96706	58
3	3 36	56 24	57451	2	42549	60750	2	39250	03299	0	96701	57
4	3 28	56 32	57482	2	42518	60786	2	39214	03304	0	96696	56
5	9 3 20	2 56 40	9.57514	3	10.42486	9.60823	3	10.39177	10.03309	0	9.96691	55
6	3 12	56 48	57545	3	42455	60859	4	39141	03314	1	96686	54
7	3 4	56 56	57576	4	42424	60895	4	39105	03319	1	96681	53
8	2 56	57 4	57607	4	42393	60931	5	39069	03324	1	96676	52
9	2 48	57 12	57638	5	42362	60967	5	39033	03330	1	96670	51
10	9 2 40	2 57 20	9.57669	5	10.42331	9.61004	6	10.38996	10.03335	1	9.96665	50
11	2 32	57 28	57700	6	42300	61040	7	38960	03340	1	96660	49
12	2 24	57 36	57731	6	42269	61076	7	38924	03345	1	96655	48
13	2 16	57 44	57762	7	42238	61112	8	38888	03350	1	96650	47
14	2 8	57 52	57793	7	42207	61148	8	38852	03355	1	96645	46
15	9 2 0	2 58 0	9.57824	8	10.42176	9.61184	9	10.38816	10.03360	1	9.96640	45
16	1 52	58 8	57855	8	42145	61220	10	38780	03366	1	96634	44
17	1 44	58 16	57885	9	42115	61256	10	38744	03371	1	96629	43
18	1 36	58 24	57916	9	42084	61292	11	38708	03376	2	96624	42
19	1 28	58 32	57947	10	42053	61328	11	38672	03381	2	96619	41
20	9 1 20	2 58 40	9.57978	10	10.42022	9.61364	12	10.38636	10.03386	2	9.96614	40
21	1 12	58 48	58008	11	41992	61400	13	38600	03392	2	96608	39
22	1 4	58 56	58039	11	41961	61436	13	38564	03397	2	96603	38
23	0 56	59 4	58070	12	41930	61472	14	38528	03402	2	96598	37
24	0 48	59 12	58101	12	41899	61508	14	38492	03407	2	96593	36
25	9 0 40	2 59 20	9.58131	13	10.41869	9.61544	15	10.38456	10.03412	2	9.96588	35
26	0 32	59 28	58162	13	41838	61579	15	38421	03418	2	96582	34
27	0 24	59 36	58192	14	41808	61615	16	38385	03423	2	96577	33
28	0 16	59 44	58223	14	41777	61651	17	38349	03428	2	96572	32
29	0 8	59 52	58253	15	41747	61687	17	38313	03433	3	96567	31
30	9 0 0	3 0 0	9.58284	15	10.41716	9.61722	18	10.38278	10.03438	3	9.96562	30
31	8 59 52	0 8	58314	16	41686	61758	18	38242	03444	3	96556	29
32	59 44	0 16	58345	16	41655	61794	19	38206	03449	3	96551	28
33	59 36	0 24	58375	17	41625	61830	20	38170	03454	3	96546	27
34	59 28	0 32	58406	17	41594	61865	20	38135	03459	3	96541	26
35	8 59 20	3 0 40	9.58436	18	10.41564	9.61901	21	10.38099	10.03465	3	9.96535	25
36	59 12	0 48	58467	18	41533	61936	21	38064	03470	3	96530	24
37	59 4	0 56	58497	19	41503	61972	22	38028	03475	3	96525	23
38	58 56	1 4	58527	19	41473	62008	23	37992	03480	3	96520	22
39	58 48	1 12	58557	20	41443	62043	23	37957	03486	3	96514	21
40	8 58 40	3 1 20	9.58588	20	10.41412	9.62079	24	10.37921	10.03491	3	9.96509	20
41	58 32	1 28	58618	21	41382	62114	24	37886	03496	4	96504	19
42	58 24	1 36	58648	21	41352	62150	25	37850	03502	4	96498	18
43	58 16	1 44	58678	22	41322	62185	26	37815	03507	4	96493	17
44	58 8	1 52	58709	22	41291	62221	26	37779	03512	4	96488	16
45	8 58 0	3 2 0	9.58739	23	10.41261	9.62256	27	10.37744	10.03517	4	9.96483	15
46	57 52	2 8	58769	23	41231	62292	27	37708	03523	4	96477	14
47	57 44	2 16	58799	24	41201	62327	28	37673	03528	4	96472	13
48	57 36	2 24	58829	24	41171	62362	29	37638	03533	4	96467	12
49	57 28	2 32	58859	25	41141	62398	29	37602	03539	4	96461	11
50	8 57 20	3 2 40	9.58889	25	10.41111	9.62433	30	10.37567	10.03544	4	9.96456	10
51	57 12	2 48	58919	26	41081	62468	30	37532	03549	4	96451	9
52	57 4	2 56	58949	26	41051	62504	31	37496	03555	5	96445	8
53	56 56	3 4	58979	27	41021	62539	32	37461	03560	5	96440	7
54	56 48	3 12	59009	27	40991	62574	32	37426	03565	5	96435	6
55	8 56 40	3 3 20	9.59039	28	10.40961	9.62609	33	10.37391	10.03571	5	9.96429	5
56	56 32	3 28	59069	28	40931	62645	33	37355	03576	5	96424	4
57	56 24	3 36	59098	29	40902	62680	34	37320	03581	5	96419	3
58	56 16	3 44	59128	29	40872	62715	35	37285	03587	5	96413	2
59	56 8	3 52	59158	30	40842	62750	35	37250	03592	5	96408	1
60	56 0	4 0	59188	31	40812	62785	36	37215	03597	5	96403	0
M	Hour P.M.	Hour A.M.	Cosine. A	Diff.	Secant. A	Cotangent B	Diff.	Tangent. B	Cosecant. C	Diff.	Sine. C	M

112° A A B B C C 67°

Seconds of time		1ˢ	2ˢ	3ˢ	4ˢ	5ˢ	6ˢ	7ˢ
Prop. parts of cols.	A	4	8	11	15	19	23	27
	B	4	9	13	18	22	27	31
	C	1	1	2	3	3	4	5

TABLE XXVII.

Log. Sines, Tangents, and Secants.

S'. G'.

23° A A B B C C 156°

M	Hour A.M.	Hour P.M.	Sine.	Diff.	Cosecant.	Tangent.	Diff.	Cotangent	Secant.	Diff.	Cosine.	M
0	8 56 0	3 4 0	9.59188	0	10.40812	9.62785	0	10.37215	10.03597	0	9.96403	60
1	55 52	4 8	59218	0	40782	62820	1	37180	03603	0	96397	59
2	55 44	4 16	59247	1	40753	62855	1	37145	03608	0	96392	58
3	55 36	4 24	59277	1	40723	62890	2	37110	03613	0	96387	57
4	55 28	4 32	59307	2	40693	62926	2	37074	03619	0	96381	56
5	8 55 20	3 4 40	9.59336	2	10.40664	9.62961	3	10.37039	10.03624	0	9.96376	55
6	55 12	4 48	59366	3	40634	62996	3	37004	03630	1	96370	54
7	55 4	4 56	59396	3	40604	63031	4	36969	03635	1	96365	53
8	54 56	5 4	59425	4	40575	63066	5	36934	03640	1	96360	52
9	54 48	5 12	59455	4	40545	63101	5	36899	03646	1	96354	51
10	8 54 40	3 5 20	9.59484	5	10.40516	9.63135	6	10.36865	10.03651	1	9.96349	50
11	54 32	5 28	59514	5	40486	63170	6	36830	03657	1	96343	49
12	54 24	5 36	59543	6	40457	63205	7	36795	03662	1	96338	48
13	54 16	5 44	59573	6	40427	63240	7	36760	03667	1	96333	47
14	54 8	5 52	59602	7	40398	63275	8	36725	03673	1	96327	46
15	8 54 0	3 6 0	9.59632	7	10.40368	9.63310	9	10.36690	10.03678	1	9.96322	45
16	53 52	6 8	59661	8	40339	63345	9	36655	03684	1	96316	44
17	53 44	6 16	59690	8	40310	63379	10	36621	03689	2	96311	43
18	53 36	6 24	59720	9	40280	63414	10	36586	03695	2	96305	42
19	53 28	6 32	59749	9	40251	63449	11	36551	03700	2	96300	41
20	8 53 20	3 6 40	9.59778	10	10.40222	9.63484	12	10.36516	10.03706	2	9.96294	40
21	53 12	6 48	59808	10	40192	63519	12	36481	03711	2	96289	39
22	53 4	6 56	59837	11	40163	63553	13	36447	03716	2	96284	38
23	52 56	7 4	59866	11	40134	63588	13	36412	03722	2	96278	37
24	52 48	7 12	59895	12	40105	63623	14	36377	03727	2	96273	36
25	8 52 40	3 7 20	9.59924	12	10.40076	9.63657	14	10.36343	10.03733	2	9.96267	35
26	52 32	7 28	59954	13	40046	63692	15	36308	03738	2	96262	34
27	52 24	7 36	59983	13	40017	63726	16	36274	03744	2	96256	33
28	52 16	7 44	60012	14	39988	63761	16	36239	03749	3	96251	32
29	52 8	7 52	60041	14	39959	63796	17	36204	03755	3	96245	31
30	8 52 0	3 8 0	9.60070	15	10.39930	9.63830	17	10.36170	10.03760	3	9.96240	30
31	51 52	8 8	60099	15	39901	63865	18	36135	03766	3	96234	29
32	51 44	8 16	60128	15	39872	63899	18	36101	03771	3	96229	28
33	51 36	8 24	60157	16	39843	63934	19	36066	03777	3	96223	27
34	51 28	8 32	60186	16	39814	63968	20	36032	03782	3	96218	26
35	8 51 20	3 8 40	9.60215	17	10.39785	9.64003	20	10.35997	10.03788	3	9.96212	25
36	51 12	8 48	60244	17	39756	64037	21	35963	03793	3	96207	24
37	51 4	8 56	60273	18	39727	64072	21	35928	03799	3	96201	23
38	50 56	9 4	60302	18	39698	64106	22	35894	03804	3	96196	22
39	50 48	9 12	60331	19	39669	64140	22	35860	03810	4	96190	21
40	8 50 40	3 9 20	9.60359	19	10.39641	9.64175	23	10.35825	10.03815	4	9.96185	20
41	50 32	9 28	60388	20	39612	64209	24	35791	03821	4	96179	19
42	50 24	9 36	60417	20	39583	64243	24	35757	03826	4	96174	18
43	50 16	9 44	60446	21	39554	64278	25	35722	03832	4	96168	17
44	50 8	9 52	60474	21	39526	64312	25	35688	03838	4	96162	16
45	8 50 0	3 10 0	9.60503	22	10.39497	9.64346	26	10.35654	10.03843	4	9.96157	15
46	49 52	10 8	60532	22	39468	64381	26	35619	03849	4	96151	14
47	49 44	10 16	60561	23	39439	64415	27	35585	03854	4	96146	13
48	49 36	10 24	60589	23	39411	64449	28	35551	03860	4	96140	12
49	49 28	10 32	60618	24	39382	64483	28	35517	03865	4	96135	11
50	8 49 20	3 10 40	9.60646	24	10.39354	9.64517	29	10.35483	10.03871	5	9.96129	10
51	49 12	10 48	60675	25	39325	64552	29	35448	03877	5	96123	9
52	49 4	10 56	60704	25	39296	64586	30	35414	03882	5	96118	8
53	48 56	11 4	60732	26	39268	64620	31	35380	03888	5	96112	7
54	48 48	11 12	60761	26	39239	64654	31	35346	03893	5	96107	6
55	8 48 40	3 11 20	9.60789	27	10.39211	9.64688	32	10.35312	10.03899	5	9.96101	5
56	48 32	11 28	60818	27	39182	64722	32	35278	03905	5	96095	4
57	48 24	11 36	60846	28	39154	64756	33	35244	03910	5	96090	3
58	48 16	11 44	60875	28	39125	64790	33	35210	03916	5	96084	2
59	48 8	11 52	60903	29	39097	64824	34	35176	03921	5	96079	1
60	48 0	12 0	60931	29	39069	64858	35	35142	03927	6	96073	0
M	Hour P.M.	Hour A.M.	Cosine.	Diff.	Secant.	Cotangent	Diff.	Tangent.	Cosecant.	Diff.	Sine.	M

113° A A B B C C 66°

Seconds of time		1s	2s	3s	4s	5s	6s	7s
Prop. parts of cols.	A	4	7	11	15	18	22	25
	B	4	9	13	17	22	26	31
	C	1	1	2	3	3	4	5

TABLE XXVII.

Log. Sines, Tangents, and Secants.

S′ 24° | A | A | B | B | C | C 155° G′.

M	Hour A.M.	Hour P.M.	Sine.	Diff.	Cosecant.	Tangent.	Diff.	Cotangent	Secant.	Diff.	Cosine.	M
0	8 48 0	3 12 0	9.60931	0	10.39069	9.64858	0	10.35142	10.03927	0	9.96073	60
1	47 52	12 8	60960	0	39040	64892	1	35108	03933	0	96067	59
2	47 44	12 16	60988	1	39012	64926	1	35074	03938	0	96062	58
3	47 36	12 24	61016	1	38984	64960	2	35040	03944	0	96056	57
4	47 28	12 32	61045	2	38955	64994	2	35006	03950	0	96050	56
5	8 47 20	3 12 40	9.61073	2	10.38927	9.65028	3	10.34972	10.03955	0	9.96045	55
6	47 12	12 48	61101	3	38899	65062	3	34938	03961	1	96039	54
7	47 4	12 56	61129	3	38871	65096	4	34904	03966	1	96034	53
8	46 56	13 4	61158	4	38842	65130	4	34870	03972	1	96028	52
9	46 48	13 12	61186	4	38814	65164	5	34836	03978	1	96022	51
10	8 46 40	3 13 20	9.61214	5	10.38786	9.65197	6	10.34803	10.03983	1	9.96017	50
11	46 32	13 28	61242	5	38758	65231	6	34769	03989	1	96011	49
12	46 24	13 36	61270	6	38730	65265	7	34735	03995	1	96005	48
13	46 16	13 44	61298	6	38702	65299	7	34701	04000	1	96000	47
14	46 8	13 52	61326	6	38674	65333	8	34667	04006	1	95994	46
15	8 46 0	3 14 0	9.61354	7	10.38646	9.65366	8	10.34634	10.04012	1	9.95988	45
16	45 52	14 8	61382	7	38618	65400	9	34600	04018	2	95982	44
17	45 44	14 16	61411	8	38589	65434	9	34566	04023	2	95977	43
18	45 36	14 24	61438	8	38562	65467	10	34533	04029	2	95971	42
19	45 28	14 32	61466	9	38534	65501	11	34499	04035	2	95965	41
20	8 45 20	3 14 40	9.61494	9	10.38506	9.65535	11	10.34465	10.04040	2	9.95960	40
21	45 12	14 48	61522	10	38478	65568	12	34432	04046	2	95954	39
22	45 4	14 56	61550	10	38450	65602	12	34398	04052	2	95948	38
23	44 56	15 4	61578	11	38422	65636	13	34364	04058	2	95942	37
24	44 48	15 12	61606	11	38394	65669	13	34331	04063	2	95937	36
25	8 44 40	3 15 20	9.61634	12	10.38366	9.65703	14	10.34297	10.04069	2	9.95931	35
26	44 32	15 28	61662	12	38338	65736	15	34264	04075	2	95925	34
27	44 24	15 36	61689	12	38311	65770	15	34230	04080	3	95920	33
28	44 16	15 44	61717	13	38283	65803	16	34197	04086	3	95914	32
29	44 8	15 52	61745	13	38255	65837	16	34163	04092	3	95908	31
30	8 44 0	3 16 0	9.61773	14	10.38227	9.65870	17	10.34130	10.04098	3	9.95902	30
31	43 52	16 8	61800	14	38200	65904	17	34096	04103	3	95897	29
32	43 44	16 16	61828	15	38172	65937	18	34063	04109	3	95891	28
33	43 36	16 24	61856	15	38144	65971	18	34029	04115	3	95885	27
34	43 28	16 32	61883	16	38117	66004	19	33996	04121	3	95879	26
35	8 43 20	3 16 40	9.61911	16	10.38089	9.66038	20	10.33962	10.04127	3	9.95873	25
36	43 12	16 48	61939	17	38061	66071	20	33929	04132	3	95868	24
37	43 4	16 56	61966	17	38034	66104	21	33896	04138	4	95862	23
38	42 56	17 4	61994	18	38006	66138	21	33862	04144	4	95856	22
39	42 48	17 12	62021	18	37979	66171	22	33829	04150	4	95850	21
40	8 42 40	3 17 20	9.62049	18	10.37951	9.66204	22	10.33796	10.04156	4	9.95844	20
41	42 32	17 28	62076	19	37924	66238	23	33762	04161	4	95839	19
42	42 24	17 36	62104	19	37896	66271	23	33729	04167	4	95833	18
43	42 16	17 44	62131	20	37869	66304	24	33696	04173	4	95827	17
44	42 8	17 52	62159	20	37841	66337	25	33663	04179	4	95821	16
45	8 42 0	3 18 0	9.62186	21	10.37814	9.66371	25	10.33629	10.04185	4	9.95815	15
46	41 52	18 8	62214	21	37786	66404	26	33596	04190	4	95810	14
47	41 44	18 16	62241	22	37759	66437	26	33563	04196	5	95804	13
48	41 36	18 24	62268	22	37732	66470	27	33530	04202	5	95798	12
49	41 28	18 32	62296	23	37704	66503	27	33497	04208	5	95792	11
50	8 41 20	3 18 40	9.62323	23	10.37677	9.66537	28	10.33463	10.04214	5	9.95786	10
51	41 12	18 48	62350	24	37650	66570	28	33430	04220	5	95780	9
52	41 4	18 56	62377	24	37623	66603	29	33397	04225	5	95775	8
53	40 56	19 4	62405	24	37595	66636	30	33364	04231	5	95769	7
54	40 48	19 12	62432	25	37568	66669	30	33331	04237	5	95763	6
55	8 40 40	3 19 20	9.62459	25	10.37541	9.66702	31	10.33298	10.04243	5	9.95757	5
56	40 32	19 28	62486	26	37514	66735	31	33265	04249	5	95751	4
57	40 24	19 36	62513	26	37487	66768	32	33232	04255	5	95745	3
58	40 16	19 44	62541	27	37459	66801	32	33199	04261	6	95739	2
59	40 8	19 52	62568	27	37432	66834	33	33166	04267	6	95733	1
60	40 0	20 0	62595	28	37405	66867	33	33133	04272	6	95728	0
M	Hour P.M.	Hour A.M.	Cosine.	Diff.	Secant.	Cotangent	Diff.	Tangent.	Cosecant.	Diff.	Sine.	M

114° | A | A | B | B | C | C 65°

Seconds of time		1ˢ	2ˢ	3ˢ	4ˢ	5ˢ	6ˢ	7ˢ
Prop. parts of cols.	A	3	7	10	14	17	21	24
	B	4	8	13	17	21	25	29
	C	1	1	2	3	4	4	5

TABLE XXVII.

S′. Log. Sines, Tangents, and Secants. G′.

25°			A		A	B		B	C		C	154°
M	Hour A.M.	Hour P.M.	Sine.	Diff.	Cosecant.	Tangent.	Diff.	Cotangent	Secant.	Diff.	Cosine.	M
0	8 40 0	3 20 0	9.62595	0	10.37405	9.66867	0	10.33133	10.04272	0	9.95728	60
1	39 52	20 8	62622	0	37378	66900	1	33100	04278	0	95722	59
2	39 44	20 16	62649	1	37351	66933	1	33067	04284	0	95716	58
3	39 36	20 24	62676	1	37324	66966	2	33034	04290	0	95710	57
4	39 28	20 32	62703	2	37297	66999	2	33001	04296	0	95704	56
5	8 39 20	3 20 40	9.62730	2	10.37270	9.67032	3	10.32968	10.04302	1	9.95698	55
6	39 12	20 48	62757	3	37243	67065	3	32935	04308	1	95692	54
7	39 4	20 56	62784	3	37216	67098	4	32902	04314	1	95686	53
8	38 56	21 4	62811	4	37189	67131	4	32869	04320	1	95680	52
9	38 48	21 12	62838	4	37162	67163	5	32837	04326	1	95674	51
10	8 38 40	3 21 20	9.62865	4	10.37135	9.67196	5	10.32804	10.04332	1	9.95668	50
11	38 32	21 28	62892	5	37108	67229	6	32771	04337	1	95663	49
12	38 24	21 36	62918	5	37082	67262	7	32738	04343	1	95657	48
13	38 16	21 44	62945	6	37055	67295	7	32705	04349	1	95651	47
14	38 8	21 52	62972	6	37028	67327	8	32673	04355	1	95645	46
15	8 38 0	3 22 0	9.62999	7	10.37001	9.67360	8	10.32640	10.04361	2	9.95639	45
16	37 52	22 8	63026	7	36974	67393	9	32607	04367	2	95633	44
17	37 44	22 16	63052	8	36948	67426	9	32574	04373	2	95627	43
18	37 36	22 24	63079	8	36921	67458	10	32542	04379	2	95621	42
19	37 28	22 32	63106	8	36894	67491	10	32509	04385	2	95615	41
20	8 37 20	3 22 40	9.63133	9	10.36867	9.67524	11	10.32476	10.04391	2	9.95609	40
21	37 12	22 48	63159	9	36841	67556	11	32444	04397	2	95603	39
22	37 4	22 56	63186	10	36814	67589	12	32411	04403	2	95597	38
23	36 56	23 4	63213	10	36787	67622	12	32378	04409	2	95591	37
24	36 48	23 12	63239	11	36761	67654	13	32346	04415	2	95585	36
25	8 36 40	3 23 20	9.63266	11	10.36734	9.67687	14	10.32313	10.04421	3	9.95579	35
26	36 32	23 28	63292	11	36708	67719	14	32281	04427	3	95573	34
27	36 24	23 36	63319	12	36681	67752	15	32248	04433	3	95567	33
28	36 16	23 44	63345	12	36655	67785	15	32215	04439	3	95561	32
29	36 8	23 52	63372	13	36628	67817	16	32183	04445	3	95555	31
30	8 36 0	3 24 0	9.63398	13	10.36602	9.67850	16	10.32150	10.04451	3	9.95549	30
31	35 52	24 8	63425	14	36575	67882	17	32118	04457	3	95543	29
32	35 44	24 16	63451	14	36549	67915	17	32085	04463	3	95537	28
33	35 36	24 24	63478	15	36522	67947	18	32053	04469	3	95531	27
34	35 28	24 32	63504	15	36496	67980	18	32020	04475	3	95525	26
35	8 35 20	3 24 40	9.63531	15	10.36469	9.68012	19	10.31988	10.04481	4	9.95519	25
36	35 12	24 48	63557	16	36443	68044	20	31956	04487	4	95513	24
37	35 4	24 56	63583	16	36417	68077	20	31923	04493	4	95507	23
38	34 56	25 4	63610	17	36390	68109	21	31891	04500	4	95500	22
39	34 48	25 12	63636	17	36364	68142	21	31858	04506	4	95494	21
40	8 34 40	3 25 20	9.63662	18	10.36338	9.68174	22	10.31826	10.04512	4	9.95488	20
41	34 32	25 28	63689	18	36311	68206	22	31794	04518	4	95482	19
42	34 24	25 36	63715	19	36285	68239	23	31761	04524	4	95476	18
43	34 16	25 44	63741	19	36259	68271	23	31729	04530	4	95470	17
44	34 8	25 52	63767	19	36233	68303	24	31697	04536	4	95464	16
45	8 34 0	3 26 0	9.63794	20	10.36206	9.68336	24	10.31664	10.04542	5	9.95458	15
46	33 52	26 8	63820	20	36180	68368	25	31632	04548	5	95452	14
47	33 44	26 16	63846	21	36154	68400	25	31600	04554	5	95446	13
48	33 36	26 24	63872	21	36128	68432	26	31568	04560	5	95440	12
49	33 28	26 32	63898	22	36102	68465	27	31535	04566	5	95434	11
50	8 33 20	3 26 40	9.63924	22	10.36076	9.68497	27	10.31503	10.04573	5	9.95427	10
51	33 12	26 48	63950	23	36050	68529	28	31471	04579	5	95421	9
52	33 4	26 56	63976	23	36024	68561	28	31439	04585	5	95415	8
53	32 56	27 4	64002	23	35998	68593	29	31407	04591	5	95409	7
54	32 48	27 12	64028	24	35972	68626	29	31374	04597	5	95403	6
55	8 32 40	3 27 20	9.64054	24	10.35946	9.68658	30	10.31342	10.04603	6	9.95397	5
56	32 32	27 28	64080	25	35920	68690	30	31310	04609	6	95391	4
57	32 24	27 36	64106	25	35894	68722	31	31278	04616	6	95384	3
58	32 16	27 44	64132	26	35868	68754	31	31246	04622	6	95378	2
59	32 8	27 52	64158	26	35842	68786	32	31214	04628	6	95372	1
60	32 0	28 0	64184	26	35816	68818	33	31182	04634	6	95366	0
M	Hour P.M.	Hour A.M.	Cosine.	Diff.	Secant.	Cotangent	Diff.	Tangent.	Cosecant.	Diff.	Sine.	M
115°			A		A	B		B	C		C	64°

Seconds of time		1ˢ	2ˢ	3ˢ	4ˢ	5ˢ	6ˢ	7ˢ
Prop. parts of cols.	A	3	7	10	13	17	20	23
	B	4	8	12	16	20	24	28
	C	1	2	2	3	4	5	5

TABLE XXVII.

Log. Sines, Tangents, and Secants.

S'. 26°			A		A	B		B	C		C	G'. 153°
M	Hour A.M.	Hour P.M.	Sine.	Diff.	Cosecant.	Tangent.	Diff.	Cotangent	Secant.	Diff.	Cosine.	M
0	8 32 0	3 28 0	9.64184	0	10.35816	9.68818	0	10.31182	10.04634	0	9.95366	60
1	31 52	28 8	64210	0	35790	68850	1	31150	04640	0	95360	59
2	31 44	28 16	64236	1	35764	68882	1	31118	04646	0	95354	58
3	31 36	28 24	64262	1	35738	68914	2	31086	04652	0	95348	57
4	31 28	28 32	64288	2	35712	68946	2	31054	04659	0	95341	56
5	8 31 20	3 28 40	9.64313	2	10.35687	9.68978	3	10.31022	10.04665	1	9.95335	55
6	31 12	28 48	64339	3	35661	69010	3	30990	04671	1	95329	54
7	31 4	28 56	64365	3	35635	69042	4	30958	04677	1	95323	53
8	30 56	29 4	64391	3	35609	69074	4	30926	04683	1	95317	52
9	30 48	29 12	64417	4	35583	69106	5	30894	04690	1	95310	51
10	8 30 40	3 29 20	9.64442	4	10.35558	9.69138	5	10.30862	10.04696	1	9.95304	50
11	30 32	29 28	64468	5	35532	69170	6	30830	04702	1	95298	49
12	30 24	29 36	64494	5	35506	69202	6	30798	04708	1	95292	48
13	30 16	29 44	64519	5	35481	69234	7	30766	04714	1	95286	47
14	30 8	29 52	64545	6	35455	69266	7	30734	04721	1	95279	46
15	8 30 0	3 30 0	9.64571	6	10.35429	9.69298	8	10.30702	10.04727	2	9.95273	45
16	29 52	30 8	64596	7	35404	69329	8	30671	04733	2	95267	44
17	29 44	30 16	64622	7	35378	69361	9	30639	04739	2	95261	43
18	29 36	30 24	64647	8	35353	69393	9	30607	04746	2	95254	42
19	29 28	30 32	64673	8	35327	69425	10	30575	04752	2	95248	41
20	8 29 20	3 30 40	9.64698	8	10.35302	9.69457	11	10.30543	10.04758	2	9.95242	40
21	29 12	30 48	64724	9	35276	69488	11	30512	04764	2	95236	39
22	29 4	30 56	64749	9	35251	69520	12	30480	04771	2	95229	38
23	28 56	31 4	64775	10	35225	69552	12	30448	04777	2	95223	37
24	28 48	31 12	64800	10	35200	69584	13	30416	04783	3	95217	36
25	8 28 40	3 31 20	9.64826	11	10.35174	9.69615	13	10.30385	10.04789	3	9.95211	35
26	28 32	31 28	64851	11	35149	69647	14	30353	04796	3	95204	34
27	28 24	31 36	64877	11	35123	69679	14	30321	04802	3	95198	33
28	28 16	31 44	64902	12	35098	69710	15	30290	04808	3	95192	32
29	28 8	31 52	64927	12	35073	69742	15	30258	04815	3	95185	31
30	8 28 0	3 32 0	9.64953	13	10.35047	9.69774	16	10.30226	10.04821	3	9.95179	30
31	27 52	32 8	64978	13	35022	69805	16	30195	04827	3	95173	29
32	27 44	32 16	65003	14	34997	69837	17	30163	04833	3	95167	28
33	27 36	32 24	65029	14	34971	69868	17	30132	04840	3	95160	27
34	27 28	32 32	65054	14	34946	69900	18	30100	04846	4	95154	26
35	8 27 20	3 32 40	9.65079	15	10.34921	9.69932	18	10.30068	10.04852	4	9.95148	25
36	27 12	32 48	65104	15	34896	69963	19	30037	04859	4	95141	24
37	27 4	32 56	65130	16	34870	69995	20	30005	04865	4	95135	23
38	26 56	33 4	65155	16	34845	70026	20	29974	04871	4	95129	22
39	26 48	33 12	65180	16	34820	70058	21	29942	04878	4	95122	21
40	8 26 40	3 33 20	9.65205	17	10.34795	9.70089	21	10.29911	10.04884	4	9.95116	20
41	26 32	33 28	65230	17	34770	70121	22	29879	04890	4	95110	19
42	26 24	33 36	65255	18	34745	70152	22	29848	04897	4	95103	18
43	26 16	33 44	65281	18	34719	70184	23	29816	04903	5	95097	17
44	26 8	33 52	65306	19	34694	70215	23	29785	04910	5	95090	16
45	8 26 0	3 34 0	9.65331	19	10.34669	9.70247	24	10.29753	10.04916	5	9.95084	15
46	25 52	34 8	65356	19	34644	70278	24	29722	04922	5	95078	14
47	25 44	34 16	65381	20	34619	70309	25	29691	04929	5	95071	13
48	25 36	34 24	65406	20	34594	70341	25	29659	04935	5	95065	12
49	25 28	34 32	65431	21	34569	70372	26	29628	04941	5	95059	11
50	8 25 20	3 34 40	9.65456	21	10.34544	9.70404	26	10.29596	10.04948	5	9.95052	10
51	25 12	34 48	65481	22	34519	70435	27	29565	04954	5	95046	9
52	25 4	34 56	65506	22	34494	70466	27	29534	04961	5	95039	8
53	24 56	35 4	65531	22	34469	70498	28	29502	04967	6	95033	7
54	24 48	35 12	65556	23	34444	70529	28	29471	04973	6	95027	6
55	8 24 40	3 35 20	9.65580	23	10.34420	9.70560	29	10.29440	10.04980	6	9.95020	5
56	24 32	35 28	65605	24	34395	70592	30	29408	04986	6	95014	4
57	24 24	35 36	65630	24	34370	70623	30	29377	04993	6	95007	3
58	24 16	35 44	65655	25	34345	70654	31	29346	04999	6	95001	2
59	24 8	35 52	65680	25	34320	70685	31	29315	05005	6	94995	1
60	24 0	36 0	65705	25	34295	70717	32	29283	05012	6	94988	0
M	Hour P.M.	Hour A.M.	Cosine.	Diff.	Secant.	Cotangent	Diff.	Tangent.	Cosecant.	Diff.	Sine.	M
116°			A		A	B		B	C		C	63°

Seconds of time		1s	2s	3s	4s	5s	6s	7s
Prop. parts of cols	A	3	6	10	13	16	19	22
	B	4	8	12	16	20	24	28
	C	1	2	2	3	4	5	6

TABLE XXVII.

Log. Sines, Tangents, and Secants.

S'. | G'.

27°			A		A	B		B	C		C	152°
M	Hour A.M.	Hour P.M.	Sine.	Diff.	Cosecant.	Tangent.	Diff.	Cotangent	Secant.	Diff.	Cosine.	M
0	8 24 0	3 36 0	9.65705	0	10.34295	9.70717	0	10.29283	10.05012	0	9.94988	60
1	23 52	36 8	65729	0	34271	70748	1	29252	05018	0	94982	59
2	23 44	36 16	65754	1	34246	70779	1	29221	05025	0	94975	58
3	23 36	36 24	65779	1	34221	70810	2	29190	05031	0	94969	57
4	23 28	36 32	65804	2	34196	70841	2	29159	05038	0	94962	56
5	8 23 20	3 36 40	9.65828	2	10.34172	9.70873	3	10.29127	10.05044	1	9.94956	55
6	23 12	36 48	65853	2	34147	70904	3	29096	05051	1	94949	54
7	23 4	36 56	65878	3	34122	70935	4	29065	05057	1	94943	53
8	22 56	37 4	65902	3	34098	70966	4	29034	05064	1	94936	52
9	22 48	37 12	65927	4	34073	70997	5	29003	05070	1	94930	51
10	8 22 40	3 37 20	9.65952	4	10.34048	9.71028	5	10.28972	10.05077	1	9.94923	50
11	22 32	37 28	65976	4	34024	71059	6	28941	05083	1	94917	49
12	22 24	37 36	66001	5	33999	71090	6	28910	05089	1	94911	48
13	22 16	37 44	66025	5	33975	71121	7	28879	05096	1	94904	47
14	22 8	37 52	66050	6	33950	71153	7	28847	05102	2	94898	46
15	8 22 0	3 38 0	9.66075	6	10.33925	9.71184	8	10.28816	10.05109	2	9.94891	45
16	21 52	38 8	66099	6	33901	71215	8	28785	05115	2	94885	44
17	21 44	38 16	66124	7	33876	71246	9	28754	05122	2	94878	43
18	21 36	38 24	66148	7	33852	71277	9	28723	05129	2	94871	42
19	21 28	38 32	66173	8	33827	71308	10	28692	05135	2	94865	41
20	8 21 20	3 38 40	9.66197	8	10.33803	9.71339	10	10.28661	10.05142	2	9.94858	40
21	21 12	38 48	66221	8	33779	71370	11	28630	05148	2	94852	39
22	21 4	38 56	66246	9	33754	71401	11	28599	05155	2	94845	38
23	20 56	39 4	66270	9	33730	71431	12	28569	05161	3	94839	37
24	20 48	39 12	66295	10	33705	71462	12	28538	05168	3	94832	36
25	8 20 40	3 39 20	9.66319	10	10.33681	9.71493	13	10.28507	10.05174	3	9.94826	35
26	20 32	39 28	66343	11	33657	71524	13	28476	05181	3	94819	34
27	20 24	39 36	66368	11	33632	71555	14	28445	05187	3	94813	33
28	20 16	39 44	66392	11	33608	71586	14	28414	05194	3	94806	32
29	20 8	39 52	66416	12	33584	71617	15	28383	05201	3	94799	31
30	8 20 0	3 40 0	9.66441	12	10.33559	9.71648	15	10.28352	10.05207	3	9.94793	30
31	19 52	40 8	66465	13	33535	71679	16	28321	05214	3	94786	29
32	19 44	40 16	66489	13	33511	71709	16	28291	05220	4	94780	28
33	19 36	40 24	66513	13	33487	71740	17	28260	05227	4	94773	27
34	19 28	40 32	66537	14	33463	71771	17	28229	05233	4	94767	26
35	8 19 20	3 40 40	9.66562	14	10.33438	9.71802	18	10.28198	10.05240	4	9.94760	25
36	19 12	40 48	66586	15	33414	71833	19	28167	05247	4	94753	24
37	19 4	40 56	66610	15	33390	71863	19	28137	05253	4	94747	23
38	18 56	41 4	66634	15	33366	71894	20	28106	05260	4	94740	22
39	18 48	41 12	66658	16	33342	71925	20	28075	05266	4	94734	21
40	8 18 40	3 41 20	9.66682	16	10.33318	9.71955	21	10.28045	10.05273	4	9.94727	20
41	18 32	41 28	66706	17	33294	71986	21	28014	05280	4	94720	19
42	18 24	41 36	66731	17	33269	72017	22	27983	05286	5	94714	18
43	18 16	41 44	66755	17	33245	72048	22	27952	05293	5	94707	17
44	18 8	41 52	66779	18	33221	72078	23	27922	05300	5	94700	16
45	8 18 0	3 42 0	9.66803	18	10.33197	9.72109	23	10.27891	10.05306	5	9.94694	15
46	17 52	42 8	66827	19	33173	72140	24	27860	05313	5	94687	14
47	17 44	42 16	66851	19	33149	72170	24	27830	05320	5	94680	13
48	17 36	42 24	66875	19	33125	72201	25	27799	05326	5	94674	12
49	17 28	42 32	66899	20	33101	72231	25	27769	05333	5	94667	11
50	8 17 20	3 42 40	9.66922	20	10.33078	9.72262	26	10.27738	10.05340	5	9.94660	10
51	17 12	42 48	66946	21	33054	72293	26	27707	05346	6	94654	9
52	17 4	42 56	66970	21	33030	72323	27	27677	05353	6	94647	8
53	16 56	43 4	66994	21	33006	72354	27	27646	05360	6	94640	7
54	16 48	43 12	67018	22	32982	72384	28	27616	05366	6	94634	6
55	8 16 40	3 43 20	9.67042	22	10.32958	9.72415	28	10.27585	10.05373	6	9.94627	5
56	16 32	43 28	67066	23	32934	72445	29	27555	05380	6	94620	4
57	16 24	43 36	67090	23	32910	72476	29	27524	05386	6	94614	3
58	16 16	43 44	67113	23	32887	72506	30	27494	05393	6	94607	2
59	16 8	43 52	67137	24	32863	72537	30	27463	05400	6	94600	1
60	16 0	44 0	67161	24	32839	72567	31	27433	05407	7	94593	0
M	Hour P.M.	Hour A.M.	Cosine.	Diff.	Secant.	Cotangent	Diff.	Tangent.	Cosecant.	Diff.	Sine.	M
117°			A		A	B		B	C		C	62°

Seconds of time		1s	2s	3s	4s	5s	6s	7s
Prop. parts of cols.	A	3	6	9	12	15	18	21
	B	4	8	12	15	19	23	27
	C	1	2	2	3	4	5	6

TABLE XXVII.

Log. Sines, Tangents, and Secants.

8h. 28° | 3h. 151°

M	Hour A.M.	Hour P.M.	Sine. A	Diff.	Cosecant. A	Tangent. B	Diff.	Cotangent B	Secant. C	Diff.	Cosine. C	M
0	8 16 0	3 44 0	9.67161	0	10.32839	9.72567	0	10.27433	10.05407	0	9.94593	60
1	15 52	44 8	67185	0	32815	72598	1	27402	05413	0	94587	59
2	15 44	44 16	67208	1	32792	72628	1	27372	05420	0	94580	58
3	15 36	44 24	67232	1	32768	72659	2	27341	05427	0	94573	57
4	15 28	44 32	67256	2	32744	72689	2	27311	05433	0	94567	56
5	8 15 20	3 44 40	9.67280	2	10.32720	9.72720	3	10.27280	10.05440	1	9.94560	55
6	15 12	44 48	67303	2	32697	72750	3	27250	05447	1	94553	54
7	15 4	44 56	67327	3	32673	72780	4	27220	05454	1	94546	53
8	14 56	45 4	67350	3	32650	72811	4	27189	05460	1	94540	52
9	14 48	45 12	67374	3	32626	72841	5	27159	05467	1	94533	51
10	8 14 40	3 45 20	9.67398	4	10.32602	9.72872	5	10.27128	10.05474	1	9.94526	50
11	14 32	45 28	67421	4	32579	72902	6	27098	05481	1	94519	49
12	14 24	45 36	67445	5	32555	72932	6	27068	05487	1	94513	48
13	14 16	45 44	67468	5	32532	72963	7	27037	05494	1	94506	47
14	14 8	45 52	67492	5	32508	72993	7	27007	05501	2	94499	46
15	8 14 0	3 46 0	9.67515	6	10.32485	9.73023	8	10.26977	10.05508	2	9.94492	45
16	13 52	46 8	67539	6	32461	73054	8	26946	05515	2	94485	44
17	13 44	46 16	67562	7	32438	73084	9	26916	05521	2	94479	43
18	13 36	46 24	67586	7	32414	73114	9	26886	05528	2	94472	42
19	13 28	46 32	67609	7	32391	73144	10	26856	05535	2	94465	41
20	8 13 20	3 46 40	9.67633	8	10.32367	9.73175	10	10.26825	10.05542	2	9.94458	40
21	13 12	46 48	67656	8	32344	73205	11	26795	05549	2	94451	39
22	13 4	46 56	67680	9	32320	73235	11	26765	05555	3	94445	38
23	12 56	47 4	67703	9	32297	73265	12	26735	05562	3	94438	37
24	12 48	47 12	67726	9	32274	73295	12	26705	05569	3	94431	36
25	8 12 40	3 47 20	9.67750	10	10.32250	9.73326	13	10.26674	10.05576	3	9.94424	35
26	12 32	47 28	67773	10	32227	73356	13	26644	05583	3	94417	34
27	12 24	47 36	67796	10	32204	73386	14	26614	05590	3	94410	33
28	12 16	47 44	67820	11	32180	73416	14	26584	05596	3	94404	32
29	12 8	47 52	67843	11	32157	73446	15	26554	05603	3	94397	31
30	8 12 0	3 48 0	9.67866	12	10.32134	9.73476	15	10.26524	10.05610	3	9.94390	30
31	11 52	48 8	67890	12	32110	73507	16	26493	05617	4	94383	29
32	11 44	48 16	67913	12	32087	73537	16	26463	05624	4	94376	28
33	11 36	48 24	67936	13	32064	73567	17	26433	05631	4	94369	27
34	11 28	48 32	67959	13	32041	73597	17	26403	05638	4	94362	26
35	8 11 20	3 48 40	9.67982	14	10.32018	9.73627	18	10.26373	10.05645	4	9.94355	25
36	11 12	48 48	68006	14	31994	73657	18	26343	05651	4	94349	24
37	11 4	48 56	68029	14	31971	73687	19	26313	05658	4	94342	23
38	10 56	49 4	68052	15	31948	73717	19	26283	05665	4	94335	22
39	10 48	49 12	68075	15	31925	73747	20	26253	05672	4	94328	21
40	8 10 40	3 49 20	9.68098	16	10.31902	9.73777	20	10.26223	10.05679	5	9.94321	20
41	10 32	49 28	68121	16	31879	73807	21	26193	05686	5	94314	19
42	10 24	49 36	68144	16	31856	73837	21	26163	05693	5	94307	18
43	10 16	49 44	68167	17	31833	73867	22	26133	05700	5	94300	17
44	10 8	49 52	68190	17	31810	73897	22	26103	05707	5	94293	16
45	8 10 0	3 50 0	9.68213	17	10.31787	9.73927	23	10.26073	10.05714	5	9.94286	15
46	9 52	50 8	68237	18	31763	73957	23	26043	05721	5	94279	14
47	9 44	50 16	68260	18	31740	73987	24	26013	05727	5	94273	13
48	9 36	50 24	68283	19	31717	74017	24	25983	05734	5	94266	12
49	9 28	50 32	68305	19	31695	74047	25	25953	05741	6	94259	11
50	8 9 20	3 50 40	9.68328	19	10.31672	9.74077	25	10.25923	10.05748	6	9.94252	10
51	9 12	50 48	68351	20	31649	74107	26	25893	05755	6	94245	9
52	9 4	50 56	68374	20	31626	74137	26	25863	05762	6	94238	8
53	8 56	51 4	68397	21	31603	74166	27	25834	05769	6	94231	7
54	8 48	51 12	68420	21	31580	74196	27	25804	05776	6	94224	6
55	8 8 40	3 51 20	9.68443	21	10.31557	9.74226	28	10.25774	10.05783	6	9.94217	5
56	8 32	51 28	68466	22	31534	74256	28	25744	05790	6	94210	4
57	8 24	51 36	68489	22	31511	74286	29	25714	05797	7	94203	3
58	8 16	51 44	68512	22	31488	74316	29	25684	05804	7	94196	2
59	8 8	51 52	68534	23	31466	74345	30	25655	05811	7	94189	1
60	8 0	52 0	68557	23	31443	74375	30	25625	05818	7	94182	0
M	Hour P.M.	Hour A.M.	Cosine. A	Diff.	Secant. A	Cotangent B	Diff.	Tangent. B	Cosecant. C	Diff.	Sine. C	M

118° | 61°

Seconds of time		1s	2s	3s	4s	5s	6s	7s
Prop. parts of cols.	A	3	6	9	12	15	17	20
	B	4	8	11	15	19	23	26
	C	1	2	3	3	4	5	6

TABLE XXVII.

S'. **Log. Sines, Tangents, and Secants.** G'.

29°			A		A	B		B	C		C	150°
M	Hour A.M.	Hour P.M.	Sine.	Diff.	Cosecant.	Tangent.	Diff.	Cotangent	Secant.	Diff.	Cosine.	M
0	8 8 0	3 52 0	9.68557	0	10.31443	9.74375	0	10.25625	10.05818	0	9.94182	60
1	7 52	52 8	68580	0	31420	74405	0	25595	05825	0	94175	59
2	7 44	52 16	68603	1	31397	74435	1	25565	05832	0	94168	58
3	7 36	52 24	68625	1	31375	74465	1	25535	05839	0	94161	57
4	7 28	52 32	68648	1	31352	74494	2	25506	05846	0	94154	56
5	8 7 20	3 52 40	9.68671	2	10.31329	9.74524	2	10.25476	10.05853	1	9.94147	55
6	7 12	52 48	68694	2	31306	74554	3	25446	05860	1	94140	54
7	7 4	52 56	68716	3	31284	74583	3	25417	05867	1	94133	53
8	6 56	53 4	68739	3	31261	74613	4	25387	05874	1	94126	52
9	6 48	53 12	68762	3	31238	74643	4	25357	05881	1	94119	51
10	8 6 40	3 53 20	9.68784	4	10.31216	9.74673	5	10.25327	10.05888	1	9.94112	50
11	6 32	53 28	68807	4	31193	74702	5	25298	05895	1	94105	49
12	6 24	53 36	68829	4	31171	74732	6	25268	05902	1	94098	48
13	6 16	53 44	68852	5	31148	74762	6	25238	05910	2	94090	47
14	6 8	53 52	68875	5	31125	74791	7	25209	05917	2	94083	46
15	8 6 0	3 54 0	9.68897	6	10.31103	9.74821	7	10.25179	10.05924	2	9.94076	45
16	5 52	54 8	68920	6	31080	74851	8	25149	05931	2	94069	44
17	5 44	54 16	68942	6	31058	74880	8	25120	05938	2	94062	43
18	5 36	54 24	68965	7	31035	74910	9	25090	05945	2	94055	42
19	5 28	54 32	68987	7	31013	74939	9	25061	05952	2	94048	41
20	8 5 20	3 54 40	9.69010	7	10.30990	9.74969	10	10.25031	10.05959	2	9.94041	40
21	5 12	54 48	69032	8	30968	74998	10	25002	05966	3	94034	39
22	5 4	54 56	69055	8	30945	75028	11	24972	05973	3	94027	38
23	4 56	55 4	69077	9	30923	75058	11	24942	05980	3	94020	37
24	4 48	55 12	69100	9	30900	75087	12	24913	05988	3	94012	36
25	8 4 40	3 55 20	9.69122	9	10.30878	9.75117	12	10.24883	10.05995	3	9.94005	35
26	4 32	55 28	69144	10	30856	75146	13	24854	06002	3	93998	34
27	4 24	55 36	69167	10	30833	75176	13	24824	06009	3	93991	33
28	4 16	55 44	69189	10	30811	75205	14	24795	06016	3	93984	32
29	4 8	55 52	69212	11	30788	75235	14	24765	06023	3	93977	31
30	8 4 0	3 56 0	9.69234	11	10.30766	9.75264	15	10.24736	10.06030	4	9.93970	30
31	3 52	56 8	69256	12	30744	75294	15	24706	06037	4	93963	29
32	3 44	56 16	69279	12	30721	75323	16	24677	06045	4	93955	28
33	3 36	56 24	69301	12	30699	75353	16	24647	06052	4	93948	27
34	3 28	56 32	69323	13	30677	75382	17	24618	06059	4	93941	26
35	8 3 20	3 56 40	9.69345	13	10.30655	9.75411	17	10.24589	10.06066	4	9.93934	25
36	3 12	56 48	69368	13	30632	75441	18	24559	06073	4	93927	24
37	3 4	56 56	69390	14	30610	75470	18	24530	06080	4	93920	23
38	2 56	57 4	69412	14	30588	75500	19	24500	06088	5	93912	22
39	2 48	57 12	69434	15	30566	75529	19	24471	06095	5	93905	21
40	8 2 40	3 57 20	9.69456	15	10.30544	9.75558	20	10.24442	10.06102	5	9.93898	20
41	2 32	57 28	69479	15	30521	75588	20	24412	06109	5	93891	19
42	2 24	57 36	69501	16	30499	75617	21	24383	06116	5	93884	18
43	2 16	57 44	69523	16	30477	75647	21	24353	06124	5	93876	17
44	2 8	57 52	69545	16	30455	75676	22	24324	06131	5	93869	16
45	8 2 0	3 58 0	9.69567	17	10.30433	9.75705	22	10.24295	10.06138	5	9.93862	15
46	1 52	58 8	69589	17	30411	75735	23	24265	06145	5	93855	14
47	1 44	58 16	69611	17	30389	75764	23	24236	06153	6	93847	13
48	1 36	58 24	69633	18	30367	75793	24	24207	06160	6	93840	12
49	1 28	58 32	69655	18	30345	75822	24	24178	06167	6	93833	11
50	8 1 20	3 58 40	9.69677	19	10.30323	9.75852	25	10.24148	10.06174	6	9.93826	10
51	1 12	58 48	69699	19	30301	75881	25	24119	06181	6	93819	9
52	1 4	58 56	69721	19	30279	75910	26	24090	06189	6	93811	8
53	0 56	59 4	69743	20	30257	75939	26	24061	06196	6	93804	7
54	0 48	59 12	69765	20	30235	75969	27	24031	06203	6	93797	6
55	8 0 40	3 59 20	9.69787	20	10.30213	9.75998	27	10.24002	10.06211	7	9.93789	5
56	0 32	59 28	69809	21	30191	76027	28	23973	06218	7	93782	4
57	0 24	59 36	69831	21	30169	76056	28	23944	06225	7	93775	3
58	0 16	59 44	69853	22	30147	76086	29	23914	06232	7	93768	2
59	0 8	59 52	69875	22	30125	76115	29	23885	06240	7	93760	1
60	0 0	4 0 0	69897	22	30103	76144	29	23856	06247	7	93753	0
M	Hour P.M.	Hour A.M.	Cosine.	Diff.	Secant.	Cotangent	Diff.	Tangent.	Cosecant.	Diff.	Sine.	M
119°			A		A	B		B	C		C	60°

Seconds of time		1s	2s	3s	4s	5s	6s	7s
Prop. parts of cols.	A	3	6	8	11	14	17	20
	B	4	7	11	15	18	22	26
	C	1	2	3	4	4	5	6

TABLE XXVII.

S'. **Log. Sines, Tangents, and Secants.** G'.

30°			A		A	B		B	C		C	149°
M	Hour A.M.	Hour P.M.	Sine.	Diff.	Cosecant.	Tangent.	Diff.	Cotangent	Secant.	Diff.	Cosine.	M
0	8 0 0	4 0 0	9.69897	0	10.30103	9.76144	0	10.23856	10.06247	0	9.93753	60
1	7 59 52	0 8	69919	0	30081	76173	0	23827	06254	0	93746	59
2	59 44	0 16	69941	1	30059	76202	1	23798	06262	0	93738	58
3	59 36	0 24	69963	1	30037	76231	1	23769	06269	0	93731	57
4	59 28	0 32	69984	1	30016	76261	2	23739	06276	0	93724	56
5	7 59 20	4 0 40	9.70006	2	10.29994	9.76290	2	10.23710	10.06283	1	9.93717	55
6	59 12	0 48	70028	2	29972	76319	3	23681	06291	1	93709	54
7	59 4	0 56	70050	3	29950	76348	3	23652	06298	1	93702	53
8	58 56	1 4	70072	3	29928	76377	4	23623	06305	1	93695	52
9	58 48	1 12	70093	3	29907	76406	4	23594	06313	1	93687	51
10	7 58 40	4 1 20	9.70115	4	10.29885	9.76435	5	10.23565	10.06320	1	9.93680	50
11	58 32	1 28	70137	4	29863	76464	5	23536	06327	1	93673	49
12	58 24	1 36	70159	4	29841	76493	6	23507	06335	1	93665	48
13	58 16	1 44	70180	5	29820	76522	6	23478	06342	2	93658	47
14	58 8	1 52	70202	5	29798	76551	7	23449	06350	2	93650	46
15	7 58 0	4 2 0	9.70224	5	10.29776	9.76580	7	10.23420	10.06357	2	9.93643	45
16	57 52	2 8	70245	6	29755	76609	8	23391	06364	2	93636	44
17	57 44	2 16	70267	6	29733	76639	8	23361	06372	2	93628	43
18	57 36	2 24	70288	6	29712	76668	9	23332	06379	2	93621	42
19	57 28	2 32	70310	7	29690	76697	9	23303	06386	2	93614	41
20	7 57 20	4 2 40	9.70332	7	10.29668	9.76725	10	10.23275	10.06394	2	9.93606	40
21	57 12	2 48	70353	8	29647	76754	10	23246	06401	3	93599	39
22	57 4	2 56	70375	8	29625	76783	11	23217	06409	3	93591	38
23	56 56	3 4	70396	8	29604	76812	11	23188	06416	3	93584	37
24	56 48	3 12	70418	9	29582	76841	12	23159	06423	3	93577	36
25	7 56 40	4 3 20	9.70439	9	10.29561	9.76870	12	10.23130	10.06431	3	9.93569	35
26	56 32	3 28	70461	9	29539	76899	13	23101	06438	3	93562	34
27	56 24	3 36	70482	10	29518	76928	13	23072	06446	3	93554	33
28	56 16	3 44	70504	10	29496	76957	13	23043	06453	3	93547	32
29	56 8	3 52	70525	10	29475	76986	14	23014	06461	4	93539	31
30	7 56 0	4 4 0	9.70547	11	10.29453	9.77015	14	10.22985	10.06468	4	9.93532	30
31	55 52	4 8	70568	11	29432	77044	15	22956	06475	4	93525	29
32	55 44	4 16	70590	11	29410	77073	15	22927	06483	4	93517	28
33	55 36	4 24	70611	12	29389	77101	16	22899	06490	4	93510	27
34	55 28	4 32	70633	12	29367	77130	16	22870	06498	4	93502	26
35	7 55 20	4 4 40	9.70654	13	10.29346	9.77159	17	10.22841	10.06505	4	9.93495	25
36	55 12	4 48	70675	13	29325	77188	17	22812	06513	4	93487	24
37	55 4	4 56	70697	13	29303	77217	18	22783	06520	5	93480	23
38	54 56	5 4	70718	14	29282	77246	18	22754	06528	5	93472	22
39	54 48	5 12	70739	14	29261	77274	19	22726	06535	5	93465	21
40	7 54 40	4 5 20	9.70761	14	10.29239	9.77303	19	10.22697	10.06543	5	9.93457	20
41	54 32	5 28	70782	15	29218	77332	20	22668	06550	5	93450	19
42	54 24	5 36	70803	15	29197	77361	20	22639	06558	5	93442	18
43	54 16	5 44	70824	15	29176	77390	21	22610	06565	5	93435	17
44	54 8	5 52	70846	16	29154	77418	21	22582	06573	5	93427	16
45	7 54 0	4 6 0	9.70867	16	10.29133	9.77447	22	10.22553	10.06580	6	9.93420	15
46	53 52	6 8	70888	16	29112	77476	22	22524	06588	6	93412	14
47	53 44	6 16	70909	17	29091	77505	23	22495	06595	6	93405	13
48	53 36	6 24	70931	17	29069	77533	23	22467	06603	6	93397	12
49	53 28	6 32	70952	18	29048	77562	24	22438	06610	6	93390	11
50	7 53 20	4 6 40	9.70973	18	10.29027	9.77591	24	10.22409	10.06618	6	9.93382	10
51	53 12	6 48	70994	18	29006	77619	25	22381	06625	6	93375	9
52	53 4	6 56	71015	19	28985	77648	25	22352	06633	6	93367	8
53	52 56	7 4	71036	19	28964	77677	26	22323	06640	7	93360	7
54	52 48	7 12	71058	19	28942	77706	26	22294	06648	7	93352	6
55	7 52 40	4 7 20	9.71079	20	10.28921	9.77734	26	10.22266	10.06656	7	9.93344	5
56	52 32	7 28	71100	20	28900	77763	27	22237	06663	7	93337	4
57	52 24	7 36	71121	20	28879	77791	27	22209	06671	7	93329	3
58	52 16	7 44	71142	21	28858	77820	28	22180	06678	7	93322	2
59	52 8	7 52	71163	21	28837	77849	28	22151	06686	7	93314	1
60	52 0	8 0	71184	21	28816	77877	29	22123	06693	7	93307	0
M	Hour P.M.	Hour A.M.	Cosine.	Diff.	Secant.	Cotangent	Diff.	Tangent.	Cosecant.	Diff.	Sine.	M
120°			A		A	B		B	C		C	59°

Seconds of time		1	2	3	4	5	6	7
Prop. parts of cols.	A	3	5	8	11	13	16	19
	B	4	7	11	14	18	22	25
	C	1	2	3	4	5	6	7

TABLE XXVII.

S′. Log. Sines, Tangents, and Secants. G′

31°			A		A	B		B	C		C	148°
M	Hour A.M.	Hour P.M.	Sine.	Diff.	Cosecant.	Tangent.	Diff.	Cotangent	Secant.	Diff.	Cosine.	M
0	7 52 0	4 8 0	9.71184	0	10.28816	9.77877	0	10.22123	10.06693	0	9.93307	60
1	51 52	8 8	71205	0	28795	77906	0	22094	06701	0	93299	59
2	51 44	8 16	71226	1	28774	77935	1	22065	06709	0	93291	58
3	51 36	8 24	71247	1	28753	77963	1	22037	06716	0	93284	57
4	51 28	8 32	71268	1	28732	77992	2	22008	06724	1	93276	56
5	7 51 20	4 8 40	9.71289	2	10.28711	9.78020	2	10.21980	10.06731	1	9.93269	55
6	51 12	8 48	71310	2	28690	78049	3	21951	06739	1	93261	54
7	51 4	8 56	71331	2	28669	78077	3	21923	06747	1	93253	53
8	50 56	9 4	71352	3	28648	78106	4	21894	06754	1	93246	52
9	50 48	9 12	71373	3	28627	78135	4	21865	06762	1	93238	51
10	7 50 40	4 9 20	9.71393	3	10.28607	9.78163	5	10.21837	10.06770	1	9.93230	50
11	50 32	9 28	71414	4	28586	78192	5	21808	06777	1	93223	49
12	50 24	9 36	71435	4	28565	78220	6	21780	06785	2	93215	48
13	50 16	9 44	71456	4	28544	78249	6	21751	06793	2	93207	47
14	50 8	9 52	71477	5	28523	78277	7	21723	06800	2	93200	46
15	7 50 0	4 10 0	9.71498	5	10.28502	9.78306	7	10.21694	10.06808	2	9.93192	45
16	49 52	10 8	71519	5	28481	78334	8	21666	06816	2	93184	44
17	49 44	10 16	71539	6	28461	78363	8	21637	06823	2	93177	43
18	49 36	10 24	71560	6	28440	78391	9	21609	06831	2	93169	42
19	49 28	10 32	71581	7	28419	78419	9	21581	06839	2	93161	41
20	7 49 20	4 10 40	9.71602	7	10.28398	9.78448	9	10.21552	10.06846	3	9.93154	40
21	49 12	10 48	71622	7	28378	78476	10	21524	06854	3	93146	39
22	49 4	10 56	71643	8	28357	78505	10	21495	06862	3	93138	38
23	48 56	11 4	71664	8	28336	78533	11	21467	06869	3	93131	37
24	48 48	11 12	71685	8	28315	78562	11	21438	06877	3	93123	36
25	7 48 40	4 11 20	9.71705	9	10.28295	9.78590	12	10.21410	10.06885	3	9.93115	35
26	48 32	11 28	71726	9	28274	78618	12	21382	06892	3	93108	34
27	48 24	11 36	71747	9	28253	78647	13	21353	06900	3	93100	33
28	48 16	11 44	71767	10	28233	78675	13	21325	06908	4	93092	32
29	48 8	11 52	71788	10	28212	78704	14	21296	06916	4	93084	31
30	7 48 0	4 12 0	9.71809	10	10.28191	9.78732	14	10.21268	10.06923	4	9.93077	30
31	47 52	12 8	71829	11	28171	78760	15	21240	06931	4	93069	29
32	47 44	12 16	71850	11	28150	78789	15	21211	06939	4	93061	28
33	47 36	12 24	71870	11	28130	78817	16	21183	06947	4	93053	27
34	47 28	12 32	71891	12	28109	78845	16	21155	06954	4	93046	26
35	7 47 20	4 12 40	9.71911	12	10.28089	9.78874	17	10.21126	10.06962	5	9.93038	25
36	47 12	12 48	71932	12	28068	78902	17	21098	06970	5	93030	24
37	47 4	12 56	71952	13	28048	78930	17	21070	06978	5	93022	23
38	46 56	13 4	71973	13	28027	78959	18	21041	06986	5	93014	22
39	46 48	13 12	71994	13	28006	78987	18	21013	06993	5	93007	21
40	7 46 40	4 13 20	9.72014	14	10.27986	9.79015	19	10.20985	10.07001	5	9.92999	20
41	46 32	13 28	72034	14	27966	79043	19	20957	07009	5	92991	19
42	46 24	13 36	72055	14	27945	79072	20	20928	07017	5	92983	18
43	46 16	13 44	72075	15	27925	79100	20	20900	07024	6	92976	17
44	46 8	13 52	72096	15	27904	79128	21	20872	07032	6	92968	16
45	7 46 0	4 14 0	9.72116	15	10.27884	9.79156	21	10.20844	10.07040	6	9.92960	15
46	45 52	14 8	72137	16	27863	79185	22	20815	07048	6	92952	14
47	45 44	14 16	72157	16	27843	79213	22	20787	07056	6	92944	13
48	45 36	14 24	72177	16	27823	79241	23	20759	07064	6	92936	12
49	45 28	14 32	72198	17	27802	79269	23	20731	07071	6	92929	11
50	7 45 20	4 14 40	9.72218	17	10.27782	9.79297	24	10.20703	10.07079	6	9.92921	10
51	45 12	14 48	72238	18	27762	79326	24	20674	07087	7	92913	9
52	45 4	14 56	72259	18	27741	79354	25	20646	07095	7	92905	8
53	44 56	15 4	72279	18	27721	79382	25	20618	07103	7	92897	7
54	44 48	15 12	72299	19	27701	79410	26	20590	07111	7	92889	6
55	7 44 40	4 15 20	9.72320	19	10.27680	9.79438	26	10.20562	10.07119	7	9.92881	5
56	44 32	15 28	72340	19	27660	79466	26	20534	07126	7	92874	4
57	44 24	15 36	72360	20	27640	79495	27	20505	07134	7	92866	3
58	44 16	15 44	72381	20	27619	79523	27	20477	07142	7	92858	2
59	44 8	15 52	72401	20	27599	79551	28	20449	07150	8	92850	1
60	44 0	16 0	72421	21	27579	79579	28	20421	07158	8	92842	0
M	Hour P.M.	Hour A.M.	Cosine.	Diff.	Secant.	Cotangent	Diff.	Tangent.	Cosecant.	Diff.	Sine.	M
121°			A		A	B		B	C		C	58°

Seconds of time		1s	2s	3s	4s	5s	6s	7s
Prop. parts of cols	A	3	5	8	10	13	15	18
	B	4	7	11	14	18	21	25
	C	1	2	3	4	5	6	7

TABLE XXVII.

S'. **Log. Sines, Tangents, and Secants.** G'.

32°			A		A	B		B	C		C	147°
M	Hour A.M.	Hour P.M.	Sine.	Diff.	Cosecant.	Tangent.	Diff.	Cotangent	Secant.	Diff.	Cosine.	M
0	7 44 0	4 16 0	9.72421	0	10.27579	9.79579	0	10.20421	10.07158	0	9.92842	60
1	43 52	16 8	72441	0	27559	79607	0	20393	07166	0	92834	59
2	43 44	16 16	72461	1	27539	79635	1	20365	07174	0	92826	58
3	43 36	16 24	72482	1	27518	79663	1	20337	07182	0	92818	57
4	43 28	16 32	72502	1	27498	79691	2	20309	07190	1	92810	56
5	7 43 20	4 16 40	9.72522	2	10.27478	9.79719	2	10.20281	10.07197	1	9.92803	55
6	43 12	16 48	72542	2	27458	79747	3	20253	07205	1	92795	54
7	43 4	16 56	72562	2	27438	79776	3	20224	07213	1	92787	53
8	42 56	17 4	72582	3	27418	79804	4	20196	07221	1	92779	52
9	42 48	17 12	72602	3	27398	79832	4	20168	07229	1	92771	51
10	7 42 40	4 17 20	9.72622	3	10.27378	9.79860	5	10.20140	10.07237	1	9.92763	50
11	42 32	17 28	72643	4	27357	79888	5	20112	07245	1	92755	49
12	42 24	17 36	72663	4	27337	79916	6	20084	07253	2	92747	48
13	42 16	17 44	72683	4	27317	79944	6	20056	07261	2	92739	47
14	42 8	17 52	72703	5	27297	79972	7	20028	07269	2	92731	46
15	7 42 0	4 18 0	9.72723	5	10.27277	9.80000	7	10.20000	10.07277	2	9.92723	45
16	41 52	18 8	72743	5	27257	80028	7	19972	07285	2	92715	44
17	41 44	18 16	72763	6	27237	80056	8	19944	07293	2	92707	43
18	41 36	18 24	72783	6	27217	80084	8	19916	07301	2	92699	42
19	41 28	18 32	72803	6	27197	80112	9	19888	07309	3	92691	41
20	7 41 20	4 18 40	9.72823	7	10.27177	9.80140	9	10.19860	10.07317	3	9.92683	40
21	41 12	18 48	72843	7	27157	80168	10	19832	07325	3	92675	39
22	41 4	18 56	72863	7	27137	80195	10	19805	07333	3	92667	38
23	40 56	19 4	72883	8	27117	80223	11	19777	07341	3	92659	37
24	40 48	19 12	72902	8	27098	80251	11	19749	07349	3	92651	36
25	7 40 40	4 19 20	9.72922	8	10.27078	9.80279	12	10.19721	10.07357	3	9.92643	35
26	40 32	19 28	72942	9	27058	80307	12	19693	07365	3	92635	34
27	40 24	19 36	72962	9	27038	80335	13	19665	07373	4	92627	33
28	40 16	19 44	72982	9	27018	80363	13	19637	07381	4	92619	32
29	40 8	19 52	73002	10	26998	80391	13	19609	07389	4	92611	31
30	7 40 0	4 20 0	9.73022	10	10.26978	9.80419	14	10.19581	10.07397	4	9.92603	30
31	39 52	20 8	73041	10	26959	80447	14	19553	07405	4	92595	29
32	39 44	20 16	73061	11	26939	80474	15	19526	07413	4	92587	28
33	39 36	20 24	73081	11	26919	80502	15	19498	07421	4	92579	27
34	39 28	20 32	73101	11	26899	80530	16	19470	07429	5	92571	26
35	7 39 20	4 20 40	9.73121	12	10.26879	9.80558	16	10.19442	10.07437	5	9.92563	25
36	39 12	20 48	73140	12	26860	80586	17	19414	07445	5	92555	24
37	39 4	20 56	73160	12	26840	80614	17	19386	07454	5	92546	23
38	38 56	21 4	73180	13	26820	80642	18	19358	07462	5	92538	22
39	38 48	21 12	73200	13	26800	80669	18	19331	07470	5	92530	21
40	7 38 40	4 21 20	9.73219	13	10.26781	9.80697	19	10.19303	10.07478	5	9.92522	20
41	38 32	21 28	73239	14	26761	80725	19	19275	07486	6	92514	19
42	38 24	21 36	73259	14	26741	80753	20	19247	07494	6	92506	18
43	38 16	21 44	73278	14	26722	80781	20	19219	07502	6	92498	17
44	38 8	21 52	73298	15	26702	80808	20	19192	07510	6	92490	16
45	7 38 0	4 22 0	9.73318	15	10.26682	9.80836	21	10.19164	10.07518	6	9.92482	15
46	37 52	22 8	73337	15	26663	80864	21	19136	07527	6	92473	14
47	37 44	22 16	73357	16	26643	80892	22	19108	07535	6	92465	13
48	37 36	22 24	73377	16	26623	80919	22	19081	07543	6	92457	12
49	37 28	22 32	73396	16	26604	80947	23	19053	07551	7	92449	11
50	7 37 20	4 22 40	9.73416	17	10.26584	9.80975	23	10.19025	10.07559	7	9.92441	10
51	37 12	22 48	73435	17	26565	81003	24	18997	07567	7	92433	9
52	37 4	22 56	73455	17	26545	81030	24	18970	07575	7	92425	8
53	36 56	23 4	73474	18	26526	81058	25	18942	07584	7	92416	7
54	36 48	23 12	73494	18	26506	81086	25	18914	07592	7	92408	6
55	7 36 40	4 23 20	9.73513	18	10.26487	9.81113	26	10.18887	10.07600	7	9.92400	5
56	36 32	23 28	73533	19	26467	81141	26	18859	07608	8	92392	4
57	36 24	23 36	73552	19	26448	81169	26	18831	07616	8	92384	3
58	36 16	23 44	73572	19	26428	81196	27	18804	07624	8	92376	2
59	36 8	23 52	73591	20	26409	81224	27	18776	07633	8	92367	1
60	36 0	24 0	73611	20	26389	81252	28	18748	07641	8	92359	0
M	Hour P.M.	Hour A.M.	Cosine.	Diff.	Secant.	Cotangent	Diff.	Tangent.	Cosecant.	Diff.	Sine.	M
122°			A		A	B		B	C		C	57°

Seconds of time		1s	2s	3s	4s	5s	6s	7s
Prop. parts of cols.	A	2	5	7	10	12	15	17
	B	3	7	10	14	17	21	24
	C	1	2	3	4	5	6	7

TABLE XXVII.

S′. Log. Sines, Tangents, and Secants. G′.

33° A A B B C C 146°

M	Hour A.M.	Hour P.M.	Sine.	Diff.	Cosecant.	Tangent.	Diff.	Cotangent	Secant.	Diff.	Cosine.	M
0	7 36 0	4 24 0	9.73611	0	10.26389	9.81252	0	10.18748	10.07641	0	9.92359	60
1	35 52	24 8	73630	0	26370	81279	0	18721	07649	0	92351	59
2	35 44	24 16	73650	1	26350	81307	1	18693	07657	0	92343	58
3	35 36	24 24	73669	1	26331	81335	1	18665	07665	0	92335	57
4	35 28	24 32	73689	1	26311	81362	2	18638	07674	1	92326	56
5	7 35 20	4 24 40	9.73708	2	10.26292	9.81390	2	10.18610	10.07682	1	9.92318	55
6	35 12	24 48	73727	2	26273	81418	3	18582	07690	1	92310	54
7	35 4	24 56	73747	2	26253	81445	3	18555	07698	1	92302	53
8	34 56	25 4	73766	3	26234	81473	4	18527	07707	1	92293	52
9	34 48	25 12	73785	3	26215	81500	4	18500	07715	1	92285	51
10	7 34 40	4 25 20	9.73805	3	10.26195	9.81528	5	10.18472	10.07723	1	9.92277	50
11	34 32	25 28	73824	3	26176	81556	5	18444	07731	2	92269	49
12	34 24	25 36	73843	4	26157	81583	5	18417	07740	2	92260	48
13	34 16	25 44	73863	4	26137	81611	6	18389	07748	2	92252	47
14	34 8	25 52	73882	4	26118	81638	6	18362	07756	2	92244	46
15	7 34 0	4 26 0	9.73901	5	10.26099	9.81666	7	10.18334	10.07765	2	9.92235	45
16	33 52	26 8	73921	5	26079	81693	7	18307	07773	2	92227	44
17	33 44	26 16	73940	5	26060	81721	8	18279	07781	2	92219	43
18	33 36	26 24	73959	6	26041	81748	8	18252	07789	3	92211	42
19	33 28	26 32	73978	6	26022	81776	9	18224	07798	3	92202	41
20	7 33 20	4 26 40	9.73997	6	10.26003	9.81803	9	10.18197	10.07806	3	9.92194	40
21	33 12	26 48	74017	7	25983	81831	10	18169	07814	3	92186	39
22	33 4	26 56	74036	7	25964	81858	10	18142	07823	3	92177	38
23	32 56	27 4	74055	7	25945	81886	11	18114	07831	3	92169	37
24	32 48	27 12	74074	8	25926	81913	11	18087	07839	3	92161	36
25	7 32 40	4 27 20	9.74093	8	10.25907	9.81941	11	10.18059	10.07848	3	9.92152	35
26	32 32	27 28	74113	8	25887	81968	12	18032	07856	4	92144	34
27	32 24	27 36	74132	9	25868	81996	12	18004	07864	4	92136	33
28	32 16	27 44	74151	9	25849	82023	13	17977	07873	4	92127	32
29	32 8	27 52	74170	9	25830	82051	13	17949	07881	4	92119	31
30	7 32 0	4 28 0	9.74189	10	10.25811	9.82078	14	10.17922	10.07889	4	9.92111	30
31	31 52	28 8	74208	10	25792	82106	14	17894	07898	4	92102	29
32	31 44	28 16	74227	10	25773	82133	15	17867	07906	4	92094	28
33	31 36	28 24	74246	10	25754	82161	15	17839	07914	5	92086	27
34	31 28	28 32	74265	11	25735	82188	16	17812	07923	5	92077	26
35	7 31 20	4 28 40	9.74284	11	10.25716	9.82215	16	10.17785	10.07931	5	9.92069	25
36	31 12	28 48	74303	11	25697	82243	16	17757	07940	5	92060	24
37	31 4	28 56	74322	12	25678	82270	17	17730	07948	5	92052	23
38	30 56	29 4	74341	12	25659	82298	17	17702	07956	5	92044	22
39	30 48	29 12	74360	12	25640	82325	18	17675	07965	5	92035	21
40	7 30 40	4 29 20	9.74379	13	10.25621	9.82352	18	10.17648	10.07973	6	9.92027	20
41	30 32	29 28	74398	13	25602	82380	19	17620	07982	6	92018	19
42	30 24	29 36	74417	13	25583	82407	19	17593	07990	6	92010	18
43	30 16	29 44	74436	14	25564	82435	20	17565	07998	6	92002	17
44	30 8	29 52	74455	14	25545	82462	20	17538	08007	6	91993	16
45	7 30 0	4 30 0	9.74474	14	10.25526	9.82489	21	10.17511	10.08015	6	9.91985	15
46	29 52	30 8	74493	15	25507	82517	21	17483	08024	6	91976	14
47	29 44	30 16	74512	15	25488	82544	22	17456	08032	7	91968	13
48	29 36	30 24	74531	15	25469	82571	22	17429	08041	7	91959	12
49	29 28	30 32	74549	16	25451	82599	22	17401	08049	7	91951	11
50	7 29 20	4 30 40	9.74568	16	10.25432	9.82626	23	10.17374	10.08058	7	9.91942	10
51	29 12	30 48	74587	16	25413	82653	23	17347	08066	7	91934	9
52	29 4	30 56	74606	17	25394	82681	24	17319	08075	7	91925	8
53	28 56	31 4	74625	17	25375	82708	24	17292	08083	7	91917	7
54	28 48	31 12	74644	17	25356	82735	25	17265	08092	8	91908	6
55	7 28 40	4 31 20	9.74662	17	10.25338	9.82762	25	10.17238	10.08100	8	9.91900	5
56	28 32	31 28	74681	18	25319	82790	26	17210	08109	8	91891	4
57	28 24	31 36	74700	18	25300	82817	26	17183	08117	8	91883	3
58	28 16	31 44	74719	18	25281	82844	27	17156	08126	8	91874	2
59	28 8	31 52	74737	19	25263	82871	27	17129	08134	8	91866	1
60	28 0	32 0	74756	19	25244	82899	27	17101	08143	8	91857	0
M	Hour P.M.	Hour A.M.	Cosine.	Diff.	Secant.	Cotangent	Diff.	Tangent.	Cosecant.	Diff.	Sine.	M

123° A A B B C C 56°

Seconds of time		1s	2s	3s	4s	5s	6s	7s
Prop. parts of cols.	A	2	5	7	10	12	14	17
	B	3	7	10	14	17	21	24
	C	1	2	3	4	5	6	7

TABLE XXVII.

Log. Sines, Tangents, and Secants.

S′. 34°			A		A	B		B	C		C 145° G′.	
M	Hour A.M.	Hour P.M.	Sine.	Diff.	Cosecant.	Tangent.	Diff.	Cotangent	Secant.	Diff.	Cosine.	M
0	7 28 0	4 32 0	9.74756	0	10.25244	9.82899	0	10.17101	10.08143	0	9.91857	60
1	27 52	32 8	74775	0	25225	82926	0	17074	08151	0	91849	59
2	27 44	32 16	74794	1	25206	82953	1	17047	08160	0	91840	58
3	27 36	32 24	74812	1	25188	82980	1	17020	08168	0	91832	57
4	27 28	32 32	74831	1	25169	83008	2	16992	08177	1	91823	56
5	7 27 20	4 32 40	9.74850	2	10.25150	9.83035	2	10.16965	10.08185	1	9.91815	55
6	27 12	32 48	74868	2	25132	83062	3	16938	08194	1	91806	54
7	27 4	32 56	74887	2	25113	83089	3	16911	08202	1	91798	53
8	26 56	33 4	74906	2	25094	83117	4	16883	08211	1	91789	52
9	26 48	33 12	74924	3	25076	83144	4	16856	08219	1	91781	51
10	7 26 40	4 33 20	9.74943	3	10.25057	9.83171	5	10.16829	10.08228	1	9.91772	50
11	26 32	33 28	74961	3	25039	83198	5	16802	08237	2	91763	49
12	26 24	33 36	74980	4	25020	83225	5	16775	08245	2	91755	48
13	26 16	33 44	74999	4	25001	83252	6	16748	08254	2	91746	47
14	26 8	33 52	75017	4	24983	83280	6	16720	08262	2	91738	46
15	7 26 0	4 34 0	9.75036	5	10.24964	9.83307	7	10.16693	10.08271	2	9.91729	45
16	25 52	34 8	75054	5	24946	83334	7	16666	08280	2	91720	44
17	25 44	34 16	75073	5	24927	83361	8	16639	08288	2	91712	43
18	25 36	34 24	75091	6	24909	83388	8	16612	08297	3	91703	42
19	25 28	34 32	75110	6	24890	83415	9	16585	08305	3	91695	41
20	7 25 20	4 34 40	9.75128	6	10.24872	9.83442	9	10.16558	10.08314	3	9.91686	40
21	25 12	34 48	75147	6	24853	83470	9	16530	08323	3	91677	39
22	25 4	34 56	75165	7	24835	83497	10	16503	08331	3	91669	38
23	24 56	35 4	75184	7	24816	83524	10	16476	08340	3	91660	37
24	24 48	35 12	75202	7	24798	83551	11	16449	08349	3	91651	36
25	7 24 40	4 35 20	9.75221	8	10.24779	9.83578	11	10.16422	10.08357	4	9.91643	35
26	24 32	35 28	75239	8	24761	83605	12	16395	08366	4	91634	34
27	24 24	35 36	75258	8	24742	83632	12	16368	08375	4	91625	33
28	24 16	35 44	75276	9	24724	83659	13	16341	08383	4	91617	32
29	24 8	35 52	75294	9	24706	83686	13	16314	08392	4	91608	31
30	7 24 0	4 36 0	9.75313	9	10.24687	9.83713	14	10.16287	10.08401	4	9.91599	30
31	23 52	36 8	75331	9	24669	83740	14	16260	08409	4	91591	29
32	23 44	36 16	75350	10	24650	83768	14	16232	08418	5	91582	28
33	23 36	36 24	75368	10	24632	83795	15	16205	08427	5	91573	27
34	23 28	36 32	75386	10	24614	83822	15	16178	08435	5	91565	26
35	7 23 20	4 36 40	9.75405	11	10.24595	9.83849	16	10.16151	10.08444	5	9.91556	25
36	23 12	36 48	75423	11	24577	83876	16	16124	08453	5	91547	24
37	23 4	36 56	75441	11	24559	83903	17	16097	08462	5	91538	23
38	22 56	37 4	75459	12	24541	83930	17	16070	08470	5	91530	22
39	22 48	37 12	75478	12	24522	83957	18	16043	08479	6	91521	21
40	7 22 40	4 37 20	9.75496	12	10.24504	9.83984	18	10.16016	10.08488	6	9.91512	20
41	22 32	37 28	75514	13	24486	84011	18	15989	08496	6	91504	19
42	22 24	37 36	75533	13	24467	84038	19	15962	08505	6	91495	18
43	22 16	37 44	75551	13	24449	84065	19	15935	08514	6	91486	17
44	22 8	37 52	75569	13	24431	84092	20	15908	08523	6	91477	16
45	7 22 0	4 38 0	9.75587	14	10.24413	9.84119	20	10.15881	10.08531	7	9.91469	15
46	21 52	38 8	75605	14	24395	84146	21	15854	08540	7	91460	14
47	21 44	38 16	75624	14	24376	84173	21	15827	08549	7	91451	13
48	21 36	38 24	75642	15	24358	84200	22	15800	08558	7	91442	12
49	21 28	38 32	75660	15	24340	84227	22	15773	08567	7	91433	11
50	7 21 20	4 38 40	9.75678	15	10.24322	9.84254	23	10.15746	10.08575	7	9.91425	10
51	21 12	38 48	75696	16	24304	84280	23	15720	08584	7	91416	9
52	21 4	38 56	75714	16	24286	84307	23	15693	08593	8	91407	8
53	20 56	39 4	75733	16	24267	84334	24	15666	08602	8	91398	7
54	20 48	39 12	75751	17	24249	84361	24	15639	08611	8	91389	6
55	7 20 40	4 39 20	9.75769	17	10.24231	9.84388	25	10.15612	10.08619	8	9.91381	5
56	20 32	39 28	75787	17	24213	84415	25	15585	08628	8	91372	4
57	20 24	39 36	75805	17	24195	84442	26	15558	08637	8	91363	3
58	20 16	39 44	75823	18	24177	84469	26	15531	08646	8	91354	2
59	20 8	39 52	75841	18	24159	84496	27	15504	08655	9	91345	1
60	20 0	40 0	75859	18	24141	84523	27	15477	08664	9	91336	0
M	Hour P.M.	Hour A.M.	Cosine.	Diff.	Secant.	Cotangent	Diff.	Tangent.	Cosecant.	Diff.	Sine.	M
124°			A		A	B		B	C		C 55°	

Seconds of time		1s	2s	3s	4s	5s	6s	7s
Prop. parts of cols.	A	2	5	7	9	11	14	16
	B	3	7	10	14	17	20	24
	C	1	2	3	4	5	7	8

TABLE XXVII.

Log. Sines, Tangents, and Secants.

S'. 35° | A | A | B | B | C | C 144° | G'.

M	Hour A.M.	Hour P.M.	Sine.	Diff.	Cosecant.	Tangent.	Diff.	Cotangent	Secant.	Diff.	Cosine.	M
0	7 20 0	4 40 0	9.75859	0	10.24141	9.84523	0	10.15477	10.08664	0	9.91336	60
1	19 52	40 8	75877	0	24123	84550	0	15450	08672	0	91328	59
2	19 44	40 16	75895	1	24105	84576	1	15424	08681	0	91319	58
3	19 36	40 24	75913	1	24087	84603	1	15397	08690	0	91310	57
4	19 28	40 32	75931	1	24069	84630	2	15370	08699	1	91301	56
5	7 19 20	4 40 40	9.75949	1	10.24051	9.84657	2	10.15343	10.08708	1	9.91292	55
6	19 12	40 48	75967	2	24033	84684	3	15316	08717	1	91283	54
7	19 4	40 56	75985	2	24015	84711	3	15289	08726	1	91274	53
8	18 56	41 4	76003	2	23997	84738	4	15262	08734	1	91266	52
9	18 48	41 12	76021	3	23979	84764	4	15236	08743	1	91257	51
10	7 18 40	4 41 20	9.76039	3	10.23961	9.84791	4	10.15209	10.08752	2	9.91248	50
11	18 32	41 28	76057	3	23943	84818	5	15182	08761	2	91239	49
12	18 24	41 36	76075	4	23925	84845	5	15155	08770	2	91230	48
13	18 16	41 44	76093	4	23907	84872	6	15128	08779	2	91221	47
14	18 8	41 52	76111	4	23889	84899	6	15101	08788	2	91212	46
15	7 18 0	4 42 0	9.76129	4	10.23871	9.84925	7	10.15075	10.08797	2	9.91203	45
16	17 52	42 8	76146	5	23854	84952	7	15048	08806	2	91194	44
17	17 44	42 16	76164	5	23836	84979	8	15021	08815	3	91185	43
18	17 36	42 24	76182	5	23818	85006	8	14994	08824	3	91176	42
19	17 28	42 32	76200	6	23800	85033	8	14967	08833	3	91167	41
20	7 17 20	4 42 40	9.76218	6	10.23782	9.85059	9	10.14941	10.08842	3	9.91158	40
21	17 12	42 48	76236	6	23764	85086	9	14914	08851	3	91149	39
22	17 4	42 56	76253	6	23747	85113	10	14887	08859	3	91141	38
23	16 56	43 4	76271	7	23729	85140	10	14860	08868	3	91132	37
24	16 48	43 12	76289	7	23711	85166	11	14834	08877	4	91123	36
25	7 16 40	4 43 20	9.76307	7	10.23693	9.85193	11	10.14807	10.08886	4	9.91114	35
26	16 32	43 28	76324	8	23676	85220	12	14780	08895	4	91105	34
27	16 24	43 36	76342	8	23658	85247	12	14753	08904	4	91096	33
28	16 16	43 44	76360	8	23640	85273	12	14727	08913	4	91087	32
29	16 8	43 52	76378	9	23622	85300	13	14700	08922	4	91078	31
30	7 16 0	4 44 0	9.76395	9	10.23605	9.85327	13	10.14673	10.08931	5	9.91069	30
31	15 52	44 8	76413	9	23587	85354	14	14646	08940	5	91060	29
32	15 44	44 16	76431	9	23569	85380	14	14620	08949	5	91051	28
33	15 36	44 24	76448	10	23552	85407	15	14593	08958	5	91042	27
34	15 28	44 32	76466	10	23534	85434	15	14566	08967	5	91033	26
35	7 15 20	4 44 40	9.76484	10	10.23516	9.85460	16	10.14540	10.08977	5	9.91023	25
36	15 12	44 48	76501	11	23499	85487	16	14513	08986	5	91014	24
37	15 4	44 56	76519	11	23481	85514	16	14486	08995	6	91005	23
38	14 56	45 4	76537	11	23463	85540	17	14460	09004	6	90996	22
39	14 48	45 12	76554	12	23446	85567	17	14433	09013	6	90987	21
40	7 14 40	4 45 20	9.76572	12	10.23428	9.85594	18	10.14406	10.09022	6	9.90978	20
41	14 32	45 28	76590	12	23410	85620	18	14380	09031	6	90969	19
42	14 24	45 36	76607	12	23393	85647	19	14353	09040	6	90960	18
43	14 16	45 44	76625	13	23375	85674	19	14326	09049	6	90951	17
44	14 8	45 52	76642	13	23358	85700	20	14300	09058	7	90942	16
45	7 14 0	4 46 0	9.76660	13	10.23340	9.85727	20	10.14273	10.09067	7	9.90933	15
46	13 52	46 8	76677	14	23323	85754	20	14246	09076	7	90924	14
47	13 44	46 16	76695	14	23305	85780	21	14220	09085	7	90915	13
48	13 36	46 24	76712	14	23288	85807	21	14193	09094	7	90906	12
49	13 28	46 32	76730	14	23270	85834	22	14166	09104	7	90896	11
50	7 13 20	4 46 40	9.76747	15	10.23253	9.85860	22	10.14140	10.09113	8	9.90887	10
51	13 12	46 48	76765	15	23235	85887	23	14113	09122	8	90878	9
52	13 4	46 56	76782	15	23218	85913	23	14087	09131	8	90869	8
53	12 56	47 4	76800	16	23200	85940	24	14060	09140	8	90860	7
54	12 48	47 12	76817	16	23183	85967	24	14033	09149	8	90851	6
55	7 12 40	4 47 20	9.76835	16	10.23165	9.85993	24	10.14007	10.09158	8	9.90842	5
56	12 32	47 28	76852	17	23148	86020	25	13980	09168	8	90832	4
57	12 24	47 36	76870	17	23130	86046	25	13954	09177	9	90823	3
58	12 16	47 44	76887	17	23113	86073	26	13927	09186	9	90814	2
59	12 8	47 52	76904	17	23096	86100	26	13900	09195	9	90805	1
60	12 0	48 0	76922	18	23078	86126	27	13874	09204	9	90796	0
M	Hour P.M.	Hour A.M.	Cosine.	Diff.	Secant.	Cotangent	Diff.	Tangent.	Cosecant.	Diff.	Sine.	M

125° | A | A | B | B | C | C | 54°

Seconds of time		1s	2s	3s	4s	5s	6s	7s
Prop. parts of cols.	A	2	4	7	9	11	13	16
	B	3	7	10	13	17	20	23
	C	1	2	3	5	6	7	8

TABLE XXVII.

Log. Sines, Tangents, and Secants.

S'. 36°			A		A	B		B	C		C 143° G'.	
M	Hour A.M.	Hour P.M.	Sine.	Diff.	Cosecant.	Tangent.	Diff.	Cotangent	Secant.	Diff.	Cosine.	M
0	7 12 0	4 48 0	9.76922	0	10.23078	9.86126	0	10.13874	10.09204	0	9.90796	60
1	11 52	48 8	76939	0	23061	86153	0	13847	09213	0	90787	59
2	11 44	48 16	76957	1	23043	86179	1	13821	09223	0	90777	58
3	11 36	48 24	76974	1	23026	86206	1	13794	09232	0	90768	57
4	11 28	48 32	76991	1	23009	86232	2	13768	09241	1	90759	56
5	7 11 20	4 48 40	9.77009	1	10.22991	9.86259	2	10.13741	10.09250	1	9.90750	55
6	11 12	48 48	77026	2	22974	86285	3	13715	09259	1	90741	54
7	11 4	48 56	77043	2	22957	86312	3	13688	09269	1	90731	53
8	10 56	49 4	77061	2	22939	86338	4	13662	09278	1	90722	52
9	10 48	49 12	77078	3	22922	86365	4	13635	09287	1	90713	51
10	7 10 40	4 49 20	9.77095	3	10.22905	9.86392	4	10.13608	10.09296	2	9.90704	50
11	10 32	49 28	77112	3	22888	86418	5	13582	09306	2	90694	49
12	10 24	49 36	77130	3	22870	86445	5	13555	09315	2	90685	48
13	10 16	49 44	77147	4	22853	86471	6	13529	09324	2	90676	47
14	10 8	49 52	77164	4	22836	86498	6	13502	09333	2	90667	46
15	7 10 0	4 50 0	9.77181	4	10.22819	9.86524	7	10.13476	10.09343	2	9.90657	45
16	9 52	50 8	77199	5	22801	86551	7	13449	09352	2	90648	44
17	9 44	50 16	77216	5	22784	86577	7	13423	09361	3	90639	43
18	9 36	50 24	77233	5	22767	86603	8	13397	09370	3	90630	42
19	9 28	50 32	77250	5	22750	86630	8	13370	09380	3	90620	41
20	7 9 20	4 50 40	9.77268	6	10.22732	9.86656	9	10.13344	10.09389	3	9.90611	40
21	9 12	50 48	77285	6	22715	86683	9	13317	09398	3	90602	39
22	9 4	50 56	77302	6	22698	86709	10	13291	09408	3	90592	38
23	8 56	51 4	77319	7	22681	86736	10	13264	09417	4	90583	37
24	8 48	51 12	77336	7	22664	86762	11	13238	09426	4	90574	36
25	7 8 40	4 51 20	9.77353	7	10.22647	9.86789	11	10.13211	10.09435	4	9.90565	35
26	8 32	51 28	77370	7	22630	86815	11	13185	09445	4	90555	34
27	8 24	51 36	77387	8	22613	86842	12	13158	09454	4	90546	33
28	8 16	51 44	77405	8	22595	86868	12	13132	09463	4	90537	32
29	8 8	51 52	77422	8	22578	86894	13	13106	09473	5	90527	31
30	7 8 0	4 52 0	9.77439	9	10.22561	9.86921	13	10.13079	10.09482	5	9.90518	30
31	7 52	52 8	77456	9	22544	86947	14	13053	09491	5	90509	29
32	7 44	52 16	77473	9	22527	86974	14	13026	09501	5	90499	28
33	7 36	52 24	77490	9	22510	87000	15	13000	09510	5	90490	27
34	7 28	52 32	77507	10	22493	87027	15	12973	09520	5	90480	26
35	7 7 20	4 52 40	9.77524	10	10.22476	9.87053	15	10.12947	10.09529	5	9.90471	25
36	7 12	52 48	77541	10	22459	87079	16	12921	09538	6	90462	24
37	7 4	52 56	77558	11	22442	87106	16	12894	09548	6	90452	23
38	6 56	53 4	77575	11	22425	87132	17	12868	09557	6	90443	22
39	6 48	53 12	77592	11	22408	87158	17	12842	09566	6	90434	21
40	7 6 40	4 53 20	9.77609	11	10.22391	9.87185	18	10.12815	10.09576	6	9.90424	20
41	6 32	53 28	77626	12	22374	87211	18	12789	09585	6	90415	19
42	6 24	53 36	77643	12	22357	87238	18	12762	09595	7	90405	18
43	6 16	53 44	77660	12	22340	87264	19	12736	09604	7	90396	17
44	6 8	53 52	77677	13	22323	87290	19	12710	09614	7	90386	16
45	7 6 0	4 54 0	9.77694	13	10.22306	9.87317	20	10.12683	10.09623	7	9.90377	15
46	5 52	54 8	77711	13	22289	87343	20	12657	09632	7	90368	14
47	5 44	54 16	77728	13	22272	87369	21	12631	09642	7	90358	13
48	5 36	54 24	77744	14	22256	87396	21	12604	09651	7	90349	12
49	5 28	54 32	77761	14	22239	87422	22	12578	09661	8	90339	11
50	7 5 20	4 54 40	9.77778	14	10.22222	9.87448	22	10.12552	10.09670	8	9.90330	10
51	5 12	54 48	77795	15	22205	87475	22	12525	09680	8	90320	9
52	5 4	54 56	77812	15	22188	87501	23	12499	09689	8	90311	8
53	4 56	55 4	77829	15	22171	87527	23	12473	09699	8	90301	7
54	4 48	55 12	77846	15	22154	87554	24	12446	09708	8	90292	6
55	7 4 40	4 55 20	9.77862	16	10.22138	9.87580	24	10.12420	10.09718	9	9.90282	5
56	4 32	55 28	77879	16	22121	87606	25	12394	09727	9	90273	4
57	4 24	55 36	77896	16	22104	87633	25	12367	09737	9	90263	3
58	4 16	55 44	77913	16	22087	87659	26	12341	09746	9	90254	2
59	4 8	55 52	77930	17	22070	87685	26	12315	09756	9	90244	1
60	4 0	56 0	77946	17	22054	87711	26	12289	09765	9	90235	0
M	Hour P.M.	Hour A.M.	Cosine.	Diff.	Secant.	Cotangent	Diff.	Tangent.	Cosecant.	Diff.	Sine.	M
126°			A		A	B		B	C		C 53°	

Seconds of time		1s	2s	3s	4s	5s	6s	7s
Prop. parts of cols.	A	2	4	6	9	11	13	15
	B	3	7	10	13	17	20	23
	C	1	2	4	5	6	7	8

TABLE XXVII.

S'. Log. Sines, Tangents, and Secants. G'.

37° A A B B C C 142°

M	Hour A.M.	Hour P.M.	Sine. A	Diff.	Cosecant. A	Tangent. B	Diff.	Cotangent B	Secant. C	Diff.	Cosine. C	M
0	7 4 0	4 56 0	9.77946	0	10.22054	9.87711	0	10.12289	10.09765	0	9.90235	60
1	3 52	56 8	77963	0	22037	87738	0	12262	09775	0	90225	59
2	3 44	56 16	77980	1	22020	87764	1	12236	09784	0	90216	58
3	3 36	56 24	77997	1	22003	87790	1	12210	09794	0	90206	57
4	3 28	56 32	78013	1	21987	87817	2	12183	09803	1	90197	56
5	7 3 20	4 56 40	9.78030	1	10.21970	9.87843	2	10.12157	10.09813	1	9.90187	55
6	3 12	56 48	78047	2	21953	87869	3	12131	09822	1	90178	54
7	3 4	56 56	78063	2	21937	87895	3	12105	09832	1	90168	53
8	2 56	57 4	78080	2	21920	87922	3	12078	09841	1	90159	52
9	2 48	57 12	78097	2	21903	87948	4	12052	09851	1	90149	51
10	7 2 40	4 57 20	9.78113	3	10.21887	9.87974	4	10.12026	10.09861	2	9.90139	50
11	2 32	57 28	78130	3	21870	88000	5	12000	09870	2	90130	49
12	2 24	57 36	78147	3	21853	88027	5	11973	09880	2	90120	48
13	2 16	57 44	78163	4	21837	88053	6	11947	09889	2	90111	47
14	2 8	57 52	78180	4	21820	88079	6	11921	09899	2	90101	46
15	7 2 0	4 58 0	9.78197	4	10.21803	9.88105	7	10.11895	10.09909	2	9.90091	45
16	1 52	58 8	78213	4	21787	88131	7	11869	09918	3	90082	44
17	1 44	58 16	78230	5	21770	88158	7	11842	09928	3	90072	43
18	1 36	58 24	78246	5	21754	88184	8	11816	09937	3	90063	42
19	1 28	58 32	78263	5	21737	88210	8	11790	09947	3	90053	41
20	7 1 20	4 58 40	9.78280	5	10.21720	9.88236	9	10.11764	10.09957	3	9.90043	40
21	1 12	58 48	78296	6	21704	88262	9	11738	09966	3	90034	39
22	1 4	58 56	78313	6	21687	88289	10	11711	09976	4	90024	38
23	0 56	59 4	78329	6	21671	88315	10	11685	09986	4	90014	37
24	0 48	59 12	78346	7	21654	88341	10	11659	09995	4	90005	36
25	7 0 40	4 59 20	9.78362	7	10.21638	9.88367	11	10.11633	10.10005	4	9.89995	35
26	0 32	59 28	78379	7	21621	88393	11	11607	10015	4	89985	34
27	0 24	59 36	78395	7	21605	88420	12	11580	10024	4	89976	33
28	0 16	59 44	78412	8	21588	88446	12	11554	10034	5	89966	32
29	0 8	59 52	78428	8	21572	88472	13	11528	10044	5	89956	31
30	7 0 0	5 0 0	9.78445	8	10.21555	9.88498	13	10.11502	10.10053	5	9.89947	30
31	6 59 52	0 8	78461	9	21539	88524	14	11476	10063	5	89937	29
32	59 44	0 16	78478	9	21522	88550	14	11450	10073	5	89927	28
33	59 36	0 24	78494	9	21506	88577	14	11423	10082	5	89918	27
34	59 28	0 32	78510	9	21490	88603	15	11397	10092	5	89908	26
35	6 59 20	5 0 40	9.78527	10	10.21473	9.88629	15	10.11371	10.10102	6	9.89898	25
36	59 12	0 48	78543	10	21457	88655	16	11345	10112	6	89888	24
37	59 4	0 56	78560	10	21440	88681	16	11319	10121	6	89879	23
38	58 56	1 4	78576	10	21424	88707	17	11293	10131	6	89869	22
39	58 48	1 12	78592	11	21408	88733	17	11267	10141	6	89859	21
40	6 58 40	5 1 20	9.78609	11	10.21391	9.88759	17	10.11241	10.10151	6	9.89849	20
41	58 32	1 28	78625	11	21375	88786	18	11214	10160	7	89840	19
42	58 24	1 36	78642	12	21358	88812	18	11188	10170	7	89830	18
43	58 16	1 44	78658	12	21342	88838	19	11162	10180	7	89820	17
44	58 8	1 52	78674	12	21326	88864	19	11136	10190	7	89810	16
45	6 58 0	5 2 0	9.78691	12	10.21309	9.88890	20	10.11110	10.10199	7	9.89801	15
46	57 52	2 8	78707	13	21293	88916	20	11084	10209	7	89791	14
47	57 44	2 16	78723	13	21277	88942	20	11058	10219	8	89781	13
48	57 36	2 24	78739	13	21261	88968	21	11032	10229	8	89771	12
49	57 28	2 32	78756	13	21244	88994	21	11006	10239	8	89761	11
50	6 57 20	5 2 40	9.78772	14	10.21228	9.89020	22	10.10980	10.10248	8	9.89752	10
51	57 12	2 48	78788	14	21212	89046	22	10954	10258	8	89742	9
52	57 4	2 56	78805	14	21195	89073	23	10927	10268	8	89732	8
53	56 56	3 4	78821	15	21179	89099	23	10901	10278	9	89722	7
54	56 48	3 12	78837	15	21163	89125	24	10875	10288	9	89712	6
55	6 56 40	5 3 20	9.78853	15	10.21147	9.89151	24	10.10849	10.10298	9	9.89702	5
56	56 32	3 28	78869	15	21131	89177	24	10823	10307	9	89693	4
57	56 24	3 36	78886	16	21114	89203	25	10797	10317	9	89683	3
58	56 16	3 44	78902	16	21098	89229	25	10771	10327	9	89673	2
59	56 8	3 52	78918	16	21082	89255	26	10745	10337	10	89663	1
60	56 0	4 0	78934	16	21066	89281	26	10719	10347	10	89653	0
M	Hour P.M.	Hour A.M.	Cosine. A	Diff.	Secant. A	Cotangent B	Diff.	Tangent. B	Cosecant. C	Diff.	Sine. C	M

127° A A B B C C 52°

Seconds of time		1s	2s	3s	4s	5s	6s	7s
Prop. parts of cols.	A	2	4	6	8	10	12	14
	B	3	7	10	13	16	20	23
	C	1	2	4	5	6	7	8

TABLE XXVII.

S'. **Log. Sines, Tangents, and Secants.** G'.

38°			A		A	B		B	C		C	141°
M	Hour A.M.	Hour P.M.	Sine.	Diff.	Cosecant.	Tangent.	Diff.	Cotangent	Secant.	Diff.	Cosine.	M
0	6 56 0	5 4 0	9.78934	0	10.21066	9.89281	0	10.10719	10.10347	0	9.89653	60
1	55 52	4 8	78950	0	21050	89307	0	10693	10357	0	89643	59
2	55 44	4 16	78967	1	21033	89333	1	10667	10367	0	89633	58
3	55 36	4 24	78983	1	21017	89359	1	10641	10376	1	89624	57
4	55 28	4 32	78999	1	21001	89385	2	10615	10386	1	89614	56
5	6 55 20	5 4 40	9.79015	1	10.20985	9.89411	2	10.10589	10.10396	1	9.89604	55
6	55 12	4 48	79031	2	20969	89437	3	10563	10406	1	89594	54
7	55 4	4 56	79047	2	20953	89463	3	10537	10416	1	89584	53
8	54 56	5 4	79063	2	20937	89489	3	10511	10426	1	89574	52
9	54 48	5 12	79079	2	20921	89515	4	10485	10436	2	89564	51
10	6 54 40	5 5 20	9.79095	3	10.20905	9.89541	4	10.10459	10.10446	2	9.89554	50
11	54 32	5 28	79111	3	20889	89567	5	10433	10456	2	89544	49
12	54 24	5 36	79128	3	20872	89593	5	10407	10466	2	89534	48
13	54 16	5 44	79144	3	20856	89619	6	10381	10476	2	89524	47
14	54 8	5 52	79160	4	20840	89645	6	10355	10486	2	89514	46
15	6 54 0	5 6 0	9.79176	4	10.20824	9.89671	6	10.10329	10.10496	3	9.89504	45
16	53 52	6 8	79192	4	20808	89697	7	10303	10505	3	89495	44
17	53 44	6 16	79208	5	20792	89723	7	10277	10515	3	89485	43
18	53 36	6 24	79224	5	20776	89749	8	10251	10525	3	89475	42
19	53 28	6 32	79240	5	20760	89775	8	10225	10535	3	89465	41
20	6 53 20	5 6 40	9.79256	5	10.20744	9.89801	9	10.10199	10.10545	3	9.89455	40
21	53 12	6 48	79272	6	20728	89827	9	10173	10555	4	89445	39
22	53 4	6 56	79288	6	20712	89853	10	10147	10565	4	89435	38
23	52 56	7 4	79304	6	20696	89879	10	10121	10575	4	89425	37
24	52 48	7 12	79319	6	20681	89905	10	10095	10585	4	89415	36
25	6 52 40	5 7 20	9.79335	7	10.20665	9.89931	11	10.10069	10.10595	4	9.89405	35
26	52 32	7 28	79351	7	20649	89957	11	10043	10605	4	89395	34
27	52 24	7 36	79367	7	20633	89983	12	10017	10615	5	89385	33
28	52 16	7 44	79383	7	20617	90009	12	09991	10625	5	89375	32
29	52 8	7 52	79399	8	20601	90035	13	09965	10636	5	89364	31
30	6 52 0	5 8 0	9.79415	8	10.20585	9.90061	13	10.09939	10.10646	5	9.89354	30
31	51 52	8 8	79431	8	20569	90086	13	09914	10656	5	89344	29
32	51 44	8 16	79447	8	20553	90112	14	09888	10666	5	89334	28
33	51 36	8 24	79463	9	20537	90138	14	09862	10676	6	89324	27
34	51 28	8 32	79478	9	20522	90164	15	09836	10686	6	89314	26
35	6 51 20	5 8 40	9.79494	9	10.20506	9.90190	15	10.09810	10.10696	6	9.89304	25
36	51 12	8 48	79510	10	20490	90216	16	09784	10706	6	89294	24
37	51 4	8 56	79526	10	20474	90242	16	09758	10716	6	89284	23
38	50 56	9 4	79542	10	20458	90268	16	09732	10726	6	89274	22
39	50 48	9 12	79558	10	20442	90294	17	09706	10736	7	89264	21
40	6 50 40	5 9 20	9.79573	11	10.20427	9.90320	17	10.09680	10.10746	7	9.89254	20
41	50 32	9 28	79589	11	20411	90346	18	09654	10756	7	89244	19
42	50 24	9 36	79605	11	20395	90371	18	09629	10767	7	89233	18
43	50 16	9 44	79621	11	20379	90397	19	09603	10777	7	89223	17
44	50 8	9 52	79636	12	20364	90423	19	09577	10787	7	89213	16
45	6 50 0	5 10 0	9.79652	12	10.20348	9.90449	19	10.09551	10.10797	8	9.89203	15
46	49 52	10 8	79668	12	20332	90475	20	09525	10807	8	89193	14
47	49 44	10 16	79684	12	20316	90501	20	09499	10817	8	89183	13
48	49 36	10 24	79699	13	20301	90527	21	09473	10827	8	89173	12
49	49 28	10 32	79715	13	20285	90553	21	09447	10838	8	89162	11
50	6 49 20	5 10 40	9.79731	13	10.20269	9.90578	22	10.09422	10.10848	8	9.89152	10
51	49 12	10 48	79746	14	20254	90604	22	09396	10858	9	89142	9
52	49 4	10 56	79762	14	20238	90630	22	09370	10868	9	89132	8
53	48 56	11 4	79778	14	20222	90656	23	09344	10878	9	89122	7
54	48 48	11 12	79793	14	20207	90682	23	09318	10888	9	89112	6
55	6 48 40	5 11 20	9.79809	15	10.20191	9.90708	24	10.09292	10.10899	9	9.89101	5
56	48 32	11 28	79825	15	20175	90734	24	09266	10909	9	89091	4
57	48 24	11 36	79840	15	20160	90759	25	09241	10919	10	89081	3
58	48 16	11 44	79856	15	20144	90785	25	09215	10929	10	89071	2
59	48 8	11 52	79872	16	20128	90811	26	09189	10940	10	89060	1
60	48 0	12 0	79887	16	20113	90837	26	09163	10950	10	89050	0
M	Hour P.M.	Hour A.M.	Cosine.	Diff.	Secant.	Cotangent	Diff.	Tangent.	Cosecant.	Diff.	Sine.	M
128°			A		A	B		B	C		C	51°

Seconds of time		1ˢ	2ˢ	3ˢ	4ˢ	5ˢ	6ˢ	7ˢ
Prop. parts of cols.	A	2	4	6	8	10	12	14
	B	3	6	10	13	16	19	23
	C	1	3	4	5	6	8	9

TABLE XXVII.

S'. **Log. Sines, Tangents, and Secants.** G'.

39° A A B B C C 140°

M	Hour A.M.	Hour P.M.	Sine.	Diff.	Cosecant.	Tangent.	Diff.	Cotangent	Secant.	Diff.	Cosine.	M
0	6 48 0	5 12 0	9.79887	0	10.20113	9.90837	0	10.09163	10.10950	0	9.89050	60
1	47 52	12 8	79903	0	20097	90863	0	09137	10960	0	89040	59
2	47 44	12 16	79918	1	20082	90889	1	09111	10970	0	89030	58
3	47 36	12 24	79934	1	20066	90914	1	09086	10980	1	89020	57
4	47 28	12 32	79950	1	20050	90940	2	09060	10991	1	89009	56
5	6 47 20	5 12 40	9.79965	1	10.20035	9.90966	2	10.09034	10.11001	1	9.88999	55
6	47 12	12 48	79981	2	20019	90992	3	09008	11011	1	88989	54
7	47 4	12 56	79996	2	20004	91018	3	08982	11022	1	88978	53
8	46 56	13 4	80012	2	19988	91043	3	08957	11032	1	88968	52
9	46 48	13 12	80027	2	19973	91069	4	08931	11042	2	88958	51
10	6 46 40	5 13 20	9.80043	3	10.19957	9.91095	4	10.08905	10.11052	2	9.88948	50
11	46 32	13 28	80058	3	19942	91121	5	08879	11063	2	88937	49
12	46 24	13 36	80074	3	19926	91147	5	08853	11073	2	88927	48
13	46 16	13 44	80089	3	19911	91172	6	08828	11083	2	88917	47
14	46 8	13 52	80105	4	19895	91198	6	08802	11094	2	88906	46
15	6 46 0	5 14 0	9.80120	4	10.19880	9.91224	6	10.08776	10.11104	3	9.88896	45
16	45 52	14 8	80136	4	19864	91250	7	08750	11114	3	88886	44
17	45 44	14 16	80151	4	19849	91276	7	08724	11125	3	88875	43
18	45 36	14 24	80166	5	19834	91301	8	08699	11135	3	88865	42
19	45 28	14 32	80182	5	19818	91327	8	08673	11145	3	88855	41
20	6 45 20	5 14 40	9.80197	5	10.19803	9.91353	9	10.08647	10.11156	3	9.88844	40
21	45 12	14 48	80213	5	19787	91379	9	08621	11166	4	88834	39
22	45 4	14 56	80228	6	19772	91404	9	08596	11176	4	88824	38
23	44 56	15 4	80244	6	19756	91430	10	08570	11187	4	88813	37
24	44 48	15 12	80259	6	19741	91456	10	08544	11197	4	88803	36
25	6 44 40	5 15 20	9.80274	6	10.19726	9.91482	11	10.08518	10.11207	4	9.88793	35
26	44 32	15 28	80290	7	19710	91507	11	08493	11218	5	88782	34
27	44 24	15 36	80305	7	19695	91533	12	08467	11228	5	88772	33
28	44 16	15 44	80320	7	19680	91559	12	08441	11239	5	88761	32
29	44 8	15 52	80336	7	19664	91585	12	08415	11249	5	88751	31
30	6 44 0	5 16 0	9.80351	8	10.19649	9.91610	13	10.08390	10,11259	5	9.88741	30
31	43 52	16 8	80366	8	19634	91636	13	08364	11270	5	88730	29
32	43 44	16 16	80382	8	19618	91662	14	08338	11280	6	88720	28
33	43 36	16 24	80397	8	19603	91688	14	08312	11291	6	88709	27
34	43 28	16 32	80412	9	19588	91713	15	08287	11301	6	88699	26
35	6 43 20	5 16 40	9.80428	9	10.19572	9.91739	15	10.08261	10.11312	6	9.88688	25
36	43 12	16 48	80443	9	19557	91765	15	08235	11322	6	88678	24
37	43 4	16 56	80458	9	19542	91791	16	08209	11332	6	88668	23
38	42 56	17 4	80473	10	19527	91816	16	08184	11343	7	88657	22
39	42 48	17 12	80489	10	19511	91842	17	08158	11353	7	88647	21
40	6 42 40	5 17 20	9.80504	10	10.19496	9.91868	17	10.08132	10.11364	7	9.88636	20
41	42 32	17 28	80519	10	19481	91893	18	08107	11374	7	88626	19
42	42 24	17 36	80534	11	19466	91919	18	08081	11385	7	88615	18
43	42 16	17 44	80550	11	19450	91945	18	08055	11395	7	88605	17
44	42 8	17 52	80565	11	19435	91971	19	08029	11406	8	88594	16
45	6 42 0	5 18 0	9.80580	12	10.19420	9.91996	19	10.08004	10.11416	8	9.88584	15
46	41 52	18 8	80595	12	19405	92022	20	07978	11427	8	88573	14
47	41 44	18 16	80610	12	19390	92048	20	07952	11437	8	88563	13
48	41 36	18 24	80625	12	19375	92073	21	07927	11448	8	88552	12
49	41 28	18 32	80641	13	19359	92099	21	07901	11458	9	88542	11
50	6 41 20	5 18 40	9.80656	13	10.19344	9.92125	21	10.07875	10.11469	9	9.88531	10
51	41 12	18 48	80671	13	19329	92150	22	07850	11479	9	88521	9
52	41 4	18 56	80686	13	19314	92176	22	07824	11490	9	88510	8
53	40 56	19 4	80701	14	19299	92202	23	07798	11501	9	88499	7
54	40 48	19 12	80716	14	19284	92227	23	07773	11511	9	88489	6
55	6 40 40	5 19 20	9.80731	14	10.19269	9.92253	24	10.07747	10.11522	10	9.88478	5
56	40 32	19 28	80746	14	19254	92279	24	07721	11532	10	88468	4
57	40 24	19 36	80762	15	19238	92304	24	07696	11543	10	88457	3
58	40 16	19 44	80777	15	19223	92330	25	07670	11553	10	88447	2
59	40 8	19 52	80792	15	19208	92356	25	07644	11564	10	88436	1
60	40 0	20 0	80807	15	19193	92381	26	07619	11575	10	88425	0
M	Hour P.M.	Hour A.M.	Cosine.	Diff.	Secant.	Cotangent	Diff.	Tangent.	Cosecant.	Diff.	Sine.	M

129° A A B B C C 50°

Seconds of time		1s	2s	3s	4s	5s	6s	7s
Prop. parts of cols.	A	2	4	6	8	10	12	13
	B	3	6	10	13	16	19	23
	C	1	3	4	5	7	8	9

TABLE XXVII.

S′. **Log. Sines, Tangents, and Secants.** G.

40°			A		A	B		B	C		C	139°
M	Hour A.M.	Hour P.M.	Sine.	Diff.	Cosecant.	Tangent.	Diff.	Cotangent	Secant.	Diff.	Cosine.	M
0	6 40 0	5 20 0	9.80807	0	10.19193	9.92381	0	10.07619	10.11575	0	9.88425	60
1	39 52	20 8	80822	0	19178	92407	0	07593	11585	0	88415	59
2	39 44	20 16	80837	0	19163	92433	1	07567	11596	0	88404	58
3	39 36	20 24	80852	1	19148	92458	1	07542	11606	1	88394	57
4	39 28	20 32	80867	1	19133	92484	2	07516	11617	1	88383	56
5	6 39 20	5 20 40	9.80882	1	10.19118	9.92510	2	10.07490	10.11628	1	9.88372	55
6	39 12	20 48	80897	1	19103	92535	3	07465	11638	1	88362	54
7	39 4	20 56	80912	2	19088	92561	3	07439	11649	1	88351	53
8	38 56	21 4	80927	2	19073	92587	3	07413	11660	1	88340	52
9	38 48	21 12	80942	2	19058	92612	4	07388	11670	2	88330	51
10	6 38 40	5 21 20	9.80957	2	10.19043	9.92638	4	10.07362	10.11681	2	9.88319	50
11	38 32	21 28	80972	3	19028	92663	5	07337	11692	2	88308	49
12	38 24	21 36	80987	3	19013	92689	5	07311	11702	2	88298	48
13	38 16	21 44	81002	3	18998	92715	6	07285	11713	2	88287	47
14	38 8	21 52	81017	3	18983	92740	6	07260	11724	3	88276	46
15	6 38 0	5 22 0	9.81032	4	10.18968	9.92766	6	10.07234	10.11734	3	9.88266	45
16	37 52	22 8	81047	4	18953	92792	7	07208	11745	3	88255	44
17	37 44	22 16	81061	4	18939	92817	7	07183	11756	3	88244	43
18	37 36	22 24	81076	4	18924	92843	8	07157	11766	3	88234	42
19	37 28	22 32	81091	5	18909	92868	8	07132	11777	3	88223	41
20	6 37 20	5 22 40	9.81106	5	10.18894	9.92894	9	10.07106	10.11788	4	9.88212	40
21	37 12	22 48	81121	5	18879	92920	9	07080	11799	4	88201	39
22	37 4	22 56	81136	5	18864	92945	9	07055	11809	4	88191	38
23	36 56	23 4	81151	6	18849	92971	10	07029	11820	4	88180	37
24	36 48	23 12	81166	6	18834	92996	10	07004	11831	4	88169	36
25	6 36 40	5 23 20	9.81180	6	10.18820	9.93022	11	10.06978	10.11842	4	9.88158	35
26	36 32	23 28	81195	6	18805	93048	11	06952	11852	5	88148	34
27	36 24	23 36	81210	7	18790	93073	12	06927	11863	5	88137	33
28	36 16	23 44	81225	7	18775	93099	12	06901	11874	5	88126	32
29	36 8	23 52	81240	7	18760	93124	12	06876	11885	5	88115	31
30	6 36 0	5 24 0	9.81254	7	10.18746	9.93150	13	10.06850	10.11895	5	9.88105	30
31	35 52	24 8	81269	8	18731	93175	13	06825	11906	6	88094	29
32	35 44	24 16	81284	8	18716	93201	14	06799	11917	6	88083	28
33	35 36	24 24	81299	8	18701	93227	14	06773	11928	6	88072	27
34	35 28	24 32	81314	8	18686	93252	14	06748	11939	6	88061	26
35	6 35 20	5 24 40	9.81328	9	10.18672	9.93278	15	10.06722	10.11949	6	9.88051	25
36	35 12	24 48	81343	9	18657	93303	15	06697	11960	6	88040	24
37	35 4	24 56	81358	9	18642	93329	16	06671	11971	7	88029	23
38	34 56	25 4	81372	9	18628	93354	16	06646	11982	7	88018	22
39	34 48	25 12	81387	10	18613	93380	17	06620	11993	7	88007	21
40	6 34 40	5 25 20	9.81402	10	10.18598	9.93406	17	10.06594	10.12004	7	9.87996	20
41	34 32	25 28	81417	10	18583	93431	17	06569	12015	7	87985	19
42	34 24	25 36	81431	10	18569	93457	18	06543	12025	8	87975	18
43	34 16	25 44	81446	11	18554	93482	18	06518	12036	8	87964	17
44	34 8	25 52	81461	11	18539	93508	19	06492	12047	8	87953	16
45	6 34 0	5 26 0	9.81475	11	10.18525	9.93533	19	10.06467	10.12058	8	9.87942	15
46	33 52	26 8	81490	11	18510	93559	20	06441	12069	8	87931	14
47	33 44	26 16	81505	12	18495	93584	20	06416	12080	8	87920	13
48	33 36	26 24	81519	12	18481	93610	20	06390	12091	9	87909	12
49	33 28	26 32	81534	12	18466	93636	21	06364	12102	9	87898	11
50	6 33 20	5 26 40	9.81549	12	10.18451	9.93661	21	10.06339	10.12113	9	9.87887	10
51	33 12	26 48	81563	13	18437	93687	22	06313	12123	9	87877	9
52	33 4	26 56	81578	13	18422	93712	22	06288	12134	9	87866	8
53	32 56	27 4	81592	13	18408	93738	23	06262	12145	10	87855	7
54	32 48	27 12	81607	13	18393	93763	23	06237	12156	10	87844	6
55	6 32 40	5 27 20	9.81622	14	10.18378	9.93789	23	10.06211	10.12167	10	9.87833	5
56	32 32	27 28	81636	14	18364	93814	24	06186	12178	10	87822	4
57	32 24	27 36	81651	14	18349	93840	24	06160	12189	10	87811	3
58	32 16	27 44	81665	14	18335	93865	25	06135	12200	10	87800	2
59	32 8	27 52	81680	15	18320	93891	25	06109	12211	11	87789	1
60	32 0	28 0	81694	15	18306	93916	26	06084	12222	11	87778	0
M	Hour P.M.	Hour A.M.	Cosine.	Diff.	Secant.	Cotangent	Diff.	Tangent.	Cosecant.	Diff.	Sine.	M
130°			A		A	B		B	C		C	49°

Seconds of time		1s	2s	3s	4s	5s	6s	7s
Prop. parts of cols.	A	2	4	6	7	9	11	13
	B	3	6	10	13	16	19	22
	C	1	3	4	5	7	8	9

TABLE XXVII.

S'. Log. Sines, Tangents, and Secants. G

41°			A		A	B		B	C		C	138°
M	Hour A.M.	Hour P.M.	Sine.	Diff.	Cosecant.	Tangent.	Diff.	Cotangent	Secant.	Diff.	Cosine.	M
0	6 32 0	5 28 0	9.81694	0	10.18306	9.93916	0	10.06084	10.12222	0	9.87778	60
1	31 52	28 8	81709	0	18291	93942	0	06058	12233	0	87767	59
2	31 44	28 16	81723	0	18277	93967	1	06033	12244	0	87756	58
3	31 36	28 24	81738	1	18262	93993	1	06007	12255	1	87745	57
4	31 28	28 32	81752	1	18248	94018	2	05982	12266	1	87734	56
5	6 31 20	5 28 40	9.81767	1	10.18233	9.94044	2	10.05956	10.12277	1	9.87723	55
6	31 12	28 48	81781	1	18219	94069	3	05931	12288	1	87712	54
7	31 4	28 56	81796	2	18204	94095	3	05905	12299	1	87701	53
8	30 56	29 4	81810	2	18190	94120	3	05880	12310	1	87690	52
9	30 48	29 12	81825	2	18175	94146	4	05854	12321	2	87679	51
10	6 30 40	5 29 20	9.81839	2	10.18161	9.94171	4	10.05829	10.12332	2	9.87668	50
11	30 32	29 28	81854	3	18146	94197	5	05803	12343	2	87657	49
12	30 24	29 36	81868	3	18132	94222	5	05778	12354	2	87646	48
13	30 16	29 44	81882	3	18118	94248	6	05752	12365	2	87635	47
14	30 8	29 52	81897	3	18103	94273	6	05727	12376	3	87624	46
15	6 30 0	5 30 0	9.81911	4	10.18089	9.94299	6	10.05701	10.12387	3	9.87613	45
16	29 52	30 8	81926	4	18074	94324	7	05676	12399	3	87601	44
17	29 44	30 16	81940	4	18060	94350	7	05650	12410	3	87590	43
18	29 36	30 24	81955	4	18045	94375	8	05625	12421	3	87579	42
19	29 28	30 32	81969	5	18031	94401	8	05599	12432	4	87568	41
20	6 29 20	5 30 40	9.81983	5	10.18017	9.94426	8	10.05574	10.12443	4	9.87557	40
21	29 12	30 48	81998	5	18002	94452	9	05548	12454	4	87546	39
22	29 4	30 56	82012	5	17988	94477	9	05523	12465	4	87535	38
23	28 56	31 4	82026	5	17974	94503	10	05497	12476	4	87524	37
24	28 48	31 12	82041	6	17959	94528	10	05472	12487	4	87513	36
25	6 28 40	5 31 20	9.82055	6	10.17945	9.94554	11	10.05446	10.12499	5	9.87501	35
26	28 32	31 28	82069	6	17931	94579	11	05421	12510	5	87490	34
27	28 24	31 36	82084	6	17916	94604	11	05396	12521	5	87479	33
28	28 16	31 44	82098	7	17902	94630	12	05370	12532	5	87468	32
29	28 8	31 52	82112	7	17888	94655	12	05345	12543	5	87457	31
30	6 28 0	5 32 0	9.82126	7	10.17874	9.94681	13	10.05319	10.12554	6	9.87446	30
31	27 52	32 8	82141	7	17859	94706	13	05294	12566	6	87434	29
32	27 44	32 16	82155	8	17845	94732	14	05268	12577	6	87423	28
33	27 36	32 24	82169	8	17831	94757	14	05243	12588	6	87412	27
34	27 28	32 32	82184	8	17816	94783	14	05217	12599	6	87401	26
35	6 27 20	5 32 40	9.82198	8	10.17802	9.94808	15	10.05192	10.12610	7	9.87390	25
36	27 12	32 48	82212	9	17788	94834	15	05166	12622	7	87378	24
37	27 4	32 56	82226	9	17774	94859	16	05141	12633	7	87367	23
38	26 56	33 4	82240	9	17760	94884	16	05116	12644	7	87356	22
39	26 48	33 12	82255	9	17745	94910	17	05090	12655	7	87345	21
40	6 26 40	5 33 20	9.82269	10	10.17731	9.94935	17	10.05065	10.12666	7	9.87334	20
41	26 32	33 28	82283	10	17717	94961	17	05039	12678	8	87322	19
42	26 24	33 36	82297	10	17703	94986	18	05014	12689	8	87311	18
43	26 16	33 44	82311	10	17689	95012	18	04988	12700	8	87300	17
44	26 8	33 52	82326	10	17674	95037	19	04963	12712	8	87288	16
45	6 26 0	5 34 0	9.82340	11	10.17660	9.95062	19	10.04938	10.12723	8	9.87277	15
46	25 52	34 8	82354	11	17646	95088	20	04912	12734	9	87266	14
47	25 44	34 16	82368	11	17632	95113	20	04887	12745	9	87255	13
48	25 36	34 24	82382	11	17618	95139	20	04861	12757	9	87243	12
49	25 28	34 32	82396	12	17604	95164	21	04836	12768	9	87232	11
50	6 25 20	5 34 40	9.82410	12	10.17590	9.95190	21	10.04810	10.12779	9	9.87221	10
51	25 12	34 48	82424	12	17576	95215	22	04785	12791	10	87209	9
52	25 4	34 56	82439	12	17561	95240	22	04760	12802	10	87198	8
53	24 56	35 4	82453	13	17547	95266	22	04734	12813	10	87187	7
54	24 48	35 12	82467	13	17533	95291	23	04709	12825	10	87175	6
55	6 24 40	5 35 20	9.82481	13	10.17519	9.95317	23	10.04683	10.12836	10	9.87164	5
56	24 32	35 28	82495	13	17505	95342	24	04658	12847	10	87153	4
57	24 24	35 36	82509	14	17491	95368	24	04632	12859	11	87141	3
58	24 16	35 44	82523	14	17477	95393	25	04607	12870	11	87130	2
59	24 8	35 52	82537	14	17463	95418	25	04582	12881	11	87119	1
60	24 0	36 0	82551	14	17449	95444	25	04556	12893	11	87107	0
M	Hour P.M.	Hour A.M.	Cosine.	Diff.	Secant.	Cotangent	Diff.	Tangent.	Cosecant.	Diff.	Sine.	M
131°			A		A	B		B	C		C	48°

Seconds of time		1s	2s	3s	4s	5s	6s	7s
Prop. parts of cols.	A	2	4	5	7	9	11	12
	B	3	6	10	13	16	19	22
	C	1	3	4	6	7	8	10

TABLE XXVII.

Log. Sines, Tangents, and Secants.

S′. 42° — G′. 137°

M	Hour A.M.	Hour P.M.	A Sine.	Diff.	A Cosecant.	B Tangent.	Diff.	B Cotangent	C Secant.	Diff.	C Cosine.	M
0	6 24 0	5 36 0	9.82551	0	10.17449	9.95444	0	10.04556	10.12893	0	9.87107	60
1	23 52	36 8	82565	0	17435	95469	0	04531	12904	0	87096	59
2	23 44	36 16	82579	0	17421	95495	1	04505	12915	0	87085	58
3	23 36	36 24	82593	1	17407	95520	1	04480	12927	1	87073	57
4	23 28	36 32	82607	1	17393	95545	2	04455	12938	1	87062	56
5	6 23 20	5 36 40	9.82621	1	10.17379	9.95571	2	10.04429	10.12950	1	9.87050	55
6	23 12	36 48	82635	1	17365	95596	3	04404	12961	1	87039	54
7	23 4	36 56	82649	2	17351	95622	3	04378	12972	1	87028	53
8	22 56	37 4	82663	2	17337	95647	3	04353	12984	2	87016	52
9	22 48	37 12	82677	2	17323	95672	4	04328	12995	2	87005	51
10	6 22 40	5 37 20	9.82691	2	10.17309	9.95698	4	10.04302	10.13007	2	9.86993	50
11	22 32	37 28	82705	3	17295	95723	5	04277	13018	2	86982	49
12	22 24	37 36	82719	3	17281	95748	5	04252	13030	2	86970	48
13	22 16	37 44	82733	3	17267	95774	5	04226	13041	3	86959	47
14	22 8	37 52	82747	3	17253	95799	6	04201	13053	3	86947	46
15	6 22 0	5 38 0	9.82761	3	10.17239	9.95825	6	10.04175	10.13064	3	9.86936	45
16	21 52	38 8	82775	4	17225	95850	7	04150	13076	3	86924	44
17	21 44	38 16	82788	4	17212	95875	7	04125	13087	3	86913	43
18	21 36	38 24	82802	4	17198	95901	8	04099	13098	3	86902	42
19	21 28	38 32	82816	4	17184	95926	8	04074	13110	4	86890	41
20	6 21 20	5 38 40	9.82830	5	10.17170	9.95952	8	10.04048	10.13121	4	9.86879	40
21	21 12	38 48	82844	5	17156	95977	9	04023	13133	4	86867	39
22	21 4	38 56	82858	5	17142	96002	9	03998	13145	4	86855	38
23	20 56	39 4	82872	5	17128	96028	10	03972	13156	4	86844	37
24	20 48	39 12	82885	6	17115	96053	10	03947	13168	5	86832	36
25	6 20 40	5 39 20	9.82899	6	10.17101	9.96078	11	10.03922	10.13179	5	9.86821	35
26	20 32	39 28	82913	6	17087	96104	11	03896	13191	5	86809	34
27	20 24	39 36	82927	6	17073	96129	11	03871	13202	5	86798	33
28	20 16	39 44	82941	6	17059	96155	12	03845	13214	5	86786	32
29	20 8	39 52	82955	7	17045	96180	12	03820	13225	6	86775	31
30	6 20 0	5 40 0	9.82968	7	10.17032	9.96205	13	10.03795	10.13237	6	9.86763	30
31	19 52	40 8	82982	7	17018	96231	13	03769	13248	6	86752	29
32	19 44	40 16	82996	7	17004	96256	14	03744	13260	6	86740	28
33	19 36	40 24	83010	8	16990	96281	14	03719	13272	6	86728	27
34	19 28	40 32	83023	8	16977	96307	14	03693	13283	7	86717	26
35	6 19 20	5 40 40	9.83037	8	10.16963	9.96332	15	10.03668	10.13295	7	9.86705	25
36	19 12	40 48	83051	8	16949	96357	15	03643	13306	7	86694	24
37	19 4	40 56	83065	8	16935	96383	16	03617	13318	7	86682	23
38	18 56	41 4	83078	9	16922	96408	16	03592	13330	7	86670	22
39	18 48	41 12	83092	9	16908	96433	16	03567	13341	8	86659	21
40	6 18 40	5 41 20	9.83106	9	10.16894	9.96459	17	10.03541	10.13353	8	9.86647	20
41	18 32	41 28	83120	9	16880	96484	17	03516	13365	8	86635	19
42	18 24	41 36	83133	10	16867	96510	18	03490	13376	8	86624	18
43	18 16	41 44	83147	10	16853	96535	18	03465	13388	8	86612	17
44	18 8	41 52	83161	10	16839	96560	19	03440	13400	8	86600	16
45	6 18 0	5 42 0	9.83174	10	10.16826	9.96586	19	10.03414	10.13411	9	9.86589	15
46	17 52	42 8	83188	11	16812	96611	19	03389	13423	9	86577	14
47	17 44	42 16	83202	11	16798	96636	20	03364	13435	9	86565	13
48	17 36	42 24	83215	11	16785	96662	20	03338	13446	9	86554	12
49	17 28	42 32	83229	11	16771	96687	21	03313	13458	9	86542	11
50	6 17 20	5 42 40	9.83242	11	10.16758	9.96712	21	10.03288	10.13470	10	9.86530	10
51	17 12	42 48	83256	12	16744	96738	22	03262	13482	10	86518	9
52	17 4	42 56	83270	12	16730	96763	22	03237	13493	10	86507	8
53	16 56	43 4	83283	12	16717	96788	22	03212	13505	10	86495	7
54	16 48	43 12	83297	12	16703	96814	23	03186	13517	10	86483	6
55	6 16 40	5 43 20	9.83310	13	10.16690	9.96839	23	10.03161	10.13528	11	9.86472	5
56	16 32	43 28	83324	13	16676	96864	24	03136	13540	11	86460	4
57	16 24	43 36	83338	13	16662	96890	24	03110	13552	11	86448	3
58	16 16	43 44	83351	13	16649	96915	25	03085	13564	11	86436	2
59	16 8	43 52	83365	14	16635	96940	25	03060	13575	11	86425	1
60	16 0	44 0	83378	14	16622	96966	25	03034	13587	12	86413	0
M	Hour P.M.	Hour A.M.	Cosine. A	Diff.	Secant. A	Cotangent B	Diff.	Tangent. B	Cosecant. C	Diff.	Sine. C	M

132° — 47°

Seconds of time		1s	2s	3s	4s	5s	6s	7s
Prop. parts of cols.	A	2	3	5	7	9	10	12
	B	3	6	10	13	16	19	22
	C	1	3	4	6	7	9	10

TABLE XXVII.

Log. Sines, Tangents, and Secants.

S'. G'.

43° | A | A | B | B | C | C 136°

M	Hour A.M.	Hour P.M.	Sine.	Diff.	Cosecant.	Tangent.	Diff.	Cotangent	Secant.	Diff.	Cosine.	M
0	6 16 0	5 44 0	9.83378	0	10.16622	9.96966	0	10.03034	10.13587	0	9.86413	60
1	15 52	44 8	83392	0	16608	96991	0	03009	13599	0	86401	59
2	15 44	44 16	83405	0	16595	97016	1	02984	13611	0	86389	58
3	15 36	44 24	83419	1	16581	97042	1	02958	13623	1	86377	57
4	15 28	44 32	83432	1	16568	97067	2	02933	13634	1	86366	56
5	6 15 20	5 44 40	9.83446	1	10.16554	9.97092	2	10.02908	10.13646	1	9.86354	55
6	15 12	44 48	83459	1	16541	97118	3	02882	13658	1	86342	54
7	15 4	44 56	83473	2	16527	97143	3	02857	13670	1	86330	53
8	14 56	45 4	83486	2	16514	97168	3	02832	13682	2	86318	52
9	14 48	45 12	83500	2	16500	97193	4	02807	13694	2	86306	51
10	6 14 40	5 45 20	9.83513	2	10.16487	9.97219	4	10.02781	10.13705	2	9.86295	50
11	14 32	45 28	83527	2	16473	97244	5	02756	13717	2	86283	49
12	14 24	45 36	83540	3	16460	97269	5	02731	13729	2	86271	48
13	14 16	45 44	83554	3	16446	97295	5	02705	13741	3	86259	47
14	14 8	45 52	83567	3	16433	97320	6	02680	13753	3	86247	46
15	6 14 0	5 46 0	9.83581	3	10.16419	9.97345	6	10.02655	10.13765	3	9.86235	45
16	13 52	46 8	83594	4	16406	97371	7	02629	13777	3	86223	44
17	13 44	46 16	83608	4	16392	97396	7	02604	13789	3	86211	43
18	13 36	46 24	83621	4	16379	97421	8	02579	13800	4	86200	42
19	13 28	46 32	83634	4	16366	97447	8	02553	13812	4	86188	41
20	6 13 20	5 46 40	9.83648	4	10.16352	9.97472	8	10.02528	10.13824	4	9.86176	40
21	13 12	46 48	83661	5	16339	97497	9	02503	13836	4	86164	39
22	13 4	46 56	83674	5	16326	97523	9	02477	13848	4	86152	38
23	12 56	47 4	83688	5	16312	97548	10	02452	13860	5	86140	37
24	12 48	47 12	83701	5	16299	97573	10	02427	13872	5	86128	36
25	6 12 40	5 47 20	9.83715	6	10.16285	9.97598	11	10.02402	10.13884	5	9.86116	35
26	12 32	47 28	83728	6	16272	97624	11	02376	13896	5	86104	34
27	12 24	47 36	83741	6	16259	97649	11	02351	13908	5	86092	33
28	12 16	47 44	83755	6	16245	97674	12	02326	13920	6	86080	32
29	12 8	47 52	83768	6	16232	97700	12	02300	13932	6	86068	31
30	6 12 0	5 48 0	9.83781	7	10.16219	9.97725	13	10.02275	10.13944	6	9.86056	30
31	11 52	48 8	83795	7	16205	97750	13	02250	13956	6	86044	29
32	11 44	48 16	83808	7	16192	97776	13	02224	13968	6	86032	28
33	11 36	48 24	83821	7	16179	97801	14	02199	13980	7	86020	27
34	11 28	48 32	83834	8	16166	97826	14	02174	13992	7	86008	26
35	6 11 20	5 48 40	9.83848	8	10.16152	9.97851	15	10.02149	10.14004	7	9.85996	25
36	11 12	48 48	83861	8	16139	97877	15	02123	14016	7	85984	24
37	11 4	48 56	83874	8	16126	97902	16	02098	14028	7	85972	23
38	10 56	49 4	83887	8	16113	97927	16	02073	14040	8	85960	22
39	10 48	49 12	83901	9	16099	97953	16	02047	14052	8	85948	21
40	6 10 40	5 49 20	9.83914	9	10.16086	9.97978	17	10.02022	10.14064	8	9.85936	20
41	10 32	49 28	83927	9	16073	98003	17	01997	14076	8	85924	19
42	10 24	49 36	83940	9	16060	98029	18	01971	14088	8	85912	18
43	10 16	49 44	83954	10	16046	98054	18	01946	14100	9	85900	17
44	10 8	49 52	83967	10	16033	98079	19	01921	14112	9	85888	16
45	6 10 0	5 50 0	9.83980	10	10.16020	9.98104	19	10.01896	10.14124	9	9.85876	15
46	9 52	50 8	83993	10	16007	98130	19	01870	14136	9	85864	14
47	9 44	50 16	84006	10	15994	98155	20	01845	14149	9	85851	13
48	9 36	50 24	84020	11	15980	98180	20	01820	14161	10	85839	12
49	9 28	50 32	84033	11	15967	98206	21	01794	14173	10	85827	11
50	6 9 20	5 50 40	9.84046	11	10.15954	9.98231	21	10.01769	10.14185	10	9.85815	10
51	9 12	50 48	84059	11	15941	98256	22	01744	14197	10	85803	9
52	9 4	50 56	84072	12	15928	98281	22	01719	14209	10	85791	8
53	8 56	51 4	84085	12	15915	98307	22	01693	14221	11	85779	7
54	8 48	51 12	84098	12	15902	98332	23	01668	14234	11	85766	6
55	6 8 40	5 51 20	9.84112	12	10.15888	9.98357	23	10.01643	10.14246	11	9.85754	5
56	8 32	51 28	84125	12	15875	98383	24	01617	14258	11	85742	4
57	8 24	51 36	84138	13	15862	98408	24	01592	14270	11	85730	3
58	8 16	51 44	84151	13	15849	98433	24	01567	14282	12	85718	2
59	8 8	51 52	84164	13	15836	98458	25	01542	14294	12	85706	1
60	8 0	52 0	84177	13	15823	98484	25	01516	14307	12	85693	0
M	Hour P.M.	Hour A.M.	Cosine.	Diff.	Secant.	Cotangent	Diff.	Tangent.	Cosecant.	Diff.	Sine.	M

133° | A | A | B | B | C | C 46°

Seconds of time		1s	2s	3s	4s	5s	6s	7s
Prop. parts of cols.	A	2	3	5	7	8	10	12
	B	3	6	9	13	16	19	22
	C	2	3	5	6	8	9	11

TABLE XXVII.

Log. Sines, Tangents, and Secants.

S'. 44° | A | A | B | B | C | C 135° G'.

M	Hour A.M.	Hour P.M.	Sine.	Diff.	Cosecant.	Tangent.	Diff.	Cotangent	Secant.	Diff.	Cosine.	M
0	6 8 0	5 52 0	9.84177	0	10.15823	9.98484	0	10.01516	10.14307	0	9.85693	60
1	7 52	52 8	84190	0	15810	98509	0	01491	14319	0	85681	59
2	7 44	52 16	84203	0	15797	98534	1	01466	14331	0	85669	58
3	7 36	52 24	84216	1	15784	98560	1	01440	14343	1	85657	57
4	7 28	52 32	84229	1	15771	98585	2	01415	14355	1	85645	56
5	6 7 20	5 52 40	9.84242	1	10.15758	9.98610	2	10.01390	10.14368	1	9.85632	55
6	7 12	52 48	84255	1	15745	98635	3	01365	14380	1	85620	54
7	7 4	52 56	84269	2	15731	98661	3	01339	14392	1	85608	53
8	6 56	53 4	84282	2	15718	98686	3	01314	14404	2	85596	52
9	6 48	53 12	84295	2	15705	98711	4	01289	14417	2	85583	51
10	6 6 40	5 53 20	9.84308	2	10.15692	9.98737	4	10.01263	10.14429	2	9.85571	50
11	6 32	53 28	84321	2	15679	98762	5	01238	14441	2	85559	49
12	6 24	53 36	84334	3	15666	98787	5	01213	14453	2	85547	48
13	6 16	53 44	84347	3	15653	98812	5	01188	14466	3	85534	47
14	6 8	53 52	84360	3	15640	98838	6	01162	14478	3	85522	46
15	6 6 0	5 54 0	9.84373	3	10.15627	9.98863	6	10.01137	10.14490	3	9.85510	45
16	5 52	54 8	84385	3	15615	98888	7	01112	14503	3	85497	44
17	5 44	54 16	84398	4	15602	98913	7	01087	14515	4	85485	43
18	5 36	54 24	84411	4	15589	98939	8	01061	14527	4	85473	42
19	5 28	54 32	84424	4	15576	98964	8	01036	14540	4	85460	41
20	6 5 20	5 54 40	9.84437	4	10.15563	9.98989	8	10.01011	10.14552	4	9.85448	40
21	5 12	54 48	84450	5	15550	99015	9	00985	14564	4	85436	39
22	5 4	54 56	84463	5	15537	99040	9	00960	14577	5	85423	38
23	4 56	55 4	84476	5	15524	99065	10	00935	14589	5	85411	37
24	4 48	55 12	84489	5	15511	99090	10	00910	14601	5	85399	36
25	6 4 40	5 55 20	9.84502	5	10.15498	9.99116	11	10.00884	10.14614	5	9.85386	35
26	4 32	55 28	84515	6	15485	99141	11	00859	14626	5	85374	34
27	4 24	55 36	84528	6	15472	99166	11	00834	14639	6	85361	33
28	4 16	55 44	84540	6	15460	99191	12	00809	14651	6	85349	32
29	4 8	55 52	84553	6	15447	99217	12	00783	14663	6	85337	31
30	6 4 0	5 56 0	9.84566	6	10.15434	9.99242	13	10.00758	10.14676	6	9.85324	30
31	3 52	56 8	84579	7	15421	99267	13	00733	14688	6	85312	29
32	3 44	56 16	84592	7	15408	99293	13	00707	14701	7	85299	28
33	3 36	56 24	84605	7	15395	99318	14	00682	14713	7	85287	27
34	3 28	56 32	84618	7	15382	99343	14	00657	14726	7	85274	26
35	6 3 20	5 56 40	9.84630	8	10.15370	9.99368	15	10.00632	10.14738	7	9.85262	25
36	3 12	56 48	84643	8	15357	99394	15	00606	14750	7	85250	24
37	3 4	56 56	84656	8	15344	99419	16	00581	14763	8	85237	23
38	2 56	57 4	84669	8	15331	99444	16	00556	14775	8	85225	22
39	2 48	57 12	84682	8	15318	99469	16	00531	14788	8	85212	21
40	6 2 40	5 57 20	9.84694	9	10.15306	9.99495	17	10.00505	10.14800	8	9.85200	20
41	2 32	57 28	84707	9	15293	99520	17	00480	14813	8	85187	19
42	2 24	57 36	84720	9	15280	99545	18	00455	14825	9	85175	18
43	2 16	57 44	84733	9	15267	99570	18	00430	14838	9	85162	17
44	2 8	57 52	84745	9	15255	99596	19	00404	14850	9	85150	16
45	6 2 0	5 58 0	9.84758	10	10.15242	9.99621	19	10.00379	10.14863	9	9.85137	15
46	1 52	58 8	84771	10	15229	99646	19	00354	14875	10	85125	14
47	1 44	58 16	84784	10	15216	99672	20	00328	14888	10	85112	13
48	1 36	58 24	84796	10	15204	99697	20	00303	14900	10	85100	12
49	1 28	58 32	84809	11	15191	99722	21	00278	14913	10	85087	11
50	6 1 20	5 58 40	9.84822	11	10.15178	9.99747	21	10.00253	10.14926	10	9.85074	10
51	1 12	58 48	84835	11	15165	99773	21	00227	14938	11	85062	9
52	1 4	58 56	84847	11	15153	99798	22	00202	14951	11	85049	8
53	0 56	59 4	84860	11	15140	99823	22	00177	14963	11	85037	7
54	0 48	59 12	84873	12	15127	99848	23	00152	14976	11	85024	6
55	6 0 40	5 59 20	9.84885	12	10.15115	9.99874	23	10.00126	10.14988	11	9.85012	5
56	0 32	59 28	84898	12	15102	99899	24	00101	15001	12	84999	4
57	0 24	59 36	84911	12	15089	99924	24	00076	15014	12	84986	3
58	0 16	59 44	84923	12	15077	99949	24	00051	15026	12	84974	2
59	0 8	59 52	84936	13	15064	99975	25	00025	15039	12	84961	1
60	0 0	6 0 0	84949	13	15051	10.00000	25	00000	15051	12	84949	0
M	Hour P.M.	Hour A.M.	Cosine.	Diff.	Secant.	Cotangent	Diff.	Tangent.	Cosecant.	Diff.	Sine.	M

134° | A | A | B | B | C | C 45°

Seconds of time		1ˢ	2ˢ	3ˢ	4ˢ	5ˢ	6ˢ	7ˢ
Prop. parts of cols.	A	2	3	5	6	8	10	11
	B	3	6	9	13	16	19	22
	C	2	3	5	6	8	9	11

TABLE XXVIII.

A TABLE OF RHUMBS,

SHOWING

THE POINTS AND QUARTER-POINTS, AND THE DEGREES, MINUTES, AND SECONDS, CORRESPONDING TO ANY COURSE.

NORTH.		Pts.	qr.	°	′	″	Pts.	qr.	SOUTH.	
		0	1	2	48	45	0	1		
		0	2	5	37	30	0	2		
		0	3	8	26	15	0	3		
N. by E.	N. by W.	1	0	11	15	0	1	0	S. by E.	S. by W.
		1	1	14	3	45	1	1		
		1	2	16	52	30	1	2		
		1	3	19	41	15	1	3		
N.N.E.	N.N.W.	2	0	22	30	0	2	0	S.S.E.	S.S.W.
		2	1	25	18	45	2	1		
		2	2	28	7	30	2	2		
		2	3	30	56	15	2	3		
N.E. by N.	N.W. by N.	3	0	33	45	0	3	0	S.E. by S.	S.W. by S.
		3	1	36	33	45	3	1		
		3	2	39	22	30	3	2		
		3	3	42	11	15	3	3		
N.E.	N.W.	4	0	45	0	0	4	0	S.E.	S.W.
		4	1	47	48	45	4	1		
		4	2	50	37	30	4	2		
		4	3	53	26	15	4	3		
N.E. by E.	N.W. by W.	5	0	56	15	0	5	0	S.E. by E.	S.W. by W.
		5	1	59	3	45	5	1		
		5	2	61	52	30	5	2		
		5	3	64	41	15	5	3		
E.N.E.	W.N.W.	6	0	67	30	0	6	0	E.S.E.	W.S.W.
		6	1	70	18	45	6	1		
		6	2	73	7	30	6	2		
		6	3	75	56	15	6	3		
E. by N.	W. by N.	7	0	78	45	0	7	0	E. by S.	W. by S.
		7	1	81	33	45	7	1		
		7	2	84	22	30	7	2		
		7	3	87	11	15	7	3		
East.	West.	8	0	90	0	0	8	0	East.	West.

TABLE XXIX.

WORKMAN'S TABLE,

FOR CORRECTING THE MIDDLE LATITUDE

Mid. Lat.	3°	4°	5°	6°	7°	8°	9°	10°	11°
°	° ′	° ′	° ′	° ′	° ′	° ′	° ′	° ′	° ′
15	0 02	0 03	0 04	0 06	0 09	0 12	0 15	0 19	0 23
16	0 02	0 03	0 04	0 06	0 09	0 12	0 15	0 18	0 22
17	0 02	0 03	0 04	0 06	0 08	0 11	0 14	0 17	0 21
18	0 02	0 03	0 04	0 06	0 08	0 11	0 14	0 17	0 20
19	0 02	0 03	0 04	0 06	0 07	0 10	0 13	0 16	0 19
20	0 02	0 03	0 04	0 06	0 07	0 09	0 12	0 15	0 18
21	0 02	0 03	0 04	0 06	0 07	0 09	0 12	0 15	0 18
22	0 02	0 03	0 04	0 06	0 07	0 09	0 12	0 15	0 17
23	0 02	0 03	0 04	0 06	0 07	0 09	0 12	0 15	0 17
24	0 02	0 03	0 04	0 06	0 07	0 09	0 11	0 14	0 16
25	0 02	0 03	0 04	0 05	0 07	0 09	0 11	0 14	0 16
26	0 02	0 03	0 04	0 05	0 07	0 09	0 11	0 14	0 16
27	0 02	0 03	0 04	0 05	0 07	0 08	0 11	0 14	0 16
28	0 02	0 03	0 04	0 05	0 06	0 08	0 10	0 13	0 15
29	0 02	0 03	0 04	0 05	0 06	0 08	0 10	0 13	0 15
30	0 02	0 03	0 04	0 05	0 06	0 08	0 10	0 13	0 15
31	0 02	0 03	0 04	0 05	0 06	0 08	0 10	0 13	0 15
32	0 02	0 03	0 04	0 05	0 06	0 08	0 10	0 13	0 15
33	0 02	0 03	0 04	0 05	0 06	0 08	0 10	0 13	0 15
34	0 02	0 03	0 04	0 05	0 06	0 08	0 10	0 13	0 15
35	0 02	0 03	0 04	0 05	0 06	0 08	0 10	0 13	0 15
36	0 02	0 03	0 04	0 05	0 06	0 08	0 10	0 13	0 15
37	0 02	0 03	0 04	0 05	0 06	0 08	0 10	0 13	0 15
38	0 02	0 03	0 04	0 05	0 06	0 08	0 10	0 13	0 15
39	0 02	0 03	0 04	0 05	0 06	0 08	0 10	0 13	0 15
40	0 02	0 03	0 04	0 05	0 06	0 08	0 10	0 13	0 15
41	0 02	0 03	0 04	0 05	0 06	0 08	0 10	0 13	0 15
42	0 02	0 03	0 04	0 05	0 06	0 08	0 10	0 13	0 15
43	0 02	0 03	0 04	0 05	0 07	0 09	0 11	0 14	0 16
44	0 02	0 03	0 04	0 05	0 07	0 09	0 11	0 14	0 16
45	0 02	0 03	0 04	0 05	0 07	0 09	0 11	0 14	0 16
46	0 02	0 03	0 04	0 05	0 07	0 09	0 11	0 14	0 16
47	0 02	0 03	0 04	0 05	0 07	0 09	0 11	0 14	0 16
48	0 02	0 03	0 04	0 05	0 07	0 09	0 11	0 14	0 16
49	0 02	0 03	0 04	0 05	0 07	0 09	0 11	0 14	0 17
50	0 02	0 03	0 04	0 05	0 07	0 09	0 11	0 14	0 17
51	0 02	0 03	0 04	0 05	0 07	0 09	0 11	0 14	0 17
52	0 02	0 03	0 04	0 05	0 07	0 09	0 12	0 15	0 18
53	0 02	0 03	0 04	0 06	0 07	0 09	0 12	0 15	0 18
5	0 02	0 03	0 04	0 06	0 08	0 10	0 13	0 16	0 19
55	0 02	0 03	0 04	0 06	0 08	0 10	0 13	0 16	0 19
56	0 02	0 03	0 04	0 06	0 08	0 10	0 13	0 16	0 20
57	0 02	0 03	0 04	0 06	0 08	0 11	0 14	0 17	0 20
58	0 02	0 03	0 04	0 06	0 09	0 11	0 14	0 17	0 21
59	0 02	0 03	0 04	0 06	0 09	0 12	0 15	0 18	0 22
60	0 02	0 03	0 04	0 06	0 09	0 12	0 15	0 19	0 23
61	0 02	0 03	0 05	0 07	0 09	0 12	0 15	0 19	0 23
62	0 02	0 03	0 05	0 07	0 09	0 12	0 16	0 20	0 24
63	0 02	0 04	0 05	0 07	0 09	0 13	0 16	0 20	0 24
64	0 02	0 04	0 06	0 08	0 09	0 13	0 17	0 21	0 25
65	0 02	0 04	0 06	0 08	0 10	0 13	0 17	0 21	0 25
66	0 02	0 04	0 06	0 08	0 10	0 14	0 18	0 22	0 26
67	0 02	0 04	0 06	0 08	0 11	0 15	0 18	0 23	0 27
68	0 02	0 04	0 06	0 08	0 11	0 15	0 19	0 24	0 28
69	0 02	0 05	0 06	0 09	0 12	0 16	0 20	0 25	0 30
70	0 03	0 05	0 06	0 09	0 13	0 17	0 21	0 26	0 31
71	0 04	0 06	0 07	0 09	0 13	0 18	0 22	0 27	0 33
72	0 04	0 06	0 08	0 10	0 14	0 19	0 23	0 29	0 35

Mid. Lat.	12°	13°	14°	15°	16°	17°	18°	19°	20°
°	° ′	° ′	° ′	° ′	° ′	° ′	° ′	° ′	° ′
15	0 27	0 31	0 35	0 40	0 45	0 51	0 58	1 06	1 14
16	0 26	0 30	0 34	0 38	0 43	0 49	0 56	1 03	1 11
17	0 25	0 28	0 32	0 37	0 42	0 48	0 54	1 01	1 08
18	0 24	0 27	0 31	0 36	0 41	0 46	0 52	0 58	1 06
19	0 23	0 26	0 30	0 34	0 40	0 45	0 50	0 56	1 03
20	0 22	0 25	0 29	0 33	0 38	0 43	0 48	0 54	1 00
21	0 21	0 25	0 29	0 33	0 37	0 42	0 47	0 53	0 58
22	0 20	0 24	0 28	0 32	0 36	0 41	0 46	0 51	0 56
23	0 20	0 24	0 28	0 32	0 36	0 40	0 45	0 50	0 55
24	0 19	0 23	0 27	0 31	0 35	0 39	0 44	0 48	0 53
25	0 19	0 23	0 27	0 31	0 35	0 39	0 43	0 47	0 52
26	0 19	0 22	0 26	0 30	0 34	0 38	0 42	0 47	0 52
27	0 19	0 22	0 26	0 30	0 33	0 38	0 42	0 46	0 51
28	0 18	0 21	0 25	0 29	0 33	0 37	0 41	0 46	0 51
29	0 18	0 21	0 25	0 29	0 32	0 36	0 41	0 45	0 50
30	0 18	0 21	0 25	0 28	0 32	0 36	0 41	0 45	0 50
31	0 18	0 21	0 25	0 28	0 32	0 36	0 41	0 45	0 50
32	0 18	0 21	0 25	0 28	0 31	0 36	0 41	0 45	0 50
33	0 18	0 21	0 24	0 27	0 31	0 35	0 40	0 44	0 49
34	0 18	0 21	0 24	0 27	0 31	0 35	0 40	0 44	0 49
35	0 18	0 21	0 24	0 27	0 31	0 35	0 40	0 44	0 49
36	0 18	0 21	0 24	0 27	0 31	0 35	0 40	0 44	0 49
37	0 18	0 21	0 24	0 27	0 31	0 35	0 40	0 44	0 49
38	0 18	0 21	0 24	0 27	0 31	0 36	0 40	0 45	0 50
39	0 18	0 21	0 25	0 28	0 32	0 36	0 41	0 45	0 50
40	0 18	0 22	0 25	0 28	0 32	0 36	0 41	0 45	0 50
41	0 18	0 22	0 25	0 28	0 32	0 37	0 41	0 45	0 50
42	0 18	0 22	0 26	0 29	0 33	0 37	0 42	0 46	0 51
43	0 19	0 23	0 26	0 30	0 34	0 38	0 42	0 46	0 51
44	0 19	0 23	0 27	0 30	0 34	0 38	0 43	0 47	0 52
45	0 19	0 23	0 27	0 31	0 35	0 39	0 43	0 47	0 52
46	0 19	0 23	0 27	0 31	0 35	0 39	0 44	0 48	0 53
47	0 20	0 23	0 27	0 31	0 35	0 40	0 44	0 49	0 54
48	0 20	0 23	0 27	0 31	0 35	0 40	0 45	0 50	0 55
49	0 21	0 24	0 28	0 32	0 36	0 41	0 45	0 51	0 57
50	0 21	0 24	0 28	0 32	0 36	0 41	0 46	0 52	0 58
51	0 21	0 24	0 28	0 32	0 37	0 42	0 47	0 53	0 59
52	0 22	0 25	0 29	0 33	0 37	0 42	0 48	0 54	1 00
53	0 22	0 25	0 29	0 33	0 38	0 43	0 49	0 55	1 01
54	0 23	0 26	0 30	0 34	0 39	0 44	0 50	0 56	1 02
55	0 23	0 26	0 30	0 35	0 40	0 45	0 51	0 57	1 03
56	0 24	0 27	0 31	0 36	0 41	0 46	0 52	0 58	1 04
57	0 24	0 28	0 32	0 37	0 42	0 48	0 54	1 00	1 06
58	0 25	0 29	0 33	0 38	0 44	0 50	0 55	1 02	1 08
59	0 26	0 30	0 34	0 39	0 45	0 51	0 57	1 04	1 10
60	0 27	0 31	0 35	0 40	0 46	0 52	0 59	1 06	1 13
61	0 27	0 31	0 36	0 41	0 47	0 54	1 01	1 08	1 15
62	0 28	0 32	0 37	0 42	0 49	0 56	1 03	1 10	1 18
63	0 29	0 33	0 39	0 44	0 51	0 58	1 05	1 12	1 21
64	0 29	0 34	0 40	0 46	0 53	1 00	1 07	1 14	1 24
65	0 30	0 35	0 41	0 48	0 55	1 02	1 09	1 17	1 27
66	0 31	0 37	0 43	0 50	0 58	1 05	1 12	1 21	1 31
67	0 33	0 38	0 45	0 53	1 00	1 07	1 16	1 25	1 35
68	0 34	0 40	0 48	0 55	1 02	1 10	1 19	1 30	1 39
69	0 36	0 42	0 50	0 58	1 05	1 13	1 23	1 34	1 44
70	0 38	0 44	0 52	1 00	1 08	1 17	1 28	1 39	1 50
71	0 40	0 46	0 55	1 03	1 12	1 22	1 32	1 44	1 56
72	0 42	0 49	0 58	1 06	1 16	1 27	1 38	1 50	2 04

TABLE XXX.

TABLE OF REFRACTIONS.

App. Altitude.	Refr. Br. 30. Th. 50°.	Diff. for 1′ Alt	Diff. for +1 B.	Diff. for −1° Fah.	App. Altitude.	Refr. Br. 30. Th. 50°.	Diff. for 1′ Alt.	Diff. for +1 B.	Diff. for −1° Fah.
° ′	′ ″	″	″	″	° ′	′ ″	″	″	″
4 0	11 52	2.2	24.1	1.70	10 0	5 20	.5	10.8	.69
10	11 30	2.1	23.4	1.64	10	5 15	.5	10.6	.67
20	11 10	2.0	22.7	1.58	20	5 10	.5	10.4	.65
30	10 50	1.9	22.0	1.53	30	5 5	.5	10.2	.64
40	10 32	1.8	21.3	1.48	40	5 0	.5	10.1	.63
50	10 15	1.7	20.7	1.43	50	4 56	.4	9.9	.62
5 0	9 58	1.6	20.6	1.38	11 0	4 51	.4	9.8	.60
10	9 42	1.5	19.1	1.34	10	4 47	.4	9.6	.59
20	9 27	1.5	19.1	1.30	20	4 43	.4	9.5	.58
30	9 11	1.4	18.6	1.26	30	4 39	.4	9.4	.57
40	8 58	1.3	18.1	1,22	40	4 35	.4	9.2	.56
50	8 45	1.3	17.6	1.19	50	4 31	.4	9.1	.55
6 0	8 32	1.2	17.2	1.15	12 0	4 28.1	.38	9.00	.556
10	8 20	1.2	16.8	1.11	10	4 24.4	.37	8.86	.548
20	8 9	1.1	16.4	1.09	20	4 20.8	.36	8.74	.541
30	7 58	1.1	16.0	1.06	30	4 17.3	.35	8.63	.533
40	7 47	1.0	15.7	1.03	40	4 13.9	.33	8.51	.524
50	7 37	1.0	15.3	1.00	50	4 10.7	.32	8.41	.517
7 0	7 27	1.0	15.0	.98	13 0	4 7.5	.31	8.30	.509
10	7 17	.9	14.6	.95	10	4 4.4	.31	8.20	.503
20	7 8	.9	14.3	.93	20	4 1.4	.30	8.10	.496
30	6 59	.8	14.1	.91	30	3 58.4	.30	8.00	.490
40	6 51	.8	13.8	.89	40	3 55.5	.29	7.89	.482
50	6 43	.8	13.5	.87	50	3 52.6	.29	7.79	.476
8 0	6 35	.7	13.3	.85	14 0	3 49.9	.28	7.76	.469
10	6 28	.7	13.1	.83	10	3 47.1	.28	7.61	.464
20	6 21	.7	12.8	.82	20	3 44.4	.27	7.52	.458
30	6 14	.7	12.6	.80	30	3 41.8	.26	7.43	.453
40	6 7	.7	12.3	.79	40	3 39.2	.26	7.34	.448
50	6 0	.6	12.1	.77	50	3 36.7	.25	7.26	.444
9 0	5 54	.6	11.9	.76	15 0	3 34.3	.24	7.18	.439
10	5 47	.6	11.7	.74	30	3 27.3	.22	6.95	.424
20	5 41	.6	11.5	.73	16 0	3 20.6	.21	6.73	.411
30	5 36	.6	11.3	.71	30	3 14.4	.20	6.51	.399
40	5 30	.5	11.1	.71	17 0	3 8.5	.19	6.31	.386
50	5 25	.5	11.0	.70	30	3 2.9	.18	6.12	.374
					18 0	2 57.6	.17	5.98	.362
					19 0	2 47.7	.16	5.61	.340

TABLE XXX.

TABLE OF REFRACTIONS.

App. Altitude.	Refr. Br. 30. Th. 50°.	Diff. for 1′ Alt.	Diff. for +1 B.	Diff. for −1° Fah.	App. Altitude.	Refr. Br. 30. Th. 50°.	Diff. for 1′ Alt.	Diff. for +1 B.	Diff. for −1° Fah.
°	′ ″	″	″	″	°	″	″	″	″
20	2 38.7	.15	5.31	.322	55	40.8	.025	1.36	.082
21	2 30.5	.13	5.04	.305	56	39.3	.025	1.31	.079
22	2 23.2	.12	4.79	.290	57	37.8	.025	1.26	.076
23	2 16.5	.11	4.57	.276	58	36.4	.024	1.22	.073
24	2 10.1	.10	4.35	.264	59	35.0	.024	1.17	.070
25	2 4.2	.09	4.16	.252	60	33.6	.023	1.12	.067
26	1 58.8	.09	3.97	.241	61	32.3	.022	1.08	.065
27	1 53.8	.08	3.81	.230	62	31.0	.022	1.04	.062
28	1 49.1	.08	3.65	.219	63	29.7	.021	.99	.060
29	1 44.7	.07	3.50	.209	64	28.4	.021	.95	.057
30	1 40.5	.07	3.36	.201	65	27.2	.020	.91	.055
31	1 36.6	.06	3.23	.193	66	25.9	.020	.87	.052
32	1 33.0	.06	3.11	.186	67	24.7	.020	.83	.050
33	1 29.5	.06	2.99	.179	68	23.5	.020	.79	.047
34	1 26.1	.05	2.88	.173.	69	22.4	.020	.75	.045
35	1 23.0	.05	2.78	.167	70	21.2	.020	.71	.043
36	1 20.0	.05	2.68	.161	71	19.9	.020	.67	.040
37	1 17.1	.05	2.58	.155	72	18.8	.019	.63	.038
38	1 14.4	.05	2.49	.149	73	17.7	.018	.59	.036
39	1 11.8	.04	2.40	.144	74	16.6	.018	.56	.033
40	1 9.3	.04	2.32	.139	75	15.5	.018	.52	.031
41	1 6.9	.04	2.24	.134	76	14.4	.018	.48	.029
42	1 4.6	.038	2.16	.130	77	13.4	.017	.45	.027
43	1 2.4	.036	2.09	.125	78	12.3	.017	.41	.025
44	1 0.3	.034	2.02	.120	79	11.2	.017	.38	.023
45	58.1	.034	1.94	.117	80	10.2	.017	.34	.021
46	56.1	.033	1.88	.112	81	9.2	.017	.31	.018
47	54.2	.032	1.81	.108	82	8.2	.017	.27	.016
48	52.3	.031	1.75	.104	83	7.1	.017	.24	.014
49	50.5	.030	1.69	.101	84	6.1	.017	.20	.012
50	48.8	.029	1.63	.097	85	5.1	.017	.17	.010
51	47.1	.028	1.58	.094	86	4.1	.017	.14	.008
52	45.4	.027	1.52	.090	87	3.1	.017	.10	.006
53	43.8	.026	1.47	.088	88	2.0	.017	.07	.004
54	42.2	.026	1.41	.085	89	1.0	.017	.03	.002

TABLE XXXI.

Dip of the Horizon.	
Height.	Dip.
Feet.	
1	0′ 58″
2	1 21
3	1 40
4	1 56
5	2 9
6	2 21
7	2 33
8	2 44
9	2 53
10	3 2
11	3 10
12	3 19
13	3 27
14	3 36
15	3 42
16	3 50
17	3 57
18	4 4
19	4 11
20	4 17
21	4 23
22	4 30
23	4 36
24	4 42
26	4 52
28	5 5
30	5 15
35	5 39
40	6 4
45	6 27
50	6 46
60	7 25
70	8 1
80	8 34
90	9 6
100	9 35

TABLE XXXII.

Diminution of the vertical semidiam. of ☉ or ☾, on account of Refraction.	
Alt.	Dim. of semidia.
5°	25″
6	19
7	14
8	11
9	9
10	8
11	7
12	6
13	5
14	4
15	4
16	3
18	3
20	2
30	1
45	1

TABLE XXXIII.

Augmentation of ☾'s semidiam.	
Alt.	Aug.
0°	0″
5	1
10	3
15	4
20	6
25	7
30	8
35	9
40	10
45	11
50	12
55	13
60	14
70	15
80	15
90	16

TABLE XXXIV.

Sun's par. in Alt.	
Alt.	Par.
0°	9″
10	9
20	8
30	8
40	7
50	6
55	5
60	4
65	4
70	3
75	2
80	2
85	1
90	0

TABLE XXXV.

Reduction of the ☾'s Equatorial parallax for the spheroidal figure of the Earth.

Lat.	Horizontal Parallax.				
	54′	56′	58′	60′	62′
°	″	″	″	″	″
0	0.0	0.0	0.0	0.0	0.0
8	0.2	0.2	0.2	0.2	0.2
16	0.8	0.8	0.9	0.9	0.9
20	1.3	1.3	1.4	1.4	1.5
24	1.8	1.9	1.9	2.0	2.0
28	2.4	2.5	2.6	2.6	2.7
33	3.0	3.1	3.3	3.4	3.5
36	3.7	3.9	4.0	4.1	4.3
40	4.5	4.6	4.8	5.0	5.1
44	5.2	5.4	5.6	5.8	6.0
48	6.0	6.2	6.3	6.6	6.8
52	6.7	7.0	7.2	7.4	7.6
56	7.4	7.7	8.0	8.2	8.5
60	8.1	8.4	8.7	9.0	9.3
64	8.7	9.1	9.4	9.7	10.0
68	9.3	9.6	10.0	10.3	10.6
72	9.8	10.1	10.4	10.8	11.2
76	10.2	10.6	10.9	11.3	11.7
84	10.7	11.1	11.5	11.9	12.0
90	10.8	11.2	11.6	12.0	12.4

TABLE XXXVI.

Reduction to the Meridian.

Argument = the Hour Angle from the Meridian.

s	0m	1m	2m	3m	4m	5m	6m	7m	8m	9m	10m	11m	12m	13m	14m
0	0	9	38	86	152	238	343	466	609	771	952	1152	1370	1608	1865
1	0	10	39	87	153	240	345	468	612	774	955	1155	1374	1612	1870
2	0	10	39	88	155	241	346	471	614	777	958	1159	1378	1617	1874
3	0	10	40	89	156	243	348	473	617	780	961	1162	1382	1621	1879
4	0	11	41	90	157	244	350	475	619	782	964	1166	1386	1625	1883
5	0	11	41	91	159	246	352	478	622	785	968	1169	1390	1629	1887
6	0	12	42	92	160	248	354	480	624	788	971	1173	1393	1633	1892
7	0	12	43	93	161	549	356	482	627	791	974	1176	1397	1637	1896
8	0	12	43	93	163	251	358	484	630	794	977	1180	1401	1641	1901
9	0	13	44	94	164	253	360	487	632	797	981	1183	1405	1646	1905
10	0	13	45	95	165	254	362	489	635	800	984	1187	1409	1650	1910
11	0	13	45	96	167	256	364	491	637	803	987	1190	1413	1654	1914
12	0	14	46	97	168	257	366	493	640	806	990	1194	1416	1658	1919
13	0	14	47	98	169	259	368	496	643	809	993	1197	1420	1662	1923
14	1	14	47	99	171	261	370	498	645	811	997	1201	1424	1667	1928
15	1	15	48	100	172	262	372	509	648	814	1000	1205	1428	1671	1932
16	1	15	49	102	173	264	374	503	650	817	1003	1208	1432	1675	1937
17	1	16	50	103	175	266	376	505	653	820	1006	1212	1436	1679	1941
18	1	16	50	104	176	267	378	507	656	823	1016	1215	1440	1683	1946
19	1	17	51	105	177	269	480	510	658	826	1013	1219	1444	1688	1950
20	1	17	52	106	179	271	382	512	661	829	1016	1222	1448	1692	1954
21	1	17	53	107	180	272	384	514	664	832	1020	1226	1451	1696	1960
22	1	18	53	108	182	274	386	517	666	835	1023	1230	1455	1700	1964
23	1	18	54	109	183	276	388	519	669	838	1026	1233	1459	1705	1968
24	2	19	55	110	184	278	390	521	672	841	1029	1237	1463	1709	1973
25	2	19	56	111	185	279	392	524	674	844	1033	1241	1467	1713	1978
26	2	20	56	112	187	281	394	526	677	847	1036	1244	1471	1717	1982
27	2	20	57	113	188	283	396	528	680	850	1039	1248	1475	1722	1987
28	2	20	58	114	190	284	398	531	682	853	1043	1251	1479	1726	1992
29	2	21	59	116	191	286	400	533	685	856	1046	1255	1483	1730	1997
30	3	21	59	117	193	288	402	535	688	859	1049	1259	1487	1734	2001
31	3	22	60	118	194	289	404	538	690	862	1053	1262	1491	1739	2005
32	3	22	61	119	196	291	406	540	693	865	1056	1266	1495	1743	2010
33	3	23	62	120	197	293	408	543	696	868	1059	1270	1499	1747	2014
34	3	23	63	121	198	295	410	545	699	871	1062	1273	1503	1751	2019
35	3	24	64	122	200	297	412	547	701	874	1066	1277	1507	1756	2024
36	3	24	64	123	201	299	415	550	704	877	1069	1281	1511	1760	2028
37	4	25	65	124	203	300	417	552	707	880	1073	1284	1515	1764	2033
38	4	25	66	126	204	302	419	555	709	883	1076	1288	1519	1669	2038
39	4	26	67	127	206	304	421	557	712	886	1079	1292	1523	1773	2042
40	4	26	68	128	207	306	423	559	715	889	1083	1295	1527	1777	2047
41	4	27	68	129	209	307	425	562	718	892	1086	1298	1531	1782	2052
42	5	28	69	130	210	309	427	564	720	896	1090	1303	1535	1786	2056
43	5	28	70	131	212	311	429	567	723	899	1093	1307	1539	1790	2061
44	5	29	71	133	213	313	432	569	726	902	1096	1310	1543	1795	2066
45	5	29	72	134	215	315	434	572	729	905	1100	1314	1547	1799	2070
46	6	30	73	135	216	316	436	574	732	908	1103	1318	1551	1804	2075
47	6	30	74	136	218	318	438	577	734	911	1107	1321	1555	1808	5080
48	6	31	75	137	219	320	440	579	737	914	1110	1325	1559	1812	2084
49	6	31	75	139	221	322	442	582	740	917	1114	1329	1563	1817	2089
50	7	32	76	140	222	324	444	584	743	920	1117	1333	1567	1821	2094
51	7	33	77	141	225	326	447	587	745	923	1120	1336	1571	1825	2099
52	7	33	78	142	226	328	449	589	748	927	1124	1340	1575	1830	2103
53	7	34	79	144	227	329	451	592	751	930	1127	1344	1580	1834	2108
54	8	34	80	145	229	331	453	594	754	933	1131	1348	1584	1839	2113
55	8	35	81	146	230	333	455	597	757	936	1134	1352	1588	1843	2117
56	8	36	82	147	232	335	458	599	760	939	1138	1355	1592	1847	2122
57	8	36	83	149	233	337	460	602	763	942	1141	1359	1596	1852	2127
58	9	37	84	150	235	339	462	604	765	945	1145	1363	1600	1856	2132
59	9	37	85	151	236	341	464	607	768	949	1148	1367	1604	1861	2136
60	9	38	86	152	238	343	466	609	771	952	1152	1370	1608	1865	2141

TABLE XXXVI.

Reduction to the Meridian.

Argument = the Hour Angle from the Meridian.

s	15m	16m	17m	18m	19m	20m	21m	22m	23m	24m
0	2141	2436	2750	3083	3434	3805	4195	4604	5031	5478
1	2146	2441	2755	3088	3441	3812	4202	4611	5039	5486
2	2151	2446	2761	3093	3447	3818	4208	4618	5046	5494
3	2155	2451	2766	3099	3453	3824	4215	4625	5053	5501
4	2160	2456	2771	3106	3459	3831	4222	4632	5061	5509
5	2165	2461	2777	3111	3465	3837	4228	4639	5068	5516
6	2170	2466	2782	3117	3471	3843	4235	4646	5075	5524
7	2175	2472	2788	3123	3477	3850	4242	4653	5083	5531
8	2179	2477	2793	3128	3483	3856	4248	4660	5090	5539
9	2184	2482	2799	3134	3489	3863	4255	4667	5097	5547
10	2189	2487	2804	3140	3495	3869	4262	4674	5105	5554
11	2194	2492	2809	3146	3501	3875	4269	4681	5112	5562
12	2198	2497	2815	3151	3507	3882	4275	4688	5119	5570
13	2203	2502	2820	3157	3513	3888	4282	4695	5127	5577
14	2208	2507	2826	3163	3519	3895	4289	4702	5134	5585
15	2213	2513	2831	3169	3525	3901	4295	4709	5141	5593
16	2218	2518	2837	3175	3531	3907	4302	4716	5149	5600
17	2223	2523	2842	3180	3538	3914	4309	4723	5156	5608
18	2227	2528	2848	3186	3544	3920	4316	4730	5163	5616
19	2232	2533	2853	3192	3550	3927	4322	4737	5171	5623
20	2237	2538	2859	3198	3556	3933	4329	4744	5178	5631
21	2242	2544	2864	3204	3562	3940	4336	4751	5186	5639
22	2247	2549	2870	3209	3568	3946	4343	4758	5193	5647
23	2252	2554	2875	3215	3574	3952	4350	4766	5200	5654
24	2257	2559	2881	3221	3581	3959	4356	4773	5208	5662
25	2262	2564	2886	3227	3587	3965	4363	4780	5215	5670
26	2266	2570	2892	3233	3593	3972	4370	4787	5223	5678
27	2272	2575	2897	3239	3599	3978	4377	4794	5230	5685
28	2276	2580	2903	3244	3605	3985	4383	4801	5237	5693
29	2281	2585	2908	3250	3611	3991	4390	4808	5245	5701
30	2286	2590	2914	3256	3618	3998	4397	4815	5252	5709
31	2291	2596	2919	3262	3624	4004	4404	4822	5260	5716
32	2296	2601	2925	3268	3630	4011	4411	4829	5267	5724
33	2301	2606	2930	3274	3636	4017	4416	4837	5275	5732
34	2306	2611	2936	3280	3642	4024	4424	4844	5282	5740
35	2311	2617	2912	3286	3648	4030	4431	4851	5290	5747
36	2316	2622	2947	3291	3655	4037	4438	4858	5297	5755
37	2321	2627	2952	3297	3661	4043	4445	4865	5305	5763
38	2326	2632	2958	3303	3667	4050	4452	4872	5312	5771
39	2331	2638	2964	3309	3673	4056	4459	4880	5320	5779
40	2335	2643	2970	3315	3680	4063	4465	4887	5327	5786
41	2340	2648	2975	3321	3686	4070	4472	4894	5335	5794
42	2345	2654	2981	3327	3692	4076	4479	4901	5342	5802
43	2350	2659	2986	3333	3698	4083	4486	4908	5350	5810
44	2355	2664	2992	3339	3705	4089	4493	4916	5357	5818
45	2360	2669	2998	3345	3711	4096	4500	4923	5365	5826
46	2365	2675	3003	3351	3717	4102	4507	4930	5372	5833
47	2370	2680	3009	3357	3723	4109	4514	4937	5380	5841
48	2375	2685	3015	3363	3730	4116	4520	4944	5387	5849
49	2380	2690	3020	3369	3736	4122	4527	4952	5395	5857
50	2385	2696	3026	3375	3742	4129	4534	4959	5402	5865
51	2390	2701	3031	3380	3749	4135	4541	4966	5410	5873
52	2395	2707	3037	3386	3755	4142	4548	4973	5417	5881
53	2401	2712	3043	3392	3761	4149	4555	4981	5425	5888
54	2406	2718	3049	3398	3767	4155	4562	4988	5433	5896
55	2411	2723	3054	3404	3774	4162	4569	4995	5440	5904
56	2416	2728	3060	3410	3780	4168	4576	5002	5448	5912
57	2421	2734	3066	3416	3786	4175	4583	5010	5455	5920
58	2426	2739	3071	3422	3793	4182	4590	5017	5463	5928
59	2431	2744	3077	3428	3799	4188	4597	5024	5470	5936
60	2436	2750	3083	3434	3805	4195	4604	5031	5478	5944

www.ingramcontent.com/pod-product-compliance
Lightning Source LLC
LaVergne TN
LVHW021316110826
845150LV00003B/589